THE PARABOLIC TEACHING OF CHRIST, A SYSTEMATIC AND CRITICAL STUDY OF THE PARABLES OF OUR LORD

THE PARABOLIC TEACHING OF CHRIST, A SYSTEMATIC AND CRITICAL STUDY OF THE PARABLES OF OUR LORD

Bruce, Alexander Balmain, 1831-1899

www.General-Books.net

Publication Data:

Title: The Parabolic Teaching of Christ, a Systematic and Critical Study of the Parables of Our Lord
Author: Bruce, Alexander Balmain, 1831-1899
Publisher: New York, Armstrong
Publication date: 1890
Subjects: Jesus Christ

How We Made This Book for You
We made this book exclusively for you using patented Print on Demand technology.
First we scanned the original rare book using a robot which automatically flipped and photographed each page.
We automated the typing, proof reading and design of this book using Optical Character Recognition (OCR) software on the scanned copy. That let us keep your cost as low as possible.
If a book is very old, worn and the type is faded, this can result in typos or missing text. This is also why our books don't have illustrations; the OCR software can't distinguish between an illustration and a smudge.
We understand how annoying typos, missing text or illustrations, foot notes in the text or an index that doesn't work, can be. That's why we provide a free digital copy of most books exactly as they were originally published. Simply go to our website (www.general-books.net) to check availability. And we provide a free trial membership in our book club so you can get free copies of other editions or related books.
OCR is not a perfect solution but we feel it's more important to make books available for a low price than not at all. So we warn readers on our website and in the descriptions we provide to book sellers that our books don't have illustrations and may have typos or missing text. We also provide excerpts from each book to book sellers and on our website so you can preview the quality of the book before buying it.
If you would prefer that we manually type, proof read and design your book so that it's perfect, simply contact us for the cost. We would be happy to do as much work as you would be like to pay for.

Limit of Liability/Disclaimer of Warranty:
The publisher and author make no representations or warranties with respect to the accuracy or completeness of the book. The advice and strategies in the book may not be suitable for your situation. You should consult with a professional where appropriate. The publisher is not liable for any damages resulting from the book.
Please keep in mind that the book was written long ago; the information is not current. Furthermore, there may be typos, missing text or illustration and explained above.

1

THE PARABOLIC TEACHING OF CHRIST, A SYSTEMATIC AND CRITICAL STUDY OF THE PARABLES OF OUR LORD

PREFATORY NOTE.

This Third Edition of "The Parabolic Teachine of Christ" has been carefully revised by me. For the benefit of those who possess the earlier editions, it may be stated that no material change has been made in the text. The changes consist chiefly in the correction of errors. I take this opportunity of returning thanks for the very appreciative manner in which this book has been received in this country by clergymen and other friends connected with all denominations. I feel as if I must, in some measure, have succeeded in reflecting the spirit of Christ our Master and Lord in these studies of His incomparable sayings. May He continue to bless them in spite of all their imperfections.

PREFACE.

No apology is deemed necessary for the publication of a new work on the Parables contained in the Gospels. Books of a devotional or homiletical character on some or all of these abound; but of works of a more elaborate and cr'tical description on the subject, the number in the English tongue is small. Without disparagement to such as exist, it is believed that a fresh attempt to unfold in a scholarly yet genial manner the didactic significance of these beautiful sayings of our Lord will not be unwelcome. How far the present publication supplies what is wanted it is for others to judge. A feature of the work is the classification of the parables under general heads, making available thought-affinities for the elucidation of their meaning. Another feature is strict adherence to the historical method of exegesis as distinct from the allegorising method pursued by the Fathers, and largely favoured by the chief English writer on the subject, whose strength and weakness both lie in the extent to which he has laid patristic literature under contribution for the interpretation of the parables and the literary enrichment of his pages. The author of this work has sought help from the moderns more than from the ancients. He has kept recent commentators steadily in view, while avo'ding the dryness of the commentaries, and abstaining from a parade of authorities. In appreciating the theological import of the parables he has had regard to the comparative method of New Testament theology, recognising distinct doctrinal types, and noting the resemblances and differences between these. In the ascertainment of the correct text, advantage has been taken of the latest labours of scholars, including, of course, the Revised Version, and the learned and most valuable edition of the Greek Testament edited by Drs. Westcott and Hort. The introduction is confined to a brief explanation of the method adopted for the distribution of the materials which form the subject of study. Occasional observations on topics usually included in general dissertations on the parables will be found scattered throughout the book.

The Author.

Glasgow, Se Umber, l8S2

CHAPTER VI.

THE SELFISH NEIGHBOUR ANDTHE UNJUST JUDGE; OR, THE Certainty of an Ultimate Answer to Persistent Prayer for the Coming of the Kingdom. i44

CHAPTER VII.

THE PARAPjlE of EXTRA SERVICE; OR, THE EXACTING Demands of the Kingdom, and the Temper needful TO meet them

CHAPTER VIII.

THE HOURS, THE TALENTS, AND THE POUNDS; OR,

Work and Wages in the Kingdom of God 178

BOOK 11.

t t arables of 6vacc.

INTRODUCTORY, 229

CHAPTER I. THE TWO DEBTORS; OR, Much Forgiveness, Much Love 237

CHAPTER II.

THE LOST SHEEP, THE LOST COIN, AND THE LOST SON; OR, the Joy of Finding Persons and Things

CHAPTER IIL

THE CHILDREN OF THE BRIDE- CHAMBER; OR,

Christ's Apology for the Joy of His Disciples. 295

CHAPTER IV.

PAca THE LOWEST SEATS AT FEASTS, AND THE PHARISEE AND THE PUBLICAN; OR, THE KINGDOM OF GOD FOR THE Humble 309

CHAPTER V. THE GREAT SUPPER; OR, the Kingdom for the Hungry 325

CHAPTER VL THE GOOD SAMARITAN; OR, Charity the True Sanctity 342
CHAPTER VIL
THE UNJUST STEWARD; OR, the Redeeming Power
OF Charity 355
CHAPTER Vin.
DIVES AND LAZARUS, AND THE UNMERCIFUL SERVANT; OR, Inhumanity and Implacability the Unpardonable Sins 37G

BOOK III.
' t iparalrles of lub m ui
CHAPTER I.
THE CHILDREN IN THE MARKET-PLACE; OR, THE
Judgment of Jesus on Jewish Contemporaries. 413
CHAPTER II.
THE BARREN FIG-TREE; OR, THE Withdrawal of Israel's Privilege in Favour of the Gentiles Foreshadowed 427
CHAPTER III.
PAG6
THE TWO SONS; OR, Israel's Leaders Charged with
THE Vice of Insincerity 438
CHAPTER IV.
THE WICKED HUSBANDMEN; OR, the Iniquity of
Israel's Leaders Exposed and their Doom Declared 447
CHAPTER V.
THE WEDDING-FEAST AND THE WEDDING-ROBE;
OR, the Doom of Despisers and Abusers of Grace. 459
CHAPTER VI.
THE UNFAITHFUL UPPER SERVANT; OR, the Judgment OF Degenerate Ministers of the Kingdom. 485
CHAPTER VII.
THE TEN VIRGINS; OR, the Judgment of foolish
Citizens of the Kingdom. Â. 496

TABLE OF THE PARABLES
CONSIDERED IN THIS WORK.
Table of the Parables,
Dives and Lazarus,.,
The Unmerciful Servant
The Children in the Market-Place
The Barren Fig-tree
The Two Sons.
The Wicked Husbandmen
The Wedding-Feast and the Wedding-Robe
The Unfaithful Upper Servant
The Ten Virgins.Â
IACB 400
PARABLE-GERMS.

The Physician
The New Patch on the Worn Garment The New Wine in the Old Skins.
The Rejected Stone
The Porter
The Waiting Servants
The Good-man and the Thief. The Wise and Foolish Builders. m
INTRODUCTORY.

The Parables of our Lord were of an incidental character'; and perhaps the best way of studying them is not to isolate them from the general history of His ministry for separate consideration, but rather to look at them as parts of a larger whole in connection with the particular occasions which called them forth. And yet it is, to say the least, a very natural and legitimate procedure to take these parables, which form so large, so peculiar, and so precious a portion of Christ's teaching, apart by themselves, and make them the subject of a special study. This, accordingly, has often been done already, and doubtless it will often be done again while the world lasts. We propose to add one more to the number of the attempts which have been made to ascertain the meaning of the parabolic utterances of Incarnate Wisdom. We enter on the task with much diffidence, yet not without the humble hope of being useful. Our one desire is to get at the kernel of spiritual truth enclosed within the parabolic shell: to get at it for ourselves, and to communicate it at the same time to others. The beauty of the parables we, in common with all readers of the Gospels, greatly admire; their fidelity to nature, and to the customs of the time in which they were spoken, we fully appreciate; but we should not think of undertaking an exposition of them if we had nothing more important to do than to play the part of an art-critic showing how skilfully the parabolic picture is painted in all its details, or of an antiquarian showing how conformable is the parabolic representation to all customs of the time and place.

In entering on an exposition of the parables, we are confronted at once with the question of method. In what order shall we consider the subjects of our study? Shall we take them up as they occur in the several Gospels, beginning with Matthew, then going on through Mark and Luke, as has been done by some writers? or shall we attempt a classification on a principle?â and if so, on what principle is the classification to be made? A merely casual method of arrangement is certainly not desirable, if there be any thought-affinities between the parables, any recognisable characteristics common to several of them, according to which they can be arranged in groups; for disregard of such affinities means loss of the light which related parables are fitted to throw upon each other. Now, several writers have thought they could discover certain resemblances between certain parables, and on the basis of such real or supposed resemblances have built schemes of classification by which they have been guided in their exposition. One writer, for example, the author of an elaborate and voluminous work on the parables, takes note of the fact that some of the parables have explanations attached to them, while others remain unexplained; and, asking himself the question what may be the reason of the difference, comes to the conclusion that the unexplained parables are allegories and prophecies meant to hide the truth,â the truth hid being not so much a doctrine as a future event, which before the time is a mystery, arcanum, or secret,â while the explained parables teach a doctrine or moral lesson having a bearing on present practice. In this way the writer referred to arrives at a distribution of the parables into two great classesâ the prophetic and the moral, â the former containing an esoteric and the latter an exoteric system of doctrine, This classification has met with very little approval, and perhaps its failure has had a considerable effect in deterring other writers from all attempts at methodical arrangement as futile. It does not follow, however, that because one attempt has proved a signal failure, all others must be equally abortive. We believe, for our part, that a grouping of the parables based on real and important resemblances, and at least approximately correct and complete,

Archbishop Trench, and after him Mr. Arnot.

Greswell: 'An Exposition of the Parables ai d of oth: r parts of the Gospels," in five vols.

is possible; and without staying to enumerate all the methods of grouping which we have met with in books, we shall proceed at once to indicate the principle of distribution on which we ourselves mean to proceed.

We observe, then, that the teaching ministry of our Lord falls naturally asunder into three divisions, Christ was a Master or Rabbi, with disciples whom He made it His business to instruct; He was an Evangelist, going about doing good among the common people, and preaching the gospel of the kingdom to the poor; and He was a Prophet, not merely or chiefly in the predictive sense of the word, but specially in the sense that He was one who proclaimed in the hearing of His contemporaries the great truth of the moral government of God over the world at large, and over Israel in particular, and the sure doom of the impenitent under that righteous government. Now, the parables may be conveniently, and as we believe usefully, distributed into three groups, corresponding to these three departments of Christ's ministry. Indeed, we might go further, and say that the whole public life of Jesus, as related in the Gospels, might without forcing be ranged under the three heads: the Master, the Evangelist, the Prophet. Undei" the first head comes all that relates to the training of the twelve for the apostolate; under the second Christ's miscellaneous activity as a Teacher and Healer among the general population, as the Good Shepherd seeking to save the lost sheep of the house of Israel; under the third, the extensive materials relating to His bitter conflict as the witness for truth and righteousness with the unbelieving political and religious leaders of Jewish society. When all that belongs naturally to these three divisions has been taken up, not much of the Evangelic narrative remains. But our business at present is with the parables only, not with the whole public ministry of Jesus; and we repeat the statement already made, that the parables may be distributed into three groups answering to the three titles, the Master, the Evangelist, the Prophet. First there is a class of parables which may be distinguished as the theoretic, containing the general truth,

Schoettgen, in his ' Horse Hebraiccc et Talmudicee," enunciates, and seeks to establish, the thesis Chfisiusrabbinoriun Siuunus: vide 'Rabbi nicarum Lectionum cap, L or what has been, called the ' metaphysic' of the Divine kingdom. Then there is a large group which may legitimately claim to be called distinctively the evangelic â their burden being grace, the mercy and the love of God to the sinful and the miserableâ in some more obviously and directly, in others by implication rather than by express statement, but none the less really and effectively. Then, lastly, there is a group which may be characterised as the prophetic; using the term, let it be once more explained, not in the predictive so much as in the ethical sense, to convey the idea that in this class of parables Jesus, as the messenger of God, spoke words of rebuke and warning to an evil time. Proceeding upon this classification, we in effect adopt as our motto the words of the Apostle Paul: " The fruit of the light is in all goodness and righteousness and truth," â the last word, ' truth," answering to the first group; the second, ' righteousness," answering to the last group; and the first, goodness," answering to the middle group. Christ was the Light of the world; and in His parabolic teaching He let His light shine upon men in beautiful prismatic rays, and the precious fruit is preserved for our use in three groups of parables: first, the theoretic parables, containing i e general truth concerning the kingdom of God; second, the evangelic parables, setting forth the Divine goodness and grace as the source of salvation and the law of Christian life; third, the prophetic parables, proclaiming the righteotisness of God as the Supreme Ruler, rewarding men according to their works.

The foregoing classification has not been got up for the occasion, but has insinuated itself into our mind without any seeking on our part, in connection with our studies on the Gospels. Nor do we lay claim to any originality in connection therewith, except such as consists in independently arriving at a conclusion which has commended itself to other minds. We are happy to find that we do not stand alone in recognising the distinctions indicated, and that there is an increasing consensus of opinion in favour of a classification based thereon. Differences of opinion, of course, may

Kcim, ' Jesu von Nazara," ii. 447.

Â Ephesians v. 9, where the approved reading is, h yap Kap- hq to 5 ii roc iv iraay ayaowavyy Kat iikaioavvy Koi akt)9ii(.

'Among writers who group the parables in a way similar to that given obtain as to the precise terms by which the different classes are to be described, or even as to the number of separate classes to be recognised, as also in regard to the class under which this or that parable is to be ranged; but there is a general concurrence among recent writers as to the reality and the importance of the threefold distinction above indicated. Not only so; another interesting fact has attracted the attention of many: viz. that the Evangelistsâ more definitely Matthew and Luke, for Mark has very few parables in his Gospelâ stand in distinct relations to the several groups of parables. Most of Matthew's parables belong to the first and third groups; most of Luke's to the second. This fact was signalised long ago by one whose name will ever be held in honour in connection with the literature of our subject; and it has recently been proclaimed with remarkable emphasis and felicity of language by Renan, in his charming chapter on the Gospel of Luke, in the fifth volume of his work on the â Origins of Christianity." " There is hardly," he remarks, " an anecdote, a parable peculiar to Luke, which breathes not the spirit of mercy and of appeal to sinners. The only word of Jesus a little hard which has been preserved, becomes with him an apologue full of indulgence and patience. The unfruitful tree must not be cut down too quickly. The good gardener opposes himself to the anger of the proprietor, and demands that the tree be manured before it be finally condemned. The Gospel of Luke is by excellence the gospel of pardon, and of pardon obtained by faith." The fact is unquestionable, though the use made of it by the Tubingen school of critics, and partly by M. Renan himself, may be very questionable indeed. We cannot approve of the opinion which regards the third Evangelist as a theological partisan, who not only selected, but manufactured or modified, facts to serve the cause he had espousedâ that of Pauline universalism as against Judaistic exclusivism. But we do most cordially above, may be named Plumptre, in Art. Parable in Smith's Dictionary and Lange, Bibelwerk," on Matthew xiii. Vide also his ' Leben Jesu, vol. I., book ii.

Archbishop Trench, Notes on the Parables," Introductory Essay, p. 29, Ed. xiv.

Les Evangiles," p. 266.

â Hilgenfeld, in his Einlejtung in das Neue Testament, p. 573, finds recognise Luke as an earnest believer in the gospel Paul preachedâ a gospel of pure grace, and therefore a gospel for all the world on equal terms; and we perceive clearly traces of his Pmilinism, using the word not in a controversial but in a descriptive sense, throughout his Gospel. In searching among the literary materials out of which he constructed his story, he manifestly had a quick eye for everything that tended to show that the gospel preached by Christ was really and emphatically good news from God, a manifestation of Divine philanthropy and grace, and a manifestation in which the whole world was interested. Hence the prominence given to such narratives as exhibited Jesus as the Friend of the poor; hence the introduction of incidents in which Samaritans appear to advantage in comparison with Jews, or as attracting Christ's compassion while objects of Jewish prejudice and hatred; hence the preservation in the third Gospel of such parables as those which together constitute Christ's apology for loving the sinful: the Two Debtors, the Straying Sheep, the Lost Piece of Money, and the Prodigal Son; and such others as the Good Samaritan, the Supper, the Pharisee and Publican, and even, we will venture to add, the Unjust Steward, and the Rich Man and Lazarus. It is of the utmost irfiportance to recognise this peculiarity of Luke's Gospel in all its breadth, not merely as a fact of literary or critical interest, but as one having a direct practical bearing on interpretation. One who leaves this fact out of view runs great risk of frequently missing the right track as an interpreter, while one who ever keeps it in his eye will often be guided at once to the true meaning of a narrative. We must, of course, be on our guard against giving a one-sided predominance to the characteristic in question, as if Luke had only one idea in his mind in writing his Gospel; and generally in our interpretation of the different Gospels we must beware of imagining the writers to have been so much under the influence of a particular piirpose as to have excluded everything that did not directly or indirectly bear thereon. It is characteristic of the negative school of criticism thus to treat the Gospels as exclusively writings of tendency, to the a trace of a dogmatic leaning to Paulinism, in the expression "lest they should believe and be saved " (Luke viii. 12).

great impoverishment of their value; even as it has more of less been characteristic of believing interpreters to ignore too much the distinctive features of the Gospels, and to treat them all as colourless chronicles of the life of Jesus. The truth lies between the two extremes. The Gospels have their distinctive features, and yet they have much in common: they have all the great essentials of Christ's teaching in common. Matthew's Gospel is theocratic; Luke's is Pauline, humanistic, universalistic. But the theocratic aspect of the Divine kingdom is not wanting in Luke, neither is the universal aspect thereof wanting in Matthew. Bearing this in mind, we shall not expect to find only evangelic parables in the third Gospel, but shall be prepared to meet with others of a different description; neither shall we be surprised if we find in Matthew not only parables didactic and prophetic, but also such as speak to us not of judgment but of mercy.

This caveat against too rigorous definition of the different Gospels in relation to the parables requires to be repeated in connection with the heads under which we propose to classify the latter. It must not be imagined that every parable so decidedly comes under one head that it could not with propriety be ranged under any other. This holds good probably of most, but not of all. Some parables are, if we may so express it, of an amphibious character, and might be ranged under either of two categories, because partaking of the nature of both. Such, for example, is the parable of the Great Supper, which, while full of mercy towards the homeless, hungry wanderers on the highway, presents an aspect of stern judicial severity towards those who accepted not the invitations sent to them; and might be classed either as an evangelic or as a prophetic parable, according as we took for its key-note the word of mercy, "Compel them to come in," or the word of judgment, "None of those men which were bidden shall taste of my supper." As another instance, we may refer to the parable of the " Unprofitable Servants," as it is commonly called, or, as we prefer to call it, the parable of " Extra Service." If we start in our interpretation from the words "We are unprofitable servants," we shall regard the parable as intended to teach that there is no room for merit in the kingdom of God, that all is of grace,â and so relegate it to the evangelic category. If, on the other hand, we regard it as the purpose of the parable to impress on the servants of the kingdom the exacting nature of the service to which they are called, and that no man is fit for that service who is disposed to murmur, or who ever thinks he has done enough, then we may not improperly range the parable under the first of the three categories, and treat it as one setting forth one of the properties of the kingdom of heaven.

After these explanations we now propose the following distribution of the parables, to be justified by the exposition.

I. Theoretic or Didactic Parables. â Under this head we include the group of seven parables in Matt. xiii.: The Sower, the Tares and the Drag-net, the Hid Treasure and the Precious Pearl, the Mustard Seed and the Leaven, with the parable in Mark iv. 26â 29, the Blade, the Ear, and the Full Cornâ in all forming a group of eight relating to the general nature of the kingdom of God. And besides these, the parables of the Selfish Neighbour and the Unjust Judge relating to the delays of Providence in fulfilling spiritual desires, or to perseverance in prayer (Luke xi. 5, xviii. l); the parable of Extra Service (Luke xvii. 7); and finally the three parables which relate to the subject of work and wages in the kingdom: viz. the Hours of Labour (Matt. XX. i), the Talents (Matt. xxv. 14), and the Pounds (Luke xix. 12). In all, fourteen.

II. Evangelic Parables. â To this class belong the four parables in Luke's Gospel which together constitute Christ's apology for loving the sinful: the Two Debtors (chap. vii. 40), the Lost Sheep, the Lost Coin, and the Lost Son (chap, xv.); the Children of the Bride-Chamber (Matt. ix. 14â 17 et parall), being an apology for the joy of the children of the kingdom. Under the same category fall the Lowest Seats at Feasts (Luke xiv. 7â 11), and the Pharisee and the Publican (Luke xviii. 9â 14), teaching that the kingdom of God is for the humble; the Great Supper (Luke xiv. 16), teaching that the kingdom is for the hungry; the Good Samaritan (Luke x. 30); the Unrighteous Steward (Luke xvi. i); the Rich Man and Lazarus (Luke xvi. 19), and the Unmerciful Servant, the two last together teaching which are the unpardonable sins. In all, twelve.

III. Prophetic or Judicial Parables. â This class includes the following: The Children in the Market-Place (Matt. xi. 16), containing Christ's moral estimate of the generation amidst which He lived; the Barren Fig-tree (Luke xiii. 6), the two Sons and the Wicked Husbandmen (Matt. xxi. 28â 44), and the Marriage of the King's Son (Matt, xxii, i), exhibiting more or less clearly the action of Divine judgment upon the nation of Israel; the Unfaithful Servant (Matt. xxiv. 45), and the Ten Virgins (Matt. xxv. i). exhibiting similar judicial action within the kingdom of God. In all, seven.

It will be observed that the foregoing groups do not include all the parabolic utterances of our Lord recorded in the Gospels. To those omitted belong the parabolic conclusion to the Sermon on the Mount, consisting of the metaphors of the wise and foolish builders, the similitudes of the inconsiderate builder of a tower, and the king who would wage war (Luke xiv. 28â 35), and the Rich Fool (Luke xii. 16), which appears in most treatises as one of the regular parables. These and the like are excluded, not chiefly because they cannot easily be brought within our scheme of distribution, but more especially because they are of no independent didactic importance. The parables we propose to consider have all this in common, that they embody truths deep, unfamiliar or unwelcomeâ " mysteries of the kingdom." Such a parable as that of the Rich Fool, on the other hand, conveys no new or abstruse lesson, but simply teaches in concrete lively form a moral commonplace. Parabolic utterances of that description were not distinctive of Christ as a Teacher: they were common to Him with the Jewish Rabbis. He spake these merely as a Jewish moralist; but the parables now to be studied were uttered by Him as the Herald of the kingdom of heaven.

BOOK r. THEORETIC PARABLES.

Sitting in a boat on the Sea of Galilee near the shore, on which a great multitude was assembled to hear Him, Jesus said:â

Behold I the sower went forth to sow. And as he sowed, some seeds fell by the wayside, and the fowls came and devoured them. And other seeds fell upon the rocky places, where they had not much earthy and forthwith they sprang up, because they had no deepness of earth j and when the sun was tip they were scorched, and because they had not root they withered away. And other fell tipon the thorns, and the thorns sprang up and choked them. And other fell upon the gooa ground, and brought forth fruit, soine an hundredfold, some sixty' fold, and sonie thirtyfold. Who hath ears, let him hear. â Matt. xiii. 3â 9.

Christ's hearers would have no difficulty in understanding the letter of this parable. At their side, as modern travellers who have been on the spot tell us,"' they might see an

We give the parable and its interpretation as contained in Matthew; all points of importance in the other Gospels will be noticed as we proceed.

2 6 (TTriipiotf â the man whose function it was to sow, or the sower of my parable.

3 inl rd. â mtpwst â not soil mixed with loose stones (which might be good), but soil resting on a rocky substratum a little below the surface.

Upon a soil with thorn or thistle seed in it, which afterwards sprang up. ' 8 fiiv, 8 Si, 8 diâ in this case, in that, and in a third case.

Vide Stanley, Sinai and Palestine," p. 425, in a chapter on the local connections and allusions of Christ's teaching.

agricultural scene which would enable them to comprehend all the details of the picture at a glance. They would know perfectly what was literally intended by the four kinds of ground distinguished in the parable: that the way-side signified the hard-trodden path running through the cornfield; that the rocky places signified that part of the field where the soil was shallow, and the rocky stratum below came near the surface; that the thorns denoted, not thorn bushes actually growing in the field at the time of sowing, but soil with thorn seeds latent in it, which in due course sprang up, disputing possession with the grain; and that the good ground meant that portion of the field which was free from all the faults of the other parts, and was at once soft, deep, and clean. They would know also that the fate of seed falling upon these different places respectively would be just such as described in the parable: that the seed falling on the hard path would never even so much as germinate, but either be picked up by the birds or trodden under foot; that the seed falling on shallow soil, with rock immediately beneath, might germinate, and even spring up rapidly for a short while, but for want of sap and depth of earth must inevitably wither under the heat of the sun, and so come to nothing; that the seed which fell on soil full of thorn or thistle seeds might not only germinate and spring up, but continue to grow with vigour till it reached the green earâ the fault of the ground not being poverty, but foulnessâ but would never ripen, being choked, smothered, and shaded by the overgrowing thorns; and finally, that seed which fell on good, generous soil, soft, deep, and clean, could not fail, under the genial influences of fostering sap beneath and of a bright sun above, to yield a bountiful harvest, richly rewarding the husbandman's pains.

But what might the spiritual meaning of the parable be Why did Jesus speak this parable What did He mean to teach These questions His hearers were not able to answer. That the parable was designed to teach something, that it meant more than met the ear, they would of course understand; for common sense would teach them that Christ was not likely to describe a sowing scene for its own sake, and the closing words, "Who hath ears, let him hear," was a hint â Â t a hidden meaning that could not fail to be understood even by the most obtuse. It is even possible that the people standing on the shore had a shrewd suspicion that the preacher was speaking about themselves, and describing the various sorts of hearers of the word of the kingdom who vere mingled together in that great crowd, and the correspondingly-diverse issues of the preaching of the word. But beyond that point we may be sure their comprehension did not go. They might have a dim impression that the various sorts of soil signified spiritual states; but they could not discriminate the spiritual soils on which the word of the kingdom fell, as they could at once and with ease apprehend the literal points of the parable. How should the multitude at large understand what even the disciples, the twelve, and others who had been constantly in Christ's company, failed to understand That even they were puzzled, the record informs us. When they were alone, we are told, the disciples asked their Master what might this parable be. One of the Evangelists gives the question thus: " Why speakest Thou unto them in parables?" â meaning, in such a parable as this of the Sower. The two forms of the question convey a pretty definite idea of the state of mind of those who put it. It was a state intermediate between perfect knowledge and total ignorance. They did not know clearly the meaning of the parable, else they would not have asked for an interpretation; they were not totally ignorant of its meaning, else they would not have asked, "Why speakest Thou unto them in parables? " They knew enough to be surprised that their Master addressed such a parable to the eagerly-listening multitude â a parable not setting forth any truth concerning the kingdom, like that of the Precious Pearl, which teaches the incomparable value of the kingdomâ but animadverting on the various classes of hearers. That, as we believe, was the cause of surprise: not the general fact of teaching in a new way (viz. in parables) taken abstractly and by itself, but that fact taken in conjunction with the peculiar character of the parable by which the new method was inaugurated.

If such was indeed the feeling in the minds of the disciples,-we cannot wonder at their question. For even now we who understand the parable, as they could not before it was

Luke viii, 9. Matt. xiii. 10.

explained to them, are constrained to ask ourselves the question, Why spake Jesus sucji a parable as that of the Sower to the crowd of people assembled on the shore of the Sea of Galileeâ a parable in which the Speaker preached not to the people, but at them, or over their heads; not about any important truth of the kingdom, but about the reception truth was likely to meet with; not glad tidings to men, but very sombre, depressing tidings concerning men in their relation to the gospel? One could at once understand how such a parable as this might at any time have been spoken to the disciples; because to them it was given " to know the mysteries of the kingdom of heaven," and specially because it was desirable that they, as the future apostles of the kingdom, should know what reception they were to meet with, to prevent disappointment when they learned by experience, as their Master had already learned, that the effect of the word was conditioned variously by the moral state of the hearer. Antecedently to experience, men of sanguine temper, ardently devoted to the kingdom, might anticipate a very different result, and expect the intrinsic excellence of the doctrine to insure in all cases a harvest of beneficent effects. A warning to the contrary was therefore by no means superfluous. But was it not wasting a precious opportunity thus to speak to the common people? and if the Preacher must speak in parabolic form, why not utter an " evangelic " parable, reserving didactic parables for the twelve, and prophetic parables for unbelieving hostile Pharisees and Sadducees? We put the question strongly, because we wish to force ourselves and our readers to reflect and go in quest of an answer; believing that the answer, when found, will lend greatly enhanced interest to the parable, and help us to understand its import, and may even lead to discoveries as to the design and what we may call the psychological genesis of the whole parabolic teaching of our Lord.

Without doubt, then, to answer our question at once, the reason why Jesus spoke such a parable as that of the Sower, and such other parables as these of the Tares and the Net, in the hearing of the multitude is to be sought in the moral situation of the hour Travellers and interpreters have been

Farrar, in his 'Life of Christ takes this view: "The great mass of

CH. I. Theoretic Parables. â The Sower. ly at great pains to explain the piyszcal situation â the natural surroundings of the Speaker that day when He began to open His mouth in parables. And this is well, though it is possible to have too much of it, leading to a sentimental style of treating the parables which is rather tiresome and unprofitable. The moral situation is undoubtedly the principal thing to be determined; for we cannot believe that Christ was led to speak as He did by merely picturesque influences, any more than we can believe that He then and there opened His mouth in parables from a merely intellectual liking for that symbolic manner of expressing thought. The motive must have come from the spiritual composition and condition of the crowd. Jesus must have lifted up the eye of His mind, and seen, not a literal field, with the characteristics described, in course of being sown with grain, but a spiritual field with analogous characteristics, which had been sown with the seeds of Divine truth by Himself,â even that very crowd which was assembled before Him, But have we any evidence that the spiritual condition of that crowd was such as this hypothesis requires We have. First there is the statement made by Jesus Himself, in reply to the question of His disciples, which presents a very gloomy picture of the spiritual condition of the people: " For this people's heart is waxed gross," etc. When Jesus said that, He did not merely quote a prophetic commonplace in a haphazard, pointless way, without meaning to imply that it had any very definite applicability to the multitude before Him. He believed, and He said, that in the case of that very multitude the spiritual state described by the prophet Isaiah was very exactly fulfilled or realized. Then, secondly, there is the great historical melancholy fact of the Capernaum crisis recorded in John vi., in which the Galilean revival came to a deplorable end: " From that time many of His disciples went back and walked no more with Him."

hearers," he remarks, "must now have been aware of the general features in the new gospel which Jesus preached. Some self-examination, some earnest, careful thought of their own, was now requisite, if they were indeed sincere in their desire to profit by His words" (vol. i. p. 322).

1 Matt. xiii. 15. Matt. xiii. 14. Kai dvan-Xijjooorat. The ava is intensive.

' John vi. 66.

And, finally, the minute particularr of information supplied by the Evangelists as to the circumstances amid which Jesus spake our parable, show that the Galilean enthusiasm is at its height, and therefore that the crisis, the time of reaction, must be near. Matthew tells us that so great were the multitudes who gathered together unto Jesus that He was obliged to go into a ship in order to escape pressure, and have a position from which He could be seen and heard of all. Mark says: "And He began again to teach by the seaside,"â implying eagerness in the people thereabouts to hear; and he characterises the audiences not merely as great, but as very great. Luke informs us that the congregation assembled was composed of people coming " out of every city," â that is, from all the towns and villages by the shores of the lake.

The crisis, then, is approaching, and it is in view of that crisis Jesus speaks the parable of the Sower. He sees it comin; j;, and is sad, and He speaks as He feels. The present enthusiasm, because He knows how it is likely to end, gives Him no pleasure,â it rather causes Him trouble. He wishes to be rid of it. We might almost say He speaks the parable for that end; using it, as He used the mystic sermon on the Bread of Life, in the synagogue at Capernaum, as a fan to separate wheat from chaff. At the least, we may say He speaks the parable to foreshadov the end. The parable is a prelude to the sermon, uttered to satisfy the Speaker's sense of truth; to throw hearers back on themselves in self-examination; to warn disciples against being imposed on by fair appearances, and cherishing romantic expectations doomed f to bitter disappointment; and to insure in all ages, for an enthusiasm of humanity' not blind to the weakness of human nature, a respect which it is impossible to accord to a shallow philanthropy without moral insight.

' Matt. xiii. 2. 0 X0? Trxftorof (ch. iv. 1).

' Ch. viii. 4- "' v Kardi ttoxiv iiriiropfvonivwv Trpof avrov.

For our view of the effect of that sermon see ' The Training of thÂ = Twelve," cap. ix., section 4.

"Godet says: " The end of Jesus is first to show that He is under no illusion in view of that multitude in appearance so attentive; next to pur His disciples on their guard against the hopes which the present enthusiasm might inspire; lastly, and above all, to fortify His hearers against the perils to which their present religious impressions were exposed " ' Comm.

So we account for the utterance of the parable of the Sower, and of at least some others of the group contained in Matt, xiii. But can the same or a similar account be given of the parabolic teaching of Christ in general? A remark of Jesus to His disciples reported by Mark seems to imply that it can: " Know ye not this parable? and how then will ye know all the parables?" 2 The remark, taken by Itself misjht be understood to mean that men who could not comprehend so simple a parable would be still more at a loss with other parables, spoken or to be spoken, more difficult of comprehension. But, taken along with the reference going before to the words of Isaiah, it seems rather to signify that the parables in general are to be regarded as asso-iated more or less with the mood of mind which these prophetic words express. And close observation of the parables recorded in the Gospels shows that this is really to a large extent the case. It will be found, on inspection, that very many of the parables are of an apologetic or defensive character. The position of Christ when He uttered them was that of one found fault with, misunderstood, or despairing of being understood; conscious of isolation, and saddened by the lack of intelligence, sympathy, and faith on the part of those among whom He exercised His ministry. Such seem to have been the psychological conditions under which the mind of the Saviour betook itself to parable-making. The question why He spoke in parables as a public teacher is a wide one, to which a full answer is not given in the Gospels. Doubtless temperament and the genius of race had something to do with it; and a certain class of writers would emphasise such sur revariglle de St. Luc," i. 396). The last remark in the sentence in the text to which this note refers may be illustrated by an anecdote told of Frederick the Great. When one of the apostles of eighteenth-century Illuminism spo'ce to him with enthusiasm of the results to be expected from an education based on the assumption of the goodness of human nature, his reply was, "You don't know the race." Christ did know the race, and yet loved man with an ardour and steadfastness to which no philanthropy, deistic or other, can be compared.â Vide Kahnis" History of German Protestantism," p. 49.

The question whether all the parables in Matt. xiii. were spoken at one time will be noticed in a future chapter, 2 Mark iv. 13.

causes. But while they may be admitted to have been Joint causes, we do not believe they were sole causes. There is not only a parabolic temperament and a parabolic genius that delights to wrap thoughts up in symbolic envelopes; but there is, moreover, a parabolic mood, which leads a man now, rather than then, to present his thoughts in this form. It is the mood of one whose heart is chilled and whose spirit is saddened by a sense of loneliness, and who, retiring within himself, by a process of reflection frames for his thoughts forms which half conceal, half reveal them,â reveal them more perfectly to those who understand, hide them from those who do not: forms beautiful, but also melancholy, as the hues of the forest in late autumn. If this view be correct, we should expect that speaking in parables would not form a feature of the initial stage of Christ's ministry. And such, accordingly, was the fact. Jesus opened His mouth first, not in parables, but in plain speeches; or if He used parables previously, it was only such as were common among Jewish teachers: figures meant to enliven moral commonplaces, like that of the wise and foolish builders at the close of the Sermon on the Mount. He uttered beatitudes before He uttered similitudes, and He uttered similitudes because the beatitudes had not been understood or appreciated. In His own words, as reported by the first Evangelist, Jesus began to speak in parables because His hearers, seeing, saw not, and hearing, heard not, neither did they understand. They had seen His miracles, and had been led by them to form false conceptions of His mission; they had heard His teaching on the mount and elsewhere, and had formed erroneous ideas of the kingdom; and therefore now He wraps His thoughts in forms by which those who do see shall be enabled to see more clearly, and to him who hath light shall come a still higher measure of illumination, and those, on the other hand, who see not shall be made still more blind, simply mystified and perplexed as to what the strange Speaker might mean.

Such, doubtless, were the results in many instances of

Ebrard maintains that the parables in Matt. xiii. were spoken before the Sermon on the Mount; but this view has met with little or no approval. See his 'Gospel History."

Matt, xiii, 12; Mark iv. 25.

Christ's parabolic teaching: some who so far already understood Him were led into a clearer comprehension of His mind; others who understood Him not were conducted into deeper darkness. Take, e. g., the parables which contain the apology for loving sinners. One who understood the motive of Jesus in frequenting the company of sinners would get a most instructive glim. pse into the heart of the Son of Man on hearing those charming, pathetic parables of the Lost Sheep, the Lost Coin, and the Lost Son. But what effect would these beautiful poetic parables have on the mind of unsympathetic, hostile Pharisees? Not to make them comprehend at last the true spirit of a much misunderstood and calumniated man, but to harden them into more intense antipathy,â the very beauty and poetry and pathos of the sayings making them hate niore bitterly one with whom they were determined not to be pleased. Such were the results in that case, and doubtless in many others. But were these resultsâ was the latter result, that is to sayâ hitendedf Did Jesus Christ, the Saviour of men, speak parables that blind men might be made blinder, and deaf men deafer, and hard hearts harder According to the report of what He said to the disciples in answer to their question " Why speakest Thou in parables " given by two of the Evangelists, we may seem forced to the conclusion that He did. For while Matthew makes Him say, "Therefore speak I to them in parables, because they seeing, see not" â suggesting the thought that the parabolic mode of instruction was adopted that men who saw not might see at least a-little, since they had failed to see on any other method, Mark and Luke ascribe to Him the sentiment, "To others (I speak) in parables, in order that seeing, they might not see, and hearing, they might not understand." Some critics, deeming the two accounts irreconcilable, prefer Matthew's as the more correct, and regard the aim ascribed to Christ by the other two Evangelists simply as " the hypochondriac construction put upon His words in Gospels written in a pessimistic spirit by men despairing of the Jewish people." But that the two points of view are not mutually exclusive may be inferred from the fact that even Mark, who puts the darker

Matt. xiii. 13. ' Mark iv. 12; Luke viii. 10, 8 So Keim, after Strauss, in Jesu von Nazara," ii. 439.

view most strongly, winds up his record of Christ's parabolic teaching by the lake-side with a reflection which plainly implies that the design of that teaching was not to produce blindness, but, if possible, vision. "And with many such parables spake He the word unto them, as they were able to hear it." And we may lay it down as a fixed principle that what is implied in Mark's reflection is the truth. The direct-primary aim of all Christ's teaching was to illuminate human minds and to soften human hearts. Such was both the aim and the tendency of His parabolic teaching in particular. The parable of the Prodigal Son, e. g. was surely both fitted and intended to enlighten the minds of even scribes and Pharisees as to the motive of the Speaker in associating with the sinful, and to soften their hearts into a more kindly tone of feeling towards Himself! But, on the other hand, that very parable might have just the opposite effects on minds full of prejudice and on hearts full of bitterness, and produce a more complete misunderstanding and a more inhuman and pitiless antipathy. And in uttering the parable Jesus could not but be aware of the possibility of such a result, and yet might utter it with that possible result consciously in view. Nay, we can conceive Him erecting the possible and undesirable result into the position of an end, and saying, "I speak such and such parables in order that they who see not may become more utterly blind." Only we must be careful not to misunderstand the temper in which such words might be spoken by Jesus, or by any true servant of God. No true prophet could utter such words in cold blood as the expression of a deliberate purpose. All prophets desire to illumine, soften, and save, not to darken, harden, and destroy; and without entering into the mystery of Divine decrees, we may add, God sends His prophets for no other purpose, whatever the foreseen effects of their labour may be. But a prophet like Isaiah may nevertheless feel as if he were sent, and represent himself as sent, for the opposite purpose. And when he does so it is not in the way of expressing direct aim or deliberate intention, but in irony, and in the bitterness of frustrated, despairing

love. Baffled love in bitter irony announces as its aim the very opposite of what it works for,
Mark iv. 33.
and it does so in the hope of provoking its infatuated objects to jealousy, and so defeating its own prophecy. " I go," says Isaiah in effect," to prophesy to this people, that hearing they may understand not, and seeing may perceive not, that I may make their hearts fat, and their ears heavy, and their eyes dim, lest they see with their eyes and hear with their ears and understand with their hearts, and convert and be healed;" and he goes forth to fulfil these strange ends by using means fitted and designed to produce just the opposite effects, warning them of the consequences of persisting in evil ways, and preaching unto them a gospel of rest for the weary with such plainness, emphasis, and iteration, as to expose himself to the mockery of drunkards, who said: " With this prophet it is ' precept upon precept, precept upon precept; line upon line, line upon line; here a little, there a little,"â wearisome iteration of lessons fit only for children." In the light of these observations we can understand in what spirit Jesus appropriated to Himself the harsh terms in which the prophet expressed his Divine mission, and how we are to view His parabolic teachings. He served Himself heir to Isaiah's commission in the ironic humour of a love that yearned to save, and was faithful to its purpose even to death. He spoke parables,â one now, another then; here a little, there a little, â if by any means He might teach men the truth in which they might find rest to their souls. The parables were neither deliberate mystifications, nor idle intellectual conceits, nor mere literary products of aesthetic taste: they were the utterances of a sorrowful heart. And herein lies their chief charm: not in the doctrine they teach, though that is both interesting and important; not in their literary beauty, though that is great; but in the sweet delicate odour of human pathos that breathes from them as from Alpine wild flowers. That He had to speak in parables was one of the burdens of the Son of Man, to be placed side by side with the fact that He had not where to lay His head.
Isaiah vi. 9, 10.
2 Isaiah xxviii. 9â 12. The words in the original are at once a clever caricature of elementary teaching for children, and an imitation of the thick, indistinct speech of an intoxicated person: Ki tsav-Ia-tsav, tsav-la tsav; kav-la-kav, kav-la-kav; zeer-shkm, zeer-shkm.
We proce-ed now to the interpretation of our parable. Christ's own interpretation was as follows:
Hear ye then the parable of the sower. In the case of every one hearing the word of the kingdom and not understanding it, cometh the wicked one and catcheth away that which has been sown in his heart. This is the one sown by the wayside?- But the one sown tipon the rocky places is he who heareth the word and anon with joy receive th it. But he hath not root in himself, but is only temporary," and wheji tribulation or persecution ariseth because of the word, straightway he is made to stumble. And the one sowtt among the thorns is he who heareth the word, and the care of this world and the deceitfulness of riches choke the word, and he becometh unfruitful. And the one sown upon the good ground is he who heareth the word and understandeth it, ivho

accorditigly bringeth forth fruit and produces now an hundredfold, now sixty, now thirty. â Matt. xiii. i8â 23.

The parable, according to this authoritative interpretation, is meant to teach that among those to whom the word of the kingdom is spoken are diverse classes of hearersâ four at least â corresponding to the four sorts of ground on which the seed falls. A record of observation in the first place, it is, moreover, a prophetic picture of the future fortunes of the kingdom. In relating under a parabolic veil His own sad experience, Jesus forewarned His disciples what they had to expect when they were called on as apostles to sow the word of the kingdom. They should find among their hearers classes of persons of which these sorts of ground were the types. Now, the matter of chief importance here is, to form just conceptions of these classes, that the moral lesson may come home to all. Many interpreters grievously offend here. Greswell, e. g., makes the wayside hearer one characterised by an absolute hardness, whose state of mind " may be the most deplorable to which human frailty is exposed and the most horrible to which human wickedness is liable to be reduced,â

Elliptical for "he who is meant in the part of the parable which speaks of seed sown by the way." Similarly in all the other cases.

irpoffkaipog.

' (5, expressive of self-evident result. See p. 36.

Greswell labours to prove that there can be no more than four classes. Such discussions are not in the spirit of the parable, which expresses facts that had come under the Speaker's observation, not necessary psychological truth.

the last stage in a long career of depravity, and the judicial result of perseverance in obstinate wickedness with impunity and impenitence." This is surely to confound weakness and wickedness, and so to render the parable useless for the purpose of warning to a very common class of hearers. Ve must remember, in the quaint words of a wiser expositor, that " the trodden path is after all not a rock," and generally give heed to the remark of a greater than either: " In order that the admonitions of the parable may benefit us the more, it must be kept steadily in view that no mention is made therein of despisers of the word, but only of those in whom appears a certain measure of docility." Doubtless there were ' wayside' hearers in the crowd to whom the parable was addressed; yet all present had come with more or less desire to hear Christ preach, and learn at His lips the doctrine of the kingdom.

We shall best learn to discriminate accurately the different classes of hearers by giving close attention to the manner in which they are respectively characterised by our Lord. '

I. The wayside hearer hears the word, but does not understand it,â or, to use a phrase which expresses at once the literal and the figurative truth, does not take it in. Thoughtlessness, spiritual stupidity, arising not so much from want of intellectual capacity as from preoccupation of mind, is the characteristic of the first class. Their mind is like a footpath beaten hard by the constant passage through it of " the wishes of the flesh and the current thoughts " concerning common earthly things. For a type of the class we may take the man who interrupted Christ while preaching on one occasion, and said: " Master, speak to my brother, that he divide the inheritance with me." He had just heard Christ utter the words, "And when they bring yo x into the synagogues, and unto 1 Parables," vol. ii. 37. ' Stier, Reden Jesus, ii. 83.

3 Calvin, ' Comment, in Quatuor Evangelistas," in loc.

"Our language is capable in this instance, like the Greek, of expressing by one phrase equally the moral and the material failure: ' Every one that hears the word of the kingdom and does not take it in (Â aj ovvikvroz)- " Arnot, 'The Parables of our Lord," p. 52.

So Mr. M. Arnold renders the Apostle Paul's phrase rh. Bixrifiara rfe aapkUQ Kal rajv Siavotojv (Eph. ii. 3). Vt'iis Literature and Dogma,"p. 202.

Luke xii. 13.

magistrates and powers," and these suggested to him the topic on which his thoughts were habitually fixed â his dispute with his brother about their patrimony. And so it happened to him according to the parable. The truth he had heard did not get into his mind, hardened as it was like a beaten path by the constant passage through it of current thoughts about money; it was very soon forgotten altogether, caught away by the god of this world, who ruled over him through his covetous disposition. It may be regarded as certain that there were many such hearers in the crowd by the lake,â men in whose minds the doctrine of the kingdom merely awakened hopes of worldly prosperity,â who, as Jesus afterwards told them, laboured for the meat that perisheth, not for the meat that endureth unto everlasting life. Such were they who " received seed by the wayside."

2. He that received seed into stony places, on the other hand, is he that heareth the word and anon with joy receivcth it. The characteristic of this class is emotional excitability, in-â 'considerate impulsiveness. They receive the word readily with joy; but without thought. The latter trait is not indeed specified, but it is clearly implied in the remark concerning the eft"ect of tribulation, persecution, or temptation on this class of hearers. They had not anticipated such experiences, they did not count the cost, there was a want of deliberation at the commencement of their religious life, and by implication a want of that mental constitution which ensures that there shall be deliberation at all critical periods of life. It is this want of deliberation that is the fault of the class now under consideration, not the mere fact of their receiving the word with joy. Joy by itself does not define the class; for joy is characteristic of deep as well as of shallow natures. Absence of joy in religious life is a sign, not of depth, but of dulness. The noble, devoted heart that attains to high measures of faithfulness has great rapturous passionate joy in connection with its spiritual experiences. But the joy of the good and honest heart is a thoughtful joy, associated with and springing out of the exercise of the intellectual and the moral powers upon the truth believed. The joy of the stony ground hearer, on the contrary, is a thought- Â Luke xii. ii. " John vi. 27.

less joy coming to him through the effects of what he hears upon the imagination and the feeungs. Joy without thought is his definition.

Of course a religious experience of this character cannot last: it is doomed to prove abortive. For tribulation, persecution, temptation in some form, will come, not to be withstood except by those whose whole spiritual beingâ mind, heart, conscienceâ is influenced by the truth; and even by them only by the most strenuous exertion of their moral energies. A man who has been touched only on the surface of his soul by a religious movement, who has been impressed on the sympathetic side of his nature by a prevalent enthusiasm, and has yielded to the current without understanding what it means, whither it tends, and what it involves,â such a man has no chance of persevering under the conditions of trial amidst which the divine life has to be lived in this world. He is doomed to be Trpoakaipos, a temporary Christian, to be scandalised by tribulation, to apostatise in the season of temptation. For he hath not root in himself, in his moral personality, in the faculties constituting personality â the reason, conscience, and willâ which remain hard, untouched, unpenetrated by the fibres of his faith; his root is in others, in a prevalent popular enthusiasm; his religion is a thing of sympathetic imitation. He is not only-npoakaipos in the sense of being temporary, but likewise in the sense of being a creation of the time, a child of the Zeitgeist)- He comes forth as a professor of religion " at the call of a shallow enthusiasm, and through the epidemic influence of a popular cause." And this fact largely explains his temporariness. When the tide of enthusiasm subsides, and he is left to himself to carry on single-handed the struggle with temptation, he has no heart for the work, and his religion withers away, like the corn growing on rocky places under the scorching heat of the summer sun.

If a type of this class is sought for in the Gospel records, it may be found in the man who said unto Jesus, "Lord, I will follow Thee whithersoever Thou goest," and to whom Jesus

So Lange, Bibelwerk'; and also Volkmar, Die Evangelien," p. 284. Edward Irving, Sermons on the Parable of the Sower." Collected writings, vol. i. p. 169.

replied, "Foxes have holes, and birds of the air have roosts, but the Son of man hath not where to lay His head." The reply clearly implies that this would-be disciple was under some sudden impulse proposing to follow Christ, without considering what the step involved. He had received the word of the kingdom with joy, and came to offer himself as a disciple in a spirit of romantic enthusiasm, without the smallest idea what he was undertaking, utterly unaware of the hardships of disciple life. But what need to point to the scribe as if he were a solitary instance of inconsiderate profession! Was not the crowd by the lake to which the Parable of the Sower was spoken full of such professors? There was a great religious enthusiasmâ what in these days might be called a ' great revival'â in Galilee, and there were many in that crowd who had come under its influence. Infected by the spirit of the time, they followed Jesus, by whose preaching of the kingdom the movement had been created, whithersoever He went; delighted to hear Him speak, feeling as if they could never hear enough of the precious words which fell from His lips. But, alas 1 their religion consisted largely in sympathy with their fellows, and in vague romantic dreams concerning the kingdom that was coming; and so when the time of disenchantment came, and they learnt that their dreams were not likely to be realised, they " went back and walked no more with Him." How often has the same tragedy been repeated in the history of religious movements of a popular character! It is persons whose spiritual natures resemble the rocky ground who are chiefly influenced by such movements. Others of deeper character and more promise may be touched in small numbers, but these are sure to be touched in large numbers. And so it comes to pass that the melancholy history of many hopeful religious movements is this: many converts, few stable Christians; many blossoms, little fruit coming to maturity.

Luke ix. 57; cf. Matt. viii. 19. ' John vi. 66.

3 "Such men," says Godet, "form in almost every awakening a considerable portion of the new converts."â 'Comment, sur Luc," i. 399. Deeper natures are less influenced by sympathy, and their religious decisions are come to for the most part ia solitude and after earnest consideration of the subject on all sides.

3. He that received seed among the thorns is so described as to suggest the idea of a doiible-niinded man â the avi p hi vyos of St. James. This man is neither stupid, Hke his brother hearer of the first class, nor a mere man of feehng, like those of the second class. He hears in the emphatic sense of the word, hears both with thought and with feeling, understanding what he hears and realising its solemn importance. The soil in his case is neither hard on the surface nor shallow; it is good soil so far as softness and depth are concerned. Its one fault (but it is a very serious one) is that it is impure: there are other seeds in it besides those being sown on it, and the result will be tzvo crops struggling for the mastery, with the inevitable result that the better crop will have to succumb. This man h s two minds, so to speak,â we might almost say he is two men. His will is dividedâ not decided for good and against evil, but now on one side, now on the other; serving God to-day, serving mammon to-morrow; very religious, and also very worldly. Such he is at the beginning, though not very obviously; such he will be more manifestly in the after course of his religious career; such he will be to the end. To the end, we say; for it is not this man's nature to begin with enthusiasm and by and by to leave off. He is too grave, too serious, too strong-natured a man, to be guilty of such levity. What he begins he will go through with. He will not apostatise, as a rule (for there may be exceptions); he will keep up a profession of religion till he dies. His leaf will not wither,â it will continue growing till it reach the ear; but the ear will be green when it should be ripe. Only in this sense is it said of him that "he becometh unfruitful."2 He bringeth forth fruit, but he bringeth " no fruit to perfection." He never attains to ripeness in his personal character. Any one can see that he is a misthriven Christian, a man not victorious over the world, but defeated by the world in one form or another,â by carking care, by the vanity and pride of wealth, by some form of selfish or sensual indulgence, such as 1 James i. 8. Double-mindedness in this text is not to be confounded "with hypocrisy, 2 Matt. xiii. 22. Mark iv. 19.

' Luke viii. 14. Kat ob rtxitrtpopovrnv. Vtde Robertson of Brighton on this point: 'Sermons," first series, on the Parable of the Sower. The â whole sermon is instructive.

inordinate affection for things lawful, sloth, or excessive use of stimulants.! You may hope for his salvation notwithstanding; nevertheless you pronounce him a spiritual failure. He is unfruitful also in his Christian activity, unfruitful in the sense of bringing no fruit to perfection. He busies himself, probably, in good works; perhaps takes a prominent part in devotional meetings, and appears duly on philanthropic and religious platforms. But his influence is zero, or worseâ mischievous; for honest men know him, and it gives them a disgust to see such as he figuring as promoters of any good work or as patrons of any worthy cause.

It may be asked, Who has a chance of bringing forth fruit unto perfection, for what character is free from thorns "i But the question is not, who is free from evil desires, or from temptation to inordinate affection? but what attitude you assume towards these. There are roots of bitterness in every man, which, if allowed to grow up, will trouble and defile him. But the attitude of the double-minded man towards these roots is very different from that of the single-minded man. The former never makes up his mind to be resolutely against evil, and to bring to bear all his moral energy to put it down; the latter, on the contrary, does make up his mind to this, and abides habitually of this mind. The single-minded man adopts as his principle the motto, "Seek ye first the kingdom of God, and food and raiment shall be added unto you;" and in adopting and acting on this principle he becomes a perfect man, and brings forth fruit unto perfection. For the perfect man in Scripture does not mean the faultless man, but the man of single mind, who loves God above all else; and the fruit of such a man's life, though not absolutely corresponding to the ideal, will be acknowledged by all competent judges to be good, his character noble, his work such as shall stand.

Of the thorny ground hearer, the man of divided mind and Â All these forms of worldliness are referred to in the records: Matthew specifies the care of the world (iiipifiva tov aliovog) and the deceit of riches (ij dirart tov irxoiirou); Mark to these adds the desires concerning other things (ai TTfpl rd Xomd ttriovfiiai). Luke also gives these categories: cares, riches, and pleasures of life vtto niptfivcjv koi vxovtov kui I'lsovoiv tov (Siov). Lisco starts this difficulty: vide 'The Parables of Jesus," p. 6i.

double heart, we have an example in him who came to Jesus and said, "Lord, I will follow Thee; but first let me go bid them farewell which are at home at my house." Apparently a most reasonable request; but Jesus discerned in it the sign of a divided heart, and therefore replied: " No man having put his hand to the plough, attd looking back, is fit for the kingdom of God." The example is all the more instructive that the man's temptation arose, not from lust after forbidden pleasure, but from inordinate affection for things lawful. How natural, how excusable that hankering after home and household! Yet just such hankerings, and nothing worse, are in many instances the thorns which, springing up, choke the word and render it unfruitful. How many men are wasting their lives at home, who might go forth to a life of abundant fruitfulness in mission fields, were it not for an attachment like that of John Mark for fathers or mothers, or native land! 4. He that received seed into the good ground is he that heareth the word and understandeth it. The description is intended to express the idea of a perfect hearer, and for that purpose seems inadequate. For the perfect hearer ought to have all the good characteristics of a hearer of the previous class, and over and above, that which he lacksâ a pure will, a single mind. Now, even the thorny ground hearer understands the word, and is impressed by it, and only comes short by not giving to that to which the word relates, the kingdom of God, its proper place of supremacy. It does not therefore sufficiently distinguish a hearer of the last class to say of him that he hears and understands, or even that he hears with understanding and feeling. The authors of the Authorized version betray a certain consciousness of this fact in their rendering of the clause relating to the fruitfulness of the fourth classâ " which also beareth fruit"â as if the words werss. meant to express an additional characteristic of the class; while in truth they express the sure, necessary result of the

    Luke ix. 6i, 62.

2 Acts xii. 25; xiii. 13; xv. 37â 39. John Mark was one who looked back, and therefore was deemed by Paul not fit for the work of the kingdom in which he was engaged. Mark appears afterwards to have regained Paul's confidenceâ a fact which reminds us that a thorny grouud hearer is under no fatal necessity of continuing such.

characteristics already specified. We naturally turn to the other Evangelists, to see whether the apparent defect is supplied in their accounts. For the ' understandeth' of Matthew, Mark gives receive," and Luke, 'keep'; and these are important words, but neither do they bring out fully the characteristic distinction of the perfect hearer. For the thorny ground hearer also receives the truth, takes it into his mind and heart; and he not only receives it, but retains it; his only fault is that he does not receive and retain it alone, but allows the cares of this world, and the deceitfulness of riches, and the lusts of other things to enter into and abide in his heart alongside of the truth. The precise distinction of the perfect hearer, on the other hand, is this,â that he does receive and retain the word alojie in his mind. He is characteristically single-minded and whole-hearted in religion. The kingdom of God has the first place in his thoughts, and everything else only the second. His motto is taken from the words of the Psalmist: " Bless the Lord, O my soul, and all that is zvitjnn me" He loves God, and seeks the kingdom of God in accordance with the high requirement, " with all thine heart, and with all thy soul, and with all thy might." He is wholly given up, devoted, to the kingdom; for him, as for the Preacher, to " fear God and keep His commandments " is " the whole of man." That the perfect hearer must be a man of 1 Mark iv. 20: Trapasfcxovrai. Luke viii. 15: (carexowffu'.

' St. Bernard has some excellent remarks on this requirement in his Sermons on Canticles." Discoursing on the duty of loving Christ "dulciter, prudenter, fortiter," he goes on to say: " Zelum tuum inflammet charitas, informet scientia, firmet constantia. Sit fervidus, sit circum-spectus, sit invictus. Nee teporem habeat, nee careat discretione, nee timidus sit. Et vide ne forte tria ista tibi et in lege tradita fuerint, dicente Deo: Dilige Dom. inum Deum tuum ex toto carde tuo, et ex tota anima tua, et ex tota virtute tua. Mihi videtur amor quidem cordis ad zelum quemdam pertinere affectionis, animse vero amor ad industriam seu judicium rationis; virtutis autem dilectio adanimi possereferri constantiam vel vigorem. Dilige ergo Dominum Deum tuum toto et pleno cordis affectu; dilige tota rationis vigilantia et circumspectione; dilige et tota virtute, ut nee mori pro ejus amore pertimescas."'â Sermo xx. 4.

Ecclesiastes xii. 13, Hterally translated. St. Bernard says: "Propter temetipsum, Deus, fecisti omnia, et qui esse vult sibi et non tibi, nihil esse incipit inter omnia. Deum time, et mandata ejtis observa: hoc est omnii homo. Ergo si hoc est omnis homo, absque hoc nihil omnis homo."â Sermo xx. i.

this sort, we know from the nature of the case; for nothing short of t'h s will yield the result desired; and we further know from the whole teaching of our Lord, which throughout sets forth single-niirded, whole-hearted devotion to the kingdom as the cardinal virtue of all genuine citizens. The only question is whether we can by fair exegesis bring the idea of such a man out of the interpretation of the parable given by Christ, or whether we do not rather bring the idea with us and put it into His words. Now, we admit that, so far as the words to which we have as yet adverted are coii-cerned, such an allegation might plausibly be made. The idea of single-minded devotion cannot be taken out of the words 'understand," 'receive," 'retain." At most we can only justify ourselves for putting that idea into them by the consideration that they are meant to discriminate the perfect hearer from the one going before, and can do so only when they are so emphasised as to imply that nothing but the seed of truth is received and retained. But what is lacking in these words is supplied in a phrase given by the third Evangelist, to which we have not yet adverted. In the case of the perfect hearer the word is received and retained in a noble and good heart Here is what we have been in quest ofâ a perfectly definite and adequate characteristic of the class of hearers who attain unto real and abundant fruitfulness. It is worthy of notice that the remarkable expression occurs in the Gospel of Luke, the Evangelist of the Gentiles, to whom it would be no objection that the phrase was one in familiar use among the Greeks to denote the beau-ideal of manhood,â the man in all respects as he ought to be. It is not assuming too much to suppose that Luke was acquainted with the Attic sense of the phrase, and that he attached to it, as used by himself in this place, a meaning akin to the idea of Kokokayabla as understood by the Greeks. In any case we are justified, even by New Testament usage, in taking out of the expression the idea of a man whose aim is noble and who is generously devoted to his aim. The epithet kokos has reference to aims or chief ends, and describes one whose mind is raised above moral vulgarity, and is bent, not on money-making and such low pursuits, but on the attainment of wisdom, holiness, righteousness. The

Luke viii. 15.

epithet ayados denotes generous self-abandonment in the prosecution of such lofty endsâ large-heartedncss, magnanimous, overflowing devotion. Of the use of the former epithet in the sense explained we have an instance in the eulogium pronounced by Jesus on the act of anointing performed by Mary of Bethany. " She hath wrought," He said, " a noble work (epyov Kaxbu) upon me." Mary's act had been blamed as wasteful, and such it was when tested by vulgar utility. Jesus defended it by calling it noble as distinct from useful in the obvious vulgar sense, and holding it up as worthy to receive throughout the whole world an admiration to which only noble things are entitled. Of the use of the latter epithet in the sense explained we have an instance which possesses peculiar weight, as occurring in the Acts of the Apostles. We refer to the character given to Barnabas in connection with the part he took in the new movement which had commenced at Antioch. Barnabas had been sent by the Church at Jerusalem to see, and, if he approved, to assist in the work; and it is reported of him that when he came and had seen the grace of God he was glad, and exhorted them all that with purpose of heart they would cleave unto the Lord. Then to explain his conduct, the author, Luke, our Evangelist, adds: " For he was a good man avr p ayados), and full of the Holy Ghost and of faith." His goodness manifestly consisted in a generous sympathy, free from all mean narrow suspicion, with the cause of Gentile evangelisation. He believed the work to be of God, though it was a strange, startling, unlooked-for phenomenon; and he entered into it with his whole heart. If we desire still further light as to the idea attached by Luke to the epithet ' good we have but to recall to our recollection two other facts recorded by him concerning Barnabas: the sale of his estate for the benefit of the Church, and his generous recognition of Paulâ first as a convert, when he was still an object of suspicion and fear, and then as the fit man to carry on the work at Antioch when he abode in his native city, inactive and eager for an opportunity of service. A good man, in Luke's vocabulary, meant a man capable of self-sacrifice for the kingdom of Godâ a man of

Matt. xxvi. 10, ' Acts xi. 24.

â Acts iv. 37. Acts ix. 26, 27; xi. 25.

large, expansive sympathies, and magnanimously trustful and o-enerous in his relations to his brethrenâ one who could forget himself and his personal interest to serve God, or to help a new struggling cause, or a friend in time of need. And the man who in a noble and good heart hears and retains the word is just such an one as Barnabas. He is a man devoted to the kingdom of God with his whole heart and soul and mind, who could part with all for its sake, who could even at Christ's bidding, though with a keen pang, leave the dead to bury the dead, even were the dead his own father.

The demand that the kingdom be put first could not be stated in stronger terms than it was in the reply of Jesus to the disciple who asked permission to discharge the last office to a deceased parent. And the man who can comply with the hard requirement therein expressed may be taken as the type of the fruitful hearer, as the man who volunteered to become a disciple may be taken as the type of the stony ground hearer, and the man who desired leave to go and bid farewell to his friends as the type of the thorny ground hearer.

That such a man should be fruitful is not to be wondered at; any amount of fruitfulness may be expected of himâ thirty, sixty, even an hundred fold. The fruitfulness of such a hearer Jesus regarded and represented as a matter of course. Such is the force of the words rendered so feebly in the Authorized version, "which also beareth fruit." The words mean "yn iooi course,

That ayaqoq bears the meaning assigned to it in the text in the New Testament appears from Luke xxiii. 50, where Joseph of Arimathea is called avtip ayaob; Kal Sikaiog. The latter epithet is explained by the clause following: " he had not consented to their counsel and deed;" the former was shown to belong to him by his generous act in burying Jesus. A similar distinction between these words is taken in Rom. v. 7, though Jowett denies it. The same distinction is made in the Clementine Homilies," xviii. iâ 3. Both Simon Magus and Peter agree that the words denote different attributes, only Simon maintains they are incompatible. Peter defines ayabug thus: syw fijui ayaoov ilvai Tov TrapckUKov = largitoty giver. Eusebius, 'Theophania," Book iv. cap. 33, referring to this parable, and to the souls that bring forth fruit, describes the latter as men whose heart is pure and whose mind is devoted, which is just our idea of the two epithets Ka og and ayaqhq. The words of Eusebius are: ot Z Ivavrius iksivoiq Siaketfxevoi, Kuqap 4' XV ' " irpoaipkati yvt ai tov awtrjpiov virost dfitvot (TTTopov, k, t,, â Luke ix. 59, 60.

certainly, without fail, bearetli fruit." The Greek particle hr conveys the idea that the result is one which hardly needs to be specified, and which any one might anticipate. We have a similar use of the word by Paul in the well-known text " Ye are not your own, for ye are bought with a price, therefore (8?) glorify God in your body." To glorify God the apostle considered the self-evident duty of men who have been redeemed by

Christ; and he was impatient at the very thought of any Christian needing to be told what was his duty.

Such, then, are the four classes of hearers pointed at in the parable of the Sower: the spiritually stupid, without thought or feeling in relation to the kingdom, in whom the seed of truth does not even germinate; the inconsiderately impulsive, whose feelings are easily moved, in whom the truth germinates and springs up, but quickly withers away; those who receive the truth into both mind and heart, but not as the one supremely important thing to which everything else must be subordinated, in whom the seed germinates, springs up, and continues to grow even to the green ear, but never ripens; and lastly, those who receive the doctrine of the kingdom with their whole heart, soul, and mind, in whom the truth takes root, grows, and in due season produces an abundant harvest of ripe fruit.

Whence these differences between hearers? and how far is

Matt. xiii. 23: Sf 5 icaptro optl. The rendering of the R. V., "who verily" is better, but not satisfactory. Passow finds the key to all the meanings of Itf in lr oq regarding the two words as derived from the same root. Hartung ('Partikel-lehre') derives li from t ij, whom Meyer and Morrison follow, the former rendering 8c 5j) " and this was the one who," the latter "who at length."' Besides this place in Matthew and that in I Cor. vi. referred to above, the particle occurs in three other places in the New Testamentâ in Luke ii. 15, Acts xiii. 2, Acts xv. 36. In the first of these the A. V. and the R. V. both render li now. The shepherds say one to another," Let us now go even unto Bethlehem." In the second they both leave it untranslated; in the third the A. V. reads ' again," the R. V. now. The best rendering in all three cases, that which brings out the emotional colouring, is come, â "come, let us go to Bethlehem;" "come, separate for me Barnabas and Saul; " "come, let us visit the brethren in every city where we preached." The particle also occurs combined with VOX) in Heb. ii. 16, when both in A. V. and R. V. it is rendered verily'j not happily, for verily conveys the idea of a very solemn assertion, whereas what is said is of the nature of a truism thrown in to relieve the argument. The meaning is: " For, you see, it is not of angels he taketh hold.

"I Cor. vi. 19, 20.

it possible that one may pass from one class of hearers to another? Such questions Christ does not answer. He would teach one thing at a time: the fact of the difference in hearers, and the corresponding difference in the result of hearing. It is no part of an expositor's duty to discuss these questions, though in omitting to do so he is not to be regarded as denying their importance. Specially interesting is the question, whence the noble and good heart,â a topic on which some have expatiated at great length, though in some instances proceeding on a mistaken understanding of what is signified thereby. There can be little doubt what answer the Evangelist, to whom we owe the preservation of the striking phrase, would have given to the question. We may learn tjiis from the manner in which he relates the history of Lydia, who may be associated with Barnabas as a good sample of the fourth class of hearers. Luke describes Lydia as one " whose heart the Lord opened, that she attended unto the things which vere spoken of Paul." The fact about Lydia was, not that up till then she had been peculiarly unsusceptible; the contrary is implied in the very fact of her, a Gentile by birth, being present at the meeting, worshipping God as a proselyte. The fact rather was that she was distinguished by a peculiar openness and receptivity of mind. She brought that openness with her to the meeting,â it was manifest in her very countenance while Paul spoke,â and the historian tells us where she got it. It was from the Lord.

We refer specially to Edward Irving, who, in his 'Sermons on the Parable of the Sower," already alluded to, goes at great length into the question of the preparation of the soil by a slow secular process in nations and in individuals for the reception of the truth. He takes the phrase "good and honest heart" as denoting a sort of natural goodness before faith, evading the charge of Pelagianism by maintaining that such goodness is the product of God's working. The discussion is very interesting, and the truth taught,â viz. that there is a Providential preparation without which Christianity is not likely to come to much, either in individuals or in nations,â in its own place very important. On this subject there are some suggestive remarks in Martensen's Dogmatics." The Providential preparation this author calls the drawing of the Father, and his doctrine is that it profits a people little that the gospel is preached to it, that the Son draws it to the Father, unless it has come to such a point in its development that the leather in turn can draw it to the Son (p. 347)1

Acts xvi. 14.

The question whether the seven parables contained in the thirteenth chapter of Matthev were all spoken at one time is one on which opinion has been much divided. If the existence of a connection more or less intimate between these parables could settle the question there would be no room for dispute. For, while setting aside as a mere exegetical extravagance the view of those who find in this group of parables, in prophetic form, an epitome of the Church's history from the time of our Lord till the end of the world, we must admit the existence of a connection between them to this extent at least, that they exhibit mutually complementary aspects of the kingdom of heaven in its general nature, and in its progress and fortunes on this earth. The first, second, and seventh of the groupâ the parables of the-Sower, the Tares, and the Netâ teach us that the kingdom of God, as a phenomenon taking its place in the world's history, is destined to be in various respects and for various reasons an imperfect and disappointing thing, coming far short of the ideal. In the first parable the shortcoming takes the form of an unsatisfactory abortive reception of the Word of the kingdom by many individual hearers, due to the moral condition of the recipients; while in the second and the seventh it takes the form of a mixture of good and evil not in the hearts of individuals, but in the society composed of the collective body of professed believers, some being genuine

Bengal, Greswell, etc.

citizens of the holy commonwealth, and others counterfeit. The third and fourth parables of the seriesâ those of the Mustard-seed and the Leavenâ exhibit the history of the kingdom on its bright side as a spiritual movement destined to advance, by a steady onward course of development, from a small beginning to a great ending, worldwide in its extent, and thoroughgoing in its intensive pervasive effect. The remaining two parablesâ those of the Hid Treasure and the Precious Pearlâ exhibit the kingdom in its own ideal nature as a thing of absolute, incomparable worth, the highest good, worthy to be received, loved, and served with the whole heart as the summium bonuin, whatever reception it may in fact meet with at the hands. f men.

The fact of a connection is thus apparent, but it does not settle the disputed question alluded to. Two alternatives are possible. The connection between the parables might have led Christ to speak them all at one time, but it may also merely have led Matthew to relate them all in one place, though not all spoken at the same time; in accordance with his habit of grouping together materials connected by affinity of thought. That we are not shut up to the former of these alternatives, is sufficiently evinced by the fact that other parables can be pointed to which are undoubtedly closely connected in their subject-matter, and which nevertheless we have no reason to regard as uttered together; as for example, those relating to the subject of work and wages in the kingdom, the parables of the Talents, the Pounds, and the Hours. These together constitute a complete doctrine on the subject to which they relate,â and a teacher of methodic habit would probably have spoken them all at once; but Christ uttered them as occasion required. And that they fit into each other is due to their truth, not to their being parts of one lesson given in a single didactic effort.

While thus content to leave the question undecided as regards the whole group of seven taken collectively, we are strongly of opinion that at least three of the seven were spoken at one time; even on the day when Jesus opened His mouth in parables sitting in a boat on the Galilean Lake. The three areâ the parable of the Sower and the two to be

Matt. XXV. 14; Luke xix. 12; Matt, xx, I.

considered in the present chapter. These three are connected not merely in a general way, as relating to the chequered fortunes of the kingdom in this world, but specially, as all illustrating the aspect of the kingdom then present to the Saviour's thoughts,â the dark, melancholy side of things; and as suitable alike to the moral and the physical situation: to the moral, as addressed to a multitude comprising examples of all the various classes of hearers described in the parable of the Sower, and exhibiting the mixture of good and evil, of genuine and counterfeit discipleship, typified by the wheat and tares in the same field, and the good and bad fish in one net; to the physical, as spoken amid scenes where agricultural and piscatorial operations were daily carried on.

Tolerably sure as to the historical connection of these three parables, we are still more confident as to the propriety of grouping together for joint consideration the latter two of the threeâ those of the Tares and the Net. They are so like that on a superficial view one might be inclined to pronounce their didactic import identical. They do certainly teach the same general truth, viz. that a mixture of good and evil will prevail in the kingdom of God on this earth while the world lasts; and that this mixture, while in itself to be deplored, is nevertheless a thing which for wise reasons is to be patiently borne with in view of the great final separation. This being

Keim takes the same view. He thinks that parables 3 and 4 (Mustard-seed and Leaven) went originally together; also 5 and 6 (Treasure and Pearl); likewise i and 2; perhaps also 7 (Sower, Tares, and Net),â thus forming one group visibly related closely in fundamental view and expression. He thinks it not improbable that the Treasure and the Pearl went along with the last group of three, because it was not Christ's way in a popular discourse to give merely the facts or the metaphysics of the kingdom, but to aim at calling forth a movement of the human will, which would be done by the parables of the Treasure and the Pearl, On the other hand, he thinks the parable of the Mustard-seed and the Leaven were certainly spoken at another time; founding not only on the fact that they occur in different historical connections in Luke's Gospel, but also on their hopeful, triumphant character, so different from those of the Sower, the Tares, and the Net Vide 'Jesu von Nazara," ii. 446-9). Farrar thinks that along with the Sower went no other parables, " except perhaps the simple and closely analogous ones of the Grain of Mustard-seed, and of the Blade, the Ear, and the Full Corn in the Ear,. perhaps with these the similitude of the Candle " ('Life of Christ," i. 324-5).

the leading lesson of both, the two parables really constitute but one theme; and to treat them in separate chapters were simply to repeat thoughts that can be most effectively uttered once for all. These parables, however, are not without their distinctive features, which forbid us to regard the one as a mere repetition of the other. A minor point of difference is that in the parable of the Tares the presence of evil in the kingdom is regarded as due to the deliberate action of an evil-minded agent, while in the parable of the Net it appears due rather to accident. A more important distinction is that while in the former parable the separation of the evil from the good is represented as for certain reasons not desirable, in the latter it is tacitly treated as impossible. The good and the bad fish' mztst remain together in the net till they have " been dragged to land. This difference if pressed would lead to another, viz. as to the character of the evil element. The tares might be held to represent manifested recognisable evil, the bad fish unmanifested hidden evilâ a distinction answering to that taken by the Apostle Paul in the words: " Some men's sins are open beforehand, going before to judgment, and some men they follow after." Another point of distinction has been indicated, viz. that while both parables teach a J present mixture of evil and good, and an eventual separation, they differ as to the truth emphasised in each respectively, the foreground of the one picture showing the temporary mixture, that of the other the ultimate separation. It is, however, possible to exaggerate this distinction; for in the parable of the Tares the future judgment is very distinctly described, and in the parable of the Net the idea that the mixture must last till the process of development is completed is not without recognition. The net is not drawn to the shore till it is full. The filling of the net answers to the ripening of the grain as the sign that the crisis has come. It is, doubtless, a far less apt sign; still the thing to be noted is that it is intended to serve that purpose. The net is not to be pulled prematurely to shore; it must be let fully out and allowed to have its full sweep, that it may catch as many as possible. We now proceed to the interpretation of the two parables.

I Tim. V. 24.

Our attention shall be first and principally occupied by the

Parable of the Tares. The place and the time being probably the same as in the case of the parable of the Sower, Jesus put before His hearers another parable, saying:

The h'tigdo7n of heaven is likened utito a man who sowed good seed in his Jield; but while men slept, his enemy came and sowed ' tares' among the wheat, and went his way. But when the blade sprang up and brought forth fruit, then appeared also the tares. So the servants of the householder came afid said unto him. Sir, didst not thou sow good seed in thy field? Whence, then, hath it tares? And he said nnto them, An enemy" did this.-And the servants say unto hitn, Wilt thou, then, that we go and gather them up? But he saith, No; lest while ye gather the tares, ye root up the wheat along with them. Let both grow together until the harvest, and in the season of harvest I will say to the reapers, Collect first the tares, and bind them into bundles to burn them; but gather the wheat into my barn. â Matt. xiii. 24â 30.

This is one of the most difficult in the whole series of our Lord's parables. As Luther remarks, it appears very simple and easy to understand, especially as the Lord Himself has explained it and told us what the field and the good seed and the tares are; but there is such diversity of opinion among interpreters that much attention is needed to hit the right meaning.3 The expositor's task is none the less arduous that the parable has been mixed up with great controversies on such momentous topics as Church discipline and religious toleration, and the duty of civil and ecclesiastical rulers in reference to heresy and heretics. On such questions a man's opinions are very apt to be influenced by the time in which he lives and the community to which he belongs, and his interpretation of any portion of Scripture that has been made to do service on either side is only too likely to exhibit 1 The Tord tares is a most misleading rendering of to. Ktkavia, and we have printed it within inverted commas to indicate the fact. The R, V, retains the rendering of the A. V., probably from the difficulty of finding another word that exactly conveys the meaning. For remarks on the mature of the plant intended see further on.

'â ixgpoe dv9i)u)irog, a hostile man.

3 Hauspostillen, ' Predigt iiber das Evangelium Matt. xiii. 24â 30.

manifest traces of the bias thence received. With reference to the parable before us it may be said that no one has any, chance of understanding it who is not prepared to admit that the Christian Church in general is in many respects very different from what her Head desired, and that the particular branch of the Church to which he himself belongsâ nay, that he himself as an individual office-bearer thereinâ may have sinned grievously against the spirit of wise patience which the parable inculcates.

Trying to bear these things duly in mind, let us inquire what is the prima facie impression produced by the parable. Is it not this? That a mixture of good and evil menâ of genuine and counterfeit disciplesâ is to be expected in the kingdom of God on earth, and to be regarded, as inevitable, with patience, though not with complacency; and that as this mixture is in itself, if not in all respects, yet at least in the main, an evil, the children of the kingdom are to comfort themselves under it with the expectation of an eventual separation, which they are assured will certainly come to pass in due season. Thus far the parable seems plain enough, but there are points on which one would gladly receive explanations. The tares, who precisely are they.-â Then, as to the toleration of the tares, is there to be no limit thereto."' and if there is, where is the line to be drawn."' Then what does the toleration amount to Does it exclude Church discipline for errors in opinion and faults in conduct."' or is Church discipline to take its course even to the extent of thrusting offenders out of the Church, the toleration prescribed consisting simply in permitting the excommunicated to remain in the world? We eagerly turn to Christ's own explanations for a solution of our doubts, but only to be disappointed. These explanations are too elementary to meet the wants of those who, like ourselves, look back over a long course of historical development, and wish to know how far that course is in accordance with Christ's mind as expressed in the parable. They were meant for those who had no idea of the import of the parable, and therefore contain little more than the mere alphabet of interpretation. A slight inspection will suffice to convince us of this. After dismissing the multitude, Jesus, in answer to a request from His disciples, gave the following interpretation of 'The Parable of the Tares of the Field."

He that soweth the good seed is the Son of man; and the field is tht wofd; aid the good seed, these are the sons of the kingdom; but the tares are the sons of the wicked one and the enemy that sowed them is the devil; and the harvest is the end of the world, and the reapers are angels. As then the tares are collected and burned iti the fire, so shall it be in the end of the world. The Son of man shall send forth His angels, and they shall gather out of His kingdom all thifgs that offend, and those who do iniquity, and they shall cast them into the furnace of fire; there shall be the weeping and the gnashing of teeth." Then shall the righteous shine out as the suit ii the kingdom of their Father. Who hath ears, let him hear. â Matt. xiii. 37â 43.

From this explanation, we learn that in the present parable the wheat and the tares 2S persons, while in the last parable â that of the Sowerâ the wheat is the word of the kingdom; and that the soil is the world in which such persons live, while in the Sower, the soil is the mind of those who hear the word. We learn, further, that the tares are the children of the wicked one, the good seed being the children of the kingdom. Now this is a very general and indefinite statement, which leaves us free to regard the tares either as spurious Christians, or as evil men, whether professing Christianity or not. If the more general meaning be taken, then the juxtaposition of wheat and tares is in the world, as the common abode of all sorts of men, not in the Church; and the lesson to Christians is the very general one of patience under the trials inseparable from life on earth. Yet, again, we learn from this explanation of the parable given by Christ, that the reapers who make the final separation are the angels; but we are not told who the servants were who inquired Whence these tares Are the angels the servants also? If so, then the parable contains no direct instruction as to the duty of the Church, but simply an intimation of God's purpose in providence to

Or of wickedness. The R. V. here, as in the Lord's Prayer, renders Tov TTovjpoi) " the evil one." Goebel (' Die Parabein Jesu,"p. 80) adduces in favour of its being neuter, that o v o r. ir. is parallel to ol v o Tijg fsaatxiiag; also that a special clause is introduced to indicate the devil as the source of the wild growth.

2 The articles indicate that these were familiar features in the picture of Gehenna.

permit a mixture of good and evil men in the world until the end of this dispensation. The only lesson for the Church is the implied one of acquiescence in God's will. The only thing in the explanation which turns the scale in favour of a more specific conception of the drift of the parable is the expression, "gather out of His kingdojn." ' If the things that offend, and they who do iniquity, are to be gathered out of the kingdom, it is a natural inference that they were previously in it; in other words, that the tares are Christians at least in profession.

We are thus thrown back on the parable itself to see wheâ ther we cannot find more precise indications of the character of the evil element. And on looking narrowly, we do find certain particulars which tend to prove that the evil element consists not of bad men in general co-existing with Christians in the same world till the state of probation closes, but of counterfeit Christians. First and chief, there is the name of the noxious plant which spoils the cropâ i avia; than which none better could be found, if the intention were to describe counterfeit sons of the kingdom, and none less felicitous, if the design were merely to denote bad men in general. The word is one for which it is difficult to find an English equivalentâ the nearest approach to it is darnel;- but there can be no doubt as to the kind of plant it is employed to designate. It is a plant so like wheat, that in the early stages of its growth the two can scarcely be distinguished; so like that it could even be imagined that the stalks of it, which appeared in fields sewn with wheat, sprang not from separate seed, but from wheat grains that had suffered degeneracy through untoward influences of soil or season. This opinion actually was entertained by the inhabitants of Palestine in our Lord's day, as it is still; and it is reflected in the Hebrew name for the plant in question, from which the Greek word is formed. The Talmudic equivalent for C C' ia is V lf, signifying the bastard plant, from- " y to commit adultery; the idea under- ' Ver. 41. avwi ovaiv Ik rrjg jsadtkiiag,

Greswell thinks we have no equivalent, and simply transfers the Greek word, putting it into English formâ zizan. Scripture botanists identify X, ix, avia with lolium temulenfum, so called because it produce vertigo.

lying the word being that the earth, in producing from good seed such a degenerate crop, played the harlot, so to speak." Those who have the best means of knowing, say that this idea is a mistaken one; but it is at least of value as a testimony to the close resemblance between the wheat and the ' tares'; implying, as it does, that the plants are so like, that the theory that tares are simply wheat in a degenerate form, sprung from good wheat seed, might be plausibly entertained. This theory is certainly not proceeded upon in the parable, which represents the tares as springing from separate seed sown after the wheat seed had been cast into the ground. But a resemblance is implied in the description of the tares not less close than if the theory were true; and this is the second point to which we ask attention. " When the blade," we read, "was sprung up, and brought forth fruit, then ' appeared the tares- also." In other words, when the wheat and the tares had got the length of being in ear, then, and not till then, did the tares appear as tares, and were clearly â seen to be tares. This description, w iich well-informed travellers declare to be very exactly in accordance with fact, surely suggests a closer connection between the two classes of men, represented by the two crops respectively, than subsists between good and bad men living together in the same world. If by the bad crop had been meant merely bad men in general, why emphasise so pointedly the non-distinguish-dbleness of the two crops till the time of the earing? and we may add, why select a plant to represent the evil element so

So Wiinsch, Neue Beitrage zur Erlauterung der Evangelien aus Talmud und Midrasch," Gottingen, 1878. He remarks: " Of the earth in â which one sows wheat, and which brings forth a bad crop, it is said that it plays the harlot."' He gives an instance of the metaphorical use of the idea, quoting a Rabbi as saying that at the time of the flood the earth proved herself faithless, because, whereas a good seed had been committed to her, she brought forth a degenerate kind (of men), (p. 165).

Thomson, The Land and the Book," p. 421, argues against the notion as incredible.

Ver. 26. rort i avij kox to. Z, C a. via. They then appeared as tares.

Thomson, 'The Land and the Book," p. 420, says: "In those parts, where the grain has headed out, they have done the same, and there a child cannot mistake them for wheat or barley; but where both are less developed, the closest scrutiny will often fail to detect them. I cannot dc it at all with any confidence."

like wheat in the early stage of growth? why not be content with the thorns, which in the parable of the Sower choked the good seed, and prevented it from bringing forth fruit unto perfection? It is impossible for any unbiassed mind to refuse acquiescence in the opinion so well expressed by Lightfoot, that the wheat and the tares signify not simply good and bad men, but good and bad Christiajts â both distinct from other men as wheat grain is distinct from all other seeds, but distinct from each other as genuine is distinct from bastard wheat.

The stthseqiient sowing of the field with tares, and the ascription of this act to an enemy, are two additional features of the parable which point towards the same conclusion. What need of an additional sowing in order to get a crop of bad men in the world, living side by side with the children of the kingdom? Bad men abounded before the kingdom of God, which Christ came to found, appeared; and they were certain to abound after its appearance, without one taking pains for that purpose. But if what was m. eant by Jesus, when He spoke of tares as likely to arise when His kingdom was planted, was counterfeit forms of Christianityâ forms of evil which would not have appeared had not Christianity appeared, and manifesting themselves as perversions of Christian truthâ then we can understand why He spoke of an after-sowing of the field. Then, too, we can understand why He said with such emphasis " an enemy " â or still more strongly in the interpretation, " the devil "â " hath done this." For it is characteristic of an enemy animated by diabolical malice, not only to do mischief, but to do it in the most vexatious possible manner. But what more vexatious than to have one's crop of wheat spoiled, not merely by a crop of noxious plants growing up in the midst of it, but by a crop which mocks the husbandman's hope by its specious resemblance to the crop of genuine grain he has taken all needful pains to raise? To do this is a feat worthy of him who for wicked

Horae Hebraicse, in Evangelium Matthsei.

2 That the tares were sown after the wheat is evident even from the T. R., which represents the enemy as sowing them among the wheat; but it is made specially prominent when, in place of the totrupe of the T. R. in ver. 25, we substitute the reading iiriainiptv approved by critics, rendered in the Vulgate superseminavit â sowed upon the wheat previously sown.

ends transforms himself into an angel of light, and who, in the quaint words of Luther, cares not to dwell in waste dry-places, but prefers to sit in heaven.

Taking these features of the parable, then, along with the statement in the interpretation that the scandals are to be gathered out of the kingdom, we cannot doubt that the mix- "i ture of good and evil elements spoken of is a mixture to be exhibited, not in the world merely, but in the kingdom itself as it appears on this earth; and that the evil element is not bad men in general, but counterfeit Christians; or, if you please, anti-Christian tendencies, perversions of Christian truth into forms of error kindred in appearance, utterly diverse in spirit; as, for example, of spiritual authority into priestcraft, of salvation by grace into Antinomian licence, or of self-denying devotion into a gloomy asceticism. We do not, of course, mean that the tares are to be restricted to corruptions in doctrine. It is more probable that Christ had in view chiefly, not to say exclusively, men of evil life, by their conduct an offence and stumbling-block to faith. It is indeed a natural enough suggestion that the two expressions, " the scandals," and " those that do iniquity," refer to two classes of evil; the former to heresies, the latter to all forms of un-Christian practice: possibly united in the same persons, men at once errorists and evil livers. But we admit that we learn to put this double construction on the words from history rather than from the vords themselves. The dogmatic idea of heresy is a creation of a later age; the word in the New Testament denotes a moral offence. At the same time it has to be remembered that there are some opinions which have their root in a corrupt moral condition, which may therefore be included under the scandals alluded to.

The tares then are in the kingdom. But if so, how is the direction to let the tares alone until the harvest to be construed? absolutely or relatively, to the exclusion of Church

Hauspostillen, Predigt iiber Matt. xiii. 24â 30."

2 So Grotius. He remarks that after the first pure stage of the Church's existence there began to mix themselves with Christians: " Duo hominum vitiosorura genera, alii prava docentes, alii puram professionem vita turpi dehonestantcs. Prioris generis homines okavlaxa hie vocantur."â Annota-tiones in Novum Testamentum. Goebel finds in the text a reference only to evil life. The scandals are the deeds of wicked men.

censures, or, these being assumed as in their own sphere valid, at once lawful, beneficial, and obligatory? This is the qiiaestio t'cxata â a question all the harddr to answer that the conflicting interests of purity and patience are both worthy of all respect, so that no solution of the difficulty which sacrifices either interest to the other can satisfy any earnest mind. Various attempts, at once historically and exegetically interesting, have been made to solve the problem. We may note some of the more outstanding.

I. First comes the Z; zrt;i" solution. The Donatists, whose aim was to make the Church as pure in reality as it is in idea, t got over the difficulty very simply, by denying the view of the tares which creates it, viz. that they signify spurious Christians known to be such, yet for certain reasons to be tolerated. The point in the parable and its interpretation on which they laid chief stress, was the statement, "the field is the world," and the lesson they drew from the parable was, Bear patiently the evil that is in the world,â a duty involving no obligation to tolerate evil in the Church. When their opponents pointed to the parable of the Net in proof that Christ contemplated a mixture of good and evil in the Church as a characteristic of its state antecedent to the end, they admitted that such a mixture was implied in that parable, but they evaded the force of the fact as an argument against their position by saying that it was only such a mixture as was due to ignorance on the part of the Church authorities. No one can tell what sort of fish are in a net while it is under the water, and in like manner there may be men in the Church of unholy character not known to be unholy, and their presence argues nothing in favour of tolerating within the Church men known to be unholy. i For the reasons already given we cannot acquiesce in this solution. The tares, we have seen, are counterfeit Christians subsisting side by side with genuine Christians within the kingdom. Nor does the statement " the field is the world " in the least invalidate the argument in support of that position. The field indeed is the world, and the statement is one of the numerous passages in the teaching

Augustine gives an account of this controversy as to the interpretation of the parable between the Catholics and the Donatists in the tract' Ad Donatistas post Collationem, of Christ which show that in His conception the kingdom of God, whose advent He announced, was designed to cover the whole earth, and the gospel He preached good news for all mankind. But while the field to be sown is the whole world,. the field actually sown is the kingdom of God, as it exists in the earth at any given time, and the tares are within it; not of the kingdom as it is in God's sight, but in the kingdom as a visible society.

2. We notice next the Catholic solution of later times. This view, while admitting that the mixture spoken of in the parable exists in the kingdom and not merely in the world, and yet contending that heretics might not merely be excommunicated but be put to death, sought to reconcile existing practice with the prohibition against pulling up the tares by laying chief stress on the reason assigned for the prohibition â 'Mest while ye gather the tares ye root up also the wheat with them; " which was interpreted to mean. Then and then only must the tares be left alone when there is a risk of the wheat being uprooted; in other circumstances the tares may be gathered up at once. Aquinas, in stating this view, adopts the language of Augustine to the following effect: " Where that fear (of uprooting the wheat) has no place, but there is perfect security for the certain stability of the wheat, that is, when the offence of every one is so known, and appears execrable to all, that it either has no defenders, or none such as might cause a schism, let not the severity of discipline slumber." Whether this conversion of an apparently absolute into a conditional prohibition be legitimate or not is a question for serious consideration, but there can be no doubt that the words quoted from Augustine by the great mediseval doctor point out a real and most important limita- tion of Church discipline. Where there is a risk of a schism being caused by severe dealing with offenders, whether in

"Cum metus iste non subest, sed omnino de frumentorum certa stabilitate certa securitas manet, id est, quando ita cujusque crimen notum est, et omnibus execrabile apparet, ut vel nullos prorsus vel non tales habeat defensores, per quos possit schisma contingere, non dormiat severitas disciplinjs." 'August, contra Epistolam Parmenian- ilib. iii., cap. ii., 13. The words are quoted by Aquinas in the 'Summa' 2 2aÂ Ques. X., Art. viii.

matters of faith or in matters of conduct, the Church is not only entitled but bound to consider the questionâ Which of the two evils is most to be feared, the toleration of reputed corruption in doctrine or practice, or a rupture in the body ecclesiastical? It is not difficult to imagine other instances in which a prudent regard to the Church's highest interests might dictate the policy of letting the exercise of ecclesiastical censures fall into abeyance. Jerome points out one, when, commenting on the prohibition against uprooting the tares, and on the reason annexed, he says: " We are exhorted not quickly to cut off a brother, because it can happen that he who to-day is depraved by noxious doctrine may to-morrow repent and begin to defend the truth." It is well for the Church when its office-bearers are able to apply wisely these two principles enunciated by two of the most esteemed among the ancient Fathers.

3. Coming down to the time of the Reformation, we may select for notice the interpretations given respectively by Luther and Beza. Luther, in a sermon on the parable, asks two questionsâ whether the Church may use her authority and excommunicate those who create scandal, and whether the civil magistrate may use the sword against heretics. The former question he answers in the affirmative; and he reconciles his view with the prohibition in the parable by remarking that what is prohibited is the destruction of the tares. Those who exercise authority in the Church may excommunicate but not kill heretics. His second question Luther also answers in the affirmative, reconciling his answer with the parable by remarking that the Lord speaks of the kingdom of God, and of what those who exercise authority there may do; so that the prohibition does not mean heretics shall not be slain, but merely they shall not be slain by the ministers of the Gospel.2 This interpretation of the great German reformer needs no elaborate refutation. It may be answered in a single sentence. What the Master in the parable prohibits is not as Luther alleges, the destruction of the tares, but their removal from the field, their separation from the wheat.

4. Beza, while acquiescing in Luther's doctrine that heretics

Comment, in Matthasum.

â Hauspostillen, 'Predigt iiber das Evang. Matt. xiii. 24â 30.

may be proceeded against by the censures of the Church and the sword of the civil magistrate, adopted an entirely different method of harmonising that doctrine with the teaching of the parable. He expounded his views of the parable in a tract in defence of the use of the sword against heresy by the civil magistrate, in connection with the burning of Servetus; his purpose being to reply to an argument drawn from the parable by his opponents in favour of religious toleration. These were, in brief, as follows:â The tares are not heretics merely, but all sorts of offenders, and therefore if the parable contains a prohibition against the killing of heretics by the civil magistrate, it equally contains a prohibition against the execution of all sorts of evil-doers,â which is absurd. But the parable in reality contains no prohibition, at least none directed either to ecclesiastical authorities or to the civil magistrate: the servants are the angels, and the parable represents God as telling them on what method He is to conduct His ordinary providential government. " As in the beginning of the history of Job, so here, the Lord is shown conversing with His angels concerning the future state of His Church in this world." That state in general is to be one of tribulation, the children of the kingdom mingling in the intercourse of life with unbelieving and ungodly men, and enduring much at their hands. The only lesson for Christians to be inferred from the parable is the duty of bearing patiently with this general condition of things. Against the appropriate punishment of individual evil-doers, whether in Church or in State, it says not a word. It is assumed that such punishment is to be inflicted as far as possible; only we are given to understand that when ecclesiastical and civil officers have done their utmost, the world will after all be a m. ost ungenial home for the children of the kingdom. After the remarks already made in discussing the question who are the tares, Ave deem it quite unnecessary to enter into detailed criticism of this interpretation. We only observe how unlikely it is that Christ should utter a parable teaching so very general and commonplace a truth at the time and in the circumstances in which there is reason to believe the parable was spoken; and how unlikely, if He desired to convey such a lesson, that He would put the truth in so unsuitable a form. Why call wicked men in general tares? â why not rather, as on other occasions, speak of them as wolves, to whose violence His sheep are to be exposed ini this world? If we desire to know how our Lord spoke to His disciples of the tribulations they should encounter in the' world, we must turn not to this parable, but to His discourse. to the twelve in connection with the Galilean mission, or to His farewell address to them on the eve of His Passion.

5. Only one other solution of the problem now under consideration calls for mention, viz. that hinted at by Jerome and favoured by many modern theologians of high reputation. This view finds the key to the interpretation of the parable in the likeness of the tares to the wheat and the risk thence arising of pulling up wheat by mistake. The words, " lest while ye gather up the tares ye root up also the wheat with them," it takes to mean, not "lest ye pull up that which though tares to-day may be wheat to-morrow," but " lest in pulling up that which ye fancy to be tares ye uproot that which in reality is wheat." The reason for the prohibition being thus understood, it is of course assumed that when there is no room for doubt as to the noxious character of the plants mixed with the wheat, they may at once be removed. Now it is undoubtedly true that there is a close resemblance between the tares and the wheat, and that there is an intention in the parable to emphasise the fact. It is meant that we should note that tares, as Bengel remarks, have a much better appearance than thorns and thistles. It may also be ad mitted, as the same writer observes, that from the toleration of tares we may not argue for the toleration of thorns and thistles, which, as we are told by another patron of this view, only a wretched farmer would suffer in his fields. Nor is it difficult to imagine forms of spiritual evil answering to the tares which have to be tolerated, as distinct from forms answering to thorns and thistles which may not be tolerated.

' Matt. X. 16. 2 John xvi, 2 Jerome says: " Inter triticum at zizania, quod nos appelhmus lolium, quamdiu heiba est, et nondum culmus venit ad spicam, grandis similitudo est, et in discernendo aut nulla aut perdifficilis distantia."â ' Comment, in Matthjeum."

"Zizania majorem speciem habentquam cardui et s-p'meyâ Gfiomon,

"A tolerantia illorum ad horum non valet consequentia."â Gnomon,

De Valenti," Die Parabeln des Herrn."

We are quite willing to accept the description of the spiritual tares given by the author last referred to: " They are the false brethren," the " dogs," the " concision," the " lying apostles " who, like the devil himself, transform themselves into angels of lightâ men, in short, whose corrupt conduct is not altogether hidden from the true servants of the Lord, but who yet, with all their badness, show a certain skill and moderation, so that no truly Christian society has the courage to subject them to Church censures." But the difficulty which stands in the way of our accepting this interpretation is that in the parable it seems plainly implied that at the stage of growth at which the crop had arrived, the difference between wheat and tares could be plainly recognised, so that if it had been desirable the servants could have taken out each individual stalk of tares without mistake, at least without mistake arising from ignorance, for of course mistakes through carelessness would be very likely to happen. And further, the evil apprehended does not appear to be that wheat may be pulled up by mistake, but that wheat may be pulled up along with the tares, owing to the intertwining of their roots in the soil. It is not said, Lest ye root up wheat instead of tares, but. Lest ye uproot the wheat along with them. We cannot avoid the conclusion, therefore, that whatever lesson our Lord desired to teach, He meant to apply not merely to forms of evil of doubtful tendency, but to forms of evil whose character-and tendency can no longer be doubted.

But how, then, are we to get over the difficulty with which all the foregoing interpretations unsuccessfully grapple? Simply by bearing duly in mind this very elementary consideration, that Christ is not here laying down a rule for the regulation of ecclesiastical practice, but inculcating the

De Valenti, i., p. 163.

' u ia aiitoig: aia is not a preposition but an adverb. Meyer translates the words "at the same time by them " (zugleich durch sie),â taking avrolg as an instrumental dative. The idea is that the uprooted tares carry along with them the wheat, owing to the solidarity of the two in the soil.

s Besides Bengel and De Valenti, may be mentioned as supporting the foregoing interpretation, Tholuck, who in an interesting discussion of the parable in the ' Literarischer Anzeiger' for 1847, in a review of Trench's work on the Parables, goes very fully into the history of opinion. Trench himself favours this interpretation, though not adopting it exclusively.

CH. ii. J The Tares and the Drag-Net, t cultivation of a certain spirit â the spirit of wise patience; a spirit to be cherished by all men in all spheres, civil and ecclesiastical, but especially by Christians, the children of the kingdom. What has been well said concerning the Sermon on the Mount applies to this parable: everything in this discourse refers us to the world of temper and disposition. Beza was not wrong in saying that the lesson of the parable is a lesson of patience; his error lay in restricting the scope of the lesson to the tribulations Christians encounter in the world. The lesson applies not only to the evils in the world, but also, and more particularly, and chiefly, to the evils in the Church; it applies to the bearing and behaviour of Christians towards these evils, however exhibited, whether in formal Church discipline, or in private and social intercourse. The parable neither prohibits nor fixes limits to ecclesiastical discipline, but teaches a spirit which will affect that part, as well as all other parts, of religious conduct; and which, had it prevailed in the Church more than it ever has prevailed, would have made the Church's history very difierent from what it is. A recent writer on the parables, who interprets this parable as Beza did, while of course having no sympathy with the persecuting principles advocated by the sixteenth century divine, tries to shut into a corner those who hold that the parable inculcates a tolerant attitude towards evil in the Church by a peremptory logic of alternatives, thus: the prohibition against pulling up the tares is absolute; therefore either Church discipline is absolutely prohibited, or it does not bear upon discipline at all.2 The futility of this Either-or logic may be very easily

Martensen, Christian Ethics," p. 382.

2 Arnot on the ' Parables of our Lord," p. 95. This respected author accuses Dr. Trench of an Erastian bias in his way of applying the parable to the subject of discipline. But bias in an opposite direction is very manifest in his own case. He assumes that the ecclesiastical practice of his own Church in such matters is unquestionably right: the possibility of the contrary does not seem to have entered into his mind. This is the secret of his partiality for the Donatist interpretation of the words, "the field is the world." This example may illustrate what we said at the commencement, that a man has no chance of understanding this parable who is not prepared to admit the possibility of his own Church, yea, of himself, sinning against the Lord's mind as set forth therein. There are shown by a parallel case. In the Sermon on the Mount the Preacher says, "Swear not at all," Are we to say, This is either an absolute prohibition of oath-taking, or it has no bearing on the subject of oaths? Certainly not. The precept does not absolutely prohibit oaths, and yet it does bear most closely on the subject of oaths. It means, let there be no occasion, so far as you are concerned, for swearing oaths; let your utterances be absolutely truthful, your yea, yea, and your nay, nay. It is a precept whose importance every Christian acknowledges, yet few dream of its being incompatible with the actual swearing of oaths on proper occasions for confirmation of one's word, and to put an end to doubt and strife. For however truthful I may be, I know that there are many false men in the world, and that therefore distrust is excusableâ distrust even towards myself, seeing it is hard to know true men from knaves. Even so, while the world lasts, there will be need and room in the Church for the exercise of discipline, that the reality of Christian life in the holy commonwealth may come as near as possible to its high ideal; and yet the lesson of our parable will always be valid as a protest against all Church censures springing out of an impatient view of the evils inseparable from the kingdom of God in its present earthly state, and as an admonition to those who have authority in the kingdom to exercise their authority in accordance with the rule so well expressed by Augustine: "Let disciphne preserve patience, and let patience temper dis- cipline, and let both be referred to charity, so that on the one hand an undisciplined patience may not foster iniquity, and on the other hand an impatient discipline may not dissipate unity."!

The philosophy of this patience with evil prevalent in the visible Church is not fully given in the parable; at most we have but a hint of the rationale, though it is a hint which suggests much more than it says to those who understand. Before remarking on this pregnant hint we cannot but advert in passing to the marked contrast between the implied teaching of the parable of the Sower and that of this parable, as to the mode of dealing with evil appearing in connection with certainly two sides to the question how far a jealous exercise of discipline is wise or unwise. Ad Donatistas post Couationem," iv. 6w

CH. II. J The Tares and the Drag-Net, y the work of the kingdom. The imph'ed teachhig of the former parable, in reference to the thorns, is: Get rid of them, else there will be no crop of good grain. The expressed teaching of the present parable with reference to the tares is: Let them alone till the good grain is ripe. Whence this difference? Hence: the evil in the one case is zvithin ourselves, in the other case it is without us, in other men. The doctrine of the one parable is. Tolerating evil in ourselves is deadly to our spiritual interest; that of the other, Tolerating evil in others is not necessarily soâ may even be profitable as an exercise promoting the growth of the graces of patience and charity. Thus viewed, the lessons of the two parables are not only mutually compatible, but in harmony with the whole tenour of our Lord's ethical teaching. On the one hand, He ever inculcated inexorable severity in self-judgment, saying, e. g. in the Sermon on the Mount, "If thy right eye or thy right hand offend thee, pluck it out, or cut it off and cast it from thee;" on the other, with reference to our fellow-men. He gave this counsel in the very same discourse, "Judge not, that ye be not judged." Many are slow to understand the grounds of these diverse counsels, and appear to think themselves as responsible for the sins of their brethren as for their own; not to say more, for there are some of whom more could be said, viz. that they behold a mote in their brother's eye, and consider not the beam that is in their own eye. It is, indeed, a question deserving serious consideration on the part of all Christians, what are the limits of responsibility in connection with the sins of fellow-members of the same religious communion That there is a certain amount of responsibility cannot be denied, for the Church is not an hotel in which men may sit side by side at table, without knowing, or caring to know, anything about the character of a fellow-guest. But, on the other hand, the responsibility is a strictly limited one, coming far short of the responsibility lying on each man for his own conduct; for if the Christian Church is not an hotel, as little is it a club whose members may claim and use the right of excluding from membership every one who is not in all respects a person according to their taste and fancy. This

Matt. V. 29, 30. See also Matt. xvjii. 8, 9, where the counsel is repeated in the sermon on Humility. 2 Matt. vii. I. ' Matt. vii. 13.

club theory of Church fellowship, however, is much to the liking of many. It was the theory in favour with the Dona-tists, who held that mixed communions were infectious, and that the pious were polluted by fellowship with the profane. Against this ultra-puritanic theory the quaint observations of Fuller may aptly be cited: " St. Paul saith, ' Bid let a man examine hnnself, and so let him eat of that bread," but enjoins not men to examine others, which was necessary if bad communicants do defile. It neither makes the cheer or welcome the worse to sit next to him at God's table who wants a wedding garment; for he that touches his person, but disclaims his practices, is as far from him as the east from the west, yea, as heaven from hell. In bodily diseases one may be infected without his knowledge, against his will: not so in spiritual contagions, where acceditur ad vititim corriiptionis vitio co tsensionis, and none can be infected against their consent." Let us now look at the hints contained in the parable at a philosophy of the patience it inculcates towards the evil existing in the visible Church. " Nay," said the householder to the servants who proposed that the tares should at once be gathered out; " lest while ye gather up the tares ye root up also the wheat with them." Then, to explain wherein the harm of such a result lay, he added: " Let both grow together until the harvest." That is, the uprooting of the wheat is an evil when it happens during the process of growth. When that process is complete no harm can be done, the time for uprooting or cutting down having arrived. The doctrine of the parable therefore is: The matter of prime importance is not that the tares be got rid of, but that the w heat pass through the natural course of development till the process of growth reach its consummation. If both ends cannot be accomplished together, beware of sacrificing the more important to the less important.

Thomas Fuller: 'The Profane State,"bk. v. chap ii., on The Rigid Donatists. The Latin quotation in the above extract is from Augustine Contra Donatistas post Collationem." In the same tract Augustine expresses the principle of limited responsibility in terms first used by the Donatists in self-defence, and then turned against them by the Catholics; " Nee causae causa, nee personae persona praejudicat."

2 Keim says, "The parable shows the deep wisdom of Jesus forbidding all violent attacks against evil as an interference not only with the Divine

But headlong zeal for purity is ready to ask, Why cannot the two ends be accomplished together? how should the growth of the wheat be imperilled by the uprooting of the tares? Thoughtful minds have suggested various answers to these questions. Perhaps the case in which the risk is most obvious is that in which the tares are represented not by a few individual instances of men holding unwholesome opinions, and indulging in unchristian practices, but by an evil tendency, widespread in society, such as the rationalism which prevailed so extensively in the churches in the eighteenth century. It is such a case that is contemplated in the parable. The wild crop is so abundant as to make the question of the servants " Didst thou not sow wheat?", implying a shade of doubt, not an impertinence. The corresponding state of things in the kingdom indicated thereby is such as to be a stumbling-block to faith, and to give rise to doubt whether it be the kingdom of God at all, and not rather the kingdom of darkness and evil; such as to demand Satanic influence for its explanation. This must be borne in mind in connection with the prohibition to uproot the tares, which has reference to the special case supposed, that of a crop of tares growing from seed sown over the whole field, and is compatible with a contrary practice when the tares are merely stray stalks growing accidentally in the field. In such a case they are actually gathered out of a growing crop at the present hour, and probably were also in our Lord's time, as the proposal of the servants to uproot them implies. If so, then we must conclude that an exceptional order of judgment, but with the order of the earthly development in good and evil; the fine thought being quietly insinuated that the undeveloped good can easily appear to the human eye as bad, and the bad as good, so that both can assume a fixed definite character only through the tolerating of the process of development." ' Jesu von Nazara," ii. 450.

' This is implied by the expression rd okavlaka, v. 41. So Goebel. No stress is to be laid on the etymological meaning of the wordâ trapstick, as if the evil men in the kingdom were deceivers, 2 So Stanley reports," Sinai and Palestine," p. 426. My esteemed friend, Dr. Robertson Smith, late Professor of Hebrew in the Free Church College, Aberdeen, now Lord Almoner's Professor of Arabic in the University of Cambridge, and Librarian of that University, informs me that during a recent visit to the East he ascertained the present practice to be as Stated above. I cannot refer to his name without expressing my deep regret that his great talents have been lost to the Scottish Church.

case is supposed in the parable, to convey an adequate idea of the extent to which corruption would prevail in the Church, and also the special need for care in the spiritual sphere not to uproot anything good.

For such a state of things as that implied in the parable tne only remedy is patienceâ a patience inspired and sustained by the hope that a new time will come, bringing a new spirit, a new faith, and a new life; a hope that maketh not ashamed, and which has never been disappointed from the beginning of the Christian era till now. In such a state of things impatience, prompting to stamping-oiit measures, is folly, and has been condemned as such by the wisest in the Church from the time of Augustine downwards. Such a policy of impatience forgets the solidarity of men living together in the same religious community: the many ties, spiritual and social, by which they are knit together; and the penalty of its heedlessness is dismemberment, schism,â the extensive uprooting of wheat and tares together. Far better tolerate the evil, even if it were in your power to get rid of it, than uproot it at such a cost. And if the evil should be so prevalent as to outnumber and overpower the goodâ and this is quite a possible caseâ equally to be condemned is the form which the policy of impatience is then apt to assume; that, viz. of the wheat pulling up, not the tares, but itself, even when the tares are quite willing to live side by side with it. In such a case the wheat should remain among the tares, and grow there as long as the tares will permit it. The Donatistic spirit dictates another course. It says, "Come out from among them, and be ye separate." Alas that it should have found so many at. all times ready to obey its summons, and forsake the Church in disgust because all goes not according to their wish, and because nowhere appears absolute purity; heedless of the warning that " they may fly so far from mystical Babylon as to run to literal Babel, bring all to confusion, and founder the commonwealth!"

â Calvin says: " Plerique zeli praetextu, plus aequo morosi, nisi omnia ad eorum votum composita sint, quia nusquam apparet absoluta puritas, tumultuose ab ecclesia discedunt vel importuno rigore earn evertunt ac perdunt."â ' Comment, in Harmoniam Evang."

Thomas Fuller: ' Profane State," bk. v. chap. u.

In pursuing this policy of impatience, whether in the way of pulhng up the tares or in the way of pulhng up itself, the wheat does itself much spiritual harm, quite distinct from the external evil of separation into sects. The policy tends to foster pride and uncharitableness, and so prevents the wheat from ripening, or causes it to degenerate into something not better than tares, whose fruit is poisonous. The children of the kingdom become too conscious of being the wheat, boast of their purity, thank God they are better than others, and by doing so make themselves worse, banish from their hearts the spirit of Christ, and bring on their souls the curse of impoverishment and barrenness. How small the harm done by the mere juxtaposition of the tares to that which self-righteous zealots thus inflict upon themselves!

For such reasons as these ought the tares to be borne with even xvhcn there is no room for doubt as to their being tares, â which is the case supposed in the parable. It is evident that from the injunction to practise tolerance even in such a case an argument a fortiori may be drawn in favour of the toleration of plants whose character is doubtful. There is an additional reason for tolerance in such a caseâ viz. that the wheat may be pulled up not along with but instead of the tares; that being mistaken for a noxious plant which is in reality a stalk of genuine grain. This danger is not imaginary; the mistake has often happened, and it may often happen again. There is a constant risk of committing the mistake arising out of this circumstance, that every new visitation of God in His grace to His Church is apt, when new, to appear anything but a good gift to those familiar with the grace of the kingdom under its old forms. " Every new thing," it has been well said, "which appears in the life of the Spirit, every thought which moves the world for the first time, looks dangerous; one knows not what to make of it, and is troubled. Even Christ with His apostles appeared to the Jews and heathens as an impious rebel against Divine and human right." 1 For this reason we should be slow to suspect new things and in no haste to judge them. "Judge nothing before the time,"â allow it to develop itself, and to reveal its character; and if it turn out to be tares, it will be time enough then Arndt, Die Gleichnissreden Jesu Christ!." ii. 204.

to consider what is to be done with it. This seems so obvious a dictate of reason, that those who act otherwise may be suspected of being actuated by by-ends, or even of being themselves tares; for there is truth in the shrewd observation of Bengel, "Often tares pass themselves off as wheat, and endeavour to eradicate wheat as if they were tares." At the least they are chargeable with great folly; for who that is wise would act like those empirics " that would cut off a man's head if they see but a wart upon his cheek, or a dimple upon his chin, or any line in his face to distinguish him from another man."

To these arguments in favour of a policy of patience towards evils prevalent in the visible Church on earth, must be added one that will carry more weight with all true Christians than all the rest, viz. the example of Christ. He who spake this parable, Himself complied with its teaching, and took patiently the marring of His work as the Founder of the kingdom by Satanic influences; of which we have a witness in His behaviour towards the counterfeit disciple Judas, whom He bore with meekly till the hour came when He was ready as a grain of wheat to fall into the ground and die. How significant in connection with this patient bearing of our Lord the name which He gives Himself in the interpretation of our parable. " He that soweth the good seed is the Son of man." It is the name we all know and value so much as the symbol and pledge of Christ's meekness and of His sympathy with men, the name appropriate to His state of humiliation and to His work as the Saviour of the lost. The use of the name here suggests an argument in support of the doctrine of the parable to this effect: " I, the Son of man, find an enemy busy sowing bad seed in the field where I have sown the good seed. It is saddening and disappointing, but I know it will be, and I am content that it should be, till the end. When the end comes, then the Son of man, who is now humbled by the counterworking of the evil one, will be glorified by being placed at the head of a kingdom wherein shall be none that

1 " Saepe et pro tritico se venditant, et triticum tanquam zizania eradicare eonantur."â Gnomon, in loc.

2 Jeremy Taylor, ' Epistle Dedicatory to the Liberty of Prophesying. Matt xiii. 37.

CH. II. The Tares and the Drag-Net, (i' offend or that commit iniquity. Be ye like Me in this: bear patiently the mixture of evil with the good in the kingdom, and the obscuration thence arising to the children of the kingdom from the difficulty of knowing who are such indeed. The time will come when ye shall at length along with Me shine out as the sun shines out from behind a clond' in the kingdom of your

Father." How happy for the Church if all the children of the kingdom felt the power of this appeal! But, alas! it is hard to imitate the patience of Christ! Need we wonder at the impatience of many young Christians, who are naturally prone to severity, and even of not a few old ones, in whom patience might have been expected to have had its perfect work, when we think of the immense contrast between Jesus and His contemporary and forerunner John in this respect? Jesus is content that good and evil should grow together during the long course of development through which He knows His kingdom has to pass. John demands an instant severance of good from evil, of wheat from chaff, and conceives of Messiah as coming with a fan in His hand for this judicial purpose, and on finding that He has come without the fan, sends to Him to ask the doubting question, "Art thou He that should come, or do we look for another?"2

The Drag-Net.

Having discussed at such length the parable of the Tares, a very few sentences will suffice to complete the exposition of the kindred parable of the Net, which is as follows:

Again, the kingdom of heaven is like taito a net, that was cast iiito the sea, and gathered of every kind; which, when it was filled, they drew ' sicxa ifowitiv wc TO ijxiog (v. 43). Calvin has a fine thought here: " Nee dubium est quin ad locum Danielis respexerit quo magis ad vivum afficeret auditores: acsi dixisset, Prophetam ubi de futuro splendore concionatur, simul notare temporalem caliginem; ideoque ut locus detur vaticinio patienter ferendam esse niixturam quae electos Dei reprobis ad tempus involvit."â 'Comment, in Harmoniam Evang."

The Jews had a doctrine concerning the shining dodies of the righteous in the life to come. Vide on this Langen, ' Judenthum in Palastina zur Zeit Christi," p. 507, where reference is made to our parable, as also to Paul's doctrine in i Cor. xv. But in the parable the glory is ethical, being the shining forth of the true character of the righteous, obscured in this world by their being mixed with counterfeits. Matt xi. 3.

vpon the beiigh; and they sat down and gathered the good into vessels, but cast the bad away. So shall it be at the end of the world: the angels shall come forth and sever the wicked from among the just atid shall cast them into the furnace of fire: there shall be wailing and gnashing of teeth.â laTTYL. xiii. 47-50.

After what has been said it is unnecessary to discuss the debated question whether the mixture of good and evil spoken of in this parable be within or without the kingdom. No one convinced by the reasoning whereby we have attempted to show that the mixture is within in the case of the parable of the Tares, will think it worth while to contend for the thesis that it is without in the case of the parable of the Net. To show how pointless and inapposite to the affairs of the kingdom the parable becomes in the hands of those who maintain that position, nothing more is needed than to allow one of its most strenuous recent advocates to state it in his own words. â The net is not the visible Church in the world, and the fishes good and bad within it do not represent the true and false members of the Church. The sea is the world. The net, almost or altogether invisible at first to those whom it surrounds, is that unseen bond which by an invisible ministry is stretched over the living, drawing them gradually, secretly, surely, towards the boundary of this life, and over it into another. As each portion or generation of the human race are drawn from their element in this world, ministering spirits, on the lip of Eternity that lies nearest Time, receive them, and separate the good from the evil." A very graphic and solemn representation, but what has it to do specially with the kingdom of God."' The process described, the drawing of human beings out of the sea of Time to the shore of Eternity, goes on all the world over, in pagan as well as in Christian lands. Doubtless the parable contains the important doctrine of an Eternal Judgment,â the only doctrine which on this view it teaches. But that doctrine is not a specific truth of the kingdom of God; it is a doctrine of natural religion, and as such was taught in the religions of Egypt, rh ffotrpd.: literally, putrid; more generally, worthless, useless for food: " aanpa Sunt nugamenta et quisquiliae piscium, quod genus ut servatu indignum videmus a piscatoribus abjici."â Grotius, 'Annotationes in Nov. lest." Arnot," The Parables of our Lord," p. 170.

Persia, and Greece. To make it a specific doctrine of the kingdom it would be necessary to point out the principle on which the final separation takes place,â as is done, for example, in the parabolic representation of the last judgment in the twenty-fifth chapter of Matthew, where men's eternal destiny is made to turn on the way in which they treat Christ, in the person of His representatives, the poor and needy. But the parable now under consideration enunciates no specifically Christian principle of judgment,â no principle of judgment at all, indeed, beyond the very general one that men shall be disposed of according to their moral characters. The parable, therefore, becomes one relating to the kingdom only when it is assumed that the casting of the net has reference to the work of the kingdom, and the goodness and badness of the fish to the moral qualities of those who are the subjects of that work.

This parable asserts even more emphatically than that ol the tares that not now but at the end of the world is the time for separation of the good and evil mixed together in the kingdom. It so puts the matter that separation is seen to be not merely undesirable but impossible; for till the fish are landed it cannot be known which are good and which are worthless. The graphic representation has a manifest tendency to act as a wholesome sedative on impatience and anxiety. Why fret over a mixture of the evil with the good, which is pronounced on authority to be in present circumstances inevitable in some form, if not in the form of open scandal, at least in the form of hypocritical religious profession on the part of men who have a form of godliness without the power? We might be better employed than in fretting over what cannot be helpedâ viz. in casting a net and in striving to bring as many as possible within the kingdom. That is the business of the present hour; not to judge or sift, but to catch fish, using a large net and giving it as wide a sweep as possible. The proportion of good fish to bad may be very small,â it was so in Christ's own experience; for of that crowd on the shore which listened to His parables, and which represented the result of His past labours, all but a few, when the day of crisis and sifting came, "went back, and walked no more with Him." It is a sad spectacle, and all the more that it may be taken not as an isolated but almost as a typical case; nevertheless, the duty of Christians is plain. It is not to ask wistfully shall many or few be saved, but to strive with might and main to bring into the Church as many as possible of such as are at least in the way of being saved. In this connection it is important to note the kind of net referred to in the parable. It is a seine-net of vast length, such as men use in the sea where there is ample scope for a wide sweep with a view to a great haul. The word is aptly chosen so as to be in congruity with the Catholic aim and hopeful spirit of Christianity, which is a religion for the world, and the Author of which gave it as His last injunction to those whom He had chosen to be fishers of men: " Go ye into all the world, and preach the gospel to every creature."

Of the final separation so solemnly asserted and described in those two parables we do not here speak. We close with a single word concerning a notion of sceptical critics as to the alleged ecclesiastical party tendencies of the parables, which scarce deserves notice save for the great names with which it is associated. The Tubingen school, who find tendency everywhere in the New Testament, will have it that traces of the great struggle between Pauline and Antipauline views of Christianity are clearly discernible here. The parable of the Tares is directed against Paul, who is the enemy that came by night and sowed bad seed in the field." On the other hand, the parable of the Net is Propauline; the capacious net taking in all sorts of fish being intended as a justification for Paul's two-leaved door of universalism thrown wide open to admit all comers. Surely this is criticism gone mad. The two parables are in perfect accord, and they both bear the stamp of one mind,â the mind of Him who soared above petty party strifes and dwelt habitually in the serene region of 1 Acts ii. 47. The Lord added daily to the community of Christians (ttTt TO alito) such as were being saved rovq aoi oilvotg).

"ayrjvri (v. 47). Vide Trench's note on this word in his work on the Parables, p. 140.

3 Mark xvi. 15.

So Volkmar and Hilgenfeld, also Renan (in Les Evangiles," p. 273). Keim refers to this opinion with disapproval, vide Jesu von Nazara ii. 449-

Renan, Las Evangiles," p. 201,

Divine wisdom and charity. The spirit of the two parables is the same,â it is the spirit of universahsm, not in the controversial sense, but in the sense in which we ascribe that attribute to all Christ's teaching. The Kingdom of God as Jesus preached it was a kingdom whose blessings were designed for the whole human race. In perfect accord with the whole drift of His teaching is the doctrine contained in these parables. The field is the world, the net is cast into the sea and the net itself is the largest possible, to be employed for the purposes of a gracious economy by men animated by Christ's own catholic spirit

These two parables constitute together but one text, and teach the same general lesson, namely, the incomparable worth of the kingdom of God. They show us how the kingdom ought to be esteemed, in whatever esteem it may in fact be held. They are thus an important supplement to the parable of the Sower. That parable teaches that the kingdom of heaven is far enough from being the chief good to many. To some it is simply nothing at all, the word of the kingdom awakening no interest whatever in their minds; to others it is but the occasion of a short-lived excitement; to a third class it is only one of many objects of desire; only to a chosen few is it the first thing worthy to be loved above all things, with pure, undivided, devoted heart. The two parables now to be considered teach us that the kingdom deserves to be so loved by all. It is a treasure of such value that all other possessions may reasonably be given in exchange for it; a pearl of such excellence that he who sells all his property in order to obtain it may not justly be accounted a fool. How quietly and simply is this momentous truth insinuated in those two little similitudes! One is tempted to say that so important a doctrine should have been taught with more emphasis and at greater length. We might have said this with some show of reason had these two sayings been the only texts in the recorded teaching of Christ containing the doctrine in question. But they are not; they are simply the only recorded instances in which the Great Teacher set forth that doctrine in parabolic form. The truth that the kingdom of heaven is the summum bo7i? ijfi to which everything else must be subordinated, and if necessary sacrificed, occupied the foremost place in His doctrinal system. He taught that truth on many occasions, to many persons, to individual followers, to the collective body of disciples, to the multitude at large, and often in most startling terms. " Let the dead bury their dead, but go thou and preach the kingdom of God." " If thou wilt be perfect, go and sell that thou hast, and give to the poor, and thou shalt have treasure in heaven, and come and follow Me." " If any man will come after Me, let him deny himself, and take up his cross, and follow Me." " If any man come to Me, and hate not his father and mother and wife and children and brethren and sisters, yea, and his own life also, he cannot be My disciple." What are these, and many other kindred sayings, but an emphatic proclamation of the truth taught in our parables that the Kingdom of heaven or its King (the two are practically one) is entitled to the first place in our regard, as at once man's chief good and chief end."

When and to whom these parables were spoken cannot with perfect certainty be decided. From the manner in which they are recorded by the Evangelist, there is, of course, a presumption in favour of the view that they were uttered at the same time as the preceding four, but to the disciples, after the multitude to which the parable of the Sower was addressed had been dismissed. But it is quite possible that they belonged originally to another connection, and formed part of a discourse having for its aim to enforce the precept, "Seek ye first the kingdom of God." The abrupt and disconnected way in which, according to the reading approved by critics, the former of the two is introduced, seems to favour this view. "The kingdom of heaven is like unto a treasure hid in a field; " so, without any mediating word like the-naxiv in the received text, does the narrative pass from the interpretation of the parable of the Tares to the wholly dissimilar pirable of the Hidden Treasure, suggesting the idea of a water-worn pebble which has been rolled away by the stream from its original bed. And as the parable might have been uttered on a different occasion, so it might have been addressed to a

Luke ix. 60. 2 att. xix. 21.
Matt. xvi. 24. Luke xiv. 26.

different audience than Matthew's narrative seems to imply; not to the disciples, but to a miscellaneous group of hearers like that which listened to the parable of the Sower, Such a view, indeed, would be inadmissible if we could attach as much importance as Origen did to the circumstance that the last three parables in the group of seven are not called parables." That Father, in his commentary on the passage, suggests as the reason of the fact stated that the last three were spoken to the disciples, not to the multitude; proceeding on the assumption that parables were meant exclusively for those without, and therefore holding that we ought not to call the three last figurative representatives of the Divine kingdom parables, but similitudes. If this opinion were correct, we might infer, from the simple fact that the name parable is not applied to these similitudes, that they were spoken not to a miscellaneous audience, but to a closer circle of the disciples. But it is not true that parables were spoken to the multitude alone, and therefore the non-use of the name in the case of the last three parables can have no such significance as Origen alleges. It is indeed incredible that the Evangelist can have seriously meant to withhold the name from these parables as inapplicable, when he had previously applied it to the equally brief similitudes of the Mustard Seed and the Leaven. The omission of the name must be regarded as purely accidental.

We proceed to the consideration of our two parablesâ those of the Treasure and the Pearl, placing them as of kindred significance side by side, and treating them in the first place as one text in the exposition of the great truth which they teach in common, reserving for the close observations on the points in which they differ.

TJie kingdom of heaven is like unto a treasure hid in the fietd, which a man having found hid, and in his joy he goeth and selleth all that he hath, and buyeth that field.

They are introduced "with otoa iarxv. ' onouoaitg from c'ioa. The same method of treatment is adopted by Greswell and Arndt.

iv Tw dyp(; " in the field in which it lies" (Meyer). "The field in which the finder was working" (Greswell). " The article implies that in the mind of hearers the idea of a hidden treasure would be associated with that of a field as the usual hiding-place " (Goebel).

' The aiTov is genit. subj., not obj. So Meyer. Vide also Trench.

Again, the kingdom of heaven is like unto a merchantman seeking goodly pearls, who when he had found one pearl of great price went and sold all that he had, and bought it. â Matt. xiii. 44â 46.

The two emblems here employed by Jesus were fitly chosen to impress an ancient Eastern audience, and to serve in their case the purpose intendedâ that of representing the kingdom of heaven as the Absolute Good, and as such worthy that all should be given in exchange for it. In our day and land such emblems would be less appropriate. The finding of a treasure hid in a field is so rare an occurrence in modern European experience that to employ it as a parabolic representation of the finding of the Divine kingdom would be to commit the mistake of making that which ought to be an object of desire and hope to all appear so improbable as to be practically unattainable. It was otherwise in the age and country when and where the parable was spoken. Then to hide treasure in the earth, in sepulchres, or any other place where the owners deemed their property would be secure, was a not uncommon practice; and to find such a hidden treasure was by no means an unexampled felicity. Equally apt to the circumstances of the time is the emblem employed in the second parable. In our day a pearl could not properly be selected as the fittest representative of the highest good. The diamond is our most precious stone. But in ancient times the diamond, though not unknown, and though highly valued, was too rare to be a suitable emblem of the kingdom of heaven in a popular discourse. The pearl was the more appropriate object for such a purpose, because it was to the ancients what the diamond is to usâ well known, highly prized, and, when of large size and pure quality, exceeding costly. The romantic theory current in ancient times respect- 1 ai0pw7r fitTopi. The idea of travelling is involved in the term tfinopog. Bengel defines ifi-n-opoq as one " qui mercaturse causa peregrinatur et navigat." Greswell says, "His proper character is that of a collector of pearls, and probably of a trader in them, though this is no necessary supposition " (vol. ii. p. 226). For additional remarlcs see p. 88.

On this view that the treasure was hidden needs no special explanation. A hid treasure was simply in those days a natural emblem of a thing of great value. Goebel thinks the kingdom is compared to a hid treasure, to describe its character in opposition to the outward and sensuous ideas of the kingdom current among the Jews.

yi The Parabolic Tcacjiing of Christ, book i.

ing the origin of pearls served to enhance their fitness to body-forth the things of the kingdom. It was beueved that the pearl was formed by the dew of heaven entering into the shell wherein it was found, the quality and form of the pearl depending on the purity of the dew the state of the atmosphere, and even the hour of the day at the time of its conception. There is reason to think that the true cause of pearl formation is of a much more prosaic character; the probable account offered by modern science being that pearls are the result of a process of animal secretion provoked by the intrusion of a foreign substance, such as a grain of sand, within the shell, the fish covering the alien particle with pearly matter to protect itself from irritation. But the ancient theory, however baseless, is still full of interest as serving to show the esteem in which pearls were held. Worthless as science, it is valuable as poetry, as a standing evidence that the pearl was to the ancients an object of admiration, wonder, almost of worship; for it is only noble, precious, worshipful things that the human mind seeks to glorify by bringing into play the resources of its imagination.

Here then were two emblems fitly chosen to set before an ancient Jewish audience the absolute worth of the Divine kingdom,â a hidden treasure, and a very precious pearl, the best of a precious kind. The former of the two is indeed not so apparently apt to the purpose, as a treasure may be great or small, and it is not said that the treasure was a great one. But that is only not said because it is taken for granted. The presumption is that a hidden treasure will be of great value â something worth hiding, and also worth finding. That the treasure in the parable was of great value is further implied in the joy of the finder. He sees at a glance the vast extent of his treasure-trove, and his cunning in hiding it, and his joy in going to take steps towards securing it for himself, unerringly reveal the estimate he has formed. The second of the two emblems is self-evidently fitly chosen. The best and Riost precious of all existing pearls signified an immense, almost fabulous sum of money. The two famous pearls possessed by Cleopatra, according to Pliny the largest known,

For an account of the opinions of the ancients on the origin of pearls, vidt Origen's commentary on the parable.

were valued each at about; 8o, ooo in our money. Surely a sum fit to represent infinite wealth to the popular mind, though the profligate Queen of Egypt could afford to drink one of the pearls dissolved in a menstruum at a supper given to her lover!

The comparisons of our parables, while naturally suggesting the thought that the kingdom of heaven is the siimmiini bomim, at the same time felicitously demonstrate the reasonableness fv) of the demand that all be sacrificed for the kingdom. The conduct of the actors in the two parables was thoroughly reasonable. Both were gainers by the transaction of selling their all for the sake of obtaining the precious object. The buyer of the field containing the hid treasure was manifestly a gainer; for the field itself, apart from the treasure, assuming that the bargain between him and the seller was a fair one, was a full equivalent for the whole of his property which he realised in order to purchase it. The hidden treasure, whose existence was unknown to the seller, and therefore not taken into account, he had into the bargain. Provided the purchase of the field made his right to the treasure-trove secure loss in that transaction was impossible. The buyer of the high-priced pearl was likewise a gainer from a mercantile point of view. It might indeed seem a precarious proceeding to put all one's property (not merely all his other jewels, but all he had) into one single article, however precious. But the very preciousness of that one article implies that pearls of excellent quality were much in demand, so that a purchaser might safely be counted on. The merchantman was sure of his money whenever he wished to realise, and in all probability would receive for the pearl a sum far exceeding what he had

For numerous particulars respecting the value of pearls in ancient times, consult Greswell's note in his work on the Parables, vol. ii. p. 220.

That it did so seems implied in the incident recorded of R. Emi, referred to by Meyer in his commentary, that he bought a rented field in â which he had found a treasure, "ut pleno jure thesaurum possideret omnemque litium occasionem preecideret." Of the treasure-finder, Alford remarks, " he goes, and selling all he has, buys the field, thus (by the Jewish law) becoming the possessor also of the treasure."

Ovk. tl-iriv ore TrttrpakE Trdvrat; ove iixiv ov yag fisvovs, ovg 6! ir)Twv leaxovc fiapyapiraq iwvrjtai, irknpaktv, dwd Kal irdpra offa tl tv. Origen, ' Comment, in Evangelium Matth."

paid for it; for he had gone to a far-off land to buy it from the pearl-fisher, at a moderate though great cost, and had brought it, let us say, from India to the Western centres of wealth, where rich men abounded and luxury prevailed. In saying this we go upon the assumption that the purchaser of the pearl in the parable was really a merchant. If he was no merchant, but only a pearl-fancier and collector, who went to the ends of the earth in quest of the rarest samples, and having found one of incomparable excellence, hesitated not, in his passion for such valuables, to give all that he had that he might become its possessor, the case is altogether different. He was then a fool from the mercantile point of view; if he was a gainer at all, it was certainly not in money, but in the gratification of aesthetic taste and romantic desire. We shall not now decide peremptorily between these two views of the pearl-collector's conduct, for in either aspect it might serve as a parable of the kingdom. He who gives all for the kingdom of God is truly wise, but in the world's view he is a fool; and of his folly a man with a craze for collecting pearls for the bare pleasure of possessing them were no unapt emblem.

If now men could only be convinced that the kingdom of heaven is like the treasure hid in the field and the precious pearl, and that in giving up all for its sake they were only acting as the buyers of the field and the pearl acted, all would be well. They would then go and do likewise. For men never hesitate to sacrifice all for what they believe to be the chief good. Devotion all the world over is reckless of expense, and acts as if it reckoned the demand of the loved object, that it be first and all else second, no grievous commandment, but a perfectly reasonable requirement. No matter what the object of devotion may be, whether earthly or heavenly, material or mental, its language is that of the impassioned lover:

"By night, by day, afield, at hame. The thoughts of thee my breast inflame, Â The best pearls were found there or in the Red Sea. On the localities where pearls were found, see Origen, as above; also Greswells note, already referred to. Among the localities is our own land or its environing sea. Origen says the second best were found here. Asurtptuowiri Ik iti iv unpyapiraiq oj Ik tov Kara pitTaviav ojktavov Xaixjiavofitvoi,

And aye I muse and sing thy name: I only live to love thee."

The devoted disciples of the Rabbis so loved the law which they studied, because they reckoned knowledge of it the chief good. Their masters expressed the sovereign claims of the law in terms not less severe than the severest ever employed by Jesus to assert the claims of the kingdom. In addressing to a certain disciple the apparently harsh injunction, "Let the dead bury their dead, but go thou and preach the kingdom of God," our Lord did, in truth, but report a saying current in Rabbinical circles. And how faithfully did some disciples of the Rabbis comply with such hard requirements in their pursuit of legal lore! Think of the famous Hillel, come all the way from Babylon to Jerusalem to learn wisdom; of whom it is recorded that he was so poor he could not pay the porter's fee to gain admission into the school, and so was obliged to listen at the window, till on a severe winter night he was almost frozen to death, and had certainly lost his life had not the darkening of the window by his body, heaped over with falling snow, attracted the attention of those within. Here was one willing to part even with life itself in his devotion to the study of the law. And was not Socrates another of kindred spirit, seeking wisdom with pure elevated heart, and cheerfully subordinating all to the knowledge of the true, the good, and the fair! Listen to his prayer, pagan in form, but thoroughly Christian in import: " O dear Pan and all ye other Gods here! grant me to be beautiful within; and may my external possessions not be hurtful to those which are internal; and may I esteem him rich who is wise; and may my treasure be such as none can carry away save one who is of sober mind." But we are under no necessity to seek illustrations among celebrities. Multitudes of instances of self-sacrificing devotion to wisdom as the chief good might be found among the ranks of poor obscure students attending our schools of learning, whose motto is

"To scorn delights and live laborious days,"

See Cunningham Geikie's Life of Christ," vol. ii. p. i6o.

Â See Barclay, ' The Talmud," p. 15; also Jost, Judenthum.

Plato, Phaedrus, at the close.

and who would gladly part with their last ten shillings to procure some favourite book, with whose contents they had long desired to become acquainted.

The difficulty is to get men to see that the kingdom of God is indeed the sunwiicjn boniim and therefore worthy to be loved as Hillel loved the law, and as Socrates loved wisdom, and as every true student loves knowledge. They are prone to ask in sceptical mood, What is this kingdom of heaven that we should seek it as men seek hidden treasure, or buy it at any price as merchantmen buy costly jewels.? And we might here attempt a detailed answer to their question; but we shall not. We are not required to do so as expositors of the parables; for the two parables under consideration do not explain to us the nature of the kingdom of heaven, or tell us why it is entitled to be regarded as the chief good; they simply teach that it is entitled, as a matter of fact, to be so regarded. And moreover the attempt were vain; if at least its object were not merely to state truth already well enough known to an ordinarily instructed Christian, but to produce conviction. For it is not man but the Spirit of God that can make any one see the kingdom of heaven and its King in their peerless beauty and worth, so that he shall be willing to part with all for their sake. Christ Himself as a human teacher could not achieve such a result. The very parables before us are possibly a result of his consciousness of inability to do so. For why did He speak to the people in parables but because they seeing saw not; because the things of the kingdom were hidden from their view, and because He all but despaired of opening their eyes

Instead therefore of repeating common-places of Christian knowledge in the vain hope of communicating spiritual vision, we prefer to confine attention to one point in which the doctrine of these parables seems inconsistent with one of the best ascertained attributes of the kingdom whose advent Jesus announced. We refer to the attribute implied in the titleâ the kingdom of grace. That the kingdom of heaven, as Christ preached it, was emphatically a kingdom of grace Â s abundantly evident from the Gospels. It is implied in the fact that Christ called the announcement of the kingdom good tidin'gs. The proclamation of its advent was in His view the Gospel. Hence the burthen of His preaching from the beginning of His ministry was: " The time is fulfilled, the kingdom of God is at hand; repent ye and believe the good news." The same truth, that the kingdom announced was a kingdom of grace, is implied in the fact that those who received Christ's message were a glad company, resembling a wedding-party, while John's followers resembled a band of pilgrims wending their weary way with sad looks toward some shrine doing penance for their sins. The cause of this difference was this: The kingdom, as John preached it, was awful news, a kingdom of law and retribution; while the kingdom as Jesus preached it was good news, a kingdom of grace and of pardon. The same truth is further implied in the familiar facts that the kingdom, as Jesus preached it, was emphatically a kingdom for the poor, the outcast, the morally degraded, the humble, the child-like: which is only to say in other words that it was a free gift of Gcd's grace to those who had no wealth, no merit, no consciousness of. desert, no pride of virtue.

But how then are we to reconcile with this outstandinsf attribute of the kingdom the representations of the parables, in both of which the material goods, which are emblems of the kingdom, are represented as obtained by purchase f The point is one which forces itself on our attention, for the buying is not a minor, accidental, or insignificant trait, but a leading feature in the parables. It is especially noticeable in the former of the two, where it almost seems as if the speaker gave an artificial turn to the story with express intent to introduce the act of buying. One is inclined to ask. Why not at once appropriate the treasure found; why that roundabout process of buying the field in order to get possession of the hidden store of gold Would not the direct appropriation of the treasure have been far more in harmony with the genius of the kingdom as a kingdom of grace Of course the reply which will be given to our query is: The buying of the field

Mark i. 15.

Goebel thinks the didactic drift of the parables is to teach the way in which men must make the kingdom their own. It is rather that they must make it their own at any price. It is worthy of this. But that it has to be bought is also taught by implication.

was necessary to set the finder right with the law. That may be so, but we question if the answer goes to the root of the matter. For in the first place the process of buying, if it set the finder right with the law, certainly did not set him right with equity: and therefore it was not worth while to ascribe to the actor a conscientiousness which after all was formal not real. Then if, as we admit, it was not necessary for the purpose of the parable to represent the man as having a regard to equity, but simply as determined by all means to obtain the desired boon, there could be no more harm in making him reach his object by a direct breach of equity than by an indirect one. Why could he not carry away his treasure-trove and say nothing about it, but quietly spend it for his own comfort? Undoubtedly the speaker wished to make the treasure-finder a buyer, even when buying was not indispensable in order to possession as it was in the case of the pearl-seeker; as if with express intent to teach that in all cases there must be a buying in order to possession of the kingdom of heaven.

But how, we again ask, reconcile this doctrine with the nature of the kingdom as a kingdom of grace, and with its catholicity as a kingdom offered to all? If the kingdom is of grace why buy, and if it is for all what of those who have not wherewith to purchase the field in which the treasure is hid, of whom the number is at all times great. The solution of the puzzle is simple. Buying, translated into other language, means showing by action that we really do esteem the kingdom of God to be the chief good; and that all who are to receive the kingdom must do, and that moreover all, however beggared in purse or character, have it in their power to do. The kingdom must be subjectively as well as objectively the siimmiim bonum, and wherever it is so, means will be found to make the fact evident. That such subjective appreciation manifested in action is quite compatible with the nature of the kingdom may be proved by a reference to the parable of the Supper. There the highest good is represented as eating bread in the kingdom of God, as the result of accepting an invitation to a feast. That the kingdom is a gift of grace could not be more clearly taught than by such a form of Vide on this point note on p. 73, ' Luke xiv. 1.

representation. Yet even here there must needs be a buying; the prophetic paradox finds its fulfilment, for even he that hath no money, the outcast of the highway and hedges, buys and eats; buys wine and milk without money and without price. The men who were first bidden did not partake of the feast because they did not buy; that is to say, because they were unwilling for a season to leave off farming operations and forego connubial bliss to enjoy the hospitality of the neighbour who issued the invitations. They did not value the feast enough to be willing to make such a sacrifice for it. And the men who were last bidden and who came, with what did they buy With a victory over the temptation to think that so great a bliss could not possibly be meant for such wretches as they were. They had to be compelled, not because they were indifferent, but because the invitation seemed too good news to be true. And the price they paid was the renunciation of their doubts, and the exchange of the humility of unbelief for the deeper, truer humility of faith, which could dare to believe that God's grace could reach even unto such as they. And as none can be poorer than they, it thus appears that it is always possible for one who is in earnest to buy the kingdom. In the spiritual world there is no risk of a man, who greatly values the hidden treasure, finding himself so poor that he cannot purchase the field in which it lies. Though the parable seems to have no consideration for the poor, it is only on the surface. Rightly understood, it is quite in harmony with the spirit of Him who declared it to be His mission to preach the Gospel to the poor. All may have wherewithal to buy the field. For all men have hearts, and he who loves the hidden treasure with all his heart can show his love, and that is all the price that is needed. The presence of the love in the heart shows itself very variously in different men; the All which is sacrificed is very diverse in degree and in kind for one from what it is for another. The price which the fishermen of Galilee paid for the kingdom of God was their fishing boats and nets; a very humble all, but quite sufficient to buy the field and the precious pearl. The price which the young man, who came seeking eternal life, was asked to pay, was his large fortune, a

Isa. Iv. I.

much larger all, yet not more than sufficient. The price paid by Saul of Tarsus was his carefully elaborated system of legal righteousness. Augustine, on the other hand, bought the kingdom by a price different from all these, viz. by parting with the darling object of a guilty passion. The price, we repeat, is various in degree and in kind. But the poorest in purse or reputation can find a price of some sort wherewith to buy the kingdom. For the kingdom, when it comes to men, finds every one of them either loving something that ought not to be loved at all, or loving some legitimate object of affection too well; and its demand is that such sinful or inordinate attachment should cease in its own favour, and when the demand is complied with, the price which buys the chief good is paid.

From the foregoing explanation of the buying of the kingdom it will be seen that it is quite compatible not only with the nature of the latter as a kingdom of grace, but with the joyous spirit which ought to characterise the citizens of such a kingdom. The sacrifice by which the kingdom is bought is made not by constraint but willingly: not in forced obedience to an outward commandment, but in free obedience to the inward constraint of love. The sacrifice is made cheerfully, gaily, whenever the kingdom is seen to be the summum boniim â when we know in their priceless worth the things that are freely given to us of God. The genuine citizens of the kingdom all say of it " all my springs are in Thee," not lugubriously but with singing and dancing; albeit one has come from Egypt, another from Babylon, and a third, a fourth, and a fifth from Philistia, Tyre, and Ethiopia; cheerfully forgetting their old country for the sake of the newfound fatherland. It will be observed how carefully the parable is constructed so as to exclude a legal cheerless view of the sacrifice as something arbitrarily exacted. The sacrifice is made to appear the natural outcome of the joy over the discovery just made of the treasure. "In his joy he 1 Psalm lxxxvii. 7. This verse of the Psalm is rendered by Delitzsch, "and singing and dancing" (they say) '-all my springs are in thee," that is,, in Zion, viewed as the metropolis of the Divine kingdom. The new-born citizens go about in the streets of the mother-city of the Divine kingdom expressing in dance and song their joy, the burthen of their song being, " all my springs in thee." What a graphic picture I goeth and selleth all that he hath and buyeth that field." This is an important touch in the picture, and it is all the more worthy of notice that it serves to correct a false impression that might easily be made by the description of the stony ground hearer in the parable of the Sower, as one who receives the word with joy, but when tribulation arises is offended. This may very readily be mistaken for a disparagement of joy as the mark of a superficial nature, and as seldom accompanied or followed by heroic fidelity. That no such insinuation was meant is manifest from this parable, which not only represents intense joy as characteristic of the treasure-finder, but further represents that joy as the direct source of self-sacrifice. From this instance we may learn to be on our guard against hasty inferences from isolated or accidental features in parabolic embodiments of spiritual truth. And the caution may be applied not only to the joy ascribed to the stony ground hearer, but to the secrecy or cunning ascribed to the treasure-finder. Some interpreters of the parables have taken this as a feature to be emphasised, drawing from it the doctrine that silence or secrecy at the commencement of the Christian life is necessary in order to make conversion thorough and stable, and pointing to Christ's withdrawal into the wilderness after His baptism, or to Paul's three years' seclusion in Arabia by way of illustration. Now it is true that sececy and silence are sometimes advantageous, and also that they often characterise men of earnest thoughtful temper at the commencement of their religious life. But in the first place it cannot be laid down as a universal rule, that wherever there is religious genuineness and thoroughness there will be such secrecy and silence; and in the second place, when these characteristics appear they have a different source from that implied in the parable. The treasure-finder hid the treasure in fear lest he should lose it. But the man who has begun to think seriously on religion hides his thoughts deep in his heart, not from fear of losing them, but from delicacy and shyness. New-born religion, like youthful love, " is a shy, retiring thing, which shamefacedly withdraws from observation. The shyness is in some respects beneficial, and

So Arndt and De Valenti. Conf. Trench on the same point in some respects it is the reverse. It is not a thing to be prescribed as part of a necessary method for insuring salvation.

We pass now from the common to the distinctive lessons of the two parables. And here it may be well to begin with a caveat against the assumption that these parables must necessarily be intended to teach distinct doctrines concerning the things of the kingdom. The assumption is one which we are naturally inclined to make from the mere fact of there being two parables and not one; especially when it is taken for granted that the two parables were originally spoken at the same time. Why speak two parables on the same theme at one time unless because, while both set forth the same general truth, each exhibits that truth under a different phase? The question is a very natural one, and yet for our part we do not deem it prudent to lay too much stress on the argument it contains, or even to be sure that the premises on which the inference rests are well-founded. We would bear in mind the possibility that these two parables which come together in Matthew's narrative were spoken on different occasions, and that therefore the difference between them may h picturesque rather than doctrinal, due to the changing forms under which a creative mind, able to bring forth out of its treasure things new and old, contemplated the same truth at different times. While we say this, however, we are not only willing but anxious to recognise whatever distinctive lessons may seem fairly deducible from the twin parables; and, though averse from over-confident dogmatism, we think that on two points their peculiarities have didactic significance.

First, it seems legitimate to emphasise, as all expositors have done, the fact that in the one parable the material good which is the emblem of the siimimnn boman, is found by accident, while in the other it is obtained as the result of a methodic persistent search. The spiritual import of this distinction has been diversely apprehended, A recent writer expresses the opinion that both traits point to the difficulty of recognising in the kingdom offered to men the highest good, the difference being that in the one case the difficulty arises from the inherent nature of the kingdom as a hidden thing; in the other from the exacting demands which the quest of the chief good involves. On this view there is no reference to a distinction between diverse classes of recipients. Most interpreters, however, have regarded the fact in question as intended to point at such a distinction, and to divide the recipients of the blessings of the kingdom into two classes: those to whom the kingdom comes without any previous thought on their part, and those to whom it is given as the reward of an earnest foregoing search. Nathaniel and the woman of Samaria have been referred to as examples of the one class, and Augustine in his intensely interesting and eventful religious history, as described by himself in his famous ' Confessions," as an out-standing example of the other. Now that there is such a distinctior between Christians as to the manner of their coming irito the kingdom of God is certainâ there are finders and there are seekers in the kingdom of heaven. Both are finders of God and the chief good, or rather are found of them, for in all cases there is something in religious experience which does not depend on man's will; but the one class find without much or any previous quest, while the other class first seek earnestly, and it may be long, and then eventually find. And the emblems of the chief good in the two parables answer very well to this distinction between the two classes of finders. A hidden treasure is not a thing that one can well set himself to seek for, though men have given themselves occasionally to such an apparently hopeless quest. But goodly pearls are things to be sought after and obtained as the result of a continued search; and one may reasonably hope at length to find the best after having previously found many good. Such finding of the best is not only probable but certain in the spiritual world, though it is not more than a probability in the natural. A literal pearl-seeker may never find the one best pearl in all the world. But in the kingdom of heaven they that seek shall find. Their quest may be long, painful, wearisome, and they may experience many disappointments; meeting now here, now there, what seems on first view a very precious pearl, but on closer inspection is found to have flaws which ' Goebel. 2 So Trench, pp. 125-6.

' The actors in both parables are described as finding: hv evputt avopi'TTOi, ver. 44, iipwv 5i, ver. 46, depreciate its value. But one day they shall find Him whom unconsciously they seek, and in Him get rest to their souls. So found the Pearl of Price Justin Martyr, so found Him Augustine, so find Him shall every faithful soul who hungers after righteousness and passionately longs for the knowledge of God and of truth.

But to return to the distinction between finders and seekers. We recognise the reality of the distinction, but wc doubt whether it is intended in the parables to teach the existence of such a distinction; at least in so far as it is understood to imply a moral difference between the two classes. For, let it be observed, the treasure-finder is not represented as indifferent to the discovery he has made. He rejoices over the happy discovery. He at once recognises its value-as one who does not now for the first time learn the use of money. He would have been a seeker for such a treasure, not less earnest and persistent than the pearl merchant, had there been any reasonable hope of finding one. It seems therefore quite beside the mark, as some have done, to make this man represent the spiritually careless, who are suddenly arrested on their godless careerâ of those who go to church to laugh and remain to pray, of youths who leave their country homes for great cities there to make their fortune, and find what they had not sought, conversion and salvation. In point of fact, the actors in the two parables seem to differ not so much in spirit as in circumstances; and the question forces itself upon the mind whether after all the design be not to make an objective distinction between men as to their xq. s' ccwvq positions, rather than a subjective distinction between them as to their respective dispositions. Does not the one parable show us the kingdom of God as a good beyond human hope and expectation, coming as a surprise to men who are not looking for it, but who gladly welcome itâ all the more gladly because it was unexpected; and does not the other parable show us the kingdom, not as something unique, unexampled, and unlooked for, but as the best of its kind, the like of which in kind already exists and is known, so as to raise an expectation that something better of the same kind than has ever yet been seen may yet be found? In the two representations there is no

So Arnot, p. 137.

apparent difiference between the parties concerned except in position. They act differently because they are differently situated; either would act like the other if he were in his circumstances.

On this ground we incline to think that the parables point io a distinction between men as to position, not as to disposition, and show us how men of the same spirit will behave towards the kingdom of heaven in their respective situations. They will both make it welcome when found,â the one as a good he had not looked for, the other as a good after which he had long been in quest. And it is not difficult to illustrate the difference in situation implied in the parables. Who were the men in our Lord's day (for it is thence we must in the first place seek our illustrations) to whom the kingdom of heaven was as a treasure hid in a field t They were such as Zacchaeus the publican,â men who had not been seeking the kingdom simply because they had been accustomed to be treated by those who deemed themselves the children of the kingdom, as persons who had no concern or interest' therein, until they had come themselves to believe this. What a surprise it was to the pariahs of Jewish society to find that Jesus took an interest in them, and to hear Him speak to them of the kingdom as if it were specially their affair 1 Here indeed was a treasure these pqor despised ones had not been looking for! not because they set no value on it, but because they had not ventured to hope, had not been able even to entertain the thought, that God loved them. And who were they to whom the kingdom of heaven was as the precious pearl found after lengthened quest."' They were those who waited, as they who wait for the dawn, for the consolation of Israel; devout men who diligently read the ancient Scriptures in search of the pearls of wisdom, and who had learned from the words of the prophets to look for one Pearl more precious than allâ Messiah, the incarnate Wisdom of God,â and who recognised Him in Jesus of Nazareth. Equally easy is it to illustrate the distinction in question from the apostolic age. The men to whom the kingdom of heaven was as a treasure hid in a field were the Gentiles who had been aliens from the commonwealth of Israel and strangers from the covenants of promise, having no hope, and without God in the world, up to the time the Gospel was preached to them, and who yet at once welcomed that Gospel as good tidings when it was proclaimed to them; their hearts having been prepared for its reception by the very misery inseparable from a life without hope. The appropriateness of a hidden treasure as an emblem of the kingdom of heaven in their case is evinced by the fact that the Apostle Paul, whether with conscious reference to our parable we cannot tell, represents the admission of the Gentiles to participation in the blessings of salvation as a mystery hid in God And of the pearl-seekers of that timo we may find good samples in such as the Eunuch ofethiopia and Lydia: Gentiles by birth, but proselytes to the Jewish religion, who in that religion and its sacred literature had already found many goodly pearls, but yet felt that there must be better still to be found, and who did at length find the best possible in Jesus the crucified.

These illustrations from the beginning of the Gospel suffice to show the reality of the distinction implied in the two comparisons of the kingdom of heaven to a hidden treasure whose existence was unsuspected, and to a pearl which j was an object of persistent quest. But we are not shut' up to draw our illustrations from the distant past. We may find parallels to the two classes, diversely situated, as described, in every age and in our own time. The Gospel comes as a hidden treasure to all converts from heathenism who had previously been yearning in dull despair for the good they comprehended not and never hoped to see; and to all among our own lapsed masses," as we somewhat heartlessly call them, who, having spent years in ignorance and wretchedness, have at length, in some happy hour, come to learn that in Jesus they have a friend, in God a father, and in heaven a home. And the Gospel is the pearl of great price to those who, having received a Christian nurture, which has fostered in them all noble affections, on reaching young manhood devote themselves to the pursuit of truth, wisdom, and righteousness, not immediately convinced that all these are to be found by retaining the faith in which tliey have been reared, perhaps for a time rejecting that

Eph. ill. 9.

faith, and going to other masters than Christ in quest of the true, the good, and the fair; but at length, after n-iuch wandering and earnest search, always well intended, however fruitless in result, find rest to their souls in accepting Christ as Master, Lord, and Saviour, in whom are stored all the treasures of wisdom, knowledge, and grace.

In all the instances alluded to we have felt justified in assuming that the difference is one of situation rather than disposition. All alike welcome and love the good when it is presented to their view. We must not leave this topic, however, without remarking that welcoming the highest good in either class of cases is by no means a matter of course. In both parables the actors are represented as rejoicing in the discovery of the chief good, but it is not intended thereby to teach that there was no temptation to act otherwise. In both situations indicated by the two parables, there is temptation so to act as to lose the good that is attainable. In the case of the treasure-finder there is the danger of being prevented by abject fear from appropriating the good within reach; in the case of the pearl-seeker, of being too easily satisfied with what has already been obtained, and giving up the quest. How ready is one in the position of the class called 'publicans and sinners' to regard the Gospel of the kingdom as too good news to be true, to treat the invitation to the feast as a jest, and not seriously meant; not because he would not gladly go, but because he cannot believe he is wanted. And how ready is one who is already in possession of goodly pearls of wisdom and virtueâ admired and envied by othersâ to congratulate himself on his treasures, and to stop short prematurely in his quest; a philosopher, a man of

The above view is in principle identical with that advocated by Greswell. He says: " To the first of these descriptions, that is, to the idea of the kingdom of heaven as represented by the treasure, I think it may be shown will correspond the privilege of becoming a Christian; and to the second, in which the kingdom of heaven is adumbrated by the pearl, the profession of Christianity, or the continuing a Christian on principle." He adds: "By the privilege of becoming a Christian, I understand the acceptance of the first offer of Christianity, the option of the Gospel terms of salvation; an offer and an option which would consequently be inseparable from the being and promulgation of Christianity, but could have no existence until it began to be preached."â Vol ii. p. 234.

science, a man of culture, but not a Christian. How many among the diverse classes of our societyâ the cultured and the uncultureda may be committing these sad mistakes even now! Happy is the man who avoids both, and is able to say amen to the sentiment of the Apostle Paul: " This is a credible saying, and worthy of all acceptation, that Christ Jesus came into the world to save sinners,"â credible not too good news to be true, though certainly very surprising; ivortjiy of all acceptation, more to be valued than all other knowledge or wisdom.

The other distinction between the two parables as to didactic import, we shall do little more than hint at, because we are by no means sure that it is not a fancy. It is this, that in the former of the two parables the sumintim bomim seems to be exhibited under the aspect of the useful, and in the latter under the aspect of the ornamental. A treasure is valuable as supplying the means of purchasing commodities; a pearl is valuable as an ornament. That the kingdom of heaven should be presented under such various aspects is not incredible, for as the siiminiim boniiin it must satisfy all man's legitimate wants; and man is not only a being who craves happiness, but also a being who has a sense of the beautiful. The beau ideal must embrace at once the true, the good, and the fair. And the kingdom of heaven does meet these various wants of human nature. It not only aims at putting man in a happy, saved condition, but at beautifying and ennobling him as the possessor of wisdom and righteousness. But it may be said there is no foundation for such a distinction in the parables, because the pearl-collector is a

merchant, and is interested in his acquisitions not as ornaments, but out of regard to the price he will get for them. That, however, is a point open to question. The woi'd Ifitiopos does not necessarily, though it may usually, denote a merchant; and even though it were conceded that a merchant is intended, merchants have been known who were more than merchants, and were so enamoured of some article they had purchased as to be unwilling to sell it again. In favour of the view that the collector in the parable is a pearl-fancier rather than a mere trader is the statement that he is seeking goodly pearls. Of course a trader, as well as an amateur collector, would seek only goodly pearls; for to what end buy small, unshapely, discoloured specimens, which could not be expected to attract purchasers? But why expressly mention what might be taken for granted, unless to indicate that the man had a peculiar exceptional love for rare and excellent specimens,â a love due to personal tastes, not to trading propensities? But it may be objected. How absurd to suppose that a man would give all he had for a single pearl he did not mean to sell again, and make a profit by I " If, after giving all that he had for the pearl, he had hung it on his neck, where could the poor man have found food and clothing?" A very plausible, if somewhat vulgar question; yet it is but the question which the world asks in reference to the demand made to leave all for the kingdom: " What shall we eat, or what shall we drink, or wherewithal shall we be clothed? " Ask no such questions, replies Christ. Seek first, and at all hazards, the kingdom of God, and these things shall be provided for you. And this is the law by which the true citizen of the kingdom is guided. It is not a rule to be mechanically acted on, but it is nevertheless the law of the spirit of a Christian life. In acting on such a law a Christian exposes himself to a charge of folly. What a fool was the man who parted with all to obtain a single pearl, which he meant to keep in his possession! It was the act of one who had a craze, who had gone mad in the pursuit of a hobby I True, yet such folly is characteristic of the seekers after God. It is the folly of the wise
    Arnot, p. 156.

    In three of our Lord's parables the kingdom of heaven is represented as the subject of growth. These parables are the two above-named, and the parable of the Blade, the Ear, and the Full Corn, preserved in Mark's Gospel. The first of the three teaches that the kingdom is destined to increase in outward bulk as a visible society; the second, that it will'" manifest itself as a spiritual power exercising a progressive moral influence, and gradually transforming the character of the individual or the community by whom or which it has been received; the third, that in its growth the kingdom will resemble corn which groweth secretly, spontaneously, gradually, passing in the course of its growth through various stages in accordance with a fixed law which cannot be set aside, and yielding fruit only in the proper season, which cannot be hurried on, but must be patiently waited for. The three parables might very legitimately be considered in one chapter, as together exhibiting Christ's teachings on one important theme. That the Evangelists regarded them as of kindred import appears from the manner in which they connect them in their narratives, the first and third Evangelist joining together the parables of the Mustard Seed and the Leaven, and the second connecting the former of these with the parable of the seed growing gradually, which he alone has recorded. And a hasty glance suffices to show that as the three parables have a common didactic purpose, so they serve one practical aim. They are designed to inspire hope and patience amid circumstances fitted to breed despondency and discouragement. In presence of the small and insignificant beginnings of the kingdom, Jesus says to His disciples: Fear not, that which now appears so small and weak will one day be a great fact and a mighty power. And lest disciples should despair of that day ever appearing because it tarried longer than they expected, or should seek to hurry it on by impatient earnestness, their Master speaks to them the third parable to teach them what to expect in regard to the kingdom of heaven from the analogy of growth "in the kingdom of nature.

It will be convenient to confine our attention for the present to the first two of the three parables concerning the growth of the kingdom, reserving the third for a future chapter.

The two parables of the Mustard Seed and the Leaven form a pair which have for their common object to exhibit the prospects of the kingdom on the hopeful side, in contrast to the parables of the Sower and the Tares, which present the dark side of the picture. Both proclaim the important truth that the kingdom of heaven is destined to advance from a small beginning to a great end. But the two parables present this common truth under diverse aspects. The one predicts the extensive the other the intensive growth of the kingdom. Each parable, also, has its own way of conceiving the kingdom answering to its peculiar mode of viewing the growth. In the one parable, that of the Mustard Seed, the kingdom is conceived of as a visible society, which is susceptible of increase in its bulk by addition to the number of its membership. In the other parable, that of the Leaven, the kingdom is conceived of as a moral or spiritual power, which is susceptible of increase in the transforming influence which it exerts on those who are subject to its operation. From the point of view of the one parable, the disciples of Jesus, few in number, a " little flock," are the kingdom in its initial stage, destined to grow from that nucleus, small as a grain of mustard seed, into the dimensions of the Christian Church. From the point of view of the other parable, not the

His parabolis (Mustard Seed and Leaven) discipulos suos animat Christus, ne humilibus evangelii exordiis offensi, resiliant.â Calvin, Comment.

disciples themselves, at least in the first place, but rather that which makes them disciples, the faith in their hearts, is the kingdom, they being in the first instance at least the mass to be leavened by its renewing influence. For the parable of the Leaven admits of two applications, a narrow and a wide, an individual and a social. The mass to be leavened may be a single Christian or a whole community, just as we have occasion to regard it; because what is intended to be taught in the parable is the transforming power of Christianity, and that may be illustrated either in the individual man or in society at large. The parable of the Mustard Seed, on the other hand, admits properly only of the wider application, for the point of the parable is, that the kingdom of heaven as a phenomenon taking its place in the world is destined to increase in outvard bulk, which can take place only by addition to the numbers of a society already existing, though small and insignificant to the world's eye as a grain of mustard seed. We may, of course, easily make this parable also susceptible of application to the individual, if with some we make the mustard seed represent the same thing as the leaven, that is, not the insignificant company of Christ's disciples, but the faith through which they became disciples. For such a view plausible ground may be found in those gospel texts in which faith is compared to a grain of mustard seed. We are persuaded, however, that the best way to understand these two parables and to extract the greatest amount of instruction from them is not to run them into each other, but to keep their points of view as distinct as possible; understanding the one to represent the kingdom as a society ' destined to extend itself more and more over the earth, and the other to represent the same kingdom as a spiritual influence destined to pervade, with ever-increasing completeness, the whole of human life whether individual or social. Thus viewed, these parables teach not only distinct, but mutually supplementary lessons, which must be taken together in order to yield a view of the Divine kingdom and its prospects which can satisfy intelligent and earnest minds. For neither an extensive society of imperfectly sanctified men, nor a small society of men completely sanctified, answers to our ideal of what the kingdom should be. What we desiderate is a commonwealth, at once vast in extent and holy in its character. Such a society it is which is offered to our hope in these two parables. The one predicts that the kingdom of heaven will eventually be a society of great dimensions, taking rank in this respect with the kingdoms of this world; the other that it will be a society animated in all its parts by the Holy Spirit, and in this respect not of this world.

The Mustard Seed. The parable as it stands in Matthew is as follows:

The kingdom of heaven is like to a grain of mustard seed, which a man took, and sowed in his field: which itideed is the least of all seeds, but when it is grown, it is the greatest among herbs, and beconieth a tree, so that the birds of the air come attd lodge in the branches thereof. â Matt. xiii. 31, 32; parall.: Mark iv. 30â 32, Luke xiii. 18, 19.

The variations in the other Gospels are of no great importance. In Mark's version we observe a tone of exaggeration in reference both to the smallness of the seed and to the greatness of the plant which springs from it. The seed is said to be the least of all the seeds that are upon the earth, and the tree is represented as shooting out great branches," so that the fowls of the air can lodge under its shadow. These peculiarities may be set down to account of the pictorial graphic style, characteristic of the second Evangelist. Luke on the other hand, makes no mention of the smallness of the seed, but adverts only to the growth of the plant into a tree large enough to be a lodging-place for the birds. This may be due in part to the connection in which he introduces the parable. Immediately before stands a narrative which exhibits Jesus triumphing over Pharisaic censors of one of His Sabbatic miracles, and winning by His reply to their objections the hearty applause of an ingenuous multitude. In the honest joy of the people over the marvellous works wrought by Jesus, and the unanswerable words of wisdom spoken by Him in self-defence, the Evangelist sees a good omen of the future, and he is reminded thereby of the parable in which Jesus had foreshadowed the growth of His kingdom luKpotcpov ov â TTuptoiv tsjv air(p j. dro)v tuiv ini TJjg yijs (iv. l)t from its small beginnings to a great magnitude; only, as there was nothing in the circumstances which recalled the parable to his recollection leading him to emphasise the smallness of the beginning, he gives exclusive prominence to that side of the parable which predicts the greatness of the end. But, indeed, in the case of the third Evangelist, the one-sided prominence given to the ultimate greatness of Christianity scarce needs so minute explanation. It is sufficiently accounted for by the one consideration that he is the Evangelist of the Gentiles, and that he magnifies his office. His specialty is to note carefully all that points towards the grand consummation of Christianity becoming the religion of the world. In view of this familiar fact one is strongly tempted to accept as genuine the reading okvhpov i. iya found in some codices, as well as in the text us receptus, though rejected by critical editors. It would certainly come very natural to Luke, if at all admissible, to say " it grew, and waxed a great tree." It is true that that would be an exaggeration, but so also is the phrase in Mark's Gospel," and shooteth out great branches," about the genuineness of which there is no room for doubt. The much more probable supposition, however, is that the jueya is a marginal gloss introduced into the text by some copyist who, failing to catch the precise drift of the parable, thought it required the tree to be great.

Whatever may be the truth as to the correct text of Luke's version of the parable, there can be no question that in Matthew's version, as compared with that of either Luke or Mark, we have the most exact account of what our Lord actually said, so that we may with all confidence make it the basis of our observations. Turning then to the parable as we find it there recorded, we remark first, that therein the declaration that the kingdom is destined to advance from a small beginning to a great end is made by Jesus in a characteristically meek and sober manner. The smallness of the beginning is much more emphatically asserted than the greatness of the end; characteristically we say, for in this parabolic utterance Jesus but repeats what we find Him elsewhere saying in other terms. In comparing the kingdom of heaven in its present initial stage to a grain of mustard Of the great uncials the Codex Alexandrinus has this reading.

seed, He says in effect the same thing as when He called the humble band of men who followed Him a " little flock," and spoke of them as, in comparison with the wise and prudent, " babes." 2 All the three sayings were the utterances of a lowly mind that shrank not from the frankest and fullest acknowledgment of all circumstances pertaining to His present state of humiliation. Of the three, that contained in our parable presents the most intense expression of the mean condition of the kingdom in its initial phase. For no apter emblem of insignificance could possibly be found than a grain of mustard seed, it being, as is declared in the parable, " the least of all seeds." In order to justify our assertion it is not necessary to take this statement in the text strictly, as if it meant that it is not possible to find anywhere upon the earth a smaller seed than that of mustard. Smaller seeds do exist, such as those of the poppy and the rye. It is not even necessary to maintain that the mustard seed is, or was at the time when and in the country where the parable was spoken, the smallest of all seeds in proportion to the size of the plant which springs from it. Even this proposition may be doubtful; it may fairly be questioned, for example, whether the disproportion between the mustard seed and the mustard tree be greater than that between the acorn and the oak. It is enough to say that the mustard seed passed in our Lord's day, and among the Jews, for an emblem of the superlatively little. " As small as a grain of mustard seed " was a proverbial phrase current at that time, of which we have evidence in the teaching of our Lord Himself, in the reproachful word which He spake to His disciples on descending from the Mount of Transfiguration: " If ye have faith as a grain of mustard seed, ye shall say unto this mountain, Remove hence to yonder place;

and it shall remove." Whatever answer, therefore, natural history may have to give to the question which is the smallest of all seeds, or which is the smallest in Â Luke xii. 32. Matt. xi. 25.

' So Bengel, his comment on fiikporipov being "Non absoluta, sed spect. ita proportione seminis ad germen."

In Adagium vulgare abiit 7l"in 2?)T3= Pro quantitate grani sinapis. frequentissime apud Rabbinos, rem vel quantitatena minutissimam innuentes.â Lightfoot," Hors Hebraicse,"

' Matt. xvii. 20, proportion to the size of the plant which springs from it, it is certain that Jesus could not more frankly have admitted the utter insignificance of the Divine kingdom in its initial state, as it appeared in Himself or in His disciples, than by comparing it to a seed which in common speech passed for the smallest of all.

When we turn from the beginning to the end, and ask ourselves how far the mustard plant after it has reached its full growth is a fit emblem of the kingdom grown to greatness, we are constrained to acknowledge that the aptness of the parable at this point to express the truth intended to be taught is by no means so manifest. For the plant at its best is only a great herb; and it can be called a tree only by a latitude in the use of words. If it be a tree at all, it is certainly not a great tree as the cedar is great, neither are its branches great as are the wide-spreading branches of the oak. In the East, where it attains monstrous proportions, it may be the greatest of all herbs, and create surprise by reaching such a size as to entitle it almost to rank among the trees of the forest. But even there it is after all a thing of puny proportions compared with the cedars of Lebanon or tne oaks of Bashan. Stories are told of mustard trees so tall that a man could climb up into their branches or ride beneath them on horseback, and modern travellers, to give us an idea of their height, tell that they have seen samples of the tree " as tall as the horse and his rider." Accepting these stories as free from exaggeration, what do they amount to Simply to this, that the mustard plant in Palestine attains to a i remarkable height for a garden herb, and especially for an herb springing from so small a seed. If they were offered as proof that the plant in question was worthy to be regarded as the equal of forest trees, they would simply remind us of the fabie of the frog striving to inflate itself into the dimensions of an ox.

Must we then say that the mustard plant is wholly unfit to be an emblem of the kingdom in its advanced stage when it has attained to greatness? Not so; we must bear in mind 1 R. Simeon ben Chalaphta dixit, Caulis sinapis erat mihi in agro meo, in quam ego scandere solitus sum, ita ut scandere solent m ficum.â Lightfoot, Horae Hebraicae."

Â Thomson, 'The Land and the Book, p. 414. He makes the state ment with reference to the plain of Akkar, where the soil is rich.

the difficulty of finding one thing which would serve both purposes, and be content if, while a specially fit emblem of the early stage of the kingdom's history, the object selected be a sufficiently apt emblem of the later stage. It would have been very easy to do justice both to the beginning and to the end by making use of two emblems, the one to represent the beginning, the other the end; hkening, e. g. y the kingdom in its beginning to a grain of mustard seed, and in its end to a cedar of Lebanon. But the truth to be taught would be far more felicitously and impressively set forth if one natural object could be found which might serve as an emblem of the kingdom in both stages; and even if the emblem should not serve both purposes equally well, it were enough if it served them both sufficiently well. Now this is the actual state of the case as regards the mustard seed. It emblems the initial stage of the Divine kingdom excellently well, and it emblems the final stage sufficiently well. It would not have been difficult to find a natural object whose emblematic capabilities would have been the inverse of the one actually adopted. An acorn, for example, would have been better fitted to convey an idea of the vast magnitude of the Christian Church in its advanced stage of growth; for out of the acorn comes the oak. But an acorn would not have served so well to convey an idea of the utter insignificance of the beginnings of the Church. It is a greater marvel that out of a rrmstard seed should come a mustard tree, than that out of an acorn should come an oak. Possibly the relative proportions between seed and tree may not be very unequal, but the outgrowth excites more surprise in the one case than in the other. We do not wonder much that the acorn grows into an oak; we do wonder when we are told that a seed so tiny as that of the mustard plant, which in its own nature is only an herb, grows to something like the dimensions of a tree. Probably such wonder helped to give currency to the proverb, "Small as a grain of mustard seed." Men were surprised that a thing so small should grow to be anything so considerable, and by the contrast between seed and plant were led to emphasise, and even to exaggerate, the smallness of the former. And this wonder was just the cause why our Lord selected the mustard seed as the emblem of the kingdom, in preference to an acorn or any other seed from which large trees grew. He preferred an emblem whose defect, if defect there must be, should He rather in the direction of inadequate representation of the end, than in the direction of inadequate representation of the beginning-. He did so partly because it was congenial to His meek and lowly spirit, but specially because it suited the mental condition of His hearers. Adapting His lesson to the spiritual capacity of His pupils, He is careful to select an emblem which shall fully recognise the mean aspect of the kingdom He has come to found in its present state, and at the same time show by a natural analogy that even a movement so contemptible in appearance might yet come to be a considerable phenomenon, commanding general attention and respect. He is not so anxious to convey an exact or adequate idea of the ultimate greatness of the kingdom. He is content with indicating that it will not always be so insignificant, that it will one day be an institution which the world can no longer treat with disdain, that it will grow till it be not only a very large herb, but even not unworthy to be classified as a tree. That it will be the greatest of trees He does not assert. He does not even say that it will rival other trees in respect of size; He deems it enough to tell disciples unable to entertain large hopes that it will outgrow the dimensions of a garden plant and attain to something like the dimensions of a tree. Even that was an unlikely event then, and quite hard enough for weak faith to believe, without making any further demand on it. To the eye ol sense, judging from present appearances, it seemed impossible that the movement to which Christ gave the name of the Kingdom of heaven could ever become a considerable phenomenon in the history of the world. The statement that it nevertheless would become such was likely to provoke, even in believing minds, incredulous surprise. How could such a state of mind be better met than by pointing out that the wonder in the spiritual world which awakened incredulity had its parallel in the natural world This accordingly is precisely what Jesus did in uttering this parable: pointing

"The rule ex minidio maximum, which is the rule of all growth in nature, is here signalised in the growth of the mustard seed; specii lly in it, because in virtue of its proverbial peculiarity, the rule is illustrated in its case with striking eftect."â Goebel.

out in the case of the mustard seed a natural object proverbially small, which grows into a plant of astonishing dimensions. No happier selection could have been made for the purpose. The mustard seed, viewed as the parent of the mustard tree, is " the most characteristic emblem, among natural objects, especially of its own class, to mark the disproportion between the first beginning and the final result of any process," and in particular of that which it was Christ's aim to illustrate, the growth of the kingdom of God. In making this selection for the purpose of parabolic instruction on this topic, the great Teacher shoved not only humility and sobriety of mind, but conspicuous wisdom and considerate sympathy with those whom He would instruct.

When we look at the parable in the light of the use it was probably intended to serve in the personal ministry of Christ, we are delivered from all temptation to catch at any means of making the emblem of the kingdom grown to greatness a greater thing than it really is, if the common mustard plant be what is intended. Attempts of this kind have been made in recent years by travellers and men of science. It has been contended that not the mustard plant, which is properly not a tree, but only a garden herb and an annual, but a real tree of considerably larger dimensions, found in some parts of Palestine, and widely diffused in the East, is the object pointed at in the parable. The tree referred to is that which in Syria goes by the name of the khardal (the Arabic for mustard), and in botanical language is called the Salvadora Persica. The first to suggest the hypothesis were the travellers Irby and Mangles, who found the kjiardal growing in the neighbourhood of the Dead Sea. The conjecture was ingenious, 1 Greswell 'on the Parables," vol. ii. p. i66.

2 'Travels in Egypt and Nubia, Syria and Asia Minor, during the years 1817 and 1818." The passage relating to the subject is as follows: "There was one curious tree which we observed in great plenty, and which bore a fruit in bunches, resembling in appearance the currant, with the colour of the plum: it has a pleasant though strong aromatic taste, exactly resembling mustard, and if taken in any quantity, produces a similar irritability in the nose and eyes to that which is caused by taking mustard. The leaves of this tree have the same pungent flavour as the fruit, though not so strong. We think it probable that this is the tree our Saviour alluded to in the parable of the Mustard Seed, and not the mustard plant which we have in the northâ for although in our journ2y

And not without plausibility, for in its favour could be alleged not only the name of the tree, but the facts that the seed from which it springs is comparatively small, possesses pungent qualities like those of mustard, and is used for the same purposes. It is therefore not surprising that the opinion hazarded by the two travellers was afterwards espoused and strenuously advocated by scientific writers, and regarded with favour by biblical scholars such as Meyer and Stanley. It is now, however, generally set aside on sufficient grounds; of which the chief are, that there is grave reason to doubt whether the khardal ever existed or even could exist in the neighbourhood of the Sea of Galilee, the leading scene of our Lord's ministry, and that the plant of the parable is expressly represented as being in its nature a garden herb, the very point of the parable being that what is in its nature an herb, becomes in dimensions something approaching a tree. We ' do not pretend to be able to speak with authority on the point, nor do we entertain any feelings but those of sincere respect for efforts to ascertain precisely what natural objects are pointed at in Scripture allusions; but we may be permitted to express the doubt whether the opinion in question would ever have been seriously entertained had men been as alive to the moral as to the scientific conditions of correct interpretation. Doubtless the khardal answers better to the designation ' tree," for it really is a tree in nature, and it attains a height of some twenty-five feet, while the mustard plant does not reach more than half that elevation. But realise the moral situation, and you see at once that the khardal, though twice as tall, is not half so appropriate as the from Bysan to Adjeloun we met with the mustard plant growing wild, as high as our horses' heads, still being an annual it did not deserve the appellation of a tree; whereas the other is really such, and birds might easily, and actually do, take shelter under its shadow" (p. 255).

Prominent among these is Dr. Royle, who first set forth his views on the subject in a paper read before the Royal Asiatic Society in 1844, and published in vol. viii. of their Transactions.

2 Vide Meyer's Commentary, and Stanley's Sinai? ind Palestine." Â Tristram says: "There is no reason to believe that at any time it grew by the Sea of Galilee, and very strong grounds for doubting that it could flourish there at all. It is in fact one of the many tropical plants whose northern limit is in these sultry nooks by the Dead Sea, and which spread no farther north."'â ' Natural History of the Bible," p. 473.

CH. IV. The Mustard Seed. loi mustard plant to be an emblem of the kingdom of God in its developed state. It is no marvel that a plant of the tree species should grow to the height of twenty-five feet, it is rather remarkable that it should grow no taller; but it is a marvel that a plant, which is by nature an herb, should in its growth even so much as approximate the dimensions and aspect of a tree. And what is required by the moral situation is just such a marvel in physical nature to inspire faith in the possibility of a like marvel in the spiritual worldâ a religious movement in its present aspect despicably mean, becoming one day a great fact of such proportions that men could no longer despise it.

The parable then, viewed as having reference to the common mustard plant, is altogether worthy of our Lord's wisdom., Avhether we consider its bearing on the beginning or on the end of the kingdom. Christ showed His wisdom in selecting a grain of mustard seed to be an emblem of the kingdom in its obscure beginnings, because the emblem was not only true to fact, but to the law or principle of the case. Worldly-minded Jews could not believe that so mean a thing as the movement with which Jesus and His disciples were identified could possibly be the kingdom of God come. But the meanness and the smallness of the movement were no argument against its Divinity, but rather a presumption in favour of its being Divine. It is the way of Divine movements in the world's history to begin obscurely and end gloriously; and it not unfrequently happens that there is more Divinity in the obscure beginning than in the glorious ending. For while the movement is obscure men are not likely to join it, except as moved by the spirit of truth and goodness; but when it has become famous, worldly men may join it from by-ends, and so make what at first was a Divine, heavenly thing, undivine and earthly enough. Therefore we may say that Jesus showed His wisdom also in making the mustard plant at its full height an emblem of the kingdom in its advanced stage, not merely in so far as He thereby accommodated His teaching to the spiritual wants and capacities of His hearers, but more especially because He thereby presented to view a kingdom large enough to satisfy the hope of devout souls, but not so large as to awaken ambitious desires and worldly expectations, and so attract unclean ravenous birds to take up their abode among the branches of the tree of life.

The allusion in the closing words of the foregoing paragraph reminds us that we have not yet noticed that part of our parable in which our Lord speaks of the birds of the air as coming to lodge in the branches of the mustard tree. The question at once arises, what amount of significance are we to attach to this feature? In answering the question it is possible to err both by excess and by defect. The least that can be said is that the fact of the birds frequenting the branches of the mustard plant is mentioned as a mark that the plant has become a tree. The construction of the sentence makes this manifest: "It becometh a tree, j-t? tjiat' the birds of the air come and lodge in the branches thereof." The size of the plant, so to speak, deceives the winged creatures, and makes them mistake a garden herb for a forest tree. The feature is not introduced merely for the sake of picturesque effect, but to define the character of the plant. There may possibly be a latent allusion to Old Testament texts, in which birds and trees are associated together, as, e. g. those in that beautiful psalm of nature, the lo6th, which speak of the birds singing among the branches and making their nests among the cedars of Lebanon; or the well-known passage in Daniel which describes the tree of Nebuchadnezzar's vision in these poetic terms: " The tree grew, and was strong, and the height thereof reached unto heaven, and the sight thereof to the end of all the earth: the leaves thereof were fair, and the fruit thereof much, and in it as meat for all: the beasts of the field had shadow under it, and the fowls of the heaven dwelt in the boughs thereof, and all flesh was fed upon it." It would, however, be going beyond the sober truth to lay much stress on these texts, as if Christ meant to suggest that the tree of His parable resembled in size the cedars of the Psalmist, or the mystic tree of Nebuchadnezzar's dream, or that the birds resorted thereto for precisely the same reason. The tree of the parable is not large enough to harbour birds of all sizes, but only small birds like linnets and goldfinches; and what they â tsffrt, with the infinitive. â Daniel iv. 11, seek therein is not a place to build their nests, but the food it supplies in its seed, which they devour with avidity. The Greek word translated in the English version " lodge," does not signify " to make nests in," but simply "to settle upon."i '- We must, therefore, as strict expositors, deny ourselves the pleasure of finding in this parable a prophecy of a time when the kingdom of heaven, now so insignificant, should become a vast empire rivalling that of Nebuchadnezzar's vision, when the tiny seed of the kingdom should develop into a great forest tree, overshadowing the whole earth, and affording harbourage for all the nations. At most it contains a slight hint at the possibility of such a consummation, suggesting by the words employed more than it says, or than the parabolic envelope of the thought admits of being said: by the word " tree " suggesting a forest tree, though the tree actually spoken of is little more than a large bush, and by the reference to the birds of the air suggesting the idea of men coming from every quarter of the heavens and taking up their abode in the Divine commonwealth. So far as this parabolic utterance strictly interpreted is concerned, the prophetic eye of Jesus cannot be said to look beyond the time when the company of His disciples should have received large accessions within the limits of Judaea, the garden in which the grain of mustard seed was originally planted. We may not stretch our horizon much beyond Pentecost, when the number of disciples Avas increased by thousands; scarcely, though we gladly would, as far as to the later movement in Antioch, when the kingdom of Christ became so considerable a phenomenon as to require a new name, so that the disciples were there for the first time called Christians. It is quite legitimate within these limits to give to the birds of the air a symbolic significance and make them represent converts to the new religion. " It is not absolutely certain that the birds were intended to have such symbolic significance assigned to them, but it seems probable that the third Evangelist at least regarded them in that light. When we read in his narrative how the people rejoiced in the wondrous works of Jesus, and then Â This disposes of one objection to the mustard plant being the object intended in the parable, viz. that at the time when birds build their nests it is too small to be used for such a purpose.

observe how he takes occasion therefrom to record the parable of the Mustard Tree, in whose branches the fowls of heaven lodged, we cannot help feeling that in his mind the fowls are identified with the well-afiected multitude. He seems to say to himself: " Behold the Lord's parable fulfilling itself: see how the birds fly to the branches of the mustard tree."

We have now noticed all the points apparent on the surface of the parable. Other points not apparent derived from the known properties of the mustard seedâ its heat, its pungency, the fact that it must be bruised ere it yield its best virtues, etc.â we do not feel called to remark on, agreeing as we do with those who think that analogies based on these properties are foreign to the purpose for which the parable was spoken. We may, however, briefly advert to an opinion strenuously maintained by Greswell, that it is intended in the parable to represent the spread of Christianity as of a miraculous character. To make this out stress is laid on the contrast between the smallness of the mustard seed, and its vegetative vigour as manifested in the size to which the plant attains; and the right to do this is proved by a reference to tlie other passages in our Lord's teaching in which the seed of mustard is spoken of. The author's contention is, that the expression " faith as a grain of mustard seed," twice employed by Christ, does not mean faith as small as a grain of mustard, but faith as vigorous in its vital power. Our Lord, it is held, did not mean to say that any degree of faith would suffice to do the wonderful things of which the removal of a mountain into the sea is an emblem, as that would involve that the disciples had no faith at allâ seeing they were unable to do the things referred toâ which, however, was not the fact. The faith that can remove mountains is a special kind of faith, viz. that which can produce miracles. It is the sort of faith which Jesus had in view when He said to His disciples: â Verily if ye have faith, and do not hesitate, not only shall ye do the miracle of the fig tree, but should you even say unto this mountain. Be thou lifted up, and be thou cast into the sea, it shall come to pass." It is the faith which, the 1 Matt. xxi. 21, as rendered by Greswell, vide his work on the Parables, f. 162.

following morning, Jesus called faith of God, a Divine faith, describing its character and power in similar terms. If then the mustard seed in Christ's teaching elsewhere be an emblem of a faith whose specific characteristic it is to possess Divine miraculous power, we are entitled to assume that it retains that significance in the parable, though it is there used not as an emblem of faith, but of the kingdom of God in its obscure beginnings. In comparing the kingdom to a grain of mustard seed, Jesus meant to say: The kingdom of heaven is now in appearance insignificant and impotent, but it has within it a Divine power, which will enable it to triumph over all hindrances, and make it ere long great and mighty. Such is the argument. It is plausible, and of course the doctrine which it seeks to establish is true, but whether the parable be intended to teach it or not is another question. On that point we will not dogmatise; only we must remark that in our judgment the exegesis of the other texts, on which the argument is based, is very doubtful. Faith, small as a grain of mustard seed, is the interpretation which would naturally be put upon Christ's words by hearers living in a land where the smallness of the mustard seed was proverbial. The objection that this interpretation implies that the disciples had no faith at all, is of no weight. It is simply a prosaic inference from a poetic impassioned utterance. There is more force in the consideration that the statement concerning faith, even thus interpreted, implies that faith is a thing of such inherent vitality and power, that even a little of it can do great things; and as the same thing is true of the mustard seed, it is not unnatural to suppose that Christ's full thought was this: If ye had but faith even of the dimensions of a grain of mustard, ye could work wonders, such is its power, even as the tiny seed has vital force sufficient to produce a plant reaching to the size of a tree. That the paraphrase contains a just and valuable thought we admit, only we cannot pretend to be quite sure that all this was suggested, or was meant to be suggested, by the words of our Lord to those to whom they were addressed.

Â Mark xi. 22. ifiorw Qeov is the expression in the Greek, rendered ia our version " faith in God," which the R. V. retains.

The kingdom of heaven is like unto leaven, which a woman took, and hid in tjiree measures of meal, till the whole was leavened. â Matt. xiii. 33; cf. Luke xiii. 20, 21.

This parable relates not to the outward, visible increase 'which the kingdom is destined to undergo, but to the inward transformation which it will effect, which is not discernible by the physical organ of vision, but by the moral sense. The action of leaven on the dough in which it is deposited is not so much to change its bulk as its condition, and the change is perceived, not by the eye, but by taste. The kingdom of heaven in this connection signifies the doctrine of the kingdom which exercises a moral influence on the heart and life of those who receive it. It is quite conipatible with this view that the recipients of the doctrine should themselves be regarded as a leaven. Christians are a leaven in the world, as they are the light of the world. But they are a leaven in virtue of the truth which they believe, and the spirit which animates them; and they act on the world through these in precisely the same way as these act on themselves.

In likening the kingdom of heaven to leaven, Jesus in effect proclaimed a great truth, which pervades all His teaching, viz. that that kingdom is in its nature spiritual. Leaven works from the centre to the circumference, and it works by the method of contagion, and the comparison may be held to imply an analogy in these respects between the emblem and the thing emblemed; that is to say, the parable teaches that the kingdom of heaven first takes possession of the heart, the seat of life, and thence proceeds outwards, to exercise sway over conduct, and communicates itself from mind to mind by the contagious power of sympathy. In these respects the Divine kingdom differs from the kingdoms of this world, which concern themselves chiefly with the outward life, and employ force, or laws with penalties annexed, to establish their authority. But it is not peculiar to the Divine kingdom to work in this way; all spiritual influence, whether good or evil, acts in the same manner. The mere fact of a religious movement resembling leaven in its mode of spreading itself settles nothing as to its truth or moral tendency. Leaven may fitly be used to denote an evil moral influence as well as a good; and in fact, in the larger number of instances in which it is named in the Newr Testament, it is employed in a bad sense. Hence some have inferred that it must be so understood always, and therefore also in this parable. In that case the parable would contain a prophecy of a corruption of Christianity through the introduction into the Church of evil tendencies, doctrinal and practical. But this idea is precluded by the simple consideration that it is the kingdom itself that is compared to leaven. It is also entirely out of keeping with the familiar facts of domestic life on which the parable is based. Leaven, as used by the housewife, is not an evil thing, but a means by which palatable food is produced from insipid dough. If, indeed, we insist on introducing into the interpretation of the parable our knowledge of the chemical character of leaven, we may produce a plausible argument in favour of the opinion referred to. Leaven is simply a ' piece of sour dough in which putrefaction has begun, and which, on being introduced into fresh dough, produces by contagion a similar condition in the whole mass. Now putrefaction is an offensive word, suggestive of a state not pleasant to think of, and we may hastily conclude that an object in which such a state is found is necessarily and essentially evil. But it is not only our privilege, but our duty, to consider this parable of our Lord, not from a chemical, but from a popular point of view. From that point of view we are entitled to regard everything as good which produces a good effect. In studying this comparison of the kingdom of heaven to leaven we must put the putrefaction out of sight, and think only of its action in causing the dough to swell, so as to be more accessible to the heat of the oven, and in imparting to it when ready to be eaten the palatable qualities of leavened bread. We may therefore dismiss the eccentric notion in question as unworthy of serious consideration.

The relation between the dough and the leaven is well brought out in the German language, the names for the two objects respectively being Teig and Sauerteig.

The hiding of the leaven in the mass of dough is a point deserving special notice. The woman took the leaven, and hid it in three measures of meal. The insertion of the piece of sour dough called leaven into the mass of fresh dough is a matter of course in the physical process of baking, but we ought not on that account to treat the hiding of the leaven in the parable as a thing of no emblematic significance. The word employed seems chosen with a view to provoke thought. Does it not point to the silent, unobserved, â stealthy manner in which the doctrine of the kingdom was I introduced into the world by the Son of man.-' In another place the Evangelist quotes as descriptive of Christ's manner of carrying on His ministry the prophetic words: " He shall not strive, nor cry; neither shall any man hear his voice in the streets." 2 The quotation is most apposite. Jesus, as the Founder of the kingdom of heaven, worked noiselessly, as the dew or the light. The kingdom, in His hands, came indeed not with observation, but in a quiet, inward manner. His doctrine dropped as the rain, and His speech distilled as the dew; as the small rain upon the tender herb, and as the showers upon the grass. As the result of His ministry of grace and truth the kingdom was there, hidden in the hearts of a few simple fishermen, tax-gatherers, and sinful women turned from their sins; and men did not know, but kept inquiring when the kingdom should come, not suspecting that it was come already, and was coming more and more by its secret but powerful influence on human spirits. It is not necessary in interpreting the parables to be always asking who is the actorâ who is the Sower in the first parable, or who the Woman in this one. A woman is the actor in this case simply because the operation described is woman's work. Yet one cannot help taking occasion from this parable to remark on the womanlike character of Christ's ministry. No masculine ambitions or passions are noticeable there, but only the quiet, incessant, patient, retiring industry of one who is never in a hurry and yet never idle; who is content with his limited, obscure sphere, and utterly indifferent to the stir Â tvlicpu f V, Matt. xiii. 33, found only here in N. T. The corresponding word in Luke is 'tk v tv, Matt. xii. 19.

and strife of the great world without. " My kingdom is not of this world," He says to Pilate, provoking from the worldly-minded governor a smile at His simplicity. His brethren, seeing His works in Galilee, say to Him: "Depart hence, and go into Judaea, that Thy disciples also may see the works that Thou doest. For there is no man that doeth anything in secret, and he himself seeketh to be known openly. If Thou do these things, show Thyself to the world." But Jesus has no desire to advertise Himself into celebrity in Jerusalem, the seat of government and of religious ceremonial, but is content to remain in the northern province, busily occupied in that humble but congenial sphere in inserting the leaven of His doctrine into the susceptible minds which yield themselves to His influence. It is not that His doctrine is esoteric, or that any cunning or cowardice characterises his method of working. He could say with perfect truth, as He did say at His trial to the high priest: " I spake openly to the world; I ever taught in the S3'-nagogue, and in the temple, whither the Jews always resort; and in secret have I said nothing." But while His doctrine was open and not cryptic. His spirit was humble and wise. He loved quiet, unostentatious ways of working, and He believed that these would in the long run prove the most effective. The words of the kingdom, hid in the hearts of a few babes, would work there like a leaven, till it resulted in their illumination and sanctification; and from them it would be communicated by contagion to others, till the little leavened mass had leavened the whole lump of Jewish and even pagan humanity. In his intercessory prayer Jesus offered up for the eleven disciples this petition; "I have given them Thy word. Sanctify them through Thy truth: Thy word is truth. As Thou hast sent Me into the world, even so have I also sent them into the world."- The words are a brief but luminous commentary on our parable, viewed as a figurative description of our Lord's own ministry and its aim. He taught His disciples the doctrine of the kingdom; through that doctrine, by the blessing of the Divine Spirit, they were at length sanctified; and when their minds had been duly enlightened, and their hearts filled with

John xviii. 36. John vii. 3, 4.
' John xviii. 20. â John xvii. 14, 17, 18.
no The Parabolic Teaching of Christ, book i.

the grace of the kingdom, they became through their words and their Hves a leaven to the world.

Till the whole was leavened: That is another point in the, parable demanding particular attention. The question naturally arises, what is the ' whole' referred to? In the parable it is the three measures of meal, which seems from an induction of Scripture instances, to have been the usual quantity prepared for use at one time, amounting to rather more than four English pecks. But is this all that is to be said? have the three measures no emblematic significance? is the number simply a part of the natural realism of the parable? It is hard to reconcile ourselves to such conclusions, especially considering the tempting analogies suggested by the three measures. If we think of the individual man as j the subject of the leavening process, we have answering to the three measures, the three parts of human nature, body, soul, and spirit, as the subjects of sanctification; the renewing process commencing at the centre, the sp-irit, passing through the soul with all its affections and faculties, and at length reaching the circumference of the man, the body with its appetites and habits. If we think of man collectively, the number three repeats itself under all the various aspects from which we regard the subject of the leavening process. Viewing man socially, there are the three forms of social existence, the family, the Church, the State; viewing him-ethnographically, there are the three sons of Noahâ Shem, Ham, and Japhethâ from which all nations of the earth have descended. To some minds the main fact that the number three re-appears under so many diverse forms will seem conclusive evidence that it was designed to have emblematic significance, while to others the circumstance that the number admits of so many interpretations will go far to show that none of them was intended. In such questions men are very apt to be influenced by their temperament, and in absence of conclusive evidence either way it is becoming to abstain from over-confident dogmatism. A man of matter-of-fact juristic mind, like Grotius, will prefer the severely literal.

Conf. Gen. xviii. 6; Judges vi. 19; i Sam. i. 24. An ephah was; equal to three seahs, so that the quantity in all three instances was the same.

prosaic interpretation, while a dreamy, idealistic commentator, like Lange, will as certainly incline to the allegorical; and it would be presumptuous in us to decide authoritatively between them. We will not therefore say positively that the idealists are right, though our sympathies are with them, nor lay it down as a certain truth that the three measures represent the world, and that this parable is one of those utterances of Christ in which the universal destination of the Gospel is clearly taught. We may, however, without presumption say this much, that leaven is one of the three symbols employed by our Lord to represent the action of His kingdom in the world, and that in the other two instances that action is expressly represented as having relation to the whole world. The three symbols are leaven, salt, and light. We find the latter two employed in the Sermon on the Mount, both in a universalistic way. Of His disciples as the children of the kingdom, animated by its spirit, enlightened by its truth, Jesus there says, "Ye are the salt of the earth. Ye are the light of the world." If, therefore. He had said, "Ye are the leaven of the world," it would only have been a statement of the same kind, in perfect sympathy with His teaching in the Sermon on the Mount; and it is at least probable that He meant to suggest such a thought by expressly naming three measures of meal as the amount to be leavened." To this view it may appear an objection that the whole, whatever it is, is represented as being leavened, so that if the whole signify the whole world of mankind at large, the parable teaches not merely the universal destination of the Gospel as a message to every human creature, but the ultimate universal salvation of all men. Without entering here into that question, we simply observe that this is pressing the words beyond what they can bear. Assuming that our Lord has in view the world as the subject of the leavening process, we must take His words as a broad statement of tendency, not as an exact statement of the historical result. The three statements. Ye are the salt of the earth. Ye are the light of the world, and 1 'S. olTa Tpia: tantum enim simul misceri solehat.â Vide his' Annotationes."

2 Matt. V. 13, 14.

This view commended itself to the sound exegetical judgment of Bengel. He says: Videtur hoc pertinere ad totum genus humanum, quod refert tria sata, ex tribus Noachi fiuis propagatum in orbe terrae.

the one implied in this parable, Ye are the leaven of the world, must all be interpreted in one way, as indicating function and not effect. Doubtless we have in the case of the leaven what we have not in the case of the other two emblems, an express declaration as to the effect. The process goes on till the whole is leavened. But the purpose of the declaration is to indicate the nature of the leaven, which is to work on incessantly till it has more or less infected the whole mass in which it has been deposited; and in this respect leaven is a very apt emblem of Christian truth, or indeed of any spiritual influence whatsoever. It is the tendency of all spiritual influence, good or evil, to diffuse itself more and more throughout society till its presence can be traced in a greater or less extent everywhere. And it may be granted that in some sense, and to some extent, it is the destination of Christianity to pervade the whole of society, and to influence in some way, and to certain effects, the whole human race. But it does not follow that the leavening process must in all cases be complete and thorough. A given quantity of leaven will not leaven thoroughly any lump of dough however large, but only the mass which is in proportion to its amount." It would influence a larger mass more or less, as a piece of sugar would tend to sweeten a whole river of water, or a candle tend to illuminate the whole world. We do not presume to prescribe limits to the influence of Christianity, we simply enter a caveat against too sweeping inferences from the words of our parable. The doctrine there taught is that it is the genius of the kingdom of God to work outwards from the centre, where it is first deposited, towards the circumference. It is a doctrine which justifies large hopes in reference to the elevation of the individual, and to the imbuing of society and the world at large with Christian principle. But these hopes must be qualified by the recollection that Christianity does not raise even all individuals who receive it Â Stier (' Reden Jesu) says that 'okov is equivalent to oawf, and gives as alternative renderings of the words fof ov t vfiwoi oxov, till the whole meal â was leavened, or till the meal was wholly leavened. But whether oxov be taken adverbially or otherwise, the statement must be understood quantitatively, not qualitatively.

Â The universalistic interpretation is objected to by Hofmann, Dai Evangelium des Lukas."

to the same moral level, and that, as a matter of fact, it has not found all peoples equally amenable to its influence. On the other hand, the children of the kingdom ought not to allow such considerations to depress their spirits, or to make them settle down contentedly in the conviction that it is only a few that are to be saved, and that all attempts to save others are vain. They are the elect of God, it is true, called out of the world. But they must remember that they have not been called for their own sakes merely, but for the sake of others. They are called to be the salt of the earth, the light of the world, the leaven of humanity, and they should ever live under the inspiring influence of their high vocation, seeking earnestly and always two things, the perfect sanctifi-cation of their own characters that their influence on others for good may be as great as possible, and the conversion of the whole world to the Christian faith. It was, in all probability, to inspire this mind that Jesus spake this parable to His disciples. He desired the small band of followers who had received His doctrine, especially the twelve, to entertain! large expectations as to what might be accomplished through their instrumentality. He said to them in effect: Ye are but a little leaven hid in the bosom of the world, so small in bulk that men are scarce aware of your existence. But, remember, a little leaven can leaven a large lump. See that you undervalue not your importance as the leavened portion of the lump of humanity, through which the rest is to be leavened. Fear not, the future is yours; it is your Father's pleasure to give you in ample measure the kingdom. I have chosen and ordained you that ye should go and bring forth fruit. Aim at bringing forth much fruit, for that is not impossible. In the light of this paraphrase we can see that the parable of the Leaven is, equally with that of the Mustard Seed, admirably fitted to inspire hope even in the day of small things and obscure, uninfluential beginnings.

The foregoing are the principal points in the parable which call for notice. The following thoughts, suggested rather than taught therein, we append to illustrate a feature of the Parables to which we will have frequent occasion to refer, and which we may call theiri?zvj.

When we recall the etymological meaning of the Greek word for leaven, and of its Latin and English equivalents, all threeâ C V? fcrmentum, leaven â pointing to the effect of the substance denoted in causing upheaving and fermentation in the mass in which it is deposited, we are naturally led to reflect on the analogous action of the kingdom of heaven upon those with whom it comes into contact. For there is a real analogy at this point. Where the truth of the kingdom comes with power, whether in the individual or in society, it produces a moral fermentation, and the amount of fermentation it produces is the measure of its influence. The more stir it causes in the heart and mind and conscience, the more completely does it ultimately bring every thought into captivity to the obedience of Christ. Christ Himself referred to the tendency of His teaching to act as a ferment in society when He said: " Suppose ye that I am come to give peace on earth.- I tell you, nay; but rather division: for from henceforth there shall be five in one house divided, three against two, and two against three. The father shall be divided against the son, and the son against the father; the mother against the daughter, and the daughter against the mother; the mother-in-law against her daughter-in-law, and the daughter-in-law against her mother-in-law." 2 Nor is the fermenting process, so graphically described in its social aspect, confined to the family or the community; it goes on in the bosom of every believing man. The new life of the kingdom not only divides a country or a house against itself; it divides a man against himself, so that a man's foes shall be not only they of his own household, but even his very selfâ the old man fighting against the new man, the natural desires and affections resisting the claim of the kingdom to the place of sovereignty in the heart. Such fermenting processes in individual experience and in the history of nations are by no means pleasant to pass through, but they are the price that has to be paid for sanctified character, and for Christian civilisation. On no other terms can these precious blessings be obtained.

The comparison of the kingdom of heaven to leaven, duly reflected on, might serve to correct crude notions as to Â T, iir, from Â a, to boil; fermentum, contracted from fervimentum, from ferveo; leaven, from levare, to lift up. Â Luke xii. SI, 53.

the effect of regeneration and sanctification on human nature. Judging from the artificial, unnatural character which the profession of religion sometimes engenders, it would almost seem as if, in the opinion of many, the new birth and the new life produced by Christian faith involved the extirpation at once of the common characteristics of human nature, and of the idiosyncrasies of the individual. But this ought not to be the case if the kingdom of heaven be indeed like leaven. For leaven does not destroy the characteristics of meal in general, or the peculiarities of particular kinds of meal. It leaves the leavened meal essentially as it found it, and there is no difficulty in distinguishing one sort of leavened meal from another, wheat from barley, and barley from rye. Naturalness is a mark of Christian maturity, the sign of a completed sanctification. In saying this we do not mean to condemn everything savouring of artificiality in religion as spurious and hypocritical. Here again our parable is helpful in checking onesidedness. There is a stage when the dough, in which leaven has been deposited, seems unlike itself, viz. when it is passing through the upheaving process of fermentation. In like manner we ought not to expect either naturalness or geniality in a Christian when he is in the fermenting stage of the spiritual life. His experiences then are not pleasant to himself; why should we be surprised if they be still more unpalatable to others Wait till the fermenting process and the baking process are complete, and then see how the bread tastes. If the character of a Christian possesses the charm of sweetness when the process of sanctification is complete, we have no right to complain that it does not exhibit it sooner,â which, however, many do, for want of due consideration of such analogies as that suggested in this parable, and, we may add, in the parable next to be studied, that of the Blade, the Green Ear, and the Ripe Corn.

Finally, one in quest of arguments to prove the supernatural character of Christianity might easily found one upon our parable. The leaven is a thing extraneous to the meal. The woman took it from another place and put it

"The meal, although leavened in all parts, retains after, as before, its own distinctive character ('Art und Gattung'), according as it is barley, rye, or wheat meal" â Arndt.

into the dough, to produce effects which the dough Itself could never bring about. In like manner, it might be argued, it has often been argued, the kingdom of heaven was brought down from above, from heaven, by the Son of God, and deposited in the lump of humanity, there to produce moral results, which human nature by itself unaided is utterly incompetent to achieve. That the doctrine is true needs no elaborate proof; its truth is attested by the experience of individual Christians, as well as by a comparative study of the effects produced in the world at large by Christianity on the one hand, and by all other religions on the other. That it was Christ's purpose to teach this doctrine, or either of the two preceding, when He uttered this parable of the Leaven, we cannot positively affirm. But if these important lessons do not belong to the primary didactic drift of the parable, they do at least attest its felicity; for surely a parable must be admitted to be felicitously constructed which suggests so much beyond what it expressly teaches.

In the culture of grain there are two busy seasons, the seed time and the harvest. Between the sowing and the reaping intervenes a period of comparative inactivity, during which the husbandman is very much a mere spectator looking on while the earth bringeth forth fruit of herself, first the blade, then the ear, and finally the full ripe corn in the ear. Is there any analogy, one naturally asks, in this respect between the kingdom of nature and the kingdom of heaven? The Great Teacher gives us to understand that there is. Jesus said:

So is the kingdom of God as if a man should cast the seed iftto the groujtd, and slioidd sleep and rise, night and day, and the seed should spring and grow, how k)io'wet i not lie Spontaneously the earth bringeth forth fruit, first blade, then ear, then is full corn in the ear.- But when the fruit permits, immediately he putteth forth' the sickle, because the hai-vest is at haiid. â Mark iv. 26â 29.

On this clause vide remarks at p. 124.

' The true reading seems to be Trxrjpijg ctitoc, eerrt being understood. The reading in the T. R., Trxjp; alrov, has all the appearance of a grammatical correction by scribes. The R. V., however, retains it, also Westcott and Hort, who think that all the variations would be accounted for if the original reading were irxi'iptiq oitov, 7rxrj(fG being indeclinable in the accusative, as "in all good MSS. of Acts vi. 5 except B." For the. nport of the change of construction 'iide the exposition.

That is, by being ripe. This rendering of â n-apa ol (or â jrapasai) is suggested by Meyer and approved by Weiss (' Das Markus-Evangelium,"p. J 59), Bleek (' Synoptische Erklarung'), Bisping (' Exegetisches Handbuch'), and Volkmar (' Die Evangelien," p. 289). The rendering can be justified from classical usage. Meyer cites the expression Ttjq wpat napadisovctji;

See next page for Note.

According to a recent writer, the didactic aim of this parable was to teach the disciples not to expect the complete development of the new life springing out of the word of the kingdom, as the result of the exercise of an external power on the part of the Messiah, but rather to regard it as a problem for the spontaneous moral activity of the believing hearer. This, however, is by no means the whole, or even the chief, doctrinal significance of the parable. It is meant to teach a doctrine of passivity not merely with reference to Christ, the First Sower of the word, but also with reference to those whose minds are the soil into which the seed of truth is cast; a doctrine to the effect that growth in the kingdom proceeds spontaneously by fixed laws, over which the subject of growth has little or no control. Of course, in uttering a parable of this import, Jesus did not mean to teach that men have nothing whatever to do in the way of promoting growth in themselves and others. In proof of this it is enough to refer to the parable of the Sower, in which total or partial failure of the spiritual crop in certain cases is attributed to preventible causes, such as the cares of life, the deceitfulness of riches, and the lusts of other things. And even without the aid of that parable we might have been sure that it could not be the intention of Christ to teach a doctrine which would encourage men in vices to which they are only too prone, viz. indolence, indiff"erence, and thoughtless security. But why then, it may be asked, speak a parable which even seems to look that way? To check vices of a different description to which men the season of the year permitting, from Polybius, 22, 24, 9. The majority of commentators prefer the rendering, "when the fruit jjzvAj" (supple. iuvtov), a sense of the word for which no certain voucher can be cited from Greek authors, but to which a parallel can be cited from Latin, e. g. the line: Mitlta adco gelidd vielius se nocte licdernui, from Virgil's Georgics, I. 287. Unger (' De Parabolarum Jesu natura, interpretatione, usu," p. no) alludes to a similar usage in the German language. In a note he remarks: Verbum vexatum neque cum Fritsch. suppleverim voce invtov, neque cum Wircro, Gt(i(rn6v vel Kaipov, sed voce oirov vcl grana, quam quidcm nostrates etiam ita omittunt, ut tanquam verbum impersonale dicant: cs giebt her.

So in R. v., and approved by Dr. Field, ('Otium Norvicense,"para Tenia). He refers to Joel iii. 13, where the verb occurs in the Sept.

AS = f rr', which means not only to send but to put forth, as the hand.

Goebel of earnest spirit are prone. Active devoted labourers in the kingdom are tempted to exaggerate their own importance as instruments; they are apt in a busybody spirit to interfere Vv'hen it were wiser to stand still and see God work; they are prone to despondency if they see not immediate results, and to impatience when they discover how slowly growth in the kingdom proceeds onward towards its consummation. And Jesus desired by this parable to check such evil tendencies in His disciples, and to foster in them the virtues of humility, dependence, faith, and patience.

That this parabolic gem, so natural and so significant, should be found only in Mark, is one of the surprises of the Gospel history. But we are not therefore to doubt either its genuineness or its importance. It is evidently a genuine logion of Jesus, and one too at first hand, in its original form, not a modification of some other parable such as that of the Tares. i It is also a parable of great didactic value, indispensable to a full doctrine concerning the nature of the Divine kingdom, and of much practical utility to its citizens. How important to know what to expect in reference to the growth of the seed of the Word, whether in the individual or in the community, to prevent Christians being scandalised when things turn out altogether contrary to expectation! None the less important is the parable, that it proclaims a truth men are slow to understand or be reconciled to; a fact whereof we have sufficient evidence in the way in which this portion of Christ's parabolic teaching has often been handled.

So Hilgenfeld after Strauss; I'ide his ' Einleitung in Das neiie Testament,"p. 516. Volkmar ('Die Evangelien," p. 288), on the other hand, holds Mark's parable to be an original utterance of Jesus which Matthew' could not accept without modification; the necessary transformation being supplied in the parable of the Tares. With him agrees Holtzman," Die Syraoptische Evangelien," p. 107. These differences of opinion are conr nected with the views entertained by the writers as to the order of time in which the Gospels were written; Hilgenfeld contending for the priority of Matthew, Volkmar and Holtzman for the priority of Mark. Volkmar represents the three parables of the Sower, the Mustard, and the Seed growing gradually, as an original group which together teach the spirituality of the kingdom. Neander remarks: "This parable wears the undeniable stamp of originahty both in its matter and form; so that we cannot consider it as a variation of one of the other parables of the growing seed." Life of Christ," Bohn's Edition, p. 346.

The law of growth in the spiritual world not be'ng duly laid to heart, has therefore not been found here; and the parable consequently has been misinterpreted, or rather scarcely interpreted at all. Few of our Lord's parables have been more unsatisfactorily expounded, as there are few in which a right exposition is more to be desired for the good of believers. It may seem presumptuous to say this, by implication censuring our brethren and commending ourselves. But a man's capacity to expound particular portions of Scripture depends largely on the peculiarities of his religious experience; for here as in other spheres, it holds true that we find what we bring. Suppose, e. g., that the experience of a particular Christian has made him intimately acquainted with the momentous business of waiting on God for good earnestly desired and long withheld. The natural result will be an open eye for all Scripture texts, and they are many, which speak of that exercise, and a ready insight into their meaning. The case supposed is the writer's own, and therefore the parable now to be studied has been to him for many years a favourite subject of thought and fruitful source of comfort, viewed as a repetition in parabolic form of the Psalmist's counsel: Wait, I say, on the Lord

In this light we have ever regarded this parable. That the progress of growth in the Divine kingdom, in all spheres, is such as to call for waiting, being gradual and slow, and fixed down to law, seems to us its scope and burden. Hence our title for the parable, the blade, the ear, and the fidl corn, which suggests progress according to natural law, and by stages which must be passed through in succession, none being over-leapt. And though it is often true that there is little in a name, in this case we deem it important to direct attention even to the title. For the title usually given to this parable in English books is unfortunate, as tending to set the mind off on a wrong tack. It is, The seed growing secretly, which emphasises a true but subordinate feature in the parable, with most pernicious effect upon the interpretation. In illustration of the mischief wrought by this falsely-placed emphasis, we imay refer to the fact that Greswell treats the part of the parable which describes the spontaneous growth of grain as Psalm xxvii. 14. Ver. 28.

a parenthesis though that it is in reahty the very kernel is sufficiently shown by the dehberate and pointed enumeration of the stages through which the grain has to pass. Equally instructive illustrations may be found in the pages of Trench and Arnot, whose exceptionally meagre discussions are mainly devoted to the question, Who is the person who sows the seed, Christ, or an ordinary minister of the word?â a question which the very opening of the parable shows to be altogether unimportant; the formula, "So is it with the kingdom of God," signalising the fact that the agent is not in this case the centreâ that the stress lies not on the person, but on the objective facts of the case. The former of these two writers finds himself in a dilemma on the point, from which he frankly confesses he " can see no perfectly satisfactory way of escape." His perplexity is caused by the twofold statement concerning the husbandman, that he knoweth not how the grain grows, and that he putteth in the sickle when the grain is ripe, the former appearing to the writer not to suit Christ, and the latter to suit Him alone. The Scotch commentator, on the other hand, finds an escape from the dilemma by denying what the English commentator had assumed, viz. that the " reaping means the closing of all accounts in the Great Day," which makes it " the exclusive prerogative of the Lord;" and maintaining that it rather means the ingathering of souls in conversion, a function within the competency of ordinary ministers of the word. If the harvest consist in conversions, one naturally wonders what is to be understood by the appearing of the blade! It is surprising that writers who are driven to such shifts, or who have to confess themselves shiftless, should not be led by their perplexities to suspect that they have missed their way altogether in the exposition of the parable. Such unquestionably is the fact 'The Parables," vol. ii. p. 125.

' So Weiss, 'Das Markus-Evangelium, p. 159.

' So Nippold, 'Die Gleichnisse Jesu von der Wacbsenden Saat, vom grossen Abendmahl, und vom Sterbenden Weitzenkorn,"p. 12.

' Notes on the Parables," p. 290.

'The Parables of our Lord," p. 316.

Still another instance of the perplexity produced by the false point of view from which the parable has been contemplated, may be found ia the suggestion of Grotius that oinc dlltv uvtoq should be rendered?, Le.

These idle, barren discussions as to the agent in the parable all arise from misapprehending the main point, which we repeat is not the secretness of the growth, but its gradualness in accordance zvith natural lazv. The key to the interpretation is to be found, not in the expression " he knoweth not how," but in the statement that " the earth bringeth forth fruit of herself, first the blade, then the ear, after that the full corn in the ear." The truth of this assertion will appear from a cursory examination of the leading clauses of the parable.

The first point to be noticed is the description of the farmer's behaviour after he has finished the work of seed-sowing. And should sleep and rise, night and day. It is not to be supposed that these words serve no purpose except to give verisimilitude and picturesqueness to the parable; they are essential to its didactic drift. They happily describe a physical and mental habit in accordance with the situation, that of one who has to pass through a protracted period of comparative idleness. The farmer sleeps and rises, sleeps and rises, night and day, and day after day, for many days in succession.

There is plenty of time for the monotonous repetition of these actions. And there is, comparatively speaking, little else to do but sleep and rise; time hangs heavy on the husbandman's hands. He rises in the morning because he has had as much sleep as he can take; otherwise he might as well lie in bed all the day long for all that he has to do. Having passed through the waking hours in a listless mood, he retires to rest in the evening again, glad to take refuge for a while from the ennui of an idle life in the unconsciousness of sleep. Then the mood of the man corresponds to his circumstances. He knows that his part is done, and that the rest must be left to the soil; therefore he resigns himself contentedly to an easy-minded passivity, leaving the earth to bring forth fruit of itself. He knows also that growth is a process that cannot be hastened; therefore he is patient, or, as St. James expresses it, "hath long patience for it." Finally, he believes that the harvest season will come eventually, having faith in the soil and the seasons; therefore he is free from feverish anxiety, and is in a state of happy, tbe grain, knoweth not how, to avoid the ascription of ignorance to Christ I James v. 7.

healthy security as to the result of his sowing, which allows him to sleep soundly by night. And it is this mood of mind, corresponding to the physical habit so felicitously described, which the parable is intended to inculcate. Christ would have His disciples understand that they must study to resemble the farmer in these respects, and that they will have need and opportunity to do so in connection with the progress of the kingdom in themselves and in the world; need and opportunity for passivity, patience, and faith. While the kingdom progresses they will find it takes its own time, and proceeds according to its own laws; and finding this it will be their wisdom, instead of fretting or trying to force on growth, to have an easy mind, and, like the husbandman, sleep and rise night and day. The mood recommended is not utter indifference or carelessness, but that which is natural to one who is interested in a process whose completion requires time. And in this mood Christ could be and was an example to His disciples; so that this part of the parable at least imposes on us no need to inquire whether the Head of the Church, or one of His servants, be the agent referred to. Christ's behaviour as the founder of the kingdom, during His earthly ministry, was in the spirit of the farmer. He sowed the seed of the kingdom, and waited patiently for the result, not expecting it soon. No need, in order to make the parable applicable to Him, to interpret this part of it as signifying that between the sowing of the seed during His sojourn on earth and the reaping time at the end of the world. He should no longer be visibly present in the field. During the earthly ministry itself we can see Jesus playing the part of the man who sowed the seed, then slept and rose, night and day. We can see Him playing that part in all departments of His ministry, and very especially in that most important department which consisted in the training of the twelve. How patient He was with those men! His manner towards them was that of one who did not expect the ripe fruit of enlightened and sanctified Christian character to appear in them forthwith, but was fully aware that between the ripe fruit and the beautiful blossom of enthusiastic devotion, under whose inspiration they left all

So Grotius: Sensus mihi videtur perspicuus, Christum a facta semente ad messis tempus agro adspectabiliter non adfuturum.

124 The Parabolic Teaching of Christ, book 1 and followed Him, must intervene a more or less protracted period during which they should be as green ears, or crude fruit, of no value except as a promise of something better to come.

The next important feature in the parable is the representation of the growth of grain as a thing of which the farmer has no cognizance. And the seed sjiould spring, and grow up, lie knozveth not Jiozv. The point intended to be emphasised here is not the mere fact of the farmer's ignorance, but his contentment therewith. This clause simply adds another trait in the description of the manner or mood of the man. Apart from any consideration of the terms employed this is antecedently probable. In a description of a farmer's way of life one hardly expects to find a grave statement to the effect that he is ignorant of the laws by which seed sown in the earth springs and grows. Of course he is, but why make so superfluous an observation.- Scientific knowledge of the laws of growth is not in his line. Life and growth are to a large extent mysteries to all, learned or unlearned, but especially to the practical-minded agriculturist, to whom it probably never occurs once in his whole life-time to ask himself, How does the seed I have sowed germinate and braird i â what is the physical cause of growth And when we come to consider closely the words of the parable, we find reason to conclude that it is no such grave statement concerning the scientific ignorance of the farmer that they are intended to convey. The words may be rendered either " when he knoweth not," or " how, knoweth not he." In the former case they simply mean that the husbandman does not observe the growth. The seed springs and grows up, he taking little or no notice; which is just what we should expect of a man in the easy mood ascribed to the farmer in the previous clause. The words so taken simply repeat in a different form of language the statement that between the sowing and the reaping the farmer is in a listless frame of mind. Taken the other way, the words do seem at first to contain a grave statement to the effect that the farmer is

The ioit may be taken in the sense either of quuin or of quomodo. The former rendering is favoured by Kuinoel. wf, he says = cum, ut in Luc. iv. 25; and the phrase, per participium reddendum X. yipso nesciente lion animadvertente.

ignorant as to the cause of growth; but on closer consideration one discovers that they more probably contain a reference to an ostentatious indifference on his part to all such questions. How knoweth not lie, so run the words; the pronoun standing at the end and being emphatic there, " as much as to say, Whoever else may know it, it is all unknown to him by whom, and for whose benefit, the seed was sown." The sower of the seed is stolidly, we may say ostentatiously, indifferent to the cause of growth; only that the ostentation k is not conscious, but is betrayed unconsciously in his manner. And what is the cause of this indifference? It is the consciousness that the growth of the seed is not under his control. The farmer is a practical man, and the only consideration that would lead him to take an interest in the question as to the cause of growth would be the possibility of his influencing the process. If it could be shown that it was in his power to accelerate growth, the air of stolid indifference would speedily vanish; but as that is not possible, he takes no thought of the matter; and his carelessness is the sign that he is aware of the impossibility. And it is in this point of view that that carelessness is referred to in the parable. The state-mentj ' the seed springeth and groweth up, how knoweth not he," really means, "the seed springeth and groweth up independently of him, and he being conscious of the fact taketh no heed." The farmer's indifference is signalised as the visible index of habitual and unqualified recognition of the truth that growth is subject to a natural law entirely beyond his control. The motive of the parabolic representation at this point is to inculcate the duty of practically recognising a similar truth in the spiritual sphere. Christ's purpose was not merely to proclaim the general truth that the beginnings and progress of life in the kingdom of God are mysterious. This, of course, is true, and in a purely homiletic treatment of this parable it would be quite legitimate to make that truth a topic of discourse. We do well at times to meditate on the mysterious miraculous character of all life, and especially of

' ' The Gospel according to Mark Explained," by Joseph Addison Alexander, D. D.

' Principal Campbell, 'The Four Gospels translates, without Aii minding it.

the Divine life in the soul of man, and more particularly of the beginning of that life in the new birth. Christ Himself invites us to such meditation in another of his sayings, that spoken to the Jewish ruler: " The wind bloweth where it listeth, and thou hearest the sound thereof, but canst not tell whence it cometh and whither it goeth; so is every one that is born of the Spirit." And we should contemplate the mystery of a new Divine life in the soul of man with the feelings with which it becomes us to contemplate all miracles; with awe, yet not with incredulity, but rather with believing wonder. When a human being begins to seek after God, to concern himself about salvation, to hunger after righteousness and wisdom, let us behold with reverent, awe-struck eye a spiritual miracle being wrought before our face. We may not look on the spectacle listlessly as if it were a thing of course, or of little significance. On the other hand, we are to beware of so magnifying the mystery as to become unbelievers in it; to take heed lest by allowing our minds to dwell unduly on the greatness of the change which takes place in regeneration we become at length unwilling to admit that in any particular case a regenerating work has been wrought, because what we observe seems small, insignificant, and far from overwhelmingly wonderful. In all probability what we observe is very small indeed, resembling the tiny blade which springs up through the earth from the seed buried beneath; but we must not forget that even the blade is in its way as wonderful as is the appearance at a later stage on the top of the stalk of a hundred grains in place of the one which has been thrown into the ground.

Such thoughts are very edifying, and practically very useful; but it was not, we imagine, such thoughts that Christ wished to suggest when He uttered this parable, and in particular that part of it now under consideration. His aim rather was to impress on his hearers that as in the kingdom of nature, so in the kingdom of God, there is a law of growth and a fixed order of development which must be recognised and respected by them, as it is by the farmer when he takes little notice of the growth of his grain, because he knows that it is entirely beyond his control. He himself habitually recognised and respected that law and order; so that the words " how knoweth not he," in the sense explained, may with perfect propriety and truth be applied to Him. He ever acted as one who knew that there was a fixed order, a course of nature, so to speak, in the Divine kingdom which could not be materially modified or set aside even by His will. He showed his respect for law and order on various occasions and in various ways. When the two sons of Zebedee desired the places of distinction in His kingdom He replied: " To sit on my right hand and on my left is not mine to give, except to those for whom it is prepared of my Father." In this case He showed respect for the moral order of the kingdom. When asked to do works of mercy beyond the bounds of the chosen people, He declined, saying, "I am not sent but unto the lost sheep of the house of Israel." Here was respect for Xhqpolitical order of the kingdom. He was fully aware that ' His religion was destined to be the religion of humanity, but He knew also that in order to an eventual spiritual conquest of the world a firm footing must first be gained in Palestine; and He acted accordingly. Once more, Christ's whole conduct and His whole teaching were influenced by the belief that the kingdom which He was engaged in founding was to have a lengthened history, and to pass through a gradual, secular process of development onwards, towards its final consummation; and here we see His respect for what we may call the physical order of the kingdom. He was not " surprised, disappointed, or chagrined because the success attending His personal ministry was small; consisting in little more than the collection of "a little flock" of twelve men, in spiritual understanding and character " babes." He looked to the future for His reward, and saw there fields white to the harvest, the outgrowth of the seed which He had sown. It is unnecessary to prove that His teaching is pervaded by the idea that the kingdom of God should ' come only slowly, gradually, as the result of a development proceeding according to law. We find the thought in this â parable, and in the two parables which inculcate perseverance in prayer, and in all the texts, and they are not kw, which contain exhortations to watch.

But what the Master ever bore in mind, the disciples were Â Matt. XX. 23. Matt. xv. 24.

128 The Parabolic Teaching of Christ, book i.

slow to understand and lay to heart, and hence the parable before us. They were ready to ask at all times the question. Why cannot the kingdom come at once, in ourselves, or in the world? They did ask at the close of their intercourse with their Lord: " Wilt Thou at this time restore again the kingdom of Israel? " â as if feeling that after years of weary waiting, now at length the time for the fulfilment of their hope had arrived. The thought contained in our parable does not appear ever to have got a firm lodgment in their minds even in the period of their apostolic activity; and the same statement may be made with regard to the whole Christian Church during the first apostolic generation. The lapse of ages has opened our minds to the truth which was hidden from the apostles, so far as the duration of the CJiristian dispensation at large is concerned. But there is reason to believe, that the bearing of the doctrine of the parable on the sanctif cation of the individual, is yet far from being generally understood. Recognition of, and respect for, the law of growth in this sphere, are still desiderata of the average Christian intelligence. The thoughts of many in regard to this subject are like those of children who cannot grasp the idea of growth subject to law, and see no reason why out of an acorn should not at once, as if by magic, come a full-sized oak. They have yet to learn that sanctification is a work carried on after the analogy of the works of nature, in which the law of slow insensible growth, development, or evolution universally obtains.

The next important part of our parable is that which enunciates the great law of growth with reference to the pro- ' duction of grain. " Spontaneously the earth produceth fruit, first blade, then ear, then is full corn in the earl' This is but the explicit statement of a truth which on a right view of the parable has already been implicitly taught in the previous clause. The sentence just quoted simply gives the formal explanation of that feature in the farmer's behaviour vividly and quaintly expressed by the words " how knoweth not he."

Â Acts i. 6.

Â Greswell thinks the point of the parable is, that the Christian Church should continue to exist and thrive through its own vitality and the providence of God; but the aim of the parable is rather to remove a feeling of surprise that in its earthly state it should last so long.

It answers the natural question, why is he so indifferent to the growth of his grain? He who spake the parable might have left his readers to divine the answer for themselves, as we have already done. But He knew how slow His hearers were to understand the analogous truth in the spiritual sphere; therefore He takes the trouble to state with the utmost deliberation the familiar fact with regard to the natural sphere, saying in effect: "The farmer is so indifferent to the growth of his grain because he knows, as you all know, that he has no control over, that he cannot accelerate, the growth, seeing that the earth of its own accord bringeth forth fruit, first the blade, then the ear, and then the full corn in the ear. Understand ye that the same law holds in the kingdom of God, and cultivate the temper of the farmer, that naturally produced by a due recognition of and respect for the law of growth." When this, the true connection of thought, is pointed out, it becomes apparent how far this part of the parable is from being a mere parenthesis; how, on the contrary, it is the very kernel of the parable in reference to its didactic import. But in order to recognise the true connection of thought, men must be willing to receive the truth, which unfortunately many are not, with the inevitable result that the teaching of the parable is evaded rather than unfolded. A distinguished American theologian, who has done more than perhaps any other writer to throw light on " the true problem of Christian experience," remarks with reference to the text from which he discourses on that important theme: " There are some texts of Scripture that suffer a much harder lot than any of the martyrs, because their martyrdom is perpetual; and this, I think, is one of the number. Two classes appear to concur in destroying its dignityâ viz. the class who deem it a matter of cant to make anything of conversion, and the class who make religion itself a matter of cant, by seeing nothing in it but conversion." To the class of martyred texts belongs this verse of our parable, not to say the parable altogether. Men will persist in treating the verse as a parenthesis, or as an irrelevance, telling us that " in this respect there is not uniformity: the spiritual growth from spring to maturity sometimes requires more than one natural

Bushnell, The New Life," p. 161, cheap edition.

season, and sometimes is accomplished in less," all because they have not the courage to grasp and boldly proclaim the truth, that in the kingdom of God, as it reveals itself in the individual soul, growth is slow not less than in the sphere of nature; nay, not only not less, but, as another distinguished American theologian has pointed out, more; it being a law that the higher the thing which grows in the scale of being, the slower its growth. We must insist, therefore, that in respect of the slowness of growth there is an analogy between the kingdom of nature and the kingdom of God, and that it was our Lord's direct purpose to teach that there is. Not only so; we must further insist that there is an analogy not only in regard to the rate of growth, but also in regard to the stages through which the grain passes from its initial condition to maturity. This is implied by the very circumstance of the stages being so carefully enumerated, and also by the manner in which the last stage is referred to. Christ says, the earth produces, first blade, then ear; then, changing the construction, he adds, then is full corn in the ear: meaning evidently to say, then, and not till then, not till the blade and the green ear have been passed through, does the stage of the full ripe ear come. The full ripe ear is what the husbandman desires, it is the end of all his labours, of all that precedesâ blade, and green ear, being merely means towards that end; and its importance as the end of all is fully recognised by the manner in which it is spoken of. But because it is the end, we are not to be impatient of the preliminary stages which lead up to it, but must be content to reach the end step by step, passing on from blade to green ear, and from green ear to ripe ear. That is what the Lord would teach us in this verse with reference to the things of the kingdom in general, and specially with reference to the sanctification of the individual.

Our view, then, is that the analogy between growth in the natural world and growth in the spiritual world must be maintained in its integrity, with regard at once to spontaneity, sloivness, and gradation. Growth in the spiritual world as in the natural is spontaneous, in the sense that it is subject to

Arnot, 'The Parables," p. 321.
' H. W. Beecher, in a Sermon on Waiting on God.

definite laws of the spirit over which man's will has small control. The fact is one to be recognized with humility and thankfulness. With humility, for it teaches dependence on God; a habit of mind which brings along with it prayerful-ncss, and which, as honouring to God, is more likely to. nsure ultimate success than a self-reliant zeal. With thankfulness, for it relieves the heart of the too heavy burden of an undefined, unlimited responsibility, and makes it possible for the minister of the Word to do his work cheerfully, in the morning sowing his seed, in the evening withholding not his hand; then retiring to rest to enjoy the sound sleep of the labouring man, while the seed sown springs and grows apace, he knoweth not how. Growth in the spiritual world, as in the natural, is, further, a process which demands time and gives ample occasion for the exercise of patience. Time must elapse even between the sowing and the brairding; a fact to be laid to heart by parents and teachers, lest they commit the folly of insisting on seeing the blade at once, to the probable spiritual hurt of the young intrusted to their care. Much longer time must elapse between the brairding and the ripening. That a speedy sanctification is impossible we do not affirm; but it is, we believe, so exceptional that it may be left altogether out of account in discussing the theory of Christian experience. Once more, growth in the spiritual world, as in the natural,; is graduated; in that region as in this there is a blade, a green ear, and a ripe ear. Those who demur to this view may ask us to specify the distinctive marks of the several stages, so that our hypothesis may be verified. We accept the challenge, and shall endeavour to discriminate the successive phases of experience which manifest themselves in the life of a Christian in the course of his growth in grace; though conscious that in the performance of the task we shall receive small help from the commentators. But before we proceed to this topic we must make a few observations on the last sentence of the parable.

But when the fruit permits (being ripe), immediately he putteth forth the sickle because the harvest is at hand. The point of importance here is not the question what or when is the harvest, but rather the marked change in the manner of ttie farmer from Ustlessness to energetic activity. The man who erewhile slept and rose and walked about during waking hours, so to speak, with his hands in his pockets, is now all alive, moving about with nimble feet, giving his orders to his servants, saying, Go forth, with sickle in hand, for, lo, the harvest is upon us; see there the whitened fields ready to be reaped. In connection with this change of mood and manner the word Trapabox taken in the sense of per-niitsy is very significant. It implies that the advent of harvest removes a restraint from pent-up energy, and lets it at length escape in action; and thus it throws an interesting light on the nature of the antecedent indifference. It was, after all, not a real radical indifference or apathy. It was latent energy biding its time; it was fervent desire well controlled by the patience of hope. That seeming listlessness was but the sluggishness of dammed-up waters, which rush forth in an impetuous current when the temporary embankment is removed; or the languor of the race-horse, who flies like an arrow in the race when the signal to start is given.

And such is the patience of Christians during that time in their spiritual history when they wait on God for the fulfilment of their desire in an enlightened and sanctified character. Their mood may seem to others, and even to themselves, apathy, indifference, death; but at worst it is but the mood of the man in whom hope deferred maketh the heart sick. They wait not in real indifference, but as they who in darkness wait for the dawn; as Paul and his shipwrecked companions waited in the Adriatic Sea that night when they cast out four anchors and wished for the day. How much spiritual life and energy were latent in them all along becomes apparent when the spiritual harvest season arrives, the time of illumination and enlargement. Then the apparently apathetic one becomes active in all good. Then the man who seemed to care for nothing but himself gives himself up in self-abandonment to a life of love. Then the Church, for the law ' The verse, however, taken along with the preceding part of the parable, does point at a great truth concerning the moral order of the world. Growth slow, harvest sudden (ti70fwt), holds good of all Divine action in Providence. Historical movements are slow in progress but sudden in their crisis. On this truth we shall have occasion to speak in next chapter.

' Acts xx'ii. 29.

applies on the great scale as well as on the small, awakes from seeming sleep, shakes herself from the dust which has gathered about her, looses herself from the bonds of human ordinances and traditions, puts on the beautiful garments of holiness, and clothes herself with the strength of a new creative time in which she reaps the results of forces which have been slowly and secretly working, and also sow the seeds of a future harvest. For it is in such great epochs that the harvest spoken of in our parable is to be sought, not merely at the end of the world. The harvest is the result of any historical development whether in the individual or in society; and there may be as many harvests in the history of the Church as there are definite spiritual movements in her career. And now we return to the topic of the Stages, that we may characterise them more definitely than we have yet done, though we have thrown out stray hints here and there. And here we shall confine ourselves to the experience of the individual, though sensible that the history of the kingdom of God at large is a far greater theme than that of any individual Christian, and ready to admit that it was probably the former which our Lord had chiefly in His thoughts when "He uttered the parable. Our apology for restricting our inquiry to the minor subject is, first, that we understand it better; second, that while the larger subject is the more inviting theme to the speculative mind, the lesser may prove the more useful to ordinary Christians; and tjiird, that while the parable in its first intention may have the wider scope in view, it does not exclude the narrower. That Christ in uttering this parable had the spiritual growth of the individual in view, as well as the larger growth of the kingdom as a whole, will seem improbable to no one who considers these three things: first, the very general terms employed in the introduction of the parable, "So is the kingdom of God," without qualification or limitation; the implied doctrine being, that wherever the kingdom of God appears there growth is in accordance with the representation in this parable; second, the fact that in the first parable, that of the sower, the growth contemplated is exclusively that which takes place in the individual hearer of the word; tjiird, that in the lesson on perseverance in prayer, recorded in the eleventh chapter of Luke's Gospel, reference is made to the Holy Spirit' dis an object of desire to individual disciples; showing that the sanctification of His disciples individually was a topic which occupied Christ's thoughts.

First the blade â or, the blossom: for it is convenient in considering the stages of spiritual growth to employ both emblems, the second having its root in Scripture not less than the first, as e. g. in that suggestive expression in the first Psalm, y7zv 171 his season. Blade, green ear, ripe ear; blossom, green fruit, ripe fruit: such are the alternative series of stages. What we have now to do is to determine the characteristics of the incipient stage, that of the blade or the blossom.

The blade or the blossom signifies the conscious apparent beginning of the Divine life in the soul. We use the epithets conscious and apparent to qualify beginning, because we do not hold that Divine life necessarily dates from the moment when it becomes a matter of consciousness and observation. There may be grace in the heart before it is understood by the subject of its influence, or recognised by others as such. This is the case in most instances of sanctification from childhood, and the fact should be borne in mind by parents and teachers more than it is. For there is a very common and increasingly prevalent tendency to disbelieve in gracious influence unless when it is seen under its ordinary form as exhibited in adults; and those who have the charge of children, taking for granted the absence of grace from the absence of marked manifestation, set themselves with a kind of desperate earnestness to develop prematurely, by a system of forcing appliances, the usual symptoms of conversion as they exhibit themselves in persons of mature years. The result of this system in the after history of children so manipulated we believe to be calamitous, consisting in effect in the premature consumption of all the spiritual fuel in the soul of a child, leaving for manhood nothing but ashes.

When the life that is in the soul begins to appear it does not manifest itself always in the same manner. It appears sometimes as a corn-blade, and sometimes as a fruit-blossom. In the former case it attracts less notice than in the latter. It may be observable to those who look attentively, but it does

Vide on this next chapter.

not arrest attention; it does not catch the eye of even the inobservant, as the blossom of an apple tree attracts the notice of even the most careless wayfarer. " The signs of new life are not obtrusive, consisting merely in a certain quiet thought-fulness, a deepening seriousness, a tendency to shun society and court solitude congenial to meditation and prayer. There is a feeling of emptiness, a longing after the object of infinite love, a melancholy craving for love, a deep drawing of the spirit towards the unknown Divine which can satisfy the craving, an indifference towards the world, a delight in earnest reading, instruction, and meditation, a liking for the company of pious men." When the kingdom of God comes like the blossom on the fruit tree the signs of its coming are much more marked. There is in such cases greater emotional excitement; great sorrow it may be first, then great joy, the joy of the soul's espousal to the mystic Bridegroom, accompanied with a love full of rapture. " The love is consciously first love, a new revelation of God in the soul, a restored consciousness of God, a birth of joy and glorified song in the horizon of the soul's life, like that which burst into our sky when Jesus was born into the world." And as the blossom is beautiful, so this beginning of the new life is altogether lovely, and may easily create the impression of an already completed sanctification. Hence the notion that spiritual, maturity may be attained per saltum, without any process of growth; hence the conceit of perfection in some who are merely beginning the Divine life. When one considers that, the watchword of the mature and experienced Christian is aspiration, zxid. his motto"! press on," it may seem strange and presumptuous in the beginner to be otherwise minded,, and to think he has already attained. But, in truth, it is quite, natural, that "in this flowering state of beauty" the soul should discover and even have "in its feeling the sense of perfection," because the flower is perfect in its way, and the beginner has no means of knowing that this is not the kind of perfection which he is called to reach as his goal. Inex-" perienced, initial Christianity is but a blossom, and what it is '

Arndt, Die Gleichnissreden." In his treatment of this parable, this thoughtful and eloquent German author shows more insight than we have met with in any other writer on the parables.

Bushnell, The New Life," p. 162. Â Ibid., p. 163.

to come to is ripe fruit, and it is to come to that through sourness and unripeness. But the blossom knows nothing of fruit either ripe or unripe; it is conscious only of itself And it is conscious of itself as something beautiful, really perfect in its kind, even fairer to look on than the ripe fruits which hang on the tree of life in the old age of Christian experience. How beautiful the first love of the heart for Christ, the newborn passion for Christian virtue, the devotional spirit which constantly dwells in the breast, sending the youthful disciple to solitary spots to pray, and setting him on efforts to think holy, heavenly thoughts all the day long! Who that has felt this, possibly at a very early period of life, does not look back on it as something hallowed, though, alas, he knows too well that it cannot be relied on as a guarantee against the commission of many faults, and the entrance into the mind of many unbelieving, bitter, bad thoughts. Across the interval of years, in spite of much that is humbling and disappointing, in spite of lapses, backslidings, heresies, scepticisms, blasphemies, he looks back on that time as an Eden in his spiritual history, as a soft balmy spring-tide when the soul blossomed into Christian faith and feeling, and the tongue was attuned to new songs. If then, even after the sobering influence of experience, a mature Christian thinks thus tenderly of his earlier state, what wonder if the inexperienced should mistake the beginning for the end, the blossom for the fruit, spring for harvest, holy feeling for holy living, ideals for performances, gushing first love for stern fidelity temptation-proof? It is a mistake, and a very great one, but do not laugh at it; do not be angry at it; do not waste time preaching against it. It is a mistake that will be soon enough corrected by experience.

For the second stage, that of the green ear, or green fruity will certainly come; whereof we must now speak, with no assistance from the commentators, for scarcely one of them gives a single hint as to what is meant by the green ear. All one can glean from their pages is a stray remark by one that the intermediate time between the brairding and the leaping is often a time of trial; and by another, that the lime when there is no apparetit growth is a time of inward

Olshausen," Commentar."

growth, Now as to the characteristics of this second stage, â it follows of course from the simple fact of its being the time of ivaitiiig, of unfulfilled desire, of unrealised ideals, of green ears and crude, sour, unpalatable fruit, that it is a time which brings experiences more profitable than pleasant. The fruit of the Spirit tastes very acid at this stage. Its experiences are such as Bunyan's pilgrim had in his passage through the Valley of Humiliation and the Valley of the Shadow of Death; such as Bunyan himself had in the years of gloom before he attained to cleai light and settled peace, and abundant joyful Christian fruitfulness. It is a time of temptation and struggle, of doubts and fears, of sadness, depression, and gloom, of stagnation and torpor. It is that phase in the believer's history whereof Newton sings, when prayers for growth in faith, and love, and every grace are answered in such a way as almost to drive one to despair. The author of the hymn represents the bitter experiences described in it as an answer to his prayer for growth. And so it really is. The green ear, the crude fruit, is really a stage in advance of the blossom, which looks so much better, as is confessed by all, in regard to natural growth. No one looking on an apple tree after the blossom is deadened and the fruit set, thinks of remarking. What a degeneracy! But men are very ready to commit such a mistake in regard to spiritual growth. The tendency is to regard transition from the blossom to the green fruit as a simple declension, or falling away from grace, and to characterise the antecedent experience as a merely temporary excitement; which in many cases is about as wise as if one were to say with regard to an apple tree when the flowering stage is past, it was only a little temporary blossom. From ignorance of the law of growth young Christians at this stage are apt to form very unfavour-able judgments of themselves. As it is characteristic of the

incipient and final stages to entertain hopeful views of one's condition, so it is equally characteristic of this stage to take desponding gloomy views. The fruit of the Spirit's work is so bitter and unpalatable that it is readily mistaken for poisonous fruit of the devil's growing. The mind clouded
Arndt, Die Gleichnissreden.
' In the well-known hymn, "I asked the Lord that I might grow.
with sceptical and evil thoughts, the conscience afflicted with all manner of morbid scruples, the heart cold and self-centred, too engrossed with its own miseries to interest itself in anything beyond, how unlike these spiritual phenomena to the love, joy, and peace of which the apostle speaks!â how natural that one in whose soul they manifest themselves should think himself an unbeliever, an apostate, even a blasphemer guilty of sin utterly unpardonable! The subject of these experiences being so liable to mistake their true character, it is all the more to be desired that others should be able to judge them more correctly. Yet how often is it otherwise! Bunyan's history supplies an instructive illustration. When he was in that stage of his religious experience which answers to the green ear, he believed he had committed the unpardonable sin, and in his distress consulted a Christian friend who was thought to be endowed with superior spiritual insight, with what result may best be told in his own words. "About this time I took an opportunity to break my mind to an ancient Christian, and told him all my case. I told him also that I was afraid I had sinned a sin against the Holy Ghost; and he told me he thought so too. Here, therefore, I had but cold comfort; but talking a little more with him, I found him, though a good man, a stranger to much combat with the devil." What an egregious blunder to mistake the painful discipline by which Bunyan was being prepared to write the Pilgrim's Progress for blasphemy against the Holy Ghost! How many mistakes of a similar kind may be committed in every generation by men of reputed wisdom and sanctity, but " strangers to much combat with the devil." In the light of Bunyan's story we can see the utility of more acquaintance with such warfare, were it only to fit Christians for speaking a word in season to him that is weary.

Yet there is some excuse for perplexity in judging of such experiences as are incident to the stage of the green ear. For while these experiences are not to be resolved into simple declension or apostasy, they are very apt to be accompanied by, and even to produce, moral retrogression. In a joyless state it is not easy to hold one's ground. When
Vide Grace Abounding to the Chief of Sinners."
doubts assail one either as to the fundamental truths of religion, or as to personal relations with God, it is not easy to hold fast a good conscience, and to keep oneself unspotted from the world. Hence, as a matter of fact, it. do get into a dull, cheerless, doubting state of mind, without losing ground spiritually. And when the conscience is troubled the Christian can see nothing in his own case but sin. His doubts are sin; his dryness and deadness in religious duties, his joylessness, depression, and inactivity are all sin. And, on the whole, this is a safe view for one to take ot himself, provided he do not so utterly misunderstand the course of religious experience as to be without hope concerning himself, like Bunyan. But, while a practically safe view, it is far from being a complete account of the matter. The word backsliding does not by any means

sum up the experience of one who is passing through the Valley of the Shadow of Death; and to speak as if it did, as is too often done, is simply to break the bruised reed, and quench the smoking taper. It is quite possible that there may be very little sin in the whole experience, but only the morbidity inseparable from the stage of development in which it appears; as in the case of Bunyan, who was never more in earnest in the fear of God, and the love of Christ, than when he thought himself guilty of blasphemy. He thought there was no fruit of the Spirit in him then, because there was none yet ripe. But there was that in him, only in crude form, whose natural outcome in due course was to be a rich harvest of wisdom and loveâ the fruit of which still remains treasured up in his immortal volume. Only one remark more need be added on this topic. It may be supposed that the experiences described as incidental to the second stage are exceptional. We believe the contrary to be the fact. The experiences peculiar to this phase are indeed by no means stereotyped in their form, but manifest' themselves under very diverse aspects in different men. But something of the kind happens to all men of definite decided religious character. And let it not be supposed that the more piety the less of these experiences. This were in effect to say, that the cause of the green ear is the presence of thorns in the soil, so that if the soil were perfectly clean, the heart altogether good and noble, the seed would reach maturity without passing through the green stage. But the true distinction between the thorny soil and the good soil is not that in the one the green ear appears, while in the other it is never seen, but rather that in the one the grain never gets beyond the green ear, while in the other it passes on from greenness to maturity. It is no sin to be in the green ear: the sin is never to pass beyond it; and as it is no sin to be in the green ear, so neither is it any privilege to be conferred on faithful souls, to escape passing through it. No; it is not the privilege of faithful noble souls to overleap the green ear. Rather it is their lot to know more of its peculiar experiences than others, as all religious biography attests. They who reap in greatest joy sow most in tears. They who know best what it is to mount up on wings like eagles, to run and not weary, to walk and not faint, know also better than others what it is to have to wait on the Lord.

For those who faithfully and patiently wait the full corn in the ear comes without fail. But how shall we describe this last highest stage, so as at once to convey an adequate and yet a sober view of its peculiar characteristics."' It is not easy; but in a few broken sentences let us try at least to suggest a rudimentary idea of what has been variously named Christian perfection, Christian maturity, the Higher Christian Life. Bunyan gives us his idea of the state in that part of his allegory where he represents the Pilgrim as arriving at the Land of Beulah, where the sun shines night and day, the land lying beyond the Valley of the Shadow of Death, and out of the reach of Giant Despair, and from which one cannot so much as see Doubting Castle; where Christians are within sight of the city they are going toâ that is, have a lively hope of eternal lifeâ where they renew their marriage contract with their God, where they have no want of corn and wine; but meet with abundance of what they have sought for in all their pilgrimage. In the day when a Christian arrives at this stage the promise of Jesus to His disciples is fulfilled: "Ye now, therefore, have sorrow, but I will see yog again, and your heart shall rejoice, and your joy no man taketh from you." The early joy of a believer is passionate and transient, this final joy is tranquil, and abides. It is the joy of a

John xvi. 22.

conscience enlightened, and freed from bondage to scruples without loss of tenderness, of a mind established in religious conviction, and in which faith and knowledge are reconciled, and of a heart delivered from concern about self and its interests, whether temporal or eternal, to serve God and man with generous devotion, and taught by sorrow to sympathise. Now at length there does appear the ripe fruit of the Spirit: love, joy, peace, long-suffering, gentleness, goodness, faith, meekness, temperance. A well-known writer on the religious affections says: " The Scripture knows no true Christians of a sordid, selfish, cross, and contentious spirit; nothing can be a greater absurdity than a morose, hard, close, high-spirited, spiteful true Christian." The statement indicates a lack of due discrimination between sincerity and maturity. There are sincere Christians of the character described, but there are certainly no mature Christians of such a character. For the mature are loving, wise, benignant, humble, patient, rich in well-doing, willing to communicate, heartily and supremely interested in the progress of the Divine kingdom, and loyal subjects of its King. Yet, withal, the mature Christian is characteristically free from self-complacency. It is not possible for him, as it is possible for the immature disciple, to think that he hath attained the goal of perfection. His ideal of the Christian life is pitched too high to allow such a fancy to enter his mind. " I know not how to describe the grandeur and simplicity of the state that is no longer self-bounded, self-referring; how great a thing to such a freed rejoicing spirit the life in Christ Jesus seems!â a temple truly ' not of thrs building," too great to be mapped out and measured; too great to be perfect here."

From these brief hints it will be seen that the last stage of Christian growth cannot be regarded as a mere repetition of or return to the first, as if the Divine life consisted in a perpetual see-saw between falls and conversions. There is an affinity but not an identity; for that which springs out of experience can never be identical with a state which precedes

Jonathan Edwards, Treatise on the Religious Affections," Part iii. sect. 8.

' ' The Patience of Hope," p. 102. This little work by the late Miss Greenwtll is full of true insight into the law of growth in the spiritual worh.

experience. A writer already referred to puts the relation between the two thus:â "The real object of the subsequent life as a struggle of experience is to produce in wisdom what is then begotten as a feeling, or a new love; and thus to make a fixed state of that which was initiated only as a love. It is to convert a heavenly impulse into a heavenly habit. It is to raise the Christian childhood into a Christian manhood â to make the first love a second or completed love; or, what is the same, to fulfil the first love and give it a pervading fulness in the soul; such that the whole man, as a thinking, self-knowing, acting, choosing, tempted, and temptable creature, shall coalesce with it, and be for ever rested, immovably grounded in it" But, perhaps, the relations between the initial and final stages by way both of resemblance and of contrast can be better understood by examples than by any abstract statement. We shall therefore conclude with a few extracts from the autobiography of one in whose religious history all the three phases of spiritual growth were well marked, and than whom no one was ever more competent to speak on the subject of Christian sanctification, or has ever spoken more wisely. In a section of that work, the author, Richard Baxter, draws a contrast between his earlier and his later views, which is altogether very instructive, and in which the following passages, taken at random, occur:â " In my younger years my trouble for sin was most about my actual failings in thought and deed, but now I am much more troubled for inward defects." " Heretofore I placed much of my religion in tenderness of heart, and grieving for sin, and penitential tears, and less of it in the love of God, and studying His love and goodness, and in His joyful praises, than now I do." " I was once wont to meditate most on my own heart, and to dwell all at home and look little higher. I was still poring either on my sins or my wants, or examining my sincerity; but now, though I am greatly convinced of the need of heart acquaintance, yet I see more of a higher work; that I should look oftener upon Christ, and God, and heaven, than upon my own heart. I would have one thought at home upon myself and sins, and many thoughts above upon the high, and amiable, and beatifying objects." " Heretofore Â Bushnell, 'The New Life," p. i66.

I knew much less than now, and yet was not half so much acquainted with my own ignorance. I had a great delight in the daily new discoveries which I made, and of the Tght which shined in upon me (like a man that cometh into a country where he never was before). But I little knew either how imperfectly I understood these very points vhose discovery so much delighted me, nor how much might be said against them, nor how many things I was yet a stranger to." "At first I was greatly inclined to go with the highest in controversies on one side or the other. But now I can so easily see what to say against both extremes, that 1 am much more inclinable to reconciling principles." "I am not so narrow in my special love as heretofore. Being less censorious I love more as saints than I did heretofore." " My soul is much more afflicted with the thoughts of the miserable world, and more drawn out in desire for their conversion, than heretofore. Yet am I not so much inclined to pass a peremptory sentence of damnation upon all that never heard of Christ." " I am deeper afflicted for the disagreements of Christians than I once was. Except the case of the infidel world nothing is so sad to my thoughts as the case of the divided churches." " I do not lay so great stress upon the external modes and forms of worship as many young professors do. I cannot be of their opinion that think God will not accept him that prayeth by the Common Prayer Book, and that such forms are a self-invented worship which God rejecteth. Nor yet can I be of their mind who say the like of extempore prayer." " I am much more sensible than heretofore of the breadth, length, and depth of the radical, universal, odious sin of selfishness, and of the excellency and necessity of self-denial and of a public mind, and of loving our neighbour as ourselves." "I am more solicitous about my duty to God, and less solicitous about His dealings with me." â In these precious fragments we recogmse the marks of spiritual maturity: a conscience tender, yet free from superstition and legalism; a heart, which to brotherly kindness adds charity; an understanding enlightened with sober, well-balanced views of truth, refusing to call any human teacher master, yet in harmony in all essentials with the wise and good of all ages.

'Reliquiae Baxterianas," Part I.

At what precise periods in the ministry of our Lord these parables were delivered we have no means of determining. There is no ground for assuming that they were uttered at the same time, or that either of them was spoken in close proximity to the parable last considered. But the kindred character of the two parables obviously justifies us in studying them together, and their didactic import equally justifies us in taking them up at this point. They form a most appropriate sequel to the parable of the blade, the ear, and the full corn, which teaches that growth in the kingdom of God, whether in the individual or in the comm. unity, is gradual and slow. For the progress of the kingdom in both spheres may be said to be the great subject of all Christian prayer, and thus retarded progress will mean delay in the answering of prayer. And it is the experience of such delay in the case of those who earnestly desire the progress of the kingdom, and the temptation thence arising to cease from praying, with which these two parables have to do. That experience is the occasion of their being uttered, and to meet the temptation springing therefrom is their common aim. Understanding this we have the key to the true interpretation of these parables; failing to understand it we shall miss the mark. The expositor must start with the assumption that an experience of delay in the answering of prayer is presupposed in both parables; that the men to whom they are spoken are men who have discovered that God has to be waited on for the fulfilment of spiritual desire. We state this categorically at the outset, because the fact may escape the notice of one who looks merely on the surface of the parables, and has regard only to their express statements. No mention is made of delay in the earlier parable; and while in the later words occur which imply the idea of delay when rightly interpreted, they are words capable of a different interpretation, and likely to receive it from one who does not come to the parable with the conviction in his mind that what makes exhortations to perseverance in prayer needful is, and can be, nothing else than experience of Divine delay in granting the things sought after. Such a conviction, therefore, it must be the first business of the interpreter to furnish himself with. And surely this ought not to be very difficult! It requires little reflection to see that no devout man can be seriously tempted to cease from prayer merely because he does not obtain what he asks in a few minutes or hours or even days. The temptation can arise only after a sufficient time has elapsed to leave room for doubts as to the intention of the Being to whom prayer is addressed to grant the desires of supplicants. In the case of the man who knocked at the door of his neighbour seeking bread, a few minutes sufficed to produce such doubts. But in the spiritual sphere a much longer time must elapse; even years may be required to put a Ciiristian in a state of mind analogous to that of the man who stood at his neighbour's doorâ in the state of mind which makes such counsel as our Lord gives in these parables eminently seasonable. How long it will require Jesus does not state; we are supposed to learn that from experience; and in point of fact those who need the comfort of these parables do so learn, and have no need that any one should tell them.

While both directed against temptations to cease from prayer arising out of the tardiness with which growth in the Divine kingdom proceeds, these two parables have nevertheless in view two distinct classes of experiences. The one contemplates experiences of delay in connection with individual sanctification, the other addresses itself to similar experiences in connection with the public fortunes of the kingdom. That

Luke xviii. 5; last clause, Kai fiakpoovixtl (or uv) Irr avtolg â though he delay in their cause: vide the exposition of the parable.

the parable of the Selfish Neighbour has in view mainly and primarily the spiritual interest of the individual may be inferred from the closing words of the great lesson on prayer of which it forms a part: " How much more shall your heavenly Father give the Holy Spirit to them that ask Him." The supposed object of desire is the Holy Spirit as the enlightener and sanctifier of individual disciples. Some critics indeed, having regard to the fact that in the parallel passage in Matthew the general expression "good things" takes the place of the more definite phrase in the third Gospel, question the authenticity of the latter, and see in it only an instance of the colouring which Luke's report of our Lord's teaching received from his familiarity with and predilection for the Pauline system of doctrine. And we admit that this reference to the Holy Spirit as the immanent ground of Christian sanctity, an almost solitary instance in the Synoptic Gospels, is fitted to arrest attention. This ethical conception of the Divine Spirit, as distinct from the Old Testament view of Him as the transcendent source of charismata, is, as Pfleiderer has pointed out, a characteristic feature in the Pauline system of thought. And probably it was due to Pauline influence that Luke recognised its importance by introducing it into his view of Christ's teaching. But we need not therefore doubt the originality of the saying as given in the text quoted. The representation of the Holy Spirit as the supreme object of desire is in keeping with the whole circumstances in which the lesson on prayer was given. The evangelist tells us that it was after hearing their Master pray that the disciples requested Him to instruct them in the holy art. The request implied a consciousness of spiritual defect; and Jesus, knowing the religious condition of His followers better than they did themselves, proceeded to make provision for their wants by suggesting subjects of prayer to meet the lack of thoughts, by putting into their mouths forms of words to meet the need of dumb souls, and finally by furnishing inducements to perseverance in prayer to meet the need of men tempted to cease praying by the discouraging

Luke xi. 13. Â ayadh: Matt. vii. II.

' So Hilgenfeld, who characterises the phrase Trytdxa uyiov as Gut Pauunisch. ' Einleitiuig," p. 503.

consciousness that the kingdom of God was coming in theif hearts at a very slow pace. We cannot doubt, therefore, that the earher of the two parables on perseverance in prayer has in view chiefly, we say not exclusively, the disappointing spiritual experiences of individual disciples. That the later parable, on the other hand, has a wider scope, and contemplates the general interests of the kingdom, is evident from the application: "And shall not God avenge His own elect, which cry day and night unto Him, though He bear long with them.- " The situation supposed is evidently that of the elect Church of God as a collective body, in a condition of widowhood, harassed and evil entreated by an unbelieving world, and receiving no succour from Providence; to all appearance abandoned to her fate by a God who, far from behaving towards her as a husband, does not even maintain the character of a just judge in her behalf.

Wherever doubts concerning the utility of prayer engendered by delayed answers are felt, there painful misgivings regarding the reality of Divine love must force themselves on the mind. Hence these parables may be regarded as an attempt to reconcile with the facts of experience the doctrine of a paternal Providence. This doctrine, we know, Jesus taught with great emphasis and unwearying iteration, applying it both to ordinary life and to the higher sphere of the Divine life. As taught by Him the doctrine of a heavenly Father is very beautiful; but one conversant with the facts of life may be tempted to ask. Is it true Beautiful words are those spoken by Jesus about a Father who will provide for those who devote themselves to His kingdom, and will give them all they need both for body and soul; words full of pathos and poetry, the bare reading of which exercises a soothing influence on our troubled spirits in this world of sorrow and care; yet are not these lyric utterances but a romantic idyll standing in no relation to real life It may be right that we be thankful for them as springs in the desert. Nevertheless, the world is a desert all the same. Providence is anything but paternal; if there be, indeed, a Providence at all, which often seems more than doubtful. Jesus knew that such

Luke xviii. 7. The more exact rendering and interpretation of the words â will be given in the sequel.

doubting; thoughts would arise in good men's minds, and He spake not a few words designed to heal them, and among these a chief place must be assigned to our two parables. These parables are, in intent, a defence of a doctrine which Christians often find hard to believeâ the doctrine of God's fatherly love; and as such they illustrate and vindicate the apologetic character which, in the commencement of these studies, we ascribed to the parables generally.

Much of the interest of the parables before us lies in their pathos as apologies for the doubted love of a heavenly Father, the deep sympathy with which the speaker enters into the moral situation supposed, and identifies Himself with and so mediates between both parties, the doubting and the doubted. Jesus, through the insight of love, knows perfectly the thoughts of His tried ones, and how God appears to them in the hour of trial; and He dares to describe the God of appearance as He seems in the midnight of temptation, taking the tempted up at the point where He finds them, and seeking to inspire hope even in desponding minds by suggesting a distinction between the God of appearance and the God of reality. And what Jesus has dared to do we must not hesitate to say that He has done. We must not shrink from saying that the selfish neighbour in bed and the unjust judge represent God as He appears to faith tried by delay. It is a great fault in an expositor to be over-anxious to say that God is not really selfish or unjust. Of course He is not, but only seems. But the point to be emphasised is that He does seem. The expositor who fails to emphasise this point is like Job's friends, who in their stupid, prosing, didactic way defended God, saying, "Remember, I pray thee, who ever perished, being innocent? or where were the righteous cut off."'" And resembling them in their stupidity, he is apt also to resemble them in their injustice to the tried one. Too anxious to vindicate God, he does wrong to the tempted, instead of helping them with sympathy and counsel, by indulging in reflections to the efi"ect, "Thus God appears to unbeliefl" No, not to unbelief only, but to faith also in 2 So the learned but pedantic Stier ('Die Reden

Jesu'). Very differently Olshausen remarks: The Saviour here places Himself on the standpoint of times of trial; to elect ones when deserted; to an elect Church widowed, helpless, desolate, her Maker for the time not her husband, or only a husband that is dead; to a Jeremiah asking leave to reason with God about His judgments; to a Psalmist whose feet well nigh slipped when he saw the prosperity of the wicked and the hard lot of good men. By all means let commentators have sympathy with God, but let it not be a one-sided sympathy; let them have sympathy with God's people also, as Jesus had when He uttered these parables; and let them not stand between His faithful ones and the comfort He designed for them in their hours of darkness and despondency.

With pathos often goes humour, and so it is in the parables before us. The spirit of Jesus was too earnest to indulge in idle mirth, but just because He was so earnest and so sympathetic He expressed Himself at times in a manner which provokes a smile; laughter and tears, as it were, mingling in His eyes as He spoke. It were a false propriety which took for granted that an expositor was necessarily off the track because in his interpretation of these parables an element of holy playfulness appears blended with the deep seriousness which pervades them throughout. With these preliminary observations we proceed to the exposition of the parables, spoken to teach that men ought always to pray, and not to faint. And first the parable of

THE SELFISH NEIGHBOUR.

Jesus said unto His disciples, Which of you shall have a friend, and shall go tinto him at midniglit, and say unto him, Friend, lend me three loaves: for a friend of mine is come to me from a journey, and I have nothing wjiich I can set before him? Atid he from within shall answer and say, Doii t trouble me: the door is already shict, and my children are with me in bed; I canh rise and give thee. I say unto you. Even if he will not rise and give him, because he is his f'iend, yet at least because of his shamelessness he will rise and give him as many as he needs. â LUKE xi. 5â 8.

tbose who experience that God oft delays long with fulfilment of prayer, and describes Him as an unrighteous Being in accordance with the subjective feeling of the praying one, and gives his counsel in conformity therewith. Jeremiah xii. I. ' Psalm lxxiii.

On the force of the particle yi see further on.

It has been remarked of this parable, as of the Unjust Judge and many others peculiar to Luke, that in it the parabolic character is not strictly maintained, the fable passing into an example of the doctrine taught. It has also been pointed out that the grammatical structure of the parable undergoes a change as it proceeds. Commencing with the interrogative form, it passes into the form of a narrative. Had the initial form been maintained throughout, the parable would have run thus: Which of you shall have a friend, and shall go and say to him thus and thus, and (if) this one shall reply so and so, (will not persist knocking and demanding until) he shall be glad to give him what he asks to get rid of him. These defects in literary form and grammatical structure do not in the smallest degree detract from the value of the parable for the purpose in hand. It admirably illustrates the power of importunity, by showing how it can gain its end even in the most unpromising situation. The ciiriosa felicitas of the parable will best be made apparent by entering into a little detail, first in reference to the situation, and next in reference to the means by which importunity makes itself master of it.

In order to show how extremely discouraging the situation is, it will not be necessary to lay stress on the hour of the night at which the petitioner for bread finds himself called on to provide for his unseasonable visitor. Travelling in the night is common in the East, and it may be said to belong simply to the natural realism of the parable that the incident related is represented as happening at midnight. One cannot but remark, however, in passing, that it belongs to the felicity of the parable to suggest what it does not

Weizsacker, Untersuchungen," p. 209.

So Godet, who further points out that if the narrative form be adopted throughout, the parable will run thus: If one of you has a friend, and say to him, c., and this one reply, c. (nevertheless), I tell you, c. Ungcr ('Deparabolarum Natura,"(S: c.) makes the IIq i. v il)v the refuser and giver, not the asker; so that the parable runs: Who is there among you, who if a friend come and make such and such a demand, though at first annoyed, will not at length, on account of his importunity, give him what he asks?

3 The journey homewards of the wise men of the East commenced during night, likewise the flight of Joseph vide Matt. ii. 12â 14). Kuinoel, in his commentary on this passage, refers to Hasselquist's ' Reise nach Palastina' in proof that the practice still prevails.

expressly teach, viz. that the comfort it is designed to convey to tried faith is available to those who find themselves in the very darkest hour of their spiritual perplexities. But passing from this, we note the discouraging circumstances in which the man in need finds himself on arriving at his neighbour's door. The difficulty which confronts him is not a physical one; that, viz., of finding his neighbour so profoundly asleep that it is impossible by any amount of knocking, however loud, to awaken him. His discouragement is, as the nature of the argument required it to be, a moral one; that, viz., of finding his neighbour, after he has succeeded in arousing him to consciousness, in a state of mind the reverse of obliging, utterly unwilling to take the trouble necessary to comply with his request. The mood of the man in bed is most graphically depicted. It is the mood of a man made heartless and selfish by comfort. Comfortable people, we know, are apt to be hard-hearted, and comfortable circumstances make even kind people selfish for the moment. Jesus holds up to our view an illustrative example. And the picture is so sketched to the life that we cannot repress a smile at the humour of the scene, while fully alive to the deep pity and pathos out of which the whole representation springs. The man is made to describe himself, and to show out of his own mouth what an utterly selfish creature he is. First an ominous omission is observable in his reply. There is no response to the appeal to his generous feelings contained in the appellation ' Friend' addressed to him by his neighbour. The man who needs his help calls him c tae, but he takes good care not to return the compliment. How true is this touch to human nature as it shows itself in every age! The rich, who need nothing, have many friends, but the poor is hated even of his own neighbour. The first words uttered by the man in bed are a rude, abrupt, surly " Don't bother me." For so undoubtedly ought they to be rendered. We find the phrase, or one very similar, occurring several times in the New Testament: as in the parable of the Unjust Judge;

On the spiritualising of tiaovvkrlov Olshausen remarks, that as Christ's parables imply a fine intuition, it is a safe canon that no trait should be overlooked if it do not disturb the image of the whole. With this I concur; only we must always distinguish between the teaching of a parable and What I have called its felicity. a Proverbs xiv. zo.

in Christ's speech in defence of Mary of Bethany against the censure of the disciples, who blamed the extravagance of her noble work, the anointing of her Lord; and in the closing words of Paul's Epistle to the Galatians. In the two last places the words must be rendered in a dignified way, in keeping with the solemn tone of the speaker and writer. Jesus says, Do not vex Mary by finding fault with what she has just done. Paul, utterly weary of the carnality of religious contention, closes his Epistle with the sentence, Henceforth let no man cause me annoyances: for I bear in my body the marks of Jesus. " I too am a crucified man; let me have a crucified man's privilege, and be done for ever with the troublers of Israel, and enter into the rest of the weary." But it would be out of keeping with the whole situation to put a dignified speech into the mouth of a m. an irritated by unseasonable disturbance of his nightly repose. We must make him speak as men usually do when they are out of humour, employing a vocabulary redolent of slang, and spiced with words not worthy to find a place in dictionaries. When he said p? i. oi kottovs irdpexe, he felt just as those do now who say in colloquial English, "Don't bother me," or " Don't fash me;" and the same remark applies to the use of a similar phrase by the unjust judge.

Next comes a comically serious detailed description of the difficulties which stand in the way of complying with the needy neighbour's request: " The door is already barred, and my children are with me in bed." Poor man, he is to be pitied! If it were only the mere matter of getting out of bed, it would be no great affair, now that he is awake. But the unbarring of the door is a troublesome business, not so Â Matt. xxvi. ID. ' Gal. vi. 17.

' So Farrar. His remarks on the parable are very racy. " He does not return the greeting ixt; the expression fii) fxoi koitovq Trapexe, ' Don't fa-. h me," is an impatient one: the door KikXnarai, ' has been shut for the night;' ov civafxai, I can't," meaning ' I won't.""â Life of Christ," vol. i. p. 453, note.

And yet it is probably the rising out of bed that he really objects to. This crops out unconsciously in his concluding words: I am not able rising to give thee (oii livafiai dva(7Taq Â ovvai aoi). On iyepoug in ver. 5, Bengel remarks, Amicitia ad dandiuti impellere poterat: impudentia pulsare perseverans ad laborem surgendi irapellit.

easily performed as the turning of a key handle, which is all we Europeans and moderns have to do in similar circumstances. And then the dear children are in bed asleep: if one were to waken them, what a trouble to get them all hushed to rest again. Really the thing is out of the question. And so he ends with a peevish, drawling " I can't rise to give thee." His "I can't" means " I won't." The circumstances which hinder, after the most has been made of them, are utterly frivolous excuses, and it is simply contemptible to refer to them seriously as reasons for not helping a friend in need. But the very fact that he does this only shows how utterly unwilling he is, how completely comfort and sleep have deadened every generous feeling in his heart. And that he is capable of adducing such considerations as grounds of refusal is the most discouraging feature in the situation of the poor suppliant. It is a poor outlook for Need when Abundance so easily excuses herself for refusing succour, Alas, how sad to think that so much misery exists in the world unrelieved for no better reason! It is not that physical resources adequate to the purpose do not exist; it is that there is so much comfortable selfishness, which regards the smallest trouble or sacrifice as an insurmountable obstacle.

But in the case of the parable comfortable selfishness for once finds itself overmatched by importunate want. The situation is desperate indeed when the person solicited for aid finds it in his heart to refuse it on such paltry grounds. But the petitioner has the matter in his own hands; he can make the unwilling one fain to give him whatever he wishes, be it three loaves or thirty: not for friendship's sake certainly, for 1 On icÂ (c ft(TraÂ Bengel remarks, Vecte olim, qui majore labore removetur.

' The idea of some commentators, that ra iraisia refers to servants, is not in keeping withtiie simple, homely character of the parable. Grotius, while rendering vaisia children, thinks that the idea meant by the reference is that there is no one at home who can without inconvenience give bread to the man at the door. But the purpose seems rather to be to suggest the risk of disturbing the children.

Bengel on oawv remarks, Quotquot, vel si plures sint panes, quam quos summanecessitas postulat. Non incommodius est multos jam dare quam ires, unumve. There is a various reading here, some MSS. having vaov. With oitov the proper rendering is " as much as he wi'sies," with '6au)v " as many as he needs."

of that there can be little hope after that contemptible " I can't rise and give thee;" but for very selfishness' sake to get rid of the annoyance and be free to relapse into slumber. How then? What are the means by which need is able to make itself master of the situation? One word answers the question. It is shamelessness, avaihua. Shamelessness, not in knocking at the door of a neighbour at such an hour, for that may be excused by necessity, and at all events it has failed. The shamelessness meant is that which consists in continuing to knock on after receiving a decided and apparently final refusal. Think of it! the petitioner pays no heed to the excuses advanced and to the denial given. He knocks on without mercy and without delicacy, continues to knock louder and louder, hoping to compel his neighbour to rise and give him what he wants even out of a regard to that very comfort which he loves so dearly. How indecent! But necessity knows no restraints of a merely conventional kind, and success covers a multitude of sins. And of course the shameless one succeeds. For comfort's sake his neighbour at first refused his request, and for comfort's sake at last he will be fain to grant it. For how can he sleep with such a noise going on without; and what chance is there even of the children, deep and sweet though their slumber be, sleeping on through it all? The best thing to be done is just to rise and do reluctantly and tardily what should have been done voluntarily and at once. How expressive that one word shamelessness, and how in-

So Bengal, noctu venientis.

Christ's purpose is not to assert dogmatically that the neighbour will not help his friend for any other reason, but to assert that he will certainly do it for the reason specified. This is the force of the particle yi in the clause kd yt Tt)v avaiseiav avtov. Klotz (in Devarium) derives ye from reQ = Â aw, or from ayf, which renders the reader or hearer attentive, and so gives more importance to the word excepted. He says that wherever anything is affirmed by yi a certain opposition is implied; not such, however, that it cpposes things contrary, z'ner se, but so that it distinguishes and makes one thing stand out more than another. Thus if we say of one of two Uilvoc ye i Ku, we do not mean the other does not come, but this one certainly comes. The use of the future tense in the previous clause, however (tl kui ov Â wau), implies that relief on the score of friendship is very improbable. The particle yi has the same force in the other parable (Luke xviii. 5). The words of the unjust judge are to be paraphrased: Though I fear not God, nor regard man, and therefore little is to hfi expected from me on that score, yet at least on account, c.

structive! It teaches us the nature of true prevailing prayer. The prayer which gains its end is prayer which knocks till the door is opened, regardless of so-called decencies and proprieties, which seeks till it obtains, at the risk of being reckoned impudent, which simply cannot understand and will not take a refusal, and asks till it receives.

In the parable importunity is completely successful, and we see for ourselves that it cannot fail to be. The seeker has only to continue knocking to gain his point. That very love of comfort evinced by his neighbour, which constitutes the initial difficulty, supplies him with the sure means of achieving a triumph. But when we come to apply the parable to the case of prayer addressed to God, it appears to lack cogency as a persuasive to perseverance, for want of parallelism in the circumstances. The spirit of doubt will have no difficulty in evading the implied argument. It may say, "This parable certainly shows that importunity may prevail in very unlikely and discouraging circumstances. But the circumstances supposed cannot occur in the case of prayer addressed to the Divine Being. We can never have God in our power, as the petitioner in the parable had his neighbour; we cannot put God in a dilemma between granting our request and losing the thing which He values more than all else, viz. His own comfort or felicity. If God be really a Being who cares more for His own felicity than for man's good. One living high up in heaven a life of ease careless of mankind, it is not in my power to disturb His serene existence by any prayers of mine, however urgent. I may cry, but He does not hear, or hears as one who heareth not. He is too remote from this world to be disturbed by its noise, or to be interested in its concerns; He stands upon the vault of heaven and looks down calmly with His arm in His bosom, a passionless spectator of the tragedies and comedies of time. And my perplexity is to know whether this be indeed the character of Deity. To me it now seems as if it were; for I cry, and receive no answer: I knock, and no door of relief is open to me. And the parable does not solve my doubt, it simply leaves me where it found me." All this is perfectly true, and Jesus in effect admitted it to be so. For after uttering the parable He went on immediately to make a solemn declaration on His personal authority, on which, and not on the parable, rfe desired the tried soul to lay the stress of its faith: " And say to you, Ask, and it shall be given unto you; seek, and ye shall find; knock, and it shall be opened unto you." Jesus pledges His word that those who act in accordance with this counsel shall find the event justify it. The Kayo) with which the sentence begins is all the more emphatic that the v Tiv Xiyca which follows occurs for the second time here, being found in the previous sentence which forms the concluding part of the parable. One might have expected the emphatic personal pronoun to be used in the first instance rather than in the second. There must be a reason why the reverse is the case, and it is not difficult to discover. The first say to you is unemphatic because the statement which follows rests not on the Speaker's authority, but on the reason of things. Any intelligent person could say what Christ says there, for it is obvious to every one on reflection how the scene described must end. The man in bed must get up and serve his neighbour. But the second statement, to the effect that those who pray to God shall likewise be heard, rests absolutely on Christ's authority. It is not given as a fact which is self-evident, but as a fact which He, the Speaker, knows to be true. Therefore in this case He says, "And say to you, Ask, and ye shall receive." But it may be asked. If we are to take this momentous matter on Christ's word, why speak the parable at all, why argue; why not simply assert.- In reply we say. Because the parable is not good for everything, it is not therefore good for nothing. It serves at least to put doubting ones into better spirits, to cast a gleam of hope athwart the landscape, to induce them to pray on in spite of discouragements, until faith has surmounted her doubts, and come to see that God is not the selfish, indifferent, heartless One He seems, but what Jesus called him in the end of this lesson on prayerâ a heavenly Father.

From the sentence in which that blessed name is used we have already learned that throughout this lesson on prayer Jesus supposes the Holy Spirit, or personal advancement in spiritual hfe, to be the chief object of desire. Hence it follows that even that best gift is not given forthwith, though certain to be given eventually; an inference in entire accordance, it will be observed, with the teaching of the parable considered in the last chapter. It will be found, that is to say, in experience, that God, the Father in heaven, seems for a time unwilling to grant to those who seek first the kingdom even the very thing they above all things desire, viz. righteousness. There will be phases of experience in which it shall seem to disciples that they ask for bread and get only a stone,, or for fish and get a serpent, or for an egg and get a scorpion. The possibility or even probability of such experiences is implied in the simple fact that Jesus thought it necessary to refer to such hypothetical cases. It is because there are times when God seems to play the cruel part described that Jesus puts the questions: " If a son shall ask bread of any of you that is a father, will he give him a stone or if he ask a fish, will he for a fish give him a serpent or if he shall ask an g, will he offer him a scorpion " He knew that such dark thoughts concerning God lurked unavowed in even good men's hearts, and therefore He put them into words, in the hope that by bringing them into the full light of consciousness doubters might see it to be utterly incredible that God could do what even evil men are incapable of, and so be prepared 1 for accepting with cordial faith the argument a fortiori with which the doctrine winds up: "How much more shall your heavenly Father give the Holy Spirit to them that ask Him?"

THE UNJUST JUDGE.

And he spake to them a parable to the effect that it is necessary that they" should always pray, and not lose heart," saying, There was in a certain city, a certain judge, who feared not God, nor regarded man. and there was a widow in that cityj and she kept coming" to him, saying. Avenge me of mine adversary. And he was not willing for a time: but afterwards he said in himself, Thougji I fear not God, nor regard man; yet on acconnt of this widow causing me trouble, I will avenge her, lest at last, coming, she sttike me. ' And the Lord

Many MSS. have avrovg after â n-poati'xtadai. It is wanting in T. R.

lykOKHv, a Pauline word; 7'ide Eph. iii. 13; 2 Thess. iii. 13; Gal. vi. 9, c. VPx TO) t he imperfect.

The-words ti'c fi og may be connected either with tpx fiivrj or with vitionidly. The construction depends on the sense assigned to the verb. Vide exposition.

said, Hear what the judge of unrighteousness saith. And shall not God avenge His elect, who cry unto Him day and night, and He delays to interpose) in their cause? I tell you that He will avem e them speedily. Nevertheless when the Sofi of man cometh, shall He find faith on the earth? â LUKE xviii. 1â 8.

In this parable the Hearer of prayer is appropriately represented by a judge, not as in last parable by a private individual, the prayers which He seems to disregard being ex hypothesi addressed to Him by the collective body of His people in His capacity of Divine Ruler, exercising a providence and government over all. The present parable shows not less felicitously than the preceding the power of importunity to prevail even in the most discouraging situation. No situation could be conceived more unfavourable than the one depicted here, whether we regard the man who occupies the seat of justice or the individual who apjdears before him as a petitioner. The judge is described as one who neither fears God Almighty, nor regards men worthy of esteem, terms proverbially current among Jews and Greeks alike to denote a person of utterly unprincipled character. He is an unprincipled, lawless tyrant, devoid of the sense of responsibility and of every sentiment of humanity and justice. The picture is not an ideal one; there were such judges in those days; there are such judges in the same quarter of the world still, if we may trust a recent writer on Palestine, who, after describing the Pasha of Damascus as an obese, gluttonous, sensual, slothful, indifferent mortal, remarks, "It is the misfortune of Turkey that the majority of the governing class are men ignorant and fanatical, sensual and inert, notoriously corrupt and tyrannical, who have succeeded only in ruining and impoverishing the countries they were sent to govern." The judge of our parable is certainly a bad sample of a low kmd, for he not only is one who fears not God, nor regards man, but describes himself as such: " Though I fear not

There are two readings here: kox nakpodunujv, as in T. R., and rai liakpoqvuh, generally preferred by critics on such good grounds that I feel justified in adopting it. For further particulars vide exposition.

Bengel distinguishes the two verbs po oviim and ivrpttrofxai thus." Solemus ipofi-uadaipotentam, ivrpitriadai existimationem.

â For examples in Greek authors vide Wetsteia.

Conder, Tent-work in Palestine," i. p. 251.

God, nor regard man." ' It is true he says this not toothers, but to himself; but it is a sign of deep depravity that he can even go this length. Ordinary villains try to hide their character even from themselves, but this consummate villain with profligate frankness acknowledges to himself that he is quite as bad as other people think him.

He does not heed the evil opinion entertained of him by other men and by his own conscience; he promulgates its truth and laughs at it as a good joke. There could not possibly be a worse character, or a more hopeless tribunal than that over which such â a man presides. This judge you have no chance of influencing except through his self-love. If he can be made to feel that it will be more advantageous or less troublesome to do right than to do wrong, he will do right, but for no other reason.

The petitioner who appears before this corrupt judge is, prirnd facie, a very unlikely person to prevail with him. She is a friendless, destitute woman, too weak to compel, too poor to buy, justice; or to say all in a single word, a widow, who in the East was a synonym for helplessness, a prey to oppressors and knaves of every description, pious or impious, as many a pathetic text of Scripture proves. Witness that stern word of the prophet Isaiah against the degenerate rulers of Israel: " Thy princes are rebellious, and companions of thieves: every one loveth gifts, and followeth after rewards: they judge not the fatherless, neither doth the cause of the widow come unto them; " and that bitter, indignant word of Christ concerning the Pharisees of His time: " Ye devour widows' houses, and for a pretence make long prayers." 2 A widow was one who was pretty sure to have plenty of adversaries if she had anything to devour, and very unlikely to find any one on the seat of judgment willing to take the pains to look into her cause and to grant protection and redress. She is therefore most fitly selected to represent a petitioner for justice who has the

Weizsacker in the place already referred to mentions soliloquising on the part of the actors in the parables as another characteristic of the later parables of Luke's Gospel.

2 Isaiah i. 23; Matt, xxiii, 14. For some good remarks on the forlora position of widows in the East, vide Trench, pp. 492-3.

worst possible prospect of success in his plea, most fitly-chosen to represent the Church or people of God in their most forlorn plight, overborne by an unbelieving, godless world, and apparently forgotten even of their God.

Yet, as the parable goes on to show, there is hope even here. Desperate as the situation is, even a widow may find means of obtaining redress even from such a profligate administrator of injustice and perpetrator of iniquity under forms of law. Corrupt judges in the East, as elsewhere, may be influenced in three ways; by intimidation, by bribery, v and by bothering. The poor, friendless widow could not wield the first two m. odes of influence, but the third was open to her. She had a tongue, and could persecute the judge with her clamour until he should be glad to be rid of her by letting her have what she wanted. And this judge, profligate though he was, feared a woman's tongue made eloquent by a sense of wrong and extreme misery. He has experienced it before, and he knows what is possible. Therefore he thinks it best not to drive the widow to extremities, and gives in in good time. He is deaf to her entreaties for a while, too indolent to listen, perhaps accustomed to treat all complaints at first with apathy, and to wait till he has roused the furies, as mules sometimes refuse to start on their journey till they have been sufficiently thrashed by the driver. He waited till he saw the storm beginning to rise, the subdued, respectful tone of supplication rising into the shriller key and more piercing notes of impatience and passion. Then he began to say to himself, "I care nothing for justice; I am neith? r pious, righteous, nor humane; I regard solely my own pleasure and comfort; but this widow threatens to be troublesome; her reiterated entreaties have already begun to bore and bother me; I will give a verdict in her favour, lest at last she, coming, strike me." And so the widow gains her cause, not through regard to justice, but through the very love of ease which at first stood in her way.

It will be observed that in our free version of the judge's soliloquy, in which he prudently made up his mind to surrender, we have put a strong sense on the words vt; oitila(r xe, rendered in the English version " weary me." In doing so we are not guided simply by the dictionary sense of the verb, for it maybe rendered either way, but by what seems required by the situation. For we must hold that the word denotes something apprehended in the future worse than anything that has yet happened. Now the judge already feels bored. He assigns as a reason for granting the widow's request that she plagues or worries him with her demands. If, therefore, we render the term in question by some such mild word as 'weary' or tease, we get something like a tautology: She worries me; I will do her right, lest by her continual coming she annoy me. How much more expressive and characteristic to make the judge say, "She bothers me; I will do her right, lest at last she, coming, go the length of using her fist instead of her tongue." This rendering, therefore, we, with Bengel, Meyer, and Godet, decidedly prefer, preferring also what goes along therewith, the construction of ets ri'ko'i with the verb, not with the participle kpyo iivr, and rendering it not 'continually," as it requires to be in the latter case, but 'at length." To this rendering it may be objected that it is not credible that the judge really feared physical violence on the part of the widow. This is a very prosaic objection. For, as Godet observes, there is pleasantry in the word." The judge humorously affects to fear the exasperated widow's fists. There is also pictorial expressiveness in the word. Striking is the symbol of a passion that spurns all control,-which, however it manifests itself, whether by words or by blows, is the thing the judge really fears. The whirlwind of a passion roused to its height by a keen sense of wrong is a thing no man cares to encounter. As for the question of fact, whether such a passion could even at last lead to physical violence, it is one we do not care to decide very confidently in the negative. It is hard to say what a poor ' It occurs again in i Cor. ix. 27, where it clearly should be rendered ' beat." I beat my body as a boxer beats an antagonist.

Bengel says vtruiwini y, siiggilet. Hyperbole, judicis injusti et im-patientis personae conveniens. He adds: Hue refer, tiq AXoq, nam tpxoi ' est quasi 7raps Kov quo praetermisso sententia tamen quodamraodo integra est, quod tamen, adhibitum, orationem facit suavem, moratam, c. Field ('Otium Norv.") objects to this view that it demands the aorist of the verb instead of the present, because it points to a concluding act, while the present expresses continuous action.

II y a dans cette parole, une teinte de plaisanterie.

widow provoked beyond endurance by the unrighteous indiffcicnce of a judge, will do.

In the case supposed in this parable then, not less than in that supposed in the other, it is evident to every one that importunity must inevitably triumph. VVc are therefore prepared to pass on to the consideration of the ap)lication made by the Speaker to the case of a suffering Church praying to God, We observe that the evangelist introduces the epilogue by the formula, "And the Lord said." It is a formula of frequent occurrence in his Gospel, and it has attracted the notice of critics, especially in connection with the title 'Lord," used where the other evangelists wouh employ the name Jesus, and not unnaturally regarded as one of the traces in this Gospel of the influence of the faith of the apostolic Church on the mind of its author. Here the formula seems intended to mark the important character of the statement which follows. The evangelist is not content that it should come in simply as the conclusion of a parable; he desires it to stand out prominently as a substantive part of Christ's teaching. Looking then into this statement as one thus proclaimed to be of great importance, we find that the nota bene of the evangelist is fully justified. The application of the parable is in effect an argument ct fortiori. If even an unjust judge can be moved to grant redress to a forlorn widow, what may not be expected of a righteous God by those who stand to Him in the relation of an elect people, chosen out of the world to be the heirs of His kingdom."' They ought to feel assured that God will not allow His purpose in their election to be frustrated, but will certainly and effectively give them the kingdom, and so possess their soul in peace, though they be but a little flock in a wilderness swarming with wolves and ravenous beasts of every description. But unhappily the 'little flock," the 'elect' race, in their actual position are not able to appreciate the force of this a fortiori argument, because God seems to them the opposite of righteous, and the very idea of their election an idle, fond dream. Deep down in their hearts there may be a faith both in God's righteousness and in His gracious purpo."-. e, but it is a faith bewildered and confounded by the chaotic condition of the world, which seems incompatible with the reality of a moral order maintained by a righteous and benisrnant Providence. Thev are in a state of mind similar to that of the prophet Habakkuk when he penned those sublime words: "Thou art of purer eyes than to behold evil, and canst not look on iniquity: wherefore then lookest Thou upon them that deal treacherously, and boldest Thy tongue when the wicked devoureth the man that is more righteous than he? And makest men as the fishes of the sea, as the creeping things, that have no ruler over them? " The prophet was distracted by the glaring contradiction between his idea of God and facts. He regarded God as a Being who could not look on vith indifference while an iniquity was being perpetrated like that wrought by Babylonian tyrants, who threw their net of conquest into the sea of the world and drew whole nations as captives away from their native land; and yet God does actually look on, a passive spectator, while that very thing is being done to Israel, His elect people. Precisely similar is the state of mind of the 'elect," whom Christ has in view. For men in this mental condition the a fortiori argument suggested can have little force, for they stand in doubt of the very things on which the d fortiori clement rests: the righteousness or faithfulness of God, and the reality of the covenant relation implied in election. And Christ was perfectly well aware of this, and showed that He was by what He said. For He is not content, we observe, with merely asking the question, "Shall not God avenge His elect ones?" as if there were no room for reasonable doubt in the matter, or as if doubt were impious. He adds words which clearly show how sensible He is of the difficulty of believing in God's judicial interposition, in the circumstances. The added words contain three virtual admissions of the difficulty. The first is contained in the description given of the elect ones as a people in the position of crying unto God day and night, and of not being heard by Him. Such we take to be the import of the second half of the seventh verse, rendered in our version, " which cry day and night unto Him, though He bear long with them." We adopt the reading ixakpodvjxd, found in the chief uncials, and approved by the critics, as the more probable just because the less obvious, and we take it as depending not Â Habakkuk i. 13, 14.

164 The Pai'abolic Teacjiing of Christ, book i.

on ov ixt itoii (Tr, the construction required if we adopt the reading uakpoovixc v, but on tu)v (ioiovrooi'. The whole sentence from this point onwards is in effect a relative clause descriptive of the situation of the elect. Their position is that of persons "who cry to Him day and night, and yet He delays interposing in their cause " (e-n-' avrois).! The same meaning comes out if we adopt the other reading and construction. What is then said is, "Shall not God eventually avenge His elect, although He delays in their case, while they cry unto Him day and night.?" Thus on either reading or construction the words undoubtedly contain the thought that there is such a delay in answering prayer as is extremely trying to faith. The elect ones are in the position of David when he complained, "O my God, I cry in the daytime, but Thou hearest not; and in the night season, and am not silent."

The second admission of the difficulty of believing in God is contained in the asseveration which follows in the ne? t verse: " I tell you that He will avenge them speedily." It is very significant that Jesus deems it necessary to make this strong assertion. It is evident that He relies more for the inspiration of faith into doubting spirits on His own personal assurance than on the a fortiori argument. It is a repetition in effect of the emphatic " I say unto you" in the former parable. It is one seeking by the emphasis with which He ' For the suggestion that fiatcpoovfiu is dependent on jsowvrwv I am indebted to Dr. Field, who kindly communicated his opinion in a letter to my colleague, Dr. Douglas, Principal of the Free Church College, Glasgow. Dr. Field's view of the whole passage, since published in 'Otium Norvi-cense," is the same as that given above. In support of the use of the verb liak(t, 9vfiti in the sense of delay (moram facere) he refers to Ecclus. xxxv. 18, and aho to the following passage in Chrysostom's works: o k otkTeipu TO yvvaiov (the Syroph. woman) awa nukpobviiil, (3ov 6niroq rhv Xavodvovra Oijtavpvv tv Ttj yvvaiki Kardst ov litraai Troirjitai. â Opp. T., iv. p. 45 â Ed. Ben. The solution of the grammatical dil culty is at once simple and satisfactory, and it is confirmed by the reference made by Dr. Field, and introduced in the text, to the experience of David, expressed in very similar terms. The passage in Ecclus. is still more closely parallel. It runs, "For the Lord will not be slack ov kÂ 7 jipacvv-g), neither will the Mighty be patient towards them " ovli 1x7) ixakpoovfiliitri tir' avrolg â said with reference to the prayers of the poor). Dr. Field proposes this translation of the clause: " Who cry unto Him day and night, and He deferreth His anger on their behalf."

declares His own belief to communicate faith to other minds, even as David sought to inspire courage and hope in the breasts of his brethren by the hearty counsel " Wait, I say, on the Lord." We must bear this in mind in interpreting the closing expression of this declaration, speedily' (ev Tax O- If, as some think, the phrase signifies'soon,"'without delay," it must be understood rhetorically, not as a prosaic statement of fact. In any case the exclusion of delay implies delay, the excuse implies that there is ground for accusation. The Speaker means to say that whatever delay there may have been in the past, there will be no further delay. But we doubt whether the phrase is thus correctly rendered. It means, we think, not soon, but suddenly. L" So taken, the expression conveys a truth which we find elsewhere taught in Scripture, viz. that however long the critical action of Divine providence is delayed, it always comes suddenly at last, "as a thief in the night." Slow but sure and sudden at the crisis, such is the doctrine of Scripture as expressed in the proverbial phrase just quoted, in reference to the action of God in history. It is a doctrine confirmed by the historic records of nations, as exemplified in the case of Israel herself, whose awful doom, foretold by ancient prophets and long delayed, at last overtook her literally like a thief in the night. It was probably to this very doom impending over Israel that Jesus referred when He said, "I tell you that He will avenge them

That this phrase does not necessarily exclude delay in the future any more than in the past appears from the final words, which contain the third implicit admission that there is much in the experience of God's people to try their faith in His righteousness and love. " Nevertheless when the Son of man cometh, shall He find faith upon the earth?" The question amounts to an assertion of the negative. It does not mean that there will be no Christianity, no piety in the earth or in Palestine when the Son of man comes to judge the enemies of His gospel and to vindicate the rights of His Â Godet also takes h ra'x" in the sense of suddenly, "non bientot mais bien vita."

Bengal on apa finely remarks: magnum rfio habet, oratione negante per interrogationem temperata.

followers. It means that the faith in demand, the faith He wishes to inspire, faith in God's providence, will have all but died out in the hearts even of the godly, even of the elect-So long will the Judge delay His coming, that it will come to this. What an ample admission of trial involved to faith in God's peculiar manner of acting in providence! And there is no exaggeration in the statement. It is often the case that God's action as a deliverer is delayed until His people have ceased to hope for deliverance. So it was with Israel in Egypt; so was it with her again in Babylon. "Grief was calm and hope was dead " among the exiles when the word came that they were to return to their own land; and then the news seemed too good to be true. They were " like them that dream " when they heard the good tidings.

This method of Divine actionâ long delay followed by a sudden crisisâ so frankly recognised by Christ, is one to which we find it hard to reconcile ourselves. These parables help us so far, but they do not settle everything. They contain no philosophy of Divine delay, but simply a proclamation of the fact, and an assurance that in spite of delay all will go well at the last with those who trust in God. It is very natural that we should desire more, that we should seek the rationale of the mystery so strikingly expressed in those words, "One day is with the Lord as a thousand years, and a thousand years as one day." Why is the Divine temper so calm that He can regard events when they happen as we regard those which happened a thousand years ago, and yet so impulsive that at the end of a thousand years He acts as suddenly and hotly as we men do when our purposes are just freshly formed in our hearts Unbelief will reply, Because God is simply a synonym for a stream of tendency which silently moves on like the river Niagara till it approaches its natural consummation, when it makes its mighty plunge, to the astonishment of all spectators. Christians cannot accept this solution. They must find a way of reconciling delay with the reality of a Divine purpose, and with the gracious-ness of that purpose. And it is not impossible to find such a way. Delay is not incompatible with grace. It is simply the result of love taking counsel with wisdom, so that the very end aimed at may not be frustrated by too great haste to attain it." Men must be prepared for receiving and appreciating the benefit God means to bestow on them, and delay is an important element in the discipline necessary for that purpose. The child cannot at once enter on its inheritance; it must be under tutors and governors in order that it may at length enjoy and rightly use the freedom to which it is destined.

On a certain occasion Jesus said to His disciples, Which of you is there, having a servant ploughing or feeding cattle, who will say to him on his returning fro7n the field, Go straightway and sit down to meat t And will not rather, on the contrary, say to him, Make ready wherewith I may sup, and gird thyself and serve me till I have eaten and drunken; aiid after that thou shall eat and drink f Doth he thank the servant because he hath done the things commanded him f J trow not So likewise ye, when ye shall have done all the things commanded you, say, We are unprofitable servants: we have but) done that which it was our dtity to do. â Luke xvii. 7â 10.

Little or no help in the interpretation of this parable can be got from the previous context. There is no apparent connection between it and what goes before, and it would only lead us out of the track which conducts towards its true meaning to endeavour to invent a connection. Critics who are ever on the outlook for traces of tendency in the Gospels tell us that the parable and the two preceding verses are connected by the Pauline bias of both. As in these two verses Jesus, in true Pauline fashion, teaches the omnipotence of faith to disciples who had asked Him to increase their share of that grace, so in the parable He inculcates the not less

The ilq'imQ is to be taken-with wapikdhjv following, not as in A. V,, with Ipii going before. Bengel truly remarks that whatever the master said He would say it at once, so that tvo'sug is superfluous as joined to iptl.

3 The words ov Soicw are omitted in some MSS., probably by mistake of the transcriber through similar ending (airy iokQ).

Pauline doctrine of the insufficiency of works. We will not deny that the Pauline character of these two sections may very possibly have been what chiefly interested the evangelist's mind, and led him to introduce them into his narrative in juxtaposition. In that case, if we were bound as expositors to have supreme regard to Luke's motive as a reporter, we should have to relegate the present parable to the second head in our classification of the parables, and to treat it as a parable of grace, designed to teach that in the kingdom of God all is of grace, and not of debt, or that merit in man before God is impossible, the key-note of the whole being the closing words, "We are unprofitable servants." But we do not feel bound to adopt as our clue the private feelings of the evangelist. It is quite conceivable that what chiefly interested his mind in reporting the parable was its bearing on the doctrine of salvation, and that nevertheless the purpose of our Lord in uttering it was more comprehensive in its scope. As the Spirit of God often meant more by a prophecy than the prophet was aware of, so Christ might mean much more by a parable than an evangelist was aware of. In this sense there is truth in the remark of Mr. Matthew Arnold, that Jesus was over the head of His reporters.

It will be best, therefore, to lay little stress either on the external connections of the narrative or on the supposed private thoughts of the narrator, and to regard this parable as a precious fragment which Luke found among his literary materials, "at the bottom of his portfolio," as a recent commentator expresses it, and which he put into his Gospel at a convenient place that it might not be lost. If by this mode of viewing it we lose the benefit of a guide to the sense in the context, we have a compensation in the reflection made by the same commentator, that the very fragmentariness of this precious morsel is a guarantee of its originality as a genuine logion of Jesus.

What then is the doctrinal drift of this striking fragment On the surface it wears a harsh and, if one may venture to 1 So Hilgenfeld, ' Einleitung." 2 Godet.

' Schleiermacher tries to make out a connection between vers. 5, 6, and 7â 10. He thinks it was quite natural that, after saying that faith would enable them to do all things required of them, Christ should go on to cach that they were not to expect outward stimuli and privileges as a reward. Uber die Schriften des Lukas," p. 154.

7 say so, unchrist-like aspect. It seems to give a legal, heartless, inhuman representation pf the relations between God and man, and of the nature of religion. God appears as an exacting taskmaster or slave-driver, who requires His servants, already jaded with a full day's toil in the fields, to render Him extra household service in the evening, before they get the food and rest which their bodies eagerly crave. And the Master is ungracious as well as unmerciful. He doth not thank His weary slaves for their extra service in the form of attendance at table, but receives it as a matter of course. Then, finally, those servants are required to submit to this merciless and ungracious treatment without complaint or surprise, as quite right and proper; nay, they must even go the length of making the abject acknowledgment that in all their toil, day and night, they have been unprofitable servants, and at most have done no more than their statutory duty. Now we may be sure that if we could only penetrate to the heart of our Lord's meaning, we should find it to be thoroughly like Himself, and thoroughly consistent with His other teaching. It is indeed a strange, hard saying, but it is not the only hard saying which fell from His lips; and just because it is so strange we may be sure it really was spoken by Him; and just because it was spoken by Him we may be sure that, like many other of His sayings, with a very hard shell on the outside, this saying has within the shell a very sweet kernel. Let us try to break the shell and to get at the kernel.

Some interpreters of note have sought an escape from the difficulties of the parable by finding in it not a prescription, but a (fscription, of legal religion. We are told, that is, not how we ought to serve God, but how men of a legal spirit, hirelings, mercenaries, such as the Pharisaic Jews, do serve God, and how their service is estimated by God. The parable is in fact a picture of the kind of religion which Jesus saw around Him. Religious people were acting like men hired to do a certain work, in return for which they were to receive their meals. They did their 'duty," the things expressly enjoined, in the spirit of drudges rather than in the generous spirit of devotion, and their work so done was of little value, and not deserving of thanks: they really were unprofitable servants. And such men are pointed at as persons not to be imitated. Jesus says in effect, "Be ye not like these; serve God in a different fashion, and ye shall receive very different treatment. Men of servile, mercenary spirit God treats as slaves; serve God liberally, and ye shall be treated as sons." On this view the parable teaches the same lesson as the parable of the labourers who entered the vineyard at different hours of the day, in Avhich those who entered in the morning and did a full day's work, and bore " the burden and heat" of the day, are represented as being paid last, and without any thanks; while those who entered at the eleventh hour are paid first, as if the master had pleasure in paying them, and are paid as much as those who had worked the whole day. Another expedient for getting out of the difficulty, proposed by a different class of expositors, is to suppose that the parable teaches not how God does deal with any of His servants, but how He might deal with all. He might treat all in justice as worthless slaves; but that He does not we know, not indeed from this parable, but from other places of Scripture. The object of the parable is not to set forth the whole truth about God's relations to men, but merely to negative the idea of human merit, and to beat down human pride. Neither of these interpretations hits the mark. The one errs in assuming that the parable has no application to the devoted servants of the kingdom; the other in assuming that the parable gives us no information as to how God does deal with men; In opposition to the former, we believe that the parable has truth for all servants of the kingdom, especially for the most devoted; and in opposition to the latter, we believe that it teaches not how God might act, but how He does act with His servants; in other words, that it shows a real phase of the actual experience of the faithful in this present life. They are treated in providence as the parable represents. Jesus spake the parable to the twelve, as the future apostles of Christianity, to let them know beforehand what to expect, and so to prepare them for their arduous task.

We believe then that the purpose of this parable is neither by implication to condemn servile religion, nor to inculcate humility for its own sake; but to set forth the exacting character of the demands which the kingdom of God makes

So Grotius. So Trench, controverting the view of Grotiu.

â n its servants, and to inculcate on the latter humility only that the work of the kingdom may be better done, and may not be hindered by self-complacency. We take the extra aervice of the slave in the parabolic representation to be the. key to the interpretation, and assume that Christ meant to suggest that something analogous to such extra service will be found in the Divine kingdom. On this reasonable assumption, the direct object of the parable will be to teach that the service of God, nay, of Christ Himself, is a very exacting and arduous one; much more arduous than human indolence cares to undertake; far exceeding in its demands the ideal of duty men are prone to form for themselves. Christ would have His disciples understand that the Christian vocation is a very high one indeed; that for those who give themselves to it, it not merely brings hard toil in the fields through the day, but also, so to speak, extra duties in the evening, when the weary labourer would fain be at rest; that it has no fixed hours of labour, eight, ten, twelve, as the case may be according to agreement, but may summon to work at any hour of all the twenty-four, as in the case of soldiers in time cf war, or of farm labourers in the season of harvest, when the grain must be secured when weather is propitious. He would have His disciples lay this to heart, that they may be on their guard against impatience when they find, in the course of their experience, that new demands of service are made upon them beyond what already seemed a fair day's work; and against such a self-complacent satisfaction with past performances, however considerable, as might indispose tliem for further exertion.

Such being the drift of the parable, there is of course no intention revealed in it to represent God in an ungracious light. Christ's purpose is not to teach in what spirit God deals with His servants, but to teach rather in what spirit we " should serve God. Doubtless the language put into the master's mouth does convey the impression that the demand for additional service arises out of a despot's caprice rather than out of a real necessary occasion. But any one acquainted with our Lord's method of teaching knows how to interpret this sort of language. Christ was ever very bold in His representation of God's apparent character, knowing as He did that God's real character could stand it, and knowing well also what a hard aspect the Divine character sometimes wears to our view. As in the parables last considered He drew pictures of a selfish neighbour and an unjust judge, meaning these to represent God as He appears to His people when He delays answers to their prayers; so here He depicts God not according to the gracious reality of His character, but according to the stern facts of Christian life. As on other occasions Jesus spake parables to teach that men ought always. o pray and not faint, showing how importunity would ultimately prevail; so here He speaks a parable to teach that men ought always to work and not faint, schooling themselves into a '-spirit of severe dutifulness which yields not readily to weariness, nor is prone to self-complacent contentment with past attainments and performances, seeing that such a spirit is demanded by the course of providence from all who serve the Lord.

The doctrine implied in our parable, that the kingdom of God makes very exacting demands on its servants, is not one that will startle any one familiar with our Lord's general teaching. How many words He uttered bearing the same import! "Seek y first the kingdom of God." "Let the v dead bury their dead, but go thou and preach the kingdom of God." " If thou wouldst be perfect, go and sell that thou hast, and come and follow Me." " He that loveth father or mother more than Me is not worthy of Me: and He that loveth son or daughter more than Me is not worthy of Me." These are hard sayings; so hard that we are strongly tempted to exercise our wits in polishing off their sharp angles, in discovering some way by which, without setting them aside as Utopian, we may ease their pressure on the conscience. One way of doing this was very early found out. It was to convert those sayings of Christ, which seem to require renunciation of property and abstinence from domestic ties, into "counsels of perfection," as distinguished from positive commandments obligatory on all. Let all who would be perfect, who would take honours, so to speak, in the Divine kingdom, part with their property and practise celibacy. It is not necessary to do these things in order to have admission into the Divine kingdom; but those may do so who choose, and if they do it will be put to their credit. As for the common herd of Christians, all they need to mind is the keeping of the commandments of the Decalogue in their plain, obvious sense. In this way Christianity was made easy for the multitude, and those who went in for a higher style of piety had the pleasure of thinking that they were doing more than was commanded, and were therefore very far indeed from being unprofitable servants. Voluntary poverty and celibacy were the extra service after the day's work of commonplace morality and religion was over, and, as such, received a higher rate of payment, in the form of praise and honour in earth and heaven.

A most ingenious and plausible theory, but not true. Monkish asceticism is not the extra service of the Christian life. The over-time duty consists rather in extraordinary demands on God's servants in exceptional times and unusual emergencies; when Christian men, already weary, must continue to work though sentient nature demands repose; when old men, who have already served God for many years, cannot enjoy the comparative exemption from toil which their failing powers call for, but must toil on till they die in harness; when liberal men, who have already given much of their substance for the advancement of the kingdom, are called on to give still moreâ it may be to give their all; when young men have to renounce the felicity of domestic life " for the kingdom of heaven's sake," that they may be free from family cares and find it easier to bear hardship when it is restricted to their own person, and falls not upon any loved ones. In ordinary circumstances such extra service may not be called for. The servant after he has done his day's work may at once sit down to meat and enjoy rest; the veteran soldier may retire on a pension; the man of wealth may retain his means; the young man may many. But when the emergency arises which calls for extra service, then the extra service is obligatory on all. That such emergencies do arise every one knows. Extreme emergencies, times of persecution, for example, are rare; but minor emergencies are frequent; in fact, it may be said that to every Christian there come opportunities which test his patience and his obedience: times when, if he be half-hearted, self-indulgent, or self-complacent, he will say, "I have done enough;" but when, on the other hand, if he be of a dutiful mind, he will say, "I may not look on the things which are behind, or speak of past performances; my Master bids me gird myself for further service, and I must run at His call."

We can now see how appropriate is this parable as a representation of an actual experience in the life of godliness. The parable is true at once to natural life and to spiritual life. In societies where slavery prevails the slave is treated as the â parable representsâ as one who has no rights, and who therefore, do what he will, can be no profit to his master, and can have no claim to thanks. The assertion implied in the phrase " unprofitable slaves," so far from being an exaggeration, is rather a truism. The emphasis is to be placed on the word "â slaves: they are unprofitable because slaves; unprofitableness is a matter of course in a slave. And as slaves deserve no thanks, they receive none; and so long as they are slaves in spirit it is best they should not. This may seem a harsh statement, but we can cite a curious illustration of its truth from a recent book of African travel. The writer, giving some of his experiences in connection with his servants, says, "Afterwards when travelling with Arabs I found that we had treated our men with too much consideration, and they in consequence tried to impose on us, and were constantly grumbling and growling. Our loads were ten pounds lighter than the average of those carried for the Arab traders. And since they do not employ askari (soldiers, servants, donkey-drivers), their pagazi (porters), besides carrying loads, pitch tents and build screens and huts required for the women and cooking, so that they are frequently two or three hours in camp before having a chance of looking after themselves. With us the work of our porters was finished when they reached camp, for the askari pitched our tents, and the task of placing beds and boxes inside was left to our servants and gun-bearers."

The parable may be transferred to the spiritual sphere with one important exception. It is not needful or desirable that the servants of the kingdom be treated in the thankless manner in which Arab traders deal with their slaves. For God's servants are not slaves in spirit, they are free men, and their

Lieutenant Cameron," Across Africa," vol. i. pp. 107, 108.

service springs out of entirely different motives fronn those which influence slavish natures.

And this observation leads us to notice the temper needful in order to compliance with the exact demands of the kingdom. Of what spirit must they be who shall prove themselves capable of rising to the heroic pitch when called on?

Two virtues at least are indispensable for this purposeâ patience and humility. Patience, lest when the demand for ' new service comes we be unwilling to respond, and so either refuse the service or do it in a grudging humour; humility, lest we think too highly of what we have already done, and so be ignobly content with past performances and attainments. Of the two vices, impatience and self-complacency, the latter is the more to be feared. There is doubtless in all a tendency to grow weary in well-doing; but when the sense of duty is strong the temptation will be resisted. The word of God will be like a fire in the bones, and will make it impossible to refrain from action. But the spirit of self-complacency is specially to be feared just because its tendency is to drug conscience, deaden the sense of duty, lower the very ideal of life, and make us think we have done exceeding well when we have done very indiff'crently. There is no enemy to all high attainment so deadly as self-satisfaction. On the other hand, and for a similar reason, there is nothing more favourable to progress than a humility which expresses itself thus: " We are unprofitable servants." This may seem servile language, not fit to be used by a spiritual freeman, however humble. But it is not servile language. It is true of slaves that they are unprofitable, but it is not true of them that they confess themselves to be such, except it may be by way of a mere facon de parler. It is only the freeman who makes such a confession, and in the very act of making it he shows himself to be free. And whence springs this confession of the free, self-devoted spirit? Is it out of an abject sense of personal demerit, or an exaggerated sense of Divine majesty? No, but rather out of a sense of redemption. It is a deep sense of Divine grace which makes a man work like a slave, yet think little of his performance. The French have a proverb noblesse oblige, which means that rank imposes obligations; so that a true noble does not require to be told his duty, but is a law unto himself. In like manner, it may be said of a true Christian that the consciousness of redemption obliges, grateful love constrains, taxes energies, time, possessions very heavily; has the greatest possible difficulty in satisfying itselfâ in truth, never is satisfied; makes one work like a slave, refusing to be limited by hours and fixed measures and proportions, and yet pronounces on all actual performances the verdict, 'unprofitable," 'nothing to boast of And thus it appears that our parable, though on the face of it ignoring or even denying the gracious character of God, and turning Him into a slave-driver, has for its unseen foundation the very grace which it seems to deny. Nothing but a belief in Divine grace can make it possible for a man to work with the devotion and the temper required of him by the service of the kingdom. A legal relation between God and man never could achieve such a result, never could make a man in spirit and conduct a hero. Legal relation can make men unprofitable servants; but it cannot make them supremely profitable, yet all the while so humble that they can honestly think and call themselves unprofitable. That moral phenomenon in which the extremes of devotion and modesty meet can be found only where God is conceived of as a God of love, freely giving, not severely exacting; in the lives of men like Paul and Luther, and the genuine offspring of their faith. Said we not truly at the commencement, that if we could only break the shell of our parable we should find it contain a very sweet kernel The implied doctrine is that the kingdom is a kingdom of grace, and that devotion is the cardinal virtue of its citizens; a devotion rendered possible by the grace of the kingdom, and necessary by its imperial tasks.

THE HOURS, THE TALENTS. AND THE POUNDS; OR, WORK AND WAGES IN THE KINGDOM OF God.

The parable of Extra Service considered in the last chapter, when superficially viewed, makes, as we saw, the unpleasant impression that in the kingdom of heaven service is rendered to a thankless, unappreciative Master, who receives all work done for Him as a matter of course, possessing no merit, and entitled to no reward. The hastiest glance at the three parables now to be studied suffices to show that this impression is a very false one. From these parables we learn that the kingdom of God is a kingdom of perfect equity; that the Lord of this kingdom is one who knows how to value and repay all faithful, devoted labour, and in all His dealings with His servants approves Himself to beat once just and generous; and that in this kingdom rewards are bestowed on principles which commend themselves to right reason as in entire accordance with the eternal laws of righteousness.

All three parables manifestly relate to the problem of Work. and Wages. Their common theme is the political economy of the kingdom. On this account alone they might fitly be made the subject of one connected study. But we have a better reason than this for taking them up together as forming conjointly a single topic. The parables do not merely bear upon the same general theme; they are mutually complementary, and constitute together a complete doctrine on the important subject of work and wages in the kingdom of God. To see this we have but to remember that three things must be taken into account in order to form a just estimate of the ethical value of men's work: viz. the quantity of work done, the ability of the worker, and the motive. Where ability is equal, quantity determines relative merit; and where ability varies, then it is not the absolute quantity of work done, but the ratio of the quantity to the ability, that ought to determine value. But however great the diligence and zeal displayed or the amount of work done may be, no work can have any real value in the kingdom of God which proceeds from an impure motive. In this world men are often commended for their diligence irrespective of their motives, and it is not always necessary even to be zealous in order to gain vulgar applause. If one does something that looks large and liberal, men will praise him without inquiring whether for him it was a great thing, a heroic act involving self-sacrifice, or only a respectable act, not necessarily indicative of earnestness or devotion. But in God's sight many bulky things are very little, and many small things are very great; for this reason, that He seeth the heart and the hidden springs of action there, and judges the stream by the fountain. Quantity is nothing to Him unless there be zeal, and even zeal is nothing to Him unless it be purged from all vainglory and self-seekingâ a pure spring of good impulses, cleared of all smoke of carnal passion; a pure flame of heaven-born devotion. A base motive vitiates all.

Each of the three parables now to be considered gives prominence to a distinct element in this complex doctrine of moral value. The parable of the Pounds illustrates the pro- ' position that where ability is equal quantity determines relative merit. In this parable each servant receives one pound, but the quantity of work done varies; one servant with the one pound gaining ten, while another gains only five. In right reason the rewards ought to vary accordingly, and so in fact they do in the parable. The first gets ten cities to govern, the second only five. Not only so, but, what is more remarkable, words of commendation are uttered by the master in addressing the first servant which are not repeated to the second. To the former he says, "Well, thou good servant, because thou hast been faithful in a very little, have thou authority over ten cities;" to the second no praise is given, but only the bare commission, Be thou also over five cities."

The parable of the Talents, on the other hand, illustrates the proposition that when ability varies, then not the absolute quantity of work done, but the ratio of the quantity to the ability, ought to determine value. Here the amount of work done varies as in the parable of the Pounds, but the ability varies in the same proportion, so that the ratio between the two is the same in the case of both servants who put their talents to use. One receives five and gains five, the other receives two and gains two. In right reason the two should be held equal in merit, and so they are represented in the parable. The same reward is given to each, and both are commended in identical terms; the master saying to each in turn, "Well done, good and faithful servant; thou hast been faithful over a few things, I will set thee over many things: enter thou into the joy of thy Lord."

The purpose of the parable of the Labourers in the Vineyard, or, to use a briefer expression, the parable of the Hours, is to emphasise the supreme importance of iwtive as a factor in determining moral value, It teaches in effect that a small quantity of work done in a right spirit is of greater value than a great quantity done in a wrong spirit. One hour's work done by men who make no bargain, but trust to the generosity of their employer, and who seek by ardent devotion to make up for lost time, is of more value than twelve hours' work done by men who regard their doings with self-complacency, and who have laboured all along as hirelings. That this is the drift of the parable will appear more clearly hereafter; meantime we content ourselves with briefly stating our opinion, our present purpose being to point out how, on the hypothesis that the view just given is correct, the parable of the Hours completes the doctrine of Christ concerning the relation of work to wages in the kingdom of heaven, by setting forth that not the quantity of work done alone, nor even quantity combined with zeal, but above all things quality, pure motive, right affection, determines moral value.

The fact just pointed out, that the three parables before us constitute together a complete doctrine on the subject of rewards, suffices to settle the question as to the originality and independence of these parables; to prove, that is, that they are three distinct parables, and not two. The question concerns the parables of the Talents and the Pounds, for the originality and distinctness of the parable of the Hours is not disputed. It is held by many interpreters that the two former parables are siinply different versions of one and the same parable, opinion being divided as to which of the two comes nearer to the original form as spoken by Jesus. The most plausible view is that of those who maintain that Matthew's version approaches nearest to the primitive form, and that Luke's parable is simply Matthew's transformed, and combined with another parable about a king and his subjects, which was spoken at a different time, and appears in Luke's narrative only in a mutilated state. With all deference to the learned commentators who treat the two parables as one which had assumed two different forms in the course of tradition, we must express our firm belief that they are two, spoken by our Lord on different occasions and for different purposes. That the parables are very similar we do not deny; we will even admit that they are simple variations on the same theme. But they are, in our judgment, variations originating with the Master Himself, not due to the blunders of reporters, or to the modifying influence of inaccurate tradition. And we base this judgment on the remarkable manner in which the three parables as they stand fit into each other, and together form

This is the vie y of Unger. He thinks that the image of the king and his subjects does not agree with the remaining image, either in itself (princeps enim bellum gesturus, et negotiatores porro, hi atque urbium prasfecturce, minus congruunt) or in illustrating the matter in hand. He makes an attempt at restoring the mutilated parable of the king and his subjects. The king goes to a distant land, to return afterwards a(3t iv I3a(ji eiaÂ he thinks belongs only to the story, not to its meaning). He commits his kingdom to his servants; to one more, to anotber fewer cities. The citizens rebel. On his return he takes account or his vicegerents, and gives them power accordingly.â 'De Parabolarum Jesu natura," p. 130. Among more recent writers who concur in this view are Strauss, Bleek, Ewald (who also attempts to construct the lost parable somewhat differently from Unger), and Meyer, and to a certain extent Reuss in 'Histoire Evangelique." Calvin also held that the parables of the Pounds and the Talents are essentially one. Matthew he thinks MOf-e suo inserts this parable among others, neglecting the order of time, which he supposes to be given by Luke.

So also Schleiermacher, who regards the inequality of endowment as an essential feature of the one parable, and equality of endowment as an equally essential feature of the other.â Uber die Schriften des Lukas."

a complete doctrinal whole. It is not by accident or blundering that variations arise which fit so well to each other and to the didactic significance of a third parable. Such fitness bears witness to a single mind in which the three parabolic representations took their origin, and formed together a whole. In saying this we but apply to these parables the well-known argument of design. Even as the theist in enforcing the teleoli. g'cal argument maintains that by the adaptations of the different parts of an organism to each other, and of the whole organism to its environment, he is constrained to rise above the action of chance or mere mechanism to a designing mind, in which the idea of this organism pre-existed, and by which its function was pre-determined; so we, having regard to the indubitable fact that these three parables as we find them in the Gospel records do form as it were an organism of thought on the subject to which they relate, feel constrained to conclude that they owe their origin not to the accidents of tradition, but simply to the fact that they constituted a unity in the mind of the Great Teacher, and were each and all spoken by Himself as occasions occurred.

While maintaining with some measure of confidence that these parables form a didactic whole, and on that ground asserting their originality, we do not therefore feel justified in asserting that the sole design of the Speaker in each case was simply to make a contribution to a scientific doctrine on the subject of work and wages in the Divine kingdom. Had Christ been animated by a purely theoretic interest, He might have uttered all three parables at one gush, as all bearing on one theme, and have taken care so to construct them that they should all be strictly confined to one topic, and serve only one end. But such was not His way as a teacher. He was never guided by a purely theoretic or scientific interest; His utterances, however capable of being systematised, were not systematic in method, but occasional; and the motive to speech being often not simple, but complex, the words spoken frequently served more than one purpose. So it was in the case of these parables. They were in all probability spoken at different times, to different audiences, and from mixed motives, and were meant to teach not one truth only, but several; and not merely to teach, but to warn, admonish, comfort, stimulate.

Having regard to these facts, we will not pursue what might be called the scientific order in studying our parables, which would require us to consider first the parable of the Talents, then that of the Pounds, and lastly that of the Hours; setting forth in connection with the first the function of ability in determiningf value, in connection with the second the function of diligence, and in connection with the third the function of motive. We will rather take them up in the order in which they occur in the evangelic records, which may with some degree of probability be regarded as also the order in which they were delivered, beginning with

THE LABOURERS IN THE VINEYARD; OR, THE SUPREME VALUE OF MOTIVE IN THE DIVINE KINGDOM.

For the kingdom of heaven is like unto a man that was an householder who went out early in the morning to hire labourers into his vineyard. And when he had agreed with the labourers for a denarius a day, he sefit them into his vineyard. And goiftg out about the third hour, he saw others standing idle in the market-place, and said unto them; Go ye also into the vineyard, atid whatsoever is right I will give unto you. And they went their way. Again going out about

This statement applies chiefly to the parables of the Talents and the Pounds.

On such questions it is unsafe to dogmatise, but there seems no good reason to doubt that Matthew gives us the parable of the Hours in its proper historical connection, though some have been led to think otherwise by the difficulty of finding in the parable an illustration of the saying, "Many that are first shall be last, and the last first" (Neander, Bleek, Reuss). There seems also good reason to regard the other two parables," from their contents, as belonging to a later time; and of the two, Matthew's is probably the earlier, though it is brought in by him at a later period. This is the opinion of Schleiermacher, who thinks that the parable of the Talents cannot be regarded either as an imperfect understanding of that of the Pounds, or as a remodelling by Christ Himself of the latter on a later occasion. The contrary he thinks the more natural. He thinks, further, that the parable in Matthew xxv., where it stands, does not suit the connection. The probability, according to Schleiermacher, is that Christ, on an unknown occasion, spoke the parable of the Talents, in which unequal endowment was an essential feature, and then took it up again, introducing the noteworthy difference of equal endowi-ment.â Uber die Schriften des Lukas."

the sixth and the ninth hour he did likcivise. Bid go in s: out about the eleventh hour, he found others standing, and saitli to tjiein, Why stand ye here all the day idle? They say unto him, Because no man hired us. He saith unto them, Go ye also into the vineyard and whatsoever is right that shall ye receive)? So when even was cotne, the lord of the vineyard saith unto his steward, Call the labourers, and give them their hire, beginning from the last unto the first. And when they came that were hired about the eleventh hour, tliey received each a dettarius. But when the first came, they supposed that they would receive more; and they likewise received each a detiarius. A nd having received it, they inurmured against the goodmati of the house, saying, These last wrought but one hour, and thou hast made them equal unto us, who have borne the burden of the day and the heat. But he answered one of them, and said. Friend, I wrong thee not: didst not thou agree with me for a denarius? Take up thine, and go. It is my pleasure to give to this last even as to thee. Is it not lawfcl to do what I will with mine own f Or is thine eye evil, because I am good? So the last shall be first, and the first last for many be called, but feiu chosen). â Matt. xx. i â 16.

The 'for' with which the parable is introduced connects it with the saying with which the previous chapter concludes, and plainly implies that the parable is, in the view of the evangelist at least, an illustration of that saying. This connection supplies us with a clue to the interpretation of the parable whereof we stand much in need; for in truth the parabolic explanation of the saying immediately preceding is harder to understand than the saying itself. Apart from the parable, there would probably have been a tolerable amount of agreement as to the meaning of the moral apophthegm. The idea it naturally suggests is that of a change of places between those who in a certain respect are first, and those who in the same respect are last. The first in one respect become last in another, the last taking their place and becoming first. The respect in which the reversal of position takes place is sufficiently clear from the connection in which the saying was spoken by Jesus. Peter had asked the question. Behold, we. have forsaken all, and followed Thee; what shall we have

The best MSS. omit apyovq here.

â A doubtful reading, omitted in R. V. and by Westcott and Hort.

' apov TO ahv. The verb imphes either that the money had been laid down by the steward to be taken up by the labourers, or that it had been thrown down by the latter in disgust. The former is the view of Morrison, ihe latter of Greswell.

tnerefore? and had received a very inspiring answer to the substance of his question, to this effect: They who make sacrifices for Me and My cause shall receive an hundred-fold of the things renounced, and in the world to come eternal life. But the spirit of Peter's question required an answer too. It was a spirit of self-consciousness, self-complacency, and bargain-making, and a faithful master could not allow such a spirit to appear in his disciples without a warning word. The warning word is to be found in the saying which forms the motto of our parable. " But," said Jesus, as if with upraised finger, and in a grave, monitory tone, " many that are first shall be last, and the last shall be first;" manifestly meanings to hint, Think not that the mere fact of having made a sacrifice, or even a great sacrifice, for the kingdom necessarily insures the great reward I have spoken of: all depends on the spirit in which sacrifices are made; and it is possible for one who is first as to the extent of his sacrifice to be last in the esteem of God and in the amount of reward, because his sacrifice is vitiated by the indulgence of a mercenary, self-righteous, self-complacent temper. A small sacrifice made in a right, i. e. a humble, self-forgetful, devoted spirit, is of more value in God's sight than a great sacrifice made in such a spirit as seems to have prompted your question.

Such is the meaning which one naturally puts upon the moral saying with which the nineteenth chapter of Matthew's Gospel closes, viewing it in connection with all that goes before. But when the reader passes on to the parable in the next chapter, which seems designed to illustrate that saying, he is tempted to doubt the correctness of his first impression. For what he finds on the surface of the parable is not a ": hange."' places, but an abolition of distinctions by putting all oa one level; not first ones in one respect becoming last in another, and last ones in the former respect becoming first in the latter, but first and last in respect of length of service becoming equal in respect of pay. This, we say, is what one finds on the surface; and the superficial aspect has misled many interpreters into the opinion that the design of the parable is to teach the doctrine that in the kingdom of God all shall be rewarded alike." But if that be indeed its design, ' So most recently Reuss in ' Histoire Evangelique." He thinks the then one of two things must follow. Either the parable as originally spoken by Christ stood in no connection with the proverbial saying in question, or that saying must be made to bear a different meaning from that which it naturally suggests. Not a few interpreters have felt themselves shut up to the adoption of one or other of these alternatives; those who adopt the latter putting upon the gnome this sense: the first shall be as the last, and the last shall be as the first; that is, first and last shall be alike, all distinctions of first and last shall disappear."

Either of these courses appears to us violent, and not to be followed except under direst compulsion. For our own part, we much prefer trying to bring the parable into conformity with the gnome as naturally understood, than to force upon the gnome a meaning which shall bring it into accord with the supposed didactic import of the parable. For of the two things, the import of the parable and the import of the proverb, the latter seems to us much the clearer. There is little room for doubt that the proverb points not at a levelling of distinctions, but at an exchange of places. Several considerations might be adduced in support of this position. In the first place, the word incmy is in its favour. " Many that are first shall be last." Why not all, if the purpose of the proverb be to teach the general truth that in God's sight the distinctions between men vanish into nothing." Does the term many not suggest the thought that what actually happens too often is what ought not to be; that it is a departure from the normal and desirable state of things due to the action of some disturbing cause; that if all things were as they ought to be, the first in respert of sacrifice would also be first in respect of reward; that in act there is no law in the Divine kingdom that all must share alike Then, secondly, it is only when thus understood that the saying has any relevancy to the question of Peter. The words are a pointless commonplace parable is not in its true place or setting, and that it is designed to teach the equality of Divine grace in face of the inequality of the human condition in respect of the gospel promisesâ diversity in hours of labour, but above all in the fact of a covenant in the case of one of the parties (the Jews).

' So Unger: per se probabiliter explicantur: postremi atque prinu pari loco erunt. Meyer takes the same view.

in the connection in which they stand if they signify, all shall be alike in respect of the reward; not to say that they are in manifest contradiction to the terms of the foregoing promise: for these are " shall receive an hundred-fold," an expression implying a proportion between the reward and the sacrifice. So manifest is the incongruity, that a recent commentator, who understands the saying when it recurs at the close of the parable as teaching the doctrine of equality, finds it necessary to invent a meaning for it in its first position different from either of those already indicated, to the following effect: Many who are first (in a worldly point of view) because they have not forsaken their goods, will be last when they lose salvation in Messiah's kingdom; while such as through sacrifice of all have become last (in a worldly point of view), will be first because they attain unto the highest salvation. That this is not the sense of the saying is proved by the simple fact that it is not introduced by a ' for' (yap), as a reflection confirmatory of the foregoing statement, but by a 'but' (8e), as a thought looking in a different direction, and qualifying the promise going before. The interpretation is interesting and valuable simply as showing what shifts men are driven to who, despairing of bringing the proverb into harmony with the parable following, desire at least to adjust it in some not quite intolerable manner to the conversation going before. Once more, in interpreting this striking saying we are entitled to attach some weight to the general ethical teaching of Scripture. Now one great thought we find running through Holy Writ, viz. that God giveth grace to the lowly, and knoweth the proud afar off; a truth of which we find many echoes in the teaching of Christ Himself, as in that word which closes the parable of the Pharisee and the Publican: " Every one that exalteth himself shall be abased; and he that humbleth himself shall be exalted." Here is taught just such a change of places as on first thought we found in the saying now under consideration; and our second and final thought concerning that saying is that our first impression was right, and that in it we ought to find a moral reflection kindred to that illustrated by the parable of the Pharisee and the Publican, and

Weiss, ' Das Matthaus-Evangelium," p. 441, â Luke xviii. 14.

in sympathy with that vein of moral doctrine which more than all other doctrines pervades the Scriptures, to the effect that God's favour is in proportion to man's humility.

We regard it as a settled point then, that what the apophthegm points to is not a levelling of distinctions, but an exchange of places, by which the first in the amount of service and sacrifice becomes, through pride, or vainglory, or self-seeking, last in the esteem of God; and what we have now to do is to ascertain by careful examination whetlier the parable cannot be brought into harmony with the saying thus understood, so as to serve as an illustration of the doctrine that quality, not quantity, determines the value of work in the Divine kingdom.

I. First we must fix our attention very closely on the 'householder; as we may find that to understand him is the. nearest way to an understanding of the parable. This man is no ordinary employer of labour; by no means the first man of the kind you happen to meet. Before the kingdom of heaven can be likened to a man who possesses a vineyard, the man has to be assimilated to the kingdom; and the man in the parable has actually been so assimilated. Such men as he may possibly be found among this world's employers of labour, but they are rare; men like the gifted author of a charming tractate on political economy, which takes its title from a sentence in our parable, and which has for its burthen that in the business relations of men you cannot without fatal results ignore the social affections, and for its unconscious scope to turn the commercial world into a kingdom of God. Our householder is not of this world, any more than Plato's republic, nor are his ways the ways of the world, or likely to be approved by the world, but rather certain to be found fault with; as in point of fact they are represented as having been found fault with by the parties who were most closely related to him, who doubtless thought they did well to be angry. Were such a man to appear among us, he would probably give similar offence to parties similarly related; and to the outside world he would, in all likelihood, appear aji ccccjitric Jmniorist, to be laughed at rather than to be imitated. And this judgment would not be very much to be wondered at.

Unto This Last," by John Ruskin.

Fv r in truth our householder is a humorist, and his ways are in some respects very peculiar. Two peculiarities especially are notable in his character. One is, that besides hiring men in the ordinary way, and at the ordinary time, to work in his vineyard, he now and then takes it into his head to go at an advanced time of the day in search of labourers, v; benevolent motives; not for his own advantage, but for the advantage of those who have the misfortune to be unemployed. For what other motive could move any one to go to the marketplace at the eleventh hour, when the working portion of the day was about to close? What evidence is there that in this procedure our householder followed ordinary usage."' Commentators have been able to cite from books of Eastern travel passages proving that the parabolic picture of an employer of labour going out in the morning to hire labourers, is in accordance with Oriental custom. But we have not met anywhere with anything tending to prove that the quest of workers at the close of the day is in accordance with the customs of any part of the world. The learned Lightfoot indeed quotes certain phrases from the Talmud which he thinks may tend to throw some light on this feature in the parable. The Tal-mudists distinguish between persons hired for the day, and persons hired for so many hours, and they direct hirers of labour to note whether those to be hired come from various places; for, say they, there are places where people come earlier to work, and other places where they come later. The author of the Horse Hebraicae' suggests that the fact referred to in this last observation may serve to explain how there came to be persons in the market-place to be hired at such different times of the day. But in any case, the fact stated cannot explain the hiring of workers at the eleventh hour, for it is not credible that it was the custom of any place to begin work at so late an hour; and besides, both the question of the master addressed to those then hired, and their reply, imply that they had been present in the market-place

Trench quotes ' Morier's Travels in Persia' to this effect, p. 177, note.

2 Distinguunt canones Hebraeorum de conducendis operariis, prout ratio postulat, inter conductos in diem, et conductos in horas quasdam.

' Observanduin an veniant ex locis variis; sunt enim loca ubi citius ad opus pergitur, et sunt ubi serius.

all the day, ready to work for any one who engaged them. The compassionate tone of the master's question suggests the true explanation of his conduct. Not custom, and not need of more labourers, but pity for the idle moved this eccentric. landlord to go at the eleventh hour in search of new labourers. The very manner in which this part of the narrative is introduced, reveals a purpose on the part of the Speaker to signalise the action of the master as something peculiar and exceptional, indicative of a moral characteristic deserving attention. The sentence begins with the adversative particle (6ej, as if to say, Note especially what follows, and consider well what it imports as to the character of the chief actor.

The other peculiarity of our householder is that he seems to attach importance not so much to the work done as to the spirit in which it is done. He delights in the spirit of grateful devotion, and he abhors with equal intensity the spirit of envious, selfish calculation. The parable supplies evidence of this assertion. The master's abhorrence of the mercenary spirit comes out very clearly in his reply to the murmuring of those first hired, in which every word breathes indignation and disgust. But not less truly, though less obviously, does the narrative reveal the action of an opposite feeling of delight in the spirit of uncalculating devotion. For, to this feeling in the breast of the employer we must ascribe the fact of his paying the last hired first, and also the fact of his paying them a full day's wage. The commentators indeed endeavour to rob both facts of all moral significance. As to the former, one commentator tells us that the expression, "beginning from the last unto the first," signifies: No order being observed among them, but so that no one may be omitted. Others assure us that the sole reason why the last are paid first, is that the first hired might observe what was done, and have their expectations awakened. But they forget that the motive leading the Speaker of the parable to tell His story in a certain way is one thing, and the motive of the actor in the

So Olshausen, with his usual insight: " Less out of need than out of pity for the idle, did the true Hausberr from time to time call new labourers into his vineyard." Similarly Goebel says: " An unusual proceeding, which shows that the master is concerned not merely about the amount of work, but about employing as many as possible." 2 Grotius. So Calvin and Bleek, parable is another. It may be that the Speaker's reason for telhng the story as He does is, that He may be able to exhibit a certain class of workers behaving in a particular way. But the landlord must be conceived to act from a motive of his own, all unconscious of the use that is to be made of his action to point a moral. And what could his motive be but a desire to manifest special interest in those who, having come into the vineyard at the close of the day, must have cherished very humble expectations as to what they were to receive, although they had done their best during their one hour of work to show their grateful appreciation of the master's kindness? And if this was indeed his motive, then the action was not so insignificant as some would have us believe. In itself, to be paid first was a small advantage to the last hired; too small to bear the chief stress in the illustration of the principle: the last first, and the first last. But the paying of the last first was a very significant circumstance as an ivdcx of-ihe master's mitid, for in that connection we have to consider not merely the action itself, but what it may lead to.

The significance of the other fact above alluded to, the paying of the last hired a full day's wage, cannot well be denied; yet here too some commentators seem bent on making the householder's action appear as commonplace as possible. Greswell, for example, adduces from Josephus, doubtless as the result of much learned research, what he regards as an instance of similar payment made to the builders of the temple by King Herod. The words of the Jewish historian are to the effect: If any one worked one hour of the day, he received straightway the reward of this; which our commentator interprets to mean that he was paid a whole day's wage for one hour's work. There is reason to believe that he has made a 1 Morrison refers to Lofler, author of a monograph on this parable, published in the early part of last century, as suggesting that the words of the murmurers concerning the last hired, osrot o taxaroi fiiav iopav ttrojjaav, are meant to convey the idea that their work was not worthy to be called work, but was a mere consumption of a little time. This is not probable, as the verb was quite commonly used to denote working for so long. But in any case, the bitter remark of. envious fellow-workers cannot be taken as a reliable statement of fact.

Â The passage cited is from Antiq. Jud.," xx. ix. 7, and is as follows:â cat yap li liau nt upav rrjc; t'lfispaq tipydaaro, tov fiiaqov imp raiitijg ivqkws mistake in rendering the Greek, and his mistake is due not to any want of scholarship, but to a perverse desire to bring the action of the owner of the vineyard into harmony with ordinary practice. An instance must be found of similar conduct, and the needful example is discovered in the most unlikely quarter. Who can believe that Herod would act so generously towards the builders of his temple; and what rational being, however generous, would make a habit of paying one hour's work with a whole day's wage; a habit which, as Alford well remarks, could only have the result of preventing work from being done.-â What egregious errors learned and ingenious men fall into when they miss the track of true interpretation! That track, in the present instance, does not lead in the direction of making our householder as like other people as possible, but rather in the direction of recognising boldly and decidedly his peculiarity and originality, or, if you will, his eccentricity. He chooses for a reason of his own to pay one hour's work with a whole day's wage. And what is hiÂ ' reason It is not benevolence, at least not exclusively; for he does not seem to have intended it at first, for when he engaged those who entered the vineyard at the eleventh hour, he said to them, as to the others, "Whatsoever is right, that shall ye receive." The reading here, it is true, is doubtful; but the omission of the words may be due to a desire to remove an apparent incongruity between the terms of engagement and the actual payment made at the end of the day. And even if, in deference to the canons of criticism laid down by the highest authorities, we regard the clause as an expansion by copyists, we may assume that it expresses correctly th;5 understanding on which the late-hired workers were allowed to enter the vineyard. The master seems to have decided to pay the last a whole day's wage after seeing them at work. The heartiness of their endeavours pleased him much, and he was in the mood to bestow on them an amount of pay out of all proportion to the amount of work done, paying them not so much for their work as for their good will.

"An eccentric man, most unlike other people, and by no means to be imitated!" Yes; but how like is this man, with l a i aviv. Greswell thinks that the use of 6 fnaqoq absolutely requires it to be understood of the wages of a day.

his strange humours, to the Divine Being as depicted by the sweet singer of Israel: " With the raerciful Thou wilt show Thyself merciful; with an upright man Thou wilt show Thyself upright; with the pure Thou wilt show Thyself pure; and with the froward Thou wilt show Thyself froward. For Thou wilt save the afflicted people; but wilt bring down high looks." How true to this poetic picture of God is the character of our householder in the parable! He, too, is froward with the froward. How sharp and curt his words to the grumbling churls. " Friend, I wrong thee not: didst thou not agree with me for a penny Lift thine, and go;" the last words accompanied, we may imagine, with an imperative wave of the hand. Then how good he is to the meek, the afflicted people who had hung about all day in the marketplace till they had become utterly disheartened because no man had hired them, and who work during the last hour like men mad with joy! His conduct towards them well entitles him to apply to himself the august title ayaq6i? For whereas he had promised at first merely to do what was just (bikutov), or at least abstained from giving any hint of a purpose to do more, he far exceeds the limits of justice, and rises to the level of heroic benignancy and magnanimity.

Such then, according to our reading of his character, were the characteristics of the householder in our parable; characteristics not only admirable, but useful, if the possessor's chief aim in life were the culture of right affections in those about him. For benevolence tends to produce in its objects gratitude, and grateful devotion generously rewarded rises to still higher heights of devotion. But if the possessor's chief aim in life were the culture of gj apes, these characteristics, however admirable, are not so obviously useful. For in that case chief importance must be attached to the work, not to the spirit of the worker; and it may be as well not to be too sentimental, lest the indulgence of good feeling breed disaffection in men who, however defective in temper, have

Psalm xviii. 25â if.

' The use of the word here (ver. 15) supplies the best evidence possible that it really represents a different idea from Sikaiog, which Jowett in his work on the Epistle to the Romans disputes; vtwe remarks on the meaning of ayaoSg at page 35- Bengel's remark on ayaoog is: qui etiam plus preestat quam justitia (ver. 4) infert.â Rom. v. 7.

nevertheless proved themselves good workers, and borne well the burden of a long day, and the scorching heat of a broiling sun. Manifestly it is right affections rather than grapes that v' this householder is mainly concerned about, and it is this peculiarity which fits him to be an emblem of the kingdom of God.

2. Having ascertained with tolerable certainty the character of the householder, we shall find little difficulty in proving that the aim and effect of the parable is to illustrate the supreme importance in God's sight of motive as a measure of value. Two objections may be taken to this view. First, that the parable itself contains no trace of

right motive in those who are favoured; and, second, that all receive the same sum, whereas the supposed design of the parable requires that the last should be not merely put on a level with the first, but placed above them.

Now as to the former of these objections, it is true that the parabolic representation contains no express allusion to the existence of right feeling in the last hired, or to the influence of such feeling on the master's conduct. But was such express mention really necessary? That such feeling existed goes without being said. It was probable, natural, almost inevitable in the circumstances. Then we must assume its existence in order to render the master's conduct intelligible and reasonable. Reasonable, we say; for although this householder was from the world's point of view eccentric, he was not foolish. He must be assumed to have acted from motives thoroughly rational, regarded from his own point of view. But if we assume that his action had no relation to the state of mind of those whom it concerned, then it ceases to be rational, and becomes purely arbitrary. But surely it is not Christ's intention to represent the principal actor as arbitrary, though He does make him use language which has a sound of arbitrariness in rebutting the pretensions of unreasonable men, when He puts into his mouth the question, "Is it not lawful for me to do what I v. all with mine own.?" We cannot, therefore, Â To 3apoc TÂ jc 7ficpac signifies the labour of the whole day; rhv Kav(T(ova the intense heat of the middle portion of the day. Yer. IS The force of this question is increased if we insert the i) at agree with the opinion expressed by a respected c(mmentator, that "when we rise above the particular sphere of ideas with which the parable deals the quality element of character comes iiito account; but the parable itself does not hft us into this sphere, it leaves us simply in the sphere of the negative ideas that the time consumed in working and the quantity of work performed do not determine absolutely the amount of glory that shall be enjoyed." It seems to us plain that the parable does lift us into this sphere. The principal actor in the parable rises into this sphere, and has his being in it, and he lifts the parable itself and all the subordinate actors therein along with him. In order that the situation may suit his character, we must assume that the first and last hired represent two classes of men morally distinct: the first being the self-complacent and calculating;. the last the humble, self-forgetful, trustful, grateful. The ' first are the Simons, righteous, respectable, exemplary, but hard, prosaic, ungenial; the last the women with alabaster boxes, who for long have been idle, aimless, vicious, wasteful of life, but at last, with bitter tears of sorrow over an unprofitable past, begin life in earnest, and endeavour to redeem lost time by the passionate devotion with which they serve their Lord and Saviour. Or, once more, the first are the elder brothers who stay at home in their father's house, and never transgress any of his commandments, and have no mercy on those who do; the last the prodigals who leave their father's house and waste their substance in riotous living, but at length come to their senses and say, "I will arise and go to my father," and having met him, exclaim, "Father, I have sinned, and am no more worthy to be called thy son."

The other objection to our view of the parable may also be disposed of without much difficulty. It is true that all receive the same sum, the denarius, which was the ordinary pay for a day's work in those times. But this fact is not fatal to the view that the purpose of the parable is to illustrate the truth that diversity of spirit may cause men to change places, so that the first in the amount of work or sacrifice shall be the beginning of the sentence found in many MSS. It then means, Do you dispute what I had thought was indisputable? Morrison, ' Commentary on Matthew," in loc.

last in the reward, and vice versa. In making this assertion we do not insist either on the fact that the last were paid first, which in itself is of no great moment, or on the fact that the last were paid at a far higher rate than the first, which nevertheless deserves serious consideration; but simply on this, that the point of importance is not what each received at the end of the day, but the will of the master manifested in making payment, and what that will involved and must lead to. In the sentence " I will give unto this last even as unto thee," the part to be accentuated is not the " even as," but the "I will" (eaoo eyo)). The denarius is not the centre of the story, as some have imagined, but the will of him who gives it to each of his labourers. The denarius is not a fixture for that will; equality of payment is not a lav by which it is bound. The master might have given more than the denarius to the last, but he sufficiently asserted his freedom and sovereignty in giving so much; and there was a certain appropriateness in fixing on the particular sumâ it was a day's wage for an hour's work. And then it must be remembered that the master's will is not limited in its action to one day. It is so limited in the parabolic representation, and hence the illustration of the apophthegm with which it begins and ends is necessarily defective; for one day is too short to exhibit fully the action of the forces which the parable sets in motion. But the master's will will burst the bonds of to day, and act to-morrow, and produce results in advance of those of to-day. The murmurers of to-day will not be employed at all to-morrow unless they change their mood; for the ominous "Go thy way" is in reality an order to quit the service, and the last-hired of to-day will be morning workers to-morrow; working in an altoge"her different spirit from the murmurers of yesterday. And so at length the last shall be first, and the first last, to a degree not visible within

The use of the future (fvovrat) in the repstition of the apophthegm at the close of the parable is worthy of notice. One would have expected rather, So the last in this case were first. May the reason not be that the parable shows a process of reversal begun, but not finished, and pointing into the future for its consummation? It cannot be said that the sentence is merely a repetition of the one at the close of the previous chapter, and that therefore the tense of the verb has no significance. It is not a case of exact repetition, for the important word â kowox is omitted. This the narrow space to which the parabohc representation is confined.

It only remains to add that no parable could possibly supply an adequate illustration of the action of the great moral law enunciated by Jesus in the close of His reply to Peter's question, for the results therein pointed at are realized only gradually, through the slow but sure operation of tendencies. In making this remark we have in view such fulfilments of the law as fall within our observation in this present life. We do not of course mean to limit the operation of the law to this life. The question has been much discussed by commentators, What does the denarius denote Does it refer to the life eternal, or to something experienced in this world? In our way of looking at the parable the question is not of such cardinal importance as some suppose. But if we must answer it, our reply is, The denarius denotes what ever comes under the category of reward, and that, as we see from our Lord's own words to Peter, embraces both the life eternal and experiences of this present life. And we believe that the law, the last first and the first last, applies to the eternal as well as to the temporal side of the reward. We do not believe in the equality of men's conditions in the life to come any more than in the life that now is. The general felicity of the life eternal common to all the saved will embrace much variety of special condition corresponding to the spiritual histories of individuals: some will receive a full reward, others a less ample recompense; and then, too, it will be seen that some last ones will take precedence of some who in this life were reputed to be first. But of the life to come and its conditions our thoughts are dim, and we are perplexed when we attempt to apply to eternity the graduated distinctions of time. The category of the absolute dominates all our thoughts of the eternal world. We think of the good as absolutely good, and of the evil as absolutely evil, and of the blessedness and misery of the two classes as admitting of no degrees. Therefore it is easier for us to understand thf application of the law to this present life, where the distinction omission is made to adapt the saying to the parable; so also is the inversion of the clauses. Why then was the tense not changed for the same purpose, so that the sentence might stand, Thus the last in the parable became first, and the first last?

of good and evil is relative, and where the action of spiritual law reveals itself in the form of tendencies. Under this form we may confidently expect to find every law, valid for the eternal world, exercising its influence unceasingly. For with respect to the action of moral law, the two spheres, the eternal and the temporal, are virtually one. As the blue sky, is but the omnipresent atmosphere projected by the eye to an indefinite distance in space, so the eternal judgment is the incessantly active moral order of the world, projected by the conscience fo an indefinite distance in future time. This general obseivation applies in full force to the law now under consideration. It is a law amply illustrated in history. In the parable the will of the householder has a very narrow platform on which to exhibit itself, but God's will has the whole history of the world in which to display its purposes. The moral order of the world serves that will, and unfolds to view its contents. And to a wise observer the a. v7, first last and last first, can be seen slowly but certainly fulfilling itself both in individuals and in communities. It is possible even to classify the cases in which the first tend to become last. The law fulfils itself in such cases as these: when those who make sacrifices for the kingdom of heaven manifest the spirit of self-devotion in occasional acts rather than in a fixed habit; when any particular species of Christian activity has come to be in fashion, and therefore in high esteem among men, involving consequently temptations to vanity, spiritual pride, and presumption; or when, as in the case of the ascetics, self-denial is reduced to a system practised, not for Christ's sake, but for its own sake. When we consider how much Christian activity comes under one or other of these heads,â occasional spasmodic efforts, good works in high esteem in the religious world, and good works done, not so much from interest in the work, as from their reflex bearing on the doer's religious interests,â we must feel that Christ did not speak too strongly when He said many that are first shall 6e last. Far from charging His language with exaggeration, we rather admire its moderation in virtually admitting that there arc exceptions. Exceptions unquestionably there arc.

â For more extended observations on this topic, vide The Training of the Twelve," cap. xvi. sec. 3.

There are some first ones who shall not be last; and there are some last ones who shall not be first. If it were otherwiseâ if to be last in length of service, in zeal, or in devotion gave one an advantage invariably and of course, it would be ruinous to the kingdom of God; as in effect putting a premium on indolence and encouraging men to stand all the day idle. But it is not so. It is no advantage in itself to be last, and it is no disadvantage to be first. The first in sacrifice may also be first in reward; the Church's noblest ones are men who have been first in both respects. But the number of such is comparatively few. " For many are called, but few are chosen," Many, that is,â for so we, with Ben gel and others, understand the reflection wherewith the parable concludes,â many are called to work in God's vineyard, and many are actually at work; but few are choice workers, few work for God in the spirit of the precepts taught by Jesus; with ardent devotion, yet with deep humility.

Taking the householder in this parable, benevolent towards those whom no man had hired, and showing favour to those who gratefully appreciated his kindness, as a type of God, the lesson taught by the parable is that God is a God of grace, and that He giveth His grace to the lowly. The lesson is a perfectly general one, susceptible of many historical illustrations,-no one of which is entitled to be regarded as the one principally intended. Some think the parable refers especially to the case of the Jews and the Gentiles; the Jews being

The words in question are of doubtful authority, and Calvin thought they should be omitted. If retained they must bear the meaning given to them in the text, as the only one in harmony with the connection of thought. It is the sense put on the words by Bengel, Grotius, Unger, Olshausen, c. Bengel says: Ikkiktoi exquisiti prse aliis. Videtur hoc loco ubi primum occurrit, non omnes salvandos denotare, sed horum excellentissimos, Grotius observes that the Greeks also used the word ikkiktov to denote what is distinguished in anything (to igapsrov), and quotes as a parallel saying, ttoxXoi jutv vaporjko opot, iravpot Sk re (cikxoi, Kuinoel, who adopts the same view, cites as a parallel sentiment from, Virgu: Pauci, quos asquus amavit Jupiter, atque ardens evexit ad sidera virtus.â ' n.," vi. 130. Olshausen says the icxjrot are all workers, even the TTpojToi. The ikXixroi are the taxaroi, who occupy a freer position to the kingdom, and work out of inner pleasure and love. Arnot, who takes the same view, refers to Rev. xvii. 14 for a similar use of the word ikxikto'i, where the Lamb's followers are spoken of as K tjtoi kqi Lexi Kroi Kai itKJToi; picked men, spiritual heroes so to speak.

represented by the men hired in the morning, the Gentiles by tjie men engaged at the eleventh hour. It has been suggested by others that the parable primarily relates to grudges within the circle of disciples on the part of the first called against those called at a later period. Such suggestions are legitimate and useful when they are put forth simply for the purpose of exemplifying the operation of a principle, but they ought not to be regarded as exhausting the scope of the parable.

THE TALENTS; OR, EQUAL DILIGENCE IN THE USE OF
UNEQUAL ENDOWMENTS EQUALLY REWARDED
IN THE DIVINE KINGDOM.

For the kingdom of heaven is as a man travelling into a far country who called his own servants, and delivered unto them his goods. A nd 1171 to one he gave five talents, to aitoiher two, and to another one; to every man according to his several ability j and then he took hisjonrney. Then he that had received the five talents went straightway and traded with the same, and made other five talents. And likewise he that had received the two, he gained other two. But he that received the one we? it away and dug in the earth, and hid his lord's money. And after a long time the lord of those servants cometh, and reckottetk with them. And he that received the five talents came and brought other five talents, saying, Lord, thoti deliveredst unto me five talents: behold, I have gained five talents more. His lord said ujito him, Well done, thou good and faithful servant: thou hast been faitliful over a few things, I will set thee over many things: enter thou into the joy of thy lord. And he also that j-eceived the two talents came and said, Lord, thou deliveredst unto jne two talents: lo, J have gained other two talejtts. His lord said unto him, Well done, thou good and faithful servatit: thou hast been faithful over a few things, I will set thee over many things: enter thou into the joy of thy lord. Then he also that received the ojie talent came and said, Lord, I knew thee 'â So Weizsacker, ' Untersuchungen," p. 429.

â There are no words in the original answering to those within brackets. We may fill up the hiatus either as in the A. V. or, as some prefer, the return of the Son of man 7vill be, so connecting the parable closely with the previous verse. The formula of the A. V. is to be preferred, js it takes nothing for granted as to the historical connection.

8 Rather into a foreign country, leaving his own.

â Vide further on for justification of this arrangement of the words.

â This does not signify a change of sphere, as in the parable of the Pounds (from-traders to rulers), but advancement within the same sphere. The rendering in the A. V. betrays the influence of the other parable.

that thou art an hard man, reaping where thou didst not sow, and gathering where thou didst not scatter: and I was afraid, and went away and hid thy talent in the earth: lo, thou hast tliine own. But his lord answered and said unto him. Thou wicked and slothful servant, thou knewest that I reap where I sowed not, and gather where I scattered not: thou oughtest therefore to have put triy money to the bankers, and at my coming I should have received back my own with interest. Take the talent from him, and give it to him who hath the ten talents. For unto every one that hath shall be given, and he shall have abundance: but from him that hath not shall be taken even that wliich he hath. And cast ye out the unprofitable servant into the outer darkness: there shall be the weeping and the gnashing of teeth. â Matt. xxv. 14â 30.

The alternative title above indicated is not proposed as an exhaustive statement of the didactic significance of the parable of the talents. The parable manifestl)'" springs out of two motives, and we run no great risk of too much, subtlety in our analysis if we represent it as the outcome ot three. It teaches these three distinct if not equally im portant truths concerning work for the kingdom of God:â 1. The consummation of the kingdom will be long enough deferred to leave ample time for work.

2. The kingdom imperatively demands work from all it? citizens.

3. The work done will be valued and rewarded according to the principle above enunciated: equal diligence in the use of unequal endowment receiving an equal reward.

I. Certain features in the parable seem intended to teach that there will be time to workâ to work as well as to wait?-The chief points bearing on this topic are the following:â â a) The householder travels into a far country, and returnsi not till after a long time The phrase is an elastic one, and may denote either a large portion of the life of an individual, or an age in the history of the world. We now naturally put the latter interpretation on the words, but it 1 Trench has some good remarks on the affinities and contrast between this parable and that of the ten virgins (Matt. xxv. iâ 12), the object of which is to inculcate the duty of watching and waiting. As we deem it un-i desirable to be over-confident as to the historical connection, we refrain from indulging in a similar line of reflection, while sensible of its fruit-fulness in edification, itrd TToxiij'-j i ovovf ver. 19.

is probable that they suggested the former sense to the first hearers of the parable." Even on the narrower interpretation they contained an important hint to those who belonged to the first Christian generation. The mind of that generation was fixed, with an intensity which we have difficulty in conceiving, on the second coming of the Lord; and some seem to have expected that event so soon that they abandoned all worldly business, and gave themselves up to an attitude of passive waiting, or to feverish, restless excitement. The demoralising effect of the belief in the near approach of the second advent manifested itself to such an extent in the Church at Thessalonica, that the Apostle Paul found it needful to interpose, and to endeavour by seasonable counsels of Christian wisdom to bring the fanaticised community to a soberer state of mind. The sum of his advice was, Work, and do not merely idly wait. The disease and the remedy are admirably hit off in a couple of verses: " We hear that there are some which walk among you disorderly, working not at all, but are busy-bodies. Now them that are such we command and exhort by our Lord Jesus Christ, that with quietness they work, and eat their own bread." Nowhere does the apostle's good sense appear more conspicuously than in his manner of dealing with the spiritual malady that had broken out in that community. We know not whether he was acquainted with our parable when, at an early stage in his apostolic career, he wrote his Epistles to the Thessalonians, but in any case he was in full sympathy with the mind of Christ as revealed in the parable. For by the use of the suggestive phrase after a lo7ig time Jesus significantly hinted just what Paul afterwards more plainly said: that the day of the Lord would not come so soon that there would be no use setting oneself deliberately to any task; that, while ever watching, disciples must also ever cultivate a sober temper, and give themselves earnestly to Christian work, as if all things were to follow their wonted course till the end of their lives.

b) There will be time enough, according to the parable, for diligent servants to double the capital entrusted to them.

' Olshausen says the phrase does not exclude a return of the Lord ia Cie time of the apostles.

â 2 Thess. iii. ii, 12. â Vers. 16, 17.

How long that process may take depends on circumstances; it may be a year, or it may be well on for a lifetime. But beforehand the longer period is more likely than the shorter one; and a prudent trader who starts with a capital equal to about a thousand pounds sterling will think of such a substantial increase only as the result of a long-continued course of industry.

if) The lapse of a considerable period ere the master's return is implied in the absence of all reference to a speedy return in the excuse of the slothful servant. It may be taken for granted that that servant would have been glad to excuse himself in a less impudent way if he could. He could not but know the risk he ran in speaking of one who had absolute power over him, to his face, as he did, calling him an hard man, reaping where he had not sowed, and gathering where he had not strawed; in other words, as an arbitrary, exacting tyrant, who expects his servants to perform impossible tasks; to make bricks without straw, to produce a harvest of results where he had not supplied them with the seed out of which such a harvest might naturally grow. It was not in wanton recklessness that he thus spoke, but because nothing more plausible in the way of excuse occurred to him at the moment. How gladly would he rather have pleaded, I was just about to begin to work when your arrival took me by surprise; I did not expect your return so soon; or, I did not think it worth while to begin trading, for I knew that you would return so soon that there would be no time to buy and sell and make gainâ that is to

The value of a talent was in round numbers about Â 200, so that five talents would amount to about; iooo.

' It is doubtful whether the two parts of this proverbial saying employed to describe a curmudgeon mean the same thing or different things. Trench paraphrases the second clause, " gatherest with the rake where others have winnowed with the fan," thus finding in it a reference to threshing. Weiss is of the same opinion; also Olshausen. It seems likely that the proverb contains reference to two forms of keen dealing: one drawn' from reaping, another from winnowing. So viewed it has a greatly intensified strength.

3 The fact that such an excuse is not represented as being advanced is used by Schleiermacher as an argument to prove that the parable is not in its proper historical place. He thinks if the parable had been spoken to enforce the duty of watching, such an excuse would have been put into the mouth of the unprofitable servant.

say, make the very same excuse for idleness with which the rehgious busy-bodies of Thessalonica justified to their own consciences their neglect of the ordinary duties of their calling.

2. The second lessonâ that the kingdom imperatively demands work from all its citizensâ is taught by several outstanding features of the parable.

a) First we note the minute but significant touch about the servant who had received five talents proceeding straightway to trade with the money lent him. For we cannot but agree with those interpreters who think that the adverb (ev ecos) is to be taken along with the verb following (Tropei' ets), rather than with the verb going before (aitâ h ixr aev). By this arrangement the word is charged with immensely increased significance. To what end say of the master that he Straightivay took his journey.- It has been suggested that the end served is to convey the idea that the lord gave no further instructions how to use the money, but left his servants to use the talents according to their own discretion. But to this it has been effectively replied that the clause "to each man according to his ability" rendered that unnecessary; and, moreover, that in that case the idle servant would have referred to the fact as an excuse. On the other hand, take the ehdms along with what follows, as even visage requires us to do, and how full of important meaning it becomes! It then teaches the great lesson of urgency and promptitude. It says to us. The demands of the kingdom are very pressing; to work then at once without delay; to be prompt in action is a cardinal virtue in the kingdom.

(d) The rigour with which the unfaithful servant is judged

We do not make a point of the fact that the talents were given to trade with, for that is not said in this parable, though a similar statement is made in Luke's parable of the Pounds. But in reality what is not said is implied in the nature of the case. The talents were not gifts to friends, but loans to slaves, who belonged themselves to the master, and traded solely for his benefit. Such a procedure as the parable supposes was in accordance with custom.

2 Ver. 16. "So Meyer.

Weiss, ' Matthiius-Evang. Fritsche takes the same view of the verbal connection.

Weiss points out that in Matthew (v9iote always stands before the verb which it qualifies.

points in the same direction. The epithets applied to him arc very significant in this connection. He is called wicked (â r: ov) p6s), slothful (oki'rjjo?),! and wiprofitable (axpetos). The fn-st epithet refers not so much to the injurious opinion expressed by the unfaithful one of his master, as to the unrighteousness of his conduct in not following a course that was open to him, even if all he said of the master were true. So far as mere personal feeling is concerned, the master can bear to be evil thought of and evil spoken of. He calmly repeats the injurious, insolent words, and instead of complaining of them, or being roused to indignation by them, or endeavouring to show how unfounded they are, he proceeds rather to point out what the servant ought to have done if he believed his own opinion of his master to be true. It is the interest of the work, not the personal insult to himself, that the lord thinks of when he calls his slave wicked. It almost seems as if he felt that there was something, if not to justify, at least to excuse the unfavourable opinion of himself cherished by the servant. He knows there is that about his requirements which may not unnaturally wear an aspect of hardness to certain men, especially to those who have received small endowments; nay, even to those who have been most liberally endowed. And his very tolerance of hard thoughts is another index of the exacting demands of his service. There is just one thing he cannot tolerateâ waste of opportunity, keeping his money lying idle, neglecting to make the most of things, sloth, unprofitableness. Mere indolence is in his view wickedness, for it is selfishness, and selfishness, as the moral opposite of that self-devotion which is the cardinal virtue of the Divine kingdom, is to the Lord of the kingdom the very essence of evil.

Then observe, as another index of rigour, the declinature to sustain any excuse on the part of the unprofitable servant. If a servant fear his master's anger in case he lose his money in some unfortunate venture, and on that account shrink from running ordinary business risks, he must find out and follow some other method of turning his capital to account. He may not content himself with digging a pit in the earth and burying his talent there, where it will be safe at least, if not Â Ver. 26. Â Ver. 30.

in the way of making increase. If the master is to be regarded as a hard man, he must get the benefit of his bad character, and his money must be laid out to usury at least, if it is not to be employed in commerce. This stern rejection of excuses is specially instructive when it is considered that the excuses are offered by the man who received only one talent. It is natural to inquire why he is selected to play the part of the unprofitable servant. The explanation which most readily occurs to one is, that those who receive small endowments are most tempted to negligence by a depressing sense of the insignificance of their powers and the valucless-ness of any results which they may be able to achieve. And there is certainly some truth in this view. Yet second thoughts breed doubt as to whether this be indeed the true rationale of the matter. For one who reflects on the history of mankind cannot but feel that sloth is by no means confined to the poorly endowed; that indeed some of the most tragic examples of negligence and unprofitableness have been exhibited among the most highly-gifted of men. Probably the true reason of the selection is to enforce the doctrine of universal and exceptionless obligation. The man of one talent is represented as playing the part of idler, just because he is the man who would be thought most easily excusable; the purpose being to teach that excuse for negligence will be accepted in no case, not even in the case of those whose power of service is a minimum.

c) Another most significant feature in this connection is the

On roi'c TpatTti irats Grotius remarks: ne dicas invenire te non potuisse quibus pecunia e set opus. Argentarii ab omnibus pecunias sumunt foenore. The words eyw (KOfiiird irjv, c. (I would have received mine own with usury, ver. 2) he paraphrases) 9ov Ko ii taqai, i. e. exegissem, and gives as the sense, non est etiam quod in couocanda pecunia periculum obtendas: mea erat. Ego earn exegissem non tuo sed meo periculo. Tuti enim sunt qui res alienas administrant quoties eis credunt quorum fidei publice creditur. It was a way by which the servant might benefit the master without incurring any risk himself. Meyer points out that the expression (fiaxdv toiq rpatr.) conveys the idea of an action involving no trouble. The servant had only to throw the gold on the table. Lightfoot ('Horae Hebraicas') anxiously defends Christ from the charge of approving of the custom of taking usury by pointing out that the lord did not give the talents at first to be put to usury, but merely referred to the money-changers in self-defence and by way of argumentum ad hominem.

So Unger.

taking of the talent from the, unprofitable servant and giving of it to him that had ten. It is taken from the one because he is unprofitable, because he has already shown that he can make no use of it; and it is given to the other because he has shown that he can make most use of it. Both facts indicate most forcibly the urgency of the demand for work and profit; and, we may add, both facts are in most exact accord with the moral order of the world as revealed in human history. It is not merely in the parable that unto every one that hath much is given more, so that he hath abundance, and from him that hath nothing which he can show as the fruit of his own industry is taken away even that which he hath in the form of stock in trade. This stern law verifies itself with inexorable rigour in the history of individuals and of communities, and in giving utterance to the remarkable saying Christ but read off accurately one of the great moral conditions of human life.

d') Note finally under this head the doom of the unprofitable servant. "And cast ye the unprofitable servant into outer darkness: there shall be the weeping and gnashing of teeth." An awful doom, however mildly interpreted. A commentator whom we often quote with approval remarks thereon, "The punishment of the slothful one is not eternal damnation. The Bible is very exact in its speech on the subject. The unfaithful children of light are cast into darkness; the children of darkness are cast into eternal fire, each being punished through his own opposite." Another commentator of sound judgment and unimpeachable orthodoxy says, "Outer darkness is opposed to domestic light; for as in ancient times feasts were held commonly in the night, Christ represents those who are cast out of the kingdom of God as thrust forth into the darkness." Be it so; the least doom of the unprofitable one is to be left out in the cold and the darkness of night, while the faithful ones who have done well share the joy of their returned lord within the bright festive halls; and while they enjoy the good cheer, there is for him, poor wight, nothing but " weeping and gnashing of teeth"â tears of regret over a wasted life and lost

The sentence is thus explained by Weiss. â Olshausen. Â Calvin.

opportunities, and bitter chagrip at thought of the joy he too might have had, had he only been faithful. And all this for no greater offence than burying his talent in the earth. He has not squandered it in riotous living, he has simply been timid, v over-cautious, too nervously afraid of responsibility, too gloomy in his views of God's character and of life's risks. How hard that the " fearful," the cowards, should fare as the vilest of sinners! How needful, this being so, to remember that God hath not given us the spirit of fear, but of power, and of love, and of a sound mind; how valuable the virtue of manly courage to face the stern responsibilities of life and the inexorable demands of the Divine kingdom!

e) One other reflection may here be added. Nothing can more strikingly evince the intense desire of Christ, in uttering this parable, to impress upon His hearers the sense of obligation than the manner in which the religious application breaks through the parabolic form of representation. Three times over in the replies of the master to his servants the figurative manner of expression appropriate to the parable is replaced by language belonging to the spiritual interpretation. " To enter the joy of the Lord, and to be cast into outer darkness, are phrases which have nothing in common with the affairs of the bank." 2

But let us not exaggerate the severity of the demands which the kingdom makes. While certainly exacting, these demands are at the same time reasonable. First, to each man is given and of each man is required only " according to his several ability" This is a very suggestive expression. If we assume that the talents signify spiritual endowments, gifts directly fitting for service in the kingdom of God, then the phrase in

Vide Rev. xxi. 8, where the cowards ttckoic) are classed with murderers, adulterers, liars, c.

2 Reuss, Histoire Evangelique."

' This is the usual view; but Weiss thinks that the talents have no reference either to spiritual gifts or to the exercise of a spiritual calling, but are perfectly general, embracing all manner of endowments. Their meaning is explained, he thinks, by the gnome " unto him that hath,"' c., and the lesson is that the right use of gifts and goods, both in nature and in the kingdom of God, is rewarded with more, and the neglect with deprivation. That this is true there can be no doubt, and it is an instance of the deep wisdom of Jesus that He thus enunciates a far-reaching moral question suggests the idea that the spiritual is shaped by the natural, so that thelovvest in the scale of natural ability is also the lowest in the scale of grace. That this is the actual fact observation attests, and though at first sight it may appear a hard law, on deeper consideration it will be seen to be merciful. For " the degree of the gift is the measure of accountability. Whether is it fairer to give to a man possessed of one degree of ability five talents or one. Is it fairer to endow him according to his ability or beyond his ability It is enough to say that in the one case failure is crime, in the other necessity."

Next, for the timid and unventuresome there is always an alternative. There are the money-changers (jpaml nac) for those who shriiik from the risks of trade. Here it is unnecessary to inquire what precisely Christ had in view when He used this remarkable expression. All we can be sure of is that He meant to teach that no man in this world is absolutely doomed to inactivity and uselessness, that there will be opportunity to every one that is willing to use his talent in a humble, obscure, if not in a heroic and conspicuous way. We may, if we choose, occupy ourselves in suggesting possible meanings for the money-changers and the bank, such as that they denote in our day the machinery of religious and charitable societies; only we must remember that in making such law. But the primary reference is to spiritual gifts, else what is meant by Kark Tr)v ISiav Svvaixiv?

' The Stewardship of Life' (p. 52), by the Rev. James Stirling, an admirable study on this parable, and a model of homiletic treatment; published by Hodder and Stoughton, 1873.

2 Tpd-n-e av, the expression in Luke's parable of the pounds (ch. xix. 23).

3 So Alford and Godet. The author of ' The Stewardship of Life," already quoted, makes the bank the Christian Church, and thinks that the idea intended is that the slothful servant might have retired from the position of leader, and fallen into the ranks of ordinary membership. "We must bear in mind," he says, "that he occupied a representative place, otherwise we are thrown into the perplexities which have vexed interpreters of the Tpawi rai, bankers. Fearing the great peril that surrounded the teacher and leader, he failed to fall into the ranks, where ordinary powers mingle with the currency of related forces. He might have retreated to a secondary place, a line of service lower in reward and less exposed to danger, without breaking loose from the living body of Christ. There is the guild of medium endowment where men of lowest grade may be woven into muscle running into higher will. The talent sugjrestions we are not, strictly speakinop, interpreting the parable, but merely making our contribution to a proof that the general doctrine of the parable is true, viz. that opportunities of using our gifts in the service of the kingdom will never be wanting. This is the truth which we have to lay to heart. It is a very cheering truth, as tending to show that the service of the kingdom, if exacting, is also reasonable and considerate;

a service in which not merely the heroic, but the timid may take part. If any one ask, How shall I know where to find the bank in which I may deposit my talent.-â we may use for reply the opinion of an esteemed commentator as to what the bank in the parable of the pounds signifies, viz. that the bank is Divine omnipotence, whereof we can avail ourselves by prayer. " Of him who has not worked the Lord will demand, Hast thou at least prayed? " This may be a fanciful interpretation, but it contains a valuable hint to those who are perplexed concerning their responsibilities. Let such pray for guidance, and the Spirit of truth will show them how they can avoid the sin and the doom of the unprofitable servant.

3. We come now to the most specific feature of the parable, its indirectly conveyed yet most definite teaching concerning the principle on which faithful service is valued in the Div ine kingdom. The principle is that equal diligence in the use of unequal endowment shall have an equal value set upon it. This principle we infer from the repetition in identical terms of the encomium pronounced on the first servant in address-ino- the second. To the servant who received five talents and gained other five the Lord said, "Well done, good and faithful servant; thou hast been faithful over a few things, I will place thee over many things: enter thou into the joy of thy Lord." To the servant who received two talents and gained divorced from kindred talents is unproductive; the associated talents constitute a power; their confederation is a bank, and that bank is the Christian Church " (p. 254). This is certainly the most definite and suggestive view we have met with. Goebel's view is somewhat similar. Assuming that the talents refer to the ministry of the word, he makes delivery of the talent to the bankers signify retiring from the ministry which one is unable to occupy with advantage, and so leaving the office to more competent parties. ' Godet on Luke.

other two he said the same thing, word for word. What now does this imply? Does it signify that both these servants are in future to be put on a level, not only as to joy, but as to power and position, no regard being henceforth had to the difference between them in respect of natural ability? We might fliirly enough put this construction on the expression " I will place thee over many things." But it has to be considered that many is an indefinite term, which m. ight mean different things for different men; and that the idea it is intended to express may be the disproportion between the past and the future position of either party, rather than the equality of the future positions of both. In both cases it might be said, "Thou hast been faithful over a few things, henceforth thou shalt have an opportunity of being faithful over many things," though the many things of the future differed in the same proportion as the few things of the past. Then, seeing that a part of the reward of faithful ministry here is opportunity of exercising a higher ministry hereafter,â for such seems to be the import of the word in question, the interests of the Divine kingdom may require that the largest scope for service should be afforded to him who has shown greatest capacity for service. It is in fact on this very ground that the talent is taken from the unprofitable servant and given to him that has ten talents. We cannot, therefore, press the view that many must be held to denote equality of position in all respects. The most we are justified in saying is that the language is so chosen as to throw into the shade any inequality which may still exist. If there is to be inequality in the future, as in the past, the speaker has no wish to emphasise it; the truth to which he desires now to give exclusive prominence is that the two men are in a spiritual point of view peers. On this point we are left in no doubt. If many be a vague word, there is no vagueness or ambiguity in the terms of commendation bestowed in common on the two servants. Both are pronounced to have done well, and both receive the honourable appellation good and faithful servant. There can be no mistake as to what the words mean. The exclamation ei is an expression of admiration. The master, hearing the reports of his two servants, is satisfied that they have done their utmost, that they have performed an amount of work which supphcs indisputable evidence of steadfast apph'cation, unflagging energy, and enthusiastic devotion, and he generously allows his feelings to appear in the utterance of that expressive monosyllable. Though not a word more had been said, we should have known what to think of the two servants. But we are not left to conjecture the character of the men. It is drawn for us by two significant adjectives, zx A faithfid ayak Koix TTtotc). The former means here, as in the parable of the Sower, devoted, enthusiastic, single-hearted. That being the import of the one epithet, the other goes along with it as a matter of course. One who is good, ayaoos, in the sense ol putting his whole heart and soul into his work, cannot fail to be faithful, Tnaros, for the very secret of fidelity is single-, heartedness, and the sole cause of unfaithfulness is a divided heart. No fear of neglect when the whole heart is engaged. No need of a taskmaster's eye to keep the devoted man at his work. Love is its own taskmaster. Such then is the common character of the two men. The discerning eye of the master detects the precious characteristics in both, and he pronounces on both the same eulogium in identical terms, with equal warmth of tone. For keen and sharp as he seems to be in looking after his interest, he does not value men merely by the amount of money they bring in. It is no drawback in his view that the second servant brings only two talents more, having received only two. He is pleased with him not less than with the other, because he too has done what he could; and he confers on him the badge of the legion of honour, in which distinctions of rank are lost sight of, and all belong to the one order of Heroes. The judgrnent is according to equity, and it is a faithful reflection of the judgment of Him with whom the citizens of the Divine kingdom have to do. For the Lord of that kingdom judges not vnen after the vulgar fashion of the world, by the mere magnitude of the results achieved. He has regard to the diligence and devotion displayed, whether the results be great or small, and He will pronounce the encomium " good and faithful" on many whom the world has regarded as comparative failures. If there be a willing mind, it is accepted by Him according to that a man hath, and not according to that he hath not. The widow's mite is more to him than the large gifts of the wealthy, because it is the offering of a devoted spirit. How blessed to serve a Master who is utterly-superior to the vulgar worship of success and quantity! How blessed, moreover, to serve one who is as generous as He is equitable! For that any servant should be praised as both these servants are, is not less noteworthy than that the one is praised as much as the other. In this respect also the parable is faithful to the Spirit of God and of Christ as exhibited in the Bible. The God of the Holy Scriptures is characteristically generous in His moral estimates of His servants. He pronounces perfect and good men in whom we have no difficulty in seeing moral defect. The epithets are freely applied wherever there is single-hearted devotion to the cause of God â to a Moses, a David, a Job, a Barnabas.

And those who serve the Lord of the kingdom ought to bear this truth in mind. It is well that we think humbly of ourselves, but it is not well that we imagine that God thinks meanly of the best endeavours of His servants. It is injurious as towards Him, and it is degrading in its effect on our ownÂ character. Religion, to be an elevating influence, must be a worship of a generous, magnanimous God. Therefore, while in the language of a former parable we say of ourselves we are unprofitable servants, so disclaiming all self-righteous pretensions to merit, let us remember that we serve One who will pronounce on every single-hearted worker, be his position distinguished or obscure, or his success great or small, the honourable sentence Well done, good and faithful servant. What the joy of the Lord into which the faithful are to be admitted may be we can only dimly guess; in what the higher ministries of eternity, with which the ministries of time are to be rewarded, consist, and under what conditions they are to be exercised, we can but feebly attempt to imagine; but the cordial approval of the Lord is something we can understand, is something to look forward to, is something which all faithful souls shall share, and share alike.

We conclude our study of this parable by drawing a contrast which enhances our sense of its beauty and wisdom. In the

Goebel makes it promotion from a servile condition to the friendship of the Lord, and to participation in his position of possession and power.

Talmud are found parables similar to this one and to that of the labourers in the vineyard, but similar only as a dead, leafless, barkless tree of stunted dimensions is to a great forest tree with wide-spreading branches clothed with foliage. The Rabbinical parable analogous to that of the labourers in the vineyard is so meagre as not to be worth quoting, and the motive is as petty as its conception is mean. The purpose is to praise a certain Rabbi who made as much progress in the law in twenty years as others could in a hundred. What an insignificant aim compared with that of Christ to illustrate the truth of the wide-reaching moral law that the first may be last and the last first! The other Rabbinical parable analogous to that of the talents is to this effect: " A certain king gave a deposit to each of his three servants. The first guarded it safely, the second lost it, the third defiled it and committed a part of it to another to keep. After a certain time the king came to demand the deposit. Him who guarded it he praised, and made prefect of his house. Him who lost it he visited with capital punishment, and ordered that neither his name nor his possessions should remain. To the third the king said. Retain him till we see what the other will do in whose hands he left a part, and meantime let him not depart from my house. If he has treated the deposit rightly, let this one be restored to liberty, but if not let him be punished." The observations of the author from whom we take this miserable sample of parabolic narratives are so just, that we feel constrained to quote them at length. " What more frigid than this parable what more insipid can be conceived? Almost the same things are related as in the parable of Jesus; but no ornaments are added which give alacrity, so to speak, and a certain vivid movement to the whole. Jesus exhibits a picture; the Talmudist presents the barest outlineâ not a picture, but a caricature. And the things are so compared as to injure rather than assist verisimilitude and the imagination. A king gave a deposit to his three servants. For what reason? No reason is given; but Jesus says that the master went away into a far distant region. And what sort of deposit was it, and how great It does not appear. Jesus says ' his goods," and accurately indicates

For this parable vide Lightfoot, Horse Hebraicae.

the number of the talents. Had the king of the Talmudlst's parable any regard to the disposition or ability of his servants in distributing the deposits? None. Our king gives five to one, two to another, to a third one, to each according to his several abihty. With what view was the deposit given. That they might keep it. Our parable says that they might trade with it. And what sentence is pronounced on the servants For simply keeping the deposit the first is praised and promoted; for losing it the second is put to death; the treatment of the third is made dependent on the behaviour of another man. What prodigality in rewarding, what cruelty in punishing, what injustice in all! Who could believe such trifles, and what influence can they have on the minds and hearts of men?" Such senilities do not deserve to be rescued from the dust of oblivion, but they help to deepen our impressions of the literary charm, and, what is more important, of the profound insight into moral and spiritual truth, displayed in the inimitable parables of Jesus.

THE POUNDS; OR, UNEQUAL DILIGENCE IN THE USE OF EQUAL ENDOWMENTS UNEQUALLY REWARDED.

A certain man noble born went into afar country to receive for himself et kingdom, and to return. And he called ten servants of his, and delivered them ten pounds, and said unto them. Occupy till I come But his citizens hated him, and sent aft ambassage after him, saying. We do not wish this persott to reign over us. And it came to pass that when he was returned, having received the kingdom, he com-maftded these servants to be called unto him, to whom he had given the money, that he might know what they had made by trading. And the first presented himself, saying. Lord, thy pound hath gained ten pounds. And he said tmto him. Well, thou good servant, because thou hast been faithful in a very little, have thou authority over ten cities. And tjie second came, saying, Thy pounds lord, hath gained five pounds. And he said also to this one, Thou also, be thou over five cities. And another came, sayittg. Lord, behold thy pound, which I had, laid up iii a napkin. For I feared thee, because thou art an austere man: thou takest up that thou layedst not down, and reapest that thou didst not sow. He saith to him, Out of thine own mouth will judge thee, wicked servant. Thou knewest that L am an austere man, taking tip

Limburg Brouvver, De Parabolis Jesu Christi."

' UpaynatEvcraaqt, occupy yourselves in business, engage in trade.

that 1 laid not down, and reaping; that I did not sow. Why then gavest not thou my money into the bank, and I on coming would have required it with usury? And he said to those standing by, Take from him the pou id, and give it to him that hath ten pounds. A fid they said unto him. Lord, he hath ten pounds. For I say unto yojc, that unto every one that hath shall be given, and from him that hath not, even that he hath shall be taken away. But those mine enemies, who â would 7iot that I should reign over them, bring hither, and slay them before w,â LUKE XIX. 12â 27.

This parable is of a more subjective and personal character than the kindred parable of the talents. It is obviously but a veiled parabolic history of the present and future fortunes of the Speaker, and so possesses all the pathetic interest attaching to the actual humiliation and the prospective hopes of the Son of man. He is the noble-born man who goes to seek a kingdom; but is hated by His rightful subjects, and loved by only a faithful few. If we keep this fact well in mind it may help us to understand the peculiarities of this parable, and solve difficulties connected with it which have been stumbling-blocks to many.

I. Foremost among the peculiar and difficult features of the parable is the union in it of two points of view, which has suggested, not only to negative critics like Strauss, but even to sober and believing interpreters, the hypothesis that, in its present form, it consists of two parables originally distinct blended into oneâ a lost parable concerning a king and his subjects, and Matthew's parable of the talents transformed. It cannot be denied that the hypothesis possesses considerable plausibility. For the parable as given by Luke combines traits so diverse, that on first thoughts one is tempted to regard them as incompatible. The main actor appears to be at once a king and a private person, a nobleman and a tradesman; the persons to whom he is related are partly subjects and partly servants; the sum he gives the latter seems unworthy of a king, and the reward he bestows on them, while such as becomes a king, seems inappropriate to the character they have hitherto sustained, which

This saying is found also in Luke viii. 18, sligbtly altered, o? xÂ being changed into 6 Zokci txÂ v; the former suits material possessions, the latter spiritual possessionsâ such as understanding of Divine truth, in which possession in the case supposed is only imaginary.

VIII. J Jie Pounds. 217 is that of traders. In presence of these incongruities it appears excusable to ask Can such heterogeneous traits have been brought together by Jesus, all whose other parabolic representations are characterised by unity, harmony, and fitness? Yet we venture to think that, if only the situation be steadily kept in view, the objections to the originality of the parable, which appear at first so formidable, may to a large extent be removed.

As to the chief difficulty, that respecting the double point of view, the fact is indisputable, and the only question is as to its psychological truth. This question resolves itself into two: first, is it likely that Jesus would attempt in one parable to express His relations to the two sections of Jewish society, those who were hostile to Him and those who were attached to Him.? and, second, is it likely that He would use the precise figures which we find employed in the parable before us.? The circumstances amid which the parable appears to have been spoken go far to answer the first question in the affirmative. Jesus found Himself surrounded by a mixed multitude of people of diverse tendencies, and variously affected towards Himself. On one side were men of Pharisaic sympathies, to whom it was an offence that He had gone to be a guest with a man like Zacchseus, who, being a chief publican, was therefore of course a chief sinner; on the other side were many who had followed him from Galilee, full of the admiration awakened in their minds by His ministry in that region, and confidently believing that the journey towards Jerusalem portended the near approach of the long and ardently expected kingdom. From the lips of the one class came sullen murmurs; in the countenances of the other were visible the traces of enthusiastic and romantic expectation. By both classes Jesus was utterly misunderstood; the one having no comprehension of, or sympathy with, the yearning love for the lost which was the key to his conduct towards Zacchaeus, the other being equally ignorant of the nature and future history of the kingdom whose coming they eagerly desired. He was alone in the midst of that great crowd. Here was a situation fitted to evoke the parabolic mood; for it was, as we pointed out in our introductory observations, when made

As is actually done by Reuss: vide his Histoire Evangelique."

conscious of isolation, by the stupid or malignant misapprehensions of men, that Jesus spake in parables. A parable, therefore, might be looked for in the circumstances. But if a parable is to be the outcome of the situation, we expect that it will be a faithful reflection of the situation; that it will show on the one hand wdiat the murmurs of the disaffected will come to, and on the other hand, how far the hopes of friends would be fulfilled or frustrated by coming events. We are not surprised, therefore, to find in the evangelic record a parable said to have been spoken at this time of the two-sided character which the circumstances called for, with one side turned towards foes, another side towards friends; warning the one of a fearful doom awaiting them if they persisted in their present mind, and seeking to moderate the ignorant enthusiasm of the other by a sober picture of the future that lay before them.

But the question remains, Were the figures employed in this two-sided parable appropriate to the purpose on hand Now there can be little doubt as to the appropriateness of one of the tableaux, that, viz. of a king and his rebellious subjects. That picture was true to the claims of Jesus to be the Messianic King, and to the future doom of Israel, which was indeed to be destroyed before the face of the Lord. It was also true, as has been pointed out by several commentators, to the external, geographical situation; for the parable was spoken in the neighbourhood of Jericho, where was the palace of Archelaus, who had done the very thing the king in the parable is represented as doing, viz. gone to a far country, to Rome, to seek a kingdom; not without opposition on the part of the Jews, who, tired of a dynasty of adventurers, besought the emperor rather to convert their country into a Roman province. But what are we to think of the other picture, that of a man noble born, and expectant of a throne, giving to his servants a pound apiece to trade with.-â Is it suitable to the dignity of a man of royal birth and hopes to be a trader, or even to be in any way connected with trade Now here we might plead that the act is the act of a nobleman, not of a trader, and that its purpose is not even to make the servants traders, but simply to test their fidelity. But it

Josephus,"Antiq.," 17, 11, I.

must be admitted that the transaction is a most unusual one for a nobleman, suggestive of trade rather than of royalty, and fitted to compromise a high-born person's dignity. But what then."' Was not this very incongruity and indignity most suitable to Christ's actual position."' Was not His life on earth filled with incongruities between His intrinsic dignity and His outward lot? Was not this Nobleman born in the home of a village carpenter Did He not Himself become a carpenter when He grew to the years of manhood If He had to endure this extreme indignity, He might well bear the minor indignity arising out of trade associations. Those who are in quest of crowns must not be too fastidious, for they are liable to encounter strange turns of fortune on their way to sovereignty.

But we may be called to vindicate the appropriateness of the figure with reference even to the followers of Jesus. It may be asked. Might not their position have been indicated in connection with the same figure of a king and his subjects by representing them as a minority of loyal subjects who had to endure oppression at the hands of the majority during the prince's absence Such, in fact, is the opinion of Ewald, who sees no necessity for the two figures, and thinks that Luke mixed the two together for no other reason than because they both referred to a journeying lord, and because they probably lay side by side in his sources. But this view, in the first place, assigns a more subordinate position to the faithful portion of the Jewish people than seems intended, if we may judge from the parable in which the place of prominence is given not to foes, but to friends. Moreover, a parable constructed as Ewald suggests, while teaching disciples one important lesson often inculcated, viz. that the joys of the kingdom could be reached only through suffering, would have failed to convey another lesson not less important, viz. that the way to the kingdom lay through a life of strenuous activity. For this purpose Jesus must have deemed the other emblem not unapt, for He certainly employed it once (in the parable of the talents); and if once, why not a second time t In the form which it takes in the parable of the pounds the fiction is peculiarly well fitted to dissipate idle dreams, and bring the Die drei ersten Evangelien," pp. 419, 420.

thoughts of enthusiastic disciples down from the cloud-land of romance to the ground of sober reality. In this connection the paltriness of the sum given to the servants to trade with is signiiicant, as suggesting that what lay before them in the immediate future was a life not merely of activity, but of obscure, inglorious activity, amid hard, necessitous circumstances. By this parable Christ says to His faithful followers, Ye are to be rulers eventually, but ye must be traders first, and for a long time, and in a very small wayâ village tradesmen, itinerant pedlars, so to speak. I give you each a pound; do with it what you can, use it as opportunity offers, so as to earn a livelihood, and if possible make a fortune. Hard lines surely to have to live upon such a pittance, not to speak of earning money for the master's benefit! Certainly the lot appointed to these servants is one involving a severe discipline; and the end contemplated is evidently not money-making, but character-making â the development of a hardi- hood of temper and a firmness of will which can be turned to good account when the obscure traders shall have been transformed into distinguished rulers. Strange transformation doubtless, yet not unexampled even in our own land. How many in this great commercial country have risen from mean obscurity and utter poverty first to wealth, and then to positions of authority, beginning with the pound, and multiplying it into ten, and repeating the process times without number; and not always bringing to the high position ultimately reached the petty vices of narrowness and hardness which are apt to be contracted in the process of building up a fortune from small beginnings, but sometimes exhibiting a truly, princely spirit of generous, free-handed benevolence!

2. These observations have already in part disposed of a second difficulty that has been found in this parable, viz. the smallness of the sum given to each of his servants by the nobleman, which seems altogether unworthy of a man in his position. It might be enough to say, as we have already in

Long enough to allow the one pound to be multiplied into ten, which implies a longer period than the doubling of the capital in Matthew's parable.

- The Attic pound was in value somewhat less than four pounds sterling, and the sixteenth part of a talent. Kuinoel refers to an opinion of effect said; by way of reply to this objection, that it was good for those who were ultimately to be promoted to positions of authority that they should first pass through a discipline ot severe hardship. But another explanation may be offered. What if the smallness of the sum given be due to the necessitous condition of the prince himself? Candidates for crowns, however noble by birth, are apt to be needy. The Nobleman of our parable is in this case. He has the highest prospects, but His present state is one of abject humiliation and poverty; and in this veiled history of Himself Jesus takes care that the picture at this point shall be in keeping with reality. To which we may add, that in any case the very smallness and meanness of the sum given to the servants is an argument for the authenticity of the parable. No one but Christ would have dared to name so small a sum, appropriately described in the parable as a v ery li ttle. He alone knew how to value the superlatively small, and to estimate the moral worth of those who have been faithful in that which is least. Christian tradition would magnify, not diminish, the amount. We could imagine tradition increasing the pound to a talent; we cannot imagine it reducing the talent to a pound.

These remarks, we trust, suffice to show the natural propriety of the parabolic representation at this point. But what, it may now be asked, is represented by the pound." Various answers have been given to the question. The pound, according to one, is the common grace of salvation bestowed on all believers; according to a second, it is the mission of all Christ's disciples to advance His kingdom;' according to a third, it is the word which Jesus had committed to His believing followers, and which Paul in his Epistles to Timothy speaks of as the trust, the noble trust, and which

Michaelis that the translator of this parable from Hebrew into Greek had confounded the Hebrew word for portion ('"130) with the word for a mina (' â?"?), and that the parable spoke not of ten mince, but of ten portions. This is another instance of learning going egregiously astray through want of insight into the moral import of the parables. Some men would be better expositors if they had less learning, as they might then take more pains to understand ideas as distinct from words.

Godet. 2 Reuss.
Hofmann, Das Evangelium des Lukas," p. 462.
I Tim. vi. 2; 20 Tim. i. 14: ij Trapaoliicn, v caxi) irapaefikti.
is spoken of in the Acts of the Apostles as increasing and multiplying. The two last opinions are nearly coincident, and may be accepted as the most probable interpretation. '" What the servants of the nobleman have to trade with and seek to multiply is the word of the kingdom. This association of the Divine word with the idea of trade is legitimated as Scriptural by a text in Paul's Second Epistle to the Corinthians, rendered in our English version, "We are not as many, which corrupt the word of God "; but which may be more exactly translated, We are not as many who deal after the fraudulent manner of huckstering merchants with the â word of God.2
3. A third peculiarity in this parable is the equality of endowmentâ all the servants receiving the same sum; whereas in the kindred parable of the Talents the servants

receive each a different sum. This feature can cause no difficulty when it is considered what is meant by the pound; for the word of Christ and the commission to teach it was one and the same for all. But without seeking aid from the spiritual interpretation, we may learn from the parable itself, taken in connection with the circumstances amid which it was spoken, the rationale of this equality. The time of trading is a time of preparation for the higher occupation of ruling, when they who have been with Christ in His temptations shall receive kingdoms, and sit on thrones. It is therefore a time of trial, when it has to be ascertained what they are fit for in the higher ultimate state, to which the lower transitory one is a stepping-stone. But the best way to ascertain this is to put all on a level to begin with, and leave them to determine by their own exertions what place they are worthy to occupy. In a race which is to settle who is to win the prize for greatest speed, all must start in a line, and at the same moment.

4. This brings us to what may be called the theoretic â Acts xii. 24.

' 2 Cor. ii. 17. The expressive word is Ka-Kr Kihovtiq. Paul claims to be a fair trader, who deals in unadulterated wares, in all simplicity and godly sincerity. In the Clementine Homilies Peter calls the apostles good merchants of the true religion, as if offering to men's choice the seeds of Plants, Hom. ix. 8.

3 Luke xxii. 28. Matt. xix. 28.

â So Schleiermacher, Uber die Scbriften des Lukas."

feature of the parable, which, though it comes i only incidentally, is worthy of the prominence we have given it in taking from it our alternative title. The servants equally endowed make an unequal use of their endowments, and unequal ise of equal endowment is unequally rewarded. He who with one pound gained ten is made ruler over ten cities, and he who with the same sum gained only five pounds is made ruler over only five cities. It may be said indeed that in bestowing unequal measures of power upon his servants the king does not indicate unequal approbation, but simply adapts their appointments to the ascertained capacity of each, in other words, that this parable ends where the parable of the Talents begins, viz. by treating men according to their several ability.- But this view, though in the abstract legitimate, is excluded by another feature in the parable, which plainly shows that what had been ascertained by the time of probation was not the varied ability of the servants, but the unequal measure of their zeal and industry and force of will. What we allude to is the withholding of all expressions of praise in addressing the second servant. He is not said to have done well, and he is not called good. Let it not be supposed that this happens as it were per iiiciiriavi. Christ was not likely to commit the mistake of withholding approbation when it was due. He was habitually careful in His use of moral epithets. He was characteristically generous in bestowing them when they were deserved; and, on the other hand, He would not only not ascribe the quality of goodness to others who possessed it not, but He would not even allow it to be ascribed to Himself by persons who were not in a position to speak with intelligence and conviction, and who meant merely to pay a flattering compliment. Why callest thou Me good.? He said sternly to the young ruler who inquired concerning eternal life; and from the second servant in this parable He withholds the epithet not inadvertently, but deliberately, because in His judgment he had not earned it. And what does this imply.? That the second servant had not done all that it was possible ' So in effect Weiss, who remarks that the ilia lvva uq in Luke comes into view in the use of the common gift, while in Matthew it is kept in view in the distribution: ' Das Matthaus-Evangelium."

for him to do; that he had been lacking in devotion, perseverance, steadfastness; that his whole heart had not been in the business he had on hand; that he had not been a hero in the struggle of life; that he had acquitted himself only fairly, respectably, not nobly. That the first servant had possessed all the virtues opposed to these defects is signified by the title ayaqo ascribed to him; and that the second servant was chargeable with all these defects is not less surely signified by the withholding of the title from him. Therefore we may legitimately represent this parable as teaching that in the kingdom of heaven unequal zeal in the use of equal ability will be unequally rewarded; a principle, just in itself, and, when added to the principles set forth in the two other parables previously considered, completing the doctrine of Christ on the great subject of the relation between work and wages."

5. It remains to advert in a sentence or two to yet another feature in this parable, viz. that in its doctrine of rewards and punishments it seems to have in view chiefly if not exclusively the temporal aspect. The rebellious subjects are slain before the eyes of the king, the allusion being obviously to the ruin which, a generation later, overtook the Jewish people; the faithful are rewarded with appointments to rule over cities, no mention being made of the joy of the Lord spoken of in Matthew's parable; and the unprofitable servant is punished simply by being deprived of an endowment which he had not known how to use, but had tied up in a napkin, whose proper use was to wipe the sweat from his brow. We read not here of the outer darkness where is weeping and gnashing of teeth.

1 The view we take as to the didactic import of the two parables of the Talents and the Pounds is advocated among others by Dr. Gray, author of a work entitled ' A Delineation of the Parables," published about the beginning of this century. He says, In the one parable we see the two industrious servants are represented as equally diligent in their respective trusts, and therefore were entitled to the same commendation and reward. But in the other, where a greater degree of industry under the same advantages is supposed to produce greater success, we see the reward assigned to each bears a proportionable respect to his diligence and improvement." Gray was parish minister of Abernethy in Perthshire.

2 Sowjdpiov is the Latin word sttdarium imported into the language of the East. The unprofitable servant wraps his money this time in 4 napkin, instead of burying it in the earth, because it is a small sum.

In all these respects the parable is obviously political rathef than religious j and it is only a perverse ingenuity which seeks to find out what its expressions mean in reference to eternity, as when it is said that the ten or five cities represent beings who are yet in an inferior moral position, but whom the faithful in glory have a mission to elevate to their destination; or the words, To him that hath shall be given, are made to bear the meaning, Such and such a pagan people, which that young Christian might have evangelised, but did not, remaining here below the slave of ease, will be intrusted in the future economy to the devoted missionary who had here used all his powers in the service of Jesus. As to what that law may mean in reference to the world to come we prefer to confess our ignorance. It is a law as mysterious as it is certain in its operation even in this world. The remark of the bystanders, "Lord, he hath ten pounds," was a very natural expression of surprise that to him who had so much already more should still be given. Who has not in his heart made the same remark many a time! The law on both sides of its operation seems partial, unjust, inhuman. But it is idle to complain of the laws of the moral universe. We shall be better employed in endeavouring to accommodate ourselves to the conditions of our existence as responsible beings, and striving so to live that they shall be for us, not against us. Let us study to be faithful in that which is least, and then we also may have an opportunity granted us of showing fidelity on the great scale, and shall be prepared to make the most of such an opportunity when it comes, ? So Godet.

In an early chapter of his Gospel Luke tells of a discourse delivered by Jesus in the synagogue of Nazareth on the Acceptable Year of the Lord, and records that His hearers wondered at the gracious words which proceeded out of His mouth. i l hat scene was thoroughly congenial to the taste of the Pauline Evangelist, and he took it out of its historical connection and put it in the fore-front of his narrative of our Lord's public ministry, assigning to it the same place in his Gospel which is occupied by the Sermon on the Mount in Matthew's, that he might introduce Christ to his readers at the very outset as the preacher of glad tidings. Not less congenial to his liking was the phrase he employs to describe the character of the Nazareth discourse: Words of Grace, koyoi TTJs xÂ ptâ Â- One recommendation of it doubtless was that it suggested a connection between the doctrine of Christ and the doctrine of Paul, in which the idea of grace occupies a very prominent place. But it was, apart from that consideration, a well-chosen title or motto. For though the word grace, xÂ P'?) is of very rare occurrence in the Gospels, the thing signified is manifest in every page: Jesus as He appeared among men in His public ministry was indeed, as the fourth evangelist says, full of grace. And of all the evangelists Luke has done most to justify the representation by the account he has given of our Lord's teaching; for many words of Jesus that are peculiarly and emphatically words of grace have been reported by him alone. Among the words of grace spoken by Jesus a prominent place belongs to the group of parables now to engage our attention, much

Luke iv. 16â 30.

the larger number of which are peculiar to Luke, among that number being some which are the very poetry and quintessence of the gospel of pardon and of Divine love; very specially those to be studied in the next two chapters, to which may be justly given by way of eminence the title of the Parables of Grace.

A peculiar charm surrounds the doctrine of grace as taught by Jesus, not in dogmatic formulae defended by controversial dialectics as in Paulinism, but in poetic utterances of exquisite simplicity and beauty, yet infinitely suggestive. The doctrine is of course less developed, less dogmatically complete, but just on that account the more attractive. To the gospel of grace as preached by Jesus belongs the charm of the dawn, which is a delight to all mankind, which our Aryan ancestors in their childish wonder even went the length of worshipping under the name of Ushas. Christ's preaching was the dawn of the era of grace, when the Dayspring from on high visited this world, to give light to them that sit in darkness and in the shadow of death, to guide our feet into the way of peace. Let us turn our eyes towards the mild sweet light of this morning of our eternal hope with awe-struck humble gratitude.

In many of the parables belonging to the class now to be considered there is a striking union of the true, the good, and the beautiful, Jesus appears in them the Artist, the Sage, the Philanthropist, and the Hero, all in one. From the parables of grace we may learn the genius of genuine evangelic piety, the beau ideal of a truly evangelic ministry. The term evangelical' ought to signify a Christ-like spirit of love for the ' lost," combined with a wide, genial culture, and a manly type of character. In actual use the term sometimes denotes something widely differentâ a type of religion which combines strenuous advocacy of the doctrines of grace with an attitude of hostility or at least of indifference to culture, and with an ethical character which, in respect of scrupulosity, censoriousness, and narrowness of sympathy, bears a painfully

Godet gives this title to the three parables in Luke xv., but the parable of the Two Debtors may well be classed along with these. The four form a distinct group connected together by one aim, as shall appear forthwith. ' Luke i. 78, 79.

close resemblance to Pharisaism as we know it from the Gospels. Going to the fountain-head of evangelic life we discover that this unattractive combination is not necessary, but only an accident; due probably to the circumstance that the evangelical faith united to such heterogeneous attributes has been received not as a revelation from heaven, but by tradition from a former generation. The parables of grace are in their substance intensely evangelical. But in the fonn of thought homage is done to aesthetics; taste, culture, art receives due recognition, not perhaps intentional but only instinctive, but for that very reason the more effectually vindicating for these things a place of their own. Whether from deliberate design or from the unconscious action of a happy genius matters not, the fact is that in these parables we find displayed a literary taste and grace unsurpassed, inimitable. Then, when we consider the occasions which called forth many of these parables, we see how utterly antagonistic to Pharisaism the true evangelic spirit is. The most remarkable were spoken in self-defenceâ in defence of a habitual disregard of superstitious scruples, and of an unconventional charity and width of sympathy most offensive to the Pharisaic mind; were, in short, Christ's apology for a way of life utterly anti-Pharisaical; holy, but not severe towards the unholy; pure, but not puritanic; conscientious, but unfettered by the commandments of men; wearing a noble aspect of liberty, and breadth, and power. This is only what we should expect from One in whom dwelt Divine charity in all its fulness. For charity brings liberty to the conscience, and largeness to the heart, and light and beauty to the mind; banishes feebleness, narrowness, and fear, and endows the character with health, vigour, and courage.

The Parables of Grace may be distributed into groups as follows: 1. The Two Debtors, and the Lost Sheep, the Lost Coin, and the Lost Sonâ four, constituting Christ's apology foi loving sinners.

2. The Children of the Bride-chamber (including the New Patch on an Old Garment, and New Wine in Old Skins) being Christ's apology for the joy of disciples.

3. The Lowest Seats at Feasts, and the Pharisee and the Pubhcan; or the kingdom of God for the humble.

4. The Great Supper, or the kingdom for the hungry and tlie needy.

5. The Good Samaritan, or charity the true sanctity.
6. The Unrighteous Steward, or that charity covers a multitude of sins.
7. The Rich Man and La7arus, and the Unmerciful Servant, or implacability and inhumanity the unpardonable sins. Twelve in all.

The first group being the evangelic parables par excellence, some general observations on them may here be added as a contribution towards the illustration of the genius of the whole class. These four parables, as already hinted, are connected together by a common aim, that being to furnish an answer to those who found fault vith Jesus for associating with the disreputable classes of Jewish society. They are Christ's apology for loving sinners, and only when this fact is steadily kept in view can they be fully understood and successfully expounded. It is somewhat difficult for us to keep the fact in view, so completely has Christian civilization advanced beyond the stage at which such conduct as was found fault with in Jesus could be regarded as needing defence. We can hardly realise that the Founder of our faith was seriously put upon His defence for an "enthusiasm of humanity" which we now regard as His glory, and as the most effective evidence of the Divinity of His doctrine. And when we do by an effort succeed in realising it, we are apt to think that the fault-finders were a peculiarly barbarous and heartless class of men. But in truth it was perfectly natural that they should find fault; they had a perfectly good conscience in doing so; they thought they did well to be angry with Jesus, and with the ideas then current in the world they could hardly do otherwise. For the charity of Jesus was a new thing under the sun, alien not only to the spirit of Pharisaism, but also to the aristocratic genius of ethnic religion. Hence Christ's love for the lost appeared a fault quite as much to the heathen philosopher Celsus as to the holy men of Jud? ea. In his attack on Christianity he alluded to it as a characteristic fact that the chosen companions of Jesus were disre- putable persons, publicans and sailors, and he represented the preachers of the gospel in his own day as saying in effect: Let no one who is wise or educated approach; but if any one is illiterate, foolish, or untaught, a babe in knowledge, he may confidently come to us; and as aiming at making converts of the silly and senseless, of slaves, women, and children. In honest amazement and disgust he asked: " Whence this preference for the sinful?" contrasting with this strange procedure of Christians the more rational practice of Pagans in inviting to initiation into their mysteries only men of pure and exemplary lives. "While Christians address to men this call: Whosoever is a sinner, whosoever is unwise, whosoever is a babe, in short, whosoever is a Kakobaiixcov, him the kingdom of God will receiveâ we, calling men to participation in our sacred rites, say: Whoso has pure hands and is wise of speech, whoso is clean from all impiety, whoso has a conscience void of offence, whoso liveth a just life, let him come hither." If Origen had to defend Christianity against such a charge brought by a philosopher of the second Christian century, we cannot wonder that Christ had to meet a similar charge as advanced by his Jewish contemporaries, who deemed it a positive religious duty to keep themselves aloof from the unholy, in accordance with the negative notion of holiness which not unnaturally had been bred in their minds by the election and the whole past history of Israel, and the peculiar character of her religious institutions. All new things have to fight for their right to existence, and there never was a greater novelty, never a more audacious innovation, than the charity of Jesus; and therefore it was, as a matter of course, violently and repeatedly assailed, and the question often asked: Why eatest thou, why consortest thou, with publicans and sinners?

Jesus was ready with His answer; and as the incapacity of those who interrogated Him to understand His conduct was great and their ignorance deep, the answer he gave was ample, and his apology varied. It is to be gathered from the four parables of the first group, and from another word which may be called a parable-germ, a prov-erbial saying needing only to be expanded into a history to become a parable;

Origen, ' Contra Celsum," lib. i., c. 62.

that, viz., spoken at Matthew's feast, in reply to those who expressed surprise at Jesus being a guest among a gathering of publicans: They that be whole need not a physician, but they that are sick

The apology embraces three great ideas, which in general terms may be expressed thus: 1. Christianity is a remedial system, and therefore it busies itself with those who most manifestly need remedy.

2. It has faith in the redeemableness of human beings however sunk in sin and misery; nay, it believes in the possibility of extremes meeting, of the last becoming first. of the greatest sinner becoming the greatest saint.

3. It thinks the meanest and lowest of mankind worth saving, has such joy in saving the lost, that it can take delight in saving one sinner repenting, not a picked sample, but any one taken at random. In other words, man at his worst is a beingof priceless worth in God's sight, as a moral personality.

The first of these thoughts was the truth hinted at by Jesus in the word spoken in the house of Matthew, under the form of a personal apology. The point of the saying lies in the suggested comparison of Himself to a physician. That comparison accepted, all the rest follows as a matter of course. No one wonders at a physician visiting most frequently the houses of those who are afflicted with the gravest maladies. In doing so he is only showing a becoming enthusiasm in his profession, an enthusiasm which all regard as a virtue, the want of which would cause him to be lightly esteemed as one whose heart was not in his vocation. Neither is any one surprised that a physician, though refined in his personal tastes and habits, is not nice and dainty in the pursuit of his calling, avoiding with disgust loathsome diseases; but goes without hesitation wherever duty calls, though every sense should be offended. All that is in the spirit of his profession. He is a physician, and therefore cannot afford to be fastidious. Even so would men have thought of Christ's behaviour, had it occurred to them to regard Him as a Spiritual Physician, and the religion He came to establish as before all things redemptive. A spiritual 'Matt. ix. 12.

physician must visit those who are spiritually diseased, and a religion of redemption cannot consistently be exclusive and dainty, but must address itself to the million, and be ready to lay its healing hand even on such as are afflicted with the most repulsive moral maladies. Kad Christ come to be a mere rabbi or teacher of the law, then He might consistently have said of the ignorant multitude: This people that know not the law are accursed. Had He come as a philosopher, He might appropriately enough have addressed Himself exclusively to the cultivated, disregarding the illiterate vulgar. Had He come offering to initiate men into a system of religious mysteries, then He might have confined His invitations to the privileged few, neglecting the many as unworthy of initiation, as Celsus thought He and His followers should have done. But He came not as a rabbi, or a philosopher, or a mystagogue, but as a Healer of human souls; and that was an occuoation with which the world was unfamiliar, and hence the need for those apologetic proverbs and parables.

The parables of the Two Debtors spoken at another feast, taken along with its application, has for its didactic kernel, the second of the three foregoing truths. That Jesus, while ostensibly defending the woman against the evil thoughts of His host, was in reality on His own defence on that occasion also, for the same offence of loving the sinful, there can be no reasonable doubt. The evangelist evidently introduces the story in the place where it occurs to illustrate by what kind of conduct He earned for Himself the sneering epithet, or nickname, "the friend of publicans and sinners," to which he alludes in the immediately preceding context, and how He justified that conduct when it was called in question. And the parable must be studied from this point of view, and when so studied it will be found to contain a most important contribution to the apologetic of redeeming love. Its drift is to teach that vast capacities for disciple-ship are latent in the depraved and despised classes of society, that thence in truth may be obtained the best citizens for the Divine kingdom. A very good reason for attending to these

Luke vii. 34.

classes, if true; and the virtue of the parable is to show how easily it may be true; for what more likely than that those who are forgiven most should love most?

The three parables concerning the joy of finding things or persons lost complete the apology of Jesus for loving the sinful, by emphasising the truth that the lowest of men are worth saving. After you have said the worst of these "publicans and sinners," whom all morally-respectable persons shun, what does it amount to? Simply to this, that they are lost; lost to God, to righteousness, to wisdom, to all the chief ends and uses of life. But if so, what a joy if they could be found! All men have joy in finding things lost; shepherds in finding lost sheep, housewives in finding lost pieces of money, fathers in finding lost sons: why then should there not be joy also in finding morally-lost men It is the desire of such joy that moves me to mix with the depraved and the disreputable. Surely a very good reason, if there be a tolerable hope of success in the quest.

These preliminary hints will prepare us for studying sympathetically the whole class of parables which are next to engage our attention, and specially the four which come first.

CHAltKR r.
THE TWO DEBTORS? OR, MUCH FORGIVENESS, MUCH LOVE.

The parade is so deeply embedded in its historical matrix that we must take as our text the v hole narrative as it stands in Luke's Gospel. It is as follows:â â

And one of the Pharisees desired Him that He would eat with him. And He went into the house of the Pharisee, and sat down to meat. And, behold, a woman who was in the city, a sinner, when she knew that Jesus sat at meat in the Pharisee's house, brought aii alabaster vase of ointment, and standing at His feet behind Him weeping, began to wet His feet with her teais, and did wipe them with the hair of her head, and ardently kissed His feet, and anointed them with the ointment. Now when the

Pharisee which had bidden Him satu it, he spake with' in himself, saying: This man, if he were a prophet, would have known who attd what manner of woman this is that toucheth Him, that she is a sinner. A7td fesits answering said unto him: Simon, I have someiuhai to say unto thee. And he saith, Master, say on. A certain creditor had two debtors: the one owed five hundred pence, and the other ffty. And as they had nothing to pay, he frankly forgave them both. Which of them, therefore, will love him most f Simon answered and said: I suppose that he to whom he forgave most. Atid He said unto Him: Thou hast rightly judged. And turning to the woman, He said icnto Simon: Seest thou this woman f I entered into thine ' On this account Goebel has not deemed this parable a suitable theme for an independent discussion, thereby missing a most outstanding feature in our Lord's parabolic teaching.

2 Kamcxier, literally lay down on the couch, the reclining posture being in use; the head towards the table, the feet stretched out behind, so that the feet of Jesus were easily accessible to the woman.

Kats ixii; the Kara is intensive, kissed tenderly; and, as appears from V. 45, repeatedly.

own ' Jioiise, iliou pouredst no water upon My feet: hit she with her tears wetted My feet, and with her hair she wiped ihetn. A single kiss thou gavest Me not; but she, since tlie time I came in, has not ceased kissing My feet. My head with oil thou anointedst not; but she with spikenard' anointed My feet. Wherefore I tell you, for-give? i are her sins, her many sins," for she loved much; but he to whom little is forgiven, loveth little. Then He said to her: Thy sins are forgiven. And His fellow-guests began to say within themselves, Who is this who also forgiveth sins? But He said to the woman: Thy faith hath saved thee, go into peace. â Luke vii. 36â 50.

Where, when, and by whom, this anointing of Jesus was performed, whether by Mary of Bethany, or by Mary of Mag-dala, or by any other Mary, are questions which cannot be answered, and which therefore it is idle to discuss. All we know of the time and place of the remarkable scene is, that it occurred in a certain city or village in the house of a Pharisee named Simon, and that the story is told by Luke at this point in his narrative because it served to illustrate how Jesus earned the honourable nickname of the sinner's friend. And all we know of the heroine of the scene is, that she had been a woman of evil life in that town, and was still in evil repute, the secret of her repentance being as yet known only to Godâ a sinner' in a sense needing no explanation, there being only one form of sin which the world takes special note of in woman. That a female of such a character should have gained an entrance into the house of a respectable member of society may seem surprising, even when we recollect the customs of the country. It was, we know, no breach of good manners for uninvited persons to enter a house when a feast was going on, and sitting down by the wall to observe and even converse with the guests; travellers report such invasions aov emphatic, to suggest that he had neglected the duty of a host.

' livpif (so in ver. 38), in contrast to the more common olive oil ixaitfi). Grotius remarks that though the Hebrews, like the Greeks, were wont to call all sorts of ointments by the name of oil, it cannot be doubted that in this place common oil is meant by txa'uj), because a contrast runs through the whole verse (est enim perpetua avtiaroi-xia).

Such is the order in the original; the significance of it will be brought out in the exposition.

01 avvavakiifiivoi.

For examples in Greek and Latin authors of the use of the generic term 'sinner' to denote the special sin of unchastity in women, see Wetstein, in loc.

of privacy, as they appear to us, as happening in Palestine in our own day. But a woman who was a ' sinner," how could she venture upon such a liberty?â what chance of her presence being tolerated even if she dared to intrude herself? Possibly her sin was an open secret known to all, yet which all could ignore if they chose: the sin not of a harlot, but only of a woman of frail virtue. In that case it was perhaps not much more surprising that she should appear in Simon's house as a spectator, than that Jesus should appear there as a guest; for there were not many Pharisees who thought well enough of Him to be willing to do Him such an honour. Both events were somewhat out of course, not every-day occurrences; but unlikely things do happen occasionally to interupt the monotony of ordinary existence; and these were of the number, perfectly credible as matters of fact, and things to be thankful for on account of the animated scene to which they gave rise. When two such persons meet the company is not likely to be dull.

The woman had a definite purpose in coming into the house of Simon. She came not to be a mere spectator, but to anoint her benefactor with a box of precious ointment. Her benefactor we must assume Jesus to have been, though we know nothing of the previous relations. It were easy to invent a past history which should account for the present situation. Jesus lived in public; He went about the land doing good, preaching the good tidings of the kingdom, and healing the sick; all had opportunities of seeing Him and hearing Him. Many of the degraded class did see and hear Him with blessed effects on their hearts, and we may safely assume that this sinful woman was of the number, and that she is here to do honour to One whose gracious words and benignant aspect have changed the current of her affections, and possibly " to 1 Vide Farrar's Life of Christ, vol. i. p. 298, where the author speaks of the custom from personal observation.

So Grotius: non publicae hbidinis victima, sed alioqui vitae parum pudicae. Against this view, however, is the reading in ver. 37, approved by critical editors: yui')) Â; ri(; ryv iv rij-koxh afiapruabc, which seems to imply that she practised a shameful calling in the city, whereas the reading in the T. R., which places rjng ijv after iroxu, implies merely that she was a â woman of evil reputation. So Godet; but the moral import of the two readings is not so certain as he represents.

240 The Parabolic Teaching of Christ, book u.

give to Him and to herself a pledge of her resolution to change her life." But in proceeding to carry out her purpose she does more than she intended. As she approaches the object of her devoted regard her heart begins to swell with contending emotions of shame, sorrow, love, and fear; she bursts into a flood of passionate tears which fall upon the feet of Jesus; the feet so wetted with ' heart-water' she dries with her flowing hair, having nothing better at hand for the purpose; then pressing them to her lips she covers them with fervent kisses; and only after her transports have thus been calmed, and she has somewhat recovered her composure, does she at length perform the more ordinary act of homage.

Conduct so unusual could not fail to create a general sensation in the guest-chamber, and especially to arrest the astonished attention of the host. Had the woman come in quietly and taken a place apart, as a spectator, her presence though unwelcome might have been overlooked b)'- Simon. But behaviour so bold, so impudent, how could he regard otherwise than with amazement, disapprobation, and disgust."' And then what was he to think of Jesus for suffering such attentions He could not think so ill of Him as to believe Him capable of receiving these with complacency had He known the character of the person bestowing them; but at the least he must gravely doubt His prophetic insight. What he felt was apparent in his face and manner to any eye of ordinary discernment. The intruder appeared to him to be simply acting her characteristic part as a ' sinner," and the behaviour of his guest cast him into a state of painful perplexity. The woman was unhesitatingly condemned, and Jesus was put upon His defence. Now to us, who are in the secret, these hard suspicious thoughts seem of course altogether groundless. Yet we must do the Pharisee the justice to say that in his circumstances, and from his point of view, they were very natural. How was he to know that a great moral change had come over this woman, whom he had hitherto known only as a person of evil life? Doubtless he might

Reuss, Histoire Evang Iique."

Luther's expression, Herzenwasser. Vide Hauspostillen." Bengal's phrase is, Lacrimas aquarum pretiosissimee.

Godet suggests, not without probability, that she unbound her hair for the purpose.

have observed those tears, which were suggestive of another hypothesis than that by which he accounted for her strange behaviour. But then how unhkely that other hypothesis! how improbable that the frail one is here in the capacity of a penitent! how rare an event is such a moral transformation! Celsus said, " to change nature perfectly is very difficult;" and holding such an opinion he was very naturally surprised at the interest taken by Christians in the vicious. Simon doubtless shared the heathen philosopher's scepticism regarding conversion, as does the world in general, and therefore we cannot wonder if the penitence-hypothesis did not even so much as occur to his mind. He grievously misjudged in consequence; but his mistake was at least quite as excusable as that of Eli, who deemed that Hannah was drunk, when she was only a woman of a sorrowful spirit. It needs an unusually delicate and sympathetic mind to judge rightly in such cases, and Eli and Simon were commonplace men.

Happily for the object of Simon's harsh judgment, there was one present who could divine the real situation. The quick loving eye of Jesus detected what escaped the observation of a Pharisee whose vision was blunted by prejudice and custom; and, reading at the same moment with equal rapidity and certainty the thoughts of His host. He forthwith proceeded to put the true interpretation on the phenomena, and so to defend at once the woman and Himself. Nor was He sorry to have the opportunity of offering the double apology. For He had felt the coldness of Simon's manner towards Himself on entering his house as a guest. He saw at once on what footing He stood; that He was regarded as a social inferior, and that He was there to be patronised by one who thought he showed condescension in inviting Him to his house, and might therefore excuse himself for neglecting the ordinary attentions paid by a host to guests of his own rank.2 Such indignity the lowly Son of man could meekly

Origen, C. Celsum," lib. iii. c. 65. haiv yap a iu-i a rtxeajs,–Kafxaktitov, 2 I Sam. i. 14, 15.

' Meyer remarks that the custom of feet washing was not an absolute rule, but was observed chiefly towards persons arriving off a journey. But there can be little doubt that a difference had been made between Jesus and other guests of higher social rank.

endure, nor did He resent it in the present instance, for the tone of the words which He spake at this time is not that of anger, but of one who, feehng His own moral superiority, can U'ith easy self-possession say what fits the occasion. " Simon, I have somewhat to say unto thee:" what composure is in that beginning! But though He cherishes no resentment against Simon for the treatment He has received, He deems it right to avail Himself of a legitimate opportunity of setting it also in its true light, in the hope that he who has hitherto been occupied in judging others, may enter upon the more profitable occupation of judging himself And with exquisite felicity. He contrives to accomplish this purpose at the same time that He is pursuing the other, that viz. of defending the w oman and Himself against Simon's unjust suspicions. One brief, simple parable serves both endsâ at once apologising for the accused, and bringing a countercharge against the accuser. Were it not, indeed, for the interpretation given by Jesus Himself, in which He makes a complaint of Simon's coldness, we might not be perfectly sure that the parable was meant to have an offensive as well as a defensive bearing. We might think that the second debtor did not necessarily represent Simon or any one in particular, but was merely introduced as a foil to the first and for the sake of contrast. But even apart from the interpretation following, there are little touches in the parable itself which seem to indicate a purpose to attack as well as to defend. There is the pointed manner in which the Speaker intimates to Simon His desire to say something to htm Then there is the question with which the parable winds up, Which of them now will love him most which looks very like a device to entrap Simon into a judgment on himself after the manner of Nathan with David. One would say, beforehand, even without reading the application, that the woman being of course the greater debtor in the parable, Simon is represented by the other, and that Jesus meant to insinuate that if the woman had loved Himself so ardently, Simon had sinned in the opposite direction, though in what precise respects he had come short we should not have known unless we had been informed.

'On 'O o0u)f tkpivaq, V. 43, Godet well observes, that it is the Udvv ipoSig of Sociates, when he had caught his interlocutor in his net.

This parable of the Two Debtors is so simple in its structure, that it needs hardly any explanation. The case put is plain, and the inference suggested is equally so. The answer of Simon to the question, Which will love him most? is the judgment of common sense. He to whom most is forgiven will certainly love most; that is, on the assumption that the two creditors are in other respects alike; for we know, of course, that a man of a generous disposition will be more erateful for a small favour than a man of selfish nature will be for a greater. The only feature that may seem a little surprising is the smallness of the sums owed, especially when compared with those named in the parable of the Unmerciful Servant. The purpose may have been to insure an unbiassed judgment on the part of Simon, by preventing the suspicion arising in his mind that he was aimed at. So important a person was not likely to think of himself as concerned in a transaction where such paltry sums. were involved as fifty and five hundred pence. If this was what was designed, the device was perfectly successful. The air of languid indifference with which Simon gave his judgment, as if the case supposed were too insignificant to awaken any interest in his mind, shows that he had no thought of its having a reference to himself. Then while the pettiness of the amounts served this purpose beforehand, the utter insignificance of the smaller amount served another purpose after-hand, when Jesus had given His own interpretation of the parable, that viz. of letting Simon see what value his lightly-esteemed guest set upon his love. You have loved me, it said in effect, as one who has been forgiven fifty pence; as one, that is, who has received a scarcely appreciable favour. On the other hand, the larger sum, though in itself of no great amount, was sufficiently great to be a measure of the penitent's gratitude both by comparison and absolutely. By comparison, for it was ten times greater than the smaller sum; absolutely, for it was a considerable amount in relation to the social position of the humbler debtor.

' The smallness of the sums owed may be an indirect indication of the prevalent poverty of the country. Hausrath, in his ' Neutestamenthche Zeitgeschichte 'â History of the New Testament Times'â has gathered together the many indications in the Gospels of the prevalence in Palestine of impoverishment produced by excessive taxation " The most frequent

The one matter regarding this parable which needs careful consideration is its aim. What purpose or purposes was it designed to serve? Now, as we have already indicated, the parable was spoken with a threefold aim; first, to defend the conduct of the woman by suggesting the point of view under which it ought to be regarded; second, to impugn the conduct of the Pharisee; and third, to defend the conduct of Jesus Himself in accepting the homage rendered. We will consider the parable in these three points of view in succession.

I, When the whole circumstances are duly borne in mind, it becomes clear that the first thing to be done was to put a right construction on the strange behaviour of the woman. That she loved Jesus, loved Him much, was evident; but the quality and motive of the love were not so apparent; they had in fact been grievously misunderstood by Simon. These therefore must first be set in their true light. And how is this done Simply by constructing a story of two debtors, and thereby suggesting that the case of the woman is the images in the utterances of Jesus are those of the creditor, the debtor, and the debtor's prison. In one parable, everybody except the king is bankrupt; the steward is in debt to the king; the servau to the steward (Matt, xviii. 23); the rich who remit to their debtors fifty or five hundred pence are rare indeed (Luke vi. 34; vii. 41); the unmerciful creditor who always has the bailiff at hand is much more frequent. In the street, the creditor seizes the poor debtor, and the judge's officer casts him into prison, out of which he does not depart before he has paid the very last farthing (Luke xii. 58); and if he cannot pay, his lord commands him to be sold, and his wife and children, and all that he has, and payment to be made (Matt, xviii. 25). Oil and wheat, the first necessaries of life, are furnished on credit (Luke xvi. (i,) ', buildings that have been commenced remain unfinished for want of money (Luke xiv. 29); the merchant puts all his means, in order to keep them safe, into a single pearl (Matt. xiii. 46); in digging in the field, one finds the treasure which another has buried to keep it from the rapacious hands of the oppressor (Matt. xiii. 44); speculators keep their corn back from the markets, and enlarge their storehouses (Luke xii. 18). With this impoverishment is connected the parcelling out of estates; in place of the plough, appears on the smaller allotments spade husbandry. " What shall I do? " says the ruined steward; " I cannot dig, to beg I am ashamed " (Luke xvi. 3). The result of this want of money is usury. The bank of exchange flourishes (Luke xix. 23); in a short time (?) the speculator multiplies his capital five-fold and ten-told (Luke xix. 16, 18). This is the economic background of the evangelic history which comes to light in a hundred places."â Vol. I. pp. 188, 189. English translation, Williams and Norgate.

case of a moral debtor forgiven. As in the saying, "They' that be whole need not a physician," the point lies in the suggestion that Jesus was a physician; so in this parable the emphasis lies in the suggestion that the accused is not merely a sinner, but a sinner forgiven, and that her love proceeds from gratitude for the remission of her debts. It is true no express mention is made of the quality of the love, but only of its quantity, but the quality is involved in the relevancy of the parable. It had been a mere impertinence to speak a parable of two debtors, unless it were meant to convey the idea that the woman was a debtor forgiven, and her love a debtor's love to her generous creditor. This indirect way of saying the thing chiefly intended is incidental to the parabolic style, and when that is remembered it is very forcible. We then see the point of the parable, as we see a star glimmering into view in the evening twilight, most clearly, by looking a little to one side of it. Unfortunately many commentators have not looked a little to one side, but have gazed too directly at the object, and so have failed to see it, and in consequence have fallen into error in the interpretation of the sentence in which our Lord explained His leading purpose in uttering the parable: ' Wherefore I say unto thee, her sins, which are many, are forgiven; for she loved much." These words have been a stumbling-block to many, logically and theologically; the latter because they seem to teach the Romish doctrine of justification by charity, as opposed to the Protestant doctrine of justification by faith; the former because, so understood, they stand in no relation to the connection of thought either before or after The logical difficulty is the more serious of the two; for one might manage to overcome the other, either by magnanimously conceding the point to the Catholic interpreter, and contenting ourselves with the philosophic reflection that in these enlightened times "we have surmounted the polemical antithesis to work-holiness,"" or by ingeniously endeavouring to attach to the verb " loved " a sense approximating to the idea of faith, making it e. g. equivalent to ' longed," so that

I Ver. 47.

So De Wette; as if feeling that the tense was against him he says, wo may add to yatrjjo-t ayair.

the didactic import of the words should be somewhat like this: He who is to believe in forgiveness must have that longing for pardon which is love in its passive or receptive side, and is at the same time substantially faith. Such ingenious devices for reducing love to faith, and so squaring Christ's doctrine with Protestant orthodoxy, do certainly leave on the mind an impression of artificiality; but one could reconcile himself to that if no better way out of the difficulty could be found. But the logical difficulty remains, the irrelevance of the words so interpreted to the situation and the connection of thought. Thus understood, the words do not contribute to the explanation of the parable, but simply contain an independent didactic thought, to the effect that the woman will receive forgiveness of her many sins, because she has a great yearning for forgiveness, as evinced by her whole behaviour. It is very hard to believe that any such incoherence characterised the utterances of Christ on this occasion. But we are not reduced to such an unwelcome necessity. If we only keep in mind the situation, the meaning, point, and appositeness of the disputed sentence become perfectly clear. Christ's purpose in uttering these words is to suggest to Simon the true point of view from which the woman's conduct is to be regarded. He says here plainly what he has already said parabolically: the case of this woman is the case of a debtor forgiven. The solemn manner of address, "Wherefore I say unto thee." indicates a purpose to correct a wrong impression, indicates that as the chief purpose of the Speaker, though it is not the first thing spoken of. The order of the words which follow

So Ohhausen. who views faith as love receptive or the negative pole, forgiving love as the positive pole. Similarly Trench, vho finds comfort in the fact that Theophylact identifies the love referred to in ver. 47 with faith. Having stated in the text that the woman's yearning love " in fact was faith," he appends the note, " very distinctly Theophylact in loc, Srt yat);Â jtoxw, avti toi ttiutiv ivisiikaro ttoxX i." It is true that Theophylact does say this, but his saying so does not settle the matter. It only shows that he felt the pressure of the difficulty.

2 I take ov xapt" as connected with Xiyu aot, not with what follows, and understand it as mediating a return to the principal thought in the mind of the speaker, from the detailed contrast between the conduct of the wom. in. and that of Simon. Taken with the clause beginning with a(ii' uivrai the phrase must be rendered "on this account "â becauie of the Jove displayed as aforesaid, her sins are forgiven.

points in the same direction: " Forgiven are her sins, hef many sins; for she loved much." The idea of forgiveness is put in the forefront, to suggest a way of regarding the woman's conduct which Simon had never thought of " She is a moral debtor forgiven, Simon "â Jesus would say: " she is forgivenâ that is the key to the strange behaviour you have so grievously misconstrued. Her sins have been forgiven, her many sins: for you are not wrong in thinking of her as a great sinnerâ that is manifest from her behaviour: for in all these acts which have awakened so much surprise, ' she loved much," and that is the way of those who have been forgiven much." Thus paraphrased, the saying which has created so much perplexity fits naturally into the whole situation. The first clause, " forgiven are her sins," corrects Simon's misconstruction and reveals the character of the woman's love; the second clause, " her many sins," concedes all that Simon can say as to the woman's past life; the third clause, " for she loved much," at once indicates the source of the knowledge that her sins were many, and the existence of a connection between the multitude of her sins and the excess of her love. For this last clause does not depend on the first clause, but on the second, not on adpi inai, but on itowac; and so connected it contains by implication the didactic statement which we expect as the counterpart to that which follows: " but to whom little is forgiven, the same also loveth little." Expanded, Christ's whole meaning is this: " Now then, Simon, let me tell you the truth about this poor woman: Her whole conduct means that she is a penitent who has been led by me to entertain the hope that her sinful life may be forgiven. That life in your opinion has been very full of sin. I can see that there you are not mistaken: that her sins are many her behaviour towards myself attests, for in all these acts she showed much love; and that much love is the sure 1 The interpretation of this verse by Grotius is not the same as ours, but he recognises that vowai is emphatic. He gives to the verse this turn: God pardons sin, great sin, in the hope of producing such great love as this woman has shown. The woman's sin was pardoned in the foresight of such love as the natural effect. This idea corresponds to the text, "there is forgiveness with thee, that thou mayest be feared," and coincides with our view as to Christ's motive in receiving publicans and sinners.

The aorist yavqfff implies a reference to the acts enumerated in the previous verses.

sign of much forgiven, just as little love, exemplified in your own conduct, is the sure sign of little forgiven."

2. The parable was spoken not only in defence of the woman, but as an attack on the fault-finder. It is in a particular instance the judgment of Pharisaism, as an ungenial soil in which the gospel of the kingdom had little chance of taking root. It is a judgment pronounced in a fair and candid spirit through a favourable sample of the class, for such Simon seems to have been. This Pharisee was of a milder spirit than the majority of his co-religionists. He cherished no unkindly feelings towards Jesus. When puzzled by His conduct, as at this time, he did not think the hardest thoughts of Him, for many would have plainly said something much more injurious than, "He cannot be a prophet." Simon was a sort of Nicodemus; he had respect enough for Jesus to invite Him to dinner, though too hampered by pride and prejudice to be cordial in his hospitality; as Nicodemus had respect enough for Jesus to visit him, but only by night. In this light Jesus seems to have regarded him. He was willing to recognise him as one who cherished towards Himself at least a little love. If He animadverted on the littleness of the love, it was in no vindictive spirit, not to gratify private resentment, but for a higher purpose. The very frankness of the complaint testifies to the absence of perturbing passions from the mind of the Speaker. The description of a little debtor's love, as exemplified by Simon, is pervaded by a triumphant buoyancy of spirit and a happy play of humour which exclude the supposition that injured feeling was the source of inspiration. Far from being angry with his host, Jesus pitied him as a soul in bonds, unable to break away from conventionalism in thought and action, and He described

The view above given, according to which on in last clause of ver. 47, points out that by which a certain fact is known, not that on account of which a certain thing is done, is that taken by Unger; Meyer (orÂ, vom Erkenntnissgrunde zu fassen); Kuinoel (who holds that the other view, even if true, is an irrelevance); Bengal on, Remissio peccatorum, Simoni non cogitata, probatur a fructu); Reuss, Stier, Godet, and most recent commentators (not Keim). The greater number make iirt depend not on iro Xa(', but on d tujvrai. The old Protestant interpretation which took on as equivalent to li6 is entirely out of date, and mriy be referred to merely as an instance of exegesis occupying a position of servile subordination tc the dogmatic interest.

his state in hope to set him free. And how significant as well as graphic the description! " Thou gavest Me no water for My feet; thou gavest Me not a kiss; My head with oil thou didst not anoint," Cold civility, no heart, no cordiality,, no spontaneity, no free play of natural affection. This in the matter of hospitality, and the same thing of course in all other departments of conduct; for the ruling spirit of a man reveals itself in all he does. The ruling spirit in this Pharisee, and in all his class, is pride, protecting from sinful excess on the one hand, but disqualifying also for heroic virtue on the other, and dooming them to moral monotony and mediocrity. The pride of virtue binds their souls in the ice of a perpetual winter, so that in their life are seen neither the devastating floods of passion nor the fertilizing streams of charity. How certain that the kingdom of heaven will draw few citizens from the ranks of Pharisaic society, and what poor citizens even the few are likely to make! Why, this man is so enslaved by caste prejudices that he dares not treat Jesus, socially his inferior, and suspected by his class, with gentlemanly courtesy and right hospitable welcome, but must needs receive Him in a style which is a miserable compromise between civility and insult. What chance is there of such an one condescending to become a disciple of Jesus, and identifying himself wholly with His cause? As we read this indictment for inhospitality we feel that Pharisaism is hopeless, and that if Jesus desires to make disciples. He must seek them not among the men that need no repentance, but among the erring and lost, who neither can boast of Pharisaic virtue, nor are enslaved by Pharisaic pride.

3. To say just this in His own defence was the third purpose Jesus had in view in uttering this parable. This purpose is indeed not so apparent on the surface of the parable, and it has been very little noticed by interpreters, nevertheless that

Hofmann states it as the aim of the evangelist in introducing at this point in his narrative the scene in Simon's house, to show by an example how the Saviour of sinners could not be their Saviour, viz. because wanting the sense of sin they had no desire for forgiveness ('Dasevang. des Lukas," p. 203). This is a defective account of the design of the narrative, but it is true so far as it goes. To show the hopelessness of the Pharisaic class as a field for evangelistic effort, and the hopefulness of the classes they despised, and so to justify in both directions the public action of Jesus, is the full purpose and effect of the narrative.

Jesus had it in view may be considered certain. For in the first place He was put on His defence by Simon's uncharitable thoughts. Then, that He meant to defend Himself may be inferred from the question with which the parable ends, "Which of them will love Him most?" the question clearly implying that the amount of debt remitted and the amount of grateful love are connected by a general law. It is in effect predicted that every debtor who is forgiven much will love much. But if this be indeed the law of the case, what more natural than that Christ, as the recipient of the gratitude, should be influenced by that law in His conduct, and pay most attention to those who, being forgiven, would have most love to give Him, as having been forgiven most, and that having a good opportunity of justifying Himself for so acting, as in the present case, He should avail Himself of it."' Further, is it not sufficient evidence of intention to defend conduct impugned that the parable serves the purpose so admirably, saying in effect: I repel not this woman, I accept gladly those demonstrations of devoted love, for I desire to be much loved: and for this very reason it is that I am drawn by powerful attraction to comparv which you Pharisees shun, and if the truth must be told prefer it to yours, for I iind that when they have been brought to repentance and to faith in the forgiveness of sins, their love is as great as their previous sinfulness. But it becomes if possible still more certain that a purpose of self-defence was in Christ's mind, when we take into consideration the pointed contrast between the penitent and the Pharisee in the application of the parable. " Water for My feet thou gavest not, but she with tears did wet My feet, and with her hair she wiped them. A single kiss to Me thou gavest not, but she, from the time I came in, hath incessantly kissed My feet. With common oil My Jiead thou didst not anoint, but she with costliest ointinent anointed My feet." Who, as he reads these impassioned sentences, does not say to himself. No wonder that Jesus Christ preferred the society of publicans and sinners to the society of Pharisees! Who would not take pains to earn such love as that of the woman Who would not rather be excused from being the recipient of such cold love as that of Simon.? And who can doubt nc. â â ayairriaii; the predictive future.

The Two Debtors, 251 that Jesus meant to suggest such thoughts as a part of His apology for loving sinners, not merely in self-defence, but in self-revelation, that all men might know where His preferences lay?

It is matter of regret to us, that in ascribing to Jesus this aim we part company with the commentators, few of whom, as already noticed, allude to it. We take comfort, however, from the fact that we have on our side one who, though no learned commentator, was as likely as any to grasp the particular truth we now insist on. Bunyan saw it, and proclaimed it with all his characteristic force and felicity. In his famous sermon on "The Jerusalem sinner saved," he specifies as one of the reasons why Jesus would have mercy offered in the first place to the biggest sinners, that " they when converted are apt to love Him most," appealing in proof to the words spoken by Jesus in the house of Simon. We would gladly give our readers the benefit of the whole paragraph, all the more that in these days i probably will think of turning to such a quarter for light upon a parable. But we can find space for only one or two sentences. " If," shrewdly remarks our author, "Christ loves to be loved a little. He loves to be loved much; but there is not any that are capable of loving much, save those that have much forgiven them." He then cites Paul as an illustration; and having given a graphic description of the apostle's intense devotion to Christ and to the gospel, he adds the quaint reflection: " I wonder how far a man might go among the converted sinners of the smaller size, before he could find one that so much as looked anything this wayward. Where is he that is thus under pangs of love for the grace bestowed upon him by Jesus Christ Excepting only some few, you may walk to the world's end and find none." Next follows another illustration, drawn from the very narrative now under consideration, but told as a story concerning Martha and Mary, which Bunyan had read in a religious book some twenty years before. The story as told is homely enough, but the moral is admirably put. " Alas! Christ has but little thanks for the saving of little sinners. To whom little is forgiven, the same loveth little." He gets not water for His feet, by His saving of such sinners. There are abundance of dry-eyed Christians in the world, and abundance of dry-eyed duties too: duties that were never wetted with the tears of contrition and repentance, nor even sweetened with the great sinner's box of ointment," And the conclusion of the whole is: " Wherefore His way is oftentimes to step out of the way, to Jericho, to Samaria, to the country of the Gad-arenes, to the coasts of Tyre and Sidon, and also to Mount Calvary, that He may lay hold of such kind of sinners as will love Him to His liking."

This declared preference of Christ is certainly very comfortable news to those whom it concernsâ to 'Jerusalem sinners," to sinners, so to speak, writ in large capitals. But moralists may suggest the expediency of treating both the preference and the ground on which it rests as esoteric doctrines, to be whispered in the ear of the select few, lest the open proclamation of them should give rise to licentious abuse, by leading men to think that the best way to qualify themselves for being eventually great saints is in the first place to be great sinners. In their laudable zeal for the interests of morality, they may even suggest a doubt whether we have correctly understood Christ's meaningâ whether He really intended to say that He expected the most devoted disciples to come from among those who had greatly erred, and on this very ground exercised His ministry chiefly among this class. Is it not permissible, they may ask, to interpret the maxim "Much forgiven, love much," subjectively, so that it shall mean, he who hath the greatest sense of sin, being forgiven, shall love most, thus making the difference between men turn not upon the comparative amount of their outward transgressions, but upon the comparative sensitiveness of their consciences, which may quite easily be found in its highest degree in him who has outwardly offended the least. Now we have

Weizsacker is of opinion that the parable of the Two Debtors does not fit into its present surroundings, and that it was spoken on some other occasion. But he thinks that its original sense certainly throws light on the procedure of Jesus with the classes of people who are represented as approaching Hira in the narrative of the palsied man, and the feast in Levi's house. " He draws gladly to Himself the distinctively sinful and the apostates from the law (Gesetzesabtrunnigen = publicans, c.), because such, from the sense of their guilt, have also a strong sense of their deliverance, and therefore can be won in a deeper, more enduring manner."â ' Untersuchungen," p. 386.

For the above view vide Trench.

the greatest respect for such scruples and for the motives from which they arise. And we admit, as Bunyan admitted, that the doctrine in question, like the kindred doctrine of justification by grace, may be abused by evil-minded men to their own hurt We acknowledge further that great devotion does not necessarily imply great antecedent misconduct, and that in point of fact, many notable Christians never were notable offenders in outward conduct against the laws of morality; as an example of whom may be cited Luther, who was not remarkable among men for crime or vice, like Augustine before his conversion, but only for the morbid intensity of his moral consciousness. And we accept it as a corollary from this fact, that Christ's words must not be so strictly interpreted as to exclude from the category of great debtors, who are greatly grateful for forgiveness, such men as the German reformer. He to whom much is forgiven may mean he who feds himself to be a great debtor, and he to whom little is forgiven may mean he who feels himself to be a small debtor; and the latter may in fact be the greater sinner of the two, as we know that many of the Pharisees were really worse men than the very publicans and harlots. Still the fact remains that the original debtors of the parable were, in the broad outward sense, great and small debtors respectively, the woman being the great debtor, and Simon the small. The further fact remains, that Jesus did really seek and find disciples chiefly among those whose lives were far from correct and exemplary, instead of among those who, as regards outward conduct, needed no repentance. Therefore, if, on the one hand, the subjective interpretation of the parable may not be altogether excluded, neither, on the other, may the objective. It must be recognised as a fact that among those who have gone furthest wrong the kingdom of God not only may find, but is likely to find, its best citizens, so that the ministers of the kingdom are justified in paying special attention to that class. And if the rationale of this fact be demanded, it is not very hard to give. In the first place, it is much easier for one who has been a transgressor, to attain unto a strong sense of his moral shortcomiig, than ' for one in whom the sinful principle has remained comparatively latent Given the same native strength of conscience, the man who has been carried headlong into evil action, will, when moral reflection commences, have a keener sense of demerit than the man who has not been assailed by, or has not yielded to, the same temptation. Then, secondly, the natural constitution of those erring ones who have great need of repentance must be taken into account. They are children of passion: endowed with powerful impulses, good and bad, unharmonised, warring against each other, the flesh against the spirit, the spirit against the flesh, the law in the members against the law in the mind, and vice versd. Such natures are capable of going far wrong, but they are also capable, when a moral crisis comes, often brought about by their very excesses, of being very decided for the right. Men of this stamp, of whom Paul may be taken as the type, being converted, become the most devoted Christians. It is not merely that, having abundant materials in their previous life to supply a strong sense of sin, they feel themselves more than other men indebted to Divine grace, and are therefore more intensely grateful. It is that they have a natural faculty of loving, of throwing themselves with abandon into all they undertake, beyond that of ordinary men. The passionate energy formerly employed in doing evil is now brought to the service of righteousness. The sinful woman hitherto the slave of unlawful passion, now transfers the whole wealth of her afl"ections to her Saviour, and loves Him with a love purified, but not less fervent than the sinful love of other days. Saul, the fierce persecutor, becomes the equally energetic apostle of the faith he once destroyed. Surely Jesus, in seeking to make disciples among

"See," says Euthymiuszigabenus ('in Quatuorevangelia'): "How with those things wherewith she was wont to hunt after toli ivi) her own destruction, she now hunted after Idljptvat) salvation; for with amatory tears and curiously plaited hair and myrrh, she bewitched youths, but what were before the instruments of sin she now makes the instruments of virtue ' (rd irpiv opyava rijQ afiapriag opyava vvv Trtjrojjk'fv opfrzf.

That Paul was once a Pharisee, may seem to militate against the view that from the ranks of Pharisaism good samples of Christians were not likely to come. But exceptio probat regiilam. Saul of Tarsus was by â education and profession a Pharisee, but he had not the Pharisaic nature and temperament. It was inevitable that a man of his moral energy should one day break with Pharisaism, bursting its bonds, as Samsoq burst the green withs of the Philistines.

such, rather than among men of frigid natures not Hkely to do either much evil or much good, acted wisely. Let us not hesitate to say so, out of fear lest some abuse the doctrine. We cannot afford to conceal the truth out of regard to such. It is misspent anxiety to have so much regard to them. For as Bunyan well remarks: " These will neither be ruled by grace nor by reason. Grace would teach them, if they knew it, to deny ungodly courses: and so would reason too, if it could truly understand the love of God. Doth it look like what hath any coherence with reason or mercy, for a man to abuse his friend Because Christ died for men, must I therefore spit in his face."'"

It thus appears that in the words which He spoke in the house of Simon the Pharisee Jesus gave, in the form of a defence of the sinful woman, and of a censure on His host's unkindness, a complete vindication of his habitual policy as the Founder of the Divine kingdom. The Son of man came eating and drinking, living in a fashion which threw Him into contact with the less reputable portion of Jewish society, and produced an ever-widening alienation between Him and the socially and morally respectable class. For this He was much blamed, but the results quaintly hinted at in the parable of the two debtors proved that he took the course best fitted to advance the great aim of His life. The wisdom of His conduct was justified at once by the great love of the sinful woman, and by the little love of Simon. And the vindication of Christ is at the same time the vindication of the course taken by Christianity at all great epochs of its history, and very specially in the apostolic age. Speaking of the progress of Christianity in such cities as Alexandria, Antioch, and Corinth, Renan remarks: " Like the socialisms of our day, like all new ideas, Christianity germinated in what is called the corruption of great cities." The observation is just, and the reflection appended to it is not less so: " That corruption, in truth, is often only a life more full and free, a more powerful awakening of the innermost forces of humanity." AH is not bad that is to be met with among " publicans and sinners;" there lies waste a wealth of moral energy which, properly directed, ' The Jerusalem Sinner Saved." ' Saint Paul," p. 334.

2. 6 The Parabolic Teacjdng of Christ, book ii.

will do excellent service for the kingdom of God. Thereforej the followers of Jesus, when they understand their true interest, are not grieved when the kingdom sufifereth violence at the hands of those whom the wise and prudent and morally respectable regard askance, and the violent take it by force, knowing that the force displayed in storming the kingdom will all be available for its advancement.

Having finished his eloquent panegyric on the sinful woman's love, Jesus turned to her and said: " Thy sins are forgiven." 2 From this it has been inferred that up to the moment when these words were spoken the woman did not know that her sins were forgiven. The inference indicates a very inadequate conception of the position in which the poor penitent was placed in the house of Simon, which was such as to make confirmation of her faith or hope of pardon very needful, even assuming that she had cherished such before, as the parable implies she had. How chilling and discouraging to the contrite heart, the unsympathetic, or even loathing, looks of the company! How hard in such a company on earth, where is no joy over a sinner repenting, to believe that there is such joy even in heaven! By our sympathy, or the want of it, we can much help or hinder faith in the forgiveness of sins. For this woman there was no sympathy in Simon's house, save in the heart of Jesus. Therefore Jesus, knowing this full well, felt it all the more necessary that He should make a decided demonstration of 1 When one considers how much profound far-reaching thought is hidden in this simple parable, he cannot but be sensible of the incomparable excellence of Christ's parables as contrasted with those of the rabbis. The rabbis also had their parable of Two Debtors to explain how it came to pass that Isra: l, v. hib loved by God more than all other nations, was most punished for her sins. In the rabbinical parable the creditor accepts payment from one of his debtors in small instalments, and so facilitates payment in full. From the other he exacts nothing till he fails, and then he demands the whole at once. The question is thereon put, Which of the two is most favourably treated? The parable in itself is passable, but its moral is commonplace. The excellence of our Lord's parables, on the other hand, is that by the most obvious analogies truths unfamiliar and hard to be believed are made to appear intelligible, rational, and credible Rabbinical parables are nuts which on being cracked are found to be empty. For the above parable see Weill, ' Le Judaisme," vol. i. p. 158.

The Two Debtors. 257

His sympathy, and assure the penitent that though there was no forgiveness with men, there was forgiveness with God; and so, with a firm, cheerful, sympathetic voice, He said, "Thy sins are forgiven."

This friendly word, like all the words spoken by Jesus, and His whole bearing on this occasion, were out of harmony with the spirit of the company. His fellow-guests showed by their looks that the thought of their heart was: Who is this who also forgiveth sins, so committing a greater offence than is that of receiving sinners, the one being an offence against piety, while the other is only an offence against morality Treating this new exhibition of the censorious spirit with magnanimous disdain, and caring only for the spiritual well-being of the penitent, Jesus repeated his assurance in another form, and bade her farewell with the cheering words: " Thy faith hath saved thee; go in peace." Certain critics, it is true, tell us that these words must be set down to the credit of the evangelist, and that we ought to see in them, as in some other features of this narrative, traces of his Paulinist tendency. Now the sentiment is certainly thoroughly Pauline, but it is also thoroughly in keeping with the teaching of Jesus. Jesus not less than Paul, according to the concurrent testimony of all the evangelists, gave great prominence to faith, and repeatedly expressed His delight in signal manifestations thereof, and this is only what we should expect when we consider that the kingdom of God, as presented to view in the teaching of our Lord, is essentially a kingdom of grace. The ideas of faith and of grace are kindred, and He who knew so well how to exhibit the gracious aspect of God was sure to magnify the importance and the power of faith. And we have here one of the instances in which Jesus did most signally magnify faith's power to save. The statement is not to be restricted to the one blessing of the forgiveness of sins, Jesus meant to say that faith would do, had already done in principle, for the sinful mortal before Him all that needed to be done in order to a complete moral rescue. Faith, working by love,

Arndt says: " This word was needed as consolation for the humiliations esperienced in the house of Simon."

Ver. so. 3 Yi g Hilgenfeld, Einleitung," p. 560.

258 Tlie Parabolic Teaching of CJirist. book ii.

would purify her heart, ennoble her life, and, what was very necessary, protect her against the demoralising influence of social scorn which dooms so many ' sinners' to perdition. It was a bold assertion to make, but the confidence of Jesus in the power of faith was justified by what it had already done. Had not a believing reception of the glad tidings filled her soul with inexpressible love to the Preacher and to the Father in heaven whose grace He revealed: had it not transformed her into a poet, a devotee, a heroine, capable of conventionality-defying demonstrations â those gushing tears, the drying of the feet of her Redeemer with her hair, the fervent kissing of His feet, and the anointing of them Avith ointment? Here already was a new spiritual creation all due to faith, producing through the nature of the thing believed and its priceless value to the recipient intense gratitude, which by deeds more eloquent than words said: " O Lord, truly I am thy servant, I am thy servant; thou hast loosed my bonds." Well might Jesus say, "Thy faith hath saved thee," for a more complete demonstration of the recuperative ennobling power of that faculty through which we let God's grace flow into our hearts cannot be imagined. And what faith had done it might easily continue to do. The main difficulty lies in the beginning. Faith has already cast out the devils of evil passion and put Christ in their place; has already dared to face Pharisaic contempt. It will be able hereafter to keep out the demons of desire which have been cast out by the expulsive power of a new affection, and to bear with equanimity the light esteem of a world which regards the sins of the past as unpardonable. Therefore we may not doubt that when she left that house she went away into abiding peace, very probably to join the company of those of whom the evangelist speaks in the commencement of the next chapter as following Jesus and ministering unto him of their substance.

Psalm cxvi. 16.

Luke viii. iâ 3. It is noticeable that the evangelist begins this chapter as if he were continuing the previous narrative. He does not name Je us but uses the pronoun: "It came to pass afterwards that Ht went," c.

THE manner in which Luke introduces these three parables is such as to indicate, not the particular occasion, but the kind of occasion on whicli they were spoken. The words, "Now there were approaching Him all the publicans and the sinners, to hear Him," could scarcely be used with reference to any one time. What is described is a prominent feature in the ministry of Jesus, ever growing more conspicuous, and arresting the attention and provoking the criticism of unsympathetic observers, viz. the interest awakened thereby in the minds of the classes in evil repute, and the gracious manner in which Jesus regarded those by whom that interest was manifested. That the Evangelist has correctly indicated the general nature of the occasion of the parables recorded in the fifteenth chapter of his Gospel, is evident at a glance. On the very face of them these charming parables are an apology for loving and receiving the sinfulâ forming a part, and, we may add, the crowning part of Christ's inimitable defence for that noble crime committed by Him against the conventional law and custom of contemporary Jewish society. The use made by Matthew of the first of the three parablesâ that of the Lost Sheepâ in introducing it into the discourse on Humility, to teach the truth that God cares for the lowly and insignificant, is legitimate; but it is easy to see that the parable, in that connection, falls short of its full significance and pathos,

Vide Hofmann, Das Evangelium des Lukas, p. 382.
â Chap, xviii. 12.

as also, and perhaps just in consequence of tliat, of its original literary grace. For Divine love is seen at its maximum, not in caring for the lozvly, but in caring for the low; and it was when speaking of this intensest and most pathetic manifestation of love, that the mind of Jesus was likely to conceive the parabolic representation of love's gracious impulses in its most felicitous form, including the feature of the shepherd carrying the erring sheep on his shoulders, omitted by Matthew, which we cannot doubt belonged to the parable as originally spoken.

We have as little doubt that these three parables, related by Luke at one gush, were all spoken at the same time; albeit the third is introduced in a very loose way with the vague phrase, "And He said," suggesting the idea that what follows is an annex to what goes before. Accumulation of parables teaching one lesson was certainly not a usual practice with Christ, but on the present occasion it was fitted to serve an important apologetic purpose. Multiplication of instances of rejoicing over things or persons lost tended to convey the impression that such joy was universal, a touch of nature in which the whole world was kin. Jesus thereby arrayed against his critics all mankind, people of all ranks, conditions, and relations: men, women, shepherds, housewives, fathers, householders, domestics; saying in effect to the sour, cynical fault-finders: Are ye not men?â have ye not human hearts that I should need to explain to you so simple a matter.? Multiplied illustration was thus an essential part of the arsfument.

'to-

Evvald remarks that Matthew's form of the parable wants den schbnen Farbenschnielz, which it has in Luke. Weizsacker, on the other hand, thinks Matthew gives the parable in at least the original connection; its design, according to him, being to apologise for despised ones against the grudges of Christ's own disciples.â ' Untersuchungen," p. 501.

2 ilitiv St, V. II.

' Hofmann thinks the third parable was spoken on a similar, but not on the same, occasion.â Das Evang. des Lu'cas," p. 386. Assuming that they were all spoken on the same occasion, the ettect would be to suggest that such illustrations might be multiplied ad libitum. Augustine, in his Confessions," cap. viii. 3, supplies a sample of how this might be done. One might have expected more from liini, a prodigal returned to his father's house, than this conmonpli: e service in such a book.

This consideration may be regarded as conclusive in favour of the view that a plurahty of parables, exemplifying the law of human nature according to which a peculiar joy is felt in connection with the finding of things lost, was a priori to be expected. But it may be asked, On what principle is the second of the three parables to be justified, which, in comparison with the first, seems inferior, and as coming after it superfluous? By itself it might be well enough, bat placed beside the other two, is it not deprived of ail interest, so as to make it very doubtful that it was uttered at the same time? Such an objection would indicate a very imperfect comprehension of the moral. situation. The very paltriness of the second parable is what gives it its value. The story of the housewife finding a piece of money worth little more than a sixpence, and rejoicing over the discovery, serves to suggest the thought, that it does not require things of great value to call into play the tendency of human nature to rejoice in finding things lost. And, be it noted, such a suggestion was most pertinent to the purpose for which all these parables were spoken, viz. to defend the conduct of Jesus in taking a warm interest in the moral recovery of the degraded. For, in the view of the fault-finders, publicans and 'sinners' were infinitely insignificant. The conversion of one belonging to these classes to wisdom and righteousness was, in their esteem, all but an impossibility, and even should it occur, of no consequence. That Christ did not share their despair and indifference was what they could not comprehend, was so incomprehensible that they felt shut up to account for the fact by imputing to Him sinister motives. As addressed to such an audience, the parable of the lost sheep was not unlikely to fail of its purpose; for in Pharisaic esteem a man of the despised classes was not so valuable as a sheep. If there were such a thing in the history of humanity as joy over the finding of a lost sixpence, a parable to that effect might serve the turn better, for probably the Pharisees would allow that a small coin was not unfit to represent the value of

Goebel thinks the parable of the lost sheep contains an argument d, fortiori, on the principle: " How much better is a man than a sheep. Unfortunately the principle was practically denied, so that the argument would not be felt to be d fortiori.

a publican. That joy of the kind described was by no means unexampled in Judaea in those days we may well believe, when we consider the many indications of abject poverty contained in the Gospels to which this same parable of the lost coin may be added. The parable, therefore, did not violate natural probability; and if not, it certainly was in other respects most apposite, as virtually involving the argument: many poor housewives have genuine joy in finding a lost coin of small amount; is it so very surprising that I should experience similar joy when a lost sinner, no matter how insignificant socially, repents, that I should deem the meanest of mankind worth saving, and his salvation a cause of satisfaction?

The two foregoing considerationsâ the cumulative force of the three parables, and the peculiar appositeness of the second to the moral situationâ are of prime importance as enabling us to understand the general drift and exact point of these parables, regarded, as they ought in the first place to be, from the apologetic point of view. If the chosen point of view were the didactic or dogmatic, we might set ourselves, after the fashion of some interpreters, to discover reasons for there being three parables, and three just such as those recorded; one about a shepherd, a second about a housewife, and a third about a father; and to ascertain the recondite theological lessons distinctively taught by each. We have no objections to such lines of study, and are willing to allow that here, as elsewhere, they may serve the good purpose of bringing out into reuef the felicity of the parables in suggesting thoughts which they are not primarily intended to teach. But for our own part, we prefer the historical to the dogmatic or mystic method of interpretation, and therefore mean to keep close throughout to the original apologetic aim, and to give greatest prominence to those thoughts which serve to show how the parables bear thereon. We do not, therefore, ask ourselves. Why precisely these parables "i We are Â Vide note in last chapter containing extract from Hausrath on this subject.

linger takes this view of the argumentative import of the second 'parable; in qua auctior adeo apparet probans ilia gradatio quatenus â intendit, soiitam in exigua adeo re perdita curam.â De Parab." p 148.

content to regard the first parable as the standard one, as it is most akin to Christ's professed character as a Shepherd who was in quest of the lost sheep of the house of Israel; and the second as a supplement to the first, rendered necessary by the contemptuous feelings of the Pharisees towards the lower orders, and meant to teach that the law of joy over things lost obtains in reference even to things of little value; and the third as meant to exemplify the action of the same law in the human sphere, and to suggest the great truth, that even the meanest of mankind is, at the worst, only a degraded son of God, whose repentance ought therefore to be an occasion of joy to all who love God. Nor do we find any mystery in the numbersâ one hundred, ten, two. The hundred sheep are the property of a shepherd of ordinary average wealth; the ten pieces of money the pecuniary possession of a woman in humble life; the two sons signify a family just large enough to supply illustrations of the two contrasted characters, and concentrate attention upon them. In one respect only do we feel disposed to accentuate the distinctive didactic significance of the parables, viz. in regard to the different senses of the term ' lost' employed in them all. We reserve our remarks on this point till the close.

There is one aspect of these parables closely connected with their apologetic use to which we have not yet referred, and of which we must here take notice. In all three there is apparent not merely a defensive, but an offensive, attitude. Christ not only apologises for His misunderstood love, but rebukes the Pharisees for their want of sympathy with such love as inspired His conduct, and the inhumanity therein revealed. The shepherd not only himself rejoices over his lost sheep, but he calls on his neighbours and friends to sympathise with his joy, and it is taken for granted that they do so. The same holds true of the woman who lost and found the piece of money. These two parables showed the Pharisees how they ought to have acted towar ds Jesus as the friend of the publicans and sinners. The third parable assails them in another way, not by showing them how they ought to have acted, but by showing them how they did act. The elder brother in the parable is the Pharisee's picture, and the elaboration of this part of the story shows how distinctly the purpose to attack and rebuke was present to Christ's mind."- But having pointed this out, we must at the same time point out another fact in a prehminary way, reserving details for a more advanced stage. The exposure of Pharisaic inhumanity, though unavoidably severe, is markedly mild and conciliatory in tone. Jesus had no wish to exasperate His critics; His heart was too sad to indulge in bitterness. Throughout, He aims, on the one hand, so to depict the publicans and sinners as to awaken pity, and on the other, so to speak of the Pharisees as, while pointing out clearly to them their characteristic vice, if possible tc win them to a better mind. The Saviour spoke these exquisite parables in a tender, gracious mood, as one who would by the very words he uttered be a healer of social breaches, and reconciler of alienated classes. These parables, and especially the last of the three, are thus, as it were, a prelude to the cross. Heavenly charity enacts in word the part of a peace-maker, which it afterwards enacted in the death on Calvary. When we read these parables we wonder not at the spectacle presented in the crucifixion; for the love which could inspire such touching utterances in the interest of redeeming love could also, if needful, die. Jesus said of the anointing in Bethany, " she did it for My burial." We may say of these irenical parables that they were spoken against the day of the Passion.

With these remarks we proceed to the consideration of the individual parables, and first that of â

THE LOST SHEEP.

He spake to tltejn this parable, saying: What man of you having an hundred sheep, and having lost one of them, doth not leave the ninety and nine in the wilderness and go after the lost one, until he find it f And having found it, he layeth it upoji his shoulders rejoicing. And on arriving at his house, he calleth together his friejids and 7tcigh-

Goebel's exposition has the merit of duly emphasising the offensive aspect of the three parables.

' tv ry ip! iix(, in the pastoral country where sheep might feed, but where grain was not cultivated. In Matthew the phrase is iirl to. opij, on the mountains.

boiirs saying to them: Rejoice with i7ie, for 1 have found my sheep which was lost. I say unto you, that likewise joy shall be in heaven over one sinner repenting, mo7-e than over ninety and nine just per-sons such as have not need of repentance. â Luke xv. 3â 7.

There is much latent pathos in this short parable which it is desirable we should make an effort to perceive, that we may be prepared to understand the shepherd's demand for sympathy, which, on a superficial reading of the story, before we have penetrated to its heart, may appear exaggerated. The chief interest, of course, centres in the shepherd, and his behaviour on one of his sheep being found missing. And in the first place, it is taken for granted that any shepherd to whom this happens will immediately set off in quest of the erring sheep. " What man of you having a flock of sheep, and losing one, will not go after it.""asks Jesus, confident that here at least He will meet with no contradiction, virtually asserting that it is a universal human instinct to go in quest of lost property. This implied assertion is in truth the radical part of His apology for Plis own conduct. As in the earliest instance in which He was put on His defence he vindicated Himself by the suggestion, "I am a Physician," so in the present instance He offers as His apology the suggestion, "I am a Shepherd;" and as in the former case so in the latter, the suggestion being once accepted all the rest follows of course. No one wonders that a shepherd goes after his straying sheep, any more than one wonders that a physician visits the sick rather than the whole, and visits most frequently those whose ailments are most serious. Neither is any one surprised at the joy of a shepherd on finding his sheep, which is the special feature insisted on in the present parable; the most cynical will admit that the finding of a lost sheep is a most legitimate occasion of satisfaction to the finder himself at least, and therefore a perfectly reasonable motive for seeking the lost. Such joy in a shepherd, and we may add similar joy in a physician on succeeding in restoring a patient to health, Christ's Pharisaic censors were not so stupid as to condemn. Their want of sympathy with Him as the friend of publicans and sinners sprang from their failure to recognise in Him a Physician and a Shepherd. And that failure again was due to their own want of love for their fellow-men. Their hearts were hardened against the social outcasts by prejudice and pride, and therefore when they saw the common people scattered and torn like a flock of sheep without a shepherd, the spectacle did not make their hearts bleed as it made the heart of Jesus bleed. And that made all the difference. Jesus, seeing the miserable plight of the lost sheep of the house of Israel, sought to be a Shepherd to them and associated with Himself in the pastoral care of the people His disciples;-while the Pharisees, on the other hand, neither cared themselves for the lost, nor sympathised with, or even so much as believed in, the loving care of others.

The next feature in the shepherd's conduct is that he seeks he finds? He is thoroughly in earnest in the search; he is determined to recover his lost property, and will spare himself no trouble for that end. This touch is omitted in Matthew's version of the parable, where we read instead the expression, " if he happen to find it;" but wdio can doubt that it belongs to the original form of the parable as first uttered.? Jesus was a very earnest Shepherd Himself, who spared no pains to find the lost sheep of God's fold, and he was not likely to omit this trait in the portrait of the shepherd's character. It is true that the most earnest quest may after all, end in failure, and therefore such a phrase as " if so be he find " is perfectly legitimate and appropriate. Jesus Himself knew too well what such failure was, and therefore it is quite possible that in repeating the parable, if He did repeat it, He gave prominence to that aspect. But it is certain that if there is to be failure it will not be for want of eff'ort and pains on the shepherd's part. There will be persistent search in every quarter where there is the least chance of the lost being found. How true is this of Christ Himself! He could say for Himself as the Shepherd of Israel, "How often would I have gathered thee! " and His failure after all His efforts broke His heart and made Him shed bitter tears. This phrase, until he find it, is a touch we owe to the pastoral love of the speaker, as the spiritual Shepherd of men.

Matt. ix. 36.

Matt. X., which relates the mission of the twelve to the people of

Galilee. S j j; t'ipy alrb, iav yevijrat ivptiv. (Matt, xviii. 13.) Matt, xxiii. 38.

Having found the straying sheep, the shepherd layeti it upon his sjwulders. This possibly he would do in any case, however short the distance the sheep had strayed from the fold, to make sure of his captive; but this feature in the picture most probably points to exhaustion produced by long-continued wandering, exposure, and lack of food. The erring sheep needs to be carried, it cannot return on its own fget; the shepherd finds it with torn fleece, lying on the ground, emaciated, helplessly weak. This is intrinsically probable, even had we nothing but the language of the parable itself to guide us; it becomes almost certain when we bear in mind the terms in which Jesus described the state of the people at the time of the Galilean mission. To His compassionate eye the lower masses of Jewish society appeared torn and scattered about,â weary, worn, abject, â like sheep without a shepherd; therefore he sent His disciples among them to preach the good tidings of the kingdom and to heal their diseases, deeming it better they should have the benefit of inexperienced care than that they should continue longer utterly uncared for. He had the same people in the same miserable condition in view when He spake this parable. The straying sheep of our parable represents the neglected, perishing masses of the people, is one of the scattered and torn. Jesus thinks of it now, as He thought of the people on that other occasion â would have His hearers so think of it, as found by the shepherd in a pitiable plight; for His own heart is now as full of compassion as it was then, and He desires to awaken compassion in the hard hearts of His audience, that they may cease to blame Him, and begin rather to imitate Him by compassionate consideration for the lost sheep of the house of Israel.

So the shepherd has to carry his captive all the way back to the fold, and has to carry it a long way. Nevertheless he lays it on his shoulders, rejoicing, heeding not the weight, nor the fatiguing journey before him, for gladness over the recovery of his lost property. Love makes the burden light, and the way short. This feature is true to natural life, and not less true to the character of the Good Shepherd, the author of the parable. The Son of man had heavy burdens

Matt. ix. 36. tffkuxisvoi cat ipptnnsvot.

laid on His heart by that unspeakable sympathy with the woes of humanity which is so conspicuous in His history. The diseases of men, their poverty, their sins, their ignorance, their pains, their hopeless misery â all pressed on His spirit " Surcl) he hath borne our griefs, and carried our sorrows," and so was a " Man of sorrows, and acquainted with grief." Yet withal there was a wondrous gladness in the heart of Christ. He experienced a perfect rapture of delight when He found a lost sheep: witness His bearing at the well of Sychar, when His joy over the repentance of the woman of Samaria made Him forget hunger, insomuch that the disciples wondered if any man had given Him to eat. That joy, hoped for or experienced, made all His burdens light; made even the cross itself, abhorrent to His sentient nature, more than bearable. Therefore, in drawing the picture of a faithful shepherd. He might with a good conscience put in this trait, 'rejoicing."

The weary, fatiguing journey at length comes to an end; and naturally, on arriving at his home, there is a new rush of emotion in the shepherd's heart, and an eventful story to tell, and a craving for friendly neighbourl '- sympathy. This accordingly is the next feature in the parable: " When he Cometh home, he calleth together his friends and neighbours, saying unto them, Rejoice with me; for I have found my sheep which was lost." This is the point in the parable at which our sense of its fitness or naturalness is apt to be weakest. Is there not, we are ready to ask, something resembling effeminate sentimentalism in that callinsj of friends and neighbours together, and that demand for sympathy with the joy of finding the lost sheep? Would it not have been more manly and more shepherd-like to have returned quietly to ordinary duties as if nothing had happened? Have we not reason to suspect that at this point the natural realism of the parable has been sacrificed to the feelings of the speaker smarting under a keen sense of the general lack of sympathy with His own aims, and eager to reproach the Pharisees on that account."' Now in meeting these objections we assume the truth of the interpretation we have put on the previous points of the parable; that is to say, that the parable has Â John iv. 31â 34.

reference to a serious occurrence, and not merely to an Insignificant everyday case of wandering for a short distance from the fold. We are entitled to assume this, for the simple reason that a trivial case would not be parallel to the circumstances which created the need for a parable. That which made apology necessary was Christ's interest in men who, in the opinion even of His critics, had gone far astray, and the parable, to serve its purpose, must put a case analogous to that of those whom the straying sheep represents. This would be perfectly understood by the parties to whom the parable was addressed.

But, even in that case, was not the shepherd's demand for sympathy overdone We think not, and in saying so we take no account of difference of temperament between Eastern shepherds and those of our own land, though doubtless this might somewhat affect the manner of parties similarly situated. Two considerations suffice to redeem the shepherd's behaviour from sentimentalism. On the one hand, it was perfectly natural that there should be a desire, at the end of an eventful journey, to give expression to the pent-up feeling connected with its object, and to talk to acquaintances about the incidents of the way; all the circumstances connected with the search, and the finding of the lost sheep. His whole interest has been concentrated upon, his whole mind absorbed by, that one sheep; it has cost him much thought, anxiety, and effort; and now that all is happily ended, there is a rush of emotion which seeks relief in the narration of the story to sympathetic hearers. All men may not speak as the shepherd is represented speaking, but all men feel as he felt, in similar circumstances. The secret thought of every human heart, on the recovery of something lost after much and painful anxiety and effort, is, "Rejoice with me, for I have found that which was lost;" and Christ makes the shepherd say what all men think, because one chief purpose of the parable is to accentuate the joy of finding things lost. Then, on the other hand, the shepherd's desire to unburden himself to his neighbours would be greatly intensified by the assurance that his tale would greatly interest the listeners. On that he might safely reckon; not merely because of the innate curiosity of mankind, or of the craving for news to relieve the dull monotony of life in a thinly peopled, pastoral country, or of the interest which human beings take in each other, especially in rural districts, where the feeling of neighbourliness is strong, making the simple, honest denizens of hills and dales mutually communicative and sympathetic; but more particularly because of the bearing of the tale on their own personal interest. For the case of their friend and neighbour might be their own, and it would greatly interest them to know the track of the wanderer, the risks it ran, where it was found, and in what condition; for such knowledge would be useful to themselves in case any of their own sheep should stray from the fold. Therefore the returned shepherd, in asking neighbours to come and hear his story, was but giving them an expected opportunity. And we are not to think of the invitation as formal, as of a host inviting guests to a feast. The words put into the shepherd's mouth scarce needed to be spoken. The home-coming of one who had been absent for days on so interesting an errand said to all the duellers around: Come hear my story; come congratulate me on the success of my quest. And the point of importance here is, that the neighbours would certainly gather around their fellow-shepherd to hear his tale, and would hear it with sympathetic ears. That is not expressly stated, but it is more impressively said by being taken for granted. Jesus pays human nature the compliment of treating neighbourly sympathy in the circumstances as a thing of course.

In the application of the parable, which we have now to notice, neighbourly sympathy could not be treated as a thing of course, for it was precisely the absence of it that had given occasion to the parable being spoken. It is therefore to this side of the subject that prominence is given. Jesus passes over in silence His own feelings as the Shepherd of morally lost men, His joy over finding even one, and His desire that others should rejoice along with Him, delicately leaving these to be inferred from the behaviour cf the shepherd in the parable; and emphasises the sympathy which He receives in the prosecution of His workâ receives, however, not from men, but from the inhabitants of the upper world. There is wonderful pathos and pungency in this reference to heaven as the scene of sympathetic joy over the restoration of erring sinners to the fold of God. It implies that Jesus meets with no such joy on earth. It is a virtual complaint against his Pharisaic critics, which is none the less effective that it is indirectly conveyed in the form of a contrast between their conduct and that of celestials. The Son of man, who was ever busy seeking the lost, finds Himself utterly isolated and misunderstood; and with His back to the wall, as it were, He is fain to go to heaven in quest of beings who shared His feelings towards the sinful. To heaven, since He could not find backing nearer hand. Where shall I go, He asked Himself, to find beings who feel as I do.'" To the righteous men of Israel No! they have no joy over poor vulgar publicans and sinners repenting; they joy only in the fact that they are not as other men. To cultivated Sadducees? No! they think men well enough as they are, and look on repentance as much ado about nothing, an unnecessary disturbance of one's happiness during his brief tenure of existence. To the world outside Judsea? No! the day will come ere long when they will be thankful to hear of Him whose countrymen brought it as a heavy charge against Him that He received sinners; but as yet the heathen know neither the joy of saving, nor the joy of being saved. Nowhere on earth can I find sympathisers. In heaven then? Yes! in heaven they understand Me; in heaven they feel as I feel; there is joy in heaven, I tell you, over sinners repenting; yea, even over one of these despised sinners repenting, more than over ninety and nine just persons that need no repentance. The Pharisaic fault-finders might well feel ashamed for compelling the object of their censure to go so far in quest of sympathy, and they might also well feel self-condemned if they reflected for a moment on the startling declaration their cynicism had provoked. For it was by no means an improbable statement, however strange it might appear; no mere justifiable; d'esprit, uttered on the spur of the moment by one who felt himself hard pressed. Kjeii d'esprit it certainly is; for the occasion is one of those in which Christ's words were apt to be full of poetry and passion; not merely rays of light, but flashes of lightning. But it is more, even sober truth. For, take the kernel of the statementâ that there is joy in heaven over the repentance of a sinner, is that incredible? The denizens of heaven are the good; and what better occasion for joy can good beings have than the turning of a sinner from evil to righteousness? Ask not sceptically:

"Is there care in heaven? and is there love In heavenly spirits to these creatures base That may compassion of their evils move?"

Why not? The angels have the same occupation as Jesus: they are ministering spirits to those who are about to inherit salvation, and they have therefore a fellow-feeling with the Good Shepherd, like the neighbours of the shepherd in the parable. Nay, hath not the Eternal Himself a most real joy over a sinner repenting? God is love, therefore He hath no pleasure in the death of a sinner, therefore He hath pleasure when a sinner turns from his evil ways; yea, even if that sinner be the meanest of viankiiid. For consider what a difference it would make to ourselves if that meanest one were related to us as a son or a brother! Now the blessed truth is, that in the meanest member of the human race repenting, God sees a prodigal child of His returning to his Father's house. That is the truth implied in the golden saying with which the first and second of these three parables end, and it is the truth expressly taught in the third. It is the great Christian doctrine concerning God which the world never has believed, and which the Church has only half-believed, and which God knew from of old men would ever be slow to believe; hence the protestation by the mouth of prophecy: " My thoughts are not your thoughts," following the declaration: " Let the wicked forsake his way, and the unrighteous man his thoughts, and let him return unto the Lord, and He will have mercy upon him, and to our God, for He will abundantly pardon."

There may appear to be more difficulty in understanding this declaration of our Lord's, taken as referring to God, when regard is had to the comparative form in which it is putâ more joy over one sinner repenting than over ninety-and-nine just persons who need no repentanceâ the reason being the peculiarly sweet pleasure connected with finding

Isaiah Iv. 7, things lost. It may. appear that this peculiar experience is due to the constitution of human nature, and that it therefore savours of anthropopathism to ascribe such joy to the Divine Being. We need not, however, trouble ourselves with this metaphysical problem; for if we are going to be sensitive about anthropopathism, we must go further back, and inquire whether we can legitimately ascribe joy in any form, or any emotion whatsoever, to God. We shall, therefore, rather ask what this comparative statement made by Christ signifies for men; or, to be more definite, for Christ Himself. What does our Lord mean, when he says in effect: I have more joy in one of these poor sinners repenting, than in ninety-and-nine just men who need no repentance? Is He sneering at the sham righteousness of the Pharisees? No! He is in too tender a mood for sneering, not to say that He has too much love in His heart, even for Pharisees, to sneer at any time. He argues with His censors on the assumption that they are as good as they think themselves. He means to say, that there is a sense in which a man may rationally rejoice more over the repentance of a notable sinner than over the righteousness of many men who have all their days lived in an exemplary manner, if not absolutely, yet comparatively, sinless. This greater joy over the penitent sinner needs no more explanation than the joy of the shepherd over the sheep which was lost. It is simply an illustration of the great law, according to which all human beings have peculiar joy over lost things found. If the Pharisees had only made use of their own human instincts as a guide to their judgment in the affairs of morals and religion, they would not have thought the statement surprising. Nay, if they had but recollected their own theoretical views, even within the moral sphere, they would have sympathised with Christ s conduct and feelings, instead of putting Him on His defence by captious criticism. For it was a doctrine of the Talmud-ists of after-days, and was probably an opinion current in Rabbinical schools even in our Lord's time, that a man who had been guilty of many sins might by repentance raise himself to a higher degree of virtue than the perfectly righteous man who had never experienced his temptations. ' Vide on this Lightfoot, ' Horse Hebraicse," and Schwab, ' Traitd des 274 The Parabolic Teaching of Christ, book ti.

If this were so, surely it was reasonable to occupy oneself in endeavouring to get sinners to start on this noble career of self-elevation, and to rejoice when in any instance he had succeeded. But it is one thing to have correct theories, and another to put them in practice. These Pharisaic faultfinders believed in a coming Messiah, but they rejected Jesus; they searched the Scriptures as writings in which they expected to find eternal life, and they listened not to Him who had the words of eternal life; they reckoned it possible for a penitent sinner not only to equal, but to excel, one that by comparison needed no repentance, and they found fault with one who not only held this view as an abstract doctrine, but acted on it, and sought to bring those who had strayed furthest from the paths of righteousness to repentance, believing that though last they might yet be first.

THE LOST DRACHMA.

Or what woman having ten drachmcb, if she lose one arachma, doth not light a lamp, and sweep the hoiise, and seek carefully till she find it; and, having fotind it, she calls together her female friends and neighbours saying: Rejoice with me, becanse I have found the drachma which I lost. â Luke xv. 8â lo.

Tphs parable suggests the case of a poor woman, living possibly in widowed loneliness, in a humble cottage in a country village, and possessing very scanty means of livelihood; and its special lesson is that the joy of finding things lost may be experienced and sympathised with even in connection with things of little intrinsic value. A housewife who loses one piece of silver out of ten, which constitutes her stock of money, quite naturally rejoices when she recovers it, and she will receive neighbourly congratulations from her acquaint-

Berackhoth," introduction, p. xxxii. There is not perfect consent as to what the Rabbinical doctrine was; but Schwab's view is that in the case of sins against God and sobriety, a man might by repentance make himself equal or superior to the parfectly just man, Zadic gamour; but in the case of sins against men, repentance, while obtaining pardon from Goj, and regaining the esteem of men, could not make the penitent equal or superior to the perfectly good man.

1 ras; 0i'Xac Kai-yhTorac, feminine, the corresponding expression in the first parable being rovg ixovg koi roiq ytirovae.

ances on her good fortune. Such is the implied assertion; but if any one has difficulty in believing that the loss of one piece of money, of the value of a sixpence, out of ten, could appear a serious matter even to the impoverished population of a Syrian village, it is easy to conceive circumstances which would give even to the one lost coin a special value. It might form part of a whole which had been hoarded, and was all needed, for a special purpose; as to pay a tax, or to defray the expenses connected with a religious festival. In such a case, to lose one coin was to be unable to meet the emergency for the sake of which the whole had been carefully scraped together, and such inability might be the occasion of no little anxiety. Our ministerial experiences have afforded opportunity of knowing into what distress a poor, but honest, Highland widow can be thrown by her inability to pay on demand the half-yearly rent for her miserable garret, amounting to the petty sum of one pound sterling, and with what joy she will receive from a friend the m. eans of satisfying her landlord. Suppose such a poor widow had succeeded in accumulating in the course of six months the twenty shillings necessary for the purpose, and that towards the end of the period, as rent-day was approaching, she had somehow lost one of the twentyâ would you wonder that the misfortune put her much about, if she spoke of it to her neighbours and to her pastor; if she searched for it day after day, and if on finding it she joyfully reported the fact to the same parties, and met with honest sympathy from them all? We can only say for ourselves that we should feel ashamed if the joy of a poor fellow-creature in the case supposed did not awaken a very hearty response in our bosom.

This little parable gives a very life-like description of the search for the lost drachma. The woman lights a lamp, sweeps the house, and seeks carefully till she finds it. The lighting of the lamp speaks to a house ill-provided with windows, perhaps having no windows at all, but receiving light only from the door. i There may be light enough in

Robinson, in his Biblical Researches," vol. iii. p. 44, mentions a house in the Lebanon in which he passed a night, answering to this description. "There was no window, and no light except from the door."

the clay hut to enable one familiar with all its corners to grope about and find all she wants, but there is not light sufficient to guide one in searching for something lost. The housewife must go, lamp or candle in hand, looking narrowl)' into the dark nooks. But this will not suffice. For in dark neglected corners there will be dust, and if the lost coin happens to have fallen into such a dusty corner it will not be visible to the eye. The besom will be necessary as well as the lamp, and instead of sweeping here and there it will be best to sweep the floor all over, in hope of sweeping up the coin along with the dust. Then, the sweeping ended, a search among the accumulated heap of dust must be commenced. And so the anxious woman commences the search, slowly, carefully examining in the heap, and looking narrowly at everything in the least degree resembling a coin. At last her patience is rewarded; there it is shining in the lamplight. She sets down her candle, rushes out of her dwelling, and into the house of her nearest neighbours, exclaiming, "Rejoice with me, I have found the piece which I lost." And of course they do rejoice with her; for doubtless they have heard of her loss ere now; they know about the missing drachma, and they have sympathised with their neighbour's anxiety, with the sympathy peculiar to fellows in poverty; and now they sympathise not less sincerely with her in her joy over the recovery of her lost property.

It scarcely needs to be remarked that the housewife of the second parable would be more demonstrative than the shepherd of the first in the expression of her joy, and in her demand for the sympathy of her female friends and neighbours. Of this diffisrence some trace may be found in the text, if we regard that as the true reading which gives the. Greek verb rendered in the English Version, " calls together," in the middle voice in the second parable, instead of in the active as in the first. With Godet we think this reading is to be preferred, but we doubt if he has correctly indicated the significance of the change in the mode of expression. He thinks that the active (o-uykaaet) is used in the first instance because the shepherd has not a monopol of the joy, the lost sheep sharing it in part, and that the middle (Tuyca etrat) is used in the second instance, on the other hand, because the joy is wholly the woman's,â that which was lost being a thing without life, incapable of any sensation of joy. In a similar way he explains the diverse terms in which the lost object is spoken of in the two parables: in the first, described as "the lost" (jo airoxcoxoi), as an object of pity; in the second, as "the drachma which I have lost," the whole sympathy being concentrated upon the loser. The suggestions are ingenious, but possibly just a little over-refined. We are inclined to explain the first of the two differences by a reference to the difference in sex between the principal characters in the two parables. The middle voice is used in the second parable, because the actor is a woman, not a man, to mark the greater intensity and subjectivity of her sex. The second difference may be explained in a similar way. The shepherd speaks of his lost sheep in an objective way, without emphasising the fact that the loss was his. The housewife, on the other hand, puts the loss which she sustained in the forefront, and says: Not my drachma which was lost, but the drachma which I lost. It is, however, questionable whether it were not better to regard the two modes of expression as equivalent.

In the application of this parable Jesus contents Himself with the positive statement that " there is joy in the presence of the angels of God over one sinner that repenteth." A comparative statement in this case would have been unsuitable, as tending to weaken rather than strengthen the sentiment expressed at the close of the first parable; seeing that it would have had to run thus: There is joy in heaven over one sinner that repenteth, more than over nine sinners that need no repentance.

Commentaire' in loc.

' To show bow much in such minute points one is apt to be influenced by fancy, it may be mentioned that Trench puts the following construction on the diverse manner of expression in reference to the two lost objects: The Shepherd, being Christ, says My sheep; the woman, being the Church, says iie drachma.

' Lightfoot (' Horse Hebraicae') gives a parable from the Talmud like the foregoing one of the Lost Piece, the aim of which is to illustrate the quest of wisdom. Here again we have to note the comparatively commonplace moral of the Talmudic parables.

But the moral as repeated here has an interest and a pathos of its own. It suggests the thought that the repentance of the meanest of mankind, however insignificant in social position or degraded in character, calls forth a sympathetic thrill in the heart of God. It teaches us that all souls and their moral history are precious in God's sight, that every human being has value in the esteem of heaven, as endowed with reason and free will, and subject to infinite moral possibilities. This was then a new doctrine concerning man, and it is still very contrary to the world's way of thinking concerning human beings. For on this earth men are still very cheap in one another's esteem for various reasons, theoretical and practical. Some regard the moral interests of humanity with comparative indifference because their philosophy teaches them to treat as insignificant the distinction between man and beast, in nature and in destiny. Others, through the lust for gain, are accustomed to regard human life as of no account in comparison with commercial profit. Jesus assures us that in heaven human beings are not valued so cheaply. There, He tells us, all souls are precious, the souls of publicans and profligates, of bondsmen and negroes; and though nothing spiritually great should come out of the repentance of any of these least ones, though they should remain least ones for ever, yet is the change implied in repentance, even in their case deemed an event of solemn interest, because the blurred image of God is restored in some degree, and the soul is at least saved, though as through fire. Surely an altogether God-worthy way of thinking! Long may it prevail on earth as well as in heaven! For if even in spite of a Christian way of thinking and. acting, the condition of many be far from satisfactory, it would certainly be infinitely worse were the way of thinking peculiar to philosophic atheism, or to brutal mammon-worship, universally prevalent. As it is, we manage to make many ignorant and erring ones imperfect Christians; as it would be then, the multitude would live unheeded in misery, and die unmourned in sin.

This is all that needs to be said on this parable. If we â were anxious to draw out our exposition to a greater length, we might easily do so, by following the example of comment-a. tors who indulge in spiritualising interpretation, telling us that the house is the Church; and the woman the indwelling Spirit; and the drachma, man with the image of God stamped upon him, but lying in the dust of sin and corruption; the candle the Word of God held forth by the Church, and the sweeping the disturbance caused by the action of the Spirit. in the individual and in society, making dust rise and fly about, and turning the world upside down. To our mind, however, this style of interpretation savours of frigidity. If we may say it without offence, it seems to us to savour, moreover, of Pharisaism. It looks as if interpreters found it impossible to discover any real interest in the story itself, taken as a natural illustration of the joy of finding things lost, and felt it necessary to fly to the spiritual sense to get something to say. What is this but Pharisaic indifference to the affairs of common humanity in a new form? The parable as a scene from ordinary life is of no account, and all the objects must be transformed into theological equivalents ere they can be worthy of attention. How much better to try first of all to feel the human pathos of the parable as a story of real life, and then to make that pathos the one link of connection between the natural and the spiritual.

THE LOST SON.

And He said, A certain man had two sons: and the younger of thejn said to his father. Father, give me the portion of the property that falleth to me as my share. And he divided between them his living."'â And not many days after the younger son gathered all together, and took his Journey into a far country, and there wasted his substance with prodigal living? And when he had spent all, there arose a mighty famine iii that land; and he began to be in want. And he went and attached himself to a citizen of that country; and he sent him into the 1 rh Â 7r(3Â Xov xepog rr c, ovaiaq: a quite classic expression; vide Wetstein i'or examples.

"Tov (iiov, practically synonymou. with the rrjc o'vaiai; going before.

(2Ji a(T0JT(Dc, living in excess, with special reference to extravagant expenditure. From this phrase comes the common title of this parable, The Prodigal Sonâ 'O vtbg daioroc, filius perditus, or prodigus. Dr. Field, with reference to the old rendering, " riotous living," retained in R. V., asks why not " with prodigal living," with reference to the familiar English title of the parable.â ' Otium Norv."

Jields to feed swine. And he was fain to fill his belly with the carob-tree pods ' that the swine did eat: and no man gave unto hini. But when he came to himself, he said, How many hired servants of my fathers have bread ejiough and to spare, and lam perishing here with hunger! I will arise and go to my father, and will say unto him, Father, I have siiuied against heaven, and before thee, I am no more worthy to be called tjiy son.â makeme as one of thy hired servaiits. And he arose, and came to his father. But when he was yet a great uay off, his father saw him, and had compassion, and ran and fell on his neck and kissed him. And the son said unto liim, Father, I sinned against heaven and befoj-e thee, 1 am no more worthy to be called thy son. But the father said to his servajits. Bring forth quickly- the best robe, afid put it on him; and put a ring on his hand, and shoes on his feet; and bring hither the fatted calf, and kill it: and let us eat and be merry: for this person, my son, was dead, and is alive again; was lost, ajid is found. And they began to be merry. But his elder son was in the field: and as he came and drew nigh to the house, he heard music and dancing. And, calling one of the servants, he asked what these things meant. And he said to him it is), Because thy brother is come; attd thy father killed the fatted calf, because he received him safe and sound. And he was angry, and would not go in: and his father came out and entreated him. And he answering said to his father, Lo, these many years do I serve thee, neither transgressed I at any time thy commandment, and thou never gavest me a kid, that I might make merry with my friends. But as soon as thy precious) soft, this fellow who devoured thy living with harlots, arrived, thou didst kill for him the fatted calf. A nd he said ujtto him, Son, thou art ever with me and all tnine is thine. It was meet that we should make merry, and be gladj for this thy dea?-) brother was dead, and is alive again, and was lost, and is found. â Luke xv. 11â 2,2.

This parable differs from the preceding two in length, in the multiplicity of picturesque and pathetic details, in heightened moral interest due to the fact of the example being taken from the sphere of human conduct, and in the manner in which 1 Kipcitia, so called from their horn-like, curved shape. On the carob or locust tree, and its fruit, and its use as food for animals and for the poor, vide Tristram's Natural History of the Bible also Smith's ' Dictionary of the Bible."

2 Tax) probably forms part of the text, though it is not found in many MSS., and is omitted by Tischendorf.

We throw this word in to bring out the tone in which the elder son referred to his brother. It is gratifying to find Dr. Field suggesting the use of the same epithet, also of the epithet ' dear' in the next verse to bring out what the returned son ought to be to his brother. The latter suggestion we have adopted from him.

Pharisaic severity is rebuked; the former parables showing the censors of Jesus how they ought to have acted, this parable showing them (through the picture of the elder brother) how they did act. It was fitting that this should be done in the last of the three parables rather than in the others because, the illustration being taken from human conduct, the term 'lost' has a moral sense, and there is a conflict of feeling towards the lost object; on the one hand resentment against folly, on the other pity awakened by misery. In this case, therefore, sympathy with one who has recovered the lost cannot be taken for granted; as it could in the case of a lost sheep, or of a lost coin; for the feeling of resentment might predominate, as accordingly it is made to do in the case of the elder brother. By conveying reproof in this instance under this form, Jesus showed His respect for the feelings of men of exemplary lives against the sinful, so far as these were based on sincere love of virtue. He said thereby in effect: " What I condemn in you is not your disapprobation of sin, but merely the excessive one-sided nature of your resentment, shutting your hearts against pity for the sinful." This tone of carefully-qualified and guarded blame, very observable in the closing part of the parable, is traceable throughout the whole, in the picture of the Prodigal, and of the Father, not less than in that of the Elder Brother. Christ's purpose evidently is not to provoke but to conciliate, not to treat moral severity as inadmissible, but to moderate its excess, and to soften it with a mixture of compassion.

The three pictures of the Prodigal Son, the loving Father, and the relentless Elder Brother, make up this parable of exquisite beauty and inexhaustible didactic significance. Let us stand and gaze upon each of them in turn, till we have become duly impressed with the inimitable skill of the Artist who drew them.

I. The prodigal is so depicted as to show us his sin and folly, and yet to awaken in us pity for his misery. He is an unfilial, thoughtless, self-willed, sensual youth, who by his follies brings upon himself many sorrows; and he excites in us just the sort of mixed feeling with which Jesus regarded the publicans and sinners whom he represents, extenuating not their guilt, yet deeply commiserating them. This foolish.

wayward one is the younger of two sons. Ke might h ve been either of them, but it was fitting to make the younger the prodigal; because the younger the more Hkely to be thoughtless, and the weaker the influences tending to give steadiness by developing the sense of responsibility; for by the Hebrew Law the younger of two sons had a claim to only one-third of the paternal inheritance, the elder receiving a double share of two-thirds, and being the more likely just on that account to conduct himself with gravity as one conscious of the dignity of birthright. The career of this younger son is exhibited in four successive scenes, in the first of which we see hi. s self-will, in the second h. s folly, in the third his misery, and in the fourth his repentance His self-will manifests itself in the request to have his share of the paternal property given into his hands at once, that he may be free to do with it what he chooses. His motive is speedily revealed by his subsequent conduct in setting off with all his means to a distant country, where he can forget his home and family, and be, as he hopes, forgotten by, and hidden from the knowledge of, his friends. There are passionate impulses and hungry appetites within him which can get no outlet in his father's house, and he is impatient to get away from it to a place where he can follow his bent without restraint. The youth is in the Byronic or Werterean vein, and he desires freedom to sow his wild oats. It is strange that the father, who, if he had any discernment, must have noticed the mood of his boy, consented to his request; but parental soft-heartedness often does what a dispassionate judgment cannot approve. Moreover, the exigencies of the parable required that he should so act, and also the role which he sustained as the representative of Divine Providence: for God in his Providence often gives to men towards w4iom He has a high purpose of grace, free rein, permitting them to go to wild excesses of riot before he breaks them in to the yoke of obedience; of which we have a notable instance in the case of Augustine, whose history supplies a far more instructive

Deut. xxi. 17.
Ver. 12; ver. 13; vers. 14â 16; vers. 17â 19. ' Ver. 13.

Legally he might either grant or refuse the request: " Fecit non quod oportebat, sed quod licebat facere."â Maldonatus.

commentary on our parable than anything to be found in his writings.

The folly of the youth is depicted in very few words. He scattered his substance, living in sensual indulgence, continuing this course of wasteful excesses till all his means were gone. Melancholy picture of enslavement to passion, and of utter thoughtlessness and absence of self-control! The fire of sinful impulse once kindled burns on till the fuel is exhausted, when the poor wretch, who in thoughtless joy kindled this fire, and for a while compassed himself about with its sparks, must lie down in sorrow. Where, all the while, is the reason firm and temperate will Alas! these do not usually keep company with self-will and lawless desire. They may return when the tempest of passion has spent its force, but meantime madness rules the hour. How the youth spent the months of folly it is not difficult to imagine. With characteristic delicacy Jesus omits details, leaving the ungracious task of filling in repulsive particulars to the elder son. It is the animus of his representation that is at fault; his statement, though brutally unfeeling, was probably too true. We may without any breach of charity conceive the prodigal as wasting his means on every form of sensual gratification, playing the fool in no half and half manner."

The inevitable end of such courses is want and misery, and these all too soon overtook the prodigal. His money is squandered, and he is now almost without the means of purchasing the necessaries of life, not to speak of hurtful pleasures. And, as evil fortune would have it, about the time

Godet refers to Rom. i. 24 as illustrating the father's consent to his son's foolish wishes.

2 Isaiah III. Â Ver. 30. ilira-Kopv av.

From a fragment of Eusebius it might be inferred that the Ebionitic Gospel went beyond the elder brother in describing the evil life of the prodigal. In that passage Eusebius refers to the ' Gospel according to the Hebrews' in connection with the parable of the Talents, and uses the expression, iita Tropviov Kai avxtirpisuv (with harlots and flute women). It is, however, not clear whether the words are a quotation from the Hebrew Gospel, or a phrase employed by Eusebius himself to describe the prodigal's conduct. The passage in question is given by Mr. Nicholson in his recently-published work on 'The Gospel according to the Hebrews p. 59.

when his resources were nearly exhausted there " arose a mighty famine in that land." This may seem a blemish in the parable, as introducing an element of an accidental character, having no necessary connection with the prodigal's misconduct. But it is not by accident that physical and moral evil meet in human history. There is a Divine teleology in the conjunction, whether appearing in individual experience, or in the life of nations, and the parable only recognises this truth in exhibiting a correspondence between moral state and outward circumstances which is often exemplified in history, and as often shown by the result to have been designed by Providence to serve a beneficent purpose. By this unhappy conjunction of exhausted personal resources with general scarcity the luckless spendthrift is reduced to a state of destitution. And at the heels of want comes degradation. The well-born and once wealthy youth is driven by need to force himself into the service of a citizen of the country, who has no better employment for him than the one of all others the most abhorrent to a Jew, that of a swineherd to a Gentile owner. A humiliating downcome, and a representation of the degradation of the publicans, Jews by birth, serving Roman masters as tax-gatherers, such as would satisfy even Pharisaic hearers.2 The sorrows of the prodigal, beginning in want and passing into degradation, reach their lowest depth in desperation. His hunger at length attains such a pitch that he has a craving " to fill his belly," according to the homely but expressive phrase of the reading we follow, with the ikowrjoq. "The word implies that the citizen of the country to whom he applied was unwilling at first to receive him, and only after persistent pressing entreaties took him into his service."â Goebel, 'Die Parabeln." Se obtrudat tkowrjotf, contemptim)â Unger, p. 148. " The term has something abject; he was, as it were, suspended on another personality."â Godet.

"Negotium quod antehac quam maxime abhorruisset subit. Judaeus porcos pascit hominis Gentilis.â Unger.

yifiiaai rfiv Koixiav. The reading in X, B, c., is xoptaaqijvai, which Godet regards as a euphemism substituted for the true reading in the Lection-aries, and thence transferred into the text by copyists. Westcott and Hort, however, regard this as the true reading, alleging that the other reading misses the point, and holding that the documentary evidence in any case is here decisive. The R. V. also adopts this reading. The American revisers, however, prefer the other, and our sympathies are with thena.

fruit of the carob tree lying on the ground, and on which the swine fed. He had Httle else to eat, for nobody thought of giving to him when all had so little to themselves.

Desperation formed the turning-point in the youth's career, and the next scene shows him returning to his senses, and beginning to think soberly and wisely. He is brought to his last shifts, but there is one course open: he may go back to his father's house. Of that house, and of the happiness of even those, in servile position therein, he begins now, for the first time for many days, to think. The thought begets a purpose, and suggests a plan. He will go home, and he will make confession of his sin in well-premeditated form, suited at once to propitiate an injured father, and to express the modesty of his present expectations. He will own that he has been an offender both against God and against his parent, and he will beg a servant's place and position, a great boon to a starving man. The picture of the penitent is not drawn in the ethereal colours of philosophy. Repentance has its source in hunger, and its motive is to get a bit of bread. How much nobler to have returned to rationality in folly's mid career, to have pulled up suddenly and said: " This will never do; I have been a fool. I will be a fool no longer; I will henceforth live a life of sobriety and wisdom." Perhaps; but the parable is true to life. Hunger, stern necessity, abject poverty, has made many a man wise who had been foolish before, and though the repentance which thus begins is somewhat impure in its source, it clears itself betimes, as reason gradually gains its ascendancy, and the moral nature grows

The words ohluq tsisov avti it is best to understand as assigning a reason why he was fain to eat of the Kipana. The prodigal got a modicum of bread in the famine, but not enough to satisfy; he was therefore glad to eke out his diet with swine's food, which he could get for the lifting (like hungry children eating turnips out of a field). So Godet. Similarly, Calvin.

2 ws 'iva Twv fiiaoicjv. Trench thinks the n'loqwi are to be regarded as occupying a lower position than even the 5oi)Xoi, so that the sense is: a place among the lowest class of servants. But the contrast suggested is rather that between the condition of the fiiadioi in his father's house, and that of the n'lnqwi in the land where he now spends a miserable existence. So Goei)el. Godet identifies the n'labioi with the pagan proselytes of the outer court, and says the prodigal, in his hope and desire, takes his position beside the publican (Luke xviii. 13).

into strength. The prodigal's repentance became purified, whether as the result of reflection on the way home, or as the effect of an unexpectedly gracious reception from his father, is matter of conjecture; but, at all events, he dropped the last part of his premeditated confession when he came into his father's presence, and made no request, but only owned his sin.

2. We have now to look at the picture of the father of this penitent prodigal. He descries his son while he is yet a great way off, at the point where the road brings a traveller first into view. He has not forgotten his son, though his son has long forgotten him. He has been thinking of him through the long period of his absence. Probably he often cast glances along the road to see if perchance the erring one was returning, thinking he saw him in every stranger who made his appearance. He has continued looking, longing, till hope deferred has made his heart sick and weary almost to despair. If he is not represented as going in search of his lost child, it is not because he cares less for that child than the shepherd for his straying sheep, or the housewife for her missing coin; but because in this case the lost one is a man, not a beast or a lifeless thing, and can return of his own accord when his mind changes; and because only when the return is his own act, has it any moral significance. The father's solicitude therefore takes the form of waiting for his son's return. He has to wait long, but at last his patience is rewarded. For lo! at length there is one who does look like the long lost one. He is much changed, wears the aspect of a beggar, and trudges along like an aged man, weak and footsore. But love is quick to discern resemblances, and there is something in the stranger's gait and bearing that recalls the lost son. The father watches his movements for a little, till in the end he feels certain that it is none other than his son. The tide of compassion rises instantaneously, sweeping every other feeling before it. There is not even a momentary struggle between pity and resentment, such as the prophet represents taking place in the Divine bosom, in

The premeditated confession was the repentance of fear; the actual confession, the repentance.of love. The discovery of the difference pro duced the Reformation.â Godet.

reference to Ephraim. He " ran, and fell on his neck, and kissed him;" kissed him not once but many times, with fervency and rapture. The moving scene over, the son gets an opportunity at length of making his confession. On arriving at the homestead together, the happy father gives orders to his servants, which indicate the completeness of his forgiveness, and the depth of his joy. First, he commands them to bring forth quickly the best robe and put it on him as the badge of distinction, and a ring for his finger, and shoes for his feet as the badges of a free man (though the shoes, and indeed all the three thingsâ robe, ring, shoes, may be regarded simply as a provision rendered necessary by the destitute condition of the beggared prodigal).

These instructions signify full reinstatement in filial position and privilege. He who has confessed himself no more worthy to be called a son is to be treated as a son, not as a servant, and as the son of such a father, attired as becomes the member of a respectable family. He receives the adoption, the vlooeaia, to employ a prominent word of the Pauline theology. This feature in the parable is of great importance in respect of its religious significance. It is designed to suggest the doctrine that God deals with sinners repenting, as the father dealt with his returning son. God receives all penitents, evert such as the publicans and sinners of Jewish society, as sons. It may become such to say: We are not worthy to be called thy sons, in the same spirit as Jewish exiles returned from Babylon are represented by the prophet as saying: We are so changed that Abraham would not know us, so degraded that Israel might be ashamed to acknowledge us. But God is

Jer. xxxi. 20.

' Katitpixriaiv, the same word as in Lulce vii. 38, 45.

(irokriv Trjv TTfxbrrjv: literally the first, whether in time or in degree must be determined by other considerations. Theophylact understood it in the temporal sense, and rendered Trpwrnv by dpxaiav, the reference being supposed to be to the pristine state of innocence before the fall. Similarly Calvin. The other view is favoured by most interpreters, and is doubtless to be preferred. For the use of wpuiroc in the sense of 'chief," vide 1 Tim. i. 15.

So Meyer. Grotius takes SakTvxtov as a sign of dignity, and refers to Gen. xli. 42. Isa. lxiii. 16.

their Father notwithstanding; regards them as His sons, whence His joy on their return; treats them as sons, not forgiving them with a grudge, or partially, or in contempt, but to all intents and purposes acting towards them as if they had never sinned. At this point the doctrine of Christ remarkably coincides with that of St. Paul, who represents the standing of sonship as the privilege of every justified man, and the spirit of sonship as the ideal of the Christian's conscious relation to God. This harmony is only what we should expect when we consider that in the teaching both of Christ and of Paul the supreme category is Grace.

Next the father gives orders that a feast be made to celebrate his son's return, not merely to express his own joy and thankfulness, but to give the whole household an opportunity of sharing his gladness. The fatted calf, vhich had been in keeping for some periodically recurring high tide, must be killed to-day, for never was there a fitter occasion for feasting and mirth than the day on which a son who has been as dead comes to life again, and who has been lost is found. So the father describes the case, and we can understand what a depth of meaning the words have for him. For the servants to whom he first utters them, they describe merely the outer aspect of the fact: a son who has been very long away from home and of whom no tidings have been received, returned to his father's house in good health. For the father, they express this outer fact, and more, the inner ethical aspect of the event, the great fact of a morally altered life. It is idle, therefore, to discuss, as some recent writers have done, the question, whether the words " dead and alive," " lost and found," have an ethical or only a physical meaning. That depends on who uses them or hears them. The father employed a mode of expression which conveyed to his servants a meaning which they could understand and appreciate, and at the same time expressed for himself a thought he hid in his own bosom, as one with which hirelings might not inter- rhv fioaxov tov atrevrov, the fatted calf. " On every farm was the calf tbat'was being fattened for the feast day. Jesus knew rural manners."â Godet.

Hofmann contends that the words are to be taken in an ethical sense; Goebel takes the contrary view, â meddle. For him such words could not but mean more than met the ear of unreflecting domestics. But what did meet their ear sufficed to make them happy. They sympathised heartily with their master's joy, promptly executed his orders for the preparation of a feast, and then " began to be merry." All in that household were in holiday humour that day,â all but one.

3. That one was the elder son. He has been "in the field " all the day long, so that he is ignorant of what has happened, till returning home towards the evening he learns, from sounds which reach him from the house, that something unusual is going on. He has been busy at work on the paternal estate, for he is a dutiful, diligent, methodical, plodding, prosaic, uninteresting man. Inquiring what the music and the sound as of dancing means, he receives from the slave to whom he addresses his question the answer: " Thy brother is come, and thy father killed the fatted calf, because he received him safe and sound." In the words we are to find neither a sneer, nor a studied reserve in reporting the facts, as if in doubt how the news would be received, but simply an honest statement of the facts as they appeared to the superficial view of the servile mind, which thought only of the outward aspect of the event related. Probably the honest slave expected that the tidings he communicated would give the elder son as much pleasure as they gave himself. If he did, he was very much mistaken. The report that a feast had been extemporised, to celebrate the return of a worthless member of the family, roused in the virtuous man a storm of indignation, and he could not endure the thought of appearing in a company where a spirit 1 Viewing the return of the prodigal simply from the outside as a finding of one lost for a time, the servants in this parable hold the place of the neighbours and friends in the other two parables. They, regarding the event from the outside, as a matter of course sympathise with their master.

2 Hofmann, yith a strange want of insight, finds in the words a sneer adapted by a cunning domestic to the manifest ill-will of the elder brother. Meyer, on the other hand, thinks the servant showed discretion in speaking only of the physical health of the returned son. Godet, with superior discernment, says, the words of the servant describe the fact without the moral appreciation which did not suit a servant.

of mirth reigned, with which he had no sympathy. Strange thiit a brother should come behind even a slave in joy over the return of the erring one! And yet we must not overlook the fact, that in his very anger the eldest son showed himself morally superior to the slave. The slave was glad because he looked merely at the exterior side of the event: a member of the family long absent from home, at length leturned. The son was angry because he looked at the moral side of his brother's history; at the cause of his absence, and the sort of life he had been living. For thinking of these he was not to be blamed; his fault lay here, that- he was readier to think of the sin than of the repentance, which in the judgment of charity might be presumed to have been the motive impelling the prodigal to return. This was the fault of the Pharisees, of whom he is the type. They thought only of the vices of the class whom Jesus loved, nev fer of their repentance, and hence their inability to comprehend the motives, and to sympathise with the feelings, of Jesus. It was a fault due immediately to the want of a Jiopefiil spirit in reference to the moral reformation of the degraded members of society. But that want of hope resolved itself ultimately into a lack of love. Charity hopeth all things. Jesus hoped for the repentance of publicans and sinners, because He loved them deeply; the Pharisees despaired of them because their hearts were cold, frozen with the pride of virtue. Even so with the elder son, to return to him. His virtue made him hard and severe, and unable to be forbearing, gentle, pitiful, or, to use the pregnant word of the author of the Epistle to the Hebrews, xerplOTradelv, towards the erring. He thought he did well to be angry, and therefore, when his father, on receiving the servant's report that he was standing without in sullen humour, came out and entreated him to come in, his respect for his sire did not prevent him from expressing himself in the tone of one who felt himself deeply injured, dwelling with not unnatural pride on the length and faithfulness of his service, and then complaining that his devotion had never been rewarded with so much as a paltry kidling to make a feast with his friends. Of this he should never have thought

Heb. V. 2.

of complaining under ordinary circumstances; but when he sees how this worthless fellow is received and honoured by the killing of the calf that was being fattened against a family high-tide, as if no worthier occasion could be found than the day of his return, it is more than he can bear in silence. Verily he seems to have a good case against his father, and one wonders how the old man will defend himself. And on scanning his reply, one is half inclined to suspect that he is conscious of occupying a somewhat indefensible position. For he speaks with wondrous mildness, seeking to appease his angry son by calling him child, and reminding him that his place in the house is such that to offer him a kid would be no compliment; for what was such a paltry gift to one who was lord of all? But this mildness does not really spring out of weakness; its true source is paternal love. The tender-hearted parent desires to soften the heart of one brother towards the other. For this purpose he first gently reminds the offended one that the returned prodigal was his own brother. " Thy son," he had called the prodigal, but the father calls him " thy brother." Then with the softness in word and tone which turneth away wrath he pled: " It was meet that there should be mirth and gladness, for thy brother was dead and is alive, and was lost and is found." It was a plea in justification of the mirth and gladness in which he and all the rest of the family had freely indulged, and also indirectly for the mirth and gladness which ought to have been, but was not, excited by the good news in the breast of the elder son himself. It was the wisest plea the worthy head of the household could have advanced, but had he been disposed to retaliate he might easily have found a vulnerable point. He might have said, what indeed his words implied, that in complaining that he had never been presented with a kid the fault-finder had degraded himself to the position of a servant." Nay, he might have said with 1 Ver. 31. Tikvov.

kzn may refer either to something which has happened as it must have, or which ou; ht to have happened but has not. Here it is used in b)th senses; in the first sense, with reference to the father and the rest of the family; in the second, with reference to the elder brother. So Goebel.

' The servile tone pervades the elder brother's words throughout, and perfect truth, that he was not the sort of man to awaken in others the festive mood. He was an eminently respectable, correct, exemplary man, but not one to be enthusiastic about. Prosaic himself, he could never excite gushes of emotion, lvric states of soul, in his fellow-men. The fountains of emotion are opened, not by moral mediocrity and correctness, but by wickedness penitent, or by heroic goodness. For a great sinner repenting, or for a moral hero who has achieved great deeds, one would readily make a feast, but scarcely for a righteous man like the elder brother would one even so much as kill a fatted calf, not to speak of dying oneself

The elder brother in the parable is the representative of the Pharisees in their good and bad points, in their moral correctness, and in their severity and pride, as the younger brother is the representative of the " publicans and sinners " in their depravity and repentance. This seems so evident to us, that we have all along taken it for granted. Some, however, and notably the critics who are always discovering traces of tendency in the Gospel, are of opinion that the two brothers represent not the Pharisees and publicans respectively, but Jews and Gentiles. But we must here, as in all cases, distinguish between the appplications of which the parable admits, and the application primarily intended. That the reference, in the first place, is to Pharisees and publicans is to us beyond question; but that the doctrine of the parable admitted of being applied to Jews and Pagans, and that Jesus, and likewise Luke, was conscious of its applicability to the wider distinction, we have as little doubt. The Pharisees themselves could hardly fail to discern in Christ's sympathy with the degraded class, and in His defence thereof, a latent universalism. The offence they took at Christ's conduct was probably due to an instinctive, half-conscious perception, that this new love for the sinful portended a religious revolution, the setting aside of Jewish prerogative, and the introduction of a religion of humanity to which Jew and Gentile should be as one. They might arrive at this in this he was a faithful picture of the Pharisees, whose religion was essentially legal and servile in spirit.

Reuss says under ' sinners ' Pagans are included, and in the sense explained above we agree with him.

conclusioii by a very simple process of reasoning. They themselves called Jesus " Friend of publicans and sinners"; but publicans were to them as heathens, and sinners' was the epithet they used to denote the Gentiles. Therefore they might readily argue that the man who took such an interest in publicans and sinners could have no objection in principle to associating with Gentiles, and that when the leaven of His influence had had time to work, the religion associated with His name would become the religion, not of the Jews, but of mankind. If they reasoned thus they reasoned rightly-Christ's love was indeed revolutionary in tendency, and so was the doctrine He taught in these apologetic parables. The doctrine that every penitent sinner, though he were the meanest of mankind, is a son of God, could only issue in the new humanity of Paul, wherein "is neither Jew nor Greek, neither bond nor free, neither male nor female, but all are one in Christ Jesus."

It remains now to make a few observations on the import of the term ' lost' which occurs in all these three parables. It was a term frequently employed by Jesus to denote the objects of His redemptive activity. " I came," He said once and again, " to seek the lost" (jo a. TToxcoxo'i). In endeavouring to appreciate the moral significance of this figurative term, it is important to note the diflterence between the second perfect participle used passively and the middle voice of the verb atToxkvixi, as employed in a sense peculiar to the New Testament, viz. to denote the future condition of the unsaved, as in the familiar text: " God so loved the world, that He gave His only begotten Son, that every one believing in Him might not perish (fxt) dtroajjrat), but have eternal life." The participle cnroxokos is used to denote a condition of peril, but the middle voice in New Testament usage denotes absolute perdition. The state indicated by the participle in question is one from which recovery is possible; the state indicated by the verb atTowvcroat or by the noun d-Trwaeia is one of irretrievable loss. Hence that which is lost, atroawao?, is represented as the object of redeeming love. The Son of man came to seek to a-nokoxos.

Gal. iii. 28. Â John iii. 16.

' On this distinction 7V? Cremer's Dictionaryofnewtestament Greek.

Luke xix. 10; cf. Matt. x. 6; xv. 24.

What, then, Is the moral condition of humanity considered as that which, while lost, is yet capable of being found and saved? The parables we have been considering help us to answer this question. Man, viewed as the object of the Saviour's solicitude, is lost as a straying sheep is lost, through thoiigjitlcssness; as a piece of money is lost to use, when its owner cannot find it; as a prodigal is lost, who in waywardness and self-will departs from his father's house to a distant land, and there lives a life utterly diverse from that of the home he has left, and so living holds no correspondence with! iis family, but is content to be as dead to them, and that they in turn should be as dead to him. Man as Most' is foolish as a straying sheep, to his own peril; lives in vain, not fulfilling the end of his existence, like a lost coin; is without God in the world, alienated from God, like a prodigal son. As a straying sheep he is not only lost, but has lost himself, bewildered like a traveller in a snowstorm, or a child in a wood. He has gone astray not in wantonness merely, but in quest of pasture, seeking after good, blindly groping after the suinmiim bonum. He has gone further astray from that which he seeks, instead of coming nearer it. As a lost piece of money, he is forgetful of his chief end, and so lives in vain, so far as the higher purposes of life are concerned. As a lost son of God, he is not only witless like a sheep, and useless like a lost coin, but positively evil-minded, disobedient, undutiful, devoid of right affection, a lover of pleasure more than of God, one who banishes God from his thoughts, and who desires that he may not be in God's thoughts, and does what he can to hide himself from God, by living a prayerless, irreligious life, behaving as a runaway who holds no correspondence with friends that he may conceal from them his whereabouts. Such were the thoughts of Jesus concerning man when He described him as ro cfnokoukos ' Bengel distinguishes the senses of the term lost," as used in the three parables respectively, thus: Ovis, drachma, filius perditus; peccator stupidus, sui plane nescius, sciens et voluntarius. Our interpretation agrees with his in the first and third cases, but diverges from it in the secondâ he emphasising the unconsciousness of the lifeless piece of money; "sve, the fact that a lost coin is lost to use.

THE CHILDREN OF THE BRIDECHAMBER; OR, Christ's apology for the joy of his disciples.

Then come to Him the disciples of John, saying, Why do we and the Pharisees fast oft but Thy disciples fast not? And Jesus satd mi to them, Can the children of the bridechamber mourn, as loftg as the Bridegroom is with them f but days will come when the Bridegroom shall be taken from them, and then shall they fast? And no one piit-teth a piece of ten filled cloth unto an old garment, for that whichfilleth ttp taketh from the garment, and a worse rent takes place. Neither do they put new wine into old skins; else the skins burst, and the wine is shed, and the skins perish; but they put new wine into new skins, and both are preserved. â Matt. ix. 14â 17. (LUKE V. 33â 39; Mark ii. 18â 22.)

It is not usual with writers on the parables to include among the number the three suggestive comparisons or illustrations contained in this remarkable section of the Gospel History. But without disputing the right of others to act otherwise, we have no hesitation in giving them a place in our studies on the Parabolic Teaching of Christ. For, if not fully developed parables, these similitudes are at least parable-germs; a fact recognised by one of the Evangelists, who applies the term ' TTowa, much: "kvkvii, in Luke (v. 33).

Luke adds Iv ikiivan; ralg rifiepaiq, " those days;" Mark, tv iktlvy rij! nsp(f, " in that day: " the repetition adds solemnity to the statement. â pukovq dyvckpov: so also in Mark.

TO ir lipofta avrov = the patch which fills the hole in the garment. I I u-: says, " that which fills up (to 7rx; p(Â a) takes from it, the new from t'. ie old (to Kaivcv Tov Traxaiov). The mode of expression in this parable, as rerorted, is somewhat obscure throughout.

Xi'ipov ffy'Tia yiveTat.

ti ce fii'iyi, or at least if they don't attend to this rule.

parable to the second and third of the three, the new patch on the worn-out garment, and the new wine in the old skins. And what is lacking in the artistic finish of these parable-germs is fully compensated for by their mimher, which is a significant hint of the importance of the subject to which they refer. Once more Jesus is put on His defence with reference to departure from the custom of the time by Himself and His disciples, and this time as usual His apology assumes the parabolic form; only in this case He does not, as in His apology for loving the sinful, seek so much to play the part of a consummate artist in the construction of exquisitely finished parables, but rather that of the suggestive original thinker, throwing out in rapid succession fruitful ideas which might be worked out by the hearers themselves. The change in the style was suited to a change in the circumstances; for the new interrogants do not seem to have been, as in the former case, captious, disaffected fault-finders, but rather men honestly perplexed by a surprising diversity in the religious habits of the disciples of Jesus as compared with those of the Pharisees, and of John's disciples. What was called for in the former case was an effort to make a m. oral and emotional impression, and hence the artistic beauty and the pathos of the parables last considered: what is needed in the present case, on the other hand, is instruction in the form of hints at the true cause of the conduct animadverted on, and at the principles applicable to such a matter as the practice of fasting. And the instruction given is admirably adapted to its purpose. No hints could be more suggestive or stimulative of thought, more pregnant with deep meanings far-reaching in their application, more illustrative of the originality of the speaker, and more surely indicative that a great outstanding characteristic of the kingdom, a cardinal feature of the new movement heralded by the Man who was such a puzzle to His contemporaries, was pointed at. We should be very sorry indeed not to have a good excuse for including in our scheme these three parable-germsâ the cjiildrcn of the bridechainber, the new patch on the worn garment, and the new wine in the ohi skins.

Of these parable-germs any one might have been selected to be the title of this chapter; but after due consideration we have deemed the first worthiest of the honour, not merely because it is the first, but specially because it gives us the deepest glimpse into the heart of the subject. For while the second and third simply illustrate the general principle that incongruous things ought not to be combined, that is, in the particular case in hand, that fasting should not be forced upon men whose mood it did not meet, the first tells us precisely what was the mood of the disciples of Jesus which made fasting an uncongenial practice, reveals to us the latent spiritual characteristic of the Jesus-circle, which accounted for this superficial divergence from religious custom. And what then was that mood and characteristic? It was JOY. Jesus and His disciples were a wedding party; He the bridegroom, they the sons of the bridechamber, the bridegroom's friends who with Him conducted the bride to her new home, and there spent a happy week in unrestrained festivity. For all this is implied in the question. Can the children of the bridechamber mourn The question is an implicit assertion, the case put is the actual case, here as in all the parables. Such then being the relations and circumstances of the parties, of course mourning, and therefore by the law of congruity fasting, is out of the question. Joy, mirth, rules the hour, and the appropriate behaviour is not fasting, but dancing and song. But whence this joy, whence in other words the relations alleged to subsist between the Galilean Master and his companions The question throws us back on the characteristics of the kingdom as preached by Jesus. There is joy in the Jesus-circle because the kingdom is a kingdom of GRACE, a kingdom the announcement of whose advent is good news, the very gospel, and whose presence is the simimuin bonum, signifying God a Father, and men His sons. This idea of the kingdom, the one ever presented by Jesus, was the true source of the behaviour of His disciples, and the radical cause of the difference between their behaviour and that of John's disciples. The difference ran up ultimately into this: the diverse conceptions of the kingdom as preached by Jesus and John respectively. The diversity of their conceptions may be very simply formulated. The kingdom as preached by Jesus was good news. As preached by John it was azvful news. In the mouth of the one it meant God regarding men as a Father ready to bestow upon them His grace, yea, willing to receive graciously, as still His children, though erring, the most depraved of men returning to Him in penitence. In the mouth of the other it meant God coming in the majesty of His justice, to execute judgment; Messiah coming with fan in hand to sift wheat from chaff, and with axe to hew down unfruitful trees. No wonder that the followers of the two preachers differed widely in their way of life, the disciples of the one resembling a wedding party making the welkin ring with laughter and song, the disciples of the other resembling a band of pilgrims trudging with rueful look and weary foot to the shrine of a saint to do penance for their sins. No wonder that the disciples of Jesus were a puzzle and a scandal to the disciples of the Baptist; for it is not easy to understand or sympathise with conduct springing out of a radically different spirit to that which animates oneself No wonder, finally, that Jesus himself was a mystery to the Baptist as he lay brooding in melancholy fashion in the prison of Iachaerus; for in His hand was no axe or fan, in His mouth no words of terror, in His heart no severity, but only gentleness and pity dictating deeds of kindness and messages of mercy.

In all Christ's teachings can be found no more decisive indication of the gracious character of the kingdom than just this parable of the Children of the Bridechamber, But we must not suppose that the joyous mood of His disciples sprang directly out of a clear conception on their part of the nature of the kingdom. A kingdom is a very complex phenomenon, and the kingdom which Jesus preached was as yet but very imperfectly understood by those who followed Him. Their conscious thoughts about it were crude and mistaken, and what knowledge of its true nature they had was of an instinctive, unconscious, and implicit character. They knew the kingdom through Jesus the King; not through His words, but through the spirit that was in Him, and that revealed itself in His whole bearing. They knew it as voyagers know the near neighbourhood of an unseen land, by the sweet odour borne thence on the breeze. They discerned the perfume of the oil of gladness emanating from their Master, and hence divined the nature of the kingdom which He came to found. And the gladness which was in

Him passed into them by sympathy. Being in His company they were infected with His spirit, and acted as they saw Him act. Their neglect of fasting was imitative in its origin, not based on reflection. They acted from impulse, not from principle. They did what they did they knew not why, and on being found fault with they would not know what to answer. Men constantly in Christ's company might be expected at length to understand the rationale of the conduct impugned, but to such insight they had not yet attained.

In the foregoing remarks we have implied that the spirit or mood of Jesus was characteristically one of joy. To some this may seem a very questionable position. Was not Jesus the man of sorrow and sadness rather than the man of gladness."' He was a man of sorrow; there was ever in Him a deep sadness, of whose presence we have a significant index in the words, " there will come days when the bridegroom shall be taken from them," which are an ominous hint of a tragic experience awaiting Him in the future that cast its shadow on His spirit now; how deep a shadow we may judge from the repeated mention of the days of mourning, in the version of the saying given by the other Evangelists. But this deep habitual sadness notwithstanding, the spirit of Jesus was emphatically joyful, and His face radiant with the oil of gladness. There was a sunny brightness in His temper as well as an undertone of melancholy. And the springs of His gladness were twofold. First there was the joy inseparable from a religion which has its source in fresh intuitions of truth and rests not on the mere traditions of men, the joy of perfect freedom combined with absolute devotion to God, a joy of which they know nothing whose souls are imprisoned in a complicated system of conventional religious observances such as those practised by the Pharisees, or even by the Baptist's disciples. What a dull, dreary, sombre existence is that of the tradition-enslaved soul, doomed to perform the daily routine of fasting and praying and almsgiving, which composes the dead carcase of works technically holy! But how inexpressibly sweet the joy of " religion new given," consisting in "a revival of intuitive and fresh perceptions." It is the joy of the lark soaring to heaven's gate, and singing ' Literature and Dogma," p. 91.

in the bright sunshine and warm air of summer. It is a joy given to men in certain ages to know in exceptional measure (happy they who live then), and to none more than to Jesus and His disciples. The sign of its presence is the term new applied by implication in our parables to the religious movement with which Jesus and His disciples were identified. Jesus in effect calls His cause a new garment and a nciv vintage. He does this, moreover, not as one apologising for His existence, but rather as one asserting His own importance. He not merely concedes, he triumphantly proclaims the novelty of His religion. What was a fault in the eyes of others was a virtue in His view. And here we have to note the affinity between Christ's spirit and that of Paul, who gloried in the novelty of the Christian religion as a merit, inasmuch as it was but the fulfilment of the prophetic oracle which proclaimed God to be the Maker of new things. Of the same mind also was the author of the Epistle to the Hebrews, whose whole argument is a vindication of the rights of the new as opposed to the prescriptive rights of the decadent old, which he regarded as cancelled and antiquated by the bare uttering of the word ' new' in the prophetic oracle of the new covenant. This joy in the new is indeed characteristic of the whole New Testament, and it is a standing characteristic of the genuinely evangelic spirit in all ages. Besides this joy of fresh religious intuition, Jesus also knew the not less intense joy of love. His passion for saving the lost brought Him wondrous gladness, as well as deep sadness. It was meat to Him to create a spring of new spiritual life in the heart of any human being, even though it were but a publican or a Samaritan woman. He drank deeply of this joy of redeeming love at the feast in Matthew's house with publicans for fellow-guests, the occasion on which our parables were spoken. " In the midst of this feast of ' publicans the heart of Jesus is overflowing with joy; it is one of the hours when His earthly life seems to His feeling like a marriage day." Generous natures can appreciate this joy of doing good; Paul showed that he appreciated it when in his catalogue of the fruits of the Spirit he placed joy next 2 Cor. V. i6: cf. Isa. xliii. 18, 19.

Heb. viii. 13. â Godet Â loco.

to love. It was a true instinct which guided him in the collocation, for where the spirit of beneficence is, there inevitably will be the spirit of gladness. Christ could not be full of grace without being also full of joy.

In a faint degree the disciples were partakers of their Master's joy in both aspects. They knew a little, as yet only a little, of the joy of fresh religious intuition, and of the liberty thence accruing; a little also of the joy of saving the lost. But they had a joy of their own distinct from that of Jesus, the joy, not of giving, but of receiving grace, the joy of faith in the love of a Divine Father to the sinful and unworthy. And in proportion as they experienced this joy would they also experience the species of joy first described, the joy of religious liberty. Faith in God's grace has for its natural issue and consummation that exultant, triumphant joy which was so marked a feature in Paul's religious consciousness, and which finds such impassioned expression in his great controversial epistlesâ the joy of the spirit of son-ship which dares to call God, Father; the joy of hope which can take an optimistic view of life, and believe that all things work together for good; the joy which can exult even in tribulation, because it only tends to develop patience and test character, and so to confirm hope; the joy last, but not least, of liberty from lazv of happy riddance from that stern tyrannical husband, to be united in blessed wedlock to the soul's true husband, Jesus Christ. There are many in our time who gravely doubt whether the companions of Jesus

Gal. V, 22. " The fruit of the Spirit is love, joy," etc.

Gal. iv. 6; Rom. viii. 15. 3 Rom. viii. 28.

Rom. V. 3. 6 Gal. iv. 5.

Â Rom. vii. iâ 4. The idea in this passage is essentially the same as in the parable of the children of the bridechamber. These children of the bridechamber are from another point of view also the bride, as the Baptist himself hinted-when he said, "He that hath the bride is the bridegroom; but the friend of the bridegroom, which standeth and hcareth him, rejoiceth greatly because of the bridegroom's voice" (John iii. 29). Olshausen remarks on it as somewhat surprising, that in the passage before us the disciples are merely the Trapaiij iot. He reconciles the representation with the other, by saying that while with all believers they were the bride, the first disciples were the first rays shed upon humanity by the rising Sun of the spiritual world, and so might be said to introduce tha heavenly Bridegroom to His earthly bride.

ever attained to the perfect Christian joy of the Pauhne 'theology, deeming it rather highly probable that to the end the original apostles, the eleven, continued to do the very thing their Master had treated as an absurdity; to combine, that is, incongruous elements in their religious faith and practice, law and grace, works and faith, the old worn-out garment of Judaism with the new garment of evangelic righteousness; the old skins of Jewish religious custom with the new wine of a gospel of mercy which God meant to be preached to every creature under heaven. If this were indeed the case, then we can only say that the eleven made little use of their opportunities during the time " they had been with Jesus." For it cannot reasonably be doubted that Pauline antinomianism, to use the word in an uninvidious sense, was the natural outcome of Christ's own teaching, and that in accustoming His disciples to disregard existing Jewish religious custom in certain particulars he was educating them for the ultimate abandonment of the whole system as superseded by, and incongruous with, the new order of things brought in with the era of grace.

This we take to be the hidden import of the two parables concerning the new patch on the old garment, and the new wine in old skins, though on the surface they merely teach the general truth that incongruous elements ought not to be united in religion. One consideration that tends to justify the ascription to the two parables of such deep significance is the fact that in uttering them Jesus was defending His disciples for divergence from the religious customs, not of the Pharisees only, but of the Baptist's followers. From this it follows, that the religious movement inaugurated by Jesus was a new thing, new wine, a new garment, in reference even to the religion of the Baptist-circle. Much is implied in this. If Christ had called his religion new as compared with Pharisaism it might have signified no more than that His religion was Judaism reformed, for Pharisaism was Judaism!tformed. But John's religion was itself a reformed Judaism; if therefore Christ's was new in comparison with it, it must have been something more than a reform, even a revolution, an absolutely new thing, having its roots in the Old Testament doubtless, but radically diverse in spirit, principle, and tendency, from the whole religious Hfe of the age whether deformed or reformed.

Passing from this let us observe the reasons by which the law of congruity is enforced in these parables. The chief reason is the incompatibility of the new with the old, leading inevitably to rupture and waste. But it is interesting to note that besides this Luke mentions another, in connection with the first of the two parables; viz. the want of correspondence or keeping between the new and the old. Besides the rending which takes place in connection with the patching of an old garment by a piece from a new one, there is the further objection to the proceeding that the new piece will not agree or harmonise with the old. It is an offence against aesthetics, objectionable on the score of taste, even if no serious result were to follow from the inharmonious combination. The garment so patched will present a grotesque aspect to be avoided by all means. This recognition of aesthetical considerations as having their own place in religion (for we may legitin. ately transfer this feature of the parable to the spiritual sphere) is well deserving notice, though in comparison with the more serious consequences resulting from disregard of the lavv' of congruity, it be but of subordinate moment. It is a word in favour of the beautifid from the author of our faith. And it is further to be noted, that the parable of the new patch, as given in Luke, conveys to us an important hint as to the true source of beauty and harmony in religion. A religious cultus will only then exhibit a fair aspect and harmonious proportions when it is all of a piece, generated from one principle, the embodiment of one spirit, not an eclectic patchwork of beliefs and practices borrowed from various sources. This is but to say that religion is only then seen in its native comeliness when it is the religion of the spirit. Then it possesses the incomparable attractions of naturalness, spontaneity, free unfettered movement, doing ' rifl TTaxtitKp ov (Tui0aii')j(TÂ t TO itrifsXtifia to cnrb rov Kaivov (v. 36)- The expression might be interpreted as referring to the stronger quality of the new cloth leading to the result pointed at in Matthew and Mark, but, as Godet reniar'; s, it much more naturally refers to a contrast in appearance between the two cloths. Besides, as we shall see, Luke's conception of the new cloth does not make room for the idea of contraction resulting from the unfuiied condition of the cloth.

304 The Parabolic Teaching of Christ, book ii.

whatever the spirit prompts, and doing it gracefully and heartily. How repulsive by comparison a religion of mechanical habits, of which no account can be given except that they are sanctioned by tradition and custom; and not less, let us add, a religion of merely negative affected spirituality, whose mechanicalism consists in avoiding everything savouring of taste as sensuous, mistaking barbarism for purity. It is an error of the same kind in worship, as that in religious life which makes the new nature consist in beincr unnatural.

Turning now to the principal reason for observing the law of congruity, viz. the damage and loss caused by the breach of it, we find here also a peculiarity in Luke's narrative, in so far as the first of the two parables is concerned; this, viz., that the injury is done not, as in Mattliew and Mark, to the old garment, but to the new one. In the first two Gospels the evil to be shunned is the rending of the old patched garment by the contraction of the new piece of unfulled cloth under the influence of moisture. In Luke, on the other hand, the evil is the spoiling of a new garment from which a piece has been cut out. This seems a somewhat unnatural turn of thought, for the procedure pointed at, that of patching an old coat by a piece cut out of a new one, seems too absurd for any human being in his senses to think of. And when we endeavour to apply the idea to the spiritual situation we find ourselves somewhat at a loss in which direction to turn. Is Jesus justifying Himself for not playing the part of a patcher as described in the parable, or is He representing John as playing that part; and in either case what is signified by the spoiling of the new garment.-' If our Lord stated the case as represented in Luke's narrative we must put upon His words some such sense as the following:â It is a folly to combine the new doctrine of the kingdom with old customs associated with a religion of an entirely different

The piece used as a patch is taken from a new garment, a-no 'iftariov Katvov, and the evil one does by such a procedure is that he rends the new (garment) to koivov (jiiariov) axi' n- The A. V. renders this "the new maketh a rent" (in the old), which brings Lu': e into harmony with Matthew and Mark. But this construction is hardly admissible. Besides, the new piece of cloth in Luke's version does not possess the propertj which causes rending, for it is taken from a Viq s garment which would not naturally be made of unfulled cloth.

spirit. The necessary effect of such a course must be to do fatal injury to the new doctrine, by obscuring its true nature and weakening its influence. We certainly can imagine Jesus saying this in reference to John's disciples, for the deprecated line of action was just that which they pursued. They believed in the kingdom preached by their Master, and so far were on the side of the new movement; but they combined this belief with Judaistic or Pharisaic practice, with the result that their faith in the kingdom was practically neutralised, or extinguished as a light put under a bushel. And we can also conceive Jesus saying the same thing concerning Himself to the effect of justifying Himself for not pursuing the policy indicated; though not without qualification, for while He disregarded Pharisaic practice in such matters as fasting and ceremonial washing. He did certainly accommodate Himself to many existing usages, which were destined to fall into desuetude when the spirit of the new religion had had time to create for itself a fitting garment of habits.

We are inclined to think that while the thought to which Luke gives prominence in the first parable may have been glanced at, it was not the one emphasised by the speaker, but rather that brought out in the version of Matthew and Mark, viz. the tearing asunder of the new from the old after the patching process has been accomplished. In this form the first parable sympathises best with the second, for then it becomes apparent that the mischief wrought in both cases is due to the forces latent in the new.

Rending in the one case is produced by the contraction of the new cloth, in the other by the fermentation of the new wine. And the great truth in the

Godet understands the parable as referring to Christ, that is, as containing a repudiation on Christ's part of the role of a patcher. Hofmann, on the other hand, thinks the reference is to the Baptist, so that the parable contains a description of what John and his disciples did. They did what Jesu5 declined to do; spoiled the new religion by using it to patch up, or reform, a worn-out religion.

" So Olshausen, who thinks that in Luke's narrative our Lord's words have undergone modification, with a view to assimilate the two parables by making Christianity in each the chief thing: the new garment and the new wine. Godet takes strongly and even enthusiastically the opposite view, 3o6 The Parabolic Teaching of Christ book. ii.

spiritual sphere thus pointed out is, that the attempt to force old behefs and customs on a new rehgious movement must ever be disastrous either to the old or to the new, probably to both, in consequence of the vital force of the new life, which will never rest till it has rid itself of bondage to foreign elements with which it has no affinity.

In the natural sphere men take the disruptive forces latent in the new into account, and so avoid the risks run by disregard of the law of congruity. No man putteth a piece of unfulled cloth on an old garment, or new wine into worn-out skins. Such prudence is so much a matter of course, that but for the sake of the spiritual application of the parables, it had been wholly unnecessary to point out the consequences of neglect. But, alas! in the spiritual sphere the exceptional man is he who has the wisdom to act on the law of congruity. The admirers of the old will insist on forcing the new wine into old bottles, regardless of the thousandfold illustrations supplied by history of the danger and folly of so doing. How is it that a prudence which is so common in natural life is so rare in religion."' It arises from failure to recognir. e in new religious phenomena a new wine of the kingdom. Once recognise the presence of a new wine, and the sense to know what to do with it may be expected to follow; just as, once recognise that Christ is a Physician and a Shepherd, and you will no longer wonder that He takes an interest in publicans and sinners. But the difficulty is to discern the true character of the novel in religion. One is so apt to regard it not as a new wine of the kingdom, but as a poisonous liquid, the fruit of levity, impiety, youthful vanity, restless love of change. That it objects to anything in the established beliefs and customs is sufficient evidence of its dangerous character. But even after the initial difficulty of discerning in the new the traces of a genuine wine of the kingdom has been got over, there are still hindrances to be overcome before the new wine shall receive wise treatment. Men are apt to say. Why cannot the new wine go into old skins.? why should not forms of belief and worship and modes of action which suited the fathers suit the children also, and what harm can result from insisting on conformity to existing custom This is the position usually assumed virtually or avowedly by the patrons of use and wont. Conservative minds have a very inadequate idea of the vital force of belief Their own faith having become a tame lifeless thing, they imagine tameness or pliancy to be an attribute of faith generally, and too often they do not find out their mistake till an irrepressible revolutionary outburst causes them to open their eyes in amazement. They insist on adherence to what is old till the new proves its inherent power by producing an explosion needlessly wasteful, whereby both wine and bottles are destroyed, and energies which might have wrought much unmixed good are perverted into blind powers of indiscriminate destruction.

The unwisdom of the old in dealing with the new has yet another source: dislike of the unamiable repulsive elements characteristic of the latter. It may be taken for granted that there are such elements in all new movements, however noble and wholesome in the main. The existence of defects, imperfections inseparable from the initial stage of the new life, is clearly implied in both the parabolic emblems. The new piece of cloth is unfulled, not fit for wear. The new wine has to go through a process of fermentation before it be drinkable, or at least in its present state it is very inferior to the old wine in flavour. In the very striking sentence with which Luke's report of our Lord's words ends, this is very frankly recognised. " And no one," said Jesus, " having drunk old wine, wishes new, for he saith, the old is mild." It is an observation full of kindly humour, rare charity, and deepest wisdom; a candid concession to the honest lovers of old ways, and, in effect, a modest appeal to them to exercise indulgence towards the new ways. Had Christians but entered fully into the spirit of this one saying of their Lord, what a difference it would have made in the history of the Church. Then men had known how to combine preference for the old with tolerance of the new, so as to give the new time to grow mellow in turn. But such wisdom is often sadly lacking even in good men, men of taste and culture, the reverent and devout, themselves excellent samples of the old vintage. Such not unfrequently make no allowance for youth and inexperience, but treat faults Â Luke V. 39, before eÂ XÂ i many copies read ivqiiig = ' straightway," A. V. For the positive xp'J' "oc some MSS. read xp'jtorfpof. The positive is to be preferred as more emphatic.

which are at worst but the escapades of noble energies not yet perfectly under the control of wisdom, as if they were unpardonable sins. Because the new wine is as yet harsh and fiery they think they do well to spill it, saying it is naught and unprofitable. How much wiser to give heed to the appeal of the new wine as uttered by the mouth of the Eternal Vine: " We know that we are unpalatable to those accustomed to the old vintage; but bear with us, do not hate us, do not destroy us, do not cast us out. Keep us, we will mend with age, and may ultimately be as good to drink as that which is at present in use."

What sweet reasonableness' is in that saying of Jesus concerning the old wine and the new! What rare qualities of mind and heart are exhibited in all the sayings spoken by Him on this occasion: what ready wit, what kindly humour, what gaiety of spirit, what profound yet homely originality of thought; what clear insight into the significance of His own position and vocation, what confidence in His own cause, what resolute determination to maintain His independence, and to decline all self-stultifying compromises; and yet withal what patience and tolerance towards all honest earnest men who in matters of religion cannot see with His eyes!

Godet finds in this saying, recorded alone by Luke, a third parable, having for its distinctive aim to teach that the organs of the new principles must not treat those of the ancient order with harshness, but remember that it is not easy to pass from a system with which one has been identified from childhood, to an entirely different principle of life. This is certainly an important truth which was often enforced and habitually acted on by Paul, and this sentence may be used for the purpose of inculcating it on Christians, as showing how kindly their Lord treated the adherents of the old order of things. But the saying seems intended primarily to show how a plea for the toleration of the new may be combined with recognition of the merits of the old, and in this view it is better to take it as a reflection appended to the preceding parable than as a new one.

At a Sabbath-day feast in the house of an influential and wealthy Pharisee, Jesus spake the following parable to His fellow-guests, when He marked how they chose out the chief places:

Whett thou art bidden of any one to a wedding, sit not down in the chief seat, lest a more honoured one than thou be bidden of him; and he that bade thee and him come and say to thee, Give place to this one; and thejt shall thou begin with shame to take the last seat. But when thou art bidden, go and sit down in the last place, that when he that bade thee cometh, he may say unto thee, Friend, come up hither: then shall thou have glory before all thy fellow-guests. For every one that exalteth himself shall be abased, and he that hunibleth himself shall be exalted. â LUKE xiv. 7â 11.

This parable has not, any more than those considered in our last chapter, the honour of being included among the parables of our Lord in many of the books belonging to the literature of our subject. This may be due to the fact that it offers few topics for remark, and that the one lesson which it teaches, the moral enunciated in the closing verse, is more ' irpogavdiiriqi; the Trpog implying approach towards the host at the head of the table. So Field, criticising the A. V. and R. V. " No account," he says, "is taken of the irpog. It must have one of two values, either of addition,â ascende adhuc superius,â or motion towardsâ ascende hue superius. The latter seems to be the case here. The host comes into the room, takes his place at the head of the table, and calls to the guest whom he intends to honour, Friend, come up higher. This view is remarkably confirmed by Prov. xxv. 7, which our Lord had in view."â ' Otium Norv."

impressively enforced in the more important parable of the Pharisee and the Pub-hcan. It deserves however at least a passing notice, if it were only to give occasion for pointing out the prominent place which the great truth that the kingdom of God is for the humble, occupied in the thoughts of Jesus, as evinced by the fact of His uttering tivo parables to enforce it. We have discovered it to be His way to multiply parables to inculcate truths either ill understood, or of cardinal importance. We have two parables setting forth the kingdom of God as the siimmiun bomim, two to teach the value of perseverance in prayer, three to declare the joy of men in finding things lost, three to vindicate the joy of those who have believed in God's grace. In like manner we have two parables to teach that he who humbleth himself shall be exalted, and he who exalteth himself shall be abased; whence we may confidently infer that, in the view of Christ, this is one of the great laws of the kingdom of God.

On the surface this portion of our Lord's table-talk at the Sabbath feast wears the aspect of a moral advice, rather than of a parable. But it does not require lengthened consideration to be satisfied that Jesus is not here performing the part of a mere censor of manners, but is following His true vocation as the Teacher of the Doctrine of the Kingdom. Through the medium of a counsel of prudence relating to ordinary social life He communicates a lesson of true wisdom concerning the higher sphere of religion. The Evangelist perceived this, therefore he called this piece of advice 2, parable; most legitimately, inasmuch as a parable has for its aim to show by an example of human action in natural life, how men should act in the sphere of spiritual life. There is indeed a manifest difi'erence between this parable and all others hitherto considered, viz. that it tells us not how men do act in the natural sphere, but how according to the dictates of prudence they should act. The guests whom Jesus saw before Him, and whose conduct called forth the parable, had been acting in a different way, not prudently sitting down in a humble place in the hope that their host would invite them to a place of greater distinction, but proudly appropriating to themselves the places which they thought due to their social importance. The morality of the advice given to them was not high, for it

simply showed them a slyer way of gratifying ambition; but low as was its moral tone, the line of action apparently recommended was too high pitched for most of those present. The prudence prescribed, though worldly in its spirit, was too like genuine wisdom to be generally practised. The truth seems to be that Christ had no serious intention to give a lesson in social deportment, and that the parabolic element in His words is confined to this, that instruction valid only for the religious sphere is couched in terms which seem to imply a reference to ordinary social life. At the table of this chief man among the Pharisees He has an excellent opportunity of witnessing the spirit of Pharisaism in full bloom; and as He notes its characteristic vanity and pride exhibiting themselves in a struggle for the chief rooms at the feast, He thinks how different the order of things here from that which obtains in the kingdom of God! Here pride grasps at distinction and gets its reward, there pride is abased and the humble are exalted. He puts His reflections in the form of a counsel how to behave at feasts, not that He expects any one present to act on the advice, or to regard it otherwise than as the whimsical utterance of an eccentric person, to be received with a smile. He knows that no proud man can ever believe that humility is the way to exaltation, and therefore that no proud man ever will take that way. He knows also that humility does not gain honour among the worldly-minded, that on the contrary the world generally takes men at their own estimate, and gives to ambition the first place, and to modesty the last. He understands, consequently, that to attempt to change the customs of society by moral advice were to waste words and to lower Himself. What He really does is to remind His fellow-guests that there is a society in which humility is held in honour and pride gets a downsetting. That He is thinking of this sacred society is apparent from His manner uf expressing Himself. The case supposed is that of an invitation to a wedding Why a wedding, instead of an ordinary feast? Because He has in mind that kingdom of heaven which He more than once expressly represented by the emblem of a marriage-feast, and which He thought of Â Â iÂ yaiouc- D. IÂ as ydxoi. Matt. xxii. I; xxv. I.

under that figure when He spake of His disciples as the children of the bride-chamber. Then the word " glory" (So' a) in the closing sentence of the parable is very suggestive: " Thou shalt have glory before all thy fellow-guests." Would Jesus use such a term in reference to the little triumph of a guest at a common feast over his fellow-guests, in being promoted to a place of distinction The expression, it has been well remarked, would be puerile, if it did not open up a glimose of a heavenly reality."

THE PHARISEE AND THE PUBLICAN.

The parable of the Pharisee and the Publican shows us the same spirit which at the Sabbath-day feast eagerly sought the first places, at work in the sphere of religion: the Pharisee confidently taking for himself the first place among the ranks of the righteous and the devout. On this account this history cannot strictly be considered a parable, for in it is no comparison between action in the natural sphere and action in the higher spiritual sphere; but rather an illustrative example of a certain kind of action in the latter sphere, with a declaration of the Divine judgment thereon. Nevertheless the Evangelist calls it a parable, and expositors with one consent have agreed to regard it as such.

To certain men who trusted in themselves that they were righteous, and were in the habit of despising others, Jesus spake " this parable:"

Two men went up into the temple to pray, the one a Pharisee afid the. other a publicati. The Pharisee, having taken up his position, prayed within himself thus: God, I thank Thee, that I ai7i not as the rest of men, extorio7iers, unjust, adulterers, or even as this publican. I fast twice in the week, J give tithes of all that I acquire." But the publican, standing afar off, would not so much as lift up his eyes 1 Godet.

arabtiq. The word implies confidence. Bengel: fidenter, loco solito. Reciprocum plus notat quam 'kjtmq neutrum (ver. 13). Similarly Unger: oraquq, elatus.

01 XoitToi Tu)v avopwtTwv, all but himself and his class.

KTuinat, not KtkTrjfxai, which it would require to be in order to bear the rendering in A. V.

efft-Gjf, vide note 2: the publican stood in a timid attitude, as if apologizing for his existence.

unto heaven, but kept smiting his breast, saying: God, be merciful to me the simter. I tell yon, this man went down to his house justified rather than the other; for every one that exalteth himself shall be abased, and he that humbleth himself shall be exalted. â LUKE xviii. 9â 14.

It is idle to ask when or to whom this parable was spoken. The Evangelist states that it was spoken to or about certain persons who trusted in themselves that they were righteous. It is evident that it might have been represented with equal propriety as spoken to or about men of an opposite spirit, such, viz., as were ready to acknowledge their shortcomings. The really important thing to note is that this is a parable which sets forth one of the great laws of the kingdom of God, viewed as a kingdom of Grace, that enunciated in the closing verse: " Every one that exalteth himself shall be abased; and he that humbleth himself shall be exalted." It was doubtless the perception of this fact which led Luke to gather up the precious fragment and preserve it in his basket. Luke was the Evangelist, as Paul was the Apostle, of the Gentiles, and in collecting materials for the composition of his Gospel he was ever on the outlook for such incidents in the ministry of Christ as tended to show that the Gospel was designed for the whole world, and that it was fit to be a Gospel for the world. A salvation to be preached to the human race, a salvation iy grace, and therefore available for Gentiles on the same terms as for Jews, these were the fundamental articles in Luke's as in Paul's creed; and in writing the life of our Lord he was ever intent on showing that these doctrines had a root in His teaching. This parable he rightly considered fitted to serve that purpose. The poor publican, though a (t v, was in Pharisaic esteem as an heathen man; and in representing a penitent publican as an object of Divine favour, Jesus in effect and in principle proclaimed the truth: " There is hope in God even for Gentiles, for all, who are objects of contempt, as aliens from the commonwealth of Israel, to the ri aficiprw p, not the only sinner, but the man who is known by his sin, the notorious sinner.

2 The reading here is very uncertain. T. R. has Â j sktlvos. The most probable reading is that of N, B, L. nap' tktlvov. Another reading adopted by Tischendorf is yap txt'ivog, which seems to be a combination of the other two, yap being a mistake for Trap. The sense in any case is clear.

proud self-righteous Jew." Then in declaring that the penitent publican was justified rather than the Pharisee who had no sins to confess, Jesus in effect proclaimed that other grand truth, that men are saved not by works of righteousness which they have done, but by God's mercy. Christ's reflection on the two men is equivalent in drift to Paul's doctrine of justification by grace through faith. It is not so clear and explicit an announcement of that doctrine as we find in the Pauline Epistles; but it tends that way, it looks in the direction of Paul's doctrine, it is Paul's doctrine in germ, and hence the interest it awakened in the mind of Luke, who was a thorough believer in the Pauline programme: salvation by grace, therefore salvation for all on equal terms, there being no difference between Jew and Gentile, for " all have sinned and come short of the glory of God."

We shall best study this parable by making our starting-point the judgment of Jesus on the two men whose characters are so graphically depicted in it, and considering in order these points: First, the import of the judgment; Second, its grounds; Third, its uses.

I. It is declared that the publican went down to his house justified rather than the Pharisee. In endeavouring to ascertain the import of this declaration we must assume that it is not intended to call in question the statements of fact made by the two parties. Neither is supposed to have borne false witness for or against himself, whether in ignorance or with intent to deceive. Even the self-laudatory statements of the Pharisee are allowed to pass unquestioned. It is not said, insinuated, or tacitly implied that he gives himself credit for actions which he has not performed, or for virtues which he does not possess. It is conceded that he is not an extortioner, or an unjust man, or an impure man, and that he fasts twice a week, and gives tithes of all he acquires, so adding works of supererogation to his virtue, doing more than the statute required. What is blamed is not his statement of

The Pharisees fasted on Mondays and Thursdays. The law prescribed only one regular fast, that on the great day of atonement. The law as to tithes prescribed that a tenth part of the produce of the fields and of the herds should be devoted to the Levites (Levit. xxvii. 30â 32; Numbers xviii. 21, 24). The Pharisee pays tithes of all he acquires, from whatever source.

facts, but the spirit in which he makes that statement, the spirit of self-complacency. There is the less reason to doubt this that the Pharisee is not represented as uttering his prayer aloud. He took up his posture and prayed thus ivith himself. Some indeed would connect the words differently, so as to make the sentence runâ he stood by himself and prayed thus, the isolated position being supposed to be the point our Lord wished to emphasise as a mark of pride. There seem to be no good grounds, however, for departing from the arrangement as it stands in our English version, which is approved by the great majority of interpreters. But if 77 09 kavrov is to be taken with irpoo-nvxero, the fact implied is that the Pharisee's prayer was mental not audible. He prayed "within himself," even as "there were some that had indignation within themselves " at the waste of precious ointment by Mary of Bethany. It has been asked what was there characteristic of a Pharisee in praying mentally."' But this trait is added not to distinguish the Pharisee from others, but to keep the account given of his prayer within the limits of verisimilitude. Even a Pharisee would hardly dare to utter such a prayer in the hearing of his fellow-men, speaking as if he were the only good man, and all the rest of the world given up to iniq' ity. Had his prayer been meant for the public ear there would probably have been in it less depreciation of others and also less praise of himself. But just on that account there would likewise have been less sincerity, less fidelity to the actual thoughts and feelings of the man. However the Pharisee might pray in public, the prayer put into his mouth shows us how he prayed in his heart. And just because it is a heart prayer it is a true prayer reflecting his real belief. He thinks as badly of the world as he is represented; he thinks as well of himself, and he does so on the ground of the virtues and pious practices for which he gives himself credit, with perfect fidelity to fact. It is his self-complacency alone, therefore, not its fact-basis, which is liable to question.

Mark xiv. 4- ayavakrovprig irpoq kavtohc.

Goebel raises this objection to the view we advocate as to the connection.

So Godet. The Pharisee, he remarks, prayed " tr s sinc rement (car la pri re tait faite interieurement)."

The publican's account of himself is also assumed to be correct. In declaring that this man went down to his house justified, our Lord does not mean to say: This publican was mistaken in imagining himself to be so great a sinner â standing in a timid, abject attitude, as if apologising for his existenceâ calling himself tjie sinner, as if sin were the one thing by which he was known, beating on his breast, and, under an overwhelming sense of guilt, not daring to lift up his eyes to heaven. It is taken for granted that the publican's confession is true, and that his whole demeanour is but an appropriate expression of contrition. He is a sinner as he says in words, a great sinner as he declares by significant gesture. The validity of the judgment pronounced concerning him, does not at all rest on the comparative smallness of his guilt. Suppose the penitent had said more against himself sincerely (sincerely, observe, for he might have said more, and in stronger terms, and meant less), the verdict had not been different. Suppose he had said: " I am what that holy man yonder thinks he is not, an extortioner, unjust, an adulterer. He points at me, to make a long story short. He has good right. I am an epitome of all the sins "; still the judgment of Jesus had been the same.

These things being so, it is clear how the judgment must be understood. It means, not the publican is a just man, and the Pharisee an unjust, but the publican is nearer the approval of God than the other who approves himself. The approval or good will of God is what both are seeking. Both address God. The one says, "God, I thank Thee;"

the other, "God, be gracious to me." The one expects God to endorse the good opinion he entertains of himself; the other begs God to be merciful to him notwithstanding his sin. And what our Lord means to affirm is, that the publican came nearer the common end than the Pharisee did; that God regarded the self-blaming sinner with more favour than the self-praising saint; that the two men in a manner changed places, the self-styled just man being in God's sight as an unrighteous man, and the self-styled sinner being in God's sight as a righteous man. In short the term "justified" (behtkaicofxhos) is used in a sense kindred to the Pauline, and the comparison between the two dramatis person(s bar. refer- ence not to character, but to the relation to God in which they respectively stand.

We must add another observation by way of determining the import of the judgment. It does not mean that the pubhcan went down to his house thhiking that God regarded him with more favour than the Pharisee. Our Lord's purpose is to point out what God did indeed think of the two men, not what they thought He thought of them. Stier affirms that our Lord meant His declaration to refer to t. consciousness of the two parties, in which the one was sensible of his justification, the other not. This is an utterly groundless assertion, and in its practical tendency most mischievous, as fitted to rob the parable of its great use as a source of comfort to contrite souls. It is moreover a very improbable assertion. It is by no means likely that the publican felt surer of God's favour than the Pharisee did. The Pharisee, it may be shrewdly suspected, went down to his house quite confident that God was as well pleased with him as he was with himself. And it may be feared the publican went down to his house still in an anxious apprehensive frame of mind, thinking it hardly possible God could have mercy on such a wretch; walking homeward with slow and melancholy step, and eyes cast down to the ground. Strange state of mind, it may be thought, for a justified man! But we must remember that God's thoughts of us do not take their complexion from our opinion of them; that they may be very gracious towards us, when we are unable to believe it, and that salvation does not depend on our changing moods, any more than the existence of the sun depends on the presence or absence of clouds. We will return to this point. Meantime let us considerâ â

Some commentators, whose minds are dominated by the theological interest, say there is no comparison, because there are no degrees in justification. This is too rigid. To the same bias is due the attempt of Trench and others to find in the publican's l atOÂ; rtioi a reference to a propitiatory atonement. This is to overlay nature by dogmatic theology. Goebel, recognising a comparison in the expression Trap' kavov, thinks that the 6tsikat(Ofiivog points back to Siicatoi, ver. 9, and that the idea is, the publican got a better righteousness than the Pharisee's.

' ' Reden Jesu." Similarly Trench affirms that the publican was not merely justified in the secret counsels of God, but had a sweet sense of forgiveness, c., c. All which is pure assumption.

2. Th grounds of the fidginent. Only one reason is expressly referred to by Christ, but there is another reason implied to which it may be well to advert. It is this: The publican's self-dissatisfaction had more truth or religious sincerity in it than the Pharisee's self complacency, and God, as the Psalmist tells us, desires and is pleased with truth in the inward parts. In making this statement we do not, any more than our

Lord, mean to call in question the correctness of the description which the Pharisee gives of his own moral and religious character. We assume that all the statements he makes, viewed as matters of fact, are true. But it does not follow from this that he had any just reason for self-complacency. For to be pleased with oneself goes a great deal further than to make some particular statements of a satisfactory nature about one's conduct. It implies a comprehensive judgment concerning one's whole spiritual condition to the effect that it is as it ought to be. Now, so far is this from being necessarily involved in an enumeration of some favourable particulars concerning myself that such an enumeration may be but the preface or prelude to a heavy charge which I mean to bring against myself, to a long catalogue of confessions which I feel constrained to make. This worshipper, e. g. might have said all he did say concerning himself, and yet have made as many confessions as would have put all self-complacent thoughts out of his mind. Every act of thanksgiving might have been followed by an act of confession, as thus: I thank Thee I have been preserved from extortion, but I confess I have coveted ofttimes what I have not laid hands on, I thank Thee I have not been an unjust man, but I acknowledge that I am far from being a generous man. I thank Thee I am not an adulterer, but I confess that my heart has harboured many wicked thoughts. I thank Thee that my lot, my opportunities, and my habits differ widely from those of the class to which this man my fellow-worshipper, who beats his breast, belongs; but I do not flatter myself that had I been in his circumstances I should have been better than he, and I deplore that I and the class of which I am a member feel so little compassion towards these much-tempted men, that we content ourselves Â Psal. li. 6.

with simply abhorring them and holding aloof from their society. I thank Thee that it is in my heart to attend punctually to my religious duties, but I acknowledge that my zeal and my liberality come immeasurably short of what is due to Thee, and contrast but poorly with thoee of him who centuries ago offered up this prayer and thanksgiving in this holy city: " Now therefore, our God, we thank Thee and praise Thy glorious name. But who am I, and what is my people, that we should be able to offer so willingly after this sort for all things come of Thee, and of Thine own have we given Thee. O Lord our God, all this store that we have prepared to build Thee an house for Thine holy name cometh of Thine hand, and is all Thine own." What are my poor tithes to the liberality of King David, or what my religious devotion compared to his whose whole heart was set upon building a temple for Jehovah such as that within whose sacred precincts I now stand."'

The self-complacent Pharisee made no such confessions, was utterly unconscious that he had any such confessions to make, and hence we may with certainty infer that if not a conscious hypocrite, he was at least an unconscious one, a self-deceived man, utterly devoid of the soul of true goodness. For all the truly good are conscious that they have confessions to make which exclude all boasting. While not indulging in indiscriminate self-condemnation, and distinguishing between occasions for thankfulness and occasions for self-humiliation, they are ever more sensible of their shortcomings than of their good performances. And speaking generally, it may be said that a man confessing sin, is nearer to true goodness than a man boasting of his goodness. Confession of sin is the homage of an awakened conscience to the moral law; boasting of goodness is the lying vanity of a foolish self-deceived heart. He who does nothing but confess, may or may not have some good qualities which he might have specified had he been in the humour; but even at the worst, supposing previous character to have been utterly bad, he who with his whole heart says, "I am a sinner," hath more of God's spirit in him, than he who makes no confession at all, and does nothing but boast.

J Chron. xxix. 13, 14, 16.

It is characteristic of this self-complacent Pharisee, and another injex of the want of truth in the deeper sense, that while apparently unconscious of any sins of his own, he is very much alive to the sins of others. With a coarse sweeping indiscriminateness he pronounces all men but himself and his class guilty, and of the grossest sins. He makes himself very good, by the cheap method of making all others very bad. It is easy to hz a saint by comparison, when all the world consists of extortioners, knaves, and adulterers. But what truth or delicacy of conscience can there be in one who can adopt the method of an unbridled censoriousness for advancincf his own reputation."' It is sad to reflect that at this point in the parable the speaker can be charged with no exaggeration, but has faithfully described a feature of the Pharisaic spirit in every age, as exhibited both in individuals and in communities. The vulgar method of self-exaltation by depreciation of others has been and is too commonly practised.

We come now to the reason expressly stated by our Lord in support of His judgment concerning the two men. " Every one that exalteth himself shall be abased, and he that humbleth himself shall be exalted." This statement is valuable as teaching that self-praise and self-condemnation produce the same effects on the Divine mind as they produce on our own minds. When a man praises himself in our hearing the act provokes in us a spirit of criticism; when, on the other hand, we hear a man condemn himself, there arises in our bosom a feeling of sympathy towards him. Just the same effects, Christ gives us to understand, do the same acts produce on the mind of God. And with His teaching all Scripture agrees. All through the Bible runs the sentiment so forcibly expressed by the Psalmist: " Though the Lord be high, yet hath He respect unto the lowly; but the proud He knoweth afar off." This Bible doctrine may

Unger: De toto hominum genere quam humillime sentit i. q. Lutherus notat) tum seinet perfectum jam superbit, quod a flagitiis humillimis liberum se sentit. Hofmann thinks the oi Xoittoi in ver. ii does not mean all other men besides himself, but men of another disposition. Perhaps, but it does not make matters much better. What is noticeable is the absence of all indications in the Pharisee's language of an anxiety to do justice to the characters of others.

Psal. cxxxviii. 6.

be said to be a part of the philosophy of justification. It does not tell us the whole truth on that subject, but it certainly gives us some insight into the Divine procedure in connection with the forgiveness of sin. It teaches us that God forgiveth sins to such as acknowledge them, and imputeth sins to such as deny them, for this among other reasons, because it gives Him pleasure to exalt those who humble themselves, and to humble those who exalt themselves. A very good reason truly, which commends itself to the common conscience, and we may say to the common sense of mankind. Let us not despise it because it is elementary, and does not belong to the more specific doctrines of Christian theology on the subject of justification. Let those who do not feel at home in these doctrines, and to whom perchance they appear not only mysterious but unreal, lay this elementary ethical truth to heart, and it will be at least one lesson learnt on a very important subject. Believe with all the heart that God forgiveth sin penitently acknowledged, because His moral nature is like our own in this, that He scorneth scorners and giveth grace to the lowly, is pleased to save the afflicted and to bring down high looks, lightly esteems those who highly esteem themselves and regards with favour those who humble themselves. It were well that men did lay these truths more to heart, and considered that he who judgeth himself shall not be judged, that he who criticises himself disarms criticism, that he who frankly says " I have sinned" shall hear no further mention of his sin. So many imagine that their interest lies in stoutly denying or extenuating sin; so few understand that policy, not to say truth, dictates rather the use of such a prayer as that of the Psalmist, "For Thy name's sake, O Lord, pardon mine iniquity, for it is great." To deny sin, wisdom! Nay, it is utter folly. Consider what a man does who denies sin. He simply identifies himself with his sin, and compels God to treat him and it as one. He makes his innermost self responsible for his sin, binds it like a millstone round his neck to sink him down to the depths of perdition, gathers it round his person like a burning garment to consume him with the fire of damnation. But confess your sin, say it is yours, and you separate yourself from it, show that though it is yours it is not you, show that there is something in the heart of your being that abhors it: you cut the cord which suspends the millstone about your neck, and escape drowning; you tear off the burning clothes from your person and escape a horrible death by fire. It is well to have the courage to acknowledge offences. It requires an effort, but it is an effort to which humility is equal; for it has been truly said by a German writer, that the essence of Demiitji, humility, is Miith courage. A proud man cannot dare to say, "I have sinned," but a humble man can, and his daring is his salvation.

3. The uses of the judgment. It may be remarked here in the first place, that it were not to use but to abuse the words of Christ to find in them a doctrinally complete statement on the subject of justification. We learn from the verdict pronounced on the two worshippers, that it is necessary, in order to please God, to be sincere and to be humble, but we may not hence infer that we are saved by our sincerity or by our humility. We are not saved by these virtues, any more than by boasting of our goodness, but by the free grace of God.

From Luke's introduction it might be inferred that the chief purpose for which the parable was spoken was to rebuke and subdue the spirit of self-righteousness. To do this effectively is not easy, though that is no reason why it should not be attempted. Another service, however, was probably also kept in view by the speaker, which was much more likely to be accomplished, viz. to revive the spirit of the contrite, and embolden them to hope in God's mercy. This is a service which contrite souls greatly need to have rendered them, for they are slow to believe that they can possibly be the objects of Divine complacency. Such in all probability was the publican's state of mind, not only before but even after he had prayed. He went down to his house justified in God's sight, but not, we think, in his own. He had not found peace," to use a current phrase. In technical language we might speak of him as objectively, but not su'ojectively, justified. In plain English the fact was so, but he was not aware that the fact was so. In saying this, we do not forget

Arndt, "Das Wesen der Demuth ist Muth." It is a pretty play upon words, but it is more, a great moral truth.

that there is an instinct, call it rather the still small voice of the Holy Spirit, which tells a penitent, " there is hope in God," " there is forgiveness with Him that He may be feared;" " wait for God, as they that wait for the dawn." But a man who beats his breast, and dares not look up, and stands afar off in an attitude which seems an apology for existence, has some difficulty in trusting this instinct. To fear and despond suits his mood rather than to hope. There are physical reasons for this, not to speak of spiritual ones. The whole behaviour of the publican speaks to a great religious crisis going on in his soul. For that beating of the breast, and that downcast eye, and that timid posture, are not a theatrical performance got up for the occasion. They bear witness to a painful, possibly a protracted, soul-struggle. But one who passes through such a crisis suffers in body as well as in mind. His nerves are sorely shaken, and in this physical condition he is apt to become a prey to fear and depression. He starts at his own shadow, dreads the postman, trembles when he opens a letter lest it should contain evil tidings, can scarce muster courage to go into a dark room, or to put out the light when he goes to bed. How hard for a man in this state to take cheerful views of his spiritual condition, to rejoice in the sunlight of Divine grace! In the expressive phrase of Bunyan, used with reference to himself when he was in a similar state, such an one is prone rather to take the shady side of the street. Is it improbable that one object Christ had in view in uttering this parable and the judgment with which it winds up, was to take such contrite and fear-stricken ones by the hand and conduct them over to the sunny side? There are some who are stupid enough to take unfavourable views of the spiritual state of such as walk in darkness and have no light, punishing them for their despondency by declaring them to be under the frown of the Almighty. But Jesus was not one who could thus break the bruised reed or quench the smoking taper. The spectacle of a publican repenting of his sin, but hardly daring to hope for pardon, would excite the deepest sympathy in His breast. Far from harshly condemning him for his despairing mood, He would witness with respect the tremendous earnestness of his repentance, and with pity the acuteness of his mental 32,4 The Parabolic Teaching of Christ, book it.

sufferings, and He would seek to convince him that God's thoughts towards him were such as His own. Think not, He would say to him, that God casts the poor, nervous, trembling, desponding penitent out of His sympathies. Nay! the Lord is nigh unto them that are of a broken heart. If they be too sad to walk in the sun, He takes the shade along with them; for He is not as the heartless men of the world, who desert a poor unfortunate in his time of need. He loves the company of the sad better than the society of the gay, and He is ever with them, though in their melancholy they know it not: with them to comfort and exalt, if not soon, then all the more effectually in the end. To suggest such thoughts, we believe, Christ spake this parable of the Pharisee and the Publican. Who can tell how many repentant ones went down to their houses cheered by the words which had fallen from the lips of the sinner's Friend! Let us use the parable for kindred purposes still; learning from it ourselves to cherish hopeful views concerning such as are more persuaded of their own sinfulness than of Divine mercy, and doing what we can to help such to believe that verily there is forgiveness with God.

On hearing the table-talk of Jesus at the Sabbath-day feast in the Pharisee's house, one of the guests took occasion, from the reference to the resurrection of the just, to make the pious reflection: "Blessed is he that shall eat bread in the kingdom of God! " Whereupon Jesus proceeded to speak the following parable, for the benefit of His fellow-guest, and all the rest who were present:â

A certam tnaft made a great supper," and bade many: and sent Ms servant at supper time, to say to them that were bidden, Come, for all things are now ready. And they all with one consent began to make excuse. The first said tmto hii7t, I have bought afield., and must needs go to see it: I pray thee have me excused. Ajid another said, I have bought five yoke of oxen, and I go to prove them: I pray thee have me excused. And another said, I have married a wife, and therefore I catmot coine. And the servant returned, and reported to his master these things. Then the master of the house, being angry, said to his servant, Go out quickly ittto the streets and la7ies of the city, and bring in hither the poor, and the maimed, and the halt, and the blind. And the servant said, Lord, what you commanded has been done, and yet there is rootn. And the lord said unto the servant. Go out into the highways and hedges, and compel them to come in, that my house may be filled. For I tell you., That none of those men, the invited, shall taste of my supper. â Luke xiv. i6â 24.

' lii-Kvov, the principal meal in the day, not necessarily the evening meal; at least that is not the point intended to be emphasised, as is evident from the first two excuses.

atto niag; yvwfiriq, Kapdiac, wv f, or some such word, being understood!.

This parable Jesus spoke for the immediate purpose of teaching those present how httle they really cared for the kingdom of heaven, whatever they might pretend. Knowing well the stony indifference with which He and His cause had been treated by the class of Jewish society to which His host and fellow-guests belonged, He heard with impatience the sentimental reflection which had just been uttered concerning the blessedness of eating bread in the kinfjdom of God. It sounded as emit to His ear, as a statement, that is, which, while true in itself, was not true for the speaker; and it is characteristic of all earnest minds to have a hearty abhorrence of cant. The prophet Jeremiah, e. g., could not bear to hear a godless generation talk glibly of the " Burden of the Lord," while the word of the Lord was in truth no burden to them as it was to his own heart; and in the name of God and of sincerity he interdicted further use of the phrase, saying,"The burden of the Lord shall ye mention no more." It made his spirit bitter, and almost cynical, to listen to such religious phraseology, as employed by men who had no comprehension of its m. eaning. Similar were the feelings awakened in the breast of Jesus by the pious reflection of the sentimental guest, and He uttered the parable as one who would say: "Think you so.-' Let Me tell you how little many such as you care for the privilege you seem to value so highly."

But it is easy to see that the parable serves a wider purpose than merely to hold up the mirror to spurious self-deceiving piety, and show it its own worthlessness. There are elements in the parable not required for that purpose, but serving admirably another, viz. the defence of the speaker's conduct in frequenting ofttimes very different company from that in which He found Himself. In that part of the parabolic representation which relates to the invitation of the poor from the streets and lanes, and of the poorer still from the highways and hedges, Jesus but describes His own conduct in preaching the Gospel to the publicans and sinners, and indirectly vindicates the policy by its success; saying in effect: " Ye wise and prudent, holy and respectable ones, despise the kingdom I preach; I invite therefore the outcasts to partici-

Jeremiah xxiii. 36.

pate in its joys, and I am justified by their prompt response to my invitations."

Viewed didactically these two uses of censure and self-defence coalesce in one lesson. The parable teaches that the kingdom of heaven is not for the full, but for the hungry. In concrete pictorial form it declares that God filleth the hungry with good things, and sendeth the rich empty away. In conveying this lesson it sets forth another most important doctrine concerning the kingdom as a kingdom of grace. Indeed we cannot over-estimate the present parable as a contribution to the illustration of the gracious aspect of the kingdom. It is, in that point of view, full of most significant features. Everything is significant of grace: the selection of a feast as the emblem of the blessings promised, the behaviour of the first invited, the character of those invited in the second and third place, and the avowed motive of the repeated invitationsâ the desire to have the house filled. How easy to read off from these indications the truths that the kingdom is a free gift of Divine grace; that therefore it is despised by those who are full, and valued by those that are empty; that being for the needy it is offered to all the needy alikeâ to the most needy, most urgentlyâ a catholic boon for the sinful suffering race of mankind! Undoubtedly we shall not err in our interpretation of this parable, if before all things we regard it as designed to exhibit the spirit of the kingdom which Christ preached, with its policy of unconventional world-w'de charity, gainsaid of men, but justified by history.

We begin our study of the parable by considering first the account which it gives of the behaviour of the men first invited to the feast. Now what strikes one at the first glance in that behaviour is its unnaturalness or improbability. Invited to what is described as a great feast on some important occasion, instead of regarding the invitation as a great honour, and making every endeavour so to arrange their aff"airs that nothing may occur to prevent them from being present at the entertainment, all lightly esteem the privilege, and begin with one consent to invent excuses for absenting themselves. It is not usual with men invited to feasts so to act; the very feast at which the parable was spoken suffices to show how far such behaviour diverges from ordinary practice. Those who had been invited to sup with " one of the chief Pharisees " appear all to have presented themselves punctually at the supper hour, and they show the value they put on the honour conferred on them by striving eagerly to obtain the best places at the table. It is no fault in the parable, however, that its representation at this point violates natural probability; the fault rather lies with those who act as represented. The story is invented to suit the facts; and if, as a mere story of natural life, it seems highly improbable, it is because men's conduct in regard to the Divine kingdom is not according to right reason. And, in passing, we may take occasion to note the contrast between those parables which apologise for Christ's conduct as the sinner's friend, and this parable which describes the conduct of many in reference to the kingdom. What perfect naturalness characterises the parables of the lost sheep, the lost coin, and the lost son! The shepherd, the housewife, and the father act exactly as we should expect; we should feel surprised if they acted otherwise. Here, on the contrary, our surprise is awakened by the behaviour depicted, and we are conscious of the need of effort to overcome distaste for the parabolic representation because it violates the law of probability. The difference is due to this, that Christ's conduct was in accordance with right reason, and that of those who despised the kingdom of heaven was not. However strange Christ's behaviour might appear to contemporaries, it was characterised by sweet reasonableness," and therefore it was easy to find parallels thereto in ordinary life, the naturalness of which would be recognised by every one. On the other hand, however common it might be for men to treat the Divine kingdom as the parable represents, such conduct was inherently unreasonable, and therefore it was difficult, if not absolutely impossible, to find a parallel to it in natural life, or to make a parabolic representation of it which should not appear highly improbable.

Professor Calderwood ('The Parables of our Lord," p. 102), remarking on the unusual character of the occurrences narrated in this parable, speaks of the expedients for supplying guests in place of those first invited as even more strange than the refusal of the latter. They are not so, however. Lightfoot and Schottgen quote the Talmud in proof that the poor and wanderers were often invited.

This being understood, it will at once be seen that it is no part of an expositor's duty to set himself to invent hypotheses for the purpose of removing, or at least alleviating, the aspect of improbability presented by the behaviour of those first invited to the feast; or to waste time in trying to account for conduct which, like the origin of sin, is really unaccountable. The unanimous refusal of the guests to come to the feast is, indeed, hard to explain on any conceivable hypothesis. â The hypothesis, for example, of a double invitation, one a good while before the feast day, and another when the festive hour was at hand, will not avail for the purpose. Whether such double invitations were customary or not, is a point on which it is difficult to arrive at a certain conclusion, and concerning which, accordingly, interpreters are divided in opinion. A double invitation is certainly implied in the parable. The guests were first bidden, and then the message was sent at supper-time: " Come, for all things are now ready." This representation is in accordance with the facts of Jewish history. The Jewish people were first invited by the prophets to participation in the blessings of the kingdom, and then when the hour of fulfilment came, and the kingdom was at hand, Jesus, as God's servant, appeared, and cried, "Come to the feast long promised, and now ready." But it would be a mistake to imagine that the double invitation is meant to bring the conduct of the invited within the limits of natural probability. It is not fitted to do this, however we conceive of the two invitations, whether with some we regard the second invitation as rendered necessary by the first being indefinite, not fixing the time, or, with others, as owing its origin to the dilatoriness of the guests, and being merely a reminder of a befinite invitation previously given. It is enough to say that no custom could live which could have such utter failure to insure the end aimed at as its natural, or even as a possible, result. The result is a reductio ad absiirdum of the method supposed to be adopted to insure attendance. The custom of issuing two invitations could only have prevailed, because on the whole it was found to work well; that is, because it usually issued in those invited to feasts presenting themselves duly at the festive hour. If

So Goebel. ' So Meyer and Hofmann.

o The Parabolic Teaching of Christ, book ii.

so, then how came it to pass in this instance, that none of the invited rendered themselves at the feast chamber, but with one consent begged off from the engagement? However the strange fact is to be accounted for, no supposed customary double invitation will suffice to explain it; so that the question as to the actual existence of such a custom possesses only an antiquarian interest. For the discussion of such a question we do not profess either special competency or great inclination; therefore we content ourselves with expressing the opinion that it has not been proved that it was usual to send a message at the last moment, and that a second message is represented as being sent, for a special reason. That reason may be, as already hinted, to make the parabolic representation correspond more exactly with the history of Israel, or it may be, as Godet suggests, to bring out the indisposition of the intended guests. The hour pre-announced, and well known to all, had arrived, and no guests had made their appearance. Therefore a second invitation is sent that no one might have it in his power to plead forgetfulness, and that it might be made apparent that the true cause of absence was indifference. With this view it accords that none of the guests does plead either ignorance or forgetfulness, as they all certainly would if they honestly could, for either plea would have been a stronger one than any of those actually advanced.

Proceeding now to consider these excuses, we observe that they are all of the nature of pretexts, not one of them being a valid reason for non-attendance at the feast. The engagements with which the guests were preoccupied were all in themselves lawful and reasonable, but it could easily have been arranged, had the parties been so minded, that they should not come into collision with the previous engagement

Goebel quotes Rosenmiiller in proof of the custom of double invitations, and Trench, after Grotius, refers to Esther, chapters v. and vi. Thomson, Land and Book," states, that a friend at whose house he was invited to dine, sent a message when the feast was ready. To the question, is this customary, he replies, "not among common people, or in cities whose manners are influenced by the West, but in Lebanon it still prevails. If a Sheik, Beg, or Emir invites, he always sends a servant to call you at the proper time." The custom he represents as confined to the wealthy (v. p 125).

to attend the feast. Even the marriage itself, the most urgent affair, could have been adjusted to the feast, and would have been by one who was in the humour. The pleas, one and all, indicate indifference. The state of mind of those who advanced them was this. They were aware that they were under invitation to a feast. They cherished no disrespect to him from whom the invitation came, and had no desire to insult him by sending a blunt refusal to accept his hospitality. On the contrary they were pleased to have that hospitality in their offer, and probably at the moment of receiving the invitation their intention was to be present at the feast. But the feast did not appear, to their minds, an affair of urgent or supreme importance. So they went on their several ways after receiving the invitation as if nothing had happened, forming new engagements, without even recalling to their thoughts the prospective feast, or asking themselves whether the engagement already made, and those which they were making from day to day, were compatible. And so it happened that when the feast-day came, one found himself in possession of a newly-purchased piece of land v; hich he greatly desired to see, another had just bought five yoke of oxen whose qualities he wished to ascertain by trial, and a third had just got married to a wife whom it would be altogether unseemly to leave so soon after. We are to assume that the facts were as stated. It is not necessary, in order to convict the intended guests of indifference, to suspect them of inventing excuses. Granting the truth of their respective allegations, it is evident that these are insufficient reasons for not going to the feast. Can the visit to the newly-bought land and the trial of the oxen not stand over till to-morrow, and what bride would object to her husband leaving her for a few hours to attend a feast in the house of one whom he held in honour, and whose favour it was important to secure.- Manifestly, those who advance such pleas have no real desire to attend the feast. Out of their own mouth they are condemned. Indifference is their common sin, and it is the sufficient explanation of their common behaviour. No need to seek for any other explanation. There may have been forgetful-ness as well as indifference; but it was forgetfulness caused by indifference. Men do not forget what they are very much interested in. No wonder the host was angry when the excuses of his guests were reported to him by his servant. The men whom he invited had trifled with him. In spite of civil phrases and flimsy pretexts, that was the manifest state of the case.

Just such as these intended guests in the parable were the hearers of Jesus, and all like-minded, in their relation to the kingdom of God. They were solemn triflers in the matter of religion. They were under invitation to enter the kingdom, and they did not assume the attitude of men who avowedly cared nothing for it. On the contrary, they were pleased to think that its privileges were theirs in offer, and even gave themselves credit for setting a high value on them. But in truth they did not. The kingdom of God had not, by any means, the first place in their esteem. And so it came to pass that when Jesus came and proclaimed the advent of the kingdom, and expounded to them its true nature, they turned a deaf ear to His message, and refused to accept His invitations, on grounds not less flimsy than those advanced by the men in the parable. The indifferent guests of the parable represent the sentimental guest of the Sabbath feast, and he, in turn, was a type of his generation, a fair sample of a large class of men who put right sentiment in place of right action; who said to God, "I go, Sir, and went not;" who talked much about the kingdom of heaven, yet cared little for it; who were very religious, yet very worldly; a class of which too many specimens exist in every age.

While altogether insufficient as excuses, these reasons for absence are very instructive as to the causes of indifference to the Divine kingdom. The samples supplied do not by any means exhaust the list of possible causes; they are only three out of many, and these such as are most suitable to be mentioned in a parable or popular story. They do not even, as some interpreters seem to think, indicate exhaustively the classes of causes of indifference. Worldly possessions, business occupations, social ties, are certainly very prevalent

Bleek assumes the first invited guests to have accepted the invitation. This, so far as the Jewish nation is concerned, is practically correct. They had accepted God's invitation in the letter, but not in the spirit sources of religious indifference, but they do not account for all the ungodliness that is in the world. It may be questioned, indeed, whether they were the chief causes of the lukewarmness in reference to the kingdom, of Christ's immediate hearers. At all events it is certain that there were other influences at work in producing the widespread unbelief with which Jewish society regarded Jesus and His teaching. The instructiveness of the excuses specified in the parable is to be found not in the exhaustiveness of the list, but in the suggestion of a general idea embracing all the various kinds of influence by which human hearts are rendered indifferent to the chief end and good of life. That general idea is preoccupation of mind. Whatever preoccupies or fills the mind prevents the hunger which is necessary to the appreciation of God's feast of grace. Among the things which fill the mind and heart are worldly goods, cares about food and raiment and business, social relationships and enjoyments. But there are preoccupations of a more spiritual kind by which even the nobler natures innocent of vulgar worldliness are kept aloof from the kingdom; preconceived opinions, philosophical or religious prejudices, pride of virtue. These fill the minds of many, and deaden the hunger of the soul for God's kingdom and righteousness. These influences were powerfully at work among the contemporaries of Jesus, producing apathy or dislike towards Himself and His teaching. He indicated His knowledge of the fact when he uttered the familiar words, "I thank Thee, O Father, Lord of heaven and' earth, because Thou hast hid these things from the wise and prudent." The words point to a very different sort of preoccupation from any named in the parableâ the preoccupation of the wisdom of the world. The wise men of Judaea in those days had their minds filled with cut and dry notions and theories about all things human and Divine; with a fixed idea about God,

The parable no more binds us down to the precise forms of preoccupation spejified than it binds us to understand the poor invited in the second place as the literally poor, as Keim very prosaically does, so finding traces of Ebionitism in the parable. The poor represent all who from any cause are empty, and need filling with the good things of the kingdom. The poor in the literal sense are referred to only in so far as their circumstances exempt them from many of the causes of self-satisfaction to which the rich are exposed.

a fixed interpretation of every important Scripture text, a fixed theory as to the notes of the true Messiah, the nature of the kingdom and its righteousness. Hence when Christ came to them with a different set of ideas on all these topics He found among them no hunger or receptivity. He came teaching that God is a Father, and His doctrine met with no acceptance, because the public mind was preoccupied with the conception of God merely as the High and Lofty One, living above the world. He came preaching a righteousness which springs out of faith in God's grace, and manifests itself in devoted love to Him who proclaims and embodies Divine grace. What chance was there of such views finding entrance into the hearts of men who conceived of righteousness as consisting in punctilious observance of a multitude of petty rules concerning matters of no ethical or intrinsic importance He came offering to his contemporaries, in His own Person, a meek, lowly, suffering Messiah, a man of sorrows and tenderest human sympathies; and He was w elcomed only by a few 'babes," ignorant, obscure, sinful persons of no social consequence, because the minds of the ' wise and understanding' were preoccupied with an entirely different Messianic ideal, that of a conquering Christ who sought and received honour from the world, and made all things serve His ambition. In a word, Jesus came offering to men these supremely valuable boons: a Divine Father, a Kingdom of Grace, a Christ who was the sinner's Friend, and a righteousness possible even for the most depraved, nay, in which precisely they might make the greatest attainment; and He found no appetite for these benefits, no eagerness to come to the feast which He had spread, because with reference to all the topics on which He discoursed men's minds were full of thoughts and beliefs of a wholly diverse character, vhere-with they were perfectly satisfied. Hence, in order to find disciples. He was obliged to seek them elsewhere than among those whom He described as the wise and knowing: not in Jerusalem, the seat of legal lore and Pharisaic influence, but in northern Galilee, where life was simpler; not among the doctors of the law, but among the mob who knew not the law; not among the elders who by long study had matured a system of opinions which had become part of themselves,

CH. v. J. The Great Supper, but among the young who had not had time to build up a system, and whose minds were empty, open, and receptive; not among the well-conducted who made a point of observing all conventional moral proprieties, and prided themselves on an orderly and blameless life, but among the social and moral outcasts who were glad to hear that God vas merciful, and that there was hope in Him even for the guiltiest. Galilean rustics, illiterate laics, open-hearted youths, penitent " publicans and sinners "â these were the likely classes to yield converts to a doctrine like that taught by Jesus. Therefore He addressed Himself chiefly to such, and was by many of them made welcome. And so it came to pass that the intellectually and morally empty and hungry were filled with the good things of the kingdom, while the rich in reputation for wisdom and sanctity turned away in indifference or disdain.

It is this state of matters, Christ's activity and success among those of least account and poor in wisdom and sanctity, that is depicted in the second half of our parable. The people in the streets and lanes who were invited in the second place are those in Judaea who, in the ways indicated, were hungry for such a feast as Jesus invited them to; those from the highways and hedges invited in the third place were all within or without Palestineâ Jews, Samaritans, and Pagans, who were needier still, and might be glad to come to the feast, could they only be brought to believe that it was meant for the like of them. It is at this point that the gracious aspect of the parable becomes most conspicuous, and it is that aspect which must now engage our attention. Our exposition will consist in pointing out how every turn of the story and every phrase serves the purpose of accentuating the grace of the kingdom.

The first point to be noted in this view is the selection of the needy and hungry to be the recipients of benefit. To the citation of this as an index of grace it may be objected that such parties are invited only in the second place. The invitation of them is an after-thought, a device forced upon the host by the refusal of those first invited, and which he will rather have recourse to than let all the precious dishes he has prepared be lost. On the surface this is indeed the state 6 The Parabolic Teaching of Chrisl book il of the case, and the fact with regard to Christ's own action was somewhat analogous. We may say that He turned Hi? attention to the pubhcans and sinners because He found, and knew instinctively beforehand that He would find, little acceptance with those who were socially and morally in repute. And when we look to the action of the apostles in after days, more particularly of Paul, we find the same line of procedure reappearing. Paul's habit was to offer the gospel to the Jew first, and then to the Gentile. But the method of procedure does not in either case derogate from the grace of the procedure, so far as those to whom the gospel was preached in the second place is concerned. For when we come to inquire why Christ met with so poor a response among the Vise and the righteous, we discover that the real cause lay in the gracious nature of His gospel. The gracious attitude of Jesus to publicans and sinners was not produced by the indifference of other classes. The grace went before the indifference, and was its cause, not its effect. Jesus came from the first preaching a God who was the Father of men, not the patron of favourites, and a kingdom into which the most depraved might find admittance on repentance; and the Scribes and Pharisees did not love such a doctrineâ it was too humane, too catholic, too revolutionary, too vulgar in its sympathies for their taste; and so Jesus, who had the lower classes in His heart from the first, was forced by the disdain of the higher orders to turn His attention more and more exclusively to them. Similar observations apply to the case of Paul. He preached first to the Jews, because that appeared the natural order of procedure. But he preached a gospel avowedly universal in its destination, and offering to all, to Jews and Greeks alike, a righteousness not of works but of faith, that is of grace. And it was because His gospel was catholic and gracious that the Jews rejected it, and compelled him to turn away from them and address himself to the Gentiles. The truth just stated, viz. that it was the gracious character of the gospel of the kingdom which caused the unbelief of tliose to whom it was first preached, does not come out in the parable. The parable depicts facts, it does not set forth the rationale of the facts; hence the defect that the second and third invitations appear as after-thoughts, and the motive appears to be not so much love to the invited as a disuke of waste, as if the host had said to himself, "As the food has been prepared, it had better be eaten than thrown away."

Most significant as indexes of the grace of the kingdom are the two phrases, "yet there is room," and "that my house may be filled." These two words indeed might be singled out as worthy to be the mottoes of the kingdom, interpretative of its genius, bearing witness to the vastness of its charity, and its desire to communicate its blessingsto the greatest possible number. Doubtless it is easy here also by plausible reasoning to rob these mottoes of their significance. It may be said of the former of the two that it is merely the word of a servant. And so indeed it is; but it were a pertinent counter-remark that it is the word of a servant who has his master's confidence, is intimately acquainted with his disposition, and fully sympathises with it. But without pressing these considerations, there is enough in the mere fact reported by the servant to indicate the gracious mind of his lord. There is still room in the guest-chamber even after all the poor and suffering of the city have been invited, and have, as we are to assume, responded to the invitation. What a great chamber that must be! What a great feast must have been prepared, and what a magnanimous man he must be who has it in his heart to prepare such a feast! The report of the servant is a sure witness to the riches of God's grace, to the boundlessness of Divine liberality, the immeasurable dimensions of redeeming love: it is put into the servant's mouth by Jesus for that end, not merely to supply the motive for the next turn in the story, in which the host commands his servant to go forth to the highways and hedges to invite those found there to fill up the still vacant places. Only a greathearted man indeed would issue such an order; any other would be content if his house were fairly well filled. " That my house may be filled," is the speech of one animated by the very enthusiasm of hospitality. But this expression, too, may seem liable to cavil, as a motto expressive of grace. It may be pointed out that the sequel seems to imply that the host's chief reason for wishing his house filled, even if it should be with vagrants and vagabonds from the highways and hedges 3j8 The Parabolic Teaching of Christ, book ii.

is to spite the first invited and exclude them from the feast by cramming the house, in case any of them should repent his declinature, and after all desire to be present. And without doubt this is how the story runs; such is the natural import of the concluding part of the host's speechâ " for I say unto you, that none of those men which were bidden shall taste of my supper." But what then After all, the revenge proposed is the revenge of magnanimity, not of meanness and malice. If so minded the host can easily exclude the first invited without bringing in any more guests. The method of revenge is that of one who has pleasure in hospitality for its own sake, and loves to exercise it as widely as possible. It may even be suspected of being the revenge of one who is not quite in earnest in his declared purpose, and who would make room even for the first bidden if they came humbly acknowledging their offence and seeking admission. We may legitimately hesitate before taking this word spoken in anger as the last word on the subject. Christ's word, as an aside from the parable, it certainly is not; to regard it as His is to invest it with much too serious and deliberate a character. It is a word put by Him into the mouth of the host very fitly, as a word spoken in anger. But it is not a word endorsed by Him as the whole truth on the subject of Israel's future. It is important to bear this in mind in order to the maintenance of harmony between the teaching of Christ and that of Paul. For Paul does not treat it as unbelieving Israel's final doom that she shall not taste of God's supper. He refuses to believe that Israel's election is absolutely cancelled, that her inheritance is finally forfeited. He does represent the evangelisation of the Gentiles as taking place to spite Israel. But he believes that the spite is the spite of love changing its method of working towards its old end, the blessing of the covenant people; casting them out and putting the heathen in their room in order. o provoke them to jealousy, and so bring them to another mind, and induce them at length to value mercies previously ' Tbe vn'iv in ver. 24 might plausibly be adduced in proof that it is Christ vvho speaks, addressing those present and pointing for their benefit the moral of the parable: " I, Jesus, say to you now present," c. But the form of expression in what follows excludes this construction. Tbe use of the plural must be accounted for by the emotional character of tbe utterance. The host in his anger addresses himself to an ideal audience.

despised." This Pauline doctrine, the fruit of a noble patriotism which hoped against hope for fellow-countrymen, must be kept in view in interpreting the present parable, if we would not make the Master and the apostle contradict each other. The parable certainly contains no hint of the Pauline doctrine, and that is one piece of evidence that this parable has not been, as some think, remodelled by Luke to bring it into closer correspondence with Paulinism. If, as certain critics imagine, the invitation to the vagrants was added by Luke to the original parable, in order to represent the call of the Gentiles, why did he stop short here in his alterations? Why not go further in accordance with the irenical tendency ascribed to him, and give such a turn to the last word of the host as to make it contain the idea not of final exclusion, which seems to be hinted, but of provocation to repentance? We see no reason to doubt the originality of this feature of our parable. We cannot certainly regard the universalism latent in it as a good reason for such doubt. That Christ's teaching was in spirit universalistic is admitted; universalism was also immanent in His conduct, for His behaviour towards publicans and sinners could be explained only on principles equally applicable to all mankind, irrespective of racial or other distinctions. The religion of one who acted as Jesus did could only be a religion for humanity. Why should it seem surprising if one whose whole bearing said, "I am a man, and nothing human is foreign to my sympathies," should occasionally speak w 7' j-universalistic in scope? And if in any department of Christ's teaching such words are to be looked for it is in His parables, wherein truth is at once revealed and hidden. We should not expect to find in the recorded sayings of the founder of our faith any such explicit statement as this: My gospel is for the Gentiles (except, indeed, in private instructions to His disciples before He left the world), because it was meet that the purpose of grace towards the outlying nations should remain a " mystery hid in God," till the drama of the Redeemer's earthly life was complete, and the materials for the gospel were fully supplied. But we are not surprised to find mystic hints of the universal destination of the gospel in Â F f Romans xi. iiâ 14. The whole passage is very instructive in its bearing on the subject of election. So Hilgenfeld, Einleitung."

such words as these: " Ye are the salt of the earth," " Ye are the h"ght of the world," " The field is the world;" or in parables of grace like this, telling of invitations to the great feast addressed even to homeless, characterless vagrants whose food was what they could pick up, beg, or steal, and whose couch was beneath the hedge on the highway.

Yet another index of the grace of the kingdom may be found in the direction given to the servant with reference to these vagrants, to " compel them to come in." What insight into the secret thoughts, what sympathy with the miseries of the abject class, is revealed in these words! True, as it stands in the parable, the direction seems to have reference rather to the exigencies of the host than to the circumstances of the intended guests. It seems to mean: Be urgent with them and bring them quickly, for time passes, and the feast is getting out of season; take. no refusal, for I wish my house filled, so that there may be no room for the men whom I first invited. But higher motives are implied, though not expressed, or capable of expression, in the parable. The beauty of the parable is, that while moving in a lower moral plane, it constantly suggests to our thoughts a higher one in which the motives are of a purely benevolent character. The speaker of the parable lives up in the higher region, though for the sake of His hearers He comes down in the parable to the lower. It is due to the unearthly charity that dwells in His bosom that mention is made of vagrants at all as possible objects of hospitality. Nothing but such charity was capable of the audacity necessary to the bare conception of such a thought. And the same charity which could conceive the idea is revealed in the injunction, "compel them to come in." The speaker knows full well that the difficulty with the parties now to be invited will be to get them to believe that such a felicity can possibly be meant for the like of them, accustomed to misery and tothe neglect of their more favoured fellow-mortals. Jesus recognises the naturalness and the excusableness of scepticism in such circumstances, and the need of compulsion to overcome doubt. He can enter into their minds and understand just how they feel.- "We are hungry, and would gladly be fed, even with the plainest fare, how much more be partakers of so grand an entertainment I

But such bliss cannot be in store for such wretches as we are: you trifle with us, you mock our misery." Christ knew that such thoughts would certainly pass through the minds of persons situated as described. Yes, He knew that there would always be many so situated that it would be natural and excusable in them to hear with incredulity the good news which He brought from God to the world; men accustomed to misery and to hard treatment from their fellows, or so profoundly sensible of their own demerit that they could hardly believe in God's love, at least in so far as it concerned themselves. And He had pity on such, and He would have all possible means employed to overcome their mistrust, and lead them from incredulity to faith. " Compel them to come in," is the word He gives forth with reference to such. Indifference He will not comipel, but will rather treat with dignified reserve. But the incredulity of men who would gladly avail themselves of God's grace if they durst. He will compel. What hope there is in this sympathy of Christ with human hopelessness I And alas, what need of the humane compulsion He mercifully enjoins! How many now live even in Christian lands whose hard lot, whose experience of inhumanity at the hands of fellow-mortalsâ sometimes even of men calling themselves Christiansâ is such as to make God's love almost incredible! How many are in danger of being driven on to deeper degrees of guilt by the thought that they have already sinned so heinously as to be beyond the reach of mercy! Nay, who does not need compulsions to faith? For is it not one of our chief hindrances to hearty faith in Divine grace that God's love, as declared in the gospel, is so unlike anything we see in this world as to be incredible.? Behold what manner of love is this, that the most high God should care for sinful and miserable men; care even for those who have rebelled against Him! Behold what manner of love is this, that God should give His Son, that whosoever- believeth on Him might not perish! We need help, we need even compulsion, to receive this truth, and to convert the wonder of incredulity into the wonder of faith; and Christ's word in this parable assures us that all who need such compulsion, have in Him a sympathetic Friend who will not fail to help them in their infirmities.

The connection in which this parable was spoken is so distinctly indicated by the Evangelist that it will be best to quote his introductory sentences as part of our text:

And, beiold, a certain lawyer stood up to tempt Him, saying; Master wliat shall I do to inherit eternal life? A 7id He said ii? ito him, What is written in the law f how readest thou? And he attswering said: Thou shall love the Lord thy God with all thy heart, and with all thy soul, and with all thy strength, and with all thy mind;- and thy neighbour as thyself. And He said unto him: Thou hast answered right: this do, and thou shall live. But he wishing to justify himself, said unto Jesus, And who is my neighbour f And Jesus answering said:

A certain man was going down from Jerusalem to Jericho, and fell in with robbers who having both stripped him of his raiment, and inflicted on him wounds went away leaving him half dead. Now by chance there came down a certain priest that way; and when he saw him he passed by on the other side. And likewise also a Levite arrived at the place, and having come and looked at him, passed by on the other side. But a certain Samaritan, on a journey, came where he was, and seeing his plight) he was moved with pity, and approaching him he bound up his wounds, pouring on them oil and

Kuinoel suggests that Christ pointed at the phylactery on which the â words of this law were written, as He spake. Unger quotes this opinion with approval.

2 There are variations in the text here, but of no iijiportance for the interpretation of the parable.

3 Field prefers this to the rendering in A. V. and R. V. on the ground that the verb is often joined with a noun in the singular number, when of course ' among' would be unsuitable; vipikiriaiv might be rendered by the one word 'encountered."

wine, and momiting Mm on his own beast he brought him to an inn, and took care of him. And on the morrow when he was departing' he took out two denarii and gave them to the host, and said: Take care of hiin, and whatsoever thou spendest more, I, on my return, will repay. Which now of tliese three seems to thee to have become neiglibour to him that fell among the robbers? And he said, He that shewed mercy on hitn. Then said Jesus unto htm, Go, do thou also likewise. â LUKEx. 25â 37.

In the interpretation of this parable great regard must be had to the original question of the lawyer. Formally an answer to the question, Who is my neighbour? evasively asked by one who was not thoroughly in earnest about the subject of his professed solicitude, the parable is really an answer to the wider question, What is the supreme duty, by the performance of which a man may hope to attain eternal life? The moral of the charming story isâ Charity the true sanctity. This is the key to the construction of the parable, especially to the selection of its dramatis personce a priest and a Leviteâ persons holy by profession and occupation, and a Samaritan stranger of a different race from that of the man in need of neighbourly succour. Through the introduction of the two former the lesson of the parable is accentuated by suggesting a contrast between the genuine holiness of love, and spnrioiis forms of holiness; through the introduction of the latter, as doing the requisite good deed, the supreme value of love in God's sight is emphasised. It means: Even in a Samaritan love is acceptable to God; wherever it is there is true goodness, and therefore eternal life; like faith, love, wherever manifested, breaks down all conventional barriers: " Every one that loveth is born of God, and knoweth God." Such being its import, our parable is emphatically a parable of grace, revealing to us the nature ot God and of His kingdom Its teaching can be true only if God be love, and His kingdom a kingdom of grace, and the Speaker, not typically, as in the Patristic interpretation, but literally, the Good Samaritan par excellence â one, that is, to whom every human being who needs help is a neighbour; one who is ever ready to render, to those who require it, seasonable succour. It was not Christ's intention, perhaps, - iiovivai; suggesting the adage, "Neighbour is who neighbour does.

under the guise of the Samaritan stranger, to describe Himself; the less we introduce the spiritual motive into the parable itself the greater our sense of its natural beauty and pathos will be. But the present parable is one of those peculiar to Luke, in which the vehicle of instruction is not a type taken from the natural sphere to teach a truth in the spiritual, but an exajhple of the very action recommended. In connection with such a parable it is legitimate exegesis to say that Jesus was the supreme example of the virtue inculcated.

The didactic drift of the parable being such as indicated, it is obvious that the appearance on the scene of the three contrasted figures is as intentional as it is admirably fitted to serve the purpose the Speaker has in view. The Priest, the Levite, and the Samaritan do not enter on the stage by accident; they are carefully and skilfully chosen to convey the moral. In apparent contradiction with this, it is indeed said that by chance' a priest went down that way; and perhaps we ought to extend the scope of the phrase to the other two travellers also, as if Jesus would say: By a singular fortuitous concurrence these three men turned up in that lonely place just at the time the poor wayfarer came to grief. But the reference to the chance character of the meeting only makes the intention of the Artist in the selection of his dramatispcrsoncz more marked. It is a virtual apology for the unlikelihood of a concurrence which the purpose of the story demands. It says in effect: That these four men should come together in such a place, about the same time, and under such circumstances, seems, I admit, a somewhat unlikely supposition; yet suffer me to make it, for I need it in order to point duly my moral. The apology will be accepted by all who are satisfied that the characters who figure in the parable are well selected for the didactic purpose. On this point, however, doubts have been expressed by some, as, e. g., by Keim, who, disbelieving in the genuineness of the

So Goebel, who points out that this parable is the first of those in Litlce in which instruction is conveyed, not by type, but by example.

Kara ov Kvplav.

' Godet remarks that there is a certain irony in the expression, by chance, as it is certainly not accidental that the narrative makes the two characters, priest and Levite, appear on the scene.

parable, adduces in support of his opinion the fact that nowhere else do we find Jesus assuming a polemic attitude towards the priests and Levitesâ the usual objects of His attacks being the scribes. But this objection has but little force, if the classes referred to laid themselves open to attack, after the manner of our parable. And who can doubt that they did? Who does not know that men holy by profession and occupation are very prone to come short in the duties of humanity?â so divorcing holiness from charity, religion from morality. Were the officially holy persons in Israel in the last stage of her degeneracy likely to be an exception? And if not, were their shortcomings likely to escape animadversion on Christ's part, due opportunity offering itself? Far from doubting the genuineness of the parable on this score, and resolving it into a mere traditional expansion of a simpler utterance of our Lord in conversation with some legal interrogant, we gladly welcome it as filling up what would otherwise have been a blank in His many-sided teaching. It was too much needed to complete the picture of the time not to have been spoken by Him who was at once the most faithful and the wisest of all the prophets; and it is too good to have been spoken or invented by any one else.

While seeing in the reference to chance an apology for a needed combination, we must be careful not to make too much of it, as if the improbability of the concurrence were so great as to mar the natural felicity of the parable. This is so far from being the case that the Speaker might quite well have omitted the expression, and probably would have done so but for His desire to fix attention on the characters He introduced, and we may add, His exquisite sense of the fitting in narration, which was such that He felt inclined to apologise for the slightest appearance of a departure from the

Jesu von Nazara," iii. 13, note 2.

Goebel says that the priest and the Levite are introduced because they were peculiarly given to literalism.

So Keim and others of similar proclivities.

Keim's doubts are only a part of his general scepticism in regard to all the Samaritan incidents and sections in the Gospels, and especially in Luke, and are entitled to all the less consideration on that account.

dictates of f ood taste. It was quite within the limits of natural possibility that all the persons alluded to should make their appearance in the scene of the deed of violenceâ the rugged, rocky pass between Jerusalem and Jericho, arduous for the traveller even on account of its physical characteristics, and dangerous as the haunt of desperadoes who lived by plunder. Travellers on various errands must have frequented that road, for there had been no robbers had there been no one to rob. Among these travellers priests and Levites might occasionally be found; for Jericho was a city of priests, and officials would come and go between that place and Jerusalem in connection with their service at the temple. The pass of Adummim was not indeed the only way from the City ol Palms to the capital, but it Avas the most direct, and would therefore be at least occasionally taken in spite of its bad renown as the "Way of Blood." A Samaritan stranger might also now and then appear there, journeying to or from Jerusalem on his private business; for his errands might require him to choose the route which lay through Jericho.

In truth, whether we have regard to the construction of the story, or to its moral aim, we must acknowledge that in the parable before us the artistic tact of the Speaker appears in a conspicuous degree. The place, the persons, and the moral, all fit into each other admirably. A situation is chosen in which the occurrence of a calamity demanding active benevolence is probable. A wounded man in the Bloody Way, how likely a phenomenon! There, too, the men from whom help in such an emergency might naturally be expected, but from whom, alas, it will not be forthcoming, may also be met with: priests and Levites punctually attending to their religious duties according to law and custom, but deaf to the call of charity. In that same grim, perilous pass might by chance be met a Samaritan, hated of the Jews, and most probably hating in turn, yet not necessarily, conceivably nearer the kingdom of God than those who proudly despised him as a heretic and alien, by the possession of a heart susceptible of

Vide the passages in Josephus and Jerome, usually referred to in the Commentaries, and modern books of travel, such as Stanley's Sinai and Palestine." Stanley's note on the pass of Adummim at p. 424 is worth consulting.

the gentle emotion of pity, and prompt to act on its benignant impulses; not staying to inquire who or what the object of pity may be, content to know that he is a human beingâ "a certain man"' in distress. Finally, in the situation chosen love will have an opportunity of showing its true nature as an heroic passioi. For the love that shall prove itself equal to the occasion must possess very uncommon attributes. It must be stronger than fear and the instinct of self-preservation which so often harden the heart. It must be superior to the prejudice which chills pity by the thought that the claimant is one of another race and religion. It must be generous and uncalculating, grudging no expenditure of time, pains, or money, which may be necessary for the effectual succour of distress. In a word, it must be a love like that of Godâ self-sacrificing, ready to die for its object, even though that object should be an enemy; a love in which is revealed the maximum of gracious possibility, and which finds its secret reward in the blessedness of its own deed.

In details, not less than in general structure, the delineations of the parable are faithful to reality. The plight of the wounded man is desperate, as the didactic purpose requires; yet the description thereof cannot at any point be charged with exaggeration. It is just thus that the victims of bandits in those regions would be treated in those days, as it is just thus they are treated still. To be robbed of his purse, stripped of his garments, wounded, and heartlessly abandoned to his fate, is the lot of any one who has the misfortune to fall into such hands. The first of these particulars is omitted in the narrative, a circumstance diversely explained by the commentators; some suggesting poverty, others that plunder is taken for granted as a matter of course. The latter view is the more probable, whether we have regard to the verbal expression at this part of the story, or to the aim of the whole. The kox before ikhvaavt s also having stripped him) seems to imply some previous act of violence, which could only have been the forcible appropriation of that which

"He was a human being (Mensch.), that is all he says; not a word about his rank, descent, or religion," quaintly remarks Amdt, whose whole treatment of the parable is spirited, graphic, and instructive, without having recourse to spiritualising.

robbers chiefly seekâ the purse. Then the supposition that this misfortune also befell the victim, harmonises best with the design of the parable to signalise the supreme worth of humanity: for the graver the case the greater the opportunity afforded for the display of that virtue. But why, then, is this feature not introduced? In reply, we ask, Is it quite certain that it is not.-' It is not indeed expressly mentioned in the description of the victim's condition; but is it not indirectly alluded to in the picture presented of the humane conduct of his benefactor "i Among the kind services of the Samaritan to the object of his care, payment of his bill at the inn is carefully specified. That implies that the wounded one was unable to pay his own way; for the services rendered by love are all supposed to be necessary, the virtue inculcated being not quixotic, uncalled-for generosity, but readiness to succour real and urgent need. Then it may further be regarded as certain, that the poverty does not belong to the man's ordinary condition, but forms a part of the calamity which has lately overtaken him; for it belongs to the felicity of the parable that all the particulars specified should arise out of the supposed situation.

The behaviour of the priest and Levite is very simply but suggestively described. They came, they saw, and they passed by. Inhuman, unnatural conduct, one is ready to exclaim. It was inhuman, but it was not unnatural. These men did exactly what all the world is inclined to do; Avhat the majority are doing in one form or another every dayâ passing by need without giving pity time to rise in the bosom.â what every one will certainly do in whom the impulses of fear and the instinct of self-preservation are stronger than the nobler instincts and impulses of benevolence. The language of the parable betrays a consciousness on the part of tiie Speaker that the conduct he describes is not exceptional but usual. Very noticeable is the repetition of the expressive word avtitTaprjxdev. The very monotony suggests the idea of what is customaryâ the way of the worldâ and, in the present case, of the religious world. The first comer passed by, the second passed by; and in nine cases out of ten that is what you may expect. It is the exceptional case when, Grotius interprets avri7rapr 9t as signifyingâ passed in the opposite instead of avrttTapyjxOe, you can say ka-nxayxi'UOr â not he passed by, but he was moved with pity. So it is with the beggar in the street; so it is with men placed in extreme danger whom you cannot help without serious risk to yourself. There is doubtless everything in so grave a plight as that of the wounded man in the pass of Adummim to rouse the dormant feelings of compassion which minor afflictions of everyday occurrence fail to touch. Yet let us not imagine that the priest and the Levite would necessarily have a bad conscience, or go away feeling that they were behaving in an altogether monstrous manner. Nothing so easy as to invent excuses for their conduct. Every commentator suggests a list of excuses, each one inventing his own listâ so plentiful are they. " Another of these robberies. How frequent they are growing! One ought to help, but what can one do? This poor fellow seems beyond help. It is impossible to attend to every unfortunate. Then one must think of himself True, these robbers do not meddle with us; they leave us holy men to go and come in the performance of our sacred duties; but we cannot expect them to act with such forbearance unless we observe a discreet silence as to their lawless deeds." " Alas, for the rarity of Christian charity under the sun!"â and alas for the multitude of plausible, prudent reasons by which that rarity can be accounted for 1

The reasons are good enough for all who want an excuse. But if one happen to have a big, tender heart he will not be able to avail himself of such reasons for neglecting a duty lying in his way. When the emotion of pity is strong, it prevents a man from acting on the suggestions of prudence; when it is very strong, amounting to a passion, it prevents these from even arising in the mind. Thanks be to God, there are always some such men in the world. Though such charity be rare it is not unexampled; therefore the good Samaritan is not an incredible character. His picture is one of unearthly beauty, yet it is not unreal or impossible. We direction. ' Praeterivit contrario itinere ab Jerichunte, scil. Hiersolyma properans." Godet, with his usual insight, renders itâ ' In face of such a spectacle they passed." The thing emphasised is surely not the direction in which they were going, but that they avoided the sufferer, gave hina a wide berth, and hurried on from the place.

exclaim as we readâ " He did as he ought to have done; as we all ought to do." It has been said of the story of the good Samaritan that it has been " the consolation of the wanderer and the sufferer, of the outcast and the heretic, in every age and country."

It may also be said of it that it has been as a conscience in the heart of Christendom condemning inhumanity, breeding shame of cowardice and selfishness, and prompting to deeds of kindness by a heavenly yet sober and practicable ideal of benevolence. This ideal is painted with a few strokes, but with consummate art, which the Limner has learnt from His own gracious spirit. The Samaritan traveller, like the two others, comes up to the half-dead victim of violence, and sees his sorrowful condition; but, unlike the two others who preceded him, he does not pass by, but feels pity. They, too, perhaps felt a little pity, but it was just enough to scare them away in horror, and to send them on their journey inventing excuses to hide from themselves their own heartlessness. But the Samaritan's pity was a passion and an agony; therefore he could not get away from the object which excited it, but was compelled rather to draw near to him, and that not to gaze but to succour. The sufferer has taken full possession of his heart, and he must do for him all that he needs. And he does all promptly, without hesitation, or intrusion of any thought or feeling that can interrupt the flow of the commanding emotion. The several acts are carefully enumerated, not for mere pictorial effect, but for the sake of moral impression; even to show the genius of true love, as that which renders help with promptitude, thoroughness, self-denial, and unwearying patience; and also with tact, doing all things in their proper order, and in the best, most considerate way: first staunching the wounds with wine and oil, which with due forethought for emergencies it has at 'hand; then conveying the patient to the inn where he can stay till he recover; and making itself answerable for

Stanley, Sinai and Palestine," p. 425.

' Arndt is good on the attributes of love developed in the conduct of the Samaritan.

3 Schottgen asks how came the Samaritan to have wine and oil, and thinks it was usual in hot countries to carry oil. Jacob had oil to anoint the pillar, and Lot had wine with him.

all charges incurred during convalescence. Noticeable yet further in this picture is the absence of all sentimentality, for this, too, is a sure mark of genuine love. All things are done without parade, and with good sense. Specially to be remarked in this connection is the pecuniary part of the transactions. The benefactor does not give to the host a large sum of money amply sufficient to pay all possible expense with a liberal margin over. He gives a limited sum, small, but sufficient to pay past outlay, and promises to pay the rest on his return. There is thrift without niggardliness, as you expect in one who is not performing a solitary act of charity in an ostentatious way, because he happens to be in the humour, but is in the habit of doing kind actions as he has opportunity, and therefore does them in sober, business style. It may indeed appear unbusiness-like to expect the host to give him credit for future expense on account of his beneficiary. But, doubtless, the host knows his man: he has been that way before, and he will come again, and he has always been a good customer.

Such is the charming tableau. How beautiful, and also how suggestive of didactic meanings 1 In the first place, it completely answers the immediate question: Who is my neighbour The whole doctrine of neighbourhood is virtually and effectively taught in the parable. First, and directly, what it is to be a neighbour, viz. to render eff"ectual succour when and where it is needed, having regard to nothing beyond the fact of need. Next, indirectly, but by obvious consequence. Who is my neighbour?â viz. any one who needs help, and whom I have power and opportunity to help, no matter what his rank, race, or religion may be. Neighbourhood is made co-extensive with humanity. Any human being is my neighbour who needs aid, and to whom I can render aid; and I am neighbour to him when I do for him what his case demands. It matters not on which of the two sides the doctrine is approached. The relation of neighbourhood is mutual; he is my neighbour to whom I am neighbour. Jesus applied the parable on the latter side of the doctrine, as leading up most directly to the' practical appeal to the

Possibly the inn in the dangerous pass (of which ruins are still trace able) was kept by a Samaritan. So Unger.

conscience of His interrogantâ " Go, and do thou likewise." ' Which of these three," He asked, " appears to thee to have become neighbour to the man who fell among the robbers?" Had the Scribe been in the mood in which he bec an the interview he might have parried the question, and raised another quibble, saying: What I want to know is, not to whom I am neighbour, but who is neighbour to me? In so doing he would have acted as reasonably as when he first put the question; for he asked it not because he did not know, but because he did not wish to act on his knowledge. But the legal quibbler has lost all his briskness and courage. The pathos of the parable has subdued and solemnized him, and for the moment called into play those feelings of nature which even in a Jewish Rabbi were only overlaid, not extinguished, by the sophistries of conventional morality. Therefore, though it went against the grain to praise a Samaritan, and his pride refused even to name him, he could not help replying: "He who showed mercy on Him." And when Jesus bade him go and practise the virtue his conscience approved he had no heart for further fencing, but went away profoundly impressed with the wisdom and moral authority of Him whom he had tried to puzzle.

The parable further answered the larger question first propounded by the lawyer: which is the virtue that saves The Scriptures teach that without holiness no man shall see the Lord, that is, have eternal life; and in this parable two kinds of holiness are set before us, the one spurious, the other genuine. The spurious holiness is that of the priest and Levite, or sanctity divorced from charity. It is not indeed formally described; but the idea is suggested by the introduction of two oificially holy persons. The very motive of their introduction is to suggest the t. ought of a religion separated from morality, and especially from that which is the soul and essence of all morality, love. The two sacerdotal characters appear on the scene as concrete embodiments of a type of piety which God abhors, sacrifice without mercy. By placing them alongside of the humane Samaritan Jesus eloquently re-utters the prophetic oracle, "I will have mercy, and not sacrifice." In the person of the Samaritan the Â Godet.

nature of true sanctity is exhibited. We are taught that the way to please God, the way to genuine hohness, is the practice of charity. It has been remarked indeed, that in applying the parable Jesus did not repeat the words, "This do, and tjioii shall live ' and that He could not do so, because charity, though necessary, is not sufficient for salvation, faith being indispensable. But it is evident that if life could be promised to him who kept the commandments, it could also be promised to one who acted as the Samaritan, for what was such action but a most emphatic keeping of the commandments In that action, it is true, only the second of the two great commandments is expressly involved, but neither of these commandments can be kept apart from the other. He that truly loveth God loveth his brother also; and conversely he that truly loveth his brother loveth God also, unconsciously if not consciously.

The claims of faith as a condition of salvation were fully acknowledged by our Lord in His teaching, and we must take care that they suffer no neglect at our hands. But there is a better way of protecting these claims than to be jealous of the life-giving power of love. That better way is to teach that charity presupposes faith; in other words, that the man whose religion consists in loving God and his neighbour, is inevitably a man who believes in a God whose nature is love. And this leads us to remark that our parable likewise answers the question which lies behind the first question of the lawyer, viz. What is God.-' The parable virtually, though not formally, solves that problem; implying, though not saying, God is love; His kingdom is a kingdom of grace; the way to please Him is to walk in love; I, Jesus, am His well-beloved Son, because I delight in saving the lost and succouring the miserable. What the parable expressly teaches is true only because these things are true. To ascribe this extended significance to the parable is not, as already hinted, to indulge in a licentious, tropical exegesis; it is merely to extend its didactic import within the same sphere. For the spiritualising interpretation of the fathers, followed by some modems, we have no taste. It seems to us frigid, trifling, even pernicious, as tending to blunt our perception of the true, natural sense. When carried far enough it becomes ridiculous; and hence the illogical moderation and discretion exercised by some patrons of this style of exegesis, as by a leading English writer on the parables, who, having gone so far with the fathers, draws the line at the two pence, which, in the tropical interpretation, denote the two sacraments! But we have no hesitation in saying that this parable is a most important contribution to Christ's general doctrine of God, and of the kingdom of God, and in that view pre-eminently a parable of grace. It is implied that God is a God of love, and that His love is catholic, not partial; a love of mankind, not of Jews only, a ikavopmnia, as it is termed by an apostle ', a love kindred in nature to that pity which moves one human being to help another in need, to which also the name pldlantjiropy is applied in Scripture, notably, too, in the case of the kindness shown by Maltese barbarians to Paul and his shipwrecked companions. How significant this juxtaposition of the love of God most high with the humane feelings to which even the most uncultured of mankind are not strangers!

The catholic scope of our parable was doubtless one of its chief attractions in the eyes of Luke, the Pauline evangelist. Invent the parable he certainly did not, for that was a task above his genius; but select it with pleasure he certainly did on account of its universalism. It pleased him that it was a Samaritan who did the good action; it pleased him that love in man, disregardful of conventional barriers, in the parable had free course and was glorified, as implying a similar love in God, wide as the world, and bringing healing without stint for its sin and misery. And the Church and the whole world have reason to be thankful that in such things Luke took delight; for to that fact we owe the preservation of one of the most precious morsels of our Lord's incomparable teaching.

Trench, who says: " It would be an entering into curious minutiae, one tending to bring discredit on this scheme of interpretation, to affirm dccid-dly of the 'two pence' that they mean either the two Sacraments, or the two Testaments, or the Word and the

Sacraments, or unreservedly to accede to any one of the ingenious explanations which have been offered for them " (pp. 325-6).

Â Titus ill. 4. â Acts xxviil 2.

Vide Renan, Les Evangiles," p. 267.

And He said also unto His disciples: There was a certain ri: h man who had a steivard; and the same was accicsed unto him as wasting his goods. And he called him, and said nnto him, How is it that I hear this of thee? give an account of thy stewardship; for thou may est be no longer stezvard. Then the steward said within himself, What shall I do, for my lord taketh away from me the stewardship? I cannot dig, to beg I am ashamed. I am resolved what to do, that when I am put out of the stewardship, they may receive me into their houses. So he called eveiy one of Ids lord's debtors, and said unto the first. How much owest thou u7ito my lord? And he said, An hundred baths of oil. And he said unto hint, Take thy bill, and sit down and write quickly fifty. Then to another he said, And thou, how much owest thou f And he said, Ati hundred cars oftvheat. He saith to him. Take thy bill, and write fourscore. A nd the lord praised the unjust stezvard, because he had acted wisely for himself; for the childrejt of this world are wiser in their generation than the children of light. And I say unto you; Make to yourselves friends with the mammon of wiright-eottsness; that when ye fail, (or it fails), they may receive you into the everlasting te? tts. â LUKE xvi. iâ 9.

The introductory formula might seem to imply that this parable was spoken at the same time as that of the Prodigal Son contained in the preceding chapter. In reality, however, it does not necessarily imply, and ought not in the exposition to be assumed to imply, anything more than that to the mind

To yoamia in T. R.; rd ypaiiixara according to approved reading, the bond or voucher which showed the amount owed.

2 Â (c row Mafitova, rendered ambiguously of in A. V.

' ec i7rqrÂ in T. R.; kxitri) in some copies, and adopted by most critics, De Wette prefers the former.

of the Evangelist the two parables had some connection, some word, or thought-affinity, which made the one suggest the other, and led him to introduce both in the same part of his narrative. What the subjective connection was we can only conjecture; it might be very slight, for often a very insignificant point of contact suffices to bring the law of association into play. The link might be the simple circumstance that both parables refer to worldly goods, and especially to the way in which these are often abused by men. In each there is a prodigal who wastes substance, in the one case his own, in the other that of another man; and the act of wasting is described in both instances by the same term, It is quite conceivable that so slender and external a tie might bind together the two parables in the Evangelist's thought, and determine him, in absence of knowledge of the historical connection, to unite them in his story. It is probable, however, that they appeared to his view bound together by more intimate relations; by affinity in their general spirit and didactic drift not less than by their superficial features. At the least it may safely be assumed that he cannot have been conscious of any incongruity between the parables in these respects. He must have discerned even in this most unevangelic-looking parable of the Unjust Steward a vein of evangelic sentiment, which made it not unfit to stand beside that parable of the Prodigal Son in which the gracious aspect of Christ's teaching is seen at its brightest. If so, then we too must try to pierce beneath the repulsive surface to the underlying stratum of Gospel truth. And we mean to make the attempt, and that in a spirit of good hope, not of despair. For we believe that in the whole of the section wherein, according to Renan, is to be found the great originality of Luke â the fifteenth and sixteenth chaptersâ the evangelic tone prevails. To this extent at least we are prepared to go in opposition to another critic, who boldly affirms that the two chapters have absolutely nothing in common. For we cannot regard Luke with some, as a mere mechanical chronicler who placed side by side in his history materials of the most heterogeneous character drawn from his â Ziidkopinaiv, Luke xv. 13; taffkoptri'Jw ', Luke xvi. I.

â ' Les Evangiles," p. 265.

â Reuss, Histoire Evang(51ique," 495.

sources; in one chapter a section radiant with the h'ght af divine love, in another a piece of cold Ebionitic morality, ascetic in tone and commonplace in thought. The writer had religious sympathy with his subject, and was guided throughout, both in the selection and in the grouping of his materials, by a warm evangelic feeling. On this account we expect to find traces of that feeling and of that which justifies it even here, as also in the succeeding parable of the Rich Man and Lazarus. In saying so we readily acknowledge that there are difficulties to be surmounted. Among these we do not reckon the selection of an unprincipled agent to be the vehicle of instruction, for there are similar instances of the same sort which show that our Lord in His parabolic teaching was wont to use great boldness and freedom in the application of that method of instruction, a fact which only gives to the doctrine taught enhanced value and piquancy in the esteem of all intelli-gent students. If a particular character was best fitted in other respects to convey the intended lesson, the mere lack of morality was not regarded as an objection to its introduction. The main difficulty in the way of one who would get to the evangelic heart of the parable is the apparently low level of the very moral lesson itself which the parable is employed to convey. It seems to be a lesson of mere prudence in the use of money with a view to the salvation of our souls in the next world. Such a low-toned, unheroic sentiment strikes one as un-Christlike, and if that were really all that was meant, we should feel strongly tempted to acquiesce in the verdict of Keim that such a gross morality of prudence never came from the lips of Jesus, and to see in this parable a foreign element that had found its way into the Gospel from extra-canonical sources current in quarters where the genuine logia of Christ had undergone corruption, or been mixed up with apocryphal additions But we should be very slow indeed to adopt any such conclusion and we do not think the facts demand it;

Pfleiderer regards this parable as Ebionitic in spirit, and cites it as illustrating the evangelist's impartiality as an author in the use of his sources, of which he finds traces in Acts also. Vide ' Paulinismus, p. 499.

2 Vide parables of Selfish Neighbour and Unjust Judge, s J(su von Nazara," ii. 40I.

â So Hiuenfeld, Weizsacker, Pfleiderer, c.

S The Pa7'abolic Teaching of Chrisi. book ii.

that is, we are persuaded that in this section of the evangelic narrative we are taught no mere morality of prudence, though the lesson may be put in prudential form, but something worthy of Him whose words were always like Himself noble, generous, unworldly.

The parable seems to us to teach not one lesson but two, one general, the other particular; the general one a lesson of prudence in the use of temporal possessions with a view to eternal interests; the special one a lesson as to the way of using these possessions which most directly and surely tends to promote our eternal interests, viz. by the practice of kindness towards those who are destitute of this world's goods. A prudent regard to the higher concerns of man, and beneficence towards the poor as a means to that end, such are the virtues which it seems the teacher's aim to inculcate. Many commentators have failed to recognise the intention to teach a double lesson, and have virtually, though probably in many instances unconsciously, proceeded on the assumption that the interpreter had to make his choice between two mutually exclusive alternatives; the result being a multitude of interpretations not altogether erroneous, but partial and one-sided. One class leans to the side of prudence, another to the side of beneficence, the fewest have clearly perceived that the two points of view are perfectly compatible, and ought to be combined in order to do justice to the thought and purpose of the Teacher. As was to be expected, the smaller number give the preference to the special lesson of beneficence, the tendency of commentators, as of men in general, being to side with the common-place in thought rather than with the original, with the mean in ethics rather than with the lofty. To the honourable band who in this case have obeyed the nobler instinct belong two men of princely rank among interpreters, Calvin and Olshausen. The Genevan divine opens his comments on the parable with this sentence: " The sum of this parable is that we should deal humanely and benignantly with our neighbours, that when we come to the tribunal of God the fruit of our liberality may return to us." It is the utterance of a man thoroughly imbued with the evangelic spirit of the Reformation, who, while zealous for faith as the instrument of justification, was not afraid Unger in his remarks on the parable adverts to this fact.

to give love its due; he being no mere scholastic theologian, but a living Christian endowed with fresh religious intuitions, and quick to discern in Scripture whatever was in sympathy with the doctrine of grace. The more modern interpreter reechoes the sentiment of Calvin when, comparing the fifteenth and sixteenth chapters of Luke, he remarks, that what in the former is taught concerning the compassionate love of God, is in the latter exhibited as the duty of man in his surroundings. The view is significant in his case also, as an index of the close connection between the exegesis of Scripture and the life of the Church. For Olshausen also, like Calvin, was the child of a new time in which the evangelic intuition was once more restored, and Christian thought, delivered from the stupefying influence of dogmatism and the blinding influence of religious legalism, could with unveiled face and open eye see for itself the fulness of grace which was in Christ Jesus.

That these two distinguished interpreters have given only a partial account of the didactic significance of our parable may perhaps be admitted. But, while defective in detail, their view is certainly right in tendency. If the duty of beneficence be not the only lesson of the parable it is certainly the chief lesson, that which gives to the parable its distinctive character, and must dominate the interpretation of the whole. We hope to show that with this key we can unlock the secret of the parabolic narration, and explain its most peculiar features. Another decided recommendation of this view is that it raises the moral tone of our Lord's teaching clear above the low level of a vulgar religious utilitarianism. For with the practice of beneficence we get into the region of love, and there we get rid of self and prudential calculation. It is true, doubtless, that the motive to beneficence is made to assume the form of a calculation. The owner of worldly goods is advised to make friends therewith of the poor, because they in turn may be able to do him a friendly turn in the world beyond. But this will not perplex any one who remembers that the parabolic form of instruction does not afford scope for the play of the highest class of motives. It is essentially popular wisdom, and it is the way of that which aims at teaching the million to make action spring from homely motives. The prodigal is moved to return home by hunger; the host whose guests refuse to come to his feast invites the beggars to take their place from no interest in them, but to spite the first invited, and to prevent waste of the food prepared. So here, Jesus, applying His parable in the terms naturally suggested by it, bids His disciples be kind to the poor, to make sure their own admission into the eternal tents. This vulgar morality is meant to suggest the doctrines of a heroic morality. The method is of kin with the employment of bad characters to teach the lessons of visdom. Both belong to the condescension involved in the parabolic form of instruction, and in that respect are in harmony with the genius of a revelation of grace. In all the above cases it is assumed as an axiom that the real motives are higher and purer than the ones suggested. If it were not so the action described would never be performed. Mere hunger would never bring the prodigal home. Mere anger would never lead any host to entertain the abjects of society. As little will mere self-interest lead a man to practise beneficence. Beneficence is not the product of the prudence, but the prudence is rather the product of the beneficence. A benignant spirit impels a man to do beneficent actions, and in that way, without being aware of it, or reflecting on it, he practises prudence with regard to his own eternal interest; secures for himself an abundant entrance into the everlasting tents after death; nay, does more than that, even brings into his soul now that blessedness which, just because it is the true life, is therefore eternal.

With this preliminary glance at the moral import of the parable, we may now proceed to notice its more salient features.

First, we advert to the peculiar case supposed. It is that of a man occupying the position of a steward or factor to a person of wealth and rank who leaves the administration of his estate wholly in his servant's hands, and systematically abusing his trust according to reports which reach his master's ears, insomuch that his summary dismissal has become inevitable. One naturally wonders that so objectionable a character should be selected as the vehicle of instruction. For though we may not insist that no bad men shall be employed to

Un grand seigneur vivant dans la capitale, loin de ses terras dont ij remis Tadministration a un intendant.â Godet.

teach wii:3dom, we may reasonably lay it down as a rule that bad men should not be used if they can be dispensed with; that is, if good men will serve the purpose equally well, or even sufficiently well. Why, then, does Jesus oblige His scholars to make the acquaintance of so immoral and unedifying a character? The answer is, because He must find a man who is placed in a situation analogous to that which the moral lesson has in view. Now the situation contemplated by the moral lesson is that of men who look forward to the certain event of death, and who are exhorted in view of that event to make due preparation for what comes after. Such a situation suggests as its analogue in this world's affairs the position of an employ about to lose his place and be deprived of his income. A factor on the point of being deprived of his stewardship is a suitable emblem of a man about to be removed from this world by death. That being so, it is obvious that an unjust steward is more naturally introduced into the parable than a just one, for the simple reason that his misbehaviour is the natural explanation of the impending dismissal. Why should a faithful steward be removed from ofhce To conceive such a case were to sacrifice probability to a moral scruple.

Clearly then we must overcome our distaste for this unsavoury character and be content to learn wisdom even from him. But what can he teach us Well, two things at least. One that dismissal, death, will certainly come; another, that some provision must be made for what is beyond. The first lesson we are taught by the simple fact that the master had resolved to put away his unfaithful servant, which is carefully indicated by the words, give an account of thy stezvardsjiip, for thou canst be no longer stetvard. The rendering of the account is not demanded as a means of enabling the employer to decide what to do. He has decided already; he is so satisfied that his agent has been utterly false to his trust. He expects him to play the knave even in this last act, and he calls for it more out of curiosity than with any hope of satisfaction. It is meet that the steward should wind up his aftairs in that way, and therefore his master will have it so; and we may add, the Maker of the parable will have it so, because the story must go on, and the steward must have his opportunity of showing how he provides for the evil day.

That provision has to be made against that dayâ the day o Dismissal â we are taught by the vivid picture of the steward reahsing the fact. He said within himself: " What am I to do? My lord taketh away my stewardship. I cannot dig; to beg I am ashamed." The future event is distinctly laid to heart, and the question what next deliberately, anxiously pondered, all possible courses being one after another weighed. Thus would the Great Teacher have His hearers lay to heart their latter end, and consider solemnly and seriously how it will be with them thereafter. The steward's soliloquy is not recorded merely for graphic effect, though it serves that end excellently, but to suggest the lesson, " go and do likewise." " Thou, too, must be dismissed," says Jesus to those who have ears to hear: " Think with thyself what thou canst do by way of providing against the fateful day." The meditations of the disgraced steward suggest rather gloomy thoughts as to the limited capacity of men to provide for the great future. " I cannot dig; to beg I am ashamed." He is too broken-down by debauchery, too effeminate in spirit to engage in honest toil, and he is too much of a gentleman to stoop to the trade of a beggar. If he is to live at all it must be in gentlemanly fashion: by cheating possibly, but by vulgar labour or by abject dependence on charity never.

Is man so helpless with regard to eternity; unable either to work for heaven or to beg for it; too broken-down by sin to work out for himself salvation as the reward of righteousness; too proud to be dependent for righteousness on another.? But we are running unawares into the vice of the spiritualisers, and must return to our parable.

Thus far the delineation serves the purpose of enforcing the lesson of prudence in providing against the day of death. What follows is to be understood in the light of the second, higher, lesson of the value of beneficence as a means towards that end. After depicting the steward engaged in rapt meditation on his approaching dismissal and the measures

The mention of digging is natural as typical of agricultural labour with which the steward's position has brought him mainly into contact. So Lightfoot," Hor. Heb."

for ameliorating the evil consequences, Jesus represents him as at length forming his resolution. " I know what I will do," he exclaims as the bright idea strikes him. " I have it at last." Then follows the explanation of his plan, which is in effect so to benefit the creditors of his lord in his account to be rendered that after his removal from office they will gladly do him the counter favour of receiving him into their houses, not as a beggar, but as one well entitled to the benefit, and therefore able to receive it without humiliation. The scheme rests on the simple principle that one good turn deserves another. It involves knavery as towards the creditor, but it involves beneficence as towards his debtors. And that is the reason xvhy the steward is made to adopt this plan of helping himself; for the Speaker of the parable has it in view to teach a lesson of the worth of beneficence as a provision against the evil day. To make this point clear, let it be considered that the scheme of the disgraced factor was by no means the only possible one in the circumstances; he might, e. g. have required the various creditors to pay him the full sum specified in their bills while altering the figures, and then have gone to his lord and paid the sums due according to the amended accounts and pocketed the balance. This would have made provision for some time to come, if not for all time, and it would have made him more independent. For after all there was something humiliating for one who had occupied his high position to be the guest of those beneath him in station, who had formerly feared him as their real master; passing from farm to farm as he tired of each host in turn, and probably each got tired of him, with the not impossible result of finding them eventually all wearied of iyvuiv, implying not habitual knowledge, but a conclusion at length arrived at as the result of consideration. " Not = tyvwica, which would be, I know, as part of my stock of knowledge, I am well aware,"â but implying, I have just arrived at the knowledge, an idea has just struck me, I have a plan.""â Alford. Lange also puts the matter well; his account of the steward's soliloquy altogether is good. He remarks that the representation is very graphic if we regard the word as spoken exabrupto. "What shall I do.? for my lord is going to deprive me of my office:. dig I can't, to beg I am ashamed. tvpjjfca. I know, I have found out what I must do."

The values due to the master were large, a bath being equal to nearly ten gallons, and the cor about fourteen bushels.

their fastidious and moody guest. All this could not fail to pass through his mind, and to appear a serious drawback to the scheme, and to recommend some other course. It has indeed been suggested that the bills were leases, and that the change of the figures meant a change in the amount of the annual rental; in which case what he would have gained by the adoption of the other plan would have borne a very small proportion to the amount of money saved to the tenants by the transaction so viewed, that amount of course being the measure of their indebtedness to him. But apart from the doubtfulness of the suggestion, it is open to the objection that if such was the nature of the transaction it is difficult to see why this great man need condescend to live under the roofs of meaner men as a homeless penniless dependent. Why not commute the advantage into a money payment, estimating the reduction of rent at a low rate which the tenants would be willing to pay, and which yet would realise over the whole a considerable sum, and having completed the nefarious business go his way, bidding good-bye to landlord and tenants alike."' Obviously the plan actually adopted, however we interpret the alteration of the documents, is the one which suits the didactic purpose of the parable, the steward being made to appear a benefactor of the debtors without any pecuniary benefit to himself, because the aim of the narrative is to teach the value of beneficence as a passport into the eternal habitations.

As helping us to understand more fully in what respect Jesus would have His hearers regard the steward as exemplary, it is important to note not only the general nature of his plan, but the manner in which it is executed. In this connection the actor in the parable exhibits certain valuable qualities of character well worthy of imitation, decision, self-collectedness, energy, promptitude, tact. Having once resolved what to do, he proceeds without hesitation to carry out his scheme undisturbed by any scruple of conscience or fear of failure. He is cool enough to perceive where the risks of miscarriage lie, and he adopts the mode of procedure best fitted to obviate them. He calls all the debtors together not merely to save

Bailey, 'Exposition of the Parables of our Lord," advocates this view.

VII. TJie Unjust Steward. 365 time and trouble, but that all may be implicated and none may mar the plot by becoming informer. The company assembled, he proceeds to business with a briskness and spirit meant to be imposing and calculated to insure co-operation. With the documents in hand he asks each debtor in turn the amount of his obligation, and handing him his bill, in a tone of authority instructs him what to do: Sit down and write quickly such and such an amount. Nor does he give to all the same instructions. Herein he shows his tact and savoir fairs. Diverse reasons have been suggested for the variation in the remission. One suggests his knowledge of the circumstances of each debtor; another his idea of the varying degrees of dishonesty the consciences of the different debtors could stand; a third his desire to show his power to do as he pleased, and so strengthen the feeling of abligation to himself. According to a fourth interpreter the reductions were in accordance with the facts of each case. This sucrsres-tion is based on the assumption that fifty and eighty were the amounts really due to the master, and that the higher numbers indicated a fraudulent over-estimate of the indebtedness by the unscrupulous agent. According to this view the steward had been a sinner against the debtors rather than against his employer. The effect of the transaction described in the parable on this hypothesis was to make the debtors under obligation to the steward by what they supposed to be a reduction of their debt, and at the same time to gain credit for him with his master by a correspondence between the bills as altered and the amounts previously reported verbally by him. This explanation has little to recommend it except that it makes the praise bestowed by the lord on his unfaithful servant less difficult to comprehend, and also exhibits the steward as in a way repenting, and by a return to honesty fitting himself to be with less impropriety the vehicle of moral instruction.

Probabl the best explanation is to be found in the lordly temper of the man. He adopts the arbitrary line as the most imposing. It is not the power of his position as the real master that he calculates on, but rather the power of Â So Alford. 8 So Alford. Â So Hofmann.

So Goebel â So Lange.

an imperious bearing. To give all the same reduction would be to act under law to a method, like ordinary men; to remit arbitrarily, and as whimsical impulse dictates, is to play the part of a magnifico, which suits his taste, and is not less likely to succeed. The world is largely governed by show, and many admire arbitrariness as princely, more than equity, which by comparison seems vulgar. The steward knew human nature, and acted accordingly.

The scheme is carried out, and the news of it have reached the employer's ears. How does he receive the report? The lord praised his tmjust steward. This alleged praise has scandalised and perplexed commentators, and put them to shifts to explain it, or rather explain it away. The most plausible method of doing so is to suggest that the praise must be regarded from the point of view of the narrator. Jesus is going to use the story for a purpose which requires that the conduct of the steward should be in some respects praiseworthy; therefore it is represented as being actually praised by the injured employer, though in reality it could hardly have been. It would compromise the natural probability of the parable were we to have recourse to this expedient for getting rid of the difficulty. But it is really not necessary. The praise is after all not so unlikely as it seems. At first sight, no doubt, it appears as if an outburst of anger at this new act of villainy had been much more appropriate. But in truth the stage of anger is past. The master has had his bitter hours over the unfaithfulness of his servant, and these have issued in a determination to be rid of him. That resolution once formed, the master will not be troubled with any further vexation. He expects doubtless additional evidence of knavery before he is done with the unprincipled man. But then he does expect it, and has discounted it already. The exposure, when it comes, will awaken no further emotions of a painful kind. Any feeling that may be called forth will be of the nature of amusement. Henceforth the degraded steward will be a kind of psychological study to him. He will be curious to know just what the fellow will do in his extremity. And if the knave show talent, dexterity, he will be quite able to appreciate it, and

So Reuss.

in the mood even to bestow on it a sort of humorous laudation. Of course the praise will have a noticeable peculiarity of tone. You are not to imagine the master setting himself seriously to pronounce a eulogy on his ex-steward; that were a very prosaic supposition. The lord looks, says Calvin, not to the person but to the deed itself. There is humour in the situation, and the praise must be understood cum grano satis. The now completed career and the character of the dismissed servant lie in full view before his lord's eye. The picture presents a strange mixture of prodigality, magnificence, cleverness, and unscrupulousness, not without its fascination, and exciting in the beholder mixed feelings of abhorrence and admiration. In the last act of the drama the hero displays all his qualities, bad and good. Kow natural that the exhibition should extort from the spectator, even though he be one who has suffered injury at his hand, such expressions of approbation as men are wont to use with reference to skill, ability, and tact, dissociated from principle. One does not need to be a " man of the world " in order to utter or appreciate such laudatory phrases; nothing more is required than the power to enjoy the display of character.

With the praise bestowed on his unrighteous servant the parable ends; all that follows is application. The moral interpretation begins properly at the ninth verse with the solemn formulaâ And I say unto you. The last clause of the preceding verse may be regarded as a parenthesis explanatory of the term (Ppoviixu s, employed to describe the action of the steward. One might be tempted to regard it as a reflection inserted by the Evangelist, similar to that which occurs in the discourse of Jesus, recorded in the seventh chapter of his Gospel. It has somewhat the tone of those explanatory enlargements by which primitive disciples might naturally unfold for the edification of themselves and their brethren the latent meaning of Christ's pregnant words; whereof we have a sample in the addition of the words, unta repentance, in the saying, came not to calt tjie rigjiteons, but sinners. For the reflection, though true and important, is not

Alford and others remark that the master is a man of the world also, to account for the praise of a clever but unprincipled person. ' Luke vii. 29, 30, absolutely indispensable. Without it we could understand what it was that the lord in the parable praised, and how it came to pass that there was that in his servant which provoked his approbation. We know that there is such a thing as practical skill and talent leading to success in life, apart from principle; and we know, moreover, that very often most unprincipled men are exceptionally endowed with such talent. Such knowledge is a part of the ethical lore which men learn by observation. It would not therefore have been surprising if Christ had left the truth in question unexpressed, to be supplied by the intelligence of His hearers. It is, however, on the other hand, by no means incredible that our Lord did wind up the parabolic narrative with the observation, that " the children of this world are wiser in their generation than the children of light." It is, as Bengel remarks, a sublime sentence most worthy of the celestial mouth of Jesus Christ! It is a weighty truth expressed in choice language. The title bestowed on those who are not of this world is especially noteworthy. It does full justice to their superior dignity. Children of the light! How much better at the worst to belong to the goodly company than to possess in the highest degree the talent which conducts to worldly success, and by the use thereof to gain a place among the chief men of the world! Children of the light, having spiritual insight into the relative worth and unvvorth of things, and therefore choosing the better part which shall not be taken away! Children of the light, walking in the sunshine of holiness, and having no fellowship with the works of darkness I Yet taking the children of the light at their best, how inferior they are in the talent for getting on as compared with the world's children! One may say, the more they are children of the light, the less of that talent they possess. On the other hand, it is the talent of the children of the world. The world is their portion, and to know the art of advancing their own interest in the struggle of life with their own kind is their study, and their frequent attainment. Thus understood, the apophthegm conveys no censure on the children of the light for not being more like the children of the world. The purpose is not to blame the former for the want of a certaia Sublimis est haec sententia, coelesti ore Iesu Christi dignissima.

quality, but to advert to the fact of the latter possessing it in a signal degree. " Praised him for his prudence; for his prudence, I say, for a prudent and skilful prosecution of self-interest is a notable characteristic of the men of the world; it is the thing which distinguishes them as compared with the children of light." If blame be intended, then we must give the saying another turn, and understand it thus: " The children of the world show more skill in the prosecution of their worldly interest (et's ti v yeveav rrjy kavrsiv â in relation to worldly men and temporal interests) than the children of light exhibit in relation to their eternal interests." The objection to this view is, that it is true only in proportion as men are 7toi children of the light. There are multitudes of so-called children of the light who are much more wise with regard to temporal than to eternal interests. But are they children of the light at all.- Would Jesus have called them by that dignified name.- Is not the true child of light one who is wise for eternity, and a fool for this world." And yet there are degrees of light: there are those who walk wholly in the day and worthily of their vocation, seeking in all things the higher goods of life, and measuring the value of all things by their bearing on the health of the spirit. There are others who walk in the moonlight, seeing dimly, groping after the siunimun boujim, aspiring to eternal life, candidates for initiation rather than epopts, and not well instructed as to what most tends to promote their eternal interest. We must suppose that Jesus has in view these specially. The advice which follows is such as suits them. If such are meant then we may see in the application to them of the epithet, ' children of the light," an evidence at once of the charity and of the wisdom of Jesusâ of His charity in conferring a title hardly deserved; of His wisdom in conveying through the use of the title an indirect admonition. " Children of light, I call you: such is your ideal position; make it a practical reality by acting on the advice I proceed to give to you."

That advice is obviously expressed, and with great felicity, in terms suggested by the parable. The swnimmi boniim is conceived of eschatologically as a state of felicity entered upon at death corresponding to the provision made for his 7Â The Parabolic Teaching of Christ, book ii.

well-being by the steward after his dismissal from office. Death is referred to in very peculiar terms: that when ye fail, or when it, your worldly good, fails youâ for it is difficult to decide between the two readings. The weight of diplomatic and critical authority is in favour of ekAtv, but the other reading given in the received text seems to sympathise best with the parabolic representation. Both forms of expression are in accordance with usage, the verb being employed to denote death in the Septuagint, as in Genesis xxv. 8, with reference to the decease of Abraham, and the corresponding adjective being applied to riches in this same Gospel. Our own preference, is decidedly for the old reading as the more impressive and poetical, as also more in keeping with the connection of thought. That when ye fail, when ye suffer the last eclipse and bankruptcy of lifeâ how significant and pathetic the allusion!â how unmistakable, too, in this respect contrasting with the other form of expression, which does not shut us up to death as the only possible interpretation, for riches may fail before death overtakes us.

Still more striking are the terms in which the future state is described. The abodes of the blessed are called the eternal te? its. The expression is paradoxical, combining two ideas apparently incompatibleâ the idea of an unchanging home, with the idea of transitoriness inseparable from tent life. A tent is the lodging of a pilgrim and stranger; heaven is the everlasting dwelling-place, the perennial house and home of the beatified. But in this very combination of apparently incongruous ideas lies the poetry and power of this remarkable phrase. It transfers the pathos of the pilgrim life of time into the life of eternity. It has been suggested with much probability that the expression is taken from the patriarchal history. " The tents of Abraham and Isaac under the oaks of Mamre are transported by the thought into that life to come which is represented by the image of a glorified Canaan. What is the future for poetry but the past idca'ised!"

The-e tents have among their occupants men whose life on earth was hard and sorrowful, and who are now enjoying eternal comfort, even the Lazaruses to whom this world was

Orjtuvpbv av'iicxiitrrov: Luke xii. 33. Godet.

a veritable vale of tears. Of these Jesus counsels His hearers who possess wealth to make therewith friends. He speaks as one who is confident that it will be worth while to follow this course; that it will prove to be true prudence. " say unto you, make to yourselves friends with the mammon of unrighteousness. Mark my wordsâ I assure you the line of action I recommend will turn out good policy. If you do those who want what ye possess a good turn now, they will be able and willing to do you a good turn hereafter. When ye get from death notice to quit they will receive you into the eternal tents where they dwell in peace and joy with Abraham. Your beneficiaries now, they will become hereafter your benefactors." 'â

The form of the thought thus quaintly expressed is that naturally arising out of the parable. The essential truth is, that genuine beneficence has value with God, the Judge of all the earth. The statement that those whom we benefit now will receive us into heaven means, that God has regard to deeds of charity, done in the true spirit of charity, in determining men's eternal destiny. The doctrine taught here is therefore substantially identical with that set forth in the parabolic representation of the last Judgment, in which those who are welcomed to the abodes of the blessed are they who have done acts of kindness to Christ in the person of the poor and needy. It is a doctrine with which we Protestants are not quite at home, and which we are apt to regard with jealousy as endangering the supremacy of faith as the grace that saves. That we should wish to bring all Scripture statements into harmony with our dogmatic formulte is natural enough, but before setting ourselves to this task it will be well to impress upon our minds how very much teaching in the same line as that of this parable there is in the Scriptures. Going back to the Old Testament we find these beautiful words in the Book of Daniel: " Wherefore, O king, let my counsel be acceptable unto thee, and break off thy sins by righteousness, and thine iniquities by showing mercy to the

Schottgen states that the Jews believed that the poor could receive the rich into heaven. Alford quotes a genial remark of Richard Baxter's: " Is there joy in heaven at thy conversion, and shall there be none at thy glorifica. von f"
poor, if it may be a lengthening of thy tranquillity." The recognition of the principle on which Daniel's counsel was based in the New Testament is very pronounced. To the pious Cornelius it is declared by a Divine message: " Thy prayers and thine alms are come up for a memorial before God." The Apostle Peter, who was sent to teach the devout proselyte the Christian faith, in his Epistle writes: " Charity covereth a multitude of sins." Paul bids Timothy " charge them that are rich in this world, that they be not high-minded, nor trust in uncertain riches, but in the living God. that they do good, that they be rich in good works, ready to distribute, wilhng to communicate; laying up in store for themselves a good foundation against the time to come, that they may lay hold on eternal lite." Finally Christ Himself said to the inquirer after eternal life: "If thou wilt be perfect, go and sell that thou hast, and give to the poor, and thou shalt have treasure in heaven." Luther reckoned the Epistle of James a strawy production, because it appeared to him to contradict Paul's doctrine of justification alone; and we could imagine an over-zealous defender of that doctrine, in possession of a courage equal to Luther's, boldly calling in question the authenticity of the above-cited utterances, and pronouncing them one and all apocryphal in source and uncanonical in tendency. The Christian of soberer mind will incline rather to make room for the doctrine they teach in his creed, and to give earnest heed to it in his conduct, believing that so doing he will be attending to matters which make for salvation. For it is a mistake to imagine that the teaching of these texts, and of the counsel appended to our parable, is Ebionitic, making poverty a virtue, and charity towards the poor, in the purely external sense of almsgiving, a passport to heaven. The mere possession of riches is not represented as an evil, but only the unwise use of them. And the wise use does not consist in making

Thes3 and other instances are enumerated in a most effective manner by M. Oilier of Lille in his excellent boo'c, ' Meditations Chr tiennes sur les Paraboles," 1880. It is a collection of sermons full of insight and eloquence.

Godet well remarks, that the sin connected with mammon consists not, according to the parable, in being the stewards of God, but in forgetting that we are.

money in unscrupulous ways, and then compounding for the iniquity by charitable donations. Our Lord's teaching concerning money may have been abused to tliat effect; but what part of His teaching has not been abused What He dimed at was to raise His disciples up to a spiritual view of the world, as not an end in itself, but only a means to an end. To those who had been slaves of the world He preached a higher life, that consisted not in the abundance of the things they possessed. But He did not merely set that higher life and earthly possessions over against each other. He taught that the lower goods could be used so as to increase one's spiritual wealth. He held this to be possible in every case. There was no man, in His view, however degraded, sordid, and even unrighteous his life had been, who could not redeem the past and insure the future by a wise, beneficent use of his means. The only hopeless character was that of the selfish man, who continued all his life to live only for himself, havinsf no solicitude to make friends with the mammon of unrighteousness.

This phrase, the mammon of unrighteousness, must therefore not be timidly interpreted. Many shades of meaning have Deen put upon it, largely with a view to avoid exegetical encouragement to licentious abuse of our Lord's words. Mammon, we are told, is called unrighteous because it is evil when it is made our chief good, however lawfully gotten; or because it is deceitful, that is, of uncertain tenure; or because there is no money which has not at some time or other been unrighteously used, although possibly not by the present possessor; or because money represents the distinction of propertyâ menni and tuinn, which is itself the fruit of sin; or because it has not been employed for charitable purposes, neglect 'of this duty being called abikia, as the practice of it was called hikaio(Tvvr. Most commentators shrink from that which might appear the most natural interpretation: the mammon which you have gotten by unrighteousness. They tell us that with reference to such a case Christ would have counselled, not charity, but restitution.

So Reuss. ' Kuinoel and others.
' Jerome, Melancthon, c. Trench, Alford, C.
' Lightfoot (' Hor. Heb."); but with hesitation.

Nevertheless we hesitate not to say that the epithet applied to money may and ought to be understood in the last sense, not to the exclusion of the others, but with very emphatic inclusion of it among the possible meanings. Its importance consists in this, that it exhibits the extreme limit of unrighteousness, and so tests the value of the principle. Beneficence must have virtue indeed if it can redeem a life of unrighteousness; if even in the case of men who have gained wealth by fraud, there be a right use of wealth possible by which they can benefit not only others, but themselves in the highest sense. Why should we hesitate to say that Jesus did contemplate such an extreme case? Among His hearers and disciples were probably not a few publicans; men like Zacchaeus, mentioned a little further on in this Gospel. What counsel was He to give them? To restore what they had gotten by false and unrighteous means? Certainly, where possible. But what was to be done in the many instances in which it was impossible? Surely the money which could not be restored should be put to the best possible use. Let the penitent publican do all the good to others he could, and so redeem the bad past as far as lay in his power; putting the poor and the needy in the place of those whom he had wronged, and to whom he could no longer give redress.

The moral sentences which follow do not appear to us to be of great importance for the interpretation of the parable; but they are of some use as giving us additional insight into Christ's way of regarding wealth. He virtually applies to money a series of epithets all tending to show how insignificant were the possessions of time in His view in comparison with the eternal riches. Wealth is the little, the unsubstantial, that which is really not ours, because we cannot retain it in the day of death; eternal life being the ' The word mammon (properly mamon) in the Syriac means money. The idea that it was the name of a god was of mediaeval origin. There is no suggestion in the text that mammon is essentially evil, though the concluding reflection in ver. 13, "Ye cannot serve God and mammon," may seem to suggest an antagonism between a good and an evil being. But it is impossible to serve two masters, whoever they be. We cannot love both God and earthlyyrzvw supremely, any more than God and earthly possessions. It would be better to replace the word mammon in out English version by money or wealth.

great boon, the true riches, that which is our own, because it abides with us for ever. The proper use, therefore, of the little that is fleeting is to use it with a view to the attainment of the much which endures.

One word more will finish what we have to say on this remarkable parable. The lesson taught here suggests an important theological inference. If kindness to the pooi have such value in the sight of God, it must be because God Himself is a Being who delights in loving-kindness. In teaching a morality of love Jesus virtually teaches a theology of grace. The two go together. Therefore, though the parable before us is ethical in its tendency rather than doctrinal, it may be legitimately reckoned among the parables of grace. The graciousness of the parable comes out in the quality of the ethics taughu

The genius of an ethical system is revealed not only by what it loves, but by what it heartily hates, and regards as deadly unpardonable sin. In the teaching of Christ the unpardonable sins are Inhumanity and Implacability. It is the selfish worldling who cares for nothing but his own comfort that goes to the place of woe; it is the unforgiving man whom the Father in heaven does not forgive. So we learn from the two parables next to be considered, the last in the present division. The doctrine is altogether congenial to a gospel of love, and fitly crowns the goodly edifice of spiritual instruction set forth in the parables of grace. Where love is regarded as the central truth of God's being, and the supreme duty and virtue qf man, there a loveless spirit must appear the thing above all things hateful and damnable. We feel, therefore, that we commit no offence against the law of congruity in including the parables of Dives and the Unmerciful Servant under the same class with those of the Lost Sheep, the Lost Coin, and the Lost Son, and treating them as contributions to Christ's doctrine of Grace. Without misgiving on this score we proceed to the exposition of these parables, taking first the more difficult, viz.:

The Parable of Dives and Lazarus.

Now there was a certain rich i vian and he-was clothed in pnrple and Jine linen, and fared sumptuously every day. And a certain beggar,

Bleek regards 7rxoii(TÂ oc as a predicate, and renders: There was a certain man who was rich.

Â Dr. J'ield criticising the revised version, says: " The Revisers have

Lazarus by twine, was laid at his gaie" covered with ulcers, aiid desiring to be fed with the crumbs' that fell from the rich man's table: yea, even the dogs came and licked his sores. And it came to pass that the beggar died, and that he was carried by the angels into Abraliatiis bosom: and the rich man also died and was buried. And in Hades, lifting up his eyes, being in torments, he seeth Abraham from afar, and Lazarus in his bosom. And he cried and said: Father Abraham, have mercy on me, and se? jd Lazarus that he may dip the tip of his finger in water, and cool my tongjcej for I arn in anguish in this flame. But Abraham said: Son, remetnber that thou receivedst thy good things in thy lifetime and Lazarus in like manner the evil things: but now here he is comforted, and thou art in anguish. And besides all this, between us and you there is a great chasm" fixed, that they which would pass from hence to you may not be able ana that none may cross over from thc7ice to us. Then he said: pray thee, therefore, father, that thou wouldest send him to my father's ho7ise, for I have five brethren, that he may testify unto them, lest they also come into this place of tormetit. But Abraham saith, They have Moses and the prophets: let them hear them. And he said, Nay, father Abraham, but if one go to them from the dead, they zvill repetit. Btit he said unto him, Lf they hear not Moses and the prophets, jieither will they be persuaded if one rise from the dead. â LUKE xvi. 19â 31.

done right in retaining the A. V. except that for ' faring' they might with advantage have substituted ' feasting." But in the margin they propose another rendering, ' living in mirth and splendour every day." Here the luxurious living of the rich man is presented to us under two different aspects; mirth, which we may suppose to consist in eating and drinking; and splendour, which suggests elegance of house and furniture. But the Greek word tv(ppcuv6fi'ivoq only contains the former idea, that of merrymaking, which is qualified by the adverb Xantrpuig, laute, sumptuously."â Otium Norvicense."

il3si3 t)To does not necessarily mean more than 'lay."

' The correct reading is rwv vnnovruiv ithe things falling. ifixio)v = 'crumbs," has probably crept in from Matt. xv. 27. Godet, however, thinks it has dropped out by confusion of the two twv and ought to be retained.

3 dwd Kal, implymg if not an aggravation of his sufferings, a heightened colouring in the description of them.

Trt KOKu, the ills of life; not his evil things, as in the case of Dives Goebel, however, maintains that the pronoun is understood.

wse: oss = this one, Lazarus, in T. R.

' This rendering answers to the reading Itti vaai tovtoiq. The read-ng approved by critics is iv Trdai roiitoii;, literally, " in all these things."

' Xaafia. Trench remarks that when the A. V. was published the word 'chasm' did not exist in English. The R. V. retains 'gulf."

The word otrwg at the beginning of this clause suggests the idea that the chasm has been fixed for the purpose of preventing transit 378 The Parabolic Teaching of Christ, Lbook n.

In the interpretation of this parable much depends on the view taken of the connection between it and the preceding portion of the chapter in which it occurs. If the connection is supposed to be with the immediately preceding context, then the main drift of the parable will be found in the concluding verses, in which the importance of Moses and the prophets as means of grace is emphasised. If, on the other hand, these miscellaneous observations contained in vers. 14â 18 be passed over as a kind of parenthesis interrupting the train of thought, and the present parable be connected with the one going before, then we shall discover the didactic significance not in the appendix, but in the main body of the story viewed as a fictitious history invented to illustrate the moral with which the parable of the unrighteous steward ends. We have no hesitation in deciding for the latter view. The imaginary narrative of the rich man and Lazarus is intended, as we think, to enforce the counsel to make friends with the mammon of unrighteousness by showing the disadvantage of not having such friends to facilitate admission into the eternal tents. It is quite likely that Christ would illustrate such a striking counsel by some such startling story; highly probable that He meant to do so irrespective of the words which He was led to speak by the derision of the Pharisees aifiong His audience; so that we may see in the introduction of the parable the resumption of the discourse at the point at which it had been broken oiif." So far from finding the key to the interpretation of the parable in the â sentences interpolated between it and the preceding one, we should rather be disposed to agree with those who think that some of these sentences at least, especially those respecting the perpetual validity of the law, have found a place here because of the turn of thought at the close of the parable. The sentences concerning the law do not explain the story Â So Olshausen. He says that the connection between the two parabhs: is unmistakable. As in the one an example is given how earthly good. â may be used for the service of God, so in the other we have an exampl â of one who uses his possessions only for his own enjoyment. In Lazani, on the other hand, appears one who could have been of service to t â,â â rich man with reference to heaven. Here, therefore, again is beneficenro, xompassionate love, commended.

jso in effect Greswell.

which follows; that story rather explains the presence of these sentences in the foregoing context. They come in at tliat point, because the story with its peculiar conclusion was to follow. "VVe do not affirm this dogmatically; we simply throw it out as a hypothesis preferable to being led astray in our interpretation by the assumption of a rigid adherence to historical sequence on the part of the narrator.

In none of the parables is the determination of the central viewpoint at once more needful and more difficult. The need arises out of the indefinite possibilities of didactic inference opened up by the scene being in part laid in the invisible world, concerning which it is of the utmost importance to draw no false conclusions. The difficulty springs from the fact that the parable itself is unusually undidactic in form. In this case the moralist retires far into the background, and only the artist comes to the front. The artistic power displayed is not inferior to anything in the whole range of the parabolic literature. In its descriptive vividness, as in its delicacy and pathos, the touch of the Limner is inimitable. But the Great Master does not in express terms tell us this time what His picture means; we are left to draw the moral lesson for ourselves. And the diversity of judgment as to the doctrinal tendency of the parable shows that this is by no means an easy task. The question. What does this story teach? has been very diversely answered. Some have found in it a proclamation, in parabolic form, of the general doctrine of future rewards and punishments for the good and evil deeds of the present life, with sundry items of information concerning the states of the saved and the lost respectively, the most momentous being that the separation between the two classes is absolute and finalâ the dialogue between Abraham and Dives having for its chief aim to proclaim this fact. And it is quite conceivable that our Lord might have spoken a parable bearing on such a topic. But then in such a parable we should have expected to find the characters of those whose future lots were to be so different more clearly indicated than they are in the one before us, in which Dives, though rich and living luxuriously, is not represented as wicked, and Lazarus, though poor and spending a wretched existence, is not represented as pious. The description would be sufficient, only if the doctrine intended were, that to be rich is a crime and to be poor a virtue. And such, in fact, in the opinion of some, is the doctrinal import of the parable. Its burden is. Woe to the rich I blessed are the poor. It is simply a vivid concrete representation of what is taught in the makarisms and woes with which Luke's version of the Sermon on the Mount begins. Something more and different, it is admitted, is contained in the concluding part, which is regarded as a supplement appended at a later date to the original parable, to rectify its Ebionitism by making Dives be damned, not for his wealth, but for his neglect of Old Testament teaching, or by giving the rich man the character of a Judaism remaining unbelieving in spite of the resurrection of Christ." Those to whom the imputation of Ebionitic tendencies to our Lord is offensive, and who nevertheless discover in this part of His teaching the doctrine of future recompenses, find themselves constrained to purge out the evil taint by bringing out of the description of the two contrasted characters more than appears on the surface. The chief effort is directed to Lazarus with the view of transforming him from a merely poor and miserable wight into a saint. This is done by imputing to his name moral significance. In the first place, importance is attached to the fact of a name being given to him, the only instance of the kind in the whole range of parabolic utterances. Then stress is laid on the composition of the name: it being equivalent to Eleazar, which means, God my Jielp? Thus the name used descriptively as so often among the Jews, conveys the intimation that Lazarus was a man who put his trust in God, and bore all the ills of life in pious patience and hope. The exegetical process is most ingenious, and it may not be altogether fanciful; only it is not satisfactory to be obliged to rest our interpretation on what at the best is only a conjecture. For that the poor man who lay at the rich man's gate is named is accounted for very simply by the consideration that a name for him i So De Wette, who denies that the parable is the counterpart of the preceding one.

"So Weizsiicker, ' Untersuchungen," p. 215, and the Tubingen school.
' So Pfleiderer, Pauhnismus," p. 449. Also Weizsacker, p. 215.
So Hilgenfeld, Einleitung," p. 566, after Zeller.

was necessary in the dialogue between Dives and Abraham. And as for the significance of the name, even granting the correctness of the derivation vindicated, it may be descriptive of state rather than of character: Lazarus, one whom God helps, that is, who has no other helper: a forlorn man-forsaken mortal,

The dogmatic interpretation of the parable, as one setting forth the doctrine of recompense, undergoes modification in the hands of those who insist on a close connection between the parable and the immediately preceding context. The rich man now becomes the representative of Pharisaism, and the parable sets forth in pictorial style the judgment of God on that system. On this view Lazarus ceases to be an independent character exhibiting the bright side of the doctrine of recompense, and subsides into a mere foil to the principal figure. In the worldly state of Dives is represented that which is high among men, and from the reversal of his fortune in the state of the dead we learn the esteem in which the same is held of God. Lazarus is introduced into the scene on this side the grave to make the grandeur of the world all the more imposing, and he reappears in the scene laid in Hades to give the damnation of pride an aspect most deeply tragic. But the main object of the scene in the invisible world is to lead up to the sentiment concerning Moses and the prophets put into the mouth of Abraham. In that sentiment is contained a virtual censure of Pharisaism as a system whose whole tendency was to weaken the authority of the very law in which it placed its trust and boast; a tendency specially apparent in connection with the precept against adultery, to which reference is made in the eighteenth verse. Thus the parable is the judgment at once of Pharisaic pride and ostentatious worldliness, and of Pharisaic laxity; in one word, the judgment of Pharisaic hypocrisy under its twofold aspect of self-indulgence veiled by petty austerities, and of moral license disguised by a scrupulous regard to legal minutiae. Christ virtually says to the Pharisees: " Ye affect an austere life, but ye are in reality luxurious men:

So Hofmann.

â Another derivation of the word is "Itjy N? = not-help.

Â Ver. 15.

ye are very jealous in appearance for the honour of the law, but 3'e do your best to make the law void. In both respects ye are an abomination in the sight of God, and your damnation is certain and just."

Tliis interpretation is open to one very obvious criticism, viz. that one does not at all readily recognise in the description of Dives the picture of a Pharisee. As you read you incline rather to say: Behold a Sadducee delineatedâ by his wealth, his splendid style of living, his outer robe of purple-dyed wool, and his inner tunic of fine Egyptian linen, pointed out unmistakably as one of the party w ho believed not in a hereafter, and therefore acted on the maxim: " Let us eat and drink, for to-morrow we die." Accordingly Schleiermacher threw out the conjecture that Dives is Herod Antipas, taking the hint from the allusion to adultery in the verse immediately preceding the commencement of our parable. On this view the parable still remains the judgment of the Pharisees, saying to them in effect: " This is what comes of your teaching; it sends the great ones of the earth to hell; by your lax interpretations of the moral law ye destroy the chief means of grace for such, and remove the restraints which might keep them from perdition." The reference being to so exalted a personage it was convenient that this should be said by a parabolic representation rather than in plain terms. The theory is ingenious. Still it

So are the words "purple and fine linen " to be distributed, the one referring to the upper, and the other to the under garment. To these, but in reverse order, reference is made in Matt. v. 40, "If any man will take away thy coat, let him have thy cloke also." Mr. Nicholon blames the authors of the revised New Testament for retaining this ambiguous and misleading rendering. He says: "The word rendered 'coat' means shirt,"a garment lying next the skin, reaching sometimes to the knee, sometimes to the ankle, kept close to the body by a girdle, and worn either by itself or with an outer robeâ the 'cloke." Of these two the ordinary dress consisted, and were a man deprived of both, he would have nothing left. But the translation of the Authorised and Revised Versions suggests that he would harfe at least 2i. shirt left.â Our new New Testament," p. 39.

2 Wetstein says: " Sadducaeum describi ex divitiis, victu, amictu et petitione patet; Pharisaii enim credebant animos esse superstit? s, jejunv bant crebro, modestius vestiebantur, et pauperiores erant."

3 Uber die Schriften des Lukas," p. 152.

confessedly leaves much unexplained; a much larger proportion of material to which no didactic significance is assigned, Schleiermacher acknowledges, than in any other parable.

In view of the unsatisfactoriness of all these dogmatic constructions, it is not surprising that some should have felt themselves driven in despair to take up the position that the parable has no doctrinal aim, and contains no definite doctrinal teaching, but is simply intended to startle men into serious thought and make them look below appearance to reality, and keep in mind the eternal future amid the enjoyments of the present.! It thus becomes a vatvQ incuicnto mori addressed to unbelieving men of all classes who do not live under the power of the world to come, but are Sadducees in heart whatever their professed creed. Of course, when the didactic drift is reduced to this vague generality, we can understand how a Sadducee might be selected to convey the lesson, even though it was addressed immediately to Pharisees. Unbelief is a leaven common to both Pharisees and Sadducees, and any one who lives a worldly life will serve the purpose of enforcing the moral: " Be wise in time." Dives is merely one of many possible illustrations of an important but much neglected commonplace.

We are very loth to come to the conclusion that such pointless generalities are all that we can extract from this remarkable portion of our Lord's teaching. As we remarked in another connection, it is characteristic of His parables, as compared with those of the Rabbis, that their lessons are not moral commonplaces, but specific truths, unfamiliar, and for the most part unwelcome. Of course moral commonplaces are impliedâ it being, as we have more than once remarked, part of the felicity of the parables that they suggest much more than they expressly teach. The parable before us is no?" exception. It implies and indirectly conveys many important ' moral lessons, such as that " the decision of the next world will often reverse the estimation wherein men are held in this; that God is no respecter of persons; that the heart must make its choice between the good things of this life, and those

So Dr. Service in Salvation here and hereafter'; also Reuss. ' This is substantially the line of thought pursued by Trench. Vide his remarks, in loc.

384 The Pa7'abolic Teaching of Christ, book ii, which the externals of this life do not affect." It presupposes and recalls to mind truths more general still and not less momentous, such as that there is a future life after death in which men will receive the appropriate recompense of the deeds done in the life that now is. But it was not to teach such truths generally believed, if little laid to heart, that Christ spake in parables, but to express doctrine more original, more distinctively Christian, more peculiar to the kingdom of God. Thus in the parabolic representation of the Judgment in the twenty-fifth chapter of Matthew's Gospel the specific lesson is not that there will be such a Judgment, but the principle on which the Judgment will proceed, viz. the great law of charity. In like manner we come to the interpretation of the parable before us quite expecting to find that its distinctive lesson is not the general doctrine of retribution, but some specific information as to the ground of condemnation in harmony with Christ's whole teaching, though not in accordance with current opinion. The general doctrine of retribution was part of the current opinion of the time, formed indeed a prominent item in the Pharisaic creed, as the parabolic form of the present discourse implies; for a parable uses things familiar to illustrate things unfamiliar. But that the suprem. e

virtue is love, and that the damning sin is selfish inhumanity, formed no part of the ethical system of the age, and it would not surprise us to find Christ speaking a parable to teach these truths.

Just such we take to be the didactic significance of the imaginary history of the rich man and Lazarus. This ' parable," for so we may continue to call it, though in strictness it is hardly entitled to the designation, has two dogmatic momenta: that inhumanity is a damning sin, and that it is a sin without excuse. The former is the burden of the first part of the parable (vers. 19â 26); the latter of the concluding portion (vers. 27â 31). This analysis, it is obvious, does not destroy the unity of the parable, because the second doctrine is clearly allied to the first, and forms its necessary complement. A sin is not damning unless it be inexcusable; when a valid plea in extenuation can be advanced judicial rigour is out of place. The only question that can be asked is, whether we

Farrar, The Life of Christ," vol. ii. p. 128.

have correctly indicated the doctrinal gist of the story in both its parts. That question shall be answered in the following exposition, in which we hope to make it appear that all details can be naturally accounted for by, and form together a harmonious picture around, these central truths which we place in the foreground.

The first point calling for notice is the character of the rich man. Our construction of the parable requires that Dives should be, by clear implication if not by express statement, accused of inhumanity. Is the fact then so.-" Now what is expressly stated is, that Dives lived a life of princely splendour and luxury, attired as princes are attired, and faring as princes fare. It is not said that he was addicted to the vices which too often accompany fulness of bread and abundance of idleness. It is not even alleged in so many words that he was hard-hearted towards the poor. Had that been charged, we could understand the'absence of all other charges, for the effect would simply be to accentuate the wickedness of an unsympathetic spirit. But if even this is not charged what becomes of our dogmatic construction.-â Before, however, we come to the conclusion that Dives is not represented as being the opposite of benevolent, we must make sure that we have taken into consideration all that is stated concerning him. Observe what follows: " There was a certain beggar named Lazarus, zvjiicji was laid at his gate." This is a fact of importance in the history of Dives. Lazarus enters on the stage not merely to present a striking contrast to the rich man's state, but as one with whom the latter had relations. Lazarus represents opportunity for the exercise of humanity. That is the chief if not the sole purpose for which he appears in the first scene. He comes before us a picture of want and woe, and says: "I was laid at this man's gate. He knew me; he could not pass from his house into the street without seeing my condition; yet as a leprous beggar I have Hved, and as a beggar I will die." And Lazarus is not to be regarded as a solitary individual; he is one of a class who abound in the ' world, and are never far from the gates even of palaces. In no place in the world can the rich man say with truth. There are no poor and needy near me whom I can feed, and clothe, and cherish. To those who plead such an excuse for a selfish life it may ever be replied: Ye have the poor ahvays ivith you. That is in effect what Christ meant to say by the introduction of Lazarus in the first part of the story. He reminds those whom He counsels to make friends with the mammon of unrighteousness that they will never lack abundant opportunities for doing so. By representing Lazarus as laid at the rich man's gate He affirms the existence of opportunities of the most obtrusive so7't, forcing themselves on men's attention, and not to be escaped; not needing to be sought out, but seeking them out and compelling them to realise their responsibilities.

When once it is understood that Lazarus is but a symbol for ample, urgent, inescapable opportunity, it is seen to be the obvious implication that Dives is one who neglects his opportunities. The assertion of opportunity is made for the very purpose of implying such neglect. It has indeed been asked by some, anxious to fasten on the parable an Ebion-itic bias, if the rich man was inhuman, why was the poor man deposited by friends at his door? And we willingly allow force to the question, so far as to admit that the natural probability of the parable requires us to think of Lazarus as getting something at the rich man's gate; at least a pittance sufficient to stave off starvation, and to make it worth while for his relatives to bring him thither. And we can afford tg admit that he did get some crumbs from the great man's table, through the hands of servants; nay, possibly by the order of their master, who, being aware that an object of pity lay at his street gate, may have given instructions to that effect, not without a feeling of satisfaction and 5elf-com-placency. To what does all this amount to? Simply to ' So De Wette; vid. note i, p. 377.

' The clause, kui ovhiq ISisov ahn, found in some cursive MSS. and versions, borrowed doubtless from Luke xv. 16, is a gloss arising out of the feeling, that even a minimum of humanity is excluded by the intention of the parable. As such it is regarded as a correct comment by Meyer and Trench. In proof that the beggar received nothing, Goebel emphasises intovmlv, and interprets, desiring m vain. In a similar strain Trench writes, speaking of the crumbs: " Even these were not thrown to him, or not in measure sufficient to satisfy his hunger." Kuinoel and Hofmann, on the other hand, think it is implied that Lazarus did receive the usual beggar's portion.

thisâ that Dives was not a monster of inhumanity. Christ had no intention of painting a monster; it was never His way to bring exaggerated and indiscriminate charges against those whose lives He disapproved, but rather to make generous admissions, even when deahng in stern condemnation. What He desired to do in the present instance was to hold up the picture of an average man of the world, living a self-centred life, coming utterly short of the true ideal, while not without such small virtues as men of the world ordinarily practise. If among these small virtues that of doling out little charities to the poor found a place, then, by all means, He would say, let this be conceded to Dives. He conceded as much to the Pharisees, whom, nevertheless, He pronounced great sinners, even in their very almsgiving. He could concede this to Dives, and yet represent him as one who neglected opportunities for the exercise of humanity. Ah, not so easily was Christ's ideal of humanity to be realised! Not by doling out crumbs to beggars could one gain the honourable name of a friend of man. He who would win that high degree must not only give alms in a small way, but bear the miseries of men as a burden on his heart, in the spirit of Him who, though rich, for our sakes became poor. He must behave towards the Lazar-uses at his gate as the good Samaritan behaved towards the wounded man. He must act as that king of whom it is written, that he ate and drank and did judgment and justice, and especially that he judged the cause of the poor and needy. He must gain the blessing of them that are ready to perish as Job gained it, who could protest that he had not withheld the poor from their desire, or caused the eyes of the widow to fail, or seen any perish for want of clothing, or any poor whose loins had not been warmed with the fleece of his sheep, or any stranger to whom he had not opened his doors. After all has been said that can be said in his behalf. Dives is obviously not a man of this heroic type: not a good Samaritan, not a benignant prince, not a generous, noble-hearted Job, not a man who knows anything of the passion for beneficence, of Â Kuinoel remarks, that though Dives gave crumbs to Lazarus, he did not thereby make himself out a humane man, or comply with the precepts of the law and the prophets as set forth in such texts as Deut. xv. 7,81 Isa. lviii. 7; Prov. iii. 27.

Jer. xxii. 15, 16. â Job xxxi. 16â 22.

388 The Parabolic Teaching of Christ, book il the'enthusiasm of humanity;' but merely a commonplace man of the world, with vulgar, self-centred aims, and no virtues and humanities, save such as are conventional.

The description given of the state of Lazarus quite answers to this view of the behaviour of the rich man. Whatever was done for the leprous beggar, left him as he was when he was first laid down at the rich man's gate. The ve-y word e3epa.; ro, though it means strictly only ' lay," might be adduced in proof of this, as implying on the part of those who brought him there and threw him down, the hard, unfeeling manner of men accustomed to misery, who had ceased to hope, and had experienced nothing at the hands of Dives to change their mood. Then the pathetic trait of the dogs licking the ulcers is very significant. Some take it as conveying the idea that the dogs showed themselves more humane than Dives, possibly their owner, cleaning and soothing the sores by their soft tongues, adducing this feature as one of the evidences that a charge of inhumanity against the rich man is intended. Others take it as an aggravation of the poor man's misery, hokiing that the effect of the canine attentions would be the reverse of soothing. We take it as expressing neither alleviation nor aggravation, but simply as giving vividness to the description of the sufferer's chronic condition. He lay there utterly helpless, so that the dogs approached him without fear, as if he were a dead carcase rather than a living being. Such he was from the first, and such he continued to be till beneficent death came and rescued him from his misery, and the manner in which his death is spoken of completes the proof that he had received no effectual attentions from his fellow-creatures during his lifetime. He died as he had livedâ a beggar, and his carcase was disposed of as if it had been that of a beast; for so we understand the absence of all reference to his burial, Meyer infers therefrom, that the body as well as the soul of the beggar was carried by the angels to Paradise. Calvin, with better exegetical tact, suggests that nothing is said as to

So Bleek, Hofmann.

Bengel says the tongue of a dog would soothe a body slightly diseased minus affecio), but would increase the pain of one covered with ulcers.

3 So Maldonatus, Grotius, c.

what happened to the body, because it was contemptuously, and without honour, thrown into a ditch.

In confirmation of the view now taken of the rich man's character, it is legitimate to take into account the words put into the mouth of Abraham as descriptive of his earthly state in contrast to that of Lazarus, "Thou in thy lifetime receivedst thy good things, and likewise Lazarus evil things." Various shades of meaning have been assigned to the words. Accentuating the verb in the former part of the sentence, some bring out of it the meaning, "Thou didst get in full, or beforehand, thy good things." Others, emphasising the pronoun ' thy," render: " Thou receivedst the things on which thy heart was set, which alone thou accountedst good." This much at least is implied â there was no communication of goods worth mentioning. Happiness was the lot of Dives, and misery of Lazarus, and the former kept all his happiness to himself, and took no pains to make his woe-stricken fellow-creature partaker of it.

On all these grounds we cannot doubt that it was the intention of our Lord to reproach Dives as one who regulated not his life by the law of love, and who utterly failed to act on the maxim of making for himself friends with the mammon of unrighteousness. But when we turn to Lazarus, and ask whether there is any indication in the first part of the parable of an intention to describe him as not only a poor, but also a pious man, we must answer in the negative. For reasons already indicated, we cannot attach any importance to the presence or the import of the name Lazarus. It may be assumed as certain, that had the design of the parable required that the beggar's piety should be emphasised in ths description of his earthly state, an epithet would have been introduced to indicate the fact unmistakably. But how, then, are we to account for the absence of such an epithet in view of the fact that Lazarus at death goes to heaven, if we are not to say, with the Tubingen critics, that his translation to bliss is the consolation for his earthly state of poverty? That is the second question we have to consider, and the answer we give to it yields, we think, a strong confirmation of our view as to the didactic drift of the parable. Lazarus, though So Meyer and Godet. ' So Hofmann.

devout,â for of course that is implied in his going to the bosom of Abraham,â is not represented as such, because the mention of the fact was not necessary to constitute him a legitimate object of charity, but was rather fitted to convey a false impression as to the grounds on which the duties of humanity rest. If we are right in the view, that to hold up the neglect of these duties to reprobation is the aim of the parable, then to speak of the piety of Lazarus, however sincere, would have been misleading irrelevance. For it is not to the pious poor alone, but to all the destitute, suffering, and miserable, of whatever character, that we owe the offices of charity. As Christ came not to call the righteous, so we are not to pick out the godly from among the children of poverty and affliction as the recipients of our sympathy and succour. Character may make a difference as to our mode of showing sympathy, but not as to the cherishing of the feeling of pity, the proper object of which is misery. It would therefore have been an impertinence in Dives to excuse his lack of compassion towards Lazarus by saying, "I did not know he was a saint." It was enough that he knew he was a sufferer. It is just because this is so that the parable is silent concerning the moral qualities of Lazarus. That silence is exactly what we should expect on our view as to the intention of the parable, and the fact is an argument in favour of that view.

On the other hand, the same reason which prescribed silence concerning the good qualities of Lazarus on earth required that prominent mention should be made of the fact, that on his decease he went to Abraham's bosom. The didactic intention fully explains both. It is not said that Lazarus lived piously, because not piety but want is the proper object of benevolence; it is said that when he died he was carried by angels to the bosom of Abraham, because he is needed there as an illustration of the advantage of having friends who can facilitate our admission into the eternal tents, For that is really the reason vhy the poor leper, who on earth lay at the rich man's gate, goes to the regions of bliss, so far as cur parable is concerned. In real life men go to heaven because they are good; in parables they may go there because the motive of the story requires them to be there. In saying this we do not of course mean to imply that it is beneficence to the pious poor alone that counts, in other words, that unless the objects of beneficence go to heaven the labour of the humane is in vain. The loving may be received into the eternal tents, when those who have been the recipients of their charity themselves fail to gain an entrance. But when the doctrine that beneficence has value in the sight of God, the Judge of men, is put in the form which it assumes in the previous parable, viz. that by beneficence men make for themselves friends to receive them into heaven, it is obviously necessary that these friends should themselves be conceived of as being there. It may be objected, that on this view the presence of Lazarus in paradise remains still unaccounted for, having a motive, indeed, but no natural cause. This is true; but it is an unavoidable defect arising out of the fact that Lazarus has to perform two roles with conflicting qualifications. On earth he represents the objects of compassion, who are the miserable, saintly or otherwise; in heaven he represents the friends who receive the benevolent into the eternal tents, who could not themselves be there unless they had been saintly as wdl as poor. The defect is no argument against our theory of the didactic significance of the parable, but is one inseparable from the parabolic style of instruction. It makes for our view, that by it we can account both for the silence concerning the piety of Lazarus on earth, and for his presence nevertheless in heaven. On the ordinary theory, according to which the parable teaches the general doctrine of eternal recompense, neither is explained; and so the presence of Lazarus in paradise remains at once without cause and without motive.

We pass now from the first scene to the second, from earth to Hades, the common receptacle of the dead. Sooner or later death overtakes all men, and so it came to pass that the beggar died, and the rich man also died and was buried. The beggar dies first, in accordance with the requirements of natural probability; for he suffers from a deadly disease which must soon cut him off, while the rich man is full of health and strength. Death brings an exchange of fortunes; the beggar formerly left to the tender mercies of dogs, is carried by angels to the bosom of Abraham; the rich man finds himself in a very different quarter of Hades, where torments are experienced. The latter fact is gently insinuated in a participial clause, partly from pity, partly because it is not the purpose of the speaker formally to teach the doctrine that there is a place of torments, which is assumed as a currently received truth, but to convey a hint as to the kind of people who go there. But, however reluctantly, the word must be spoken. " Being in torments,"â where else could such an one as Dives be." Not surely in Paradise, the home of the loving; in the bosom of Abraham, the father of the faithful! The torments of the fires of Gehenna teach Dives a lesson, which, in the fulness of earthly felicity, he had never needed to learnâ the value of a friend, "Oh for one able and willing to bring to me the faintest alleviation of this pain!" So the tormented man is represented as raising his eyes, and seeing in the distance, across the abyss that divides the two regions of Hades, Lazarus nestling in the bosom of the patriarch, and requesting that his former petitioner might be sent to distil a little water, drop by drop, with the tips of his fingers on his burning, parched tongue. Insignificant boon, corresponding to the morsels of food which was all that the Jaeggar desired; but misery is thankful for small mercies. What a vastly greater benefit Dives might have gained through Lazarus, had he only turned his acquaintance with him to account in good time! Had he made of him a friend with his worldly possessions he might have been his companion in Paradise. But now, so far from attaining that felicity, he cannot even obtain the little favour he craves. All or nothing is the rule. So Abraham tells him in effect in the sequel of this Dialogue of the Dead, in words whose very gentleness and courtesy make them a message of despair rather than of comfort. Two reasons are given for the refusal: the law of equity, and the impossibility of complying with the request. What was fitting had happened to both ' Brouwer, speaking of the decorum of Christ s parables, as exemplified in the one before us, contrasts the mild terms in which Abraham addressed Dives with the harsh language which is addressed to the lost in the parables of the Talmudists, such as: "0 most foolish man that ever iived."â ' De Parabolis Jesu Christi," p. 91.

parties. The one had received his full share of felicity on earth and was now in sorrow; the other had drunk a full cup of misery and was now comforted. The rich man had done nothing for the poor man in bygone days, why should the poor man be asked to do anything for him now."' It was fair that every one should have his turn. But even if Lazarus were willing to render the service it was not in his power. Between the two regions of Hades was fixed a great ravine impassable either way. The former reason is of the nature of an argianentiim ad hominem, deriving a large part of its force from the very fact of its being addressed to a selfish man. One who had not troubled himself about Lazarus, could not but feel the point of the retort: why then should Lazarus trouble himself about you It was but paying him back with his own coin, applying to him the lex talionis of the dispensation under which he had lived, and of which he had taken due advantage. Hence he makes no attempt to argue the matter with Abraham, as in the case of the request for his brethren, and this fact supplies another proof that we have rightly conceived the character of his life on earth, as that of a man who had lived for himself. Conscience makes him a coward, and he has no spirit left to say even this much: " I own I have no claim, but may I not receive this small service as a matter of grace t" To this question however, though not asked, Abraham replies in the second reason for refusal. Willingness on the part of Lazarus to go on an errand of mercy is not denied, it is rather tacitly conceded; what is asserted is the impossibility of intercommunication. The assertion provokes in us many questions: What is this dreadful chasm."' Why is it fixed? For how long.? Cannot it be bridged over.? What is impossible to love or to penitence.â " Could not the one find its way to yonder side, and the other to the hither side? These questions the parable was not meant to answer, therefore they are not raised. Dives acquiesces in the reasoning, and pressed his request no further. In any case it was not meet to put such questions in his mouth, not merely because they were not questions of the age, but specially because they were not questions for the like of him. He was of too low a n'oral type to feel the pressure of such problems. Had he been 394 ' ' Pa7'abolic Teaching of Christ, book ii.

capable of that he would never have been where he was. And being where he was, he could not easily rise above his former moral level. That difficulty perhaps furnishes the best clue to the mystery of the fixed gulf. What is impossible to penitence, is it asked? But what if penitence itself be impossible? Difficult it certainly is. The difficulty is implied in the very acquiescence of Dives in Abraham's reasoning. That reasoning is by no means exhaustive. It does not say the last word on the subject raised; it does not anticipate and dispose of all questions; at most it settles the matter in hand only from the lex talionis point of view. But it is conclusive for Dives because it is adapted to his moral tone. The first reason has irresistible force for him because his conscience tells him that he has been a selfish man; the second has equal cogency, because he is incapable of entertaining the thought of bridging the gulf by self-condemnation. The acquiescence of Dives in Abraham's reasoning thus does more than show, as we have said, that he was a man for whom self has been the chief end. It shows, moreover, that to escape from the perdition to which such a life surely conducts is difficult, not to say impossible. The loving and the beneficent make for themselves friends to receive them into the eternal tents. But the unloving and inhuman banish themselves to a realm of darkness and pain out of which they shall hardly be delivered, not because of any external barriers, but because of obstacles presented in their own hearts. The gulf which divides the two classes is as wide as the difference between selfishness and self-sacrifice, and is so fixed because these moral characteristics tend to permanence. In 'hell' are they who have loved themselves; in heaven are they who have loved others as themselvesâ how hard to go over from the one class to the other; to be transformed from a Dives into a good Samaritan I

Before passing on to the closing section of the parable, we may here briefly remark that the phraseology employed by Christ in describing the place of the dead is mostly borrowed from the current dialect of the time. The ' bosom of Abraham' was a title for the abode of the blessed in common use among the Jews. The ministry of angels in conveying the spirits of the just thither had also its place in the popular belief. Dialogues of the dead formed a part of the entertainment which the Rabbis provided for their pupils. Paradise, Abraham's bosom, Hades, Gehenna were not so closely-shut that the voices of the blessed and the pains of the tormented could not penetrate from either region to the other, and also to the ears of the teachers who could report what they heard for the benefit of their disciples. The Divine Artist who painted the startling picture before us, adopted a traditional theme, and dipped His brush in conventional colours, departing from use and wont only in the one particular of the fixed chasm; thereby making the separation wider than in the Rabbinical representation, according to which the two regions are divided only by a wall, or even by a hair's breadth; a fact worthy of notice as showing that, Jesus had no disposition to minimise the gravity of the outlook in the state beyond the grave. But, on the whole, the picture of the invisible world here presented is not to be taken as didactically significant. The one point of doctrinal instruction in the parable thus far, is that set forth likewise in the account of the last Judgment, viz. that men like Dives are excluded from the goodly fellowship of those who spent their lives on earth in deeds of love.

In the close of tl p parable, the additional but connected and subordinate lesson is taught, that for the life of selfishness there is no excuse on the score of ignorance. In making this the lesson of the concluding part, we assume that the request of Dives in behalf of his brethren is indirectly self-excuse. This may seem an ungenerous assumption, especially in view of the construction put on the request by enthusiastic advocates of ' the Eternal Hope' as an indication that Dives, under the purgatorial fires of the intermediate state, is undergoing rapid moral improvement. We have all respect for the motives of those who thus argue, and we have no wish to make Dives appear worse than he is. As in forming a judgment of his life on earth, we did not accuse him of Â Vide Lightfoot, Hor. Heb."

2 Hausrath, ' Zeitgeschichte," ii. 278.

= " What is the distance between Paradise and Gehenna? According to Johanan, a wall; according to Acha, a palm-breadth; according to other Rabbis, only a finger-breadth." Midrash on Koheleth, quoted by Dr. Farrar in ' Mercy and Judgment," p. 205.

refusing crumbs to Lazarus, so we are willing to give him full credit for the solicitude he manifests after his decease for his surviving brethren. And we gladly note, as one more index of the geniality of the parable, that no anxiety is evinced to rob Dives of this praise. Only we must add that it does not amount to much. The humanity of Dives in Hades is not charity, but only such love as even publicans and harlots practise; natural affection for an extended self, indicative therefore of continuity of character rather than of radical change. And we question whether in the intention of the speaker it be even this much; whether love for the extended self be not at bottom love for the unexte'nded self. That is, we think Christ's aim in introducing this trait is not to show that unblessed spirits cherish natural affections, but to take away all ground of excuse from those who live the life that has exclusion from bliss for its penalty. The speaker's-real purpose is to tell the living that they are without excuse if they so live as to forfeit bliss. But instead of doing this in abstract terms, he prefers to do it through the machinery of the parable, as in the case of the parable of the Lost Son, where the elder brother represents the Pharisees who blamed Christ for His sympathy with the leper. Therefore he makes Dives proljer a request which leads up to the declaration, that in Moses and the prophets men have sufficient means of grace to teach them how to live. The answer pointedly excludes all self-excuse on the score of defective aids to piety, and so implies self-excuse as the motive of this request. The secret thought of Dives is: Had I been warned it might have been otherwise. In like manner we cannot so far stretch our charity as to give Dives credit for the peculiar urgency he shows in behalf of his brethren. It is certainly a curious circumstance, that whilst abstaining from pressing his petition for himself, he ventures to expostulate with Abraham in pleading for his brethren, after the manner of Abraham himself in pleading for Sodom. We are not inclined to see in this a reflection of the spirit of Rabbinical dispute and

Pharisaic impudence. But neither can we see in it a trace of disinterested love. The repetition of the demand is meant merely to supply a

So Godet.

motive for the utterance of the sentiment, that those who are not moved to piety by the means actually available, would not be moved by any means, however extraordinary. Doubtless the law of probability requires that this should be done in a natural way; but this remark cuts two ways. It may "imply that Dives was particularly anxious for the welfare of his brethren; but it may also imply that he was very desirous to justify himself by some such reflection as this: Had only some one come from the dead, with the calm, clear light of eternity shining in his eyes, to inform me that the life beyond is no fabie, that Paradise is a place or state of unspeakable bliss, and Gehenna a place or state of unspeakable woe, had I not then renounced my voluptuous, selfish ways, and entered on the path of piety and charity? If one had come to me from the dead I had surely repented, and so would not have come to this place of torment.

The didactic point then here is, that the selfish life is inexcusable, and therefore justly visited with penalties. But how does this appear t The reply of Abraham is: " They have Moses and the prophets, let them hear them." It is a reply addressed to a Jew, and exactly adapted to the actual religious practice in the synagogue, in which precisely the parts of the Old Testament named the law and the prophets (those only, not the Hagiographa) were regularly read. It implies that these books were sufficient as a guide of life to all men of right dispositions, without any further extraordinary means of grace, and that when they failed, a better result could not be reached by any conceivable means. To the men of right mind a messenger from the dead was wholly unnecessary, and to the men of wrong mind he would be utterly useless. It was a reply not to be gainsaid by any Jew, the truth of the implied affirmations being sufficiently proved by the lives of the saints who lived under the old dispensation, and had not more than the law and the prophets for their rule of faith and practice, and many of them, such as Abraham himself, not even so much. One thing very noticeable about these books is the little prominence they give to the life to come. The fact of a future life is recognised, but so obscurely that Paul could truly speak of immortality as being brought

See Lightfoot.

to light through the Gospel. It is to miss the point of Abraham's reference to the Old Testament entirely to suppose that it means that the doctrine of immortality is there taught with sufficient clearness. It is nearer the mark to say, that what is meant is rather that the knowledge of that doctrine is not indispensable to the life of piety. Certainly the doctrine in question is not clearly set forth or strongly insisted on in the Hebrew Scriptures. And if the future life occupied a quite subordinate place in Old Testament teaching, we may safely assume that it occupied a still less prominent place in the thoughts and motives of Old Testament saints. They tested theories of life by their bearings on this world much more than by their bearings on the next. Hence their perplexities respecting the mysteries of human life, their querulous complainings, e. g. concerning the sufferings of the righteous. But in spite of their comparative ignorance of the life to come, and their consequent misreading of the riddles of the present life, we find no traces of dubiety as to the comparative merits of the two opposed schemes of lifeâ â the way of godliness and the way of the world. They might find difficulties in such facts of Providence as are pictured in this parable: a low-minded voluptuary, prosperous, rich, happy according to his taste, on the one hand; a saintly man in beggary, diseased, starved, homeless, on the other. They might, in vie v of such phenomena, sometimes ask, "Why doth the way of the wicked prosper?" But they never had any doubt whether it were better to be good or evil, to be righteous or to be wicked, to be a humane merciful man, or to be a sordid, selfish, heartless worldling. Nor did they hesitate to walk in the way of godliness in spite of all drawbacks. They chose the way that is everlasting; they could not do otherwise; the spirit of God in them would not permit them. They needed no messenger from the dead to convince them of the superiority of a life of justice, mercy, and piety over a life of unrighteousness, inhumanity, and sensuality. Far from that, they needed not to know that there was a life to come. The godly life appeared to them superior intrinsically, on its own merits, apart altogether from the question of duration. It was self-evident to them that in any case, whatever betide it is better to be a wise good man, doing justly, loving mercy, walking humbly with God, and holding all appetites and passions in strict subjection to conscience anii reason, than to be clothed in purple and fine linen, and to fare sumptuously every day, doing nothing else worth speaking of. Even if they knew certainly that there was no hell to fear, they could not live as Dives lived; it would be hell enough to be compelled to attempt it.

It thus appears that the Jew had amply sufficient means of grace, and was therefore without excpse if he chose the wrong way of life. But it is not the Jew alone that is required to hve the life of piety and charity. Christ taught that He should judge all the nations, and that the principle of judgment would be the law of charity. Are the Pagans also without excuse, though not having the law and the prophets Yes; because the law of humanity is written on their hearts, and they need no book, any more than an Old Testament Jew needed a clear doctrine of immortahty, to impose obligation to fulfil that law. This position obviously underlies the representation of the Judgment, and it is even not obscurely implied in the words put into the mouth of Abraham in this parable. For what is the meaning of the assertion, that if they believe not Moses and the prophets, neither will they believe though one rose from the dead t Simply this, that you cannot by any means compel faith in men morally indisposed to believe. That is, everything turns on moral disposition. In absence of that, neither Bible nor messenger from the dead will do me any good. I will find plausible reasons for disregarding even the most potent and miraculous aids to faith. A messenger from the dead! He would have a preliminary difiiculty to deal with ere he delivered his message. He would find it hard to get himself recognised as a visitor from the other world. Instead of listening with awestruck hearts to what he had to say, men of unbelieving temper would begin to discuss whether the supposed visitant from the world of spirits could ever have been dead, or were not a mere phantasm; nay, refusing to treat the matter seriously, they would probably receive vith shouts of merriment the very idea of one returning from the grave to preach to them of repentance and judgment to come. On the other hand, does a man of right disposition require a Bible, not to speak of a messenger from the dead, to tell him that he ought to love his neighbour? Let the Pagan who has no Bible consult his heart, and he will find that law written there. This is the one law for the neglect of which all men everywhere are without excuse. No need, in order to obligation to fulfil this law, of special supernatural inducements; no need of knowledge of the life to come; no need either of Moses, prophets, or gospels; the light within is enough. Those who have the benefit of such special means of grace, and yet neglect this law, are certainly blameworthy in a peculiar degree; but even those who have no such privileges are for the like neglect without excuse. Such in spirit is the teaching of our parable. It declares love to be the supreme duty, and it declares the disregard thereof to be, without exception, a deadly damning sin, because it is a duty which shines in the light of its own self-evidence. What Abraham said to Dives was what it w as fitting to say to Jews. But so much could be said to them because it is fitting and fair to say to all; " Ye have the voices of conscience, hear them."

THE UNMERCIFUL SERVANT.

Therefore is the kingdom of heaven likened ttnto a certain man, a king, who would make a reckoning with his servants. And when he had begun to reckon, there was brought unto him one who was a debtor to the extent ofteti thousand talents. Ajid seeing he had not wherewith to pay, his lord commanded that he should be sold, and his wife, and his children, and all that he had, and payment to be made. The servant therefore fell down and did obeisance to him, saying. Lord, have patience with me, and I will pay thee all. And the lord of that servatit, being tnoved with compassion, released him, and forgave him the debt. But that servatit going out, fotind one of his fellow-servants who owed him a hundred denarii: attd he laid hold on him, and took him by the throat, saying, Pay wiat thou owest. And his fellow-servant fell down and besought him, saying. Have patience with me, and I will pay thee And he would not, but zuent and cast him into prison, till he should pay that which was due. His fellow-servants, therefore, seeing what was done, were exceedingly sorry, and catne and told their lord all that was done. Then his lord called him unto him, and said unto him, Thou wicked servant, I forgave thee all

TO laviiov, literally, the loan.

Â Mo5t MSS. omit iravra. It may have crept in from ver. 26.

that debt, because thou bewnghtest me: oughtest thou not also to have had inercy on thy fellow-servant, even as I had mercy on thee? And being wroth, his lord delivered him to the tormentors, till he should pay all that was due to him. So shall also my Heavenly Father do unto you, if ye forgive not every one his brother from your hearts â Matt, xviii. 23â 35.

There is no difficulty in ascertaining the didactic drift of this parable. The moral it is intended to teach is indicated with perfect distinctness by our Lord Himself in the last sentence, in which He applies the narrative to the hearts of His hearers, the disciples. Even without that application we could easily deduce the lesson from the parable itself, viewed in connection with its surroundings. It forms the fitting conclusion of a conversation between Jesus and His disciples, arising out of their dispute as to who should be greatest in the kingdom of heaven. That dispute evinced the presence among them of the spirit of ambition, whose characteristic tendency it is, at once to be prone to do wrong, and to be very unforgiving towards wrong done by others. Jesus, therefore, fitly took occasion to warn His disciples against giving offences, especially to the weak, and to instruct them how to behave when they were the receivers, not the givers, of offences. The general tenor of the instructions given was â be meek and merciful, not prone to resentment, hard to appease, but good and ready to forgive. The counsel-to cherish a spirit of love bent on overcoming evil with good found its culminating expression in the reply to Peter's question, "How often must I forgive.-'" " Until seven times.?" the disciple added, tentatively answering his own question, and in doing so showing how far the benignant spirit of his Master had already influenced him, raising him above the ideas current in rabbinical circles, which fixed the limit at three times, But Jesus went as far beyond Peter as Peter went beyond the rabbis; nay, infinitely further, for He said, "Not till seven times, but until seventy times seven." That is, times without number; your forgivenesses must be as numerous as the implacable man's revenges; you must never weary 1 TO. irapaitTwuara airdv (their trespasses) seems to be a gloss from Matt. vi. 15.

2 Vide Lightfoot and Wetstein in loc.

â Some, not without probability, have found in our Lord's words an pardonin; offences. By this strong utterance Christ's thought concerning forgiveness was raised to the high level at which parabolic speech becomes natural and needful: natural on the part of One who was conscious that His thoughts on such matters were not those of the world; needful to familiarise the minds of hearers with truths lofty and novel. Therefore Jesus spake at this time the parable of TJie Umnercifiil Servant, the obvious aim of which is to expose the odiousness and criminality of an implacable temper in those who are citizens of the kingdom of heavenâ a kingdom of grace in which they themselves occupy the position of forgiven men. Having this for its burden, it is emphaticall) a parable of grace, forming a worthy ending of Christ's discourse in Capernaum and of His whole ministry of love in Galilee; teaching His disciples that the kingdom of heaven was a kingdom of grace; a kingdom among whose blessings pardon occupied a foremost place; a kingdom, therefore, in connection with which ambitious disputes concerning places of distinction, and still more, vindictive passions, were unseemly and intolerable.

A certain severity of tone is observable in the present parable as compared with the one last considered. " His lord was zuroih, and delivered him to the tormentors, till he should pay all that was due to him. So likewise shall My heavenly Father do unto yon, if ye forgive not every one his brother fro)n yonr hearts." The reason is that Jesus speaks here to offending disciples, members of His own family circle whom He loves dearly, therefore rebukes and chastens faithfully; and, moreover, to future apostles, on whose behaviour the well-being of the Church about to be founded largely depends. He anticipates the time, no longer distant, when He shall be personally removed from the earth, and He is anxious to prepare His chosen companions for playing worthily the part of His representatives. This He knows they cannot do so long as the spirit of ambition and vainglory, which has recently manifested itself, animates their breasts. Therefore He subjects them to the wholesome discipline of pathetic allusion to the speech of Lamech in Gen. iv. 24: " If Cain shall be avenged sevenfold, truly Lamech seventy and sevenfold."

The final separation from Galilee is recorded in the commencement of the next chapter.

example, heroic counsel, and stern warning, that by admiration, quickened sense of duty, and godly fear, they may become morally transformed by the renewing of their minds. Not merely the concluding parable, but the whole discourse on humility savours of this unwonted rigour: witness that saying, "Whoso shall offend one of these little ones which believe in Me, it were better for him that a millstone were hanged about his neck, and that he were drowned in the depth of the sea; " or that still more stern saying concerning the cutting off an offending hand, or foot, or eye. In this homily on lowliness Jesus seems Himself to perform the part of a surgeon, operating with the sharp knife of rebuke on the diseased parts of the souls of rlis disciples. We shall best understand the parable with which the homily closes by regarding it from this point of view.

This parable has for its specific aim not merely to inculcate the general duty of forgiveness, which is a part of natural ethics, but to inculcate that duty on men who are themselves forgiven of God, and living under a reign of grace. Hence the unforgiving man is in the first place represented as himself the object of pardoning mercy. And in this part of the parabolic representation we note the apparently exaggerated statement of the amount forgivenâ ten thousand talents, equivalent to millions sterling. The enormous sum is formally explained by conceiving of the offender as a farmer of revenue on a great scale, or as the satrap of a province, whose duty it is to remit the tribute of the country under his jurisdiction to the sovereign. But this explanation only throws us back on the previous question: Why is such a magnate selected to represent the foi-given one wdio forgives not? A satisfactory answer to this question is necessary to vindicate the verisimilitude of the parable. Now the fitness of the representation appears in various ways. It is fitting, in the first place, as a statement of the magnitude of all men's indebtedness to God as compared with the insignificant extent of the moral indebtedness of any one man to any other, represented

The exact amount will vary according to the particular talent meant; but the intention is not to state precisely the amount due, but to convey the idea of an immense sum, the payment of which was hopeless.

Vide Trench, who gives illustrative examples, p. 153, note.

by the hundred denarii. It is further fitting in some special respects more closely connected with the particular purpose of the parable. It suits the character in which the disciples are addressed, as men destined ere long to occupy princely position in the kingdom of God. It also suits the temper of those who are likely to be guilty of harsh, merciless dealing towards such as have done them wrong. Implacability is the sin of pride. But pride is high-minded, and just because it is so it is a great sinner against God. Therefore it is fit that the implacable man should be represented as occupying high station, and likewise as a great debtor to his lord. Once more, the vastness of the debt owed and forgiven is a just tribute to the gracious magnanimity of God, who 'abundantly pardons," and from whose mercy even the most wicked of men are not excluded.

The conduct of the lord toward his deeply-indebted servant is a second point in which the parable seems chargeable with exaggeration. At first it appears unduly severe, then after the debtor has presented his petition, unduly lenient. 'Forasmuch," we read, "as he had not to pay, his lord commanded him to be sold, and his wife, and children, and all that he had, and payment to be made." Yet after the debtor has pled for time, his lord suddenly changes his tone, and grants not time to pay, but a free remission. Is it credible, we are ready to inquire, that one who issued such an order would confer so great a favour; or, conversely, that one capable of such magnanimity would entertain thoughts of such pitiless rigour And, without doubt, the parabolic representation does wear an aspect of double improbability. Nevertheless, here it is the improbable that happens. In the first place, as respects the truculent command, it faithfully reflects the attitude of the law of antiquity towards debt. The Roman law permitted a debtor (in the literal sense) to be so treated, and the law of Moses seems not to have been behind it in rigour; i indeed the rude practice of selling a man and his whole belongings for debt appears to have been a common feature in the judicial system of ancient nations. Therefore in issuing such an order the king was simply acting as the

Vide Exod. xxii. 3; Levit. xxv. 39, 47; Amos ii. 6; viii. 6.

mouthpiece of the law apart altogether from personal feeling; and it is observable that no such feeling is imputed to him at this stage. He could not well do otherwise in the first place, whatever compassionate sentiments or purposes might be latent in his breast. On the other hand, in the free pardon of the debt we see the moral individuality of the monarch displaying itself. In the command is revealed the rigour of the ruler, in the remission of the debt the humanity of the man. A very unusual humanity truly, and most unlikely to be practised by men, whether kings or subjects, living under barbaric codes of law. But the improbability at this point is inevitable; for the humanity must be very unusual indeed which is to represent the mercy of God. For the Divine magnanimity passes all human example; His ways in forgiving rise above the ways of men high as heaven rises above earth.

"For the love of God is broader

Than the measures of man's mind, And the heart of the Eternal Is most wonderfully kind."

Viewed with reference to the history of revelation, the rigour and benignity combined in the behaviour of the king represent the relation between law and gospel. The command, Sell the debtor and all he hath, that the debt may be paid, exhibits the legal attitude towards sin; the free forgiveness of the debt exhibits the grace that came in with Jesus Christ. The one prepared for the other; the rigour of the law for th grace of the gospel. That rigour brought the debtor to his knees, with a petition coming far short of the grace in store, asking only for time to pay, for a hired servant's place; for men are unable to imagine and dare not hope for the good which God has prepared for them. The rigour was meant to lead up to the mercy through the way of repentance; it was but a means to an end, for had it been otherwise the more beneficent dispensation had never come. The law was but a pedagogue to conduct to Christ.

Euthymius Zigabenus expresses this thought. Speaking of. the cora-mand to sell for the debt, he says, Ovk i mhottitoq Sk rovro EKsxeiffji, a (K (TvixTraqt'iag, "va tu ni3r 9(iq ikiivog ri v Toiavrrjv atr6(paaiv (tkextvarj) Kal Tv-) r, Ttiq ckpeaeaiq' il yap fxr) ha ToiitO Toiavrtjv i'(t vtyktv dwoipaaip oiik av ikirtvaavn TO xpÂ '0C d(pijKtv.

When Christ came the World entered into a state of objective grace, under which God imputeth not to men their trespasses; and it becomes all who have attained to the knowledge of this truth to imitate the Divine charity in their relations to their fellow-men. But the wranglings of His disciples gave Jesus too good ground for the apprehension that an implacable spirit might be by no means a rare phenomenon in the era of grace; therefore, having in the first part of the parable depicted the mercy of God, He proceeded in the second part to describe the unmercifulness of so-called Christian men. The picture drawn is unspeakably repulsive, and bears witness to the deep abhorrence with which the Speaker regarded an unforgiving spirit in one who confesses his own need, and has experienced the benefit of forgiveness. The great debtor goes forth from the presence of his benignant master, straightway meets a fellow-servant who owes a petty debt to himself, in the most truculent manner lays hold of him and demands immediate payment, and on hearing from his debtor's lips the same appeal he had previously made to the king, refuses his request, unmoved by the august presence from which he has just come, by the memory of a recent benefit, and by the repetition of the words of his own prayer; and with brutal ferocity drags him to prison, there to lie till he has paid the paltry sum. Shall we say there is exaggeration here too? It were a comfort to be able to think so, and perhaps it may be said truly that Christ draws the picture in the darkest possible colours, that His disciples and all who bear His name might be scared into a holy fear of offending in such wise, and a godly jealousy lest they should bear the most distant resemblance to so odious a character. Yet we cannot flatter ourselves that the picture is a purely ideal one. It is not possible to conceive one conscious that his own moral debt is great,. and believing in the forgiveness thereof, deliberately so acting,

The act denoted by ttrviytr, seizing by the throat, though ferocious, â was legal according to Roman law. The approved reading in the next clause, tt rt 604(fieâ literally, "if you owe aught"â must be understood in sympathy with the truculent spirit displayed in that act. The Â rt, as Meyer remarks, is neither courteous nor problematical, but logical = if you owe you must pay. Unger puts it, "Conditio dicta pro causa." Grotius says, "Solet t! sane non conditionem sed generautatem significare."

for, foreiven much, he will love much both God and his fellow-men. But it is only too possible to be under the objective reign of grace, and to take advantage of the benefits of the era of grace, not without a certain appreciation of their value, yet to regulate our relations to our brethren by the strict regime of law, aggravated by the superadded horrors of violent temper and brutal passion when the slightest opposition is offered to the immediate execution of our selfish will. How many members of Christian Churches may rise from the communiontable to go forth on the following day to the perpetration of such atrocities in connection with their secular business! The sin of merciless hardness is one which easily besets us all, and instead of asking. Is thy servant a dog, that he should do such a thing? we do well to ask, rather, Is it I?

Even those who might themselves be guilty of such conduct would readily condemn it in others, and hence the fellow-servants of the two who stand in the relation of debtor and creditor are fitly represented as interesting themselves in the case, and reporting it to the common lord in a spirit of compassion towards the sufferer. Their sympathies are roused simply by the spectacle of excessive severity, without reference to the glaring inconsistency of the wrong-doer, of which they are not supposed to be aware. But that inconsistency is what arrests the attention of the king. Now for the first time he is angry, and he gives expression to his wrath in terms of unmitigated condemnation, followed up by a sentence of unqualified rigour. He calls the offender ' wicked," using the epithet not with reference to his own great debt, but to stigmatise the mercilessness he had shown towards his brother who owed him a small debtâ a mercilessness to be reprehended in any one, and utterly inexcusable in him, who had himself been forgiven so immensely greater a sum. And the sentence pronounced on this wicked ' one is, that having shown no mercy, he should receive none. The pardon granted is revoked, and he is remitted to the custody of the roughest, most ruthless, gaolers, who will rather take pleasure in tormenting him than in mitigating the discomforts of his imprisonment, and will take good care that he do not get out till he have paid all that he owed,

Most interpreters take the ' tormentors' in this general sense gaolers of the rudest order.

The language of the parable here, as throughout, is strong, but there is no occasion at this stage for any suggestion of exaggeration. Intensity of utterance, the characteristic of the whole parable, is discernible in this part also, but not extravagance. The words put into the mouth of the king find a response in every healthy conscience. Who will call in question the appropriateness of the epithet ' wicked '? Must we not rather acknowledge the moderation of judgment evinced in applying the terra to the offender not qua debtor, but qua creditor? It is not easy to imagine how any man could amass such an amount of debt without culpability approaching to wickedness. But, with fine discrimination, the word is not brought in till the party characterised has been guilty of conduct whose unmitigated iniquity could be doubtful to no one having the slightest pretensions to moral discernment. Then, as to the sentence, it is doubtless inexorably stern, but it is undeniably equitable and just. The case described is one of those in which the public conscience would feel aggrieved were a severe sentence not pronounced, and a lenient punishment would appear little short of an outrage.

We are not surprised, therefore, to find our Lord expressing His deliberate approval of the sentence pronounced on the unmerciful servant, and solemnly assuring His disciples that after the like manner should they themselves be treated if they followed his bad example. Such is the import of the closing sentence: So shall also My heavenly Father do unto you, if ye forgive not every one his brother front your hearts. Nothing could be more explicit than the declaration here made that a policy of severity will be pursued against all the unforgiving. And Christ's personal approval of that policy is equally pronounced. Specially worthy of notice in this view is the designation given to thef Ruler and Judge of men. One not in sympathy with the rigour of Divine government might have said. So shall the Judge of all the earth do to you. Not so." peaks Christ here. He gives to God, even in this sombre connection, the endearing title of Father. Not only so, He calls God My Father, as if to express in the most emphatic manner His perfect sympathy with the Divine mind. At other times He called God your Father, with reference to His disciples; but here He takes the Divine Father from them, as if to imply that between Him and them so acting there could be nothing in common, and appropriates Him to Himself, as if to say," I and My Father are one in this matter." Obviously Jesus has no sense of incongruity between the Fatherhood of God and the strange work of stern judgment on the unmerciful. Neither was there room for such a feeling. Just because God is a Father, and because His inmost spirit is love, He must abhor a spirit so utterly alien from His own. It is only what we should expect, that under the government of a gracious God the spirit of mercilessness should have judgment without mercy. Some good men think that it is due to the Divine love that we should cherish a hope of ultimate mercy even for the merciless in the long course of the ages. It may be so, though there is little either in the letter or in the spirit of this parable to encourage such a hope. On this dark subject we do not incline to dogmatise so freely as is usual on either side, but would be swift to hear and slow to speak. Whether the ' tormentors' and the imprisonment be ceonian merely, or strictly everlasting, may, for aught we know, be a fair question; but it is one we had rather not discuss, especially in connection with a class of sinners who have so little claim on our sympathy.

BOOK lit.

THE PARABLES OF JUDGMENT.

The little similitude of the Children in the Market-place does not usually find a place in treatises on the parables. Nevertheless it seems to us fit and worthy to stand at the head of the division on which we now enter as an introduction to the study of those parables in which Christ appears as a Prophet, speaking words of warning and of doom to His contemporaries in Israel. For it sets forth the judgment of Jesus on that generation, the opinion which He entertained of their character; an opinion from which it is easy to see that they were in a bad way: blind, wanting spiritual insight,â incapable of appreciating goodness when it showed itself among them, not knowing the time of their merciful visitation; a generation saying now, "Not this Man, but the Rabbis," and likely to say ere long, to their own hurt, 'Not this Man, but Barabbas."

The whole section of the gospel history in which this parable occurs may be described as a chapter of moral criticism. Its contents are given in greatest fulness in the eleventh chapter of Matthew, wherein we find Jesus expressing His opinion, first of John the Baptist, then of the Jewish people of that time, and finally of Himself. Of John He says that he is a great prophet of moral law, yet less than the least in the kingdom of God; the reason of the latter part of the judgment being that the Baptist did not understand or appreciate the kingdom of heaven as a kingdom of grace. To him it was a kingdom of law, demanding of men righteousness, not a kingdom of mercy, offering itself to men's acceptance as the siiminum bomim. Therefore Jesus Himself was a stumbling-block to him, for he expected Messiah to come with axe and fan, to judge, hew down, and sift; and lo, He had come in the spirit of love, patience, and pity. So he stood aloof from the new movement inaugurated by Jesus, wondering what it all might mean; a true man of God, yet outside the kingdom as a new historical phenomenon. Of Himself Jesus said, "I am despised and rejected by the wise and understanding ones, and received only by babes. Nevertheless those who despise Me cannot do without Me. I am the way to the knowledge of the Father. Nor does their contempt harm Me; for though men know Me not nor value Me, the Divine Father knoweth Me, and I know Him, and Heloveth Me, and hath committed all thingsâ the sovereignty of the futureâ into My hands. I can do without them, though they cannot do without Me."

Of the Jewish peopleâ that is, of those then living in Judaea who were under the influence of the spirit of the time, forming the great bulk of the nationâ Jesus pronounced the opinion which is contained in our parable, which, as it stands in St. Matthew's Gospel, is as follows:

Whereiinto shall I liken this ge7tcration? It is like iinfo childfcn sitting in the market-place who, calling iinto their fellows say: We piped unto you, and ye daficed not; we wailed, and ye mourned not. For John came neither eating nor drinking, and they say: He hath a devil. The Son of man came eating and drinking, and they say: Behold a gluttonous man, and a winebibber, a friend of publicans and sinners; a7td wisdom is justified' by her children? â Matth. xi. 16-19.

1 italpoiq, the reading in T. R. retained in R. V. N- B., c., have irepoiq, â which is adopted by Tischendorf, and Westcott and Hort. Alforj thinks irkpoig came into texts through mistake of the earâ a case of itacism, the â words being pronounced the same way. But of course this cuts both ways. Lange adopts inpotg, and assigns to it a moral significance = a different set not in the mood to play, representing Jesus and John, who were too earnest to trifle.

2 isiicaiwor, the aorist whose distinctive force is to be retained wherever possible. But we may regard the present as a case of the use of the gnomic aorist, iadicating a law of the moral order analogous to the same use of the aorist to denote facts belonging to the physical order, as in James i. 11.

3 Tikvwv, as in T. R. The R. V., Westcott and Hort, and Tischendorf adopt the reading Ipyuiv, found in N. B. Alford suggests that this reading may have been substituted for Tixvuv, which might easily have arisen from

The parable proper occupies only a single sentence, the remainder of the passage quoted giving its application, whence we learn that the opinion express- d by Jesus in the parable concerning His contemporaries had reference to the reception they had accorded to Himself and to John. But though very short, it is very significant. It hints that the contemporaries of Jesus and John, in judging these messengers of God, judged themselves; had shown themselves to be children. " To what shall I liken this generation?" asked the Divine Critic of His age, and His reply to His own question was: " They are like unto children." In one respect it was a mild judgment, but it was also very ominous. For it is a serious thing when men are like children, not in the good sense, but in the badâ not children, but childish. A generation like children in this evil sense is a generation in its spiritual dotage, or second childhood, in a state like that of the Hebrew Christians of after days so pathetically and graphically described by the writer of the Epistle addressed to them, as, "become such as have need of milk, and not of strong meat." When this state of senility is reached death is not far off. This condition of spiritual dotage had been reached by the generation to which our parable refers. Their senses were blinded by age so that they were unable to discern between good and evil. They were blind to true wisdom and goodness, and could not recognise these when they presented themselves to view under various forms, as in Jesus and John. They were blind to their own true interest, and could not discern the signs of the time, the weather signs portentous of the coming storm. They were on the wrong tracks, and had not the sense to allow themselves to be put right. There was no salvation for them in any of the guidances in which they put their trustâ â in Rabbinism. in Phariseeism, or in patriotism; yet they would follow these blind guides, and turned a deaf ear to the still voice of wisdom behind them, saying, "This is the way, walk ye in it." That such was the spiritual state of Israel Jesus

Tikviav, by the change of k into x- Readings found in i. B. together are, on the grounds so ably stated by Westcott and Hort in the valuable introduction to their edition of the Greek Testament, always entitled to serious consideration; but we do not feel called upon in every case, and as a matter of course, to introduce such into our text. Heb. v. 12.

was fully aware when He likened His generation to children. We could imagine Him using the comparison for the express purpose of pointing out such a condition; it would have been natural to have employed it in this sense when speaking with reference to the unappreciative attitude of contemporaries towards either Himself or John separately. But on the present occasion He thought of Himself and John together, and of the marked difference in their whole manner of life between the two messengers of God to that time, and of the impartiality with which their fellow-countr3'-men had dealt out to both an equal measure of disesteem, and other points of resemblance to children suggested themselves, for which He found a fit emblem in the scene from the market-place of children playing at marriages and funerals. The figures convey the idea that the men of that timeâ the generation of men under the influence of the characteristic Zeitgeist, and specially the more religious folk â the Phariseesâ were merely playing at religion. While He and John were both consumed with earnest zeal about the things of the kingdom, each striving after his own mode to promote its interests, they were only amusing themselves with pious works. Then, further, the similitude suggests that the parties depicted were like children in the fickleness of their temper. They were changeable in their humour; fastidious, difficult to please, much given to peevish complaining and fault-finding, after the manner of self-willed children. As one might see children in the market-place playing at their games and quarrelling with each other, never all in the same humour at the same moment, one set wishing to play at marriages when another wanted to play at funerals; so could one with spiritual vision see that childish generation behaving itself with reference to Jesus and John. The two men w'ere very diverse in their spirit and mode of life and method of working; and it might have been expected that if either was disliked the other would be a favourite. But no; they were both alike unpopular. When people saw John's austere garb and heard him preach repentance, they were in the mood to wish for something less severe. When they observed the genial way of Jesus, how He ate and drank and dressed as other men, and heard the gentle, pitiful words He addressed to the sinful, they turned away unsympathising, deeming that a sterner mood was called for.

Both the great ones, full of love and originality, sinned against the law of the mean expressed in such proverbs as 7ie quid iwnis, ij. rfi v liyav, and so incurred the penalty of being blamed by those, at all times the majority, to whom whatever was not characterised by tameness, half-and-halfncss, and mediocrity was an offence.

Such is the general drift of the parable, and in a broad sketch of the Parabolic Teaching of Christ it might not be necessary to add anything more by way of interpretation. But in a systematic exposition such as we have on hand there are some particular points adverted to by the commentators of which some notice must be taken. The questions have been discussed: Who are the complainants and who the complained of.- Who say "We piped, we wailed "." and who are they who danced not and mourned not.-' The settlement of these questions depends on another: Does Jesus, with wondrous condescension, as Bengel thinks, include Himself and John among the children If so, then they may be regarded either as the complainers or the complained of, the former alternative being that in favour with the older interpreters. According to this view those who call to their companions are Jesus and John, and their complaint, a just one, against their countrymen is that they had not responded to their call, and danced when they had piped, or wept when the Baptist mourned. It is in favour of this view that it assigns to Jesus and John the initiative, and puts their generation in the position simply of not sympathising with their work, in accordance with the historical state of the case. But against it is the consideration that it ascribes to the two prophets a role which was not characteristic of them, but which was eminently characteristic of the Pharisaic religionists of the timeâ that of complainingâ and so mars the literary felicity of the parable. The prophets had a good right to complain; but it was not their way to complain. We therefore concur in the opinion held by many modern commentators, viz. that the children who were so unfortunate as never to be able to get other children to play with them were not the two great ones of the time, but their small-souled critics.

"Jesus non solum Judasos, sed etiam se et Joannem diversis modis com-parat cum puerulis, mirabili, quod ad Jesus attinet, facilitate." Gnomon.

418 The Parabolic Teaching of Christ, book hi.

If then Jesus and John be among the children, they must represent the parties who would not dance and weep. But these, though all complained of, are not all complained of for the same reason. There are those whose fault is that they will not dance; and there are others whose fault is that they will not weep. Which of these two classes is represented by Jesus, and which by John.-" Diverse views have been expressed on these points. Some, e. g. Alford, think that the former class is represented by Jesus and the latter by John. On this view the cause of complaint is not that Christ and His followers were not of glad humour, and that John and his disciples were not of sad humour, but that the gladness of the one and the sadness of the other were not of the kind their contemporaries liked. This view appears so artificial that it is hardly worth while arguing against it; but it may be pointed out that the stress laid on the kind of joy or sorrow is not in keeping with the variation in the Evangelic reports of our Lord's words." It can hardly be doubted that John represents the group who will not dance, and Jesus the group who will not mourn. The negatives have the force of emphatic positives. Ye danced not, means not, ye danced otherwise than we wished, but ye did the opposite of dancing â went to culpable excess, in sadness. Ye mourned not, means not, ye gave no place to the element of sadness, but, on the contrary, indulged in a measure of mirthfulness and joy with which we could not possibly sympathise. The situation implied in the parable is thus that Jesus and John went to extremes in opposite directions, and so offended the taste of those who loved moderation in all things, and who deemed that the just, wise way of life in which gladness and sadness are duly blended. When men of this temper heard the Baptist preach with awful earnestness the necessity of repentance, they felt that he offended against the law of the mean by taking too gloomy a view of human conduct, and practising too ri; id a way of life; and they said, He hath a devil; he is a monomaniac with a fixed idea in his brainâ " Repent, repent, repent." When the same sort of man came into contact with the society of Jesus on any peculiarly significant,

Lu'. e vii. 32:' Wprjvijaaiitv vfuv koi ovk UXavaatt; Matt. xi. IJ: ioprjv))-eafiiv Kai ol'K tki'. paa9i.

characteristic occasion, as at Matthew's farewell feast, they were shocked by the exuberant joy, and said, Surely these revellers forget the sadness that is in human existence. Such was the actual state of the case as we know from the gospel records, and it is to this state that Jesus alludes in the parable of the children in the market-place, when He makes one set of children, representing the bulk of Jewish religious society, complain of another set, representing Himself and John and his disciples, that they would not dance or mourn; if, that is to say, we are to assume that Jesus and John are among the children.

But we must now say that we do not believe this assumption to be correct. The supposition is one which is due to a microscopic way of interpreting the parables against which we have steadily protested. The truth in this case, as in so many others, is hit by Olshausen, who finds in both classes of childrenâ the complainants and the complained ofâ representatives of the fickle generation among whom Jesus and John lived. The drift of the parable is: This generation is like a company of peevish children with whom nothing goes right,â one half wishing this, the other that, so that activity with a fixed aim is impossible among them. Both sets of children are alike unreasonable; they are well-matched playmates, fellows in spirit as well as in years; and they are photographed together, caught in the act of play, to form a picture of the grown-up children of the time, who behaved towards Jesus and John as unreasonably as the children in the market-place behaved towards each other. It is immaterial which of the two readings, Iratpot? or erepot?, we adopt; for even if with the critics we adopt the latter and emphasise its distinctive meaning so as to make it signify a different set of children, still it will remain true that the two sets were fellows; their differences superficial, their agreement radical. All the sects and societies of that time in Judaea were under the influence of one and the same spiritâ the spirit of a decadent age approaching dissolution. The only party in which there was any life or light or hope for the future was the party of Jesus, in which for the present we may include that of John and his disciples; for John was Christ's forerunner, and when his work had its proper effect it issued in 420 The Parabolic Teaching of Christ, book hi.

his disciples joining the society of Jesus. Pharisees, Sadducees, Herodians, were all in servile subjection to the old, the customary, the morally commonplace; and therefore they all instinctively agreed to hate the movement led by Jesus, characterised as it was by originality, poetry, passionate earnestness, and creative energy destined to make many things new. All alike were, under diverse guises, children of the world, and such wisdom as they could boast of was but worldly wisdom, which abhors enthusiasm, is incapable of making allowance for the faults real or seeming that accompany it, and devoid of the power to appreciate great characters; insomuch that it could commit the almost incredibly stupid mistakes of deeming such an one as the Baptist a madman, and such an one as Jesus a profligate, and of finally putting both to death as intolerable nuisances of whom it did well to rid itself.

Though Jesus and John are not included among the children the parable is so constructed as to exhibit them very clearly in their distinctive peculiarities, in the picture of the time This is effected by the simple device of representing the children not merely employed in play and quarrelling ovei their games, which would have sufficed as a picture of thi Jewish people, but as playing at marriages and funerals; the former symbolising the joy of the company of Jesus; the latter the sadness of the Baptist's circle. And thus it appears that in a single sentence the Divine Artist has given us a photograph of His age, including among the figures of the tableau, though not in the foreground, the two greatest characters of the ageâ John and Himself. We see in this picture a fickle peevish generation behaving themselves in religion like the children of a village gathered together in the marketplace at the hour of play; not without a certain keen interest in religious and moral movements, taking note of them as they made their appearance, observing their characteristics, going out in crowds to hear and see the preacher of repentance in the wilderness, and watching with curious eye the strange, eccentric, and unconventional behaviour of the Prophet of Nazareth; fascinated yet repelled by both, hoping for a moment to find in them that which might satisfy the obscure uncomprehended cravings of their hearts, only to be immedi- ately disappointed by traits of character and modes of action not to their taste. Behind the motley group in the forefront vve perceive the two great ones whose appearance has created the stir and disturbance in the pubhc mind. One is attired in a garment of camel's hair, gathered up with a leathern eirdle. and wears a sad, austere countenance, as of one who feels it to be his vocation to be a standing protest against the iniquities of an evil time. The other wears no external badge of isolation or singularity, and in His face is a strange blending of sadness and gladness. All that His companion knows of the world's evil is known to Him, and is a constant burden to His spirit, but He knows also of a cure for it, and the predominant expression of His countenance is one of hope and joy and enthusiastic devotion to a Saviour's calling. These two are the rudiments of a new era. All else in Judsa is of the old era and doomed to perish, too hopelessly degen crate to be capable of salvation, too blind to know the time of its gracious visitation, proved to be incurably bad by its treatment of those who could have led it in the way of peace. "All else," we have said, not forgetful that in the worst of times there are always some exceptions to the general corruption. Such there were in Judaea in the time of Christ â contemporaries of the generation animadverted on in the parable, but not belonging to it; children of wisdom, though babes in respect of Rabbinic lore, and of no account with the sages of the age. To these, as to the tribunal of true wisdom, Jesus appealed from the harsh, unsympathetic judgment of the worldly wise. The Son of man came eating and drinking, and they said. Behold a gluttonous man and a winebibber, a friend of publicans and sinners, and the quiet reply to such savage censure by the object of it was, Wisdom is justified by her children. The way in which the reflection is introduced has all the effect of humour. It is connected with the reference to the slanders of a prejudiced public by Kat', ' and," conveying the idea that the two things are wont to go together; the censure of the blind and the approbation of the wise: " They say such things of John and Me, and of course we are justified by true wisdom." The censure of folly is the negative test of goodness, the praise of wisdom is the positive; where the one is the other is to be looked for.

Thus viewed, the reflection with which the parable concludes is the statement of a moral axiom, and as such is properly rendered," Wisdom is justified," though the tense is the aorist. Not that it would be difficult to put a good sense on the sentence viewed as a statement of historical fact with reference to Jesus and John. So taken it would suggest this train of thought: John came and was evil entreated; Jesus came and was likewise evil entreated. Both were rejected by their generation, though for superficially opposite reasons; yet in the case of both wisdom was justified of her children. The wisdom of God, the Sender of the two badly-received prophets, and the wisdom of the sent were recognised by a small minority in an evil time, by those, viz. who were themselves the children of wisdom. But it is better to take the aorist, ebikatworj, as the gnomic aorist, expressing, in the form of an historical fact, that which belongs to the usual course of things.

We are shut up to this interpretation of the tense if we adopt the reading 'works' rexvciv) instead of 'children' (t4kv(ov). Then the meaning will be: Men blame, but the result justifies those blamed; the issue will show that both John and I were in our right, both in different ways inspired by wisdom. Historical in form, the statement is in reality a prophecy. So taken, the saying contains an important truth often verified in history, that proscribed causes in the long run are justified by their effects, and obtain general recognition as having their origin, not in folly, but in wisdom. That Christ should make such an appeal to the future is nowise unlikely, only it may be doubted whether this was all He had in view. It is probable He had the present and even the past in His thoughts when He uttered this pregnant saying, and it is not difficult to give such a wide sense to 'works' as to cover such a reference, and indeed make the two readings practically coincide. Among the works of wisdom we may reckon the children of wisdom, those who possess spiritual insight into the nature of moral phenomena. These see at the beginning what all see at the endâ that movements which give rise to criticism are of God, and by their insight those movements are justified. But if we may reckon among the works of wisdom the few who at an early stage detect the character of spiritual movements, a foi'tioj-i we may reckon in the same category the chief agents in those movements whose conduct is the principal subject of criticism. And confining our view to them we may say: " Wisdom is justified by her works,"â meaning, wisdom is justified in all her diverse ways of working; in the two instances in question, in particular.

Thus understood, the saying is demonstrably true. Wil dom was indeed justified in the diverse modes of life and methods of work characteristic of Jesus and John respectively. John came neither eating nor drinking, and inculcating an ascetic habit; Jesus came both eating and drinking, and initiating His disciples into a life of liberty and joy; and wisdom revealed itself in bothâ God's wisdom in sending them such as they were, their wisdom in being what God meant them to be. Both had one end, and were devoted to that end, but their manner of life and action were very diverse; yet both were legitimate and wise, because they were adapted to the gifts, the opportunities, and the tasks of each respectively. Wisdom dictates that means correspond to ends, and that men be like their work, and this law of congruity was complied with in the case of Jesus and John. John standing at the threshold of the new era of grace was yet a man of the old era, and his vocation was that of a Hebrew prophet, viz. to show the people their transgressions. He was indeed the last of the prophets, and the harbinger of the new era, but that function demanded the same type of man. The work of a forerunner of Messiah involved rough tasks, and needed a stern will. He had to prepare the way of the Lord, levelling the hills of pride, rousing dormant consciences, and so preparing men for receiving the, Redeemer when He came in the fulness of grace. It became one having such a vocation to live austerely, and by the very exaggerations of his self-denial to be a living protest against all forms of sensualism. His very dress served his vocation, giving emphasis to his ministry of repentance, speaking to the eye of the people, and telling them that this was another Elijah, a representative of moral law isolated from them, raised above them, and from Sinai's peak thundering down a stern "Thou shalt not" against the vice of the world below. The garment of camel's hair girt with a leathern girdle was thus a most legitimate 424 The Parabolic Teaching of Christ, book hi.

piece of ritualism. It is very easy to criticise this man, and point out faults. His austerity is excessive, his aspect is grotesque, his speech uncourtly, his whole way so eccentric, that men, at a loss what to think of him, might very excusably solve the problem by the hypothesis of demoniacal possession. Nevertheless John, wanting these peculiaritiesâ call them faults if you willâ would not have done his work so well. They were at least proofs of his utter sincerity; proofs that he zvas a man possessed, not indeed, as the critics imagined, with an evil spirit, but with the sublime spirit of righteousness; so utterly possessed by the noble passion for right as to disturb the balance and mar the symmetry of his character, and make him appear, to a superficial view, a one-. sided, extreme, singular, even absurd man, unendurable except to those who sympathised with his work, and understood its requirements.

The same law of congruity made it meet that Jesus should be as like other men as possible within the limits of the innocent; for thus only could He get close to them and win His way into their hearts with His gospel of mercy. He did well to come eating and drinking. Not eating and drinking riotously did He come, as He was slanderously reported to have done. His accommodations to existing customs sprang from love, not from laxity, and were the outward symbol of that sympathetic spirit which led Him to call Himself Son of man; and, having this end, they were accommodations in accordance with wisdom. The life of Jesus suited His vocation as one sent to preach a gospel to the poor, the fallen, the miserable; for it helped Him to win the confidence of those whom He sought to benefit. It becomes the Sanctifier to be in all possible respects like those whom he would sanctify; the more points of contact the better. This is the key to many features in Christ's conduct, and especially to that part of His public conduct which was so much blamed â His intercourse with the tax-gatherers, and the morally suspicious or disreputable class with whom they were associated. In that instance wisdom was justified by Christ's own lips in those beautiful apologies for loving the sinful which we had occasion to expound in studying the parables of grace.

And wisdom was further justified by her worksâ by the actual results. For Christ's open, genial bearing did win the confidence of many social outcasts; and the faith thus inspired exercised a redeeming influence upon their spirit, and led them to peace and purity. Wisdom was justified by children of folly transformed into children of wisdom, and as time went on, and the new movement unfolded itself, and its tendencies were revealed by its effects, the vindication grew more and more complete.

If the critics of Jesus had foreseen all that was to come out of His work they might possibly have abstained from faultfinding; for the world respects results, and recognises that which by these has fully vindicated its right to exist. But it is the misfortune of worldly wisdom that it has exclusive regard to results, and at the same time wants the prophetic prescience that can divine what these will be, and so is liable to be misled by present appearances into false and injurious judgments. In both respects it differs from true wisdom, which is not guided in its judgment solely by results seen or foreseen, but looks into the heart of things, and when it can recognise in conduct the expression of sincere conviction, the forth-putting of Divine force, does homage thereto irrespective of consequences. In this spirit the truly wise judge others; in this spirit they act themselves. They show their wisdom not by calculating consequences, but by being faithful in word and deed to the best impulses within them. So they play the hero; while worldly wisdom, in its anxiety to please all, to obviate immediate difficulties, to gain temporary advantages, stifles conviction, chills enthusiasm, and cuts itself off from the possibility of a heroic career permanently influential. But again, true wisdom has clear insight into the ultimate consequences of conduct. It has confidence in the moral order of the world, and knows that the final issues of all right action must be good. Worldly wisdom, in its blindness, can only infer from ascertained effects the quality of the cause. Genuine wisdom, from insight into the quality of the cause, can predict the nature of the effects. The one can only judge of the tree by its fruit; the other can judge of the fruit by the tree.

The people of Judaea, unhappily for themselves, did not even possess the former and easier of these faculties of moral 42.6 The Parabolic Teaching of Christ, book hi.

judgment. They persisted in entertaining a poor opinion of Jesus and His work even after it had attained to the measure of development manifested in the Apostohc Church. They were still unconvinced of their own sin, and of Christ's righteousness. And so there remained for them nothing but a fearful prospect of the wrath to the uttermost that came upon them in the first Christian century, from which Jesus and John would gladly have saved them.

Jesus spake this parable:

A certain man had a Jig-tree planted in Ins vineyard; and he came seeking fruit on it, and found not any. And he said unto the vinedresser, Behold, these three years I come seeking fruit on this fig-tree, and 1 find it Jtot: cut it down; why doth it also ' jnake the land useless? And he answering saith unto him, Lord, let it alone this year also, till I shall dig about it, and dung it, and if it bear fruit next year, well; but if not, thou shall cut it down. â LUKE xiii. 6â 9.

If it be assumed that the conception and delivery of this parabolic speech sprang out of the incidents previously ' The omission of this word in the A. V. is a grave fault, as it is essential to the meaning. The R. V. corrects the error.

2 (carapyft. The rendering cumbereth' in A. V. retained in R. V. is objectionable as too vague, not to mention that the verb cumber is used in another place of the same Gospel for a wholly different Greek word (Luke X. 40). The same word should certainly not be used in both places. The idea intended by carapyÂ seems to be that the land is rendered Of yog = atpyo.

In the T. R. ti t6 iexXoi comes after li Sk iviye. The rendering 'henceforth' in the R. V., replacing the 'after that' of the A. V., is too general, trog is understood after fxkwov. So Bengel, Meyer, and Hof-mann. Also Dr. Field, who, criticising the R. V., remarks: " Here trog occurs in the preceding verse, but even without that the idiom is well established. Plutarch frequently uses it of magistrates designate " (' Otium Norvicense," Part III). The correct rendering of the phrase was given early in last century by the Cambridge scholar, Jeremiah Markland, to whom reference is made by Dr. Field, and also by Bos in 'Ellipses Graecas' under the word iroe.

narrated, its judicial character is self-evident. In that case the obvious purpose of the parable is to enforce the warning: " Except ye repent, ye shall all likewise perish; " to intimate, that is to say, that the judgment of the Jewish nation was impending. But even if, as is most likely, the connection between the parable and what goes before is subjective only, in the mind of the writer, rather than in the actual course of events, the sombre and threatening nature of the utterance is still very apparent. The unfruitful tree, which we may safely assume to be Israel, is about to be cut down. It is on its last trial, the issue of which, judging from the past, is far from hopeful. There is, indeed, mercy in the petition that it may have a last trialâ another year of grace. This circumstance, however, throws no shadow of doubt on the judicial character of the parable; or, if it does, then we must conclude that it is a mistake to speak of a separate class of parables of judgment. For none of our Lord's parabolic sayings are so purely judicial as to show no trace of the grace that dwelt in Him. The grace is visible enough here in the intercession of the vinedresser. Nevertheless, judgment preponderates. The very intercession is ominous. The vinedresser shows His mercifulness by deprecating immediate cutting down, but the careful specification of conditions, and the limitation of the period within which experiments are to be made, intimate that peril is imminent.

The object of judgment, already hinted at, is Israelâ that would be so obvious to the hearers that it was quite unnecessary to explain it; and what is threatened is exclusion from the kingdom of God, forfeiture of privilege as the elect people. As in most parables belonging to the present group, the threatening against Israel is accompanied by hints at the replacing of the chosen people by other recipients of Divine favour. The most obvious hint is contained in the words: Why also rendereth it the land useless The owner reo-ards the occupation of the land by an unproductive tree as a serious evil, and one reason of his desire to cut down the tree is that another fertile tree may be planted in its room. It thus appears that in one aspect a parable of judgment, the present parable,â and a similar remark may be made with reference to all belonging to the same group,â is in another aspect a parable of grace. A parable of judgment as towards Israel, it is a parable of grace as towards the Gentiles, intimating God's purpose to put them in the place of an unfruitful elect people.

In this fact, doubtless, lay the attraction of this parable for the third Evangelist, who has alone recorded it. The doom of Israel by itself was an unpleasant subject of contemplation to a Christian mind; and had there been nothing but that to be found in the parable, Luke might have kept it out of his gospel. But his quick Pauline eye detected much more in it than that. He found there, to his comfort, a hint that Israel's doom was to be the opportunity of the Gentiles; that the sunset of Israel's day of grace was to be the sunrise of a day of grace for the outside nations.

The parable before us is one of those parts of our Lord's teaching in which is latent Pauline universalism. This element is its specialty, and only when we keep it steadily in view can we do full justice to all the features of the representation, or enter sympathetically into the spirit of either the speaker or the narrator. We understand the story of the unfruitful fig-tree only when we see in it an anticipation of Paul's apologetic for his Gentile Gospel, as apparently liable to the objection of setting aside the election of Israel, in the ninth, tenth, and eleventh chapters of his Epistle to the Romans. So at least we read the story, and we hope to justify the reading by the exposition following.

The lesson of the parable then being, on our view, not merely the doom of Israel, but that doom as accompanied by the in-bringing of the Gentiles, let us see how the details fit into the hypothesis.

The first point claiming attention is the subject of the parabolic narrationâ d. fig-tree in a vineyard. That requires explanation. A fig-tree is not the thing we look for in a vineyard. The peculiarity has not escaped the notice of commentators, and they have tried to account for it. Some point out that a fig-tree does not conflict with the prohibition in Deut. xxii. 9 â Thou shalt not soiv thy vineyard with divers seeds lest the fruit of thy seed zvhicji thou hast sown, atid the fruit of thy vineyard, be defiled, inasmuch as trees are not referred to in the passage. Others conversant with the present practice in

So Meyer.

the East tell us that a fig-tree in a vineyard is by no means an uncommon phenomenon. One who writes with authority on all that relates to the Natiwal History of the Bible, states that the corners and irregular pieces of ground in a vineyard are generally occupied by a fig-tree. Such observations prove that a fig-tree in a vineyard is not contrary either to law or to usage; but they do not explain why our Lord selected a fig-tree instead of a vine, as we should have expected, to be the vehicle of instruction. However legal or usual the presence of a fig-tree in a vineyard may be, it is not, as in the case of a vine, a matter of course, and Christ must have had a reason for introducing it, and the reason can only be found in the didactic significance of the emblem. What, then, was the reason On our view of the drift of the parable it is not difficult to answer the question. The fig-tree is chosen to represent Israel as a tacit yet effective protest against the notion of her possessing a prescriptive right to occupy in perpetuity the place she held in God's favour. The supposition is directed against the pride and self-importance of an elect race, prone to think that Israel and God's kingdom were synonymous, or as intimately and essentially related to each other as are vineyard and vine. To have used the vine as an emblem of Israel might have seemed to concede this claim, but by selecting the fig-tree as an emblem Christ said to his countrymen in effect, "Ye have no natural or necessary place in the sphere within which God's grace manifests itself, like a vine in a vineyard, without which the vineyard can hardly be conceived: Ye are but a fig-tree in the vineyard, legitimately, suitably enough there, yet there by accident, or by free choice of the owner, and there only so long as ye serve the purpose for which he put you there." Much the same thing indeed could be said even of a vine. For

Vide Stanley," Sinai and Palestine," p. 421.

2 Tristram, 'The Natural History of the Bible,"p. 352. Godet remarks t'lat the soil of a vineyard is very good for fruit-trees, as if the point of the parable were to teach that God had done all for Israel that He could (so Arnot). This is not the moral lesson of the parable, and the observation concerning the goodness of the soil, besides being irrelevant to the didactic scope, leaves the selection of a fig-tree as emblem unexplained. The land was good for any fruit-tree; why then name this one in particular?

II. J The Barren Fig-Tree, 431 while vines are necessary to the idea of a vineyard, this or that particular vine is not, and the introduction of any individual plant is a matter of choice, and its continuance depends on its fruit-bearing qualities; for no owner of a vineyard recognises a prescriptive right in a vine to remain in its place even when it has proved unfruitful. But what may be said even of a vine may be said a fortiori of a fig-tree, and to select a fig-tree as the emblem of Israel was a way of provoking reflections of this kind in a people not by any means inclined thereto. The Jewish people would not of their own accord think of themselves as a fig-tree in a vineyard. They would rather think of themselves as God's vine, which He brought from Egypt and planted in the goodly land of promise; and they would flatter themselves that as God had taken so much pains to elect them, and as they had been so long in possession, they would continue in the vineyard for ever. It was because the Jews cherished such thoughts that necessity was laid on Paul to reconcile his Gentile Gospel, not only with ethical interests and with the claims of the Mosaic la v, but with the election of Israel. They had the same thoughts in our Lord's time, and it was to provide an antidote to such self-deception and self-flattery that He called Israel a fig-tree in a vineyard; so by a single word accomplishing the same end which Paul sought to serve by an elaborate process of argument, designed to show that in election God is free, that therefore it confers no prescriptive rights, that what God freely began He may freely end, so far as human claims are concerned; and that Israel, so far from having any prescriptive right, had justly forfeited her privilege as the elect people by her utter failure to realise the Divine purpose in her election. All this is hinted by one short parable, and even by the single word fig-tree; all this, and yet more, for the comparison of Israel to a fig-tree suggests forcibly the thought that God's vineyard is a much more comprehensive category than the chosen race. Doubtless it was intended to suggest this thought, and when we keep this fact in view we can have no

Sucb is the scope of Rom. ix., x. Chap. xi. qualifies the severity of the previous argument by showing that the cancelling of Israel's election is not absolute or final.

2 Bengel had a glimpse of this, as appears from his suggestive remark: cvmiv, arborem cui per se nil loci est in vinea.

43a The Parabolic Teaching of Ch'ist. book hi.

difficulty in answering the question: If Israel be the fig-tree, what is the vineyard? The question has puzzled commentators and received various and even curious answers. Some say the vineyard in this instance must mean the world. One expositor, unable to accept this view, and at a loss to suggest any other, on the assumption that the fig-tree denotes Israel, in despair makes the tree represent individual Israelites, the vineyard being Israel collectively. The truth is, that the vineyard is the kingdom of God, the sphere within which God manifests Himself in grace; always in idea and Divine purpose distinguishable from and wider than the Jewish people, and now on the eve of becoming a much more comprehensive thing in reality through the calling of the Gentiles, after which it would become apparent to all that the place of Israel in the kingdom was as that of a fig-tree in the corner of a vineyard, small at the best, and by no means secure.

By no means secure, for the fig-tree has been iinfrnitful: that is the outstanding fact in its history. ' Behold, these three years I come seeking fruit on this tree, and find not any." The three years signify the time sufficient for ascertaining the tree's fruit-bearing qualities, after the lapse of which one may infer incurable barrenness. Possibly, as has been suggested, the number of years has been fixed with reference to the precept in the law directing that the fruit of young trees should for three years not be eaten, but be reckoned uncircumcised. There is little reason to believe that Jesus meant to refer to the years of His own personal ministry, though this view, in favour with many, certainly helps to remove the appearance of harshness in limiting the trial to so short a period, as in that case the meaning would be, that during a time of special means of grace Israel should have been exceptionally fruitful. Similar service is rendered by the suggestion that the three years represent the three epochs of the judges, the kings, and the high priests; each year in the parable signifying a period of many centuries in the Â So Euthymius Zig. Trench, Oostersee, Arnot.

Stier in ' Die Reden Jesu."

Â So Hofmann and Goebel. The vineyard, says Hofmann, is "die Anstalt des Hells."

So Godet. â Leviticus xix. 23. So Hofmann.

history. Certainly the time of trial does seem short, and in so far conveys an unfavourable impression as to God's patience towards Israel, not justified by the actual facts; for Jehovah had borne long with the unfruitfulness of His chosen people. But the time is made short because the purpose is not to emphasise the Divine patience, but to give prominence to the thought that fruitas the thing looked for, the reason of the fig-tr: g's presence in the vineyard. It belonged to the didactic drift of the parable to emphasise this point, for it tended to justify the threatened excision of Israel. Hence is explained the limitation of the period of trial to the barely sufficient number of years. The same bias comes out in the use of the present pxoij. at, in speaking of the owner's quest for fruit " I am coming," he says: he is continually on the outlook for fruit, and on its becoming apparent to him that a particular tree is not likely to be fruit-bearing, he has but one thought concerning it, viz. to cut it down or remove it, and plant another in its place. The point meant to be insisted on obviously is not the patience of God, but His impatience with a spiritually unfruitful people, even though it were an elect people. Christ would teach His countrymen, presuming on their privilege, that election was only a means to an end, and that if the end were not attained it would be sternly cancelled.

The restriction of the intercession of the vinedresser for a prolongation of the experiment to a single year indicates Christ's own sympathy with this Divine rigour. He is the vinedresser, and His ministry of grace and truth is the means whereby it is faintly hoped Israel may yet, at the eleventh hour, be made spiritually fruitful. But, full of grace though He be. He neither expects nor desires an indefinite extension of Israel's day of grace. He knows that though God is long-suffering, yet His patience, as exhibited in the history of His dealings with men, is exhaustible; and that in Israel's case it is now all but worn out. And He sympathises with the Divine impatience with chronic and incurable sterility. For though He preaches with enthusiasm a gospel of grace. He does so with the aim of producing in the recipients of the good tidings holiness, and in the conviction that belief in the gospel is the most efficient cause of holiness. A kingdom of God must be a kingdom of righteousness, and if Jesus presented it to view as a kingdom of grace, it was because He believed that was the most direct way of reaching the ideal. It was made a kingdom of grace to begin with, that it might become a kingdom of righteousness to end with. In this respect there is absolute agreement between Christ and Paul. The Herald of the kingdom, not less energetically than the apostle of the Gentiles, repudiates the idea that men might sin with impunity because grace abounded. The intercession put into the mouth of the vinedresser is a solemn act of repudiation, similar in import to Paul's protest in the sixth chapter of his Epistle to the Romans. "Let it alone this year also, till I shall dig about it, and dung it; and if it bear fruit next year, well; and if not, thou shalt cut it down." What words could more clearly or forcibly declare that grace is meant to lead to holy living, and that when it fails to do that it will be and ought to be exchanged for judicial rigour.-' The words of the vinedresser naturally make no reference to what may follow the cutting down of the unfruitful tree. And yet from the respect which he shows for the owner's urgent demand for fruit, as well as from that demand itself, it is easy to infer what is to be expected. The place of the barren tree will be filled by another tree in the hope of its proving fruitful. The owner of the vineyard must have fruit, and if he cannot get it from one quarter, he will provide that it be forthcoming from another. The thought suggested by the stress laid throughout on fertility is distinctly expressed by the words put into the mouth of the proprietor, "Why maketh it the land useless.-'" That the tree occupied un-profitably soil which might otherwise be productive is held to be sufficient condemnation. Some interpreters, ancient and modern, put a pregnant sense on the verb Karapy l, so as to make it cover not only the idea of profitless occupation, but that of injuring the land by intercepting the sun's rays, and sucking out of it its nutritive juices. This heaping of accus- â So Gregory the Great, and, almost as a matter of course, after him Trench; also. Bengal, who thus pithily sums up the case against the tree:â "Non modo nil prodest, sed etiam laticem avertit, quern e terra sucturae erant vites, et soles interpellat, et spatium occupat." To the same effect Maldonatus.

ations on the devoted tree arises out of a latent feeling that the owner's tone appears unduly severe, and stands in need of vindication. A strong case must be made out against the tree, that the owner may be cleared from the charge of unreasonableness. Therefore three sins are imputed to it, over and above that of unfruitfulnessâ it occupies space, it shuts out the sun, it impoverishes the soil. But this looks very like a repetition of the sin of Job's theorising friends, that of playing the part of special pleaders for God. The interpreters, missing the point of the parable, have been decidedly too hard upon the poor fig-tree. For, after all, it is a young tree, and cannot do very great harm by its leaves casting shade, or by its roots sucking moisture out of the land. No doubt the nation of Israel, which it represented, was an old tree, and did serious harm by its hypocritical profession of piety, causing the name of God to be blasphemed among the Gentiles, as Paul solemnly declared. But the parable is not so constructed as to bring out these facts, and we are not entitled to foist them into it. The fig-tree of the parable is a young tree of comparatively small dimensions and short roots. It has just lived long enough to show that it is not likely to be fruitful, and therefore uselessly occupies a place in the vineyard. And the point of the parable is, that that alone is sufficient to justify removal. To accumulate charges against the tree is simply to teach by implication that the one reason of profitless occupancy is not enough, and to obscure the moral lesson, which is that the supreme motive of Providence in its dealings with men is a regard to fruitful-ness. The attempt to make out a strong case only issues in making out a weak case. The true interest of the interpreter, therefore, is to concentrate attention on the one point, and to set forth as the lesson of the parable, that as soon as it has been definitely ascertained that a tree planted in the Divine vineyard is barren, and therefore idly occupies the ground, it ought to be removed and another planted in its room. In the history of nations a long time is allowed for ' The Vulgate renders icarapyÂ by occupat. Trench pronounces the rendering inadequate; in our view it hits the meaning intended exactly. The fact that xarap- uv is a favourite Pauline word might tempt us to put a Pauline sense on a word which occurs here only outside of Paul's the ascertainment of the fact; but it holds good, nevertheless, that such is the principle on which nations are dealt with by Providence, and, in particular, that such is the principle on which the people of Israel were dealt with.

The means proposed by the vinedresser for the cure of barrenness are characteristic. They are means of grace; such means as from the gospel records we know to have been employed by Christ to win His countrymen to repentance and true piety. " I shall dig about it, and dung it." These processes began with the ministry of John the Baptist, and were carried on faithfully and lovingly by Jesus till the hour when He uttered the pathetic lament over Jerusalem, because she had defeated all His efforts to save her. The doctrine of the Kingdom was the chief ingredient in the fertilising matter laid at the roots of the barren tree. That doctrine was supremely well fitted to regenerate Israel, and cause her to bring forth fruit to God, in place of mere foliage and wood. Yet it signally failed to do so; the Jewish people, as a whole, treated the good tidings with contempt, and became worse rather than better. And it is a melancholy reflection, that this is apt to be the case with a people after it has attained a certain stage of spiritual decay. The goodness of God leadeth it not to repentance; it rather despises the riches of His goodness and forbearance and long-suffering. This fact in the spiritual world has its analogue in the physical world. It is a well-known fact, that both in the animal and in the vegetable kingdom fertility is frequently better promoted by starving than by fattening. A barren tree, gone to leaf and wood, is rendered fertile, not by dunging, but by cutting the roots. Severe treatment restores to fruit-bearing more readily than generous gardening. Poor populations are more prolific than well-to-do classes. It is a remarkable law

Epistles, or to suppose that Luke, the Pauline evangelist, must have understood it in a Pauline sense. But even if we were to yield to this iuipulic, it would not conduct to a sense widely different from that assigned to the word in our exposition. A prevalent Pauline sense of the term is "to ma': e void." That is just what an unfruitful tree does to land. The land is as good as non-existent which is occupied by a barren tree.

Qui vinitor eximia imago est ejus qui il v Ttjv noxtv ttttxxavatv In aitr v. Unger.

2 Vide Doubledas Law of Population."

this, according to which impoverishment is the condition of abundant reproduction, and nature is compelled to make an effort at self-preservation, by having its continued existence threatened. The law, ever active alike in the physical and in the spiritual spheres, was exemplified in Israel. The manuring process utterly failed, and there was nothing left but to try the cutting process. This process was tried when Israel was cut off, and the Gentiles were put in her place. Then means of grace gave place to measures of severity, to which Paul applied the expressive name of atiotO iia According to the apostle, these measures were means of grace under a different guise. They were only a new way towards the old endâ that of making Israel in truth a people of God. Such is the drift of the last part of the great argument by which Paul seeks to reconcile his gospel with the election of Israel. God, he says, hath not totally or finally cast off His people. He has only adopted a new method of accomplishing the purpose of the election. It is a comforting doctrine, whether we have regard to the case of Israel or to the dark, judicial side of God's dealings with men generally. It is a doctrine not taught in our parable. The cutting down spoken of there is final and irretrievable. For if a tree be felled with the axe it cannot grow again. The fact reminds us of the relativity and partiality of many individual Scripture statements, and of the need for combining mutually complementary texts in order to a just, full, and balanced view of Bible teaching on matters of fundamental moment.

Romans xi. 22.

2 Vide remarks on this topic in connection with the parable of the Great Supper, at p. 338.

THE TWO SONS; OR, tsRAEL'S LEADERS CHARGED WITH THE VICE OF INSINCERITY.

During the conflicts of the Passion-week Jesus spake the following parable, one of the three directed one after the other against the ecclesiastical leaders of the Jewish people, now become His relentless adversaries:

But what think ye? A man had two sons; and coming to the Jirst, he said, So7t, go work to-day in the vineyard. And he answered and said, J go, sir; and went not. And comiiig to the second, he said likewise. And he answered and said, I will not; but afterwards, repenting, he went. Which of the two did the will of his father f They say the second. Jesus saith to them, Verily I say unto you, that the publicans and the haj'lots go into the kingdojn of God before you. For John came to you in the way of righteousness, afid ye believed him not; but the publicans and the harlots believed him: and ye, when ye saw it, did not even afterwards repent, that ye jnight believe hitn. â St. Matt. xxi. 28â 32."

This parable, like that of the Children in the Market-place, is also a parable of moral criticism, associated here as in the earlier instance with the name of the Baptist. It arose naturally out of the preceding discussion in which Jesus, put upon His defence, with controversial tact made use of John to put to silence His opponents. John's career was finished; his name belonged to history; and public opinion had pronounced on him its final verdict, to the effect that he was

We give the parable as it stands in the text of the Vatican Codex, and as given in Westcott and Hort; the order in which the two sons are named being the inverse of that in the T. R. For remarks in vindication of this order, see the exposition.

a true prophet of God, entitled to speak in God's name to his fellow-countrymen. This judgment the religious heads of the people could not afford to gainsay, and as prudent men of the world they bowed to it. But they did not recognise the claims of the Baptist while he lived and carried on his work. Then they found fault with him, not less than with Jesus, though on different grounds. Of this fact Jesus, interrogated concerning His prophetic authority, takes care to remind them now, putting them in an awkward dilemma by asking the question: " The baptism of John, whence was it? from heaven or from men.-â " The effect of the question was to rob their doubt or unbelief in regard to Himself ot all moral weight. It meant: " You bow to the opinion of the public now, concerning John, but you know how you thought and spoke of him not long ago. Your adverse opinion against a man does not count for much. He may be a genuine messenger of God, and yet be evil spoken of by you. I do not think it worth while to answer your question about my authority. If ever you recognise it, it will be after the world has done so, for your way is not to lead but to follow opinion."

Having first used John in self-defence, Jesus next proceeded to turn him into a weapon of attack against His foes by relating in parabolic form the treatment which His fellow-prophet received at their hands. The parable and its interpretation amount to a charge of insincerity against the Pharisaic class, as manifested in their behaviour towards the Baptist. Animadversion on this Pharisaic vice was natural in the circumstances; for the opponents of Jesus had just shown themselves guilty of it by their evasive answer to His question concerning John's baptism and its source. "We know not," replied they, because it was inconvenient to give a more distinct answer. Had they spoken according to the thoughts of their own hearts they would have given one answer; had they followed their inclination to echo the voice of the nation they would have returned an opposite answer. They in fact said both yes and no to the assertion that John was a prophet; yes, by their deference to the vox populi; nj, by their deepest sympathies. The design of the parable is to declare that what these men did then they had been doing all alongâ assuming a yes-and-no attitude towards the Baptist's public vocation and ministry, seeming to approve his general aim yet utterly out of sympathy with his spirit. The parabolic discourse seems to charge a twofold insincerity against the parties animadverted on; one of the past, and one of the present. They had said yes and no while John exercised his ministry, approving of his way so far as it was a way of legal righteousnesss, disapproving of his spirit; they say yes and no still, saying with the general public, ' John is a prophet," and so appearing at length to believe in him: yet all the while disliking his moral temper as much as ever, so retaining their secret conviction altogether unrepented of.

Insincerity, then, deep, habitual, incurable, is the vice with which the Pharisaic character is here branded. It is a much more serious charge than that brought in the earlier parable of moral criticism. There the fault animadverted on is simply childish caprice and whimsicality, which can be pleased with nothing, and regards with equal dislike the most diverse moral tendencies. There also the censure is mitigated by the employment of children as an emblem of the objects of censure, for who is much surprised at the peccadilloes of children, however naughty Here the emblem of an evil generation is a son grown to man's estate, who may be expected to realise the responsibilities and to address himself seriously to the duties of life. And w hat is charged against this son is that he recognises his responsibilities in word or sentiment only, not in deed, and so trifles with and wrongs those to whom he owes relative duties. Yet the vices exposed in the two parables are more closely connected than at first appears. The child of the earlier parable is the father of the young man of the later. The child's fault is playing at religion; the man's fault is still that of playing at religion, only in a theatrical, hypocritical sense.

The two parables, while linked together by the common reference to John in the interpretation, have this difference, that, whereas in the earlier both John and Jesus are alluded to in the interpretation, in the latter John alone comes in. This is easily explained by the difference in the didactic drift. The earlier parable, having for its aim to convict the contemporaries of Jesus and John of unreaso7iable caprice, naturally , The Two Sons, 441 employs for this purpose both prophets, so diverse in their way of Hfe and work, yet equally disapproved of by the men of that generation. The present parable, being intended to establish a charge of insincerity, could not with effect refer to the behaviour of the parties censured towards Jesus. For they had never even pretended or seemed to s'de with Him. From the first they had regarded Him and His ways with surprise and distrust, which as time went on deepened into disgust, hostility, and hatred. He and they lay too far apart, not only in spirit but in fundamental principles. They might be wrong and He right, but their dissent could not convict them of insincerity, but only of spiritual blindness. Reference to the case of John, on the other hand, was peculiarly apposite in connection with an attempt to establish such a charge. For John and the Pharisees and Scribes had much in common. Their 'way'â using the term as it is sometimes used in the New Testament, in the sense of a religion â and John's was essentially the same. John came neither eating nor drinkingâ that is, practising ascetic fasting â observing the rules regarding purification, and teaching his disciples forms of prayer; just as the Pharisees did, who fasted oft, scrupulously attended to ceremonial washing, and said many prayers. The watchword of both parties was righteousness, and their professed aim to keep the law in all its parts. This agreement in principle and aim is what is referred to in the expression, "John came unto you in the way of righteousness." The phrase is not employed to express the common-place truth that John was a righteous man. It means: " John came in your own way; the way you loved and professed to walk in, the good old way as you might think it, comparing it with mine which might appear to you a new way involving objectionable innovations: neglect of fasting and ablutions. Sabbath desecrations, and the like." The implied assertion is that they had no excuse for not believing in John such as they might plausibly allege for not believing in Himself. If they disbelieved

in John it could not be on account of his principles or his practice; it must be solely on account of the earnestness with which he pro-
Vide Acts ix. 2 j xix. 9, c. Matt. ix. 14; xi. 18.
' John iii. 25. Luke xi. I. Matt. xxi. 32.
claimed his principles, and insisted on their being carried out in conduct.

Yes! the earnestness of John was his one grand offence in the eyes of his contemporaries. He came in their own way of righteousness and that they approved of, but he came with such consuming earnestness that, zealots though they were, they were repelled and shocked. The man seemed out of his senses: possessed, so to speak, with a demoniac zeal for holiness. Such zeal was unwholesome, and also uncomfortable, for it attached supreme importance to moral law, while scrupulously attentive to ritual. It rebuked vice in kings; yea, even in Pharisaic zealots themselves. So they condemned the Baptist, and in doing so convicted themselves of insincerity; exhibited themselves playing the part of the son in the parable, saying to his father bidding him go work in the vineyard, "I go, sir," and after all not going. They said, ' I go, sir," by agreeing with John's general aim, and busying themselves about righteousness. They " went not," by disapproving of John's spirit of downright moral earnestness and behaving as moral triflers, attending seriously to minutiae, neglecting the great matters of the law.

It would have been possible to represent the religionists of Judaea in this light, in parabolic form, without introducing a second son. The parable might have run, "A certain man had a son, and he said to hifn, ' Go, my son, work to-day in my vineyard;' and he said, ' I go, sir, and went not;' " and the interpretation: " John summoned you to walk in the way of legal piety, and ye affected great zeal for that way; nevertheless ye walked not in it." But the introduction of a second figure serves several good purposes. The picturesque interest of the parable is immensely increased by contrast. The character which it is the chief object of the speaker to describe is more exactly defined and estimated by com- 1 So Olshausen. Trench refers in general terms to his view, without naming him, and explains its import without saying whether he approves it or not. "An emphasis," he remarks, "has been sometimes laid on the words, in the way of rtghteoustiess."' " This is a most unsatisfactory way of disposing of a view which is either a conceit, or the key to the interpretation of the parable. We have no doubt at all that it is the latter.

parison with another type, also faulty but not so criminal. Then by this device it is made possible to present to view the whole behaviour of the Pharisaic class towards John, from the days of his appearing in the desert till now. They are exhibited not only as giving a hypocritical response to the Baptist's summons, but as persisting in their first mood when the course of events seemed to demand a change of mind. When the class represented by the publicans and the harlots had responded to John's call and repented, and when by general consent he had been accepted as a prophet, their inmost thoughts remained unaltered. For prudential reasons they might have changed their tone, and ceased to complain of the Baptist's extreme and unreasonable temper as an excuse for keeping aloof from his movement, but they had not changed their heart. Finally the use of comparison gave a natural occasion for the question by which the auditors were drawn unwittingly into self-condemnation.

In these remarks we have virtually assumed that one of the two sons—the one who represents the degraded classes—is introduced as a mere foil to the other, that representing the religious leaders of the people. If this assumption be correct, then we should expect to find the latter first mentioned in the parable. The principal character naturally takes precedence of the foil; the main object of censure of the figure introduced merely to give point to the censure. For this reason we have without much hesitation adopted the order in which the two sons are named in the Vatican text. Our chief feeling indeed is one of surprise that there should have been any considerable variation in the manuscript readings of the passage. The difficulty is not so much to decide which is the more probable reading, as to account for the variations from the Vatican text which exist, that, viz. of Codex Bezae which puts the son who represents the publicans first, but retains the Vatican reading in the answer to Christ's question, "Which did the will of his father.?" and that of the Textus Receptus, which puts the same son first, and gives the answer as that order naturally demands, the first Yet on reflection we see several things which might mislead copyists and tempt them to try their hand at ' rectifying' what This reading is found in N CLX.

444 The Parabolic Teaching of Christ, book hi.

we regard as the true text. In the first place it might easily be assumed th; it the father wanted only one son to go to work in the vineyard, in which case the first asked must refuse in order to supply a motive for asking the second. Then the solemn manner in which the interpretation commences with a verily I say unto you, might be supposed to imply that Christ was not merely confirming a right answer, but correcting a wrong one given impudently in flagrant contradiction to common sense: the answer, viz. that the son who said, I go, sir, and went not, did the will of the father. This idea would account for the textpf Codex Bezae, which places first the son who said, go not, and afterwards ivent, yet puts into the mouth of the audience the reply to Christ's query who did the will of his father—tjie second. A third misleading element probably was the expression, i? before you â npoayovac), applied by Christ to the publicans and harlots with reference to the Pharisees; which m'ght be interpreted thoughtlessly as applying to the order in which the two sons were named in the parable. Finally, in a similar way the word afterwards (varepov), in the clause ye, when ye had seen it, repented not afterwards, might react upon the arrangement by misleading copyists into the notion that the representative of the class to whom these words refer must come second. When once under these influences the order had been fixed as in the Textus Receptus, the change of the answer given by the audience from the second into the rj" was almost a matter of course, as a rectification to bring the whole passage into harmony with itself.

While these considerations seem to explain the deviations from the Vatican text as errors not unnatural on the part of mechanical copyists, that text itself is recommended by all the probabilities of the case. It was natural that the Pharisees should be mentioned first, not merely as the more important class socially, but because they are the direct object of ' Tregelles (on the printed text of the Greek Testament," pp. 106-8) suggests as the meaning of ovart oq in Codex Bezae, ver. 31, "the man who afterwards repented," which would reconcile the ans. er with this son occupying the first place in the parable. But this view was not likely to occur to copyists or at least to satisfy them. The adoption of Trpisroc along with that order was ultimately certain. Vide on the whole passage Ihe notes of Weatcott and Hort.

animadversion. It has indeed been suggested that the Vatican order had its origin in the fact, that the current interpretation of the parable made it refer to Jews and Gentiles. But the suggestion is gratuitous, because the order in question is equally congruous to the narrower reference. Whether we apply-the parable to Pharisees and publicans on the one hand, or to Jews and Gentiles on the other, it was most fitting that the son who answered insincerely should take precedence of the son who answered rudely. And that this was the actual order seems to be certified by the fact that it is in this order the parties are spoken of in the interpretation. "John came unto you' said Jesus to the men whose conduct He was criticising, "in the way of righteousness, and ye believed him not, but the publicans and harlots believed him." It only remains to add, that the order which we defend corresponds to that in which the same parties are introduced in the parable of the Great Supper.

If the introduction of a second son representing the lowest class of society as a foil to the first representing the higher orders added greatly to the literary and moral value of the parable, it also very manifestly enhanced immeasurably its offensiveness. To tell the proud self-satisfied zealots for righteousness that the moral scum of society was nearer the kingdom of God than they, was to offer them a mortal and unpardonable insult. Publicans and harlots! Why the phrase was proverbial to denote all that was vile, loathsome, and alien to the feelings of the pure, the respectable, and the patriotic. The analogous phrase in Corea, another Judaea in exclusiveness, is " pig-stickers and harlots." In either case the words are so unsavoury as to be unfit to be spoken to polite ears. Barely to use the phrase was a sin against conventional good taste. But to speak of such people, and to add, " bad as they are in their moral rudeness and licentiousness, they are better than you, for they have repented, and that you, with not less need, have not done;" what a deadly offence, surely provocative of bitter resentment and murderous intents!

So Trench.

2 Vide 'History of Corea, Ancient and Modern,"p. 311, by the Rev. John Ross.

Even so, Jesus knew it; and yet He felt constrained to speak this parable and its interpretation. The truth must be spoken, however it might offend, because it concerned more than those to whom it was first addressed. For while mercilessly severe as towards them, this utterance is full ot precious truth as regards the kingdom of God, and the depraved members of the human family. It tells us what we have already learned, but what we cannot hear too often, that the kingdom of God is open to all comers irrespective of their moral antecedents; that there is hope even for the most depraved; nay, that so far from their case being desperate, there are great possibilities of good in them. In telling us so much, it implicitly tells us more: viz. that the kingdoni ot God is not for Jews only but for mankind. For a kingdom that can go so low as publicans and harlots, must be prepared eventually to go to the ends of the earth in quest of citizens. In this parable, as in so many others, there is latent Christian universalism: a parable of judgment in its bearing towards the insincere and hollow-hearted, it is a parable of grace in its bearing towards the sinful everywhere, whom it makes welcome to all its privileges on the one condition of repentance.

In continuance of His prophetic discourse, Jesus addressed to His captious hearers another parable of judgment, saying:

Hear another parable: There was a man, a householder, who planted a vineyard, and set a hedge about it, and dug in it a winepress, and built a tower and let it out to husbandmen, and went abroad. And when the fruit season drew near, he sent his servants to the husbandmen to receive its fruits And the husbaiidmen took his servants and beat one, and killed another, and stoned to death) another. Again he sent other servants more than the first,"" and they did unto them likewise. But afterwards he sent unto them his son, saying. They will reverence my son. But the husbandmen, when they saw the son, said among themselves. This is the heir; come, let us kill him and seize his inheritance. And laying hold of him, they cast hi7n out of the vineyard and slew him. When therefore the lord of the vineyard shall have come, luhat will he do to those husbandmen f They say unto Him, He will miserably destroy those miserable men and will let out the vineyard to other husbandmen who shall render hitn the fruits in their seasons. â Matt. xxi. 33â 41 (Mark xii. iâ 9; LUKE xx. 9â 17).

The abrupt, imperative manner in which the parable is introduced betrays the emotion of the Speaker. He is aware what deep offence the words last spoken have given, and proceeds to reveal His knowledge by foreshadowing His own ' Or his, the ahrov may refer either to the vineyard or to the owner.

2 Trxtt'ovae might refer to quality as well as to number, and is so understood by some. Vide Exposition.

' Kakovc icakttic airok'tah. The play of words in the Greek has been variously done into English by commentators. The attempt of the R. V. adopted above is good enough.

448 The Parabolic Teacjihig of Christ, book hi.

fate. He is aware also that insincerity never stands alone, that when pressed by moral earnestness to cease trifling and become real it resents the demand as an impertinence; and He proceeds with stern resolution, and at all hazards, to show the triflers the truculent side of their character. Yet again He regards the inquiry concerning His authority as a mere affectation, one more manifestation of the Pharisaic vice of insincerity; and He proceeds to show how little His interrogators and their predecessors cared for authority insisting in God's name on anything being done which they did not feel inclined to do. The parable rises to the sublime height of tha sacred passion of prophetic indignation which animated the soul of Jesus during the days immediately preceding His crucifixion. It is by no means a pleasant parable to read, the tragic history to which it relates appearing too clearly through the parabolic veil. But the fault is not the Speaker's, it is that of those whose conduct and doom He describes. It may be a question whether the parabolic form is of much use in such a case; whether when it comes to speaking so plainly as is done here, it were not better to speak more plainly still, and to describe in undisguised, unfigurative terms the repulsive facts of the past, and the not less repulsive events about to happen; as Stephen d'd in after days, whose speech before the Sanhedrim, as has been remarked, is but the commentary and development of the parable before us. One unavoidable result of the adoption of the parabolic form is improbability in the fictitious narrative; for who ever heard of husbandmen, even in the worst governed countries, behaving as these vinedressers."'

The parable is true to Israel's history, but it is not true to natural probability; and for the reason stated in connection with the parable of the Great Supper, to which the same observation applies, viz. that the conduct animadverted on is itself thoroughly unnatural. But why speak in parables when by the nature of the case probability is excluded? Is it that men whose self-complacency will prevent them from seeing the drift of the story may be led on to condemn themselves? We can hardly lay much stress on that, especially when we consider that in the narratives of Mark and Luke the answer to the question, What shall be done to these men?

Sabatier, ' L'Apotre Paul."

Is not ascribed to the audience. Or is it that the Speaker shrinks from referring to Himself without disguise as the Son of God? There is more force in this consideration, for such delicacy and reserve was characteristic of the Son of man, and suitable to the state of humiliation. But perhaps the true explanation is that in this instance Jesus did not so much invent a new parable as use an old one whose words were familiar to Jewish ears, and its meaning generally understood â that, viz., contained in Isaiah's song of the vineyard. At most, our parable is but an old theme worked up with new variations. Every one who heard it knew what the vineyard with its hedge, winepress, and tower signified, and who the vine-dressers were, and who the servants sent for the fruits. These phrases belonged to the established religious dialect of Israel as much as the words pastor, flock, lambs of the flock, Zion, c., do to ours, used by us all without consciousness that we are speaking in figures. In adopting this form of presentation, therefore, Jesus was not so much speaking in parables as using the recognised authority of written prophecy against His opponents, a most appropriate procedure when the question at issue respected His personal authority. It was saying in effect, Let me take Isaiah's familiar parable of the vineyard and expand it a little that I may show you how it stands with you as regards this matter of authority, that we may see whether ye have as much respect for the ascertained will of God as ye pretend, so that ye should be sure to submit to Me if only ye were satisfied that I was an accredited messenger of God.

The parable, it will be observed, does more than show what amount of respect the parties to whom it was addressed had for prophetic authority. It shows that disregard for authority going counter to inclination had been a characteristic of Israel's leaders and representative men all through her history. This does not indeed appear from the mere structure of the parable, for the events described might all fall within the compass of a single fruit season, the servants being sent one after another to demand the produce due in one and the same year, for anything that is said to the contrary; though

Mark xii. 9; Luke xx. 16. Isaiah v, iÂ 450 The Parabolic Teaching- of Christ, book hi.

the number of messengers sent seems hardly compatible with the brief period of a single fruit season, and suggests as the more natural hypothesis a succession of seasons, when the demand for fruit was renewed as the time came round. But the self-evident interpretation of the parable as referring to the prophets under the servants, makes it certain that the mtention of the Speaker was to characterise the behaviour of Israel throughout her long history towards God's messengers. And this broadening of the charge of iniquitous dealing so as to include the misbehaviour of the past, was well fitted to serve Christ's purpose to bring home such a charge to the consciences of His hearers. It raised a strong presumption against these hypocritical inquirers after His authority to show that they belonged to a race whose habit it had all along been to treat authority with contempt, except when it chimed in with their own wishes. In the parable of the Children in the Market-place Jesus had spoken of this generation. He now speaks of all the generations of Israel's headmen as one generation morally, with rebellion in its blood, the original sin transmitted from sire to son. The fact as to the past representatives of this moral generation was indubitable, and the onns probandi lay on the present representatives to show that they were free from. the taint. The likelihood was all the other way, viz. that they would consummate the iniquity of their fathers by committing a greater offence of the kind denounced than any previously committed, and so, filling up the measure of their sin, serve themselves heir to their guilt, and bear its bitter penalty. That this would be the actual fact it is the aim of the latter part of the parable to declare, the reference being to the approaching crucifixion of Jesus, the Christ, and the Son of God, and the subsequent ruin which overtook the Jewish nation.

A very noticeable feature in the parable is the dark picture it presents of the behaviour of the vine-dressers towards the servants sent to demand the fruit. The most violent acts are selected as typical. One is flayed by stripes, another is slain by the sword, a third is put to death by stoning iâ the three instances forming an ascending series of atrocities. So in Matthew's version, and similarly in Mark and Luke, the con-1 Vide Lightfoot, Horae Hebraicae.

duct of the criminals advances from bad to worse, though the stages are not so distinctly marked. In this description Christ's audience would not recognise their own likeness; for as yet they had been guilty of nothing so truculent, thoug'a they were on the point of committing even greater atrocities. They had not treated the 'servant' of their time, John the Baptist, in so barbarous a fashion. He had indeed been beheaded, but not by them. All they had done was to look on him as a madman, and so excuse themselves for disregarding his summons to repentance. The triflers hgd not found John's ministry sufficiently provoking or formidable to carry their opposition beyond depreciatory speech and cold neglect. The implied allegation of the parable is that they would have gone greater lengths had they been forced to it by circumstances. The direct assertion is that their predecessors had gone greater lengths; had actually beaten, insulted, and killed their prophets. They had also committed offences of a less aggravated character. They too had manifested their hostility to the prophetic order under the minor forms of evil speaking, mockery, and ridicule. The drunkards of Ephraim mocked Isaiah's reiterated warnings and expostulations by comparing him to a teacher of children, with his everlasting tsav-la-isav, tsav-la-tsav, kav-la-kav, kav-la-kav? But they had often shown themselves capable of worse things than banter and blasphemy; even of down-right brutality, as in the case of Zechariah stoned to death in the court of the house of the Lord. And acts of this more aggravated character are singled out for mention to show what the spirit of rel'gious insincerity tends to and culminates in. This is what ultimately comes of that temper which beg'ns by saying politely, "I go, sir," and not going. Press insincerity a little, and the politeness gives place to rudeness; press it still more, and rudeness in word gives place to rudeness in act; press it still further, and minor indignities, such as smiting with the hand, spitting, pulling off the hair, give place to more serious forms of violence, such as the inflicting of wounds with lethal weapons; press it yet

> Especially is this true of Luke, whose version is somewhat toned down throughout. Isaiah xxviii. lo. Viie remarks on this passage at p. 23.
> 2 Chron. xxiv. 21.

further, and violence culminates in murder. Behold the polite but false-hearted gentleman, transformed by degrees into a ruffian. Who could have believed it.-' yet how natural it all is. " Is thy servant a dog."' " asked Hazael of the prophet, quite sincerely possibly, and yet he did all the atrocious acts specified. History supplies ample material for illustrating the strange transformation, and proving the humbling truth that refinement and savagery do not lie far apart in human nature. The most startling example is supplied in the case of the very men to whom this parable was addressed. In their ordinary relations with their fellow-men, the religious heads of Israel were, without doubt, courteous and gentle, pleasant, if not sincere, in speech, and duly attentive to all social proprieties. Yet these same men were responsible for all the indignities, iniquities, and brutalities of the crucifixion and its accompaniments.

Another significant feature in the parable is the particularity with which the details connected with the construction of the vineyard are specified. For the general purpose of the story it might have been enough to have said, A certain householder planted a vineyard, and let it out to husbandmen. The introduction of the processes of hedging, digging a winepress, hewing out a place for a vat, and building a tower, is not a mere affair of word-painting for picturesque effect; considering the circumstances and the mood of the Speaker, such merely literary play was very unlikely. The design is to signalise the contrast between the spirit of the owner and that of the men to whom the vineyard was entrusted. The owner has an eye to fruit; the details depicting the construction of the vineyard all point towards fruit as the chief end, and they are enumerated for no other reason. There is a hedge that the vines may not be spoiled by wild beasts; a press and vat that the grapes may be squeezed and the juice preserved; a tower that the ripe fruit may not be stolen. The didactic significance of these particulars is not, as in the original form of the allegory in Isaiah, that all has been done that could be done for the vineyard, so as to make the owner free from blame, but that all has been done with

Mark speaks of a viroxi'ivtov, which signifies the vat for receiving the juice running into it from the press above.

one object in view, viz. the production of fruit. In keeping with this emphasising of fruitfulness as the reason of the existence of the vineyard fully equipped for the purpose, is the reiterated persistent demand for the fruit when the season came round, as also the intimation of the owner's purpose, on conclusively ascertaining that no fruit was to be forthcoming, to entrust his vineyard to other husbandmen, who should render the fruits in their seasons. On the other hand, what was the temper of the vine-dressers Was it that of men who wished to keep the fruit to themselves instead of giving it to the owner? No; but rather that of men who never thought of fruit, but only of the honour and privilege of being entrusted with the keeping of the vineyard.

They were triflersâ men utterly devoid of earnestness, and the practical purpose of the property committed to their charge they habitually forgot. The hedge and the press and the tower might as well not have been there. When the servants came for the fruit they were simply surprised. " Fruit, did you say we have occupied the position of vine-dressers, and duly drawn our wages; what more do you want?" Such was the actual fact in regard to the spiritual heads of Israel. They had been entrusted with a valuable institution; an elect nation furnished with good laws, and meant to be a holy nation, a people to God's praise. And speaking generally, they had lost sight of the end of Israel's calling, and had made no use of the means provided for its attainment. They had occupied their position for their own glory; taken pay and done no work. They had neglected the vineyard, so that it brought forth no grapes, or at least only wild grapes. In a word, they had committed the sin to which privileged classes have ever been prone, that of thinking only of privilege and forgetting duty. All through Israel's history her spiritual guides, priests, scribes, and elders, not to speak of her princes, ' In the following similitude of the Rejected Stone, these others' are called a'nation," which seems to point to the rejection of Israel, and tho call of the Gentiles; the nation being the true, spiritual Israel of God in every land. (So Olshausen.) Keim ('Jesuvon Nazara,"iii. 119) thinks that a reference to the Gentiles is not in keeping with the scope of the parable which animadverts on the sin, not of Israel, b'jt of her rulers;, and that the ' others' are Messiah's faithful followers in Israel.

had been saying, ' I go, sir," without going, professing to keep a vineyard which they did not keep.

Nothing is more remarkable in the history of Israel than the constant co-existence within her pale of two entirely opposite classes of menâ that of the moral triflers, too numerously represented among those exercising official influence, and that of the men of consuming zeal for righteousness, that is, the prophets. It is strange indeed that a people so prone to baseness should have so many noble men, who made it their duty to remonstrate with it for its baseness, and summon it to a better life. The parable accentuates this fact in order to show the enormity of Israel's guilt and the justness of her doom. In the versions of Matthew and Mark the multitude of servants sent is very expressly alluded to. After stating, by way of sample, how these were treated, the first Evangelist adds, "Again he sent other servants, more than the first." Mark in like manner uses the significant phrase, " and many others." Luke's version is defective at this point, making mention only of three, and giving no hints that more were sent. There can be no doubt as to which account is most in keeping with the didactic drift of the parable. It has been suggested that the expression Trkeiovas in Matthew refers not to number but to quality, and that the purpose is to set forth an enhancement of Israel's guilt, by exhibiting her as treating with indignity a higher order of prophets sent subsequently to those first spoken of. On this view the parable would specify three stages or degrees of criminality: first, evil treatment of a certain number of servants; second, similar treatment of servants of higher grade; third, the same misconduct towards one who was not a servant, but a son. Now, it is perfectly true that the word Trkilovas might mean, not more in the numerical sense, but more respectable, of higher rank. Nor is the objection to this view insuperable that no such distinction as is implied existed between the earlier and later Old Testament prophets, for the

The view above given excludes the idea that the vine-dressers were engaged on the metayer system of paying rent with part of the produce. On our view there was no produce. The sin of the husbandmen was not dishonesty, but neglect,

So Morrison.

reference might be to John the Baptist,! or even to John and Jesus together; for the latter, though referred to as the son, might also be referred to as one of the prophets, and on a level with John, as in the earlier parable of the Children in the Marketplace. The contemporaries of Jesus sinned against Him as a prophet, as well as in His higher capacity as the Messiah, and they committed the one offence earlier than the other. But the interpretation in question, nevertheless, is not to be approved. It is uncertain at the best, and it is not required by the didactic drift of the parable. To aggravate Israel's guilt, it was enough to refer to the number of her prophets without insisting on any distinction between them as to rank or importance, which, though real, might not be apparent to the parties concerned; as indeed, if John, or even Jesus, be referred to, it was not, for their contemporaries did not see in them greater prophets than Elijah, or Isaiah, or Jeremiah. They thought they paid them very great respect in putting them on a level with the great prophets of the olden time.

The last point in the parable is the mission of the son, in connection with which the guilt of the vine-dressers reaches its highest measure. In the narratives of Mark and Luke the value set upon this son by the owner, his father, is emphasised. Luke represents the father as calling him ' beloved'; Mark adds that he was an only son. These particulars are not added to enhance the criminality of the occupants of the vineyard, but to show the intensity of the owner's desire for fruit. He has found by many experiments that the tenants are utterly regardless of his claims, but before arriving at the conclusion that to bring them to their senses is hopeless, he resolves to try once more, in the most effective way possible, by the mission of his son. He is aware of the risk run; for the probability is that the men who have habitually treated his messengers with disrespect will not be restrained by any feeling of reverence from repeating their misbehaviour towards his son, and in case they do, his sorrow will be great for the loss of a beloved and only son. Never-tlieless, there is a possibility, and he will run the risk, so: aixious is he to bring them to reason. But the result, as 1 So Goebel, who, like Bengel, Campbell, c., takes Trxtiovac as an adjective of quality.

45 6 The Parabolic Teaching of Christ, book hi.

was to be expected, is unhappy. The mission of the son only brings a new opportunity of outrage, and a temptation to more audacious and complete acts of rebellion than any hitherto perpetrated. Seeing this last messenger, and discovering somehow that he is not a servant but a son, the vinc-dressers say to each other, "This is the heir; come, let us kill him, and seize his inheritance;" and forthwith proceed to carry the nefarious scheme into effect, casting him out of the vineyard as a place he had no right to enter, and putting him ruthlessly to death. Their calculation is that they will be no longer troubled with messages about fruit; they will now enjoy their position without molestation, and be practically not tenants, but landlords. Their presumption is based upon long experience of impunity in connection with their habitual insubordination. They make the natural and common mistake of imagining that because sentence against an evil work is not executed speedily it will never be executed at all; and so their heart is fully set in them to do evil.2 But the truth is that they have only exhausted the patience of their employer, and his resources for bringing them to repentance, and filled up the measure of their iniquity by committing an unpardonable offence; and in accordance with the laws by which the moral order of the world is regulated, condign punishment must speedily overtake them. This, accordingly, is what is announced in the closing sentence of the parable, in which it is declared that he who has sent so many messengers will at length come himself, and inflict on the criminals a punishment closely answering to their offenceâ consisting in their ejection from the vineyard which they thought to make their own, and their utter destruction.

The representation is in accordance with the facts of Israel's subsequent history, however improbable it may appear in the parable. Certainly it does strike one as strange that the owner of a vineyard should act as representedâ coming to judge and visit with doom unfaithful servants, acts which seem appropriate not to a landowner, but to a king. On this account this part of the parable has been regarded as an. allegorising addition by the evangelists. But if we are to

In Mark the act of murder precedes the casting out.

Ecclesiastes. viii. Ji. So Weiss, ' Das Markus-Evangelium."

be guided by such considerations then the authenticity of the whole parable must be called in question. For everything in it is improbable: the behaviour of the vine-dressers, the long patience of the owner under a series of unparalleled outrages, not less than the ultimate judicial rigour with which the offenders are visited by the same person, he being merely a landowner and not a king. Throughout, the natural probabilities of the story are sacrificed to the requirements of its moral interpretation.

The account given in the parable of the mission of the son has an important bearing on two topics, viz. the personal self-consciousness of Christ, and the knowledge possessed by the Jews of His peculiar claims. The son is described as the only and well-beloved son of his father, and it is natural to suppose that as that son represents the Speaker, He claims for Himself all that he ascribes to the former. In that case this text must be associated with the remarkable one in the eleventh chapter of Matthew as vindicating for Jesus a unique position in relation to God. The vine-dressers are represented as knowing the son and heir. Is it implied that the men to whom the parable is addressed knew the Speaker to be the Christ, the Son of the living God 1 In that case Jesus virtually charges them with being on the point of putting to death one whom they admitted to be Divine, or at least invested with Messianic dignity. But probably all that is strictly implied is that they might have known who the Speaker was, and would have known had their hearts been pure. In asking Him as to His authority they affected not to know who He was, and perhaps it was not a mere affectation, for prejudice and passion had blinded their eyes. But they were not on that account without blame, for they had resisted evidence and crushed down rising conviction. Had they been sincere and single-minded, their hearts would have yielded to the" force of truth, and hailed Jesus as their king. They were not, therefore, sinning in ignorance simply against the Son of man, they were sinning against light, and dangerously near the mortal sin of blasphemy against the Holy Ghost. Hence the severity of tone in the sentences appended to our parable concerning the Rejected Stone, which might be regarded a3 forming another parable. Availing Himself of a well-known 4-5 8 Tlie Parabolic Teaching of Christ, book hi.

text in a psalm, Jesus happily describes His own fortunes and those of His hearers in terms borrowed from the art of house-building. The men who have just been compared tu vine-dressers now become builders, and the heir cast out of the vineyard and murdered is now a stone thrown aside as useless. But the new figure enables the Speaker to give a glimpse of what is to happen to Himself after evil men have wrought their worst. The text from the psalm declares that the stone which the builders refused is to become the head of the corner. The reference is to despised Israel, restored to her former glory, by God's grace, a marvel to all beholders. But Jesus, appropriating the prophecy to Himself, thereby intimates to His hearers that in killing Him they will not be done with Him: He will be raised to a place of power, an object of admiration to friends, a source of dismay to foes. Woe, then to the builders who had scornfully rejected Him. Then their case would not be that of men stumbling against a stone, as many had done in ignorance, sinning against the Son ot man to their hurt and loss, but not unpardonably. It would be that of men on whom a great stone falls, descending in judgment to grind them to powder.

Jesus, we are told by the Evangelist, spake again to the people in parables, saying:

The kingdom of heaven is likened utito a certai7i king who made a marriage feast for his son. And he sent forth his servants to call the called to the feast, and they would not come. Again he sent forth other servants saying, Tell the invited: Behold, I have made ready my difiner," my oxen and my fed beasts are slain, and all things are ready, come to the feast. But they made light of it, and wetit their ways, one to his own farm, atiother to his merchandise; and the rest laid hold on his servants, and entreated them shamefully, and killed them. But the king was wroth, and he sent his armies and destroyed those murderers, and burned their city. Then saith he to his servaitts. The wedding is ready, but those who were invited were not worthy. Co ye therefore unto the thoroughfares and as many as ye shall find bid

Koxiaai roiiq KikXrjiikvovg.

2 apiotov, the midday meal, "with which the series of marriage festivities would begin."â Meyer.

3 The akoioaq of the T. R. is omitted in the best MSS.

Some texts have the singular to ar drtv a, a reading probably due to a feeling that armies were not needed for such an expedition, or to the knowledge that the Romans used only one army against Jerusalem. So Fritsche. There is a certain tone of exaggeration in the expression, or perhaps we should rather say vagueness and inexactitude.

5 6 yaioc; the plural in ver. 2 refers to the festivities connected with the wedding.

rdc liil, olovq, rwv osihv, literally the outlets of the ways, exitus viarum, Vulg. The word lu o oq occurs only once in the N. T., and it is impossible to determine with certainty what is meant by the expression in the text. It may either signify the roads leading out from the town into the to the marriage feast. â A7id those servants going out into the roads, gathered together all as manjy as they found, both bad and good; and the wedding chamber was filled with guests. But when the king came in to behold the guests he saw there a man not clad with a wedding garment. And he saith unto him, Friend, how camest thou in hither not having a wedding garme7it? And he was speechless. Then the king said to the ministers Bind him hand and foot and cast him out into the outer darkness; there shall be the weeping and the gnashing of teeth. For many are called, but few chosen.â Si. Matt. xxii. 1â 14.

The manner in which this parable is introduced does not imply any strict view as to the connection with what goes before, and it is not likely to have come in just at this point. It may be too much to say that it occupies an impossible position; but it certainly does seem to interrupt the course of the history as indicated in the narratives of the other Synoptical Evangelists. From internal evidence, however, it is manifest that the parable belongs to the last days of our Lord's life, and is to be regarded as one of the memorable utterances of the Passion week. In its first part it has a close affinity with the preceding parable of the vine-dressers, presenting a gloomy picture of similar misconduct visited with similar doom. That parable exposes Israel's neglect of covenanted duty; this her contempt of God's grace. The two are mutually complementary, and present together a full view of Israel's sin. The parable now to be ccmsidered bears a still more obvious resemblance to one already studied under the second division, that of the Great Supper in the fourteenth chapter of Luke. The common features are so numerous and striking as to have led many to regard the two as one parable differently reported by the first and third Evangelists. The opinion is one which can hardly fail to suggest itself, and yet it is based on a very superficial, country, or the crossings of such, or the streets leading into open places and squares in the town. The general idea is: places where men are likely to be found, whether in town or in country. wovq. Westcott and Hort adopt the reading ovq.

6 vvn(pu)v, the reading of S. B. L.; 6 yafioq in T. R.

' Siokovoiq. 4 So Keim.

Keim admits that the materials out of which the parable is constructed (by the Evangelist) suit that late period.

This opinion is held, among others, by Calvin and Maldonatus.

outward view of the narratives. Without doubt the theme is one and the same, but it is a theme twice handled by the same artist, and for diverse purposes. If the essence or soul of a parable lie in its didactic drift, then these two parables are broadly distinct, while in several circumstances or features strikingly like. The earlier of the two is a parable of grace, having for its aim to show what sort of men care for and shall enjoy the blessings of the kingdom; the later is a parable of judgment, having for its aim to show the doom of those who in any way despise, abuse, or undervalue these blessings. There is indeed both grace and judgment in each parable, but in very different proportions, and with differently-placed emphasis. The host in the earlier parable declares that the first invited shall not taste of his feast; that is the amount of the judicial element, and even this comes in not so much as a threatening of punishment, but rather as an indirect intimation that they are not the kind of men for whom the joys of the kingdom are designed, these being reserved for the hungry. In the later parable the host shows his grace by inviting and re-inviting to his feast, and even humbling himself to extol the entertainment in prospect with a view to excite desire; but all this takes place only to enhance the culpability of those who after all refuse to come, and to justify the severity with which they are visited.

The difference just indicated in the didactic drift of the two parables explains at once their resemblances and their points of contrast. Common to both are a feast, a refusal from the first invited, and a subsequent invitation to a lower class. These resemblances arise out of the fact that the two parables deal in different ways and to different intents with the grace of the kingdom; the one showing who are its chosen objects, the other the danger of despising it. A feast is a most appropriate emblem of the kingdom as a kingdom of grace, likely to be employed as often as there was occasion to speak of that topic. The refusal of the first invited shows the tendency of preoccupation to produce indifference, and supplies a motive for inviting persons not at first contemplated as guests, though more likely from their circumstances to welcome the benefit put within their reach. That final invitation thus brought about, for the first time brings into 462 The Parabolic Teaching of Christ, book hi.

light the true genius of grace, accrediting it with a benignant will to make its blessings free to all, and if possible freest to those who most urgently need them. On the other hand, the parables differ in these respects, that in the earlier the feast is given by a private individual, in the later by a king to his subjects, and on a very important occasionâ the marria' e of his son; in the one the invitation to the first invited is not repeated after it has been refused, in the other it is repeated with such descriptive accompaniments as are fitted to awaken desire; in the one the first invited are simply indifferent, in the other they not only show indifference, but some of them at least proceed to deeds of violence, and these are visited with violent penalties. All these variations are accounted for by the simple consideration that the later parable is a parable of judgment. The feast is one given by a king on a solemn occasion, because such a feast gives scope for a kind of offences and of punishments which could have no place in connection with a private feast. It is a feast possessing political significance, presence at which is a mark of loyalty, absence from which indicates a spirit of disaffection which is sure to manifest itself in deeds of rebellion, making vengeance inevitable. The invitation is repeated to make the king's patience conspicuous, to bring more fully into the light the latent hostility of his subjects, and to exhibit their persistent refusal as utterly inexcusable. Acts of violence are ascribed to some of the invited because such enormities were the actual reply of Israel's representatives to God's overtures of love, and the mention of them prepares the hearer for sympathising with the doom pronounced against them. That doom is inexorably severe, but it is only an exact anticipation of the fact, and a parable setting forth the judgment of Heaven on contempt of grace could not, if it aimed at adequate statement, say less. In all these respects the variations are only such as we should expect from any expert in the use of the parabolic style. And the method of variation is also what we should expect such an one to employ in such a case; that is, the adaptation of an old theme to a new case, rather than the invention of an entirely new theme. The common theme forms the link of connection between two parables, both of which relate to grace; the variations in the later form from the earlier point it out as a parable setting forth the judgment of grace despised. What is common gives emphasis to what is peculiar, and bids us mark what it is that is judged. Why-should we hesitate to ascribe such skilful variation for so important a purpose to the Great Master rather than to the Evangelist."' Why refuse to Christ the use of a method which seems not to have been unknown even to the Rabbis t One point in the variation of the later from the earlier parable we have purposely overlooked in the foregoing remarks; that, viz., relating to the guest without a wedding robe. In Luke's parable there is nothing but welcome for the poor without exception, while in Matthew's, judicial rigour is exercised even on one of them who is found unsuit-ably attired. At this point the difference between the two parables in didactic scope becomes specially apparent. We feel that such a feature would altogether mar the beauty of the former, whose aim throughout, and in every phrase, is to emphasise the graciousness of the kingdom. In the case of the latter, on the other hand, the wedding-robe scene, however unwelcome, is in keeping with the general tenor of the story.

Wunsche cites no less than three parables from the Talmud more or less like the one we are considering. The first is of a king who asks guests to a feast, not telling them when it was to be, but bidding them prepare for it by bathing, washing their garments, c. Those anxious to be present watch at the door of the palace for the symptoms of the feast approaching; the easy-minded go about their business and are taken by surprise, and come in every-day attire to be rejected. The moral isâ â Watch, for ye know not the day of death. The second is of a king who invited to a feast and bade the guests bring each a seat. The guests brought all sorts of thingsâ carpets, stools, pieces of wood, c. The king ordered that each should sit on what he had brought. Those who brought poor seats complained: Were these seats for a palace? The king replied, they had themielves to blame. Moralâ we shall fare as we deserve. The third is of a king who distributed costly robes among his servants; the wise folded them up and took care of them, the foolish wore them. The garments were demanded back; the wise render up their trust with approbation; the foolish had to send the garments to the washing, and were put in prison. The garment is the soul given to man by God, pure, and to be rendered back pure. ' Neue Beitrage zur Erlauterung der Evangelien aus Talmud und Midrasch," p. 252. For the first of these parables vide also Meuschen, Nov. Test, ex Talmud illustratum."

464 The Pa7'abolic Teachijig of Christ, book hi.

It, too, is a story of grace indeed, but of grace unworthily met, and manifesting itself in judicial severity against those who commit the wrong. And just because it is a parable of judgment, there must be judgment whenever it is called for. There must be no partiality. If the first invited are to be punished because they sin against grace in one way, the guests invited in the second place must be punished if they sin against grace in another way. The relevancy of the wedding-robe scene in a parable of judgment vindicating grace against injury can be legitimately denied only if it be impossible for the recipients of grace to commit any offence against it, which, as we shall see, is far enough from being the case. The lesson taught in the second scene is thoroughly germane to the lesson taught in the first. The first shows the judgment of those who despise and reject grace, the second the judgment of those who receive it, but in a disrespectful manner. The only question that can reasonably be raised is whether it is likely that Christ would combine the two lessons in dne parable, and speak them at the same time and to the same audience. That is a question affecting the literary rather than the doctrinal character of the parable. It may plausibly be alleged that literary tact would dictate that only one of these lessons should be taught at one time, so as to insure that it should receive due attention; and as no such want of tact may be ascribed to Christ, it may hence be inferred that the combination is due to the Evangelist: another instance of Matthew's habit of joining together sayings of kindred doctrinal import. If such were the case, we should have to admit that the joining has been very well done. But it is so well done, the dovetailing is so complete, and the parable is so manifestly a doctrinal unity, that we are constrained to doubt the alleged want of tact, and the inference founded on it. Why should not Christ have joined these two lessons together Each gives point to the other, rather than weakens its force. The second, taken along with the first, says, that so determined is God that His grace shall not be scorned, that even those who receive it shall be punished for disrespect. The first, taken along with the second, says, if God be so severe towards those who despise His grace, let those who receive it, but not with due reverence, beware. The two tofjether vindicate the Divine impartiality, and form a complete doctrine on the subject to which they relate.

With these preliminary observations we proceed to consider in detail the two parts of the parable in which these distinct lessons are taught.

I. The judgment of grace despised set forth in

THE FIRST SCENE (vers. Iâ 9).

The emblem selected to represent the grace of the Kingdom is a fit one. It is that of a marriage-feast. The term yctxouj might indeed mean any great feast resembling a wedding-feast in magnitude and importance; as, for example, a feast celebrating the event of an heir to an estate arriving at his majority, or of a king delivering his kingdom into the hands of his son. But the proper sense of the word is a marriage feast, and we can have the less hesitation in ascribing to it this meaning here, that the same emblem was employed by Jesus at other times to denote the kingdom of heaven, especially on the memorable occasion when He was interrogated concerning the neglect of fasting by His disciples. No fitter emblem could be found at once to exhibit in brightest lustre the benignity of God, and to test the spirit of men. It suggests the most intimate union possible between the Head of the Church and the members, that of wedlock; for the guests are also the Bride. And if men refuse an invitation to a marriage-feast, what favour are they likely to accept,"'â what more certain indication of ill-will can there be than such refusal

Those who are invited to the wedding-feast are represented as persons already invited. The servants are sent forth to call Tom Kekkrjixivovs. This term connects the New Testament history of Israel with that of the Old Testament, and denotes the position in which the chosen race were placed by the ministry of the prophets. For the prophets performed a

In Esther (ix. 22) the word ydfioi is used for the feast by which the Jews commemorated their deliverance from the plot of Raman. Kuinoel thinks the occasion referred to in the text is that of the delivery of the kingdom into the hands of the son. Meyer, on the other hand, contends that ydfioi is never used for anything else than a marriage-feast.

double function. They were on the one hand servants of moral law, demanding in God's name the fruit of genuine righteousness; and on the other servants of the promise or purpose of grace, preaching under various forms a Messianic Hope, an ideal bliss to come in the end of the days. Through this eloquent ministry of the Better Hope the people of Israel were called to participation in the Messianic wedding-feast. But they were merely called; while the fulfilment of Messianic prophecy tarried, it could not be ascertained how the offered privilege would be received. Their attitude towards the prophetic ministry of righteousness could be, and was, ascertained at once. Throughout her whole history the chosen people showed plainly that the Divine demand for righteousness was one she did not mean to comply with; and the damning verdict of the record is endorsed in the preceding parable of the Vinedressers. But all the while she might flatter herself that she was welcoming the Messianic Hope, and looking with eager expectancy for the advent of the era when all the glowing ideals of the prophets should be realised. Whether that was so indeed could only be tested when the era of fulfilment arrived, and the parable before us describes the result of the experiment. The test is supposed to apply not merely to the generation who witnessed the fulfilment, but to all the generations going before to whom the Messianic prophecies had been addressed. Here, as in the last parable, the moral solidarity of all the generations of Israel is recognised, and the spirit of the past is judged from the behaviour of the present. It is assumed that former generations would have acted as the one then living, if placed in the same circumstances. Therefore the servants are represented as calling the called, though the called of the prophetic era were distinct from the called of the era of fulfilment.

The ' servants' are Jesus and His disciples. The call covers the period of Christ's personal ministry, and its substance isâ The kingdom of heaven in all the fulness of grace is here; come, and participate in its joys. The Baptist we do not include among the servants, because he was a minister of law rather than of grace; like all the prophets doubtless performing a function in relation to the Messianic Hope, still belonging in spirit and tendency to the era of expectation rather than to the era of fulfilment. He had his place in thi. last parable as one of the many messengers whom God sent to demand fruit; but he has no place in this, except as one ol those through whom the first preparatory call was addressed to Israel. On the other hand, we have no hesitation in including Jesus among the servants who are sent forth to invite the guests to the feast, long expected, now at hand. Though He be the son whose marriage is about to be celebrated, yet is He also a servant, the chief of the callers to the feast. There may be an incongruity in this union of two such opposite characters in the same person, but it is not greater than that resulting from the same parties be'ng at once bride and guests. However incongruous, both combinations are matters of fact; nor do they mar the propriety of the parabolic narrative, for neither is allowed to appear therein. So far as the parable is concerned, the son and the servant are distinct, as are also the bride and the guests, though in reality the two in either case are one.

The result of the invitation to the feast, briefly told, is that the invited are not inclined to come. In these mild, simple terms does Jesus describe the reception He had met with at the hands of His countrymen, as the Herald of the kingdom of grace. The account stands in striking contrast with the view presented in the last parable of the reception given to the last messenger of the owner of the vineyard, his son and heir. How is this contrast to be explained Partly by the consideration that the two parables contemplate the history of Israel from different positions, the one looking on it from the Old Testament view point, and the other from the New. In the one case, what is done to the last messenger forms the climax of a long series of iniquities, and is therefore drawn in as dark colours as possible, and made the ground of Israel's doom. In the other the New Testament history of Israel ceases to be the background and comes into the foreground, and so resolves itself into several distinct scenes, in which, in accordance with fact, she gets a second chance after her misbehaviour towards the ' son' of the former parable, before being visited with her final doom. This second chance coincides with the ministry of the apostles, after Christ's death and final departure from the earth. And as Israel was tc get this second chance, a signal proof of the patience of God, and clearing His final severity of all appearance of undue rigour, it was fitting that her misbehaviour towards the first callers should be described in mitigated terms, to leave room, as it were, for a further day of grace. Had the first callers in this parable been treated as the heir was treated in the last, the proper sequel had been not a second invitation, but judgment. But this explanation does not go to the root of the matter. It amounts to this, that the structure of the parable required the facts as to the reception given to the first callers to be understated, implying of course that the facts were worse than represented. The true key to the solution of the difficulty is to bear in mind the different capacities in which Jesus acts in the two parables. In the Vine-dressers He, like all His predecessors, is a prophet of moral law, demanding in God's name true righteousness. In the Weddi7ig Feast He is a minister of grace preaching the gospel of the kingdom. Now His reception in these two distinct capacities was respectively as represented. It was as a prophet of duty that He was maltreated by His countrymen. He provoked them to wrath by His exposure of their sham sanctities in punctilious performance of ritual ablutions, fastings, prayers, tithe-paying, c., accompanied by scandalous neglect of the great matters of the law. The key to the crucifixion is utterances by the Prophet of Nazareth such as those collected together in the great antipharisaic discourse in the twenty-fourth chapter of Matthew. On the other hand, the reception given to Jesus as the Minister of grace was just that indicated in our parable. He invited His countrymen to a great feast and they would not come. They did not hate Him or visit Him with violence for His invitations. They simply were not attracted by what He offered, and turned heedless away, as from an idle dreamer. At times the boon He held up to view for a moment appeared tempting,â a kingdom and a kingship of this world, real and worth having; but the deluded soon discovered that they were mistaken, to their disappointment and disgust. In this indifference towards the Minister of grace the people of Israel were far less culpable than in their hostility to the Prophet of

The above is, in effect, Goebel's view.

law. For righteousness was a thing familiar to them. It was their own watchword and 'way." But the kingdom of heaven, as Jesus presented it, was a new phenomenon, strange, puzzhng even to honest minds, even to the Baptist himself. Shyness, doubt, misunderstanding for a time were pardonable, and were. so regarded by Jesus. He did not denounce those who stood in doubt of this new movement. He only said,

"Blessed is he that is not offended in Me." The parable before us is in full sympathy with that considerate, gentle utterance. Of those to whom the Author of the parable preached the gospel of the kingdom it is said simply they were not willing to come. And their unwillingness is, by implication, treated as a pardonable misunderstanding when the king is represented as sending forth other servants to renew the invitations, with instructions to appraise the feast, so as to awaken desire. It is a notable instance of the 'sweet reasonableness' of Christ, as well as a faithful reflection of the patience of God.

The ' other servants," who receive this new commission, are of course the apostles, whom Jesus had chosen to carry on His work after He left the world, and of whose agency He could not but think much at this time when His own end was so near. The kingdom of heaven was not to disappear when He personally left the world; it would go on its course in spite of all that men might do to Himself, not to say in consequence thereof, and the preaching of His companions whom He had sought to embue with His spirit, would give Israel another opportunity of receiving thankfully the things freely bestowed by God. Very notable, in connection with the mission of the apostles, is the special direction given to the second set of ' callers ': " Say to those invited, ' Behold, I have prepared my dinner, my oxen and fed beasts slain, and all things ready; come to the feast.'" The second ' callers' are not merely to invite to, they are to commend the feast, with a view to create desire. The fact suggests a contrast between the ministry of Christ and that of His apostles. The apostles differed from their Master in two respects. They were more aggressive or urgent in their manner of preaching, and they preached a more developed gospel. Jesus went forth into the world and said quietly 470 The Parabolic Teaching of Christ, book hi.

The kingdom is come. Nor did He explain fully or elaborately wherein the kingdom consisted, and what blessings it brought; at most He conveyed only hints of these by aphorism or parable, or by kind words and deeds to sinful and sorrowful men. He did not strive, or cry, nor did any one hear His voice in the streets. He did not aim at teaching the multitude the mysteries of the kingdom, but spoke these into the ear of a select few. These privileged ones, on the other hand, when the time arrived for commencing their apostolic career, did not appear before the world as imitators of their Master. They did not affect His calm, lofty tone, they did not speak in parables, they did not select from the crowd a band of disciples to be taught an esoteric doctrine. They became street preachers in temper and style, they spoke from the house-top, they addressed the crowd, they. proclaimed a more explicit, definite, common-place gospel of forgiveness and salvation from wrath, talked as it were of oxen and fed beasts and the other accompaniments of a feast, with an eloquence less dignified but more fitted to impress the million with a sense of the rkhes of Divine grace

And what was to be the result of this new aggressive declamatory ministry Surely it will be more satisfactory than that of the first servants, to which all but a few simple folks turned a deaf ear.? Alas, no! The result of this second effort was to be worse rather than better. The majority were to imitate the indifference of their predecessors, and the rest were to be guilty of insolence and violence towards the King's messengers. Such is the picture presented in the words of our parable. " They went away, taking no heed; one to his own field, another to his merchandise, and tlie rest laid hold of his servants, and treated them shamefully and killed them." It is in a few words a correct description of the treatment received by the apostles at the hands of the Jews. The bulk of the people, preoccupied with secular affairs, finding their satisfaction in possessions, or in the

Beyond this general idea no significance is to ba attached to the ravpoi and (TitK-TTii. Theophylact makes the ravpoi signify the Old Testament, and the airiara the I ew. The interpretation in the latter case he justifies by the consideration that loaves are offered on the altar which are properly called aitiara, as made from wheat.

pursuit of gain, took no interest in the spiritual goods which the preachers of the gospel brought within their reach. The heads of the nation, whom we may assume to be represented by ' the others' in the parable, persecuted the missionaries of the new religion, fearing evil consequences from its progress to the established civil and religious order. So we learn from the familiar narratives of the Acts of the Apostles. That Christ should predict so distinctly beforehand what was to happen cannot appear surprising, as it scarcely needed prophetic prescience to enable Him to do so. He had but to reason from what happened to the Master to what would happen to disciples. For though it be true that the indignities which He suffered at the hands of men came upon Him rather as a prophet of law than as a minister of grace, yet His experience contained ominous indications of the antagonism which might be provoked even by the bringer of good tidings when he involuntarily offended against the prejudices of his hearers. How significant in this connection the incidents in the synagogue of Nazareth recorded by the Evangelist Luke. Jesus discourses on the acceptable year of the Lord in ' words of grace' which excite general admiration; yet in a few minutes after His life is endangered by one or two historical references, which wound the self-love of villagers animated by the bigoted exclusive spirit of their race. That sudden ebullition of patriotic wrath was prophetic of the fate which awaited the heralds of the new era of grace at the hands ot Jewish pride. For, however acceptable the good tidings might be in themselves, it would be impossible to publish them without in some way giving offence. And as time went on offences would increase. If the Nazarenes persecuted their fellow-townsman, the Jewish people were sure to persecute more bitterly His followers while engaged in their apostolic calling, and that on account precisely of those characteristics by which their ministry was distinguished from His; its greater aggressiveness, and its more explicit style of announcement. More energetic action would provoke more violent reaction, and a more developed and intelligible gospel would provoke more emphatic contradiction. When

The words ti'c tov llwv ay ov suggest the idea of landed property. â Luke iv. i6.

the gospel of the kingdom, set forth in enigmatic aphorisms, took the form of a gospel of salvation by a crucified man, offences would not be wanting! It was a matter of course, therefore, that the second class of servants should be insulted, assaulted, imprisoned, and even put in danger of their lives. And it was natural that, in a parable setting forth the judgment of Israel for her contempt of grace, allusion should be made to these prospective experiences to make it clear that, on every ground, the guilty nation was ripe for doom. For a people not only persistently negligent of duty, and practising habitual violence against those who reminded it of its obligations, but equally insensible to God's overtures of mercy, and equally insolent towards the ministers of reconciliation, what could be hoped.-â Even Paul, patriot though he was, capable of wishing himself accursed for his countrymen's sake, was forced to despair, and to describe Israel as a people which despising the riches of God's grace, forbearance, and long-suffering, and misunderstanding their meaning with a hardened, impenitent heart, treasured up for itself wrath in the day of wrath and of the revelation of the righteous judgment of God.

This wrath the parable proceeds to describe in these terms: " But the king was angry; and sending his armies, he destroyed those murderers and burned their city." The words foreshadow the ruin of the Jewish state and the holy city, a generation later, by the might of imperial Rome, employed by Providence to punish Israel for her sins. It is startling to find so distinct an anticipation of the event in a parable spoken so long beforehand. But Christ says here only what he repeated with equal distinctness in the discoursb on the last things in a subsequent chapter of the same Gospel; even as in the description of the fate awaiting the apostles He but briefly hints what, on various occasions. He had already said to His disciples by way of forewarning, and was to say again in the farewell discourse.

The concluding sentence of the first part of the parable intimates the king's resolve to transfer his favour from those vho had been guilty of such grievous misconduct to such as

Rom. ii. 4, 5, Ver. 7. Matt. xxiv.

Matt. X., xvl John xvl were more likely to value them. This purpose, while an act of grace towards those next to be called, is an act of judgment towards the first invited. It is the natural sequel of the dread visitation spoken of just before. Israel, ruined as a nation, is at the same time to be cast oft" as a people; as no longer worthy of the prerogatives and privileges of the elect race. Of these indeed she had never been worthy, but in view of her contempt of God's grace, and judicial blindness in regard to her spiritual opportunities, her demerit might be spoken of with an emphasis that in other circumstances might appear excessive. By such behaviour as the parable depicts, the Jewish people, as Paul declared in the synagogue of Antioch, judged themselves unworthy of eternal life, and justified the transference of despised privilege to the Gentiles. Of this transference our parable speaks in very general terms. " Go ye," says the king to his servants, " to the outlets of the ways, and call to the marriage feast whomsoever ye find." We have already alluded to the vagueness of the expression employed to denote the quarters where the new guests are to be found. Much diff'erence of opinion prevails as to its meaning, and many interpreters express their views in a tone of dogmatism which is altogether unwarrantable. Some are sure that the reference is to the streets or squares of a city,2 others pronounce with great confidence in favour of the country roads, or crossings of the highways. One asserts that the city in which the new guests are to be sought is the same as that which is to be burned; another informs us that it is another city, that of the king; " not Jerusalem, but God's world." There is nothing in the text to justify such confidence, or to help us to a certain conclusion. The expression is vague; perhaps it is purposely so; it may have been selected to embrace in its scope the localities visited in the two missions to the poor in Luke's parableâ the streets and lanes, and likewise the highways and hedges. The single mission to the poor in Matthew's parable is another point in which it differs from Luke's. Both have a double mission; but Matthew's is to the first called, while Luke's is to

Acts xiii. 46. 2 Kypke, Kuinoel, Trench, c. ' Fritsche after Fischer, De Wette, Meyer, Goebel.

Trench. Â Alford.

those called in the second place. This difference is to be accounted for in the same way as all the rest; viz. by the consideration that the parable before us is a parable of judgment. Its aim is not to set forth with distinctness and emphasis God's purpose of grace to the outlying peoples, but to justify the withdrawal of His grace from the chosen race. Therefore the calling of those without is referred to only in indefinite terms: even as in the close of the parable of the Vine-dressers, where it is said that the kingdom of God should be taken from Israel, and given to a nation eouei.) yielding the fruits thereof. We shall best reflect the spirit of the parable by allowing the terms to remain indefinite, and not binding them down to any particular reference. If the Speaker had meant to fix the reference down either to town or country, to the Jewish or the Gentile world, He could easily have done so, as in the parable of the Supper, where one set of phrases are employed clearly referring to the town, and then another as clearly referring to the country. Good, or at least plausible, arguments have been advanced by respectable authorities on both sides of the question, and that fact suggests that the wisest course may be to be on both sides. The phrase, le outlets of the ways, has a suggestive vagueness about it which stimulates the imagination, and craves room and scope and largeness of interpretation, so that it may embrace at once the outcasts of Israel and the Pagans. The king's dining-hall was ample, and the servants were to bring as many as they could find, and there are plenty of servants about a king's palace to search for guests in all directions, in town or country. This, accordingly, the servants seem to have done; for it is written that they went out into the ways (68ovs), the peculiar expression in their directions not being repeated in the record of the execution.

1 Matt. xxi. 43.

' Farrar (' Life of Christ) finds in this a delicate " reference to tbe imperfect work of human agents,"' the words within inverted commas being quoted from ' Lightfoot on Revision," p. 68. We would rather find in the change of expression a tacit admission that the phrase first used, while suitable enough in the mouth of the king giving general instructions, was too vague to be used with propriety in describing what was actually done.

II. The judgment of grace abused.

The tenth verse appropriately introduces the new tableau of the guest without a wedding-robe. That a fresh start in the narration, with a distinct didactic aim, is being made is apparent from the simple fact that the messengers who go out to collect guests from the highways are spoken of as those servants ol hovkoi ikclvoi). If the verse had been merely the conclusion of the preceding narrative, the servants would have been the appropriate expression. But that the story is about to take a new turn is chiefly indicated by the significant expression employed to characterise the guests gathered together by this mission. Those servants, we read, going forth, collected together all whom they found, doth bad and good. We must not, with Bengel, minimise the force of the phrase, as if it were a proverbial expression signifying ' indiscriminately." It is intended to emphasise the fact that the invitation was indiscriminate with special reference to the moral character or reputation of the parties, and that with an obvious regard to the scene which follows in the wedding-chamber. The terms applied to the guests are all the more significant when compared with those employed in the corresponding parable in Luke. There what is accentuated is the abject poverty of the guests. It is the children of misery and want that are invited; the desperately needy, the very beggars on the highway, when it is found that there is still room. Here, on the other hand, there is no reference to poverty; a fact overlooked by many commentators, with the result that unnecessary difficulty is introduced into the part of the parable relating to the wedding-robe. How unreasonable, it is argued, to visit with severe penalties the want of such a robe on the part of a poor man, who was not in possession of one or able to purchase one; and to get over the difficulty it is deemed necessary to assume that the guests must have been furnished with wedding-attire out of the royal wardrobes. We shall come to that question by and hy; meantime, let it be noted that there is not a word about poverty in the text. The guests are not a crowd of paupers and beggars; they are a congregation of men and women got together without reference to their moral antecedents. In 1 So Goebel 476 The Parabolic Teaching of CJu'ist, book hi the esteem of society some of them might be good, and some bad; but of such distinctions the servants took no account. They invited all they met without question or hesitation as to character or antecedents; although it might be evident at a glance from dress, features, and bearing, that some were suspicious enough. Doubtless, among the invited would be some poor,â probably the majority were of that class; but of that fact no note is taken. What is remarked on is that the guests were a motley crew as to character; some respectable, others disreputable: ragged not in their outward attire, but in their name and fame, like the Corinthian Church of after days, of which Paul remarked: " Such were some of you ": drunkards, adulterers, thieves, and the like.

When we realise distinctly the import of the phrase " bad and good," we are prepared for some such offence as is reported in the sequel. In such a crowd, swept together from street and highway, rudeness, irreverence, insensibility to the claims of the royal presence and the solemn occasion might be looked for. These guests have not been accustomed to appear in such a place, and it will be strange indeed if they comport themselves, without exception, as becomes a palace and a royal marriage. We should rather expect irreverence to be the rule, and decorum the exception. Yet in the parable only one of the guests appears guilty of rudeness. Why is this? Because if the parable at this point had followed natural probability, there would have been a risk of guests being few, a great difficulty in getting the feast-chamber filled. The chamber was filled with guests because the messengers invited all regardless of antecedents; but it might have been emptied again, if the scrutiny had complied with the requirements of probability. Many were called, but few might have been allowed to remain. To avoid this result, and to keep the chamber full, the number of off"enders is reduced to one.2 One was enough to suggest the fact, and illustrate the principle of scrutiny. In consequence of this restriction, the representation of the parable, as has been

I Cor. vi. II.

2 One or two interpreters have found the explanation in the supposition that Christ h: id Judas Iscariot in view. Even Olshausen speaks of this prosaic hypothesis as possible.

remarked, is not in keeping with the concluding apophthegm: " Many are called, but few are chosen "â all being chosen but one. The incongruity cannot be helped, for the feast must go on with a number of guests answering to the importance of the occasion. Therefore one guest is selected to represent a class.

When we consider how far short the parabolic statement at this point comes of natural likelihood, we see that it cannot have been the intention of Christ to represent the king as entering the chamber with the express purpose of scrutinising the guests. He enters not to scrutinise but to welcome; any other supposition would give to his appearance among his guests an ungracious aspect, altogether out of keeping with the occasion. The discovery of a man without a wedding-robe is an accident, an unpleasant incident not looked for beforehand, though a thing which cannot be overlooked once it has been observed. Had the intention been to make the king enter for the purpose of a scrutiny, it would have been necessary either greatly to multiply the numbers, to give the scrutiny an aspect at once of reality and of probability, or to make the concluding aphorism run. Many are called, but not all are chosen.

But now, what is the offence of which the solitary representative of the disapproved is guilty? We can have no difficulty in answering the question if we bear in mind the composition of the multitude collected in the marriage-chamber. Answers very wide of the mark have been returned by commentators approaching the subject from the dogmatic, instead of the natural and historical, point of view. The sin of the offending guest, we are told variously, is self-righteous-ness,2 disloyalty, intrusion into a feast to which he has not been invited. All these views are connected witlx a theory as to the wedding-garment being the gift of the king. The guest was self-righteous, because he preferred his own garment to that offered him from the royal wardrobe; he was disloyal, because he refused the garment which etiquette required all guests to receive and wear, in mere rudeness and wantonness; he was an intruder, because had he been

D'Eichthal, Les Evangiles." Arndt, Alford.

â Arnou Baumgarten-Crusius, 478 The Parabolic Teaching of Christ, book hi.

invited he would doubtless have been offered a wedding-robe, and of course would have put it on. These suggestions are all out of keeping with the circumstances. Self-righteousness is not the sin which besets people such as those guests swept indiscriminately from street and road. As little is disloyalty to be imputed without urgent reason to men who have so far shown loyalty by coming to the feast in response to the invitation. And as for the idea that the offending guest was an uninvited intruder, it is simply absurd. IMerely to hear of the feast, even at second-hand, was to be invited, for the commission to the servants was to bring as many as they could find. " Let him that heareth say come, and whosoever will, let him take of the water of life freely."

Of what kind of fault were those guests likely to be guilty Surely of unmannerliness, coming without decoration, not from want of loyal feeling, or from conceit, or because they had no suitable apparel, but from pure want of thought and refined feeling. The moral fault answering to this is an unethical license, taking advantage of God's goodness, without taking pains to cultivate the virtue that becomes those who are admitted into close relations with the Divine Being. This is one of two forms under which men may sin against grace. It is the form under which those can so sin who accept God's invitations; the other being that under which those offend who decline the invitations. Paul speaks of both offences in his Epistle to the Romans. The one, that of the refusers of God's invitations, he calls despising God's grace, which he charges upon the self-righteous Jews; the other he calls sinning because grace abounds- which is the sin of what we might describe as unregenerate faith.

That Jesus should take occasion to enter a protest against this sin, the licentious abuse of grace, as well as against the other offence, proud contempt of grace, cannot appear surprising. For though He ever gave great prominence to the gracious character of the kingdom. He was always zealous likewise for its righteousness. He set forth the kingdom as a kingdom of grace to begin with, because He wished it to be a kingdom of righteousness to end with. He deemed the proclamation of free grace the best way to produce holiness.

1 Rom, ii 4. Rom. vi. I.

If He offered the grace of God to the chief of sinners, it was because He believed that such might become the chief of saints; on the principle that much forgiveness breeds much love. The lesson of the wedding-robe is thus in keeping with the general spirit of His teaching. And let it be observed that this is not the only parable in which a zealous regard to the interests of holiness is manifested. The same zeal comes out, not so obtrusively perhaps, but not less unmistakably, in the parables of the Fig-tree and the Vine-dressers. The barren tree is removed because it unprofitably occupies the ground, which implies that any tree which is planted in its place is put there for the purpose of bringing forth fruit. Then in the sentences appended to the Vine-dressers, it is stated that the kingdom of God is to be taken from the Jews and given to a x-Si! dox producing tjie fruits thej'cof.

The broad lesson then of the sub-parable of the Wedding-robe is that the recipients of Divine grace must live worthily of their privilege. The wedding-robe represents Christian holiness, and the demand is that all believers in the gospel hall sedulously cultivate it. This being so, it is useless to discuss, as a matter of life and death, the question whether, according to ancient custom, the wedding-robe was a gift of the king. The point is of no consequence to the didactic significance of the parable, but merely a curious question ot Biblical archaeology. So far as we can judge from the extracts cited by commentators from works relating to Oriental customs, we should say that a probable case has been made out in favour of the alleged custom. But that is not enough to justify us in making that custom the hinge of the interpretation. Had the didactic significance of the wedding-robe turned on its being a gift, the fact that it was presented to each guest to be worn on the occasion would have been mentioned." It will not do to say that the custom was so familiar to Christ's audience that the point might be taken for granted. Facts are not specified or omitted in parables according to the ignorance or the knowledge of hearers, but according as they do or do not bear on the purpose of the story. Thus the parable of Dives passes over the piety of Lazarus, not because it might be assumed as

So Meyer and Neander (' Life of Christ'), Bleek, c.

known but because the mention of it would have been an irrelevance. Similarly here: suppose it were not a matter of inference merely, but a certainty that the wedding-garment was a robe similar to the kaftan presented now in the East by kings to persons appearing before them, the absence of all allusion to the custom must be held to be conclusive evidence that it is irrelevant to the lesson intended to be taught. The silence means that the Speaker wishes to accentuate the duty of each guest seeing to it that he appeared at the feast in proper attire. In short, as has been remarked, prominence is given to the ethical view-point which emphasises man's responsibility, rather than the religious which represents all as depending on God. To prove ever so cogently that the wedding-garment came from the king's stores does not invalidate this statement, but only confirms it. The conclusion to which these observations point is, that there is no foundation in the parable for the good old Protestant interpretation, according to which the wedding-garment is the righteousness of God given to faith. Vestis est justitia Christi, says the devout and scholarly Bengel, and we should gladly agree with him; but we feel that the idea of an objective righteousness given to faith lies outside the scope of this parable, and, indeed, except in the most general form, is not to be found in the whole system of truth contained in the records of our Lord's teaching. That idea is distinctively Pauline. It is the form under which he presents to view the summnm bonum, or the gift of grace. The equivalent 1 De Wette.

2 While a circumstance of such didactic importance as that the wedding-garment was a loan from the king could not properly be onittedt it is otherwise with the circumstance that the guests gathered from the highways were allowed an opportunity to make a change of raiment soimhow. That might be taken for granted as a matter of course. Storr, while pointing this out, yet concurs in the opinion that it is not necessary to determine whence the wedding-garment was to be procured; the intention being to teach merely the general lesson that the soul must be clothed anew with righteousness, not the method of procuring the necessary vesture ('De Parabohs Christi," translated in the 'Biblical

Cabinet," vol. ix.).

3 The nearest approach to it in the Synoptical Gospels is in the expressions, "The kingdom of God, and His righteousness"' (Matt. vi. 33); and "Justifiedx2X i x than the other" (Luke xviii. 14).

in Christ's teaching is the kingdom of God. These two ideas are not opposed to each other; on the contrary, they are intimately related, and in full sympathy with each other. Still their relation is one of co-ordination, not of sub-ordination. The righteousness of God is not, as is implied in Bengel's interpretation of the wedding-garment, a detail under the general head of the kingdom of God. It is another name for the same thing. The doctrine of Christ and that of Paul are essentially one. In both, man's relation to God is represented as based upon grace. That view is implied in this parable; but it is important to note at what point it comes in. The grace of the kingdom is set forth by the selection of a wedding-feast to be its emblem. The wedding-robe represents the holiness of the kingdom which ought to accompany and flow from the reception of grace. Its equivalent in the Pauline system is not the righteousness of faith, which answers to the feast in the parable, but those parts of the Apostle's teaching in which he insists on holiness as the outcome of faith in God's grace, and so guards his doctrine against objections springing out of concern for ethical interests. The passages in Paul's writings which come nearest in import to the sub-parable of the Wedding-garment are those in his Epistle to the Romans where he protests against the impious idea that we may sin because grace abounds, and warns the Gentile believers to beware lest through spiritual shortcomings the same fate befall themâ the wild olive branches, which had overtaken the natural branches, the elect people of Israel.

We pass now to the sequel of the scene. The king saith to the offending guest: " Friend, how earnest thou hither not having a wedding-garment."' " The guilty one made no reply; in the expressive language of the parable he was muzzled. His speechlessness was the product of confusion 1 Rom. vi. I.

2 Rom. xi. 16â 22. We may here, at the conclusion of the discussion as to the wedding-garment, note that in the 'Clementine Homihes," viii. 22, the garment is supposed to be Baptism: tvsvfia yufiov, otrtp iorip fsclTTTKrua. (In the same place the Su osot rwv osiov are identified with the Gentile world, hsxivasv r'ifih; dg rag' Sii osovg riov uswv tkOovtiv o irrriv irphg vnac) The Fathers generally made the wedding-robe holiness. Thus Origen calls it to txpacriia rqf upirrii.

in the august presence of the king. Till that moment the habit ijf irreverence had prevailed; for he had not realised, had never even thought, what it was to be confronted with royalty. But when the king actually appears, fixes his eye on him and speaks to him, he is confounded and struck dumb. Thus may the manner of the man be most naturally explained. It is unnecessary to ascribe to him any deliberate intention to insult by any act of rudeness or disloyalty. His offence was one of thoughtlessness, as was likely to be the case in a man of his class. The severity of his punishment naturally tempts us to make his fault appear as aggravated as possible by laying stress on every word that can be supposed to imply deliberate purpose, and by imagining circumstances fitted to deprive him of all excuse, such as that the missing article of apparel was simply an inexpensive badge or symbol which the poorest could have procured for himself But instead of thus striving to magnify the offender's criminality, it is better to direct attention to the solemn truth that even sins of thoughtlessness are no light matters in those who bear the Christian name, and profess to bel'eve in God's grace. In this connection it is important to remember that it is this class of sins the writer of the Epistle to the Hebrews seems to have in view when he exhorts his readers to follow peace with all men, and holiness as an indispensable condition of seeing God. For he goes on immediately to refer to Esau as the type of those who through neglect of holiness fall short of the grace of God. The sin of Esau was heedlessness. He was dying of hunger, and what was a birthright to a starving man t When appetite was satisfied he regretted his rash, thoughtless act, for he had not deliberately despised his birthright. The writer of the Epistle would-have his brethren understand that through nothing worse than such moral rudeness might Christians miss salvation. And that is the lesson taught in our parable. We see here a man who falls from the king's grace not Â Thus Trench points out that the particle of negation in the king's question is not os, as in the previous verse, but a"), m ' X ' vlv xa yaiou not having (and knowing that thou hadst not) a wedding-garment.

2 So Arnot, who refers in illustration to the bride's favour given tr guests at marriages in this country.

through self-righteous pride, or bold disloyalty, or deliberate disrespect, but by the rude behaviour of one who has never been accustomed to restraint, and who without thought carries his unmannerly ways into the royal presence.

The doom of one guilty of such an offence, as described in the parable, appears unduly severe. Enough for such an one, we are inclined to think, that he be unceremoniously turned out of a company in which he is not fit to appear. Was it worth while, one is apt to ask, for the king to get angry over the unmannerliness of this clown who had strayed into the marriage-hall, or to issue such peremptory instructions as to how his ministers should deal with him Was not such wrath and such preciseness undignified in a royal person? Certainly, on first thought, it does seem so. At the very least the king's action seems to stand in need of apology, and the apology that comes readiest is that the king's temper has been so ruffled by the contempt of the first invited that he is naturally very jealous of any fresh manifestations of irreverence, and prone to resentment when such appear. And such an explanation of the king's behaviour is quite legitimate, for we are not bound to vindicate the actions of characters in parables from all charges of infirmity. In studying the parable of the Great Feast in Luke's Gospel we saw that the motive of the host for filling his dining-hall with beggars from the highways was by no means an elevated one. Even so here we may imagine the king to be simply giving way to one of those sudden ebullitions of anger in which eastern rulers so frequently indulge, under whose influence they issue the most ruthless orders on comparatively slight provocation. In this way we should at all events justify the parabolic representation as in accord with natural probability. But the royal wrath and the order in which it issues have more than picturesque significance. They convey the thought that a heedless life on the part of a believer in Divine grace may be attended with fatal consequences; the same thought which Paul sought to impress on the Corinthians, and the writer of the Epistle to the Hebrews on Jewish Christians, by reminding them of the melancholy fate which overtook the people of Israel in the wilderness, notwithstanding that they had participated in the grace of Jehovah in connection 484 The Parabolic Teaching of CJn-ist. book hi.

with the Exodus. The passages in which these solemn warnings are given are the best possible commentary on the command of the king. They refer to historical facts which prove that what seem very pardonable sins of unbelief, murmuring, and hankering after forbidden enjoyments, may be mercilessly punished, leaving no room for repentance, even though it be sought carefully and with tears. Christ, ever faithful, and truly desirous of the salvation of all His followers, draws His picture in accordance with the facts of experience, at the risk of seeming to make God appear a harsh tyrant, and Himself less pitiful than we love to think Him. For if, as we have no reason to doubt, the concluding reflections of the parable were spoken by Him, then He must be understood as acquiescing in the rigour of Providence. " There shall be the weeping and the gnashing of teeth," says He, in reference to the ejected guest; suggesting the picture of a poor wight lying in darkness bound and helpless, lamenting his exclusion from joy, and the folly which occasioned it. " Many are called, but q. v chosen," He adds, to suggest that the sad fate of the one may befall many, the number of the heedless being at all times great,

I Cor. X.; Heb. ul

In the two parables which remain to be considered ere we bring these studies to a close, judgment appears active within the kingdom of grace. In the second scene of the last parable we already see the judicial activity of Christ beginning to manifest itself in this sphere. But the sub-parable of the Wedding-robe is only a prelude to the judgment of the house of God. There is judged a class who never realised the responsibilities of those who receive God's gracious favour, who entered the kingdom in the rudeness of nature, untouched by any regenerative influence. But in the parables now to be studied we witness the judgment not of the unregenerate, but of the degenerate, who made a fair start, but have undergone a demoralising process, and declined from their initial spiritual condition as believers. They begin by recognising the claims of holiness, but they do not persevere in this mind.

In every process of declension or degeneracy time enters as an element. The phenomena resulting can appear only after the movement with which they are associated has lasted for a while. Perseverance in holiness in the individual and in the community is tested by the occurrence of a period of trial. The parable first considered, that of the Sower, taught us this. Jesus speaks there of those who receive the word with joy, but when tribulation cometh are offended. It is not 486 The Parabolic Teaching of Christ, book ni.

surprising, therefore, that the parables before us are found connected in the record with an eschatological discourse, in which the consummation of the kingdom, while represented as an event to be looked for at any moment, is at the same time spoken of as an event likely to be deferred so long as to involve a great trial of faith and patience. The virtue specially called for by such a situation is watchfulness. Were the near advent of the consummation certain, watching would not be needed; being possible, yet not certain, that habit is at once necessary and difficult. For delay brings temptation to relax zeal, and yielding to the temptation exposes to the risk of surprise. The discourse on the last things, accordingly, contains frequent exhortations to watchfulness. " Watch, therefore, for ye know not the day nor the hour," comes in at intervals like a solemn refrain. And the lesson is enforced not merely by repetition of the counsel, but by the use of figurative representations exhibiting vividly the need of watching, and the danger of neglecting it. We find a whole group of parabolic sayings embedded in the eschatological discourse, all having for their moral: " Watch, for you may be thrown off your guard by delay, and be surprised by the sudden (for sudden it will be) coming of the long expected." In Matthew's version of the sermon there are three: the Good-man and the Thief, the Unfaithful Upper Servant, and the Ten Virgins. The second of the three is given by Luke in a different connection, prefaced by another parable, that of the Waiting Servants who expect their absent lord with loins girt and lights burning, which was probably spoken at the same time as the others. Mark gives a fifth, that of the Porter; its peculiarity being that the duty of watching, which in the other parables is enjoined on all the servants, is assigned in the distribution of offices to a particular functionary." It is possible, however, that this is not a distinct parable, but an amalgam of the Waiting Servants and the Talents, the watching porter representing the lesson taught in the former, and the assignment of tasks to the servants individually representing the distribution of talents in the latter. Omit-

Luke xii. 35â 37. Mark xiii. 34.
So Weiss, ' Das Markus-Evangelium.

ting it, there remain four parabolic utterances bearing on the same theme, and all, there is little doubt, spoken at the same time; a sufficient index of the prominent place which the subject of watching occupied in Christ's thoughts in His last days, in its bearing on the spiritual welfare of His disciples.

Of these four parables only two, those of the Unfaithful Upper Servant, and the Ten Virgins, call for detailed study. The two others merely inculcate in a general manner the duty of watching; these show the evil tendency of delay to demoralise character in different ways, and the doom of such as yield to the baleful influence. The Waiting Servants and the Good-man and the Thief may be regarded as introductory to the parable which is first to engage our attention, as indeed they appear in Luke's narrative. In the former the coming of the Son of man is compared to the return of an householder from a marriage-feast to his own home at an unseasonable hour of the night, when, in the ordinary course, all the inmates would be asleep. But on such an occasion, when their master is expected, dutiful servants will not retire to rest, but will patiently wait for His arrival, at whatever hour it may take place, with garments tucked up in readiness for service, and with the lights burning brightly in the chambers. Such an attitude Jesus desired His disciples habitually to maintain. " Let your loins be girt about," He said, " and your lamps burning, and be ye yourselves like unto men who wait for their lord." He indicated how difficult He deemed it to carry into effect the counsel by appending to the parable the reflection: " Blessed are those servants whom their lord, when he cometh, shall find watching; verily I say unto you, that he shall gird himself, and make them sit down to meat, and shall come and serve them." When our Lord used this epithet ' blessed," He always meant to represent the thing spoken of as high and rare. Rare virtue," He here exclaims in effect, in reference to the conduct of the waiting servants. So rare does He reckon it, that He represents the master as not expecting it; counting rather on finding the house dark and his servants in bed, with hardly one left to open the door when he knocks. Finding the facts otherwise, observing the cheery appearance of lights in the windows, sure indication' that the household is on the outlook, he is so delighted that, instead of accepting service from his dutiful slaves, he is rather in the mood to turn servant to them, and supply them with refreshment, and so reward rare virtue with equally rare felicity and honour.

The scene next changes from servants waiting for their absent lord to a householder whose house is in danger of being broken into by thieves. In this instance ve are told, not what the man does or ought to do, but what he vould do in a supposed case. If he knew when the thief would come he would watch to protect himself against the risk of having his property carried off. If only he, like the waiting servants, knew the day, it would not matter what the hour was, he would gladly keep awake through all the watches of the night to avoid the threatened danger. But he does not know the day any more than the hour; for while it is for the interest of an absent master that his servants should know at least the day of his return, it is the thiefs interest, on the contrary, that his victim should be ignorant as to the day, as well as the hour, of his attack. Therefore the good-man of the house cannot help himself; he must go to bed and take his risk; for it is physically impossible to do Without sleep, and watch night and day all his life long. He acts so from necessity, not because he is indifferent; not even trusting to his poverty as a sufficient protection. A poor man he is, for he lives in a mud house, which can be dug through, so that a barred door is no sufficient defence. But even poverty does not lull him into security; for the little he has is valuable to him, and it would be valuable also to a thief, probably poorer than himself, and tempted by want to steal. The moral is: Let disciples do always what the good man of the house would do if he could, or does on occasion. They have need; for the end is apt to come thief-like, tarrying long, as if it would never arrive, then overtaking men by surprise. They can; for though they know neither the day nor the hour, watching in the moral sense is possible at

The term employed to denote the mode by which the thief gets in is all times; there is no necessity in the spiritual sphere for being at the mercy of the thief.

Such urgent exhortations to watchfulness, spoken doubtless with great earnestness of tone, must have fallen with startling effect on the ears of hearers. We can readily believe, therefore, that Peter, speaking for the twelve, asked such a question as is put into his mouth by the third Evangelist. The question is vaguely expressed,â " Speakest Thou this parable.?" he said, though two had been uttered,â and without any indication of motive. Peter doubtless had in view the whole discourse about watching, and his question probably arose out of a feeling of surprise at the severe tone pervading it. His thought fully expressed was probably something like this: "Master, you seem to consider watchfulness very difficult, as well as very needful. Whom have you specially in view when you speak thus? Do you think that we, your chosen companions, need to be particularly exhorted after this fashion, or are you not speaking to us at all, but merely addressing general exhortations to the crowd.?" Probably Peter's feeling was that he and his brethren did not need to be spoken to so, but were superior to the vulgar vice of heedlessness. In that case there was indicated in his question the same spirit of self-confidence which revealed itself on the night before the Passion in connection with the declaration of Jesus, "All ye shall be offended in Me this night." If, as is probable, the putting of the question formed an incident in the delivery of the eschatological discourse during Passion Week, we have two characteristic manifestations of Peter's infirmity occurring within a few days of each other, in one of which he asks, with a tone of injured virtue, "Speakest Thou thus to us?" and in the other declares, "Though all shall be offended in Thee, I will never be offended." In the light of this juxtaposition we can better understand the stern tone of Christ's reply, which must have sounded almost as harsh to Peter's ear as the word which foretold his fallâ "Verily I say unto thee, that this night thou shalt deny Me thrice." Taking the two together, the announcement of the impending fall and the parable of the Unfaithful Upper Servant, they convey this lesson: The demoralising effect on character of a sudden crisis overtaking 490 The Parabolic Teaching of Christ, book hi.

an inexperienced disciple is bad enough, but that produced by long delay is still worse. The one leads to humiliating denials of the Lord, the other may lead to shameless profligacy: habitual denial in life, more culpable far than the momentary denials of the tongue. â

The parable which teaches this lesson is as follows:

Who then is the faithful and wise servant whom his lord set over his household to give thetn their food in due season? Blessed is that servant whom his lord when he cotneth shall find so doing. Verily J say to you, that he will place him over all his goods. But if that evil servant shall say ifi his heart, My lord tarrieth, and shall begin to beat his fellow-servants, and shall eat and drink with the drunken; the lord of that servant shall cojne in a day when he expecteth not, and in an hour when he knoweth not, and shall cut him asunder, and appoint his portion with the hypocrites: there shall be the weeping and the gnashing of teeth. â Matt. xxiv. 45â 51.

The reply of Jesus to Peter's question is indirect but clear. Without saying in express terms, "I mean you as well as others, nay, you very specially," by selecting an upper servant as the subject of the parable He shows that the duty of watching is one to which men called to be apostles are specially summoned, and the neglect of which in their case involves peculiar dangers. In its main drift the parable is the judgment of ministers of the kingdom demoralised even to profligacy by the delay of the second advent. From the parable thus viewed two inferences may be confidently drawn: that Christ must have expected His kingdom to pass through a lengthened history before reaching its consummation; and that He regarded perseverance in grace through a protracted period as exceedingly difficult for the individual and for the community. Only in the light of these inferences can the salient features of the representation be understood and appreciated.

l The version of the parable in Luke is nearly the same as in Matthew. For Tpoi fiv, ver. 45, Luke has aitonirpiov. Instead of " to eat and drink â with the drunken," Luke reads, "to eat and to drink and to be drunken." For vtTokQitwv Lulce has cnriatinv. Luke adds a reflection on the difference as to the amount of penalty between those who know their lord's will and those who know it not.

First we notice the black picture of the upper servant's misconduct during his lord's absence. He becomes a brutal tyrant and a drunken profligate, a man utterly unworthy of his trust, and absolutely indifferent to his master's interests, whatever he may pretend; whose proper place in character, as in penalty, is among the faithless and the hypocritical. Consider what this means in the spiritual sphere. A profligate clergy lording it over God's heritage, dissolute in life, sceptical in reference to the future glory of the kingdom and all great Christian verities, and guilty of grossest hypocrisy in combining the exercise of sacred functions with a total lack of personal faith and holiness. It takes a long time to develop such a deplorable state of matters. Not at the beginning of a religious movement, not in its creative epoch, do such scandalous phenomena make their appearance; but when the spiritual force has to a large extent spent itself, and its effects have taken their place among the institutions of the world, as at the conversion of the Roman empire under Constantine, and the 'establishment' of Christianity as the religion of the State. When He drew the dark picture Christ must have been looking far beyond the apostolic age; for any one of ordinary sagacity, not to speak of prophetic prescience, might understand that the degeneracy depicted could not appear then in a form intense and extensive enough to make it worth while to construct a parable concerning it. The delay of the master's coming must have meant for Him a lengthened period, during which the kingdom was to pass through a secular process of development, in the course of which hideous forms of evil, as well as new forms of good, would manifest themselves. It is true that in the parable only a single instance of degeneracy is mentioned, which might occur even in the best of times, even in the earliest or apostolic age. It is true also that the case is put hypothetically. If the servant act thus and thus he will be treated accordingly. But parabolic speech suggests more than it says, and it is due to its dignity and gravity to assume that a more serious state tsv airivtiov, Luke xii. 46.

â TWI VTTOKpitWV, Matt. Xxiv. 51.: j â dmaroe may mean either faithless or unbelieving.

492 The Parabolic Teaching of Christ, book hi.

of things than a sohtary, exceptional instance of depravity-would amount to is signified, even a widespread declension; and further, that such declension is not only possible, but probable or even certain.

If this be so, then the second inference above stated is abundantly justified, viz. that Jesus must have had a profound sense of the difiiculty of persevering in grace through a protracted period. But this more plainly appears from the manner in which fidelity is spoken of in the opening sentences of the parable. Who, it is asked, is the faithful and wise servant who, being appointed to a place of trust and responsibility in his master's house, shall act as is expected of him as i; such a person were hardly to be found. Who is he where is he what would one not give to see him That such a one is pronounced blessed signifies the same thing; for, as already stated, this word as used by Christ always denotes something high, exceptional, rare. Applied to conduct, it signifies virtue arduous, heroic, and therefore uncommon. Applied to state, it signifies felicity out of the common course. " Blessed is that servant" means he is a rare man, a hero, one among a thousand. It means further, great shall be his reward, and of this accordingly the parable goes on next to speak. " Verily I say unto you, that he shall make him ruler over all his goods." Having proved himself trusty, he shall be rewarded with unlimited trust, and promoted to a position next to his lord, which can be occupied by one only, the first man in the house, the prime minister in the state.

It may appear strange that our Lord took so sombre and discouraging a view of the capabilities of the average disciple to persevere in faith and fidelity amidst the temptations arising out of the mere lapse of time, not to speak of other more positive forms of trial. But it is not necessary to suppose that He meant to represent time in itself as a source of trial. Time is a mere abstraction, and the lapse of time tries men simply by affording scope for the play of influences within or without hostile to their spiritual interest. The real thought underlying the parabolic representation is: the diffi-culty of persistence in spiritual life throughout a curriculum of trial such as the lapse of years and ages inevitably brings, one of the sorest temptations involved being the disappointment of early hopes for the speedy consummation of devout desires. Even when thus put the doctrine is hard enough, and were it to be found only in this parable, we might well doubt the correctness of our interpretation. But it pervades our Lord's teaching, and we do not need to go beyond the discourses of the Passion Week to meet with words of kindred import to that now under consideration. In the very same discourse of which our parable forms a part we read, "Because iniquity shall abound, the love of many shall wax cold. But he that shall endure unto the end, the same shall be saved," a statement implying that endurance is hard, and therefore rare, at least in times when wickedness is rampant. Then on the Passion eve Jesus said to the eleven, "Ye are they which have continued with Me in My temptations," so gratefully acknowledging a fidelity which had been far from easy; and to indicate still further His sense of the heroic character of their behaviour. He added, "And I appoint unto you a kingdom." Ye have done nobly, and noble shall be your rewardâ such is the import of the pathetic utterance. It is in full sympathy with the didactic drift of our parable, though it implies a more genial appreciation of the behaviour of Peter and his fellow-disciples than that which seems to be insinuated in the latter.

The punishment awaiting the wicked servant is dreadful. His lord, coming on a day when he expects him not, and at an unknown hour, will cut Juvi asunder. Whatever the word 8txorop)(ret may signify in the spiritual sphere, it is to be interpreted literally when we seek to determine the exact character of the parabolic representation. It means in plain terms to cut the body into two, as by a saw or other instrument, a barbaric and revolting mode of putting to death practised among the Hebrews and other nations of antiquity. One is inclined to wonder that Christ did not shrink from using a word suggestive of such horrible associations. But â Matt. xxiv. 12. 2 Lukexxii. 28, 29.

3 Vide I Sam. xv. 33; 2 Sam. xii. 31; Heb. xi. 37. For classical references vide Wetstein.

doubtless He did shrink, and forced Himself nevertheless to employ the term, with an eye to moral effect. The strong word served several good purposes. It conveyed, in the first place, as has been happily pointed out by Bengel, the idea of a punishment congruous to the character of the criminal on whom it is inflicted, that, viz., of a iiypucrite. " A hypocrite divides soul and body in the worship of God; wherefore his soul and his body are divided in eternal destruction." Then, secondly, the Dantesque expression adequately indicates the intense abhorrence with which Jesus regarded conduct on the part of professed fouovers by which the house of God was turned into a house of Belial. Finally, it was well fitted to scare and terrify the twelve disciples to whom the parable was first spoken, and so effectually prevent them from being guilty of misconduct pronounced worthy of such punishment. In this connection it is important to point out that Christ's strongest, harshest words occur in speeches addressed to His di. sciples. It is in the discourse on Humility that we find the viillstone suspended by the neck; it is in the parable of the Unmerciful Servant that mention is made of the tormetitors; it is in the parable of the Wicked Upper Servant that the horrible punishment of cutting in two is alluded to: the audience in all three instances being the twelve. The purpose is plain: strong language is used to render hated sin impossible.

With the punishment of the unfaithful one, the parable as given in Matthew ends. Luke appends a reflection intended to meet a feehng naturally arising out of the parabolic representation. Declension into faithlessness is difficult to resist, and its penalty is rigorous: such I's the drift of the whole. "Who then can be saved.?" is the question which suggests itself to every sincere disciple. Such despair is dangerous; for nothing is more demoralising than to be told at once that virtue is next to impossible, and that the want of it will be'inexorably punished. Jesus hastened to obviate the evil effect by making a distinction between those who sin with full knowledge of their

Lord's will, and those who sin in comparative ignorance thereof A milder word also is employed to denote the penalty in either case. Stripes take the place of cutting asunder. The stronger word denotes the inherent turpitude of the offence, the weaker is used out of compassionate regard to the infirmity of human nature, which often causes men not wicked in will to fall grievously before the assaults of temptation, whereof the denial of his beloved Master by Peter is an instructive example.

CHAPTER VII.
THE TEN VIRGINS; OR, THE JUDGMENT OF FOOLISH CITIZENS OF THE KINGDOM.

Theti shall the kittgdotn of heaven be likened unto ten virgins, who took their lamps, and went forth to meet the bridegroom. And five of them were foolish, and five were wise?" For the foolish, when they took their lamps, took no oil with themselves. But the wise took oil in their vessels with their own lamps. Now while the bridegroom tarried, they all nodded and slept. But at midnight is raised a cry, Behold the bridegroom; come ye forth to meet him." Then arose all those virgins, and trimmed their lamps. And the foolish said unto the wise, Give us of your oil, for our lamps are going out. But the wise answered, saying, Lest there be not enough for us and you, go rather to them thai sell, and buy for yourselves. And while they were going away to buy, the bridegroom came; and the virgins that ' a i. Tzaloz, properly torches. Probably the 'lamps' consisted of a short wooden stem held in the hand, with a dish at the top in which was a piece of cloth dipped in oil or pitch. Lightfoot (' Hon Heb.") gives from the Talmud an account of torches used at marriages among the Ishmaelites answering to this description. They carry before the bride "decem baculos ligneos, in uniuscujusque sunimitate vasculum instar scutellse habentes, in quo est segmentum panni cum oleo et pice." The number ten is noticeable.

â Such is the order in the chief uncials, and adopted by Tischendorf, Westcott and Hort, and the R. V.

3 'ivvaralav. The nodding was transient, the initial stage, hence the aorist; the sleeping was continuous, hence tkciqivlov, the imperfect. Nodded is a familiar word, but it has the merit of stating exactly what happened, and conveys the idea that as the night advanced the virgins were overtaken with drowsiness.

Wc airuvttiaiv: literally, "unto meeting:" a familiar and important ceremony.

nijitott ovk, which Goebel renders 'never," making the refusal unnecessarily peremptory. The rendering above given is Campbell's, after the Vulgate.

were re dy went in with him to the marria e-feast and the door was shjit. Afterwards came also the other virgins, saying, Lord, Lord, open to us. But he answered and said, Verily say iittto yoit, I knoiv you not. Watch, therefore, for ye know not the day nor the hour. â Matt. xxv. i â 13.

The last of the parables is one of the most beautiful and touching. The arts have been made to minister to its illustration: poetry, painting, and the drama have combined to give it an exceptional hold on the Christian imagination. The weird pathos of the story is unspeakable. The occasion is so happy, the agents so interesting, the issue so tragic. It is a wedding that is on hand; the characters brought on the stage are virgins, young, bright, and fair; the fate of some of them is so hardâ exclusion from the marriage festivities at which they so longed to be present, and for so slight a cause â a little too late. One's heart is sore for those five witless, luckless girls.

A parable like this one would rather silently read than expound; for exposition is almost certain to mean turning poetry into prose. For another reason one shrinks from the interpreter's task in the present instance. No parable has been so completely taken possession of by allegorising theology. The natural story has been buried beneath a heap of spiritual meanings which have been accumulating from the patristic period till now. To every wordâ virgin, bridegroom, lamp, oilâ has been assigned its emblematic significance. A comparatively sober Catholic commentator counts fifteen parts which have their spiritual equivalents, not reckoning among these the part in which the foolish virgins are represented as going to buy, which he regards as a mere ornament. To go against the exegetical tradition of well-nigh two thousand years is not only audacious, but almost profane. And yet there is no parable in which preliminary discussion of the story apart from the moral interpretation seems more urgently needed. Convinced of this, we must decline to ask such questions as what does the oil signify, until we have formed a clear idea of what persons whose oil-supply had run out would be likely to do at an ordinary wedding. The result ax 1701(101 = the ready ones, viz. the wise virgins. Maldonatus.

498 T. c Parabolic Teaching of Christ, book hi.

of our inquiry may be to place us in the undesirable position of an almost solitary dissenter. Yet what can one do but state honestly the opinions which, after much reflection, commend themselves to his mind?

The situation, or course of events, is by no means clear. The movement of the narrative is rapid, many details are omitted, only the salient points necessary to the moral lesson being given; and, as has been remarked, the information supplied by travellers and writers on antiquities concerning Jewish customs do not afford much help towards filling up the picture. Such information carries us little beyond the generality of a torchlight procession, which was not peculiar to Judaja, but formed a feature in the marriage customs also of Greece and Rome. We read of ten virgin-companions of the bride, whose function it was to go forth with lamps to meet the bridegroom. But from what point did the torchlight night journey start."' and how are we to conceive its progress To these queries no less than four distinct answers are given by the commentators. They may be briefly stated thus:â 1. The virgins set out from their own homes with lamps in hand, arrive one after the other at the bride's home, there wait for the announcement of the bridegroom's approach, whereupon they prepare to accompany him, with his bride, to his house, where the nuptial festivities are celebrated.

2. The virgins meet at the bride's home, their rendezvous. How or when they get there is a matter of indifference to the parable. There they wait till the approach of the bridegroom is announced; then,(? r tjie fij'st ;;i?, they proceed to light their lamps, that with these they may go forth to meet the bridegroom and conduct him to the bride's house, where, and not in his own house, the marriage takes place.

3. The virgins, assembled at the bride's house, set out with

So Fritsche and Bengel.

2 Vide Wetstein for references to classic usage.

' amvtc, ver. I, implies that the clause following describes the kind of nr ins meant. They are bridesmaids.

Bornemann in 'Studien und Kritiken," 1843, Ewald, Greswell. ' Goebel their lights to meet the bridegroom without waiting for the announcement of his approach, expecting him to come at a certain time. When they have gone a certain length on the way it becomes apparent to them that he is not coming so soon as was expected, and, weary with the journey, they turn aside to some halting-placeâ an inn, a private dwelling, or the roadsideâ to rest, and are soon overpowered with sleep, from which they are aroused by the cry, The bridegroom is at hand; whereupon they join his party and return with them to the bride's house.

4. The virgins join the procession of the bridegroom and the bride coming from the house of the latter and going to the house of the former; meeting the bridal party at some convenient point on the road at which they have gathered.

The difference which chiefly concerns us in these four hypotheses is that between the second and all the rest. That view implies that the foolish virgins had no oil at all, while all the others imply that they took with them from their homes oil enough to last for the time which they expected to elapse before the arrival of the bridegroom. On the one view their folly consisted in never thinking of oil, and merely taking the empty lamps; on the other it consisted in taking only as much as was usually sufficient, and making no provision for the possible case of the delayed arrival of the bridegroom. The author of the second hypothesis insists, in support of it, on the reflexive pronoun kavrhw after Aa(x7ra8as in ver. i, and before exawv in ver. 3. The foolish virgins took their own lamps, but they took not their own oil; for that, or for the light that oil gives, they trusted to others; it would be enough to be in the company of those who had light-giving lamps. The expression, "Our lamps are going out," in ver. 8, he thinks does not mean the oil in our lamps is exhausted, but simply implies that wicks had been kindled in oilless lamps, which of course were no sooner lighted than they began to go out. Against the more common view he argues that it makes the wise far too wise, for how should they be able to guess that the arrival of the bridegroom might possibly be delayed a considerable time Moreover, he contends that in any case l Bleek, Meyer, (Stc. a Trench Amot, Lange.

500 The Parabolic Teaching of Christ, book hi.

there was no need for an extra supply of oil. The lamps were not needed till the arrival of the bridegroom was announced, and the procession of virgins to meet him went only a short distance, and lasted only a short time. The idea of the virgins setting out in a haphazard way, without any announcement, to meet the bridegroom, is altogether unlikely, and the halt on the road for rest absurd, and contrary to all notions of propriety.

The argument is ingenious, and in some points, especially the last referred to, cogent; but the hypothesis in question has its assailable points also. If some of the other views make the wise too wise, it in turn makes the foolish too foolish. It is surely possible to be as foolish as the moral of the parable requires without being so foolish as to take lamps without ever thinking of oil! In fact, the folly of the foolish virgins on this view has no relation to the moral lesson. Suppose the bridegroom had not tarried, the foolish virgins would have been equally at fault. But the point of the parable is to illustrate the effect of delay, or of the unexpected, in. qsx- ng forethought, which is the chief part of wisdom. Besides, on this view it is difficult to see why the foolish virgins trimmed, that is to say, lighted, their lamps. They knew they had brought no oil, they knew why they had neglected to do so, viz. because they reckoned it enough that their companions should have lamps that gave light. Why did they not continue to be of this mind, and join the procession with lamps unlit,? Were they so foolish as not to know that a wick without oil to feed the flame would not continue to burn? One other objection may justly be taken to the hypothesis in question. It seems intended to obviate the difficulty in the spiritual interpretation arising from the fact of the foolish having oilâ faith, hope, love, yet after all failing to attain salvation. The hard problem is solved by the simple method of degrading the foolish virgins into mere formalists. They have their own lamps, and probably are ' Greswell, adopting the reading iv roiq ayytoig lav-Siv fxtrd. rwv Xai-rrasojv in ver. 4, makes a point of the fact that the vessels for extra supply of oil were the property of the virgins, while the lamps are not said to be. " Though their lamps might have been received from any other quarter, very conscious of the fact; but they have not that without which lamps of religious profession are of no use, viz. the oil of grace-On the whole it appears certain that the general tenor of the story and its didactic purport demand that we should suppose that all the virgins alike were furnished with a certain amount of oil, such as would have sufficed for ordinary circumstances, and that the distinction of the wise virgins and the proof of their wisdom consisted in their taking with them an extra supply in vessels used for that purpose, whether attached to the torch handle or carried separately. In all other particulars we are willing to adopt the second hypothesis and to conceive of the circumstances thus: The virgins come from their own homes to that of the bride with lamps burning, there rest waiting for the announcement of the bridegroom, their lamps still burning or blown out. When the cry is raised, they all rise and trim their lamps, the wise pouring in more oil, the foolish lighting theirs as they were, to discover soon that the oil was exhausted. The procession goes forth to meet the bridegroom, to conduct him to the bride's house, where the marriage takes place. Usually the marriage-feast was celebrated in the house of the bridegroom, but the practice does not appear to have been uniform, exceptions occurring in the sacred history, as in the cases of Jacob and Samson, and reasons readily suggest themselves why the parabolic representation should follow the exceptions rather than the rule.

Having settled one question respecting the oil, in finding that the folly of the foolish virgins consisted not in bringing no oil, but in not bringing enough, we have now to deal with another more difficult and delicate, viz. was the oil indispens- the vessels in question must have been provided for themselves. The original provision of the lamps, with their ordinary supply of oil, conveying as it did the privilege of an invited guest, or being an evidence thereof, might be due to a cause independent of themselves; but the provision of vessels, at the same time, was a precaution which emanated from the wise virgins themselves."

1 This fact may account for the reading of D in ver. l, which adds to the text icat r c vvfitpttg = to meet the bridegroom and the bride.

Gen. xxix. 22; Judges xiv. 10.

502 The Parabolic Teaching of Chrisi, book hi.

able? Would the foolish virgins have been excluded from the feast supposing they had joined the procession and arrived in good time, simply on the ground that they carried lamps which gave no light? This question the commentators do not so much as ask themselves, yet with one consent they virtually answer it in the affirmative. They come to the parable with the foregone conclusion that the oil, like the wedding garment, signifies some necessary grace, faith, love, c., without which no man can see the Lord, and of course they find themselves shut up to the conclusion that the foolish virgins were placed in the fatal dilemma of being obliged on the one hand to procure oil somehow, and on the other to make themselves too late for the feast by their endeavour to obtain the needed article. It is an extreme instance of exegesis dominated by homiletic preoccupation. The bondage is so complete that it may appear almost an impiety to claim the liberty to hold a different opinion. And yet there are good reasons for doubting the soundness of the exegetical tradition at this point. One is the endless diversity of opinion as to the emblematic significance of the oil. Every interpreter has his own conjecture. The oil is faith, charity, almsgiving,, desire for the praise of God rather than the praise of men; good works in general, the Holy Spirit, diligence in the culture of grace, religious joy. In short, it is anything you please; each conjecture is purely arbitrary, one is as legitimate as another, and the multiplicity of opinions justifies the inference that they are all alike illegitimate. Another reason for doubt is the fact that in the parable the ground of exclusion is not want of oil, but lateness. They that were ready went in with the bridegroom to the marriage-feast. They were ready by being present, while the others were away in quest of oil. Had these absent ones been present and gone on with their sisters, they would, for anything that appears to the contrary, have been admitted also. But the chief consideration that weighs with us is that drawn from the natural probabilities of the case. Suppose it were the story of an ordinary wedding,

Weiss, Das Matthaus-Evangelium," says that the want of oil does not, any mere than the sleep, cause exclusion from the feast. It mocks, he adds, eery allegorising interpretation.

not intended to convey any spiritual lesson. A number of young women are about to set out on a torchlight procession in the evening to escort the bridegroom. Some of them have mislaid their torches, and cannot find them in the hurry when the cry is raised The bridegroom is at hand! or, as in the parable before us, their torches are rendered useless for want of oil. What are they to do.-' Run the risk of making themselves too late by searching for their torches or going in quest of oil, or fall into the procession.- Of course they go on with their companions, and of course they are admitted to the feast with the rest. For though the carrying of a lighted torch is a part of the festive ceremonial, and belongs to the conventional proprieties of the occasion, it is not the essential element. The essential element is the welcoming of the bridegroom; the carrying of lights is an accident due to the fact that the procession takes place by night. If this be a correct representation of what would happen in natural life, and all that we learn from those conversant with Eastern customs confirms it, then it was simply a second act of folly on the part of the foolish virgins to disqualify themselves for showing honour to the bridegroom, and to make themselves late for the feast by going away to buy oil, so turning an accessory into an essential, and imperilling substantial interests by scrupulous regard to ceremony. Had they been wise they would have gone on as they were, and so gained an admission to the festive hall.

According to this view the foolish virgins act in character from first to last. They are fools all through. They are foolish first in taking only a limited supply of oil, assuming that the usual will happen; while the wise with characteristic forethought make provision for the unusual, that is, for the ' The passage cited from Ward's 'View of the Hindoos' by Trench, ana after him by Morrison, is quite in accordance with our view. Ward mentions that, at a certain marriage ceremony which he witnessed, the bridegroom, coming from a distance, kept the party waiting for him several hours. Then, his arrival being announced in words similar to those in the parable, all lighted their lamps, and ran to join the procession. Some, however, lost their lamps. What then? The author saysâ "It was too late to seek them, and the cavalcade moved forward,"' not saying, but implying, that those who had lost their lamps did not waste time in seeking them, but went on without them ide vol. iii. p. 171).

possible case of unexpected delay. They are foolish next in going away at an unseasonable hour to purchase oil instead of taking their place in the marriage procession as they were, a little put to shame by their dark lamps, nevertheless making sure their part in the main events of the occasion, the welcoming of the bridegroom, and admission to the wedding feast. Such consistency of character commends itself as intrinsically probable. The only serious objection to the hypothesis is the fact that the suggestion to go and buy oil comes from the wise virgins. How, it may be asked, could they advise their sisters to do a foolish thing? Does not the very fact of their giving such advice imply that to procure a supply of oil was indispensable to admission Now it is not necessary in order to meet this difficulty to adopt the suggestion of Augustine, that the advice of the wise was only an exemplification of that mockery of wisdom at the calamity of folly spoken of in the book of Proverbs. There is certainly not a little in the circumstances to give plausibility to this view. The hour was midnight, and the bridegroom was at hand, what likelihood of being able to get oil at all when the shops of those who sold were shut, and their owners in bed.-' What chance of getting it at least in time, however near the houses of the vendors might be.-' To say in such circumstances. Go and buy, was very like heartlessly advising to do the impossible. But the conduct of the wise can be explained without ascribing to them cruelty. Sudden emergencies bring into play a certain element of selfishness. Then it is every one for himself. The sharp loud cry is raised. Behold, the bridegroom is at hand! Excitement and hurry pervade the house, each one is engrossed with her own business, and when help is sought by the shiftless from the shifty it is declined with the best answer that occurs at the moment. In natural life one might say to another, "Go and buy for yourself," without expecting the advice to be taken seriously, yet without intending to mock. Objectively the advice of the wise virgins to the foolish was a mockery; subjectively it was nothing more than a declinature to be burdened with their neighbours' affairs.

Augustine's-vrords are, Non consulentium, sed irridentium, est ista j-esponsio (Serm. xciii. 8); similarly in Epist. cxl 31.

If the foregoing view be correct, the oil, hitherto regarded as a symbol of grace, under one aspect or another, ought rather to be reckoned a symbol of the means of grace; and the action of the virgins who went to buy oil will represent the superstitious importance attached to such means by a certain class of religionists to the peril of their spiritual interests. Taking together the two acts of folly committed by the foolish virgins, the neglect to take a sufficient supply of oil, and the unseasonable attempt to provide what was lacking, the resulting character is marked by two salient featuresâ lack of forethought and superstitious regard to form, or, to express it otherwise, vain regard to appearance. That is to say, folly reveals itself in this parable under the same guise as in another parable, in which a contrast is drawn between the foolish and the wise, that, viz. with which the Sermon on the Mount concludes; and the fact confirms us in the belief that the view we venture to take is correct. The foolish builder is a man who thinks not of the future, and who has regard only to appearances; while the wise builder keeps in view the uncertainties and dangers of the future, and is not content with mere appearance. The characteristic differences come out in connection with the cardinal question of the foundation. The one builder, the wise one, makes the foundation of his house a matter of serious consideration; the other begins to build without ever thinking of a foundation, and therein shows his folly. His mistake does not consist, as is often imagined, in making a bad choice of a foundation; but in acting as if a foundation were a matter of no consequence, beginning to build anywhere, on the loose sand, on the banks, or even in the bed of a river, dried up by summer heat. This appears very clearly from Luke's report of our Lord's words. i He that heareth and doeth is there compared to a man who " built a house and digged deep and laid a foundation 2 upon the rock;" and he that heareth and doeth not to a man that, " without a foundation built a house upon

Luke vi. 46â 49.

2 BiiibXiov, without the article, implying that a foundation is not, as usual, a matter of course.

3 X ptc 6Â lx40tb the earth." That is, the one takes great pains with the foundation of his houseâ digs below the surface, and goes deep in diggingâ digs till he reaches the rock; the other takes no pains about a foundation, provides none indeed, but begins at once to build at haphazard on the surface of the ground. It is thus not a case of choosing well between two possible foundations, one good, the other bad; but rather a case of attending to or neglecting the foundation. And the question to be considered by the expositor or preacher is not what are the two foundations represented respectively by the rock and the sand, but what are the qualities of character implied in attending to or neglecting the foundation of a house. The rock and the sand have no independent significance, the one didactically important point is the contrast of character brought out by the difference indicated in the respective ways of disposing of the question of a foundation.

In what respects, then, do the characters of the two builders, behaving as represented, stand in contrast Obviously in two respects. First, the wise builder has a prudent regard to the future. He anticipates the coming of storms, and aims at being well provided against these. The foolish builder, on the other hand, thinks only of the present. It is sunshine to-day, and he recks not of to-morrow and the storms it may bring. Then, secotidly, the wise builder looks not merely to appearance. The question with him is not what will look well, but what will stand. The foolish builder, on the contrary, cares for appearance alone. A house without a foundation looks as well as one having a foundation; it may even be made to look better. These distinctions have their counterpart in the spiritual sphere, which form the salient characteristics of two classes of men both professing religion. There are those who have forethought, and those who have none; those who think of the trial which the future may bring, those who think only of to-day and its bright sunshine. The one class count the cost when they meditate becoming disciples of Christ; the other receive the word with joy, leaving out of view the 'tribulations' they are likely to encounter in the career on which they are entering. Again, the one class looi to what is not seen by men in religious character, the hidden foundation of inward disposition; while the other consider only what can be seen by men, the outward act. The outward acts of both may be the same, but the motives are entirely different. The motive of the one is love of goodness; that of the other, vanity. Both pray, but a man of the one class prays in secret, his desire being not to be known as a praying man, but to get the favour he asks of Heaven; a man of the other class prays by preference at the corner of the street, desiring chiefly to get credit for a devotional spirit. Both practise beneficence; but the one from love or pity, and with modesty; the other not so much sympathising with the poor, as seeking a reputation for philanthropy.

Such are the distinctive attributes of the wise and the foolish, the genuine and the counterfeit, in religion. The marks of the one are forethought and sincerity, or depth; the marks of the other thoughtlessness and insincerity, or superficiality. The two sets of attributes always keep company. Sincerity implies forethought, and forethought sincerity; and in like manner the two other attributes imply each other. The man who has regard only to appearances would never profess religion at all, if he considered the future. He acts from impulse, imitation, and fashion, and the use of religion as a support in trial is not in all his thoughts. Hence it was that Christ so often presented the difficulties of the spiritual life to those who offered themselves as disciples. It was His way of ridding Himself of counterfeit discipleship originating in by-ends or thoughtless sentiment, and of securing that His circle of followers should include only men whose religion was an affair not of sentiment alone, but of reason and conscience, of reason looking well before, and of conscience realising moral responsibility.

The parable of the two builders shows us the respective fates of these two classes. Looking to appearances it would be difficult to say which was to be preferred; perhaps the verdict would be in favour of the counterfeit, for they make appearances their study, and it is not wonderful if they excel in their own line; But the eemenis judge infallibly and ruthlessly. The rains descend, the floods rush, and the winds blow, and the house built on a rock stands, "it fell not;" btit the house built on the sand " fell, and great was the fall of it." The elements are trials of all sorts, by providential calamities, by religious doubts, by sinful desires, by tribulations connected with profession of religion. Such trials the man of forethought and sincerity stands; before them the man whose piety imitative and impulsive goes down.

Such are the lessons to be learnt from the parable of the Wise and Foolish Builders, and they seem to us fitted tc throw light on the parable of the Wise and Foolish

Virgins. It is to be presumed that wisdom and folly have fixed characteristics in Christ's teaching, so that if we have correctly determined their respective attributes in any one place, we may expect to find them reappearing in all other places where they are spoken of. They do reappear in the parable of the virgins if we decide to regard the going to buy oil as an act of folly, not otherwise. On that assumption we have in the parable two characteristic acts of the foolish virgins close ol kin to each other. There is the initial act of taking an inadequate supply of oil, wherein is revealed characteristic want of forethought. As the foolish builder did not anticipate storms, but acted as if the usual good weather were to last always, and without exception; so the foolish virgins did not anticipate delay, but acted as if the usual at marriages was sure to happen, the prompt arrival of the bridegroom at the appointed time. Then there was the lurther act of folly consequent on discovering the evil result of the first, that, viz., of going away to buy oil, instead of doing without it, and joining the procession so as to insure admission to the feast. This act corresponds in general character to that of the foolish builder in having regard only to appearances, and so neglecting to provide a foundation. It is the act of persons to whom custom is an inviolable law. These foolish virgins must be in the fashion, must attend to all the usual ceremonies, must have their lighted lamps as well as the rest. The accidental though interesting accompaniment of the bridal procession, is to their custom-ridden minds the essence of the matter. It would look so ill to meet and escort the bridegroom with dark lamps in their hand. The two acta of folly are obviously of kindred character, so that those who do the one are likely to do the other; they both denote enslavement to the usual, which is a characteristic mark of the morally commonplace, in contrast to the wise, who show their wisdom by the ability to anticipate the unusual as possible, and to disregard custom when it stands in the way of the attainment of a great end. The parable affords no scope for the display of the latter phase of wisdom, for the wise virgins having oil enough were in a position to follow the usual custom, and of course did it; for to set aside even the least commandment of fashion unnecessarily is no part of wisdom. But it is true, nevertheless, that the wise are distinguished by freedom as well as by forethought in reference to the usual. They are incapable of being enslaved by superstitious regard for that which is only of secondary importance, a means to an end, an affair of decorum rather than of principle. Such freedom belongs to wisdom both in social life and in religion. On the other hand, the lack of such freedom is a sure mark of the weak and unwise. They are superstitiously devoted to the fashion of their time in religion as in other spheres. Means of grace, forms of worship, take the place of absolutely binding laws in their minds, and so become hindrances rather than helps in the Divine life. They understand not that "as ceremonies, such as men have devised, are but temporal; so may and ought they to be changed when they rather foster superstition than edify the Church using the same." They think all change impious, and the very thought converts the risk into a baleful reality.

It may appear strange, if the going to buy oil was an act of folly, that Jesus did not distinctly indicate the fact. But was it not enough to say, once for all, " five were foolish " The omission to characterise the second act as foolish is a significant recognition of the persistency of character, more instructive than the repetition of the epithet foolish. It signifies: " Take care to possess the spirit of wisdom, for remember the spirit that is in you will dominate all your conduct. Ye cannot be foolish to-day, and wise to-morrow;

Old Scotch Confession of Faith," ch. xxi.

foolish in this action, wise in the next. Character tends to fixity, and to get the benefit of wisdom at any time ye must be under its guidance at all times." A great, solemn truth,, to be seriously pondered by all, and too often overlooked.

As now explained, the present parable obviously points to a species of degeneracy to be manifested in the Church in the course of ages very difie'-ent from that spoken of in the parable last considered. There the evil foretold is a hideous combination of hypocrisy, tyranny, and sensuality; here the evil hinted at is religious superstition. The two evils manifested themselves together in the Church, the one among the clergy, the other among the illiterate. The latter is the less evil, and its doom accordingly is milder. The foolish virgins are simply shut out from the feast, the unfaithful upper servant is cut in two. The lesser doom is serious enough, and it is one to which all are exposed who resemble the foolish virgins in their religious character. The slaves of use and wont are ever in peril of their souls, ever exposed to the risk of exclusion from the joys in store for those prepared to receive the Bridegroom at His coming at each crisis in the Church's history. So were the Pharisees excluded from the society of Jesus, which was a veritable wedding party. So were the Hebrew Christians, clinging to venerable Jewish customs and ordinances, in danger of forfeiting all share in the blessings of the Kingdom of Grace. As their faithful Teacher warned them, there was a risk of their being carried by the strong current of old custom away from Christ, as a boat is carried down a river past the landing-place on the opposite shore. While they went to buy at the Jewish synagogue the Bridegroom might come, and the door be shut.

The slumber of the virgins is a feature in the parable which cannot fail to attract the attention of all thoughtful readers. To the allegorising interpretation which strives to discover a spiritual equivalent for every feature in a parable, this slumber denotes the negligence which overtakes all more or less with reference to the eternal, venial and remedial in the case of the wise, fatal in the case of the foolish; or, the common sleep of death. To others, unable to acquiesce in either of these suggestions, and

Heb. ii. i, i Trori Trapapwwitv. "lest haply we drift away."â R. V.

averse from the allegorising method of exegesis, the introduction of this feature appears simply a device for bringing about a situation involving a surprise which brings disaster to the unprepared. The foolish have to sleep, because had they kept awake they would have observed that their oil was getting done, and have provided a fresh supply in good time. The wise have to keep their foolish sisters company in slumber, that they may escape the charge of unkindness in allowing the sleepers to sleep on till it was too late to attend to the necessary preparations. The truth lies between these extremes. The sleep of the virgins is not of such grave significance as the allegorisers imagine, and on the other hand it is something more than a mere device for bringing about a situation necessary to the moral of the parable. It is a meagre view which sees in the delay of the bridegroom, only a contrivance to make room for slumber, and in the slumber in turn only a contrivance to give occasion for a surprise. The delay of the bridegroom represents a spiritual fact; the protracted endurance of the period of development, and the consequent indefinite postponement of the consummation of the kingdom. And the sleep of the virgins represents the natural inevitable occupation with the present which ensues when through long delay hope or expectation of a future good has been all but extinguished. The relevancy of the parable requires that the sleep should have some such counterpart in the spiritual sphere; for if the fact were otherwise we should have a situation described to which there is no parallel in religious experience. The sleeping scene, therefore, besides being thoroughly true to the natural, has an important didactic significance. It teaches that there is a certain sleep of the mind with regard to the future and the eternal which is unavoidable, in itself perfectly harmless, yet fraught with danger to such as are not ever ready for any event, so that the m. ost sudden crisis cannot overtake them unawares. The inevitableness of this sleep is very happily brought out in the delineation of the scene. The word all itself implies it; the universality suggests the idea of necessity. Then the way in which sleep comes on is significant. They grow drowsy, then 1 So in effect Storr, 'De Parabolis Christi' 512 The Parabolic Teaching of Christ, book hi, begin to nod, then fall into deep slumber. The sleep is involuntary, the virgins do not go to bed with deliberate intent to sleep, they are overtaken with sleep while maintaining an attitude of waiting, like the disciples in the garden, like weary sentinels on the battle-field, like devout worshippers in church. Fatigue, advancing night, the demands of nature, prevail over all wakeful influences. Yet these are by no means wanting. For the virgins, one and all, are full of the excitement of the occasion. To see them one would say that though the bridegroom should tarry till daybreak sleep will be impossible till he arrive and the wedding festivities are over. That is not said, but it goes without being said; it is enough to remember that the occasion is a marriage, and that the actors in the drama are young maidens. The innocence of the sleep follows of course from its being unavoidable, but it is also taught by implication when in the sequel the wise virgins are represented as having time to trim their lamps between their awaking and the arrival of the bridegroom. Sleep in their case does not interfere with the efficient performance of all needful ofiices. Yet that this sleep, though innocent, may be dangerous appears from what befalls the hapless maidens. They awake and discover that neglected tasks have to be attended to when there is no time for their performance.

The parabolic representation at this point is characterised in a conspicuous degree by that felicity on which we have often had occasion to remark. It suggests more lessons than it is expressly designed to teach. It illustrates, for example, the 'sweet reasonableness' of Christ's teaching, in so far as it exhibits an ideal of waiting, not too exacting for human nature under the conditions of this present life. When Christ requires of His disciples to watch, as He does in the closing sentence of this parable. He does not demand exclusive preoccupation of mind with the future. The watching required, we learn from the parable, is such as is compatible with a very complete engrossment with the present. It signifies timely preparation, ordering life on a right principle deliberately adopted once for all. It involves not continuous straining of the attention towards the eternal, but fixed intention active even when we are unconscious. The tension of the mind may innocently and must naturally vary, it is enough that its intention is ever the same, enough that we live under the power of the future and the eternal even when not thinking of it. This is quite possible. All know what it is to sleep under the power of the thought of having to rise at a particular hour in the morning. The slumber is light; there is a certain semi-consciousness all through the night. The slightest whisper, the calling of one's name ever so gently, suffices to awaken him; nay, in some mysterious way the latent thought of the engagement in prospect, the journey to be undertaken, suffices of itself to perform the part of an alarutn clock, and to rouse the sleeper at the appointed time. So wise virgins sleep, as those who lie down with the thought in their minds that at any moment they may hear the thrilling call: " Behold the Bridegroom! come ye forth to meet Him."

Christ's ideal of watching, though eminently and characteristically reasonable, is too high for many. In the parable one half of the virgins fail to realise it, but in real life the proportion of defaulters is much larger. The number of those who understand the art of watching, providing for the uncertain future, for the unusual, for the eternal, while living healthily and heartily in the present, is small. The multitude are the slaves of the usual; the wise man who can anticipate the unusual and prepare for it is one among a thousand. How many accidents by land and sea are due to the rarity of such wise forethought! Railway accidents happen because they are exceptional, and officials get accustomed to their not happening. Sailors on the outlook observe something before them, but take no alarm. They think it is a cloud when it is an iceberg, for icebergs are not usually met with at that time of the year. Their mind is asleep under the soporific influence of the usual, though their physical senses are awake. The same cause works disastrously in the spiritual sphere. Here it is specially difficult to expect the unexpected, and specially dangerous to lack the power to do so, and many there be who fail. The young Christian does not expect the difficulties and delays connected with the fulfilment of his hopes which he is destined to encounter, and when they occur he is scandalised and becomes an apostate. Or he is not prepared to find the life of the spirit passing through phases markedly different from each other, and he clings to the initial stage and remains a babe, superstitiously attached to forms which, once means of grace, degenerate into mere fetishes. So also does it fare oftentimes with religious communities. They lack the wisdom to anticipate and provide for changes in the course of development. These when they come find them enslaved by the past, and unprepared to meet the new situation, and the inevitable result is decay and death.

In parabolic language, the doom of those who are guilty of such folly is that the door is shut not to be opened again to them when they arrive too late and seek admission. Taking the parable as a story of natural life, this feature seems arbitrary. Children ask their parents the hard question, "Why could he not open the door " and learned interpreters ask the same question and acknowledge themselves unable to answer. When the representation is viewed in connection with the final judgment it becomes too awful to speak of, and very difficult to construe with other Scriptural teaching. A recent writer remarks that the exclusion of the belated virgins allegorically interpreted leads to the wholly unbiblical thought that even the most earnest desire for salvation is in vain when the hour of decision has struck. " The irreparabile dani7min of the 'too late' in this sense is not a Biblical doctrine." When one thinks of the penitent thief, he is conscious that the difficulty is not imaginary. Then one cannot but remember the supplement in the Pauline teaching to the doctrine of exclusion taught in the parable of the Great Supper. " None of those men which were bidden shall taste of my supper," says the parable. The Jews are cast ovx pro tempore, and the Gentiles brought in to provoke the former to jealousy, that they may also at length be brought in, says the Apostle Paul. Applying Paul's doctrine to the present parable in the case of

Reuss speaks of the virgins going to buy oil and their exclusion as features introduced with a view to the application In natural life they could have got oil in the house of the bride, and they would have been admitted though late.

Weiss, Das Matthaus-Evangeliunx the Jews, it would imply that that people, prevented by their prejudices from taking part in the bridal procession, would nevertheless gain admittance to the feast when arriving late they cried, "Lord, Lord, open to us." Without doubt the judgment of exclusion in its temporal application is not in this parable, any more than in the parable of the Supper, absolute. It merely indicates tendency. It is not on that account trivial. Even the temporal losses entailed by the lack of the wisdom commended in this parable are grave enough to justify serious solicitude. Leaving the eternal reference out of account, that wisdom is highly to be prized. In view of eternity its value is unspeakable.

Tns BNSk
Clj-p
University of Toronto Library
REMOVE
CARD
FROM
THIS
POCKET
Acme Library Card Pocket LOWE-MARTIN CO. limited

Lightning Source UK Ltd.
Milton Keynes UK
14 March 2011

169256UK00001B/59/P

9 781151 772848